W9-CPQ-090

CasebookConnect.com

REGISTER NOW to access the Study Center for:

- Hundreds of practice questions
- Selections from popular study aids
- Progress trackers to save you time
- Tutorial videos

Combine this wealth of resources with an **enhanced ebook** and **outlining tool** and you will **SUCCEED** in law school

Use this unique code to connect your casebook today

Access Code: EPST989371377336

Go to www.casebookconnect.com and redeem your access code to get started.

ASPEN CASEBOOK SERIES

ELEVENTH EDITION

CASES AND MATERIALS ON TORTS

RICHARD A. EPSTEIN

Laurence A. Tisch Professor of Law
New York University School of Law
Peter and Kirsten Bedford Senior Fellow
The Hoover Institution
Stanford University
James Parker Hall Distinguished Service Professor of Law
Emeritus and Senior Lecturer
The University of Chicago

CATHERINE M. SHARKEY

Crystal Eastman Professor of Law
New York University School of Law

 Wolters Kluwer

Published by Wolters Kluwer in New York.

Wolters Kluwer Legal & Regulatory US serves customers worldwide with CCH, Aspen Publishers, and Kluwer Law International products. (www.WKLegaledu.com)

To contact Customer Service, e-mail customer.service@wolterskluwer.com, call 1-800-234-1660, fax 1-800-901-9075, or mail correspondence to:

Wolters Kluwer
Attn: Order Department
PO Box 990
Frederick, MD 21705

Printed in the United States of America.

1 2 3 4 5 6 7 8 9 0

ISBN 978-1-4548-6825-5

Library of Congress Cataloging-in-Publication Data

Names: Epstein, Richard Allen, 1943- author. | Sharkey, Catherine M., author.
Title: Cases and materials on torts / Richard A. Epstein, Laurence A. Tisch
  Professor of Law, New York University School of Law, Peter and Kirsten
  Bedford Senior Fellow, The Hoover Institution, Stanford University, James
  Parker Hall Distinguished Service Professor of Law Emeritus and Senior
  Lecturer, The University of Chicago, Catherine M. Sharkey, Crystal Eastman
  Professor of Law New York University School of Law.
Description: Eleventh edition. | New York: Wolters Kluwer, [2016]
Identifiers: LCCN 2016010098 | ISBN 9781454868255
Subjects: LCSH: Torts—United States—Cases. | Liability (Law)—United
  States—Cases. | Damages—United States—Cases.
Classification: LCC KF1250 .E655 2016 | DDC 346.7303—dc23
LC record available at http://lccn.loc.gov/2016010098

Certified Chain of Custody
Promoting Sustainable Forestry

www.sfiprogram.org
SFI-01042

SFI label applies to the text stock

About Wolters Kluwer Legal & Regulatory US

Wolters Kluwer Legal & Regulatory US delivers expert content and solutions in the areas of law, corporate compliance, health compliance, reimbursement, and legal education. Its practical solutions help customers successfully navigate the demands of a changing environment to drive their daily activities, enhance decision quality and inspire confident outcomes.

Serving customers worldwide, its legal and regulatory portfolio includes products under the Aspen Publishers, CCH Incorporated, Kluwer Law International, ftwilliam.com and MediRegs names. They are regarded as exceptional and trusted resources for general legal and practice-specific knowledge, compliance and risk management, dynamic workflow solutions, and expert commentary.

To the next generation

Bella Catherine Pianko
Noah David Pianko
Ethan Saul Pianko
Caleb Emmett Sharkey
Phoebe Lila Sharkey

SUMMARY OF CONTENTS

Contents   xi
Preface   xxiii
Acknowledgments   xxv
Introduction   xxxi
Torts *Treatise: List of Chapters*   xxxix
List of Abbreviations   xli

PART ONE

PHYSICAL AND EMOTIONAL HARMS   1

 1. Intentional Harms: The Prima Facie Case and Defenses   3
 2. Strict Liability and Negligence: Historic and Analytic Foundations 71
 3. Negligence   137
 4. Plaintiff's Conduct   275
 5. Causation   341
 6. Affirmative Duties   467
 7. Strict Liability   539
 8. Products Liability   641
 9. Damages   759
10. Tort Extensions: Insurance and No-Fault Systems   815

PART TWO

TORTS AGAINST NONPHYSICAL INTERESTS   881

11. Defamation   883
12. Privacy   985
13. Misrepresentation   1051
14. Economic Harms   1099
15. Tort Immunities   1169

Table of Cases   1205
Table of Restatement Sections   1231
Table of Secondary Authorities   1237
Index   1251

CONTENTS

Preface   xxiii
Acknowledgments   xxv
Introduction   xxxi
Torts *Treatise: List of Chapters*   xxxix
List of Abbreviations   xli

PART ONE

PHYSICAL AND EMOTIONAL HARMS   1

CHAPTER 1

INTENTIONAL HARMS: THE PRIMA FACIE CASE AND DEFENSES   3

Section A. Introduction   3
Section B. Physical Harms   4
    1. Trespass to Person and Land   4
       Vosburg v. Putney   4
       Dougherty v. Stepp   12
    2. Defenses to Intentional Torts   14
      a. Consensual Defenses   14
       Mohr v. Williams   14
       Canterbury v. Spence   22
       Hudson v. Craft   22
      b. Mental Disability   28
       McGuire v. Almy   28
      c. Self-Defense   32
       Courvoisier v. Raymond   32
      d. Defense of Property   36
       Bird v. Holbrook   36
      e. Necessity   41
       Ploof v. Putnam   41
       Vincent v. Lake Erie Transportation Co. 44
       Thomson, The Trolley Problem   50
Section C. Emotional and Dignitary Harms   52
    1. Assault   52

I. de S. and Wife v. W. de S. 52

Tuberville v. Savage 53

Blackstone, Commentaries 53

2. Offensive Battery 56

   Alcorn v. Mitchell 56

3. False Imprisonment 58

   Coblyn v. Kennedy's, Inc. 58

4. The Intentional Infliction of Emotional
   Distress: Extreme and Outrageous Conduct 63

   Wilkinson v. Downton 63

CHAPTER 2

STRICT LIABILITY AND NEGLIGENCE: HISTORIC AND ANALYTIC FOUNDATIONS   71

Section A. Introduction 71

Section B. The Formative Cases 72

   The Thorns Case (Hull v. Orange) 72

   Weaver v. Ward 78

Section C. The Forms of Action 82

   1. The Significance of the Forms 82

   2. Trespass and Case 83

      Scott v. Shepherd 84

   3. The Breakdown of the Forms of Action 88

**Section D. Strict Liability and Negligence in the Second Half
   of the Nineteenth Century** 91

   Brown v. Kendall 92

   Fletcher v. Rylands (1865) 97

   Fletcher v. Rylands (1866) 100

   Rylands v. Fletcher 102

   Brown v. Collins 108

   Powell v. Fall 112

   Holmes, The Common Law 114

Section E. Strict Liability and Negligence in Modern Times 122

   Stone v. Bolton 122

   Bolton v. Stone 123

   Hammontree v. Jenner 132

CHAPTER 3

NEGLIGENCE   137

Thayer, Public Wrong and Private Action Green,
   Judge and Jury 137

Section A. Introduction 137

Section B. The Reasonable Person   139
    Vaughan v. Menlove   139
    Holmes, The Common Law   144
    Roberts v. Ring   146
    Daniels v. Evans   148
    Breunig v. American Family Insurance Co.   153
    Fletcher v. City of Aberdeen   157
    Denver & Rio Grande R.R. v. Peterson   159
Section C. Calculus of Risk   160
    Blyth v. Birmingham Water Works   160
    Terry, Negligence   162
    Seavey, Negligence — Subjective or Objective?   163
    Osborne v. Montgomery   164
    Cooley v. Public Service Co.   166
    United States v. Carroll Towing Co.   170
    Ross, Settled Out of Court   178
    Andrews v. United Airlines   179
Section D. Custom   181
    Titus v. Bradford, B. & K. R. Co.   182
    Mayhew v. Sullivan Mining Co.   184
    The T.J. Hooper (1931)   186
    The T.J. Hooper (1932)   187
    Lama v. Borras   193
    Murray v. UNMC Physicians   200
    Schuck, Rethinking Informed Consent   205
    Canterbury v. Spence   206
Section E. Statutes and Regulations   218
    Anon.   219
    Thayer, Public Wrong and Private Action   219
    Osborne v. McMasters   221
    Martin v. Herzog   227
    California Businesss & Professions Code §25602   231
    Uhr v. East Greenbush Cent. Sch. Dist.   232
Section F. Judge and Jury   235
    Holmes, The Common Law   238
    Baltimore and Ohio R.R. v. Goodman   240
    Pokora v. Wabash Ry.   241
Section G. Proof of Negligence   248
    1. Methods of Proof   248
    2. Res Ipsa Loquitur   249
        Byrne v. Boadle   249
        Colmenares Vivas v. Sun Alliance Insurance Co.   255
        Ybarra v. Spangard   263

CHAPTER 4

PLAINTIFF'S CONDUCT   275

Section A. Introduction   275
Section B. Contributory Negligence   276
  1. Basic Doctrine   276
       Butterfield v. Forrester   276
       Beems v. Chicago, Rock Island & Peoria R.R.   277
       Schwartz, Tort Law and the Economy in Nineteenth-Century
            America: A Reinterpretation   278
       Gyerman v. United States Lines Co.   281
       LeRoy Fibre Co. v. Chicago, Milwaukee & St. Paul Ry.   289
       Derheim v. N. Fiorito Co.   292
  2. Last Clear Chance   296
       Fuller v. Illinois Central R.R.   296
Section C. Imputed Contributory Negligence   301
Section D. Assumption of Risk   303
       Lamson v. American Axe & Tool Co.   303
       Murphy v. Steeplechase Amusement Co.   308
       Dalury v. S-K-I Ltd.   315
Section E. Comparative Negligence   322
  1. At Common Law   322
       Lombard Laws, King Liutprand   322
       Beach, Contributory Negligence   323
       Prosser, Comparative Negligence   323
       Li v. Yellow Cab Co. of California   324
  2. By Legislation   336
       Federal Employers' Liability Act   336
       New York   337
       Pennsylvania   337
       Wisconsin   337

CHAPTER 5

CAUSATION   341

Section A. Introduction   341
Section B. Cause in Fact   343
  1. The "But For" Test   343
       New York Central R.R. v. Grimstad   343
       Zuchowicz v. United States   348
  2. Joint and Several Liability and Multiple Causes   353
       a. Joint and Several Liability   353
            *Union Stock Yards Co. of Omaha v. Chicago, Burlington,
                 & Quincy R.R.*   354

California Civil Procedure Code §§875-877.5 356
American Motorcycle Association v. Superior Court 358

    b. Multiple Sufficient Causes 367
        Kingston v. Chicago & N.W. Ry. 367

  3. Indeterminate Causes 372
    a. Alternative Liability 372
        Summers v. Tice 372
    b. Market Share Liability 376
        Sindell v. Abbott Laboratories 376
    c. Loss of Chance of Survival 387
        Herskovits v. Group Health Cooperative 387

  4. Proof of Factual Causation 394
    General Electric Co. v. Joiner 394

Section C. Proximate Cause (Herein of Duty) 403
  1. Physical Injury 403
    Bacon, The Elements of the Common Lawes of England 403
    Street, Foundations of Legal Liability 403
    Ryan v. New York Central R.R. 403
    Berry v. Sugar Notch Borough 407
    Brower v. New York Central & H.R.R. 412
    Wagner v. International Ry. 417
    In re Polemis & Furness, Withy & Co. 419
    Overseas Tankship (U.K.) Ltd. v. Morts Dock &
    Engineering Co., Ltd. (Wagon Mound (No. 1)) 423
    Palsgraf v. Long Island R.R. 431
    Marshall v. Nugent 444
    Virden v. Betts and Beer Construction Company 448
    Hebert v. Enos 450
  2. Emotional Distress 451
    Mitchell v. Rochester Ry. 451
    Dillon v. Legg 455

CHAPTER 6

AFFIRMATIVE DUTIES   467

Section A. Introduction 467
Section B. The Duty to Rescue 469
    Luke 10:30-37 (King James Translation) 469
    Buch v. Amory Manufacturing Co. 470
    Hurley v. Eddingfield 472
    Bohlen, The Moral Duty to Aid Others as a Basis of Tort Liability . 473
    Ames, Law and Morals 473
    Epstein, A Theory of Strict Liability 475
    Posner, Epstein's Tort Theory: A Critique 476

	Bender, An Overview of Feminist Torts Scholarship	477
	Montgomery v. National Convoy & Trucking Co.	481
Section C.	**Duties of Owners and Occupiers**	486
	Robert Addie & Sons (Collieries), Ltd. v. Dumbreck	486
	Rowland v. Christian	494
Section D.	**Gratuitous Undertakings**	505
	Coggs v. Bernard	505
	Erie Railroad Co. v. Stewart	507
	Moch Co. v. Rensselaer Water Co.	512
Section E.	**Special Relationships**	518
	Kline v. 1500 Massachusetts Avenue Apartment Corp.	519
	Tarasoff v. Regents of University of California	528

CHAPTER 7

STRICT LIABILITY 539

Section A.	**Introduction**	539
Section B.	**Trespass to Chattels and Conversion**	540
	1. Trespass to Chattels	540
	Intel Corp. v. Hamidi	541
	2. Conversion	549
	Poggi v. Scott	549
	Moore v. Regents of the University of California	553
Section C.	**Animals**	563
	Gehrts v. Batteen	563
Section D.	**Ultrahazardous or Abnormally Dangerous Activities**	572
	Spano v. Perini Corp.	572
	Indiana Harbor Belt R.R. v. American Cyanamid Co.	582
Section E.	**Nuisance**	590
	1. Private Nuisance	590
	Vogel v. Grant-Lafayette Electric Cooperative	590
	Michalson v. Nutting	596
	Fontainebleau Hotel Corp. v. Forty-Five Twenty-Five, Inc.	600
	Rogers v. Elliott	604
	Ensign v. Walls	608
	Boomer v. Atlantic Cement Co.	612
	2. Public Nuisance	621
	Anonymous	621
Section F.	**Vicarious Liability**	624
	Ira S. Bushey & Sons, Inc. v. United States	624
	Petrovich v. Share Health Plan of Illinois, Inc.	632

CHAPTER 8

PRODUCTS LIABILITY   641

Section A. **Introduction**   641
Section B. **Exposition**   645
      Winterbottom v. Wright   645
      MacPherson v. Buick Motor Co.   648
      Escola v. Coca Cola Bottling Co. of Fresno   656
Section C. **The Restatements**   666
    1. A Tale of Two Texts   666
      Restatement (Second) of Torts §402A   666
      Restatement (Third) of Torts: Products Liability §§1-2   670
    2. The Theory of Products Liability: Tort or Contract   671
      Casa Clara Condominium Association, Inc. v.
        Charley Toppino & Sons, Inc.   671
    3. Proper Defendants Under Section 402A   678
Section D. **Product Defects**   682
    1. Manufacturing Defects   682
      Speller v. Sears, Roebuck and Co.   683
    2. Design Defects   687
      Campo v. Scofield   687
      2 Harper and James, Torts §28.5   687
      Wade, On the Nature of Strict Tort Liability for Products   687
      a. Development of the Negligence Test   688
        Volkswagen of America, Inc. v. Young   688
      b. Consumer Expectations versus Risk-Utility Tests 697
        Barker v. Lull Engineering Co.   697
      c. Third Restatement and the Alternative Design Test   704
    3. The Duty to Warn   708
      MacDonald v. Ortho Pharmaceutical Corp.   709
      Vassallo v. Baxter Healthcare Corp.   719
      Hood v. Ryobi America Corp.   725
Section E. **Plaintiff's Conduct**   731
      Daly v. General Motors Corp.   731
Section F. **Federal Preemption**   740
      Geier v. American Honda Motor Co.   741
      Wyeth v. Levine   747

CHAPTER 9

DAMAGES   759

      Sullivan v. Old Colony Street Ry.   759
      Zibbell v. Southern Pacific Co.   759
Section A. **Introduction**   759
Section B. **Recoverable Elements of Damages**   760

      1. Pain and Suffering   760

        McDougald v. Garber   760

      2. Economic Losses   768

        O'Shea v. Riverway Towing Co.   768

        Duncan v. Kansas City Southern Railway   776

Section C. Wrongful Death and Loss of Consortium   782

      1. Wrongful Death   783

        a. History   783

        b. Measure of Damages   785

      2. Survival of Personal Injury Actions   786

      3. Actions for Loss of Consortium   786

        a. History   786

        b. Parents and Children   787

        c. Nontraditional Families   788

        d. Damages in Consortium Cases   789

Section D. Punitive Damages   790

      Kemezy v. Peters   790

      State Farm Mutual Automobile Insurance Co. v. Campbell   796

Section E. Litigation Financing   805

      1. Contingent Fees   805

      2. Class Actions   807

      3. Fee Shifting   808

      4. Sale of Tort Claims   808

      5. Litigation Insurance   809

      6. Alternative Litigation Financing   809

Section F. Collateral Benefits   810

      Harding v. Town of Townshend   810

CHAPTER 10

TORT EXTENSIONS: INSURANCE AND NO-FAULT SYSTEMS

815

Section A. Introduction   815

Section B. Liability Insurance   816

      1. Automobile and Other Basic Lines of Insurance   816

        a. The March to Compulsory Insurance   816

        b. The Standard Provisions of the Automobile
          Insurance Contract   818

          i. The Omnibus Clause   818

          ii. "Drive the Other Car" Clauses   819

          iii. Uninsured Motorist Coverage   819

          iv. Medical Payments   820

          v. Misrepresentation and Nondisclosure   820

          vi. Notice and Cooperation   821

      2. Ambiguities of the Insurance Carrier   822

        a. The Duty to Defend   823

b. The Obligation to Settle in Good Faith	823
Crisci v. Security Insurance Co.	823
3. Modern Tort Litigation	827
Dimmitt Chevrolet, Inc. v. Southeastern Fidelity	
Insurance Corp.	827
4. Cumulative Trauma Cases	835
Section C. The No-Fault Systems	837
1. Workers' Compensation	837
a. Historical Origins	838
b. The Scope of Coverage: "Arising Out of and	
in the Course of Employment"	844
Clodgo v. Rentavision, Inc.	844
Wilson v. Workers' Compensation Appeals Board	852
c. Benefits Under the Workers' Compensation Statutes	855
d. Exclusive Remedy	857
Rainer v. Union Carbide Corp.	857
2. Automobile No-Fault Insurance	862
a. The Basic Reform Proposal	862
American Bar Association, Special Committee on	
Automobile Insurance Legislation, Why the Statistical	
Studies Critical of the Fault System Are Flawed	864
Epstein, Automobile No-Fault Plans: A Second	
Look at First Principles	865
b. The Challenge of Implementation	865
3. No-Fault Insurance for Medical and Product Injuries	869
Section D. The 9/11 Victim Compensation Fund	871
Section E. The New Zealand Plan	873
Report of the Royal Commission of Inquiry,	
Compensation for Personal Injury in New Zealand	874
Accident Compensation: Options for Reform	875

PART TWO

TORTS AGAINST NONPHYSICAL INTERESTS 881

CHAPTER 11

DEFAMATION 883

Section A. Introduction	883
Section B. Publication	885
Mims v. Metropolitan Life Insurance Co.	885
Firth v. State of New York	889
Blumenthal v. Drudge	893
Section C. False or Defamatory Statements	898
Parmiter v. Coupland	898

	Muzikowski v. Paramount Pictures Corp.	898
	Wilkow v. Forbes, Inc.	906
Section D.	**Libel and Slander**	912
	Varian Medical Systems, Inc. v. Delfino	912
Section E.	**Basis of Liability: Intention, Negligence, and Strict Liability in Defamation**	918
	E. Hulton & Co. v. Jones	918
Section F.	**Damages**	920
	1. Special Damages	920
	Terwilliger v. Wands	920
	Ellsworth v. Martindale-Hubbell Law Directory, Inc.	922
	2. General Damages	925
	McCormick, Damages	925
	Faulk v. Aware, Inc. (1962)	925
	Faulk v. Aware, Inc. (1963)	926
	3. Other Remedies	928
	a. Injunctions	928
	b. Retraction	928
	c. Reply Statutes	929
	d. Declaratory Relief and "Libel Tourism"	930
Section G.	**Nonconstitutional Defenses**	931
	1. Truth	931
	Auvil v. CBS 60 Minutes	931
	2. Privileges in the Private Sphere	937
	Watt v. Longsdon	937
	3. Privileges in the Public Sphere	943
	a. Legal Proceedings and Reports Thereon	943
	Kennedy v. Cannon	943
	b. Reports of Public Proceedings or Meetings	949
	Brown & Williamson Tobacco Corp. v. Jacobson	949
	c. Fair Comment: Artistic and Literary Criticism	952
	Veeder, Freedom of Public Discussion	954
Section H.	**Constitutional Privileges**	957
	1. Public Officials and Public Figures	957
	New York Times Co. v. Sullivan	957
	Curtis Publishing Co. v. Butts	964
	2. Private Parties	972
	Gertz v. Robert Welch, Inc.	972
	Obsidian Finance Group, LLC v. Cox	980

CHAPTER 12

PRIVACY

		985
Section A.	**Introduction**	985
Section B.	**Historical Background**	986

Warren & Brandeis, The Right to Privacy   986
Prosser, Privacy   988
Kalven, Privacy in the Tort Law — Were Warren and
    Brandeis Wrong?   990
Prosser, Privacy   992
Section C. **Intrusion Upon Seclusion**   993
Nader v. General Motors Corp.   993
Boring v. Google Inc.   1000
Desnick v. American Broadcasting Co., Inc.   1003
Section D. **Public Disclosure of Embarrassing Private Facts**   1011
Sidis v. F-R Publishing Corp.   1012
Cox Broadcasting Corp. v. Cohn   1016
Haynes v. Alfred A. Knopf, Inc.   1022
Section E. **False Light**   1027
Time, Inc. v. Hill   1027
Section F. **Commercial Appropriation of Plaintiff's Name**
or Likeness, or the Right of Publicity   1032
In re NCAA Student-Athlete Name and Likeness Litig.   1033
Factors Etc., Inc. v. Pro Arts, Inc.   1045

CHAPTER 13

MISREPRESENTATION   1051

Section A. **Introduction**   1051
Section B. **Fraud**   1052
Pasley v. Freeman   1052
Vulcan Metals Co. v. Simmons Manufacturing Co.   1060
Swinton v. Whitinsville Savings Bank   1065
Laidlaw v. Organ   1069
Edgington v. Fitzmaurice   1072
Laborers Local 17 Health and Benefit Fund v. Philip Morris, Inc.   1081
Section C. **Negligent Misrepresentation**   1087
Ultramares Corp. v. Touche   1087

CHAPTER 14

ECONOMIC HARMS   1099

Section A. **Introduction**   1099
Section B. **Inducement of Breach of Contract**   1100
The Statute of Labourers (1351)   1100
Lumley v. Gye   1101
Asahi Kasei Pharma Corp. v. Actelion Ltd.   1111

Section C. **Intentional Interference with Prospective Advantage**   1117
    Tarleton v. M'Gawley   1117
Section D. **Negligent Interference with Economic Relationships**   1120
    People Express Airlines, Inc. v. Consolidated Rail Corp.   1120
    532 Madison Avenue Gourmet Foods, Inc. v. Finlandia Center, Inc.   1129
Section E. **Unfair Competition**   1136
    Mogul Steamship Co. v. McGregor, Gow & Co.   1136
    International News Service v. Associated Press   1145
    The National Basketball Association v. Motorola, Inc.   1152
    Barclays Capital Inc. v. Theflyonthewall.com   1156
    Ely-Norris Safe Co. v. Mosler Safe Co.   1159
    Mosler Safe Co. v. Ely-Norris Safe Co.   1161

CHAPTER 15

TORT IMMUNITIES   **1169**

Section A. **Introduction**   1169
Section B. **Domestic or Intrafamily Immunities**   1170
    1. Parent and Child   1170
        a. Suits Between Parent and Child   1170
        b. Third-Party Actions   1174
    2. Spouses   1175
Section C. **Charitable Immunity**   1176
Section D. **Municipal Corporations**   1178
    1. At Common Law   1178
    2. By Statute   1180
        745 Ill. Comp. Stat. (2016)   1181
    3. Under the Constitution   1183
Section E. **Sovereign Immunity**   1185
    Federal Tort Claims Act §§2671-2680   1186
    Berkovitz v. United States   1187
Section F. **Official Immunity**   1196
    Clinton v. Jones   1196

Table of Cases   1205
Table of Restatement Sections   1231
Table of Secondary Authorities   1237
Index   1251

PREFACE

The eleventh edition of this casebook marks yet another change in the four short years since Catherine M. Sharkey joined Richard A. Epstein as a coeditor of the casebook. The most conspicuous changes in the eleventh edition of the casebook are visual, as the physical book has been redesigned in light of the new sensibilities of the age. For the first time the book contains pictures, cartoons, tables, and charts that are set off from the main text to supply visual background information about the persons, places, and things that hold center stage in the cases and materials of the book. The design of these materials has been spruced up with red headings to mark transitions and with boxes that contain key provisions of the various Restatements of Torts and other materials. The text, too, has been revised in light of the reduced number of credits allocated to torts in the first year curriculum. In response to these pressures, we have shortened the material somewhat by thinning out the notes and eliminating some of the principal cases. We have also consolidated the materials of the insurance contract and the no-fault systems into a single chapter that touches both.

That said, we have strived to preserve those key intangibles, the basic character and feel of the book. Accordingly, its basic organization and structure are consistent with the broad objectives of the first edition of the casebook, which first appeared in 1959 by the late Professors Charles O. Gregory and Harry Kalven, Jr., both exceptional and imaginative scholars. Their second edition followed some ten years later, and was in fact the book from which Professor Epstein first taught torts at the University of Southern California in 1969. In 1972, he joined the faculty of the University of Chicago Law School. In January 1974, with Gregory in retirement, Professor Kalven asked Epstein to collaborate with him on the third edition of the casebook. Kalven's tragic death in October 1974 cut short that brief collaboration before it began. Thereafter Professor Gregory reentered the lists to read and comment on the drafts of the third edition that Epstein prepared, which appeared in 1977. The preparation for the fourth edition of Epstein, Gregory and Kalven, which appeared in 1984, was done by Epstein alone. Gregory died in April 1987, after a rich and full life. Epstein was then the sole editor of the fifth (1990), sixth (1995), seventh (2000), eighth (2004), and ninth (2008) editions on ever shorter cycles. Even after so much time and revision, much of the case selection and organization of this book reflect the initial judgments of Gregory and Kalven, whose pioneering spirit and rich imagination brought so much to the study of torts.

The tenth edition reflected the new partnership between Epstein and Sharkey, who initiated a new set of changes. That edition merged the material on joint and several liability into the chapter on causation. The material on vicarious liability was inserted at the end of the now-Chapter 7 on strict liability, to which was also added the materials on trespass to chattels and conversion that had formerly been included in Chapter 1. Extensive references were made to the key provisions of the Third Restatement of Torts: Liability for Physical and Emotional Harm, approved by the American Law Institute in 2011. To these were added the changes in both appearance and organization for the eleventh edition, as set out above. Even with these changes, the casebook also carries over many of the features from earlier editions, including extensive historical materials on the evolution of tort law, the expanded treatment of public nuisance law, recent developments in products liability law, expansion of the materials on various types of injuries in damage cases, and the heavier emphasis on web-based communications under the law of defamation and privacy.

As with earlier editions, however, our intention has been to update the materials while preserving historical and conceptual continuity between the present and the past. In so doing, we have sought to keep one of the distinctive features of this casebook, which is to stress the alternative visions of tort law as they developed in the nineteenth (and the now complete) twentieth centuries. Toward that end, we have retained in the eleventh edition those great older cases, both English and American, that have proved themselves time and again in the classroom, and which continue to exert great influence on the modern law. But by the same token, we reviewed in detail the many major changes in tort law that took place in the years between 1968 and 1980. Although many of those developments continue to remain important, others have been either modified or rejected in favor of more traditional doctrines. It is no longer likely in 2016 that strict liability rules will exert greater sway in medical malpractice cases, or that market share liability will expand much beyond the original DES cases. We have sought to keep pace with these new developments both through common law and, increasingly, through legislation.

Five previous editions of this book were dedicated to the memory of Charles Gregory and Harry Kalven. Time has moved on. In 2004, Epstein dedicated the eighth edition of the book to the memory of his contemporary, the late Gary Schwartz, who died in 2001, one of the most insightful, learned, and fair-minded tort professors of any generation. For many years his kindness, generosity, and insight helped improve the earlier editions of the casebook. The ninth edition was dedicated to the late Bernard D. Meltzer, himself a casebook author of great distinction, who passed away at age 92 in 2007. In the tenth edition, we moved from the past to the future, and dedicated jointly this edition to the next generation, our grandchildren and children, respectively. We have done the same in the eleventh edition, happy that their expanded ranks (by one) are all happy and well.

Richard A. Epstein
Catherine M. Sharkey

New York
April 2016

ACKNOWLEDGMENTS

In preparing the tenth edition of this casebook, we have been fortunate enough to draw on the comments of many teachers and students who have used the book. Over the years we have received additional assistance and suggestions on various points of this volume from Kenneth Abraham, Jennifer Arlen, Vincent Blasi, William Cohen, Michael Corrado, Richard Craswell, Theodore Eisenberg, Robert Ellickson, Cindy Estlund, Stephen Gillers, James Henderson, Gail Heriot, Morton Horwitz, Keith Hylton, Jason Johnston, Spencer Kimball, Alvin Klevorick, Stanton Kraus, William Landes, Fred McChesney, Thomas Miles, Marc Miller, Cornelius Peck, Malla Pollock, Richard Posner, Glen Robinson, Howard Sacks, Gary Schwartz, Paul Schwartz, Perry Sentell, Ken Simons, Geoffrey Stone, Alan Sykes, Aaron Twerski, Ernest Weinrib, and Jerry Wiley. We should also like to thank in addition all the unnamed casebook users who have filled in their forms to explain what they did and did not like about earlier editions of the book.

Our largest debt, however, goes to the team of diligent research assistants who helped in the preparation of this book. Phoebe King, Gabriel Panek, and Samuel Schoenburg of NYU School of Law and Rachel Cohn, Craig Fligor, Julia Haines, Madeline Lansky, Krista Perry, and Manuel Valle of the University of Chicago Law School provided immense assistance in gathering materials and working on the revisions of the Eleventh Edition. We also thank John Devins for seeing this project through at Wolters Kluwer, and Tom Daughhetee and Cindy Uh for overseeing production with their team at The Froebe Group. We would also like to thank the authors and copyright holders of the following works:

Articles & Books

American Bar Association, Special Committee on Automobile Insurance Legislation, Automobile No-Fault Insurance (1978).

American Law Institute, Restatement (Second) of the Law of Torts §§13, 18, 20, 21, 46, 85, 218, 222A, 223, 286, 315, 328D, 332, 339, 402A, 431, 433A, 448, 449. Copyright © 1965 by the American Law Institute. Reprinted with permission of the American Law Institute.

American Law Institute, Restatement (Second) of the Law of Torts §§519, 520, 522, 523, 524, 524A, 538, 549, 559, 575, 577, 611, 652B, 652C, 652D, 652E. Copyright © 1977 by the American Law Institute. Reprinted with permission of the American Law Institute.

Photographs & Illustrations

Exxon Valdez. Photograph. Copyright © Chris Wilkins/AFP/Getty Images. Reprinted by permission.

Fish meal. Photograph. Copyright © Julio Etchart/Alamy. Reprinted by permission.

Guido Calabresi. Photograph. Copyright © Robert Benson Photography. Reprinted by permission.

Henrietta Lacks. Photograph. Copyright © The Henrietta Lacks Foundation. Reprinted by permission.

Henry J. Friendly. Photograph. Copyright © The Estate of Fabian Bachrach. Reprinted by permission.

Hugh McCalmont Cairns, 1st Earl Cairns c. 1860. Photograph. Copyright © John Watkins/National Portrait Gallery, London. Reprinted by permission.

"If you're so enlightened, how come you can't lick that slice?". Illustration. Copyright © Sam Gross/The New Yorker Collection/The Cartoon Bank. Reprinted by permission.

"It's a mixed-use facility: retail space". Illustration. Copyright © Sidney Harris/ The New Yorker Collection/The Cartoon Bank. Reprinted by permission.

"It's my fault—I wasn't worrying enough" Illustration. Copyright © Tom Cheney/The New Yorker Collection/The Cartoon Bank. Reprinted by permission.

Jacob Lawrence, The Migration Series, Panel 1/The Jacob and Gwendolyn Knight Lawrence Foundation, Seattle/Artists Rights Society (ARS), New York.

Jacqueline Kennedy Onassis. Photograph. Copyright © Ron Gallela/Wire Image/Getty Images. Reprinted by permission.

Joanna Wagner. Illustration. Copyright © The Print Collector/Getty Images. Reprinted by permission.

Ken Hamidi. Photograph. Copyright © Ken Hamidi for Governor. Reprinted by permission.

Kenneth Feinberg. Photograph. Copyright © Alex Wong/Getty Images. Reprinted by permission.

King Canute. Illustration. Copyright © Hulton Archive/Getty Images. Reprinted by permission.

Kivalina, Alaska. Photograph. Copyright © Don Bartletti/Los Angeles Times via Getty Images. Reprinted by permission.

"Let's just say you both went up this hill to fetch a pail of water". Illustration. Copyright © Michael Maslin/The New Yorker Collection/The Cartoon Bank. Reprinted by permission.

Matt Drudge. Photograph. Copyright © Evan Agostini/Getty Images. Reprinted by permission.

Meryl Streep. Photograph. Copyright © Hulton-Deutsch Collection/Corbis. Reprinted by permission.

Motorola Sports Trax. Photograph. Copyright © Eric E. Johnson/Konomark. Reprinted by permission.

Ortho-Novum Dialpak dispenser. Photograph. Copyright © B Christopher/ Alamy. Reprinted by permission.

Paula Jones. Photograph. Copyright © Jamal A. Wilson/AFP/Getty Images. Reprinted by permission.

People Express. Photograph. Copyright © Scott McKiernan/ZUMA Wire/zumapress.com/Alamy Live News. Reprinted by permission.

Ralph Nader in 1967. Photograph. Copyright © AP Images. Reprinted by permission.

Richard Posner. Photograph. Copyright © University of Chicago Law School. Reprinted by permission.

Roger J. Traynor. Photograph. Copyright © Law School Archives, University of California, Berkeley. Reprinted by permission.

"Safety Last". Illustration. Copyright © Guy & Rodd/Distributed by Universal Uclick for UFS via CartoonStock.com. Reprinted by permission.

"Screens out harmful ultraviolet rays". Illustration. Copyright © Edward Frascino/The New Yorker Collection/The Cartoon Bank. Reprinted by permission.

Sidney Blumenthal. Photograph. Copyright © Tim Sloan/AFP/Getty Images. Reprinted by permission.

Sir Nicholas Conyngham Tindal. Copyright © Thomas Philips/National Portrait Gallery, London. Reprinted by permission.

Sir Thomas Littleton (Lyttleton). Illustration. Copyright © National Portrait Gallery, London. Reprinted by permission.

The Eden Roc and Fountainebleau hotels. Photograph. Copyright © Jordan Cerruti. Reprinted by permission.

The Empire State Building, New York City Blackout of 1977. Photograph. Copyright © Dan Farrell/New York Daily News Archive via Getty Images. Reprinted by permission.

The Return of the Pink Panther. Photograph. Copyright © AF Archive/Alamy. Reprinted by permission.

Tugboat John A. Bonker. Copyright © Atomic/Alamy. Reprinted by permission.

"Vioxx?" billboard. Photograph. Copyright © Bob Daemmrich/Corbis. Reprinted by permission.

Wagon Mound. Photograph. Copyright © Auke Vissier/Bulkers/Photobucket. Reprinted by permission.

"Well, gentlemen, I must say this is a coincidence". Illustration. Copyright © I. Klein/The New Yorker Collection/The Cartoon Bank. Reprinted by permission.

"We've got a class-action suit if ever I saw one". Illustration. Copyright © Mischa Richter/The New Yorker Collection/The Cartoon Bank. Reprinted by permission.

"Why carry malpractice insurance if you don't malpractice once in a while". Illustration. Illustration. Copyright © Peter Steiner/The New Yorker Collection/The Cartoon Bank. Reprinted by permission.

William Prosser. Photograph. Copyright © Law School Archives, University of California, Berkeley. Reprinted by permission.

Wisconsin State Journal staff in 1924. Photograph. Copyright © Wisconsin State Journal Archive. Reprinted by permission.

"You've got termites". Illustration. Copyright © Matthew Diffee/The New Yorker Collection/The Cartoon Bank. Reprinted by permission.

INTRODUCTION

The eleventh edition of this casebook appears four years after the tenth edition, and some 57 years after Charles O. Gregory and Harry Kalven, Jr., published the first edition of this casebook in 1959. Those 57 years have been marked by both continuity and change in the law. From the late 1950s until the mid-1980s, these changes tended to move largely in one direction. With the exception of the law of defamation and privacy, tort liability expanded on almost all fronts. Today, however, the picture is far more clouded. In the traditional areas of physical injuries, tort liability appears to have reached its high water mark, and in some jurisdictions—California and New York—the tides have been receding. There are now many cases in which eyebrows should be raised because liability has been denied, not because it has been found.

In the midst of these ebbs and flows in tort liability, certain questions have remained with us in more or less the same form in which they were faced by the earliest generations of common law lawyers. The tension between the principles of negligence and strict liability in stranger cases surely falls into this class. The debates framed in the nineteenth-century cases have largely shaped the subsequent analysis in important areas of the law, such as those dealing with abnormally dangerous activities and with private and public nuisances, all of which continue to take on additional importance in an age that shows greater preoccupation with environmental harms and toxic torts.

Yet in other areas we have witnessed major transformations, both in the types of cases brought to litigation, and in the choice of legal theories used to decide them. In 1959—the year of the first edition—the paradigmatic tort action was still the automobile collision. When one thought of institutional tort defendants, the railroads came first to mind. The areas of products liability and medical malpractice cases were, when viewed with the benefit of hindsight, still in their early childhood, while mass torts and toxic torts (the two often go together) still lay a decade or more in the future.

The emergence of new types of litigation has taken its toll on traditional tort theory. The question of "proximate cause"—whether a remote consequence could properly be attributed to the wrongful conduct of the defendant—was the dominant issue of causation in 1959 and the major source of contention among academic writers. That is no longer true today. Increasingly, modern tort litigation concentrates on two other problems. The first involves the difficult questions of evidence and statistics necessary to establish the factual connection between, for example, the defendant's drug or waste discharge and the medical injuries of the plaintiff. The second involves the rules designed to deal with multiple causation when two or more parties are charged with responsibility for all or part of the same harms, which happens in many nuisance and toxic tort cases. Both of these shifts in emphasis have accelerated in the past generation, and continue to be taken into account in this edition.

Notwithstanding the enormous substantive changes, the educational aims of this casebook are much the same as those of the previous ten editions. The primary goal remains one of giving to the student an accurate sense of both the legal evolution and the current legal position of tort law. In this context, that means incorporating into the book the output of the American Law Institute, which has now published multiple volumes of a Third Restatement dealing with Liability for Physical and Emotional Harm, Liability for Economic Harms, Apportionment of Liability Among Multiple Defendants, and Products Liability. It also means taking into account repeated rounds of legislative initiatives, which, not by coincidence alone, have taken place in the same areas that have generated the new Restatement output.

This casebook, however, would fail in its essential mission if it did not accomplish two other tasks. First, it should provide the student an opportunity to examine the processes of legal method and legal reasoning, with an eye to understanding the evolution of legal rules, and the huge impact that these changes have had on our social institutions. Second, it should give the student some sense of the different systematic and intellectual approaches that have been taken to the law of torts over the years.

The importance of understanding method and historical evolution cannot be underestimated in legal education. A casebook—certainly this casebook—is not a reference book, much less a treatise. Indeed with the rise of the online services, internal case and page references are cut back to a minimum, typically with no explicit indication of omitted citations, in order to improve the flow of the text. The great problem of legal work today does not lie in finding too little law, but in being overwhelmed by too much. A click on a single principal case puts you on a trail that branches off in a thousand directions. Faced with this surfeit of information, the standard legal curriculum, by necessity, touches on only a small fraction of the huge and ever-growing body of judicial decisions, Restatement provisions, statutory material, and academic literature, much of which will change with time. The education of the lawyer of the future therefore rests on an ability to isolate the key documents from a mass of legal materials, to identify the underlying assumptions, to determine possible implications for analogous cases, and, above all, to deal with the persistent uncertainty, ambiguity, and at times downright confusion in the law.

To help with these tasks, it is essential to trace the development of a legal principle over time, through a line of cases that illustrates its application and tests its limits. To that end this casebook contains many cases from the nineteenth century and before, even some that have long ceased to represent the current law. Much of the material in the eleventh edition does not represent modern cases, but earlier decisions whose intellectual value has survived the passage of decades, or even centuries, including one short but insightful passage from the Lombard laws on comparative negligence that dates from 733 A.D.! Likewise, in order to capture the nature of legal debate, in many principal cases we have reproduced not only the opinion of the court but those of concurring or dissenting judges. With Fletcher v. Rylands, *infra* at 97, for example, five separate opinions from three different courts are reproduced, because each adds something to the total picture. These cases are often of exceptional value because their interesting facts invite examination of subtle variations in judicial reasoning. The quality of the judicial arguments has also made these cases focal points for analysis in subsequent judicial opinions. Likewise in legal scholarship, modern treatments of complex issues tend to gravitate to the discussion of the classic cases that have already been studied by previous generations of scholars.

A sound legal education requires more than attention to doctrinal and analytical skills. The law of torts in particular is one of the richest bodies of substantive law, and it has been examined and explored from historical, philosophical, and institutional perspectives by judges and scholars alike. It is essential for all students to gain some sense of the diverse possible approaches to tort law, lest the constant probing with the Socratic method lead to an unhappy form of intellectual nihilism. The materials selected are designed, wherever possible, to allow torts to be confronted not only as a collection of discrete rules but also as a systematic intellectual discipline.

For the past four or five decades, judges and scholars have voiced fundamental disagreement about the proper orientation toward the tort law and about the proper choice of its key substantive rules. Speaking first to the question of intellectual orientation, it is possible to identify three major positions. The traditional view—which had unspoken dominance at the time when the first two editions appeared in 1959 and 1969—looked upon the law of torts as a study in corrective justice, that is, as an effort to develop a coherent set of principles to decide whether *this* plaintiff was entitled to compensation or other remedy from *this* defendant as a matter of fairness between the parties. Issues of public policy and social control were of course never absent from the judicial or academic discourse, but they did not dominate judicial or academic attitudes toward either particular cases or general theory. Fairness, justice, and equity, however elusive, were the dominant themes. Most laypeople, and many judges, instinctively approach most tort cases in just this fashion.

Over the past 40 or 50 years, the traditional approach has been under attack from two flanks. On the one hand there is continued insistence, which is sometimes expressly articulated in the cases, that the compensation of injured parties is in itself a valid end of the tort law, such that the doctrines of tort law that frustrate that objective must be hedged with limitations or totally eliminated unless strong justification is given for their retention. The older presumption that the plaintiff had to show "good cause" to hold a defendant liable (roughly speaking) has yielded in some quarters to a new presumption that the defendant who has demonstrably caused harm must show why liability should not be imposed. That shift in presumptions, which is today hotly contested, has two major implications. First, the risk of "inevitable accidents" shifts. These were usually borne by the plaintiff under the dominant view from the late nineteenth to the mid-twentieth century, both for private and institutional defendants. Yet once the presumption shifts, especially with institutional defendants (corporations, hospitals, professional practice groups), the risk of inevitable accidents tends to be shifted to defendants for both physical and emotional harm. Charging institutional defendants with tort liability, it is said, allows for the orderly shift of these individual losses to society at large, either by altering the nature and type of products sold and services provided, or by spreading the risk through liability insurance. Second, in suits against institutional defendants, defenses based on plaintiff's conduct—notably contributory negligence and assumption of risk—receive a narrower interpretation and rarely bar, but typically reduce, the plaintiff's recovery.

The second critique of the traditional approach comes from a different quarter, that of economic theory. Looking first at the tort law as a system of social control, advocates of the economic approach have generally argued that the proper function of the tort law is to lay down workable liability rules that create incentives for both individuals and firms to minimize (the sum of) the costs of accidents, the costs of their prevention, and the administrative costs of running the legal system. In this view of the subject, the compensation of individual parties is not an end in itself, but only a means to enlist private parties to help police the harmful activities of others. Tort law is thus understood as a part of a complex system that necessarily interacts with the criminal law and legislative and administrative regulation, not to mention contractual and customary limitations on proper conduct. Given its systematic orientation, this economic approach tends to downplay both the importance of corrective justice in the individual case and compensation for individual victims of accidents, treating the first as largely question-begging and the second as better achieved through voluntary first-party arrangements for life, health or disability insurance. Until very recently, its importance was largely academic, but today its influence in the decided cases is increasing. But it would be a mistake to state that current judicial decisions are dominated by the law and economics approach, or that it has displaced the traditional intuitive reliance on fairness—except perhaps with the hardy band of law professors turned judges.

The diversity of opinions on the proper approach to the tort law carries over to disputes about the proper substantive basis of tort liability. From the earliest times until today courts have entertained three main theories—each subject to many variants—for recovery in tort. There is, first, recovery for harms intentionally inflicted by the defendant on the person or property of the plaintiff. Second, there is recovery for harms negligently inflicted, that is, through the want of reasonable or ordinary care. Last, there is recovery under a theory of strict liability, that is, for harms inflicted on the plaintiff by a defendant who acts without negligence and without any intention to harm.

In dealing with these three theories it is important to keep in mind several recurrent themes. One set of issues concerns the relationships between the

TORTS: LIST OF CHAPTERS

TORTS
Richard A. Epstein
(Aspen Law & Business, 1999)

1 Intentional Torts
2 Defenses to Intentional Harms
3 Strict Liability and Negligence: History
4 Strict Liability and Negligence: Conceptual Foundations
5 Negligence: Reasonable People and Unreasonable Risks
6 Negligence: Custom and Statute
7 Proof of Negligence
8 Plaintiff's Conduct
9 Multiple Tortfeasors
10 Causation
11 Affirmative Duties
12 Owner's and Occupier's Liability
13 Traditional Strict Liability
14 Nuisance
15 Products Liability: Theory and History
16 Modern Products Liability Law
17 Damages
18 Defamation
19 Privacy
20 Misrepresentation
21 Economic Harms
22 Immunities

general approach to the law of torts and the choice of specific theories of liability in particular cases. When does a concern for corrective justice require the use of a strict liability principle, a negligence principle, or an intentional tort principle? What about theories based on the need for individual compensation or on the use of the tort law as a device for minimizing accident costs by channeling scarce resources to their most efficient use? Conversely, it is important to ask which *limitations* on recovery are consistent with the basic theories of liability and with their basic orientation to the subject matter. In this connection it is important to ask the extent to which recovery should be denied because of the plaintiff's own conduct — be it called contributory negligence or assumption of risk — the conduct of a third party, or an act of God when plaintiff has otherwise made out a good cause of action.

Finally, it is crucial to consider what might conveniently be termed the "boundary" questions in the law of torts. As stated, any of the three theories of liability — strict liability, negligence liability, or liability for intentional harms — could apply to any case involving physical, emotional, reputational, or economic harm. How do these different theories coexist across the full range of tort cases? To anticipate for a moment, does, for example, the commitment to a theory of strict liability in classical trespass cases — those involving the direct application of force on the person or property, both real and personal, of another — require (or allow) the use of a similar theory in cases involving slips and falls on business or residential premises or for the harm caused by those engaged in abnormally dangerous activities or the manufacture of dangerous products? Similarly, it must be asked whether the choice of a negligence theory in medical malpractice cases commits us to that theory for routine traffic accidents or whether a theory of intentional harms in assault cases commits us to that theory in defamation cases.

With our major conceptual dimensions identified, it is perhaps desirable to close this introduction with a brief summary about the organization of this book. The subject matter of the law of torts can be approached from a large number of different perspectives, and the order of organization is by no means "neutral," since instructors with one outlook are apt to gravitate to certain materials in one order while those with a different outlook are apt to gravitate to yet another. Here we have tried to adhere to traditional modes of presentation that can, it is hoped, be varied with minimum confusion to suit the tastes of different instructors.

Chapter 1 begins with an exploration of the principles of intentional harms to persons and land. This study can be conveniently concluded before turning to the bulk of the materials, which deal with physical harms caused by accident. The chapter covers first and foremost the cases of physical injuries to the person and to land. We have postponed the discussion of conversion and trespass to chattels to Chapter 7, where they are linked with other specific forms of strict liability. Once the analysis of the prima facie case is completed, the book addresses such distinctive defenses as consent, mental disability, self-defense, and private and public necessity. Once that is completed the chapter addresses the various harms associated with wrongful imprisonment and the intentional infliction of emotional distress.

Chapter 2 introduces the recurrent tension between negligence and strict liability in the context of accidental physical injuries by examining the two alternatives in both their historical and analytical aspects. The study spans nearly 500 years from the mid-fifteenth to the mid-twentieth century, first in England and then in the United States.

Chapter 3 then undertakes a detailed analysis of the negligence principle, which addresses the different interpretations that can be attached to the idea of unreasonable conduct, the role of custom and statute, and the issues of proof, with special attention to the doctrine of res ipsa loquitur, and to the role of judge and jury in trying negligence cases.

Chapter 4 turns to plaintiff's conduct, including contributory negligence, assumption of risk, and comparative negligence.

Chapter 5 then deals with two of the major issues of causation, cause-in-fact and proximate cause, as seen through both traditional and modern theories.

Chapter 6 addresses affirmative duties, most notably the duty to rescue people in distress. It examines this problem both in connection with strangers and then for persons with whom the defendant stands in some special relationship. This last category includes the full range of entrants onto land from invitees, licenses and trespassers. It also covers situations in which the defendant exercises some degree of control over other people, including children, students, tenants and even psychiatric patients.

Chapter 7 then deals with strict liability torts: animals, trespass to chattels, conversion, abnormally dangerous activities, and nuisance. It concludes with a discussion of the role of strict liability in dealing with vicarious liability.

Chapter 8 examines the evolution of products liability from its nineteenth-century preoccupation with privity to its modern applications in dealing with the three major classes of defects: namely those in manufacturing, design, and warning. It also addresses the ever more important question of whether and when federal regulation displaces the rights of action in duty to warn and design defect cases, which has been the subject of intense litigation in the U.S. Supreme Court in recent years.

Chapter 9 completes the exposition of the elements of the basic tort with an analysis of the rules for governing damages, both compensatory and punitive.

Chapter 10 goes beyond the tort system narrowly defined and deals with two topics: insurance and alternatives to the tort system. The insurance portion covers the rule of insurance in dealing with tort cases, including today's major coverage disputes for pollution and asbestos-related industries, as well as the conflicts of interest that arise between the insured and its insurers. The chapter then turns to alternatives to the tort system, workers' compensation and the various forms of no-fault insurance for automobiles, products (especially vaccines), medical accidents, as well the special scheme of compensation put into place for the victims of the 9/11 attacks. It concludes with a short discussion of the displacement of the tort law by New Zealand's comprehensive system of no-fault insurance.

Chapter 11 covers defamation from its common law origins to its constitutional complications, dealing both with the prima facie case of liability and the possible defenses to it, covering both truth defenses and the privileges available in suits brought by various persons against private and media defendants.

Chapter 12 then takes up the closely related issue of rights of privacy, both as they relate to the right of individuals to resist intrusions from the external world, and to control the use of their name and likeness, the so-called right of publicity.

The next two chapters of the book deal with more traditional economic relationships:

Chapter 13 is devoted to the law of misrepresentation (with a peek at modern securities law) under both theories of fraud and negligence.

Chapter 14 is directed to the general subject of economic harms, here defined as those harms that do not flow from either bodily injury or property damage to the plaintiff, but which covers inducement of breach of contract, interference with advantageous relations, and unfair competition.

Chapter 15 rounds out the discussion by dealing with immunities from all sorts of torts for private persons and for public bodies and officials under both state and federal law.

We have consciously edited the materials with an eye toward smoother reading. Unless the context otherwise seems to require, we have followed a loose convention of using the female pronoun for plaintiffs and the male pronoun for defendants. Citations to cases (and to cases within cases), footnotes, and other quoted material have been eliminated or simplified without any special indication, solely to remove clutter and preserve readability. The few footnotes that have been retained keep their original numbering for easier reference to the original materials. Footnotes added by the editors are indicated by an asterisk.

References to W. Prosser and W. Keeton on Torts (5th ed. 1984) are simply to Prosser and Keeton on Torts. References to F. Harper, F. James, and O. Gray, The Law of Torts (3d ed. 2007) are simply to Harper, James and Gray, Torts, unless an earlier edition is explicitly mentioned. Epstein has written a treatise on the law of torts (Torts, Aspen Law & Business 1999), but we have refrained from giving citations to it in this volume, lest they appear with monotonous regularity. But we have included a List of Chapters for that book, which indicates its coverage (see page xxxix). Virtually all of the issues that are covered in this casebook are also covered in *Torts.*

LIST OF ABBREVIATIONS

Abbreviation	Full Citation
A.C.	Appeals Cases (to the House of Lords)
C.F.R.	Code of Federal Regulations
ILCS	Illinois Compiled Statutes
K.B.	King's Bench
MPC	Model Penal Code
Q.B.	Queen's Bench
RT	Restatement of Torts
RST	Restatement (Second) of Torts
RTT: LEH	Restatement (Third) of Torts: Liability for Economic Harm
RTT: LPEH	Restatement (Third) of Torts: Liability for Physical and Emotional Harm
RTT: PL	Restatement (Third) of Torts: Products Liability
RTUC	Restatement (Third) Unfair Competition
RSA	Restatement (Second) of Agency

CASES AND MATERIALS ON TORTS

PART ONE

PHYSICAL AND EMOTIONAL HARMS

Intentional Harms:
The Prima Facie Case
and Defenses

SECTION A. INTRODUCTION

It is best to begin our study of tort law with intentional harms. At first blush, these torts are the easiest to comprehend, because no society can survive if all of its individual members are free to kill and injure strangers whenever they wish to do so. But even though most people think they understand a punch in the nose, it is only on reflection that it becomes clear punches in the nose come in all sizes and shapes. Intuitively, then, deliberate injuries are the first order of business. However, conceptual and practical complications immediately arise. First, the law often distinguishes between the intent to commit an act that causes harm and the intent to cause the harm itself. Why and how is that distinction important? How does the tort conception of intention differ from the criminal conception of mens rea (the guilty mind)? Second, once the plaintiff has established her prima facie case for liability, what excuses and justifications are available to the defendant, and to what qualifications are they subject?

The intentional harms have traditionally covered a wide range of interests. Most obviously, the law guards against physical harm to person or property. It also protects people against forcible dispossession of their land and against the taking, or conversion, of their personal property. Finally, it extends its protection against assaults, defined as threats, even if not acted on, to use force against the person, and (somewhat more haltingly) to affronts to personal dignity and emotional tranquility. The first part of the chapter discusses physical harms, which include the torts of battery (or trespass to the person) and trespass to real property. In addition, it examines the full range of defenses based on consent, insanity, defense of person and property, and necessity. The second part of the chapter examines the torts designed to protect dignitary or emotional interests:

assault and offensive battery, false imprisonment, and the intentional infliction of emotional distress, as well as the interplay between the plaintiff's prima facie case and the available defenses.

SECTION B. PHYSICAL HARMS

1. Trespass to Person and Land

Vosburg v. Putney
50 N.W. 403 (Wis. 1891)

The action was brought to recover damages for an assault and battery, alleged to have been committed by the defendant upon the plaintiff on February 20, 1889. The answer is a general denial. At the date of the alleged assault the plaintiff was a little more than fourteen years of age, and the defendant a little less than twelve years of age.

The injury complained of was caused by a kick inflicted by defendant upon the leg of the plaintiff, a little below the knee. The transaction occurred in a schoolroom in Waukesha, during school hours, both parties being pupils in the school. A former trial of the cause resulted in a verdict and judgment for the plaintiff for $2,800. The defendant appealed from such judgment to this court, and the same was reversed for error, and a new trial awarded.

[A more complete statement of the facts is found in the earlier opinion by Orton, J., 47 N.W. 99, 99 (Wis. 1890), on the initial appeal to the Wisconsin Supreme Court: "The plaintiff was about 14 years of age, and the defendant about 11 years of age. On the 20th day of February, 1889, they were sitting opposite to each other across an aisle in the high school of the village of Waukesha. The defendant reached across the aisle with his foot, and hit with his toe the shin of the right leg of the plaintiff. The touch was slight. The plaintiff did not feel it, either on account of its being so slight or of loss of sensation produced by the shock. In a few moments he felt a violent pain in that place, which caused him to cry out loudly. The next day he was sick, and had to be helped to school. On the fourth day he was vomiting, and Dr. Bacon was sent for, but could not come, and he sent medicine to stop the vomiting, and came to see him the next day, on the 25th. There was a slight discoloration of the skin entirely over the inner surface of the tibia an inch below the bend of the knee. The doctor applied fomentations, and gave him anodynes to quiet the pain. This treatment was continued, and the swelling so increased by the 5th day of March that counsel was called, and on the 8th of March an operation was performed on the limb by making an incision, and a moderate amount of pus escaped. A drainage tube was inserted, and an iodoform dressing put on. On the sixth day after this, another incision was made to the bone, and it was found that destruction was going on in the bone, and so it has continued exfoliating pieces of bone. He will never recover the use of his limb. There were black and blue spots on the shin bone, indicating that there had been a blow. On the 1st day of January before, the plaintiff received an injury just above the knee of the same leg by coasting, which appeared to be healing up and drying down at the time of the last injury. The theory of at least one of the medical witnesses was that the limb was in a diseased condition when this touch or kick was given, caused by microbes entering in through the wound above the knee, and which were revivified by the touch, and that the touch was the exciting or remote cause of the destruction of the bone, or of the plaintiff's injury. It does not appear that there was any visible mark made or left by this touch or kick of the defendant's foot, or any appearance of injury until the black and blue spots were discovered by the physician several days afterwards, and then there were more spots than one. There was no proof of any other hurt, and the medical testimony seems to have been agreed that this touch or kick was the exciting cause of the injury to the plaintiff. The jury rendered a verdict for the plaintiff of $2,800. The learned circuit judge said to the jury: 'It is a peculiar case, an unfortunate case, a case, I think I am at liberty to say that ought not to have come into court. The parents of these children ought, in some way, if possible, to have adjusted it between themselves.' We have much of the same feeling about the case."]

The case has been again tried in the circuit court, and the trial resulted in a verdict for plaintiff for $2,500. . . .

On the last trial the jury found a special verdict, as follows: "(1) Had the plaintiff during the month of January, 1889, received an injury just above the knee, which became inflamed, and produced pus? *Answer.* Yes. (2) Had such injury on the 20th day of February, 1889, nearly healed at the point of the injury? *A.* Yes. (3) Was the plaintiff, before said 20th of February, lame, as the result of such injury? *A.* No. (4) Had the tibia in the plaintiff's right leg become inflamed or diseased to some extent before he received the blow or kick from the defendant? *A.* No. (5) What was the exciting cause of the injury to the plaintiff's leg? *A.* Kick. (6) Did the defendant, in touching the plaintiff with his foot, intend to do him any harm? *A.* No. (7) At what sum do you assess the damages of the plaintiff? *A.* $2,500."

The defendant moved for judgment in his favor on the verdict, and also for a new trial. The plaintiff moved for judgment on the verdict in his favor. The motions of defendant were overruled, and that of the plaintiff granted. Thereupon judgment for plaintiff for $2,500 damages and costs of suit was duly entered. The defendant appeals from the judgment.

LYON, J. The jury having found that the defendant, in touching the plaintiff with his foot, did not intend to do him any harm, counsel for defendant maintain that the plaintiff has no cause of action, and that defendant's motion for judgment on the special verdict should have been granted. In support of this proposition counsel quote from 2 Greenl. Ev. §83, the rule that "the intention to do harm is of the essence of an assault." Such is the rule, no doubt, in actions or prosecutions for mere assaults. But this is an action to recover damages for an alleged assault and battery. In such case the rule is correctly stated, in many of the authorities cited by counsel, that plaintiff must show either that the intention was unlawful, or that the defendant is in fault. If the intended act is unlawful, the intention to commit it must necessarily be unlawful. Hence, as applied to this case, if the kicking of the plaintiff by the defendant was an unlawful act, the intention of defendant to kick him was also unlawful.

Had the parties been upon the play-grounds of the school, engaged in the usual boyish sports, the defendant being free from malice, wantonness, or negligence, and intending no harm to plaintiff in what he did, we should hesitate to hold the act of the defendant unlawful, or that he could be held liable in this action. Some consideration is due to the implied license of the play-grounds. But it appears that the injury was inflicted in the school, after it had been called to order by the teacher, and after the regular exercises of the school had commenced. Under these circumstances, no implied license to do the act complained of existed, and such act was a violation of the order and decorum of the school, and necessarily unlawful. Hence we are of the opinion that, under the evidence and verdict, the action may be sustained.

Certain questions were proposed on behalf of defendant to be submitted to the jury, founded upon the theory that only such damages could be recovered as the defendant might reasonably be supposed to have contemplated as likely to result from his kicking the plaintiff. The court refused to submit such questions to the jury. The ruling was correct. The rule of damages in actions for torts was held [in a prior case] to be that the wrong-doer is liable for all injuries resulting directly from the wrongful act, whether they could or could not have been foreseen by him. The chief justice and the writer of this opinion dissented from the judgment in that [prior] case, chiefly because we were of the opinion that the complaint stated a cause of action ex contractu [out of contract], and not ex delicto [out of tort], and hence that a different rule of damages—the rule here contended for—was applicable. We did not question that the rule in actions for tort was correctly stated. That case rules this on the question of damages.

[Judgment was reversed, and the case was remanded for a new trial because of error in a ruling on an objection to certain testimony.]

NOTES

1. *Vosburg v. Putney: the backstory and aftermath.*   For well over 100 years, *Vosburg* has remained one of the most storied cases in American law. In *Vosburg v. Putney: A Centennial Story*, 1992 Wis. L. Rev. 877, Professor Zile probes every aspect of the legal proceedings and their social setting. The plaintiff, Andrew Vosburg, was a sickly boy from an ordinary farming background, whereas the defendant, George Putney, was the scion of a wealthy and prominent Wisconsin family whose ancestors arrived in Massachusetts in 1637. Zile further describes the newspaper publicity surrounding the case, its political overtones, the low-level criminal proceedings in justice court brought against the defendant, and the possible medical malpractice action lurking in the background.

And what happened to Andrew Vosburg and George Putney after that fateful day at the schoolhouse? Putney finished his education at Union School, graduated from high school, enrolled at University of Wisconsin, but left during sophomore year. He returned to Waukesha, clerked at his family's general store, got married, moved to Milwaukee, and eventually became a salesman, first of clothing, then of cars. He died on June 13, 1940. Andrew Vosburg, in 1900, was hired by the Milwaukee Electric Railroad, rose to foreman, married, had three children, and, along with his wife, made a living buying, refurbishing, and selling homes. Although a laced leather brace limited his activities, he otherwise led a normal life and died on October 4, 1938, at 64.

2. Defendant's intention and plaintiff's conduct.   Which, if any, of the jury's answers to the first six questions may be incorrect in light of the medical evidence? Given the jury's response to the sixth question, can the defendant's act be treated as an intentional tort? Does it make a difference that the teacher had already called the class to order when the kick landed? If the pupils typically tapped each other on the leg under the desk to get each other's attention after the class had been called to order, should defendant's act be excused by the "implied license of the classroom"? Should a defendant's actual malice, wantonness, and negligence all be treated the same way for playground injuries? Should plaintiff have worn a shin guard to protect his leg from further injury? Should he have stayed home from school?

3. Whither "unlawful" intent?   In Garratt v. Dailey, 279 P.2d 1091 (Wash. 1955), and 304 P.2d 681 (Wash. 1956), the plaintiff, an adult woman, brought a battery suit against Brian Dailey, a boy five years and nine months old, who caused her fractured hip when he was a guest in her backyard. Sharp factual disputes required two trials and two appellate decisions to resolve. The defendant claimed that he had tried to help the plaintiff by placing a chair under her as she was about to fall, but that he was too small to move it properly into place. His version was accepted by the trial judge at the first trial. However, the plaintiff's sister, who was present at the occasion, testified that the plaintiff, an "arthritic woman[,] had begun the slow process of being seated when the defendant quickly removed the chair and seated himself upon it, and that he knew, with substantial certainty at the time, that she would attempt to sit in the place where the chair had been."

On appeal from the first judgment, 279 P.2d 1091, 1093-1094, the Washington Supreme Court addressed the issue of intent in the tort of battery:

> It is urged that Brian's action in moving the chair constituted a battery. A definition (not all-inclusive but sufficient for our purpose) of a battery is the intentional infliction of a harmful bodily contact upon another. . . .
>
> We have here the conceded volitional act of Brian, i.e., the moving of a chair. Had the plaintiff proved to the satisfaction of the trial court that Brian moved the chair while she was in the act of sitting down, Brian's action would patently have been for the purpose or with the intent of causing the plaintiff's bodily contact with the ground, and she would be entitled to a judgment against him for the resulting damages. Vosburg v. Putney. . . .
>
> A battery would be established if, in addition to plaintiff's fall, it was proved that, when Brian moved the chair, he knew with substantial certainty that the plaintiff would attempt to sit down where the chair had been. . . .
>
> The mere absence of any intent to injure the plaintiff or to play a prank on her

or to embarrass her, or to commit an assault and battery on her would not absolve him from liability if in fact he had such knowledge. Without such knowledge, there would be nothing wrongful about Brian's act in moving the chair and, there being no wrongful act, there would be no liability.

On remand, the trial judge accepted the testimony of the plaintiff's sister, and awarded the plaintiff $11,000. That judgment was upheld on the second appeal. Is removing a chair tantamount to striking the plaintiff?

4. The Restatement account of intention in battery cases.   The common law of torts has been "codified" in the Restatement of Torts [RT], which was published in 1934 by the American Law Institute, an organization founded in 1923 following a study conducted by the Committee on the Establishment of a Permanent Organization for the Improvement of the Law, a group composed of 40 American judges, lawyers, and academics.

The Restatement of Torts was prepared by a large and distinguished team of judges, practicing lawyers, and academics, with Professor Francis H. Bohlen as its chief reporter. The Restatement, as its name implies, emphasizes "restating" rather than "reforming" the law, but interstitial reform often occurs whenever the law is in flux or some conflict persists among the various states. The Restatement (Second) of Torts [RST] appeared in four volumes, published between 1965 and 1979. The first 280 sections of the Second Restatement are devoted to every aspect of intentional torts.

In contrast, the Restatement (Third) of Torts [RTT] has not been organized as a unified project. Instead, different volumes of the RTT dealing with discrete topics have been released at different times. At present, the major volume dealing with physical harms is the Restatement (Third) of Torts: Liability for Physical and Emotional Harm [RTT:LPEH]. The other finished volumes, to date, include Apportionment of Liability (Reporters William Powers, Jr. and Michael Green) and Products Liability (Reporters James Henderson and Aaron Twerski). A further volume, Liability for Economic Harm (Reporter Ward Farnsworth), is in tentative draft form as of 2015. Portions of the draft of a fifth volume, Intentional Torts to Persons (Reporter Kenneth Simons), were approved at the 2015 Annual Meeting of the ALI. In 2015, the ALI announced the launch of a Property Torts project (Reporters Henry Smith and John Goldberg).

It is instructive to compare the definitional provisions of the RST with those of the RTT.

How does RST §13 square with the results in *Vosburg* and *Garratt?* The Restatement uses the term intention "to denote that the actor desires to cause consequences of his act, or that he believes that the consequences are substantially certain to result from it." RST §8A; RTT:LPEH §1. Note also that both the Second and Third Restatements approve of the result in *Vosburg,* which the former describes as follows: "Intending an offensive contact, *A* lightly kicks *B* on the shin." RST §16, comment *a,* illus. 1. Did the court in *Vosburg* treat the case as one of offensive battery?

Restatement of the Law (Second) of Torts

§13. BATTERY: HARMFUL CONDUCT

An actor is subject to liability to another for battery if
(a) he acts intending to cause a harmful or offensive contact with the person of the other or a third person, or an imminent apprehension of such a contact, and
(b) a harmful contact with the person of the other directly or indirectly results.

Restatement of the Law (Third) of Torts: Liability for Physical and Emotional Harm

§1. INTENT

A person acts with the intent to produce a consequence if:
(a) the person acts with the purpose of producing that consequence; or
(b) the person acts knowing that the consequence is substantially certain to result.

Illustration 2: Wendy throws a rock at Andrew, someone she dislikes, at a distance of 100 feet, wanting to hit Andrew. Given the distance, it is far from certain Wendy will succeed in this; rather, it is probable that the rock will miss its target. In fact, Wendy's aim is true, and Andrew is struck by the rock. Wendy has purposely, and hence intentionally, caused this harm.

Although the Restatement provisions are powerful authority, sometimes courts reject them. In White v. University of Idaho, 797 P.2d 108 (Idaho 1990), the defendant Neher, a music professor, was a social guest in the house of the plaintiff, one of his piano students. While she was writing, "Professor Neher walked up behind her and touched her back with both of his hands in a movement later described as one a pianist would make in striking and lifting the fingers from a keyboard." The plaintiff claimed she suffered a strong adverse reaction, which necessitated the removal of a rib, and damage to her brachial plexus nerve that required the severing of her scalenus anterior muscles. The professor claimed he touched Mrs. White to show her the sensation of certain forms of playing, but meant no harm. She countered that the touching was nonconsensual. The court held that she stated a valid claim for battery even though the defendant had not meant to either harm or offend her. The court brushed aside any attempt to incorporate the requirement of offensive intent, noting curtly that "we have not previously adopted the Restatement (Second) in Idaho and decline any invitation to do it now." Given that the University had immunity from suits arising out of intentional torts committed by its employees, the court's battery holding amounted to a finding of no liability on the part of the University. The Restatement (Third) of Torts: Intentional Torts has embraced *White*'s "single intent" standard. See RTT:IT §102.

Restatement of the Law (Third) of Torts: Intentional Torts to Persons (Tentative Draft No. 1, Apr. 8, 2015)

§102. BATTERY: REQUIRED INTENT

The intent required for battery is the intent to cause a contact with the person of another. The actor need not intend to cause harm or offense to the other.

Comment b. Single intent v. dual intent: . . . The single-intent approach affords greater protection to the plaintiff's interest in bodily integrity, and can be understood as imposing a modest degree of strict liability, insofar as the actor is liable although he might have genuinely and even reasonably believed that the contact he caused would not cause harm or offense. By contrast, the dual-intent approach is more consistent with the view that liability for battery should exist only when the actor is especially culpable—and in particular, more culpable than a negligent or strictly liable actor. . . .

Illustration 2: Stephanie approaches Carol, a new coworker in her office, from behind. "You look tense!" Stephanie declares, and immediately begins giving Carol a vigorous neck massage. When Carol objects, Stephanie promptly ends the massage. The massage injures Carol's neck and requires her to miss several weeks of work. Stephanie is subject to liability to Carol for battery.

---

5. *Transferred intent.*   In Talmage v. Smith, 59 N.W. 656, 657 (Mich. 1894), the plaintiff was struck in the eye by a stick that the defendant threw at two of the plaintiff's companions while they were trespassing upon the defendant's property. The defendant asserted that he did not see the plaintiff, much less intend to hurt him. The court held this contention immaterial: "The right of the plaintiff to recover was made to depend upon an intention on the part of the defendant to

hit somebody, and to inflict an unwarranted injury upon someone. Under these circumstances, the fact that the injury resulted to another than was intended does not relieve the defendant from responsibility." Does it matter whether the injured plaintiff was trespassing on defendant's property? See generally Prosser, Transferred Intent, 45 Tex. L. Rev. 650 (1967).

6. Governmental immunity. The traditional form of sovereign immunity for the United States was waived by the Federal Tort Claims Act, 28 U.S.C. §§2671-2680 (2012), which contains an important exception for "[a]ny claim arising out of assault, battery, false imprisonment, false arrest, malicious prosecution . . ." 28 U.S.C. §2680 (h). In Sheridan v. United States, 487 U.S. 392, 403 (1988), that exception insulated the government from liability when an obviously intoxicated off-duty serviceman fired several rifle shots that injured the plaintiffs, while riding in their automobiles. But that exception did not apply to the plaintiffs' further claim that three naval corpsmen were negligent when, having previously discovered the serviceman "lying face down in a drunken stupor" with a loaded weapon, they failed to take him into custody or to alert the appropriate officials that he was on the prowl.

Similar results have obtained at the state level. In City of Watuaga v. Gordon, 434 S.W.3d 586, 592 (Tex. 2014), a police officer was sued for placing handcuffs too tightly on an arrestee. The plaintiff sought to frame his case in negligence in order to avoid exemption for assault and battery in the Texas Tort Claims Act, but was rebuffed by Devine, J., who gave a broad definition to the tort:

> Although a specific intent to inflict injury is without question an intentional tort, and many batteries are of this type, a specific intent to injure is not an essential element of a battery. . . . [A] battery does not require a physical injury, and thus it follows that an intentional physical injury is also not required. In fact, even a harmful or offensive contact that is intended to help or please the plaintiff can be actionable as a battery.

The Utah sovereign immunity for the tort of assault was in play in Wagner v. State, 122 P.3d 599, 601-602 (Utah 2005), in which the plaintiff insisted that Sam Giese, a mentally disabled man in the care of the Utah State Development Center, did not form an intention to harm her when he attacked her inexplicably in a K-Mart store. The court held that the state could claim sovereign immunity because Giese's conduct constituted an assault under the Restatement definition of battery: "A person need not intend to cause harm or appreciate that his contact will cause harm so long as he intends to make a contact, and that contact is harmful." The opposite view concerning intention was taken in White v. Muniz, 999 P.2d 814, 818 (Colo. 2000), in which a mentally disabled Alzheimer's patient, not in government care, was sued for assaulting and battering her caregiver. There the court held that Colorado law "requires the jury to conclude that the defendant both intended the contact and intended it to be harmful or offensive." See also McGuire v. Almy, *infra* at 28.

Dougherty v. Stepp

18 N.C. 371 (1835)

This was an action of trespass quare clausum fregit [wherefore he broke the close], tried at Buncombe on the last Circuit, before his Honor Judge MARTIN. The only proof introduced by the plaintiff to establish an act of trespass, was, that the defendant had entered on the unenclosed land of the plaintiff, with a surveyor and chain carriers, and actually surveyed a part of it, claiming it as his own, but without marking trees or cutting bushes. This, his Honor held not to be a trespass, and the jury, under his instructions, found a verdict for the defendant, and the plaintiff appealed.

RUFFIN, C.J. In the opinion of the Court, there is error in the instructions given to the jury. The amount of damages may depend on the acts done on the land, and the extent of injury to it therefrom. But it is an elementary principle, that every unauthorised, and therefore unlawful entry, into the close of another, is a trespass. From every such entry against the will of the possessor, the law infers some damage; if nothing more, the treading down the grass or the herbage or as here, the shrubbery. Had the locus in quo been under cultivation or enclosed, there would have been no doubt of the plaintiff's right to recover. Now our Courts have for a long time past held, that if there be no adverse possession, the title makes the land the owner's close. Making the survey and marking trees, or making it without marking, differ only in the degree, and not in the nature of the injury. It is the entry that constitutes the trespass. There is no statute, nor rule of reason, that will make a wilful entry into the land of another, upon an unfounded claim of right, innocent, which one, who sat up no title to the land, could not justify or excuse. On the contrary, the pretended ownership aggravates the wrong. Let the judgment be reversed, and a new trial granted.

Judgment reversed.

NOTES

1. Traditional forms of trespass to real property. Trespass quare clausum fregit (or trespass q.c.f.) has long been granted to protect the plaintiff's interest in the exclusive possession of land and its improvements. It has been long settled that a trespass to real property takes place not only on the surface, but also with respect to any intrusion above or below the surface of the land. Thus in Hutchinson v. Schimmelfeder, 40 Pa. 396, 397 (1861), the Supreme Court of Pennsylvania upheld the following jury instruction:

> If two persons own adjoining lots which lie below the grade of the street on which they front, and either wishes to grade his lot up to the street, he must build a wall on his own ground, or in some other way keep the dirt within his own line. He cannot so fill up his own lot as to let the earth pass over his line on the lot of his neighbor.

Is there any direct act of trespass? Should it matter? In Smith v. Smith, 110 Mass. 302 (1872), the defendant was adjudged a trespasser when the eaves of his barn overhung the plaintiff's land. Further, in Neiswonger v. Goodyear Tire and Rubber Co., 35 F.2d 761 (N.D. Ohio 1929), airplane overflights within 500 feet of the ground, in violation of air traffic rules established by the Department of Commerce, were also treated as common law trespasses. The strict nature of the prima facie case should not exclude any justification for entry onto the land. Could the plaintiff in *Dougherty* have pleaded some necessity for entrance given his desire to determine whether he in fact owned the land? Or should he have gotten a court order to make the survey?

2. *Intention and damages in trespass to real property.* Owing to the passive and immovable nature of real property, the courts have generally adopted stringent standards of liability whenever the trespass results in actual harm. In Brown v. Dellinger, 355 S.W.2d 742, 747 (Tex. Civ. App. 1962), two children, aged seven and eight, were held liable for the loss of the plaintiff's $28,000 home. The court observed:

> The acts of the minor defendants in bringing matches onto the premises of [plaintiff] and igniting the fire in the charcoal burner in [plaintiff's] garage were all voluntary and purposeful and were acts which they even at their tender years had sufficient capacity to do, as evidenced by the fact that they did do such acts. Undoubtedly they did not intend for the fire to escape from the grill and spread to the curtain canvas and burn and damage the garage, house and contents thereof. However their acts of igniting an unauthorized fire on [plaintiff's] premises made them trespassers, and they must be held civilly liable for the consequences which directly flowed from their unauthorized acts of igniting the fire in question.

If the plaintiff's charcoal burner had been defective and the defendants had used it with all possible care, should the plaintiff still recover? If the defendants had been burned while using the defective burner, could they recover from the plaintiff for their personal injuries? If the defendants had started the fire on their own property, could the plaintiff recover under *Brown* if the fire had spread to his premises?

In Cleveland Park Club v. Perry, 165 A.2d 485, 487-489 (D.C. 1960), the plaintiff operated a social club for the benefit of its members. One day while the defendant, a nine-year-old boy, was using the swimming pool, he dove down to a depth of seven feet, "and thinking there was no suction at the time," removed the drain cover and inserted a rubber ball. The ball was caught in a narrow portion of a pipe where it caused extensive damage, requiring the pool to be closed for repairs. The judgment for the defendant at trial was reversed on appeal, and a new trial ordered. The court stressed that in trespass cases "the intent controlling is the intent to complete the physical act and not the intent to cause injurious consequences." Did the defendant intend to place the ball in the mouth of the drain, or in the middle of the pipe? What weight should be given to his mistaken belief that there was no suction? Should it make a difference if the defendant was on the premises with the plaintiff's permission? Could the defendants in *Garratt*, *Brown*, and *Cleveland Park* be held liable on a negligence theory? See *infra* Chapter 3, Section A.

See generally Epstein, Intentional Harms, 4 J. Legal Stud. 391 (1975), for an account of the role that different understandings of intention play in shaping the substantive tort law.

3. Intangible trespasses.   In Public Service Co. of Colorado v. Van Wyk, 27 P.3d 377, 390 (Colo. 2001), the plaintiff sued in trespass for the harm attributable to the noise, radiation, and electromagnetic fields that resulted from an upgrade in Public Service's utility system that had been approved by the state Public Utility Commission. Martinez, J., distinguished this case from physical trespasses in which particulate matter is deposited on the plaintiff's land despite no visible intrusion, and held that, unlike claims for physical invasions,

> . . . an intangible intrusion may give rise to a claim for trespass, but only if an aggrieved party is able to prove physical damage to the property caused by such intangible intrusion.
>
> Our holding here is consistent with the historical requirement of an entry or use that interferes with possession for trespass liability to be established. The requirement that the intangible intrusion be intentional, and that a plaintiff prove physical damage caused by the intrusion, safeguards against the concern that allowing trespass claims against intangible intrusions would produce too much liability. Moreover, a property owner forced to prove damage will be further limited to seeking redress in cases of serious or substantial invasions. The difficulty in proving a connection between a minor damage and an intangible intrusion is too great to support mass litigiousness on the part of pestered property owners.

Martinez, J., also sustained plaintiff's nuisance claim that the defendant's actions depreciated the value of their property, caused mental distress, and deprived them of the quiet use and enjoyment of their land. Why do those not count as consequential losses from the trespass? See *infra* Chapter 7, Section E.

In Bickerstaff v. Halliburton Energy Services, Inc., 2015 WL 4208702 (W.D. Okla. 2015), the question before the court was "whether [perchlorate groundwater] contamination . . . should be considered a tangible or an intangible trespass." Miles-LaGrange, J., held that "because the perchlorate contamination at issue in this case is impalpable and imperceptible by the senses, plaintiffs' trespass claims should be analyzed as an intangible trespass," which required showing "substantial damage to their properties." Is the definition of intangible trespass in *Bickerstaff* the same as in *Van Wyk*?

2. Defenses to Intentional Torts

a. Consensual Defenses

Mohr v. Williams
104 N.W. 12 (Minn. 1905)

BROWN, J. Defendant is a physician and surgeon of standing and character, making disorders of the ear a specialty, and having an extensive practice in the city of St. Paul. He was consulted by plaintiff, who complained to him of trouble with her right ear, and, at her request, made an examination of that organ for the purpose of ascertaining its condition. He also at the same time examined her left ear, but, owing to foreign substances therein, was unable to make a full and complete diagnosis at that time. The examination of her right ear disclosed a large perforation in the lower portion of the drum membrane, and a large polyp in the middle ear, which indicated that some of the small bones of the middle ear (ossicles) were probably diseased. He informed plaintiff of the result of his examination, and advised an operation for the purpose of removing the polyp and diseased ossicles. After consultation with her family physician, and one or two further consultations with defendant, plaintiff decided to submit to the proposed operation. She was not informed that her left ear was in any way diseased, and understood that the necessity for an operation applied to her right ear only. She repaired to the hospital, and was placed under the influence of anaesthetics; and, after being made unconscious, defendant made a thorough examination of her left ear, and found it in a more serious condition than her right one. A small perforation was discovered high up in the drum membrane, hooded, and with granulated edges, and the bone of the inner wall of the middle ear was diseased and dead. He called this discovery to the attention of Dr. Davis — plaintiff's family physician, who attended the operation at her request — who also examined the ear and confirmed defendant in his diagnosis. Defendant also further examined the right ear, and found its condition less serious than expected, and finally concluded that the left, instead of the right, should be operated upon; devoting to the right ear other treatment. He then performed the operation of ossiculectomy on plaintiff's left ear; removing a portion of the drum membrane, and scraping away the diseased portion of the inner wall of the ear. The operation was in every way successful and skillfully performed. It is claimed by plaintiff that the operation greatly impaired her hearing, seriously injured her person, and, not having been consented to by her, was wrongful and unlawful, constituting an assault and battery; and she brought this action to recover damages therefor.

The trial in the court below resulted in a verdict for plaintiff for $14,322.50. [The trial judge set aside the verdict as excessive and ordered a new trial. Both parties appealed from those orders. On appeal Brown, J., first refused to overturn the jury's finding of no emergency. He then held that plaintiff's consent to the operation could not be implied, and said in part:]

The last contention of defendant is that the act complained of did not amount to an assault and battery. This is based upon the theory that, as plaintiff's left ear was in fact diseased, in a condition dangerous and threatening to her health, the operation was necessary, and, having been skillfully performed at a time when plaintiff had requested a like operation on the other ear, the charge of assault and battery cannot be sustained; that, in view of these conditions, and the claim that there was no negligence on the part of defendant, and an entire absence of any evidence tending to show an evil intent, the court should say, as a matter of law, that no assault and battery was committed, even though she did not consent to the operation. In other words, that the absence of a showing that defendant was actuated by a wrongful intent, or guilty of negligence, relieves the act of defendant from the charge of an unlawful assault and battery.

We are unable to reach that conclusion, though the contention is not without merit. It would seem to follow from what has been said on the other features of the case that the act of defendant amounted at least to a technical assault and battery. If the operation was performed without plaintiff's consent, and the circumstances were not such as to justify its performance without, it was wrongful; and, if it was wrongful, it was unlawful. As remarked in 1 Jaggard, Torts, 437, every person has a right to complete immunity of his person from physical interference of others, except in so far as contact may be necessary under the general doctrine of privilege; and any unlawful or unauthorized touching of the person of another, except it be in the spirit of pleasantry, constitutes an assault and battery. In the case at bar, as we have already seen, the question whether defendant's act in performing the operation upon plaintiff was authorized was a question for the jury to determine. If it was unauthorized, then it was, within what we have said, unlawful. It was a violent assault, not a mere pleasantry; and, even though no negligence is shown, it was wrongful and unlawful. The case is unlike a criminal prosecution for assault and battery, for there an unlawful intent must be shown. But that rule does not apply to a civil action, to maintain which it is sufficient to show that the assault complained of was wrongful and unlawful or the result of negligence. . . . Vosburg v. Putney, 80 Wis. 523, 50 N.W. 403.

The amount of plaintiff's recovery, if she is entitled to recover at all, must depend upon the character and extent of the injury inflicted upon her, in determining which the nature of the malady intended to be healed and the beneficial nature of the operation should be taken into consideration, as well as the good faith of the defendant.

Orders affirmed.

NOTES

1. Determining the scope of consent.   Did the physician in Mohr v. Williams violently attack or batter his patient solely because he did not obtain the requisite consent to perform the operation? Should Dr. Davis be treated as the plaintiff's agent? Why did the trial judge conclude that the jury awarded excessive damages? (On remand, the jury awarded only nominal damages.) More modern cases take a less rigid view of the consent requirement. In Kennedy v. Parrott, 90 S.E.2d 754, 759 (N.C. 1956), the defendant surgeon, while performing an appendectomy on the plaintiff, discovered several large cysts on the plaintiff's left ovary. Exercising his best medical judgment, he intentionally punctured the cysts, without negligence. Unfortunately, the puncture cut one of plaintiff's blood vessels, from which she developed a painful phlebitis in her leg. The court rejected her claim for trespass even though she did not consent to the puncturing of the cysts, noting that in modern hospital settings surgeons could no longer turn to the guidance of family members. It concluded:

In major internal operations, both the patient and the surgeon know that the exact condition of the patient cannot be finally and definitely diagnosed until after the patient is completely anesthetized and the incision has been made. In such case the consent—in the absence of proof to the contrary—will be construed as general in nature and the surgeon may extend the operation to remedy any abnormal or diseased condition in the area of the original incision whenever he, in the exercise of his sound professional judgment, determines that correct surgical procedure dictates and requires such an extension of the operation originally contemplated. This rule applies when the patient is at the time incapable of giving consent, and no one with authority to consent for him is immediately available.

Does *Kennedy* support the conventional view that "the absence of consent is a matter essential to the cause of action, and it is uniformly held that it must be proved by the plaintiff as a necessary part of his case"? RST §13, comment *d*.

To avoid many of the factual issues in cases like *Mohr* and *Kennedy*, physicians and hospitals often resort to a form similar to that put out by the American Medical Association, including authorization for different procedures. See, for example, Paragraph 2 of the sample form on page 18. These forms are commonly modified in individual cases to prohibit from the outset certain kinds of procedures. In Hoofnel v. Segal, 199 S.W.3d 147, 151 (Ky. 2006), the plaintiff, a woman aged 56 and of limited education, came to the defendant physicians needing the removal of a lesion from her colon. The surgeon, Dr. Galandiuk, recommended that she be allowed to perform an operation to remove both plaintiff's uterus and ovaries, but the plaintiff insisted that she did not want "any of my female parts removed." Nonetheless, she later signed a consent form that authorized both procedures if necessary. During surgery Dr. Galandiuk consulted with Dr. Segal, and both agreed that the organs had to be removed because of their enlarged size and possible cancerous condition. Graves, J., held that the "clear and unambiguous words of the consent form" superseded the prior conversations.

The essence of [appellant Hoofnel's] argument is that she did not actually intend for her signature to grant consent. Appellant testified that she told Dr. Galandiuk, during an initial consultation, that she did not want her ovaries or uterus removed. Even assuming this conversation to be accurate, her signature on the consent form directly authorized one of these procedures and thus superseded this previous intention. The additional surgical procedure to remove the uterus became medically necessary once the enlarged uterus was observed as it impaired and impeded Dr. Galandiuk's ability to resect the lesion in the colon. The existence of a signed consent form gives rise to a presumption that patients ordinarily read and take whatever other measures are necessary to understand the nature, terms and general meaning of consent. To hold otherwise would negate the legal significance to written consent forms signed by the patient and render the consent form completely unreliable.

Cooper, J., in dissent, protested the excessive reliance on the consent form relative to the entire "process" that preceded and followed the signing. On the majority view, what overrides the "presumption" that attaches to the form? Why

                                                                    A.M.
                    Date_____ Time_____P.M.

     1. I authorize the performance upon _____
                            ╱   *(myself or name of patient)*
of the following operation   _____
                              (state nature and extent of operation)
to be performed by or under the direction of Dr._____.
     2. I consent to the performance of operations and procedures in
addition to or different from those now contemplated, whether or
not arising from presently unforeseen conditions, which the above-
named doctor or his associates or assistants may consider necessary
or advisable in the course of the operation.
     3. I consent to the administration of such anesthetics as may be
considered necessary or advisable by the physician responsible

for this service, with the exception of   _____
                                    (state "none," "spinal anesthesia," etc.)
     4. The nature and purpose of the operation, possible alternative
methods of treatment, the risks involved, the possible consequences,
and the possibility of complications have been explained to me by
Dr._____ and by _____.
     5. I acknowledge that no guarantee or assurance has been given
by anyone as to the results that may be obtained.
     6. I consent to the photogaphing or televising of the operations
or procedures to be performed, including appropriate portions of my
body, for medical, scientific or educational purposes, provided my
identity is not revealed by the pictures or by descriptive texts accompanying them.
     7. For the purpose of advancing medical education, I consent to
the admittance of observers to the operating room.
     8. I consent to the disposal by hospital authorities of any tissues
or body parts which may be removed.
     9. I am aware that sterility may rsult from this operation. I know
that a sterile person is incapable of becoming a parent.
     10. I acknowledge that all blank spaces on this document have
been either completed or crossed off prior to my signing.
              (Cross Out Any Paragraphs Above Which Do Not Apply)

Witness_____   Signed_____
                                        *(Patient or person
                                         authorized to
                                         consent for patient)*

Consent form
Source: American Medical Association, Medicolegal Forms with Legal Analysis 46 (1991)

is this not a case of informed consent? On informed consent, see *infra* Chapter 3, Section D.

In those cases in which the consent form is ambiguous, however, summary judgment may not be obtained. Thus in Musgrove v. McCray, 834 N.W.2d 82 (Iowa Ct. App. 2013), it was unclear whether the consent form covered the removal of all plaintiff's remaining upper teeth, or all plaintiff's remaining upper *and* lower teeth. This raised a genuine issue of fact that required a jury trial.

2. Consent implied in fact. Although consent is normally expressed in words, it may also be inferred from conduct. In O'Brien v. Cunard Steamship Co., 28 N.E. 266, 273-275 (Mass. 1891), the plaintiff was an immigrant to the United States whose entry into this country required vaccination against smallpox. She stood in line with many other female passengers and held out her arm to the defendant's surgeon, who inspected it and noted the lack of the typical mark found after smallpox vaccinations. Thereafter he told her that she had to be vaccinated, and she replied that her previous vaccination had left no mark. The physician did not respond further, and the plaintiff held up her arm and allowed the vaccination to take place, after which she received her entry ticket. The alternative to vaccination was detainment and quarantine. The court held that her consent barred her cause of action:

> If the plaintiff's behavior was such as to indicate consent on her part, the surgeon was justified in his act, whatever her unexpressed feelings may have been. In determining whether she consented, he could be guided only by her overt acts and the manifestations of her feelings. . . . [Plaintiff] was one of a large number of women who were vaccinated on that occasion, without, so far as appears, a word of objection from any of them. They all indicated by their conduct that they desired to avail themselves of the provisions made for their benefit. There was nothing in the conduct of the plaintiff to indicate to the surgeon that she did not wish to obtain a card which would save her from detention at quarantine, and to be vaccinated, if necessary, for that purpose.

Would it have been rational for her to refuse treatment? How should we take into account these additional facts found in the record:

> The plaintiff, an Irish immigrant in steerage, was seventeen years old at the time of the vaccination. Signs announcing the vaccinations were posted around the ship, but contained language the plaintiff did not understand. The passengers in steerage were rounded up, divided into lines by gender, and herded down the steps to the doctor. No one was allowed to leave without the doctor's permission.

Vogel, Cases in Context: Lake Champlain Wars, Gentrification and Ploof v. Putnam, 45 St. Louis U. L.J. 791, 796 (2001).

3. Emergency rule. Normally a patient has the right to accept or reject the proffered medical treatment, making an unauthorized operation a technical assault and battery even if no damage ensues. Schloendorff v. Society of New York Hospital, 105 N.E. 92, 93 (N.Y. 1914), stated the general rule:

> Every human being of adult years and sound mind has a right to determine what shall be done with his own body; and a surgeon who performs an operation without his patient's consent, commits an assault, for which he is liable in damages. This is true except in cases of emergency where the patient is unconscious and where it is necessary to operate before consent can be obtained.

It follows that a conscious patient can refuse consent even in an emergency situation. That principle was at play in Cooper v. Lankenau Hospital, 51 A.3d 183, 186 (Pa. 2012), in which the plaintiff mother, herself a pediatric cardiology anesthesiologist, fell while 27 weeks pregnant. When taken to the hospital, her treating physicians thought that the fetus was suffering from a low heart rate that could lead to fatal consequences and proceeded to operate without consent. The jury found that the defendants had not committed a battery. Baer, J., upheld the verdict after approving the following instructions:

> A physician's performance of surgery in a nonemergency without consent, or the performance of surgery in an emergency when the patient has refused consent is considered a battery under the law. A battery is an act done with the intent to cause a harmful or offensive contact with the body of another, and directly results in the harmful or offensive contact with the body of another.
>
> If you find [the defendant] operated on the plaintiff in a nonemergency without consent, or in an emergency where the plaintiff refused consent, then you must find that [the defendant] committed a battery; otherwise no battery occurred.

Is there any need to include the phrase "harmful or offensive contact with the body of another" in the instruction?

Whenever actual consent cannot be given, however, "medical treatment also will be lawful under the doctrine of implied consent when a medical emergency requires immediate action to preserve the health or life of the patient." Allore v. Flower Hospital, 699 N.E.2d 560, 564 (Ohio Ct. App. 1997). This implied consent is a legal fiction, justified by the assumption that the plaintiff, as a rational agent, would have consented to the operation if she could have been asked. This rule thus protects otherwise helpless patients by encouraging others to assist them in time of need. Should the bystander whose quick intervention saves the plaintiff's life receive compensation? What about the surgeon who operates, even if unsuccessful? See Cotnam v. Wisdom, 104 S.W. 164 (Ark. 1907), allowing the action, but only for a successful outcome, while barring higher fees based on the physician's special knowledge of the decedent's wealth. Why are these two conditions attached to the compensation right?

4. Substitute consent and judgment for the benefit of others. How ought physicians treat minors and incompetents who are unable to give consent? The standard rule requires physicians to obtain, except in emergencies, the consent of a guardian. See Bonner v. Moran, 126 F.2d 121, 122 (D.C. Cir. 1941).

Substituted consent is also needed for adult incompetents who lack any capacity to make medical decisions on their own behalf. Generally, the law protects the guardian's good-faith decision from any judicial challenge or review. For example, in Brophy v. New England Sinai Hospital, Inc., 497 N.E.2d 626 (Mass. 1986), the court allowed the wife and family of a man left in a permanent vegetative state to cut off all nutrition and hydration over the objections of his treating physicians, when everyone agreed that he would have requested termination if he had been competent. Similarly, in In re Guardianship of Tschumy, 853 N.W.2d 728, 752 (Minn. 2014), Gildea, J., held that a statutory guardian "may consent to remove the ward from life-sustaining treatment when all the interested parties agree that such removal is in the ward's best interests" without first obtaining a court order but that such court intervention would be required when interested family members are not in agreement as to what that best interest is. In dissent, Anderson, J., insisted that the statutory powers of a guardian "to enable the ward to receive necessary or medical or other professional care" did not include the power to terminate treatment.

5. Constitutional claims over consent to medical treatment. The autonomy principle at work in the medical consent cases does not compel the constitutional acceptance of the right to voluntary euthanasia. In Cruzan v. Director, Missouri Department of Health, 497 U.S. 261, 281 (1990), Rehnquist, C.J., noted that the sacredness of life under the law of homicide justified the use of "heightened evidentiary requirements" before cutting off life-sustaining treatment.

At the opposite extreme, how should courts respond to claims that individuals have a right to accept risky treatment, not to end, but to save their lives? In Abigail Alliance for Better Access to Developmental Drugs v. Eschenbach, 495 F.3d 695, 703-707 (D.C. Cir. 2007), Griffith, J., held that claims of personal autonomy did not support a constitutional right to compel the FDA to allow terminally ill cancer patients to use new therapies that had passed Phase I clinical trials—those which establish only that the drugs were not toxic in large doses—but which the FDA had not yet licensed as "safe" and "effective." The dissent of Rogers, J., relied on *Schloendorff, supra* Note 3, to support the conclusion that if every individual has an absolute autonomy right to refuse treatment, every person should have the absolute right knowingly to accept risky treatments. For a defense of the outcome in *Abigail Alliance*, see Annas, Cancer and the Constitution—Choice at Life's End, 357 New Eng. J. Med. 408 (2007).

Substituted judgment becomes more delicate when the proposed treatment or operation is for the benefit of another. In Lausier v. Pescinski, 226 N.W.2d 180, 183 (Wis. 1975), the court held that it did not have the power to permit the removal of one of the incompetent's kidneys, which was needed to save the life of his brother, even though the risk of harm to the incompetent was slight. The incompetent's guardian, his sister, opposed the operation because it "brought back memories of the Dachau concentration camp in Nazi Germany and of medical experiments on unwilling subjects." Similarly, in Curran v. Bosze, 566 N.E.2d 1319, 1326 (Ill. 1990), the court upheld the right of a mother of two 3½-year-old twins to refuse to have her children tested to see if they could make bone marrow transplants to their 12-year-old half-brother who was dying of leukemia. The court stated that "it is not possible to determine the intent of a 3½-year-old child with regard to consenting to a bone marrow harvesting procedure by examining the child's personal value system." Should the consent of the incompetent's guardian make a difference? How persuasive is the argument that the incompetent will benefit by the survival of his brother?

Canterbury v. Spence
464 F.2d 772 (D.C. Cir. 1972)

[The text of the opinion and notes thereto are found beginning on page 206.]

Hudson v. Craft
204 P.2d 1 (Cal. 1949)

CARTER, J. [The plaintiff, an 18-year-old boy, was solicited by the defendant promoter to participate in an illegal prize fight for which he received a $5 fee. The fight was neither sanctioned by the State Athletic Commission nor conducted in accordance with its rules. During the fight, the plaintiff sustained personal injuries from a blow by his opponent. Plaintiff sued both his opponent and the promoter, but did not serve process on his opponent. The trial court dismissed his complaint.]

The basis and theory of liability, if any, in mutual combat cases has been the subject of considerable controversy. Proceeding from the premise that, as between the combatants, the tort involved is that of assault and battery, many courts have held that, inasmuch as each contestant has committed a battery on the other, each may hold the other liable for any injury inflicted although both consented to the contest. [The court cited many cases, including Teeters v. Frost, 292 P. 356 (Okla. 1930).] Being contrary to the maxim volenti non fit injuria [the willing suffer no injury], the courts have endeavored to rationalize the rule by reasoning that the state is a party where there is a breach of the peace, such as occurs in a combat, and that no one may consent to such breach. There are cases expressing a minority view and severe criticism has been leveled at the majority rule, such as, that it ignores the principle of pari delicto [equal wrong] and encourages rather than deters mutual combat. See Hart v. Geysel, 159 Wash. 632[, 294 P. 570]; Bohlen, Consent as Affecting Civil Liability for Breaches of the Peace, 24 Colum. L. Rev. 819 [1924]; . . . The Restatement adopts the minority view. An assent which satisfies the rules stated "prevents an invasion from being tortious and, therefore, actionable, although the invasion assented to constitutes a crime." (Rest., Torts, §60.) An example given thereunder is a boxing match where no license was had as required by law. The only case discovered involving the liability of a third-party promoter of the combat such as we have in the case at bar, is Teeters v. Frost, supra, where the court, following the majority position as to the liability of the participants as between themselves, was not confronted with any difficulty in deciding that the instigator was liable as an aider and abettor.

There is an exception to the rule stated in the Restatements, reading: "Where it is a crime to inflict a particular invasion of an interest of personality upon a particular class of persons, irrespective of their assent, and the policy of the law is primarily to protect the interests of such a class of persons from their inability to appreciate the consequences of such an invasion, and it is not solely to protect the interests of the public, the assent of such a person to such an invasion is not a consent thereto." (Rest., Torts, §61.) It is evident that the so-called exception and the foregoing discussion has to do only with consent as refuting liability, not with the basic tort upon which the liability is rested, assault and battery. Concerning the bearing of the factor of consent or assumption of risk on liability, the instant case, as will more fully appear from the later discussion herein, clearly falls within the exception stated in section 61 (supra) by reason of the declared public policy of the state.

If liability is predicated on the tort of battery, it might seem to follow that in order to hold the promoter liable, it would be necessary to impose responsibility upon the combatants as to each other on the theory that they are the principals while the instigator is only the aider and abettor. In view of the public policy of this state as expressed by initiative, legislation, rules of the Athletic Commission, and the Constitution, the promoter must be held liable as a principal regardless of what the rule may be as between the combatants.

From the beginning, this state has taken an uncompromising stand against uncontrolled prize fights and boxing matches.

[The court then reviewed the extensive history of boxing regulation in California from 1850 through 1942. When this fight took place, the law forbade any person under 18 from participating in a fight, it required all fighters to undergo physical examinations before fighting; it prescribed a maximum number of rounds and a minimum weight for gloves; it required a physician to be in attendance at the fight; and it required that a referee supervise the match and stop the fight if there were "too great a disparity between the boxers." The statute also authorized the boxing commission to adopt rules to set weight classes for fighters, define fouls in the ring, and provide for inspection and physical examination of the premises. Many, if not all, of these requirements were violated in the instant case.]

The foregoing declarations by the people, the Legislature, and the commission evince an unusually strong policy, obviously resting upon a detailed study of the problems relative to boxing matches. While there are other purposes underlying that policy, it is manifest that one of the chief goals is to provide safeguards for the protection of persons engaging in the activity. It may be that the actual participants, as well as the promoter, are liable criminally for a violation of the provisions, but insofar as the purpose is protection from physical harm, the chief offender would be the promoter—the activating force in procuring the occurrence of such exhibitions. It is from his uncontrolled conduct that the combatants are protected. Secondarily, the contestants are protected against their own ill-advised participation in an unregulated match. This is especially true in the case at bar where plaintiff is a lad of 18 years.

The foregoing policy compels the conclusion that the promoter is liable where he conducts boxing matches or prize fights without a license and in violation of the statutory provisions above discussed, regardless of the rights as between the contestants, and that the consent of the combatants does not relieve him of that liability. Manifestly the doctrine of pari delicto is not pertinent inasmuch as one of the main purposes of the statutes is to protect a class (combatants) of which plaintiff is a member. It may be observed that the basis of such liability finds some support in principle in the doctrine of negligence per se . . . , and strict liability arising from the nature of the conduct and its consequences . . . , the seriousness of which is here established by a statute with comprehensive regulatory features aimed at the goal of especial protection for a certain class. The end result is the same and the controlling factor is whether or not the expressed public policy is sufficiently urgent, explicit and comprehensive.

It is not necessary in the instant case to state a general rule inasmuch as each situation must have individual consideration. The nature and scope of the legislation here involved and above shown requires liability, especially when we consider that it calls for continuous and "on the spot" supervision of boxing matches. That feature alone is sufficient to distinguish it from such cases as a person operating a car without an operator's license and the like. Moreover, we have more here than the mere failure to obtain a license. While it could have been more accurately pleaded, it may be inferred that the defendants did not comply with the statutes from the allegation that they failed to so comply therewith in that they did not obtain a license and did not observe the rules and regulations of the Athletic Commission.

For the foregoing reasons, the judgment is reversed.

NOTES

1. Minority view on consent to illegal acts.   Why is the fight promoter in *Hudson* responsible for blows inflicted by a third party if the other combatant is entitled to a defense of consent? Should violations of the legislative scheme be sufficient to impose liability per se on the promoter? See *infra* Chapter 3, Section E.

In Hart v. Geysel, 294 P. 570, 572 (Wash. 1930), the plaintiff's husband was killed by a blow struck in an illegal prizefight in which he consented to participate. In adopting the minority and Restatement view, the court in *Hart*, over vigorous dissent, first noted that both fighters had violated the criminal statute, and therefore "it is not necessary to reward the one that got the worst of the encounter at the expense of his more fortunate opponent." The *Hart* court relied on two basic legal doctrines that the majority view implicitly rejected: (1) *volenti non fit injuria,* and (2) *ex turpi causa non oritur actio,* or no action shall arise out of an improper or immoral cause. Is the private action for damages a sensible aid to criminal enforcement? Does the denial of a private action encourage or discourage participation in illegal prizefights? Does the action against the promoter discourage prize fighting? Reduce the size of the purses? Both? For an excellent defense of the Restatement's adoption of the minority rule, see Bohlen, Consent as Affecting Civil Liability for Breaches of the Peace, 24 Colum. L. Rev. 819 (1924), reprinted in Studies in the Law of Torts at 577 (1926).

2. *Private rights of action for statutory rape.* In Barton v. Bee Line, Inc., 265 N.Y.S. 284, 285 (App. Div. 1933), an underage plaintiff, age 15—18 was the legal age of consent—brought an action for damages even though she had fully consented to sexual intercourse with the defendant's chauffeur, for which he was guilty of statutory rape, a crime then punishable by up to ten years of imprisonment. The court refused to allow her to sue:

> Should a consenting female under the age of eighteen have a cause of action if she has full understanding of the nature of her act? It is one thing to say that society will protect itself by punishing those who consort with females under the age of consent; it is another to hold that knowing the nature of her act, such female shall be rewarded for her indiscretion. Surely public policy—to serve which the statute was adopted—will not be vindicated by recompensing her for willing participation in that against which the law sought to protect her. The very object of the statute will be frustrated if by a material return for her fall we should unwarily put it in the power of the female sex to become seducers in their turn.

Barton was repudiated in Christensen v. Royal School District, 124 P.3d 283, 288 (Wash. 2005), where a 13-year-old girl brought suit against both the teacher with whom she had sexual relations and the school district that employed him. A divided court allowed the action on the ground that the girl was "too immature to rationally or legally consent." The majority of courts today follow *Christensen*. Are the statutory rape cases distinguishable from the illegal boxing cases? Why does the RST take the alternative view and allow liability for statutory rape cases, but not for illegal boxing cases? See RST §892A.

3. *Athletic injuries: formal settings.* The legal remedy for persons deliberately or recklessly injured in professional athletic contests has been the subject of frequent litigation. In most sports it is generally held that plaintiffs consent to injury from blows administered in accordance with the rules of the game, but not when the blows are deliberately illegal. In Hackbart v. Cincinnati Bengals, Inc., 601 F.2d 516, 520-521 (10th Cir. 1979), Dale Hackbart, a defensive back for the Denver Broncos, was injured by a blow struck by Charles "Booby" Clark, an offensive halfback for the Bengals. After the Broncos intercepted a pass, Clark, "acting out of anger and frustration, but without a specific intent to injure . . . stepped forward and struck a blow with his right forearm to the back of the kneeling plaintiff's head and neck with sufficient force to cause both players to fall forward to the ground." Although Hackbart suffered no immediate ill effects from the blow, he shortly thereafter experienced severe pains that, after two more brief game appearances, forced him to retire, ending a successful 13-year career. The trial court dismissed the action, chiefly on the ground that in the absence of legislation it was inappropriate to impose upon one professional football player a duty to care for the safety of another. The Tenth Circuit through Doyle, J., reversed:

> Contrary to the position of the court then, there are no principles of law which allow a court to rule out certain tortious conduct by reason of general roughness of the game or difficulty of administering it.

Indeed, the evidence shows that there are rules of the game which prohibit the intentional striking of blows. Thus, Article 1, Item 1, Subsection C, provides that: "All players are prohibited from striking on the head, face or neck with the heel, back or side of the hand, wrist, forearm, elbow or clasped hands." Thus the very conduct which was present here is expressly prohibited by the rule which is quoted above. . . . Therefore, the notion is not correct that all reason has been abandoned, whereby the only possible remedy for the person who has been the victim of an unlawful blow is retaliation.

What result in the absence of a specific rule such as that referred to in the opinion? What if the owners of all teams agree that no tort actions should be brought for injuries suffered on the playing field? What about an agreement among the players to the same effect?

Courts have applied similar principles to high school and college athletic contests. In Nabozny v. Barnhill, 334 N.E.2d 258, 261 (Ill. App. Ct. 1975), the plaintiff soccer goalie sustained severe and permanent injuries when kicked in the head inside the penalty area even though the defendant could have easily avoided any contact. The game was played under football association rules, under which any contact with the goalkeeper and any attempt to kick a ball in his possession while in the penalty area are infractions, even if such contact is unintentional. The court, while concerned about the negative impact of tort liability on legitimate athletic activities, held that "a player is liable for injury in a tort action if his conduct is such that it is either deliberate, wilful or with a reckless disregard for the safety of the other player so as to cause injury to that player, the same being a question of fact to be decided by a jury."

Today *Nabozny* has spawned the so-called contact sports exception to the general rules of negligence, precluding liability for ordinary negligence. See Karas v. Strevell, 884 N.E.2d 122, 134 (Ill. 2008), arising out of a hard hockey body check from behind, holding that "a participant breaches a duty of care to a coparticipant only if the participant intentionally injures the coparticipant or engages in conduct totally outside the range of the ordinary activity involved in the sport." How ought that exception apply?

In Avila v. Citrus Community College District, 131 P.3d 383, 392-393 (Cal. 2006), the defendant's pitcher hit the plaintiff, a varsity baseball player, in the head with a pitch, cracking his helmet and causing serious, unspecified injuries. The plaintiff alleged that "the pitch was an intentional 'beanball' thrown in retaliation for [a] previous hit batter or, at a minimum, was thrown negligently." Werdegar, J., showed no patience with either allegation, holding that the defendant school had a duty "to, at a minimum, not increase the risks inherent in the sport." Even so, the home team was not liable because intentional beanballs were an "inherent risk of the sport." Should beanballs be allowed as "an integral part of pitching tactics"? How does the purported justification for throwing beanballs tie in with the Third Restatement's definition of recklessness?

> **Restatement of the Law (Third) of Torts: Liability for Physical and Emotional Harm**
>
> **§2. RECKLESSNESS**
>
> A person acts recklessly in engaging in conduct if:
>   (a) the person knows of the risk of harm created by the conduct or knows facts that make the risk obvious to another in the person's situation, and
>   (b) the precaution that would eliminate or reduce the risk involves burdens that are so slight relative to the magnitude of the risk as to render the person's failure to adopt the precaution a demonstration of the person's indifference to the risk.
>
> **Comment a. Terminology and Scope:** . . . Taken at face value, [gross negligence] simply means negligence that is especially bad. Given this literal interpretation, gross negligence carries a meaning that is less than recklessness.

In Turcotte v. Fell, 502 N.E.2d 964, 969-970 (N.Y. 1986), the plaintiff, a professional jockey, sued in negligence when injured in a race by the defendant, a fellow jockey, who had violated track rules. The court refused to allow the action, contrasting this case with *Hackbart* and *Nabozny* as follows:

> Although the foul riding rule is a safety measure, it is not by its terms absolute for it establishes a spectrum of conduct and penalties, depending on whether the violation is careless or willful and whether the contact was the result of mutual fault. As the rule recognizes, bumping and jostling are normal incidents of the sport. They are not, as were the blows in *Nabozny* and . . . *Hackbart,* flagrant infractions unrelated to the normal method of playing the game and done without any competitive purpose. Plaintiff does not claim that Fell intentionally or recklessly bumped him; he claims only that as a result of carelessness, Fell failed to control his mount as the horses raced for the lead and a preferred position on the track. While a participant's "consent" to join in a sporting activity is not a waiver of all rules infractions, nonetheless a professional clearly understands the usual incidents of competition resulting from carelessness, particularly those which result from the customarily accepted method of playing the sport, and accepts them.

4. Athletic injuries: informal settings. In Marchetti v. Kalish, 559 N.E.2d 699, 701-703 (Ohio 1990), plaintiff and defendant were playing a backyard game called "kick the can" in which players attempt to reach the home base, or can, before they are spotted by the player designated as "it." Once "it" sees another player, he places his foot on the can, and calls out the player's name, yelling "kick the can—one, two, three." (The rules of the game were sufficiently well articulated that the parties set them out in a joint appendix to the opinion.) On this occasion plaintiff, a 13-year-old girl, placed her foot on the ball, used in place of a can, and announced that the defendant, a 15-year-old boy, was "it." The defendant continued to run straight at the plaintiff, and collided with her as he was kicking the ball out from under her foot. The plaintiff staggered to the ground, and found that she had broken her right leg in two places.

The plaintiff conceded that her injuries were neither intentionally nor recklessly inflicted. The Ohio Supreme Court entered a summary judgment for defendant, relying on both *Nabozny* and *Hackbart*. "[Plaintiff] argues that these cases from other jurisdictions are distinguishable from the present case because we are dealing with children involved in a simple neighborhood game rather than an organized contact sport." But the court held the distinction immaterial so long as the children "were engaging in some type of recreational or sports activity. Whether the activity is organized, unorganized, supervised or unsupervised, is immaterial to the standard of liability. . . . [B]efore a party may proceed with a cause of action involving injury resulted from a recreational or sports activity, reckless or intentional conduct must exist." And in Gentry v. Craycraft, 802 N.E.2d 1116, 1118 (Ohio 2004), the recklessness standard was applied to spectators so long as they were old enough to appreciate the inherent risk in the activity. "To hold otherwise would be to open the floodgates to a myriad of lawsuits involving the backyard games of children." Any liability for the parents for negligent supervision?

b. Mental Disability

McGuire v. Almy
8 N.E.2d 760 (Mass. 1937)

Qua, J. This is an action of tort for assault and battery. The only question of law reported is whether the judge should have directed a verdict for the defendant.

The following facts are established by the plaintiff's own evidence: In August, 1930, the plaintiff was employed to take care of the defendant. The plaintiff was a registered nurse and was a graduate of a training school for nurses. The defendant was an insane person. Before the plaintiff was hired she learned that the defendant was a "mental case and was in good physical condition," and that for some time two nurses had been taking care of her. The plaintiff was on "twenty-four hour duty." The plaintiff slept in the room next to the defendant's room. Except when the plaintiff was with the defendant, the plaintiff kept the defendant locked in the defendant's room. There was a wire grating over the outside of the window of that room. During the period of "fourteen months or so" while the plaintiff cared for the defendant, the defendant "had a few odd spells," when she showed some hostility to the plaintiff and said that "she would like to try and do something to her." The defendant had been violent at times and had broken dishes "and things like that," and on one or two occasions the plaintiff had to have help to subdue the defendant.

On April 19, 1932, the defendant, while locked in her room, had a violent attack. The plaintiff heard a crashing of furniture and then knew that the defendant was ugly, violent and dangerous. The defendant told the plaintiff and a Miss Maroney, "the maid," who was with the plaintiff in the adjoining room, that if they came into the defendant's room, she would kill them. The plaintiff and Miss Maroney looked into the defendant's room, "saw what the defendant had done," and "thought it best to take the broken stuff away before she did any harm to herself with it." They sent for one Emerton, the defendant's brother-in-law. When he arrived the defendant was in the middle of her room about ten feet from the door, holding upraised the leg of a low-boy as if she were going to strike. The plaintiff stepped into the room and walked toward the defendant, while Emerton and Miss Maroney remained in the doorway. As the plaintiff approached the defendant and tried to take hold of the defendant's hand which held the leg, the defendant struck the plaintiff's head with it, causing the injuries for which the action was brought. [After noting that the Massachusetts precedents had not settled the rules governing the liability of an insane person, the court continued:]

Turning to authorities elsewhere, we find that courts in this country almost invariably say in the broadest terms that an insane person is liable for his torts. As a rule no distinction is made between those torts which would ordinarily be classed as intentional and those which would ordinarily be classed as negligent, nor do the courts discuss the effect of different kinds of insanity or of varying degrees of capacity as bearing upon the ability of the defendant to understand the particular act in question or to make a reasoned decision with respect to it, although it is sometimes said that an insane person is not liable for torts requiring malice of which he is incapable. Defamation and malicious prosecution are the torts more commonly mentioned in this connection. A number of illustrative cases appear in the footnote. These decisions are rested more upon grounds of public policy and upon what might be called a popular view of the requirements of essential justice than upon any attempt to apply logically the underlying principles of civil liability to the special instance of the mentally deranged. Thus it is said that a rule imposing liability tends to make more watchful those persons who have charge of the defendant and who may be supposed to have some interest in preserving his property; that as an insane person must pay for his support, if he is financially able, so he ought also to pay for the damage which he does; that an insane person with abundant wealth ought not to continue in unimpaired enjoyment of the comfort which it brings while his victim bears the burden unaided; and there is also a suggestion that courts are loath to introduce into the great body of civil litigation the difficulties in determining mental capacity which it has been found impossible to avoid in the criminal field.

The rule established in these cases has been criticized severely by certain eminent text writers both in this country and in England, principally on the ground that it is an archaic survival of the rigid and formal medieval conception of liability for acts done, without regard to fault, as opposed to what is said to be the general modern theory that liability in tort should rest upon fault. Notwithstanding these criticisms, we think that as a practical matter there is strong force in the reasons underlying these decisions. They are consistent with the general statements found in the cases dealing with the liability of infants for torts. Fault is by no means at the present day a universal prerequisite to liability, and the theory that it should be such has been obliged very recently to yield at several points to what have been thought to be paramount considerations of public good. Finally, it would be difficult not to recognize the persuasive weight of so much authority so widely extended.

But the present occasion does not require us either to accept or to reject the prevailing doctrine in its entirety. For this case it is enough to say that where an insane person by his act does intentional damage to the person or property of another he is liable for that damage in the same circumstances in which a normal person would be liable. This means that in so far as a particular intent would be necessary in order to render a normal person liable, the insane person, in order to be liable, must have been capable of entertaining that same intent and must have entertained it in fact. But the law will not inquire further into his peculiar mental condition with a view to excusing him if it should appear that delusion or other consequence of his affliction has caused him to entertain that intent or that a normal person would not have entertained it.

We do not suggest that this is necessarily a logical stopping point. If public policy demands that a mentally affected person be subjected to the external standard for intentional wrongs, it may well be that public policy also demands that he should be subjected to the external standard for wrongs which are commonly classified as negligent, in accordance with what now seems to be the prevailing view. We stop here for the present, because we are not required to go further in order to decide this case, because of deference to the difficulty of the subject, because full and adequate discussion is lacking in most of the cases decided up to the present time, and because by far the greater number of those cases, however broad their statement of the principle, are in fact cases of intentional rather than of negligent injury.

Coming now to the application of the rule to the facts of this case, it is apparent that the jury could find that the defendant was capable of entertaining and that she did entertain an intent to strike and to injure the plaintiff and that she acted upon that intent. See Am. Law Inst. Restatement: Torts §§13, 14. We think this was enough. [The court then rejected the argument that the plaintiff had consented to or assumed the risk as a matter of law. In its view the risk became "plain and obvious" only after she entered the room, just before the assault, when an emergency sufficient to deny voluntary consent had already been created.]

Judgment for the plaintiff on the verdict.

NOTE

Intention and mental disability.   What mental state must the defendant have toward her victim to be held liable? What result if Almy had thought she was striking a creature from outer space? That her actions were in self-defense against an imagined assault by McGuire? Looking at the other side of the case, was the court right to reject defendant's assumption-of-risk defense in light of the elaborate preparations plaintiff took before entering defendant's room? In light of her role as a paid caretaker?

The vast majority of the decisions on insanity defense have hewed to the uncompromising line set out in *McGuire*. For a justification of this position, see Gould v. American Family Mutual Insurance Co., 543 N.W.2d 282, 285 (Wis. 1996), *infra* Chapter 3 at 156:

> [W]here a loss must be borne by one of two innocent persons, it shall be borne by him who occasioned it, and it has also been held that public policy requires the enforcement of the liability in order that those interested in the estate of the insane person, as relatives or otherwise, may be under inducement to restrain him and that tortfeasors may not simulate or pretend insanity to defend their wrongful acts causing damage to others.

The insanity defense also proved futile on the grisly facts of Polmatier v. Russ, 537 A.2d 468, 472 (Conn. 1988). The defendant Russ and his two-year-old daughter visited his father-in-law's house. The defendant sat astride his father-in-law, beating him over the head with a beer bottle. He then searched two bedrooms in the house, found 30-caliber ammunition and a Winchester rifle, and returned to the living room where he killed his father-in-law with two shots. The defendant was later found naked, sitting on a stump in a wooded area about two miles from the decedent's home, carrying his blood-soaked clothing and cradling his daughter in his arms. He was diagnosed as "suffering from a severe case of paranoid schizophrenia that involved delusions of persecution, grandeur, influence and reference, and also involved auditory hallucinations." The defendant was found unfit to stand for a criminal trial, but was held responsible for an intentional tort:

> We note that we have not been referred to any evidence indicating that the defendant's acts were reflexive, convulsive or epileptic. Furthermore, under the Restatement (Second) of Torts §2, "act" is used "to denote an external manifestation of the actor's will and does not include any of its results, even the most direct, immediate, and intended." Comment b to this section provides in pertinent part: "A muscular reaction is always an act unless it is a purely reflexive reaction in which the mind and will have no share." Although the trial court found that the defendant could not form a rational choice, it did find that he could make a schizophrenic or crazy choice. Moreover, a rational choice is not required since "[a]n insane person may have an intent to invade the interests of another, even though his reasons and motives for forming that intention may be entirely irrational." Restatement (Second) of Torts §895J, comment c.

The court rejected any further requirement that the defendant must have "acted for the *purpose* of causing," or with a "desire to cause the resulting injury."

What result in cases of automatism, where the sleepwalking defendant has done *no act* at all and thus cannot have committed any tort, intentional or otherwise? See, for the evolution of the insanity defense, Kelley, Infancy, Insanity and Infirmity in the Law of Torts, 48 Am. J. Juris. 179 (2003).

c. Self-Defense

Courvoisier v. Raymond
47 P. 284 (Colo. 1896)

Hayt, C.J. It is admitted or proven beyond controversy that appellee received a gunshot wound at the hands of the appellant at the time and place designated in the complaint, and that as the result of such wound the appellee was seriously injured. It is further shown that the shooting occurred under the following circumstances:

That Mr. Courvoisier, on the night in question, was asleep in his bed in the second story of a brick building, situated at the corner of South Broadway and Dakota streets in South Denver; that he occupied a portion of the lower floor of this building as a jewelry store. He was aroused from his bed shortly after midnight by parties shaking or trying to open the door of the jewelry store. These parties, when asked by him as to what they wanted, insisted upon being admitted, and upon his refusal to comply with this request, they used profane and abusive epithets toward him. Being unable to gain admission, they broke some signs upon the front of the building, and then entered the building by another entrance, and passing upstairs commenced knocking upon the door of a room where defendant's sister was sleeping. Courvoisier partly dressed himself, and, taking his revolver, went upstairs and expelled the intruders from the building. In doing this he passed downstairs and out on the sidewalk as far as the entrance to his store, which was at the corner of the building. The parties expelled from the building, upon reaching the rear of the store, were joined by two or three others. In order to frighten these parties away, the defendant fired a shot in the air, but instead of retreating they passed around to the street in front, throwing stones and brickbats at the defendant, whereupon he fired a second and perhaps a third shot. The first shot fired attracted the attention of plaintiff Raymond and two deputy sheriffs, who were at the Tramway depot, across the street. These officers started toward Mr. Courvoisier, who still continued to shoot, but two of them stopped when they reached the men in the street, for the purpose of arresting them, Mr. Raymond alone proceeding towards the defendant, calling out to him that he was an officer and to stop shooting. Although the night was dark, the street was well lighted by electricity, and when the officer approached him defendant shaded his eyes, and, taking deliberate aim, fired, causing the injury complained of.

The plaintiff's theory of the case is that he was a duly authorized police officer, and in the discharge of his duties at the time that the defendant was committing a breach of the peace, and that the defendant, knowing him to be a police officer, recklessly fired the shot in question.

The defendant claims that the plaintiff was approaching him at the time in a threatening attitude, and that the surrounding circumstances were such as to cause a reasonable man to believe that his life was in danger, and that it was necessary to shoot in self-defense, and that defendant did so believe at the time of firing the shot. . . .

The next error assigned relates to the instructions given by the court to the jury and to those requested by the defendant and refused by the court. The second instruction given by the court was clearly erroneous. The instruction is as follows: "The court instructs you that if you believe from the evidence, that, at the time the defendant shot the plaintiff, the plaintiff was not assaulting the defendant, then your verdict should be for the plaintiff."

The vice of this instruction is that it excluded from the jury a full consideration of the justification claimed by the defendant. The evidence for the plaintiff tends to show that the shooting, if not malicious, was wanton and reckless, but the evidence for the defendant tends to show that the circumstances surrounding him at the time of the shooting were such as to lead a reasonable man to believe that his life was in danger, or that he was in danger of receiving great bodily harm at the hands of the plaintiff, and the defendant testified that he did so believe. [The court then reviewed the injured plaintiff's sworn version of the facts of the case and continued:]

. . . He then adds: "I saw a man come away from the bunch of men and come up towards me, and as I looked around I saw this man put his hand to his hip pocket. I didn't think I had time to jump aside, and therefore turned around and fired at him. I had no doubts but it was somebody that had come to rob me, because some weeks before Mr. Wilson's store was robbed. It is next door to mine."

By this evidence two phases of the transaction are presented for consideration: *First,* was the plaintiff assaulting the defendant at the time plaintiff was shot? *Second,* if not, was there sufficient evidence of justification for the consideration of the jury? The first question was properly submitted, but the second was excluded by the instruction under review. The defendant's justification did not rest entirely upon the proof of assault by the plaintiff. A riot was in progress, and the defendant swears that he was attacked with missiles, hit with stones, brickbats, etc.; that he shot plaintiff, supposing him to be one of the rioters. We must assume these facts as established in reviewing the instruction, as we cannot say what the jury might have found had this evidence been submitted to them under a proper charge.

By the second instruction the conduct of those who started the fracas was eliminated from the consideration of the jury. If the jury believed from the evidence that the defendant would have been justified in shooting one of the rioters had such person advanced towards him as did the plaintiff, then it became important to determine whether the defendant mistook plaintiff for one of the rioters, and if such a mistake was in fact made, was it excusable in the light of all the circumstances leading up to and surrounding the commission of the act? If these issues had been resolved by the jury in favor of the defendant, he would have been entitled to a judgment. Morris v. Platt, 32 Conn. 75.

[Judgment was reversed.]

NOTES

1. Mistake and self-defense. Note that the *Courvoisier* court held that the defendant could plead self-defense even if he mistakenly thought that he was under attack. In other cases of intentional harms, including cases of trespass and conversion, the risk of an innocent mistake usually falls on the party who makes it. What accounts for the different result in this case?

In Morris v. Platt, 32 Conn. 75 (1864), the court held that the accidental harming of an innocent bystander by force reasonably intended in self-defense to repel an attack by a third party is not actionable. The Second Restatement concurs, noting that the defendant is liable to the innocent third party "only if the actor realizes or should realize that his act creates an unreasonable risk of causing such harm." RST §75. Is *Morris* consistent with the trial judge's approach in *Courvoisier*? The appellate court's, given that the defendant in *Morris* had no intention to strike the plaintiff? Does the plaintiff in *Morris* have a cause of action against the defendant's assailant?

With *Morris*, contrast the Roman law approach in Justinian's Digest 9.2.45.4:

> Persons who do damage because they cannot otherwise defend themselves are innocent; for all statutes and legal systems allow one to repel force by force. But if in order to defend myself I throw a stone at my adversary, but hit, not him but a passer-by, I shall be liable under the Lex Aquilia [the general Roman tort statute for wrongful damage]; for one is allowed to strike only the person who uses force, and then only when it is done for the purpose of protection and not revenge as well.

Even though self-defense is universally recognized as a justification for intentionally inflicting harm, there is a persistent debate over whether it can be raised against all actors, regardless of their mental state. May a social outcast use force to protect himself from attack by a prominent businessman or scientist, who has gone temporarily mad, if both are trapped together in an elevator? If so, how does one measure the claims to personal integrity against those of social welfare? Second Restatement §64, in a caveat, takes a discreet pass: "The Institute expresses no opinion as to whether there is a similar privilege of self-defense against conduct which the actor recognizes, or should recognize, to be entirely innocent." How ought the question be resolved?

2. Self-defense against actual attacks. The defense of self-defense is far more secure when the plaintiff has in fact attacked the defendant. But even here critical questions can arise: Who struck the first blow, and was the force excessive under the circumstances? In Boston v. Muncy, 233 P.2d 300, 301, 303 (Okla. 1951), the defendant encountered the plaintiff in a domino parlor after work and asked what had happened to an automobile heater—difficult to obtain because of post–World War II rationing—that he had promised to put aside for the defendant. The plaintiff denied having made such a promise. According to the plaintiff, the defendant then called plaintiff a liar and, without provocation, struck him over the right eye, causing serious damage. According to the defendant, "when he reminded plaintiff that he had promised to save a heater for him plaintiff called him a liar and made an attempt to hit him with his fist; that he then struck the plaintiff in self-defense." Plaintiff and defendant each had witnesses to support his version of the events. The defendant then asked for instructions that provided "the defendant had the right to exercise and use such reasonable force as may have reasonably appeared to him in good faith to be necessary to protect himself from bodily harm, even though he may not have been actually in danger." But the trial court, in instruction No. 8, said:

> . . . if at the time the defendant is alleged to have assaulted and struck the plaintiff the defendant in doing what he did was acting in an effort to protect his own person or life, and the circumstances then surrounding the defendant were such [that] the exercise of reasonable judgment would justify or induce in his mind an honest belief that he was in danger of receiving some great bodily harm, judging from the standpoint of the defendant, then the defendant would be justified in doing what he did, and your verdict should be for the defendant.

The Oklahoma Supreme Court held that instruction No. 8 was prejudicial error because it "too narrowly" limited the right of self-defense. It remanded the case for a new trial, saying:

> The evidence is highly conflicting as to who was the aggressor. The jury might have found that plaintiff was the aggressor, but it also might have further found that defendant was not justified in apprehending or believing that plaintiff intended to inflict upon him some great bodily harm, and under the instruction it might have concluded that the defendant therefore had no right to stand his ground and defend himself against the attack and it was therefore its duty to render a verdict for plaintiff.

Does removing the word "great" from the trial judge's instructions entitle the defendant to use the minimum force necessary to protect himself, even from trivial harm? Should a squeamish and nervous person be held to a standard of "ordinary firmness and courage" that he could not meet in practice? If armed, could he have used a gun when an ordinary man could not have done so? See RST §63, comments *i* and *j*. For the complex rules governing self-defense, see RST §§63-76. For an excellent discussion of the problem, see Fletcher, Proportionality and the Psychotic Aggressor: A Vignette in Comparative Criminal Theory, 8 Israel L. Rev. 367 (1973).

3. Stand-your-ground laws.   Recently many states have adopted stand-your-ground laws that allow people to resist attacks with force even when they have the option to retreat. These laws uniformly apply to attacks that take place within the home, but often are extended to any place where a person has a lawful right to be. Thus Fla. Stat. Ann. §776.032 creates an immunity against both criminal prosecution and civil action for anyone who uses force in defense of either person or property against anyone except a police officer. The scope of that privilege is then broadly defined by Fla. Stat. Ann. §776.012(2) (West 2015):

> A person is justified in using or threatening to use deadly force if he or she reasonably believes that using or threatening to use such force is necessary to prevent imminent death or great bodily harm to himself or herself or another or to prevent the imminent commission of a forcible felony. A person who uses or threatens to use deadly force in accordance with this subsection does not have a duty to retreat

and has the right to stand his or her ground if the person using or threatening to use the deadly force is not engaged in a criminal activity and is in a place he or she has a right to be.

The Florida law also states, subject to some qualifications, that an individual may threaten or use deadly force against individuals who are in the process of unlawfully and forcefully entering, or who have already unlawfully and forcefully entered, "a dwelling, residence, or occupied vehicle," Fla. Stat. Ann. §776.013(1)(a), and may use all force, "except deadly force," to prevent trespasses against real property. Fla. Stat. Ann. §776.031(1). Why no duty to retreat?

4. Defense of third parties.   Under what circumstances may a person intervene in defense of a third party? What if he hurts the plaintiff in the mistaken, but reasonable, belief that a third party needs assistance? See RST §76, which notes that a person is privileged to defend a third party "under the same conditions and by the same means as those under and by which he is privileged to defend himself if the actor correctly or reasonably believes" that the third party is entitled to use force in self-defense and that his own intervention is necessary to protect that party. How should the issue be decided under *Courvoisier, Morris,* and Justinian's Digest 9.2.45.4?

d. Defense of Property

Bird v. Holbrook
130 Eng. Rep. 911 (C.P. 1825)

[The defendant had rented and occupied a walled garden in which they grew valuable tulips. The garden was located about a mile from his home, and it contained a single-room summer-house in which he and his wife slept from time to time. Shortly before the present incident, the defendant's garden had been robbed of flowers and roots worth 20 pounds:] in consequence of which, for the protection of his property, with the assistance of another man, he placed in the garden a spring gun, the wires connected with which were made to pass from the door-way of the summer-house to some tulip beds, at the height of about fifteen inches from the ground, and across three or four of the garden paths, which wires were visible from all parts of the garden or the garden wall; but it was admitted by the Defendant, that the Plaintiff had not seen them, and that he had no notice of the spring gun and the wires being there. [The plaintiff, a 19-year-old youth, had gone into the garden between six and seven in the afternoon on March 21, 1825, for an innocent purpose—to get back a pea-fowl that had strayed—at the request of the servant of its owner. The plaintiff climbed on the wall at the back of the garden and called out several times before jumping down into the garden. As he approached the summer-house, he triggered the spring gun, which discharged heavy shot that caused a severe wound above the knee.]

A witness to whom the Defendant mentioned the fact of his having been robbed, and of having set a spring gun, proved that he had asked the Defendant if he had put up a notice of such gun being set, to which the Defendant answered, that "he did not conceive that there was any law to oblige him to do so," and the Defendant desired such person not to mention to any one that the gun was set, "lest the villain should not be detected." The Defendant stated to the same person that the garden was very secure, and that he and his wife were going to sleep in the summer-house in a few days. . . .

Merewether, Serjt. [i.e., highest order of counsel] for the defendant. . . . The main ground of the defence, however, is, that the Plaintiff cannot recover for an injury occasioned to him by his own wrongful act. Commodum ex injuria non oritur [an advantage cannot arise out of a wrongful act] and it is equally the principle of our law, that jus ex injuria non oritur [no right arises from a wrong]. If a man place broken glass on a wall, or spikes behind a carriage, one who wilfully encounters them, and is wounded, even though it were by night, when he could have no notice, has no claim for compensation. Volenti non fit injuria [To a willing person, no injury is done]. The Defendant lawfully places a gun on his own property; he leaves the wires visible; he builds a high wall, expressly to keep off intruders; and if, under those circumstances, they are permitted to recover for an injury resulting from their scaling the wall, no man can protect his property at a distance.

Wilde in reply. . . . No illustration can be drawn from the use of spikes and broken glass on walls, & c. These are mere preventives, obvious to the sight,—unless the trespasser *chooses* a time of darkness, when no notice could be available,—mere preventives, injurious only to the persevering and determined trespasser, who can calculate at the moment of incurring the danger the amount of suffering he is about to endure, and who will, consequently, desist from his enterprise whenever the anticipated advantage is outweighed by the pain which he must endure to obtain it.

Best, C.J. I am of opinion that this action is maintainable. . . .

It has been argued that the law does not compel every line of conduct which humanity or religion may require; but there is no act which Christianity forbids, that the law will not reach: if it were otherwise, Christianity would not be, as it has always been held to be, part of the law of England. I am, therefore, clearly of opinion that he who sets spring guns, without giving notice, is guilty of an inhuman act, and that, if injurious consequences ensue, he is liable to yield redress to the sufferer. But this case stands on grounds distinct from any that have preceded it. In general, spring guns have been set for the purpose of deterring; the Defendant placed his for the express purpose of doing injury; for, when called on to give notice, he said, "If I give notice, I shall not catch him." He intended, therefore, that the gun should be discharged, and that the contents should be lodged in the body of his victim, for he could not be caught in any other way. On these principles the action is clearly maintainable, and particularly on the latter ground. . . . As to the case of Brock v. Copeland, Lord Kenyon proceeded on the ground that the Defendant had a right to keep a dog for the preservation of his house, and the Plaintiff, who was his foreman, knew where the dog was stationed. The case of the furious bull is altogether different; for if a man places such an animal where there is a public footpath, he interferes with the rights of the public. What would be the determination of the court if the bull were placed in a field where there is no footpath, we need not now decide; but it may be observed, that he must be placed somewhere, and is kept, not for mischief, but to renew his species; while the gun in the present case was placed purely for mischief. The case of the pit dug on a common has been distinguished, on the ground that the owner had a right to do what he pleased with his own land, and the Plaintiff could shew no right for the horse to be there.

. . . But we want no authority in a case like the present; we put it on the principle that it is inhuman to catch a man by means which may maim him or endanger his life, and, as far as human means can go, it is the object of English law to uphold humanity and the sanctions of religion. It would be, indeed, a subject of regret, if a party were not liable in damages, who, instead of giving notice of the employment of a destructive engine, or removing it, at least, during the day, expressed a resolution to withhold notice, lest, by affording it, he should fail to entrap his victim.

BURROUGH, J. The common understanding of mankind shews, that notice ought to be given when these means of protection are resorted to; and it was formerly the practice upon such occasions to give public notice in market towns. But the present case is of a worse complexion than those which have preceded it; for if the Defendant had proposed merely to protect his property from thieves, he would have set the spring guns only by night. The Plaintiff was only a trespasser: if the Defendant had been present, he would not have been authorised even in taking him into custody, and no man can do indirectly that which he is forbidden to do directly.

NOTES

1. An economic interpretation of Bird v. Holbrook.   Writing from an economic perspective, Judge Posner has analyzed *Bird* as follows:

> The issue in the case, as an economist would frame it, was the proper accommodation of two legitimate activities, growing tulips and raising peacocks. The defendant had a substantial investment in the tulip garden; he lived at a distance; and the wall had proved ineffective against thieves. In an era of negligible police protection, a spring gun may have been the most cost-effective means of protection for the tulips. But since spring guns do not discriminate between the thief and the innocent trespasser, they deter owners of domestic animals from pursuing their animals onto other people's property and so increase the costs (enclosure costs or straying losses) of keeping animals. The court in *Bird* implied an ingenious accommodation: One who sets a spring gun must post notices that he has done so. Then owners of animals will not be reluctant to pursue their animals onto property not so posted. A notice will be of no avail at night, but animals are more likely to be secured then and in any event few owners would chase their straying animals after dark.

Posner, Economic Analysis of Law 240 (9th ed. 2014). For his more extensive analysis, see Posner, Killing or Wounding to Protect a Property Interest, 14 J.L. & Econ. 201, 208-211 (1971).

Exhibit 1.1 **Spring Guns**

As Richard Posner notes, "[s]pring guns were something of a *cause célèbre* in early nineteenth century England." Spring guns were often used by large landowners to trap or deter armed bands of poachers. Market gardeners, of whom Holbrook was one, were particularly troubled by the poachers. Their businesses were located on the outskirts of London and they claimed that an efficient municipal police force had driven London's thieves into their neighborhoods. They viewed spring guns as an easy and inexpensive way to protect their farms. See Posner, Killing or Wounding to Protect a Property Interest, 14 J.L. & Econ. 201, 202 & n.5 (1971).

Parliament enacted strict regulations on the use of spring guns a year before *Bird* was decided. The central provision of the statute stated:

> That from and after the passing of this Act, if any Person shall set or place or cause to be set or placed, any Spring Gun, Man Trap, or other Engine calculated to destroy human Life, or inflict grievous bodily Harm, with the Intent that the same or whereby the same may destroy or inflict grievous bodily Harm upon a Trespasser or other Person coming in contact therewith, the Person so setting or placing, or causing to be so set or placed, such Gun, Trap, or Engine as aforesaid, shall be guilty of a Misdemeanor....

The Act exempted spring guns and similar devices set in dwelling houses between sunset and sunrise. It also "declared and enacted" that the Act did not apply to anything done prior to its passage.

Spring gun – Birmingham, 19th century
Source: Museum Victoria Collections

Some members of Parliament argued that market gardeners should be allowed to set spring guns to protect their property until they were afforded greater police protection.

Suppose a person sets a spring gun in violation of the statute. If the gun is triggered by an individual against whom the application of direct force is warranted (e.g., a would-be assailant who enters a home during the day), does the statute override the homeowner's defense to the intruder's cause of action for personal injuries? Should it excuse the payment of the statutory fine? Note that the statute was repealed in its entirety, 24 & 25 Vict. c. 95 §1 (1861).

What result if an injured child cannot read English? Is it ever proper to use spring guns on property that is not surrounded by a fence or protective wall? Should a landowner be entitled to set spring guns to protect a warehouse as well as a dwelling house? For an affirmative answer, see Scheuermann v. Scharfenberg, 50 So. 335 (Ala. 1909).

2. The malicious use of spring guns. In Katko v. Briney, 183 N.W.2d 657, 659, 663 (Iowa 1971), the defendants owned an old, boarded-up house located several miles from their home, where they stored various old bottles, fruit jars and the like, which they considered to be antiques. Several times the windows in the house had been broken and the entire place "messed up." The defendants first posted "no trespass" signs, but the break-ins continued. Shortly before the injury to the plaintiff, the defendants placed a "shotgun trap" in one of the bedrooms. The gun was first positioned so as to hit an intruder in the stomach, but Mr. Briney, at his wife's insistence, lowered it to hit at the legs. He said that he set the gun "because I was mad and tired of being tormented," but insisted that he "did not intend to injure anyone." The plaintiff was shot in the legs and permanently injured when he entered the defendant's bedroom shortly after the gun was set. He had been to the place several times before, and had intended to steal some of the defendant's possessions. The plaintiff pleaded guilty to a charge of larceny and paid a fine of $50. He also sued the defendant for personal injuries and was awarded $20,000 in actual damages and $10,000 in punitive damages.

At trial the jury was instructed as follows: Instruction No. 5: "You are hereby instructed that one may use reasonable force in the protection of his property, but such right is subject to the qualification that one may not use such means of force as will take human life or inflict great bodily injury. Such is the rule even though the injured party is a trespasser and is in violation of the law himself." Instruction No. 6 stated that the rule was not changed even if "the trespasser may be acting in violation of the law," except that "setting a 'spring gun' or a like dangerous device is justified . . . when the trespasser was committing a felony of violence or a felony punishable by death, or where the trespasser was endangering human life by his act."

The Iowa Supreme Court approved these instructions on appeal and affirmed the judgment for the plaintiff without addressing the question of punitive damages, which had not been raised below. Larson, J., protested against awarding large "windfall" damages to a criminal defendant, noting that "where the evidence is sufficient to sustain a finding that the installation was intended only as a warning to ward off thieves and criminals, I can see no compelling reason why the use of such a device alone would create liability as a matter of law."

Katko stirred up great protest in Iowa and throughout the nation. Hundreds of strangers, including prison inmates, sent checks and cash totaling over $10,000 to the Brineys. Briney remained unrepentant: "They used booby traps in Viet Nam, didn't they? Why can't we use them here to protect our property in this country?" Asked if he would do it again, Briney replied, "There's one thing I'd do different, though, I'd have aimed that gun a few feet higher." See a fuller account in the Chicago Tribune of April 25, 1975, at 1, col. 1.

3. *Wounding or killing in defense of property.* The Second Restatement takes a fairly permissive approach toward the use of force in defense of property.

Restatement of the Law (Second) of Torts

§85. USE OF MECHANICAL DEVICE THREATENING DEATH OR SERIOUS BODILY HARM

The actor is so far privileged to use a device intended or likely to cause serious bodily harm or death for the purpose of protecting his land or chattels from intrusion that he is not liable for the serious bodily harm or death thereby caused to an intruder whose intrusion is, in fact, such that the actor, were he present, would be privileged to prevent or terminate it by the intentional infliction of such harm.

Illustration 1: A, who owns a field adjacent to a golf course, is constantly annoyed by caddies coming into his field for balls driven out of bounds. To prevent these intrusions A installs spring guns upon his land. B, a caddy entering in search of a ball, is shot by one of these guns and has his eye put out. A is subject to liability to B whether he has or has not posted warnings or personally warned the caddy who was injured.

As RST §85 notes, issues surrounding the defense of property also arise when the defendant is present. In these cases should the privilege to use force be broader or narrower than in the spring gun case? In M'Ilvoy v. Cockran, 8 Ky. (2 A.K. Marsh) 271, 275-276 (1820), the defendant, M'Ilvoy, shot and severely wounded the plaintiff, Cockran, while the latter was attempting to tear down a fence on M'Ilvoy's land. The court first held that the defendant did not have to request the plaintiff to leave when he was engaged in the active destruction of property, as would be the case for a simple entrance. However, it rejected the defendant's plea that this wounding was justified in defense of property, noting that

> in cases of *actual force,* as breaking open a gate or door, it is lawful to oppose force with force; and if one breaks down a gate, or comes into a close with force and arms, the possessor need not request him to depart, but may lay hands upon him immediately, for it is but returning violence with violence: so if one comes forcibly and takes away my goods, he may be opposed immediately, for there is no time to make a request: but, say the court, where one enters the close without actual force, although his entry will be construed a *force in law,* there must be a request to depart before the possessor can lay hands upon him and turn him out.
>
> But although a wounding cannot be justified barely in defence of possession, yet if, in attempting to remove the intruder, or prevent his forcible entry, he should commit an assault upon the person of the possessor, or his family, and the owner should, in defence of himself or family, wound him, the wounding may, no doubt, be justified; but then, as the personal assault would form the grounds of justification, the plea should set out, specifically, the assault in justification.

e. Necessity

Ploof v. Putnam
71 A. 188 (Vt. 1908)

MUNSON, J. It is alleged as the ground of recovery that on the 13th day of November, 1904, the defendant was the owner of a certain island in Lake Champlain, and of a certain dock attached thereto, which island and dock were then in charge of the defendant's servant; that the plaintiff was then possessed of and sailing upon said lake a certain loaded sloop, on which were the plaintiff and his wife and two minor children; that there then arose a sudden and violent tempest, whereby the sloop and the property and persons therein were placed in great danger of destruction; that to save these from destruction or injury the plaintiff was compelled to, and did, moor the sloop to defendant's dock; that the defendant by his servant unmoored the sloop, whereupon it was driven upon the shore by the tempest, without the plaintiff's fault; and that the sloop and its contents were thereby destroyed, and the plaintiff and his wife and children cast into the lake and upon the shore, receiving injuries.

This claim is set forth in two counts; one in trespass, charging that the defendant by his servant with force and arms wilfully and designedly unmoored the sloop; the other in case, alleging that it was the duty of the defendant by his servant to permit the plaintiff to moor his sloop to the dock, and to permit it to remain so moored during the continuance of the tempest, but that the defendant by his servant, in disregard of this duty, negligently, carelessly and wrongfully unmoored the sloop. Both counts are demurred to generally.

There are many cases in the books which hold that necessity, and an inability to control movements inaugurated in the proper exercise of a strict right, will justify entries upon land and interferences with personal property that would otherwise have been trespasses. A reference to a few of these will be sufficient to illustrate the doctrine. . . .

In trespass of cattle taken in *A*, defendant pleaded that he was seized of *C*, and found the cattle there damage feasant [causing damage], and chased them toward the pound, and that they escaped from him and went into *A*, and he presently retook them and this was held a good plea. 21 Edw. IV, 64 Vin. Ab. Trespass, H. a. 4 pl. 19. If one have a way over the land of another for his beasts to pass, and the beasts, being properly driven, feed the grass by morsels in passing, or run out of the way and are promptly pursued and brought back, trespass will not lie. See Vin. Ab. Trespass, K. a. pl. 1.

A traveller on a highway, who finds it obstructed from a sudden and temporary cause, may pass upon the adjoining land without becoming a trespasser, because of the necessity.

An entry upon land to save goods which are in danger of being lost or destroyed by water or fire is not a trespass. 21 Hen. VII, 27 Vin. Ab. Trespass, H. a. 4, pl. 24, K. a. pl. 3. In Proctor v. Adams, 113 Mass. 376 (1873), the defendant went upon the plaintiff's beach for the purpose of saving and restoring to the lawful owner a boat which had been driven ashore and was in danger of being carried off by the sea and it was held no trespass.

This doctrine of necessity applies with special force to the preservation of human life. One assaulted and in peril of his life may run through the close of another to escape from his assailant. 37 Hen. VII, pl. 26. One may sacrifice the personal property of another to save his life or the lives of his fellows. In Mouse's Case, 12 Co. 63, the defendant was sued for taking and carrying away the plaintiff's casket and its contents. It appeared that the ferryman of Gravesend took forty-seven passengers into his barge to pass to London, among whom were the plaintiff and defendant; and the barge being upon the water a great tempest happened, and a strong wind, so that the barge and all the passengers were in danger of being lost if certain ponderous things were not cast out, and the defendant thereupon cast out the plaintiff's casket. It was resolved that in case of necessity, to save the lives of the passengers, it was lawful for the defendant, being a passenger, to cast the plaintiff's casket out of the barge; that if the ferryman surcharge the barge the owner shall have his remedy upon the surcharge against the ferryman, but that if there be no surcharge, and the danger accrue only by the act of God, as by tempest, without fault of the ferryman, every one ought to bear this loss, to safeguard the life of a man.

It is clear that an entry upon the land of another may be justified by necessity, and that the declaration before us discloses a necessity for mooring the sloop. But the defendant questions the sufficiency of the counts because they do not negative the existence of natural objects to which the plaintiff could have moored with equal safety. The allegations are, in substance, that the stress of a sudden and violent tempest compelled the plaintiff to moor to defendant's dock to save his sloop and the people in it. The averment of necessity is complete, for it covers not only the necessity of mooring, but the necessity of mooring to the dock; and the details of the situation which created this necessity, whatever the legal requirements regarding them, are matters of proof and need not be alleged. It is certain that the rule suggested cannot be held applicable irrespective of circumstance, and the question must be left for adjudication upon proceedings had with reference to the evidence or the charge. . . .

Judgment affirmed and cause remanded.

NOTES

1. Necessity and self-help. While still at sea, were the plaintiffs entitled to use force to land on the dock if the defendant's servant had resisted them? To keep their boat moored to the dock? Note that under the general common law rules, the defendant's servants, while they may not resist plaintiff's entry to dock in conditions of necessity, are not obliged to lend a helping hand. See *infra* Chapter 6, Section B. Why the difference? Why should the master have to pay for his servant's torts? See *infra* Chapter 7, Section F.

2. General average contribution. Mouse's Case, 77 Eng. Rep. 1341 (K.B. 1609), discussed in cryptic form in *Ploof*, held "that in a case of necessity, for the saving of the lives of the passengers, it was lawful for the defendant, being a passenger, to cast the casket of the plaintiff out of the barge, with other things in it." Mouse's Case hints at the elaboration of the necessity principle in the law of admiralty under the rubric of general average contribution. Suppose a vessel is carrying cargo owned by a number of different parties when its master is confronted with a sudden emergency that jeopardizes the safety of the ship and cargo. Under the law of general average contribution, the master may jettison some of the cargo in order to save the ship and the remaining cargo. In order to prevent some property owners from being relatively disadvantaged by the loss of their cargo, they receive pro rata compensation from other parties, including the owner of the hull, so that the

Exhibit 1.2   "The Pirates of Lake Champlain"

Photo of a boat similar to one that may have belonged to the Ploofs. The original had its boiler and machinery removed to be used as a houseboat.
Atomic / Alamy

The official presentation of the facts conveys the impression that Sylvester Ploof was a complete stranger who happened to be traveling on the lake when he was caught in the storm and then just happened to sail to the defendant's island and dock. The local lore about this case is quite different. The Ploofs were a poor, landless family who lived and worked on their boat. They earned their living transporting firewood and other goods on the lake and were well known and disliked by the lakeshore inhabitants. Known as the "pirates" of Lake Champlain, they were often accused of raiding and stealing from vacation homes on the lake. When they were seen in the area, homeowners generally went on the alert and even chased them off with guns. Henry Putnam's caretaker untied the Ploofs' boat because he knew them and he was aware of their reputation as thieves, not simply because the Ploofs were using the dock without the owner's permission.

Vogel, Cases in Context: Lake Champlain Wars, Gentrification and Ploof v. Putnam, 45 St. Louis U. L.J. 791, 798 (2001).

total loss from property damage is prorated across all owners. In effect, in time of emergency all are treated as joint owners of all the property in question. This rule gives the master a desirable incentive to minimize the aggregate loss to all concerned. As each owner is placed, as it were, behind a veil of ignorance, he can do best by himself only if he does best by all owners of hull and cargo alike. On the complexities of the law of general average contribution, see Gilmore & Black, The Law of Admiralty §§5.1, 5.2 (2d ed. 1975). See also Landes & Posner, Salvors, Finders, Good Samaritans, and Other Rescuers: An Economic Study of Law and Altruism, 7 J. Legal Stud. 83, 106-108 (1978).

Vincent v. Lake Erie Transportation Co.
124 N.W. 221 (Minn. 1910)

O'BRIEN, J. The steamship Reynolds, owned by the defendant, was for the purpose of discharging her cargo on November 27, 1905, moored to plaintiff's dock in Duluth. While the unloading of the boat was taking place a storm from the northeast developed, which at about ten o'clock P.M., when the unloading was completed, had so grown in violence that the wind was then moving at fifty miles per hour and continued to increase during the night. There is some evidence that one, and perhaps two, boats were able to enter the harbor that night, but it is plain that navigation was practically suspended from the hour mentioned until the morning of the twenty-ninth, when the storm abated, and during that time no master would have been justified in attempting to navigate his vessel, if he could avoid doing so. After the discharge of the cargo the Reynolds signaled for a tug to tow her from the dock, but none could be obtained because of the severity of the storm. If the lines holding the ship to the dock had been cast off, she would doubtless have drifted away; but, instead, the lines were kept fast, and as soon as one parted or chafed it was replaced, sometimes with a larger one. The vessel lay upon the outside of the dock, her bow to the east, the wind and waves striking her starboard quarter with such force that she was constantly being lifted and thrown against the dock, resulting in its damage, as found by the jury, to the amount of $500.

We are satisfied that the character of this storm was such that it would have been highly imprudent for the master of the Reynolds to have attempted to leave the dock or to have permitted his vessel to drift away from it. One witness testified upon the trial that the vessel could have been warped into a slip, and that, if the attempt to bring the ship into the slip had failed, the worst that could have happened would be that the vessel would have been blown ashore upon a soft and muddy bank. The witness was not present in Duluth at the time of the storm, and, while he may have been right in his conclusions, those in charge of the dock and the vessel at the time of the storm were not required to use the highest human intelligence, nor were they required to resort to every possible experiment which could be suggested for the preservation of their property. Nothing more was demanded of them than ordinary prudence and care, and the record in this case fully sustains the contention of the appellant that, in holding the vessel fast to the dock, those in charge of her exercised good judgment and prudent seamanship.

It is claimed by the respondent that it was negligence to moor the boat at an exposed part of the wharf, and to continue in that position after it became apparent that the storm was to be more than usually severe. We do not agree with this position. The part of the wharf where the vessel was moored appears to have been commonly used for that purpose. It was situated within the harbor at Duluth, and must, we think, be considered a proper and safe place, and would undoubtedly have been such during what would be considered a very severe storm. The storm which made it unsafe was one which surpassed in violence any which might have reasonably been anticipated.

The appellant contends by ample assignments of error that, because its conduct during the storm was rendered necessary by prudence and good seamanship under conditions over which it had no control, it cannot be held liable for any injury resulting to the property of others, and claims that the jury should have been so instructed. An analysis of the charge given by the trial court is not necessary, as in our opinion the only question for the jury was the amount of damages which the plaintiffs were entitled to recover, and no complaint is made upon that score.

The situation was one in which the ordinary rules regulating property rights were suspended by forces beyond human control, and if, without the direct intervention of some act by the one sought to be held liable, the property of another was injured, such injury must be attributed to the act of God, and not to the wrongful act of the person sought to be charged. If during the storm the

Reynolds had entered the harbor, and while there had become disabled and been thrown against the plaintiffs' dock, the plaintiffs could not have recovered. Again, if while attempting to hold fast to the dock the lines had parted, without any negligence, and the vessel carried against some other boat or dock in the harbor, there would be no liability upon her owner. But here those in charge of the vessel deliberately and by their direct efforts held her in such a position that the damage to the dock resulted, and, having thus preserved the ship at the expense of the dock, it seems to us that her owners are responsible to the dock owners to the extent of the injury inflicted. . . .

In Ploof v. Putnam, 71 Atl. 188, the Supreme Court of Vermont held that where, under stress of weather, a vessel was without permission moored to a private dock at an island in Lake Champlain owned by the defendant, the plaintiff was not guilty of trespass, and that the defendant was responsible in damages because his representative upon the island unmoored the vessel, permitting it to drift upon the shore, with resultant injuries to it. If, in that case, the vessel had been permitted to remain, and the dock had suffered an injury, we believe the shipowner would have been held liable for the injury done.

Theologians hold that a starving man may, without moral guilt, take what is necessary to sustain life but it could hardly be said that the obligation would not be upon such person to pay the value of the property so taken when he became able to do so. And so public necessity, in times of war or peace, may require the taking of private property for public purposes; but under our system of jurisprudence compensation must be made.

Let us imagine in this case that for the better mooring of the vessel those in charge of her had appropriated a valuable cable lying upon the dock. No matter how justifiable such appropriation might have been, it would not be claimed that, because of the overwhelming necessity of the situation, the owner of the cable could not recover its value.

This is not a case where life or property was menaced by any object or thing belonging to the plaintiffs, the destruction of which became necessary to prevent the threatened disaster. Nor is it a case where, because of the act of God, or unavoidable accident, the infliction of the injury was beyond the control of the defendant, but is one where the defendant prudently and advisedly availed itself of the plaintiffs' property for the purpose of preserving its own more valuable property, and the plaintiffs are entitled to compensation for the injury done.

Order affirmed.

Lewis, J. I dissent. It was assumed on the trial before the lower court that appellant's liability depended on whether the master of the ship might, in the exercise of reasonable care, have sought a place of safety before the storm made it impossible to leave the dock. The majority opinion assumes that the evidence is conclusive that appellant moored its boat at respondents' dock pursuant to contract, and that the vessel was lawfully in position at the time the additional cables were fastened to the dock, and the reasoning of the opinion is that, because appellant made use of the stronger cables to hold the boat in position, it became liable under the rule that it had voluntarily made use of the property of another for the purpose of saving its own.

In my judgment, if the boat was lawfully in position at the time the storm broke, and the master could not, in the exercise of due care, have left that position without subjecting his vessel to the hazards of the storm, then the damage to the dock, caused by the pounding of the boat, was the result of an inevitable accident. If the master was in the exercise of due care, he was not at fault. The reasoning of the opinion admits that if the ropes, or cables, first attached to the dock had not parted, or if, in the first instance, the master had used the stronger cables, there would be no liability. If the master could not, in the exercise of reasonable care, have anticipated the severity of the storm and sought a place of safety before it became impossible, why should he be required to anticipate the severity of the storm, and, in the first instance, use the stronger cables?

I am of the opinion that one who constructs a dock to the navigable line of waters, and enters into contractual relations with the owner of a vessel to moor the same, takes the risk of damage to his dock by a boat caught there by a storm, which event could not have been avoided in the exercise of due care, and further, that the legal status of the parties in such a case is not changed by renewal of cables to keep the boat from being cast adrift at the mercy of the tempest.

JAGGARD, J., concurs.

NOTES

1. Private necessity, assumption of risk, and unjust enrichment. Under traditional law, *Vincent* represents a case of "conditional" or "incomplete" privilege. The defendant may use or damage the plaintiff's dock, which he could not do deliberately in the absence of necessity, but, in contrast to self-defense, he must pay for the privilege by tendering reasonable rental value or compensation for lost or damaged property, as the case may be. See RST §197. A case of incomplete privilege usually occurs between strangers, but it may also arise where a business invitee or social guest remains on an owner's property, after being asked to leave, to avoid facing the necessity. Does the majority opinion ever come to grips with the dissent's contention that the case turns on how the mooring contract allocated the risk of loss? How does one decide which risks the shipowner assumed when the contract does not expressly cover the problem? Contrast Epstein, A Theory of Strict Liability, 2 J. Legal Stud. 151, 157-160 (1973) (defending *Vincent*) with Weinrib, Causation and Wrongdoing, 63 Chi.-Kent L. Rev. 407, 425-429 (1987) (criticizing it).

The outcome in *Vincent* may also be justified under a theory of "unjust enrichment," which requires the boat owner to compensate the dock owner for the benefit that he received from the use of the dock. How does that theory work if the shipowner's benefit is $10,000, and the harm to the dock $500? When the figures are reversed? When the ship is lost and the dock damaged? See generally, on unjust enrichment, Keeton, Conditional Fault in the Law of Torts, 72 Harv. L. Rev. 401, 410 (1959).

2. Necessity and bilateral monopoly. The private necessity issue also has an important contractual dimension. Suppose that a vessel in distress at sea seeks to dock where the normal mooring fee is $100. In a world in which prices are determined solely by private agreement, the dock owner may "hold out" for a larger fee, perhaps one approaching the value of the boat and cargo. If the boat owner complies with the demand, should he be held to the contractual price when the dock owner practiced neither fraud nor duress? The standard response, both in admiralty and at common law, is to void the contract and restrict the dock owner's recovery to a reasonable fee relative to the cost, as adjusted for risk, of the services rendered.

The point has been made most forcefully with contracts for salvage, or rescue at sea by professional salvors. In Post v. Jones, 60 U.S. 150, 159, 160 (1856), the *Richmond*, laden with oil and whalebone, ran aground in heavy fog in the Bering Sea on a barren shore in an area populated by "few inhabitants, savages and thieves." In distress its master sold at auction about 800 barrels of oil and large quantities of whalebone to the Elizabeth Firth and the Panama. On their return home the owners of the oil and whalebone sought to modify the terms of those sales over claims from the respondents that "this sale was a fair, honest, and valid sale of the property." Grier, J. set aside the transaction, writing:

> The contrivance of an auction sale, under such circumstances, where the master of the Richmond was hopeless, helpless, and passive — where there was no market, no money, no competition — where one party had absolute power, and the other no choice but submission — where the vendor must take what is offered or get nothing — is a transaction which has no characteristic of a valid contract. . . .
>
> It has been contended, also, that the sale was justifiable and valid, because it was better for the interests of all concerned to accept what was offered, than suffer a total loss. But this argument proves too much, as it would justify every sale to a salvor. Courts of admiralty will enforce contracts made for salvage service and salvage compensation, where the salvor has not taken advantage of his power to make an unreasonable bargain; but they will not tolerate the doctrine that a salvor can take advantage of his situation, and avail himself of the calamities of others to drive a bargain; nor will they permit the performance of a public duty to be turned into a traffic of profit. The general interests of commerce will be much better promoted by requiring the salvor to trust for compensation to the liberal recompense usually awarded by the courts for such services.

In practice, the holdout problem at sea is often averted by the common practice of referring salvage awards to arbitration, often through Lloyd's of London, where they are resolved in accordance with standard industry practice. Formerly, the salvor's award had been limited to the rescue of hull and cargo. Now that liability for pollution has become a major economic risk, salvage awards specifically include "liability salvage" for preventing spillage, notwithstanding the obvious measurement problems involved. See Brough, Liability Salvage — By Private Ordering, 19 J. Legal Stud. 95 (1990).

3. Public necessity. When are private or government agents privileged to destroy private property to protect the interests of the community at large? The problem has arisen chiefly in two contexts: first, where property is destroyed in order to prevent the destruction of a city by fire and, second, where weapons and facilities are destroyed to keep them from falling into enemy hands in time of war. In Mayor of New York v. Lord, 18 Wend. 126, 129-130 (N.Y. 1837), the court held that it was "well settled" that the privilege was absolute so that "in cases of actual necessity, to prevent the spreading of a fire, the ravages of a pestilence, the advance of a hostile army, or any other great public calamity, the private property of an individual may be lawfully taken and used or destroyed, for the relief, protection or safety of the many, without subjecting those, whose duty it is to protect the public interests, by or under whose direction such private property was taken or destroyed, to personal liability for the damage which the owner has thereby sustained." In the words of Bohlen, "since the benefit is solely social, there is no reason why one who acts as a champion of the public should be required to pay for the privilege of so doing." Bohlen, Incomplete Privilege to Inflict Intentional Invasions of Interests of Property and Personality, 39 Harv. L. Rev. 307, 317-318 (1926). Should the person whose property is converted to the public use be required against his will to become the champion of the public?

To understand the scope of the doctrine, it is important to distinguish two types of cases. In one type of public necessity case, the property destroyed would have been lost anyway. The city fire would have consumed the homes demolished in order to prevent its spread; the industrial installations blown up would have been taken or destroyed by the enemy. In these cases, the plaintiff loses not because the privilege is complete, but because virtually all the loss is caused by a third party.

In the second type of case, however, the property would *not* have been destroyed without the defendant's intervention. The fire died out before it reached the demolished homes; the enemy was unable to capture the installations. In these cases, the defendant must rest solely on the privilege. The Pennsylvania Supreme Court in Respublica v. Sparhawk, 1 U.S. (1 Dall.) 357, 363 (Pa. 1788), justified the complete privilege for these cases in this way:

> We find, indeed, a memorable instance of folly recorded in the 3 Vol. of Clarendon's History, where it is mentioned, that the Lord Mayor of London, in 1666, when that city was on fire, would not give directions for, or consent to, the pulling down forty wooden houses, or to the removing the furniture, &c. belonging to the Lawyers of the Temple, then on the Circuit, for fear he should be answerable for a trespass; and in consequence of this conduct half that great city was burnt.

Sparhawk reveals the asymmetrical incentives found in all cases of public necessity. The public official who wrongly orders the destruction of property bears all the loss if his prediction that the fire will spread proves false, but captures none of the gain if correct. Why then should he act at all? As the official cannot recoup his losses from the owners of the saved property, the only way to balance his incentives is to insulate him from liability, at least when he acts reasonably and in good faith. But this approach, taken alone, does not compensate the individual owners who suffer enormous private losses for the benefit of the community at large. Should an aggrieved landowner be allowed an action for restitution against the benefited landowners? From the government? If so, should it pay out of general revenues, or from special assessments levied against the parties benefited? On the general merits of personal and official immunity, see the Symposium, Civil Liability of Government Officials: Property Rights and Official Accountability, 42 Law & Contemp. Probs. 8 (1978).

4. Public necessity and just compensation. The complete privilege for public necessity is in constant tension with the basic constitutional principle that requires the government to compensate private owners whose property is taken for public use. For a vivid example that tests the line between the two doctrines during wartime, see United States v. Caltex, Inc., 344 U.S. 149 (1952), where the Court refused to order compensation for the demolition of an oil company's terminal facilities in Manila before the Japanese takeover, Black and Douglas, JJ., dissenting. Likewise, in National Board of Y.M.C.A.s v. United States, 395 U.S. 85 (1969), the Court found no compensable taking when U.S. Army troops occupied the plaintiff's buildings located in the Panama Canal Zone after they had been placed under siege by rioting Panamanians who had already caused substantial damage to the structures.

That position has held firm in the years since then. In Brewer v. State, 341 P.3d 1107, 1115-1116 (Alaska 2014), major forest fires swept through Fairbanks, Alaska, and threatened to burn the structures of several landowners. The Alaskan Forest Service deliberately set backfires that destroyed the landowners' vegetation but saved the structures. The landowners' tort claim was emphatically rejected on statutory grounds that gave the Forest Service immunity "for the purpose of preventing, suppressing, or controlling a wildland fire." The constitutional takings claim was in turn rejected under the general police power on grounds of necessity, regardless of whether the fires were intended to save the plaintiff's property or other state lands:

> Public necessity acts as a defense to property torts such as trespass and conversion and allows a person to enter land and destroy property where there is "[a] necessity that involves the public interest." Public necessity "completely excuses the defendant's liability." While the privilege of public necessity is an individual one, state officials can exercise it. Thus, the state generally does not have to pay compensation where "the destruction or damage was, or reasonably appeared to be, necessary to prevent an impending or imminent public disaster from fire, flood, disease, or riot."

Should the Forest Service be entitled to send the landowners a bill for the property saved?

Judith Jarvis Thomson, The Trolley Problem
94 Yale L.J. 1395 (1985)

Some years ago, Philippa Foot drew attention to an extraordinarily interesting problem. Suppose you are the driver of a trolley. The trolley rounds a bend, and there come into view ahead five track workmen, who have been repairing the track. The track goes through a bit of a valley at that point, and the sides are steep, so you must stop the trolley if you are to avoid running the five men down. You step on the brakes, but alas, they don't work. Now you suddenly see a spur of track leading off to the right. You can turn the trolley onto it, and thus save the five men on the straight track ahead. Unfortunately, Mrs. Foot has arranged that there is one track workman on that spur of track. He can no more get off the track in time than the five can, so you will kill him if you turn the trolley onto him. Is it morally permissible for you to turn the trolley?

Everybody to whom I have put this hypothetical case says, Yes, it is. Some people say something stronger than that it is morally *permissible* for you to turn the trolley: They say that morally speaking, you *must* turn it—that morality requires you to do so. Others do not agree that morality requires you to turn the trolley, and even feel a certain discomfort at the idea of turning it. But everybody says that it is true, at a minimum, that you *may* turn it—that it would not be morally wrong in you to do so.

Now consider a second hypothetical case. This time you are to imagine yourself to be a surgeon, a truly great surgeon. Among other things you do, you transplant organs, and you are such a great surgeon that the organs you transplant always take. At the moment you have five patients who need organs. Two need one lung each, two need a kidney each, and the fifth needs a heart. If they do not get those organs today, they will all die; if you find organs for them today you can transplant the organs and they will all live. But where to find the lungs, the kidneys, and the heart? The time is almost up when a report is brought to you that a young man who has just come into your clinic for his yearly check-up has exactly the right blood type, and is in excellent health. Lo, you have your possible donor. All you need do is cut him up and distribute *his* parts among the five who need them. You ask, but he says, "Sorry. I deeply sympathize, but no." Would it be morally permissible for you to operate anyway? Everybody to whom I have put this second hypothetical says, No, it would not be morally permissible for you to proceed.

Here then is Mrs. Foot's problem: *Why* is it that the trolley driver may turn his trolley, though the surgeon may not remove the young man's lungs, kidneys, and heart? In both cases, one will die if the agent acts, but five will live who would otherwise die—net saving of four lives. What difference in the other facts of these cases explains the moral difference between them? I fancy that the theorists of tort and criminal law will find this problem as interesting as the moral theorist does.

NOTE

Moral and legal theories. Having restated Professor Foot's problem, Professor Thomson then explores some possible responses. If, morally speaking, it is worse to kill than to let die, the surgeon should not act while the trolley driver can turn the wheel because his only choice is between killing one and killing five. But suppose, as Thomson next suggests, a bystander is able to throw a switch that will divert the trolley from its original track, but can choose to do nothing, in which case the trolley will kill five. Is the bystander not justified in doing what the trolley driver may do?

Note that one difference between the two cases rests on the observation that the crisis "suddenly" struck the driver, but not the surgeon. Accordingly, an alternative approach shifts attention to the long-term incentive effects of adopting one rule or the other. So long as the trolley driver is held responsible whether he kills one or five, he faces two separate incentives: the first, which is the subject of the Thomson inquiry, is to minimize the number of deaths *once* the emergency occurs. The second is to check the brakes to prevent the emergency from arising in the first place—an incentive that remains in place so long as the liability rule remains fixed in ways that hold the driver responsible in tort for whatever harm he causes. Quite simply, we should expect fewer brake failures.

The effects on the famous surgeon in the prior period, however, are quite different, for she will never be able to attract patients in the first place if she is intent on cutting them up to help others. Over the long haul, it might be possible to organize a voluntary market for the sale of organs either during life or after death, which has none of the downside of coerced transfers. Yet while organ donations are legal today, their sale is flatly prohibited by federal law. See National Organ Transplant Act (NOTA) §301, 42 U.S.C. §274e (2012), which prohibits the payment or receipt of "valuable consideration," in either cash or kind, in exchange for organs used for human transplantation. For a trenchant critique, see Cohen, Increasing the Supply of Transplant Organs: The Virtues of a Futures Market, 58 Geo. Wash. L. Rev. 1 (1989). The case for a regulated market in organ transplants is made by Williams, Finley & Rohack, Just Say No to NOTA: Why the Prohibition of Compensation for Human Transplant Organs in NOTA Should Be Repealed and a Regulated Market for Cadaver Organs Instituted, 40 Am. J.L. & Med. 275 (2014). As of November 2015, over 122,000 people were on the transplant list. For continuously updated numbers, see OPTN: Organ Procurement and Transplantation Network, U.S. Dep't of Health & Human Services, http://optn.transplant.hrsa.gov/.

SECTION C. EMOTIONAL AND DIGNITARY HARMS

1. Assault

I. de S. and Wife v. W. de S.
At the Assizes, coram Thorpe, C.J., 1348 [or 1349] Year Book,
Liber Assisarum, folio 99, placitum 60

I. de S. & M. uxor ejus querunt de W. de S. de eo quod idem W. anno, & c., vi et armis, & c., apud S., in ipsam M. insultum fecit, et ipsam verberavit, & c. [I. de

S. and his wife, M., sue W. de S. concerning that which in the year, etc., by force and arms, etc., at S. has made insults of the aforesaid M., and has beat her.] And W. pleaded not guilty. And it was found by verdict of the inquest that the said W. came in the night to the house of the said I., and would have bought some wine, but the door of the tavern was closed; and he struck on the door with a hatchet, which he had in his hand, and the woman plaintiff put her head out at a window and ordered him to stop; and he perceived her and struck with the hatchet, but did not touch the woman. Whereupon the inquest said that it seemed to them that there was no trespass, since there was no harm done.

THORPE, C.J. There is harm, and a trespass for which they shall recover damages, since he made an assault upon the woman, as it is found, although he did no other harm. Wherefore tax his damages, & c. And they taxed the damages at half a mark.

THORPE, C.J., awarded that they should recover their damages, & c., and that the other should be taken. Et sic nota, [And thus it was noted] that for an assault one shall recover damages, & c.

Tuberville v. Savage
86 Eng. Rep. 684 (K.B. 1669)

Action of *assault, battery,* and *wounding.* The evidence to prove a provocation was, that the plaintiff put his hand upon his sword and said, "If *it were not assize-time [i.e., if the judge were not in town], I would not take such language from you.*" — The question was, If that were an assault? — The Court agreed that it was not; for the declaration of the plaintiff was, that he would not assault him, the Judges being in town; and *the intention* as well as *the act* makes an assault. Therefore if one strike another upon the hand, or arm, or breast in discourse, it is no assault, there being no *intention* to assault; but if one intending to assault, strike *at* another and miss him, this is an assault: so if he hold up his hand against another in a threatening manner and say nothing, it is an assault. — In the principal case the plaintiff had judgment.

William Blackstone, Commentaries
Vol. 3, p. 120 (1765)

[A]ssault [is] an attempt to offer to beat another, without touching him: as if one lifts up his cane, or his fist, in a threatening manner at another; or strikes at him, but misses him; this is an assault, insultus, which Finch describes to be "an unlawful setting upon one's person." This also is an inchoate violence, amounting considerably higher than bare threats; and therefore, though no actual suffering is proved, yet the party injured may have redress by action of trespass vi et armis; wherein he shall recover damages as compensation for the injury.

Exhibit 1.3   Sir William Blackstone

Bio source: *William Blackstone*, Encyclopaedia Britannica, http://www.britannica.com/biography/William-Blackstone Image source: Wikimedia Commons

Sir William Blackstone (1723-1780), English jurist and judge, is best known as the author of the Commentaries on the Laws of England, a four-volume treatise that chronicled the state of English law in the eighteenth century. Soon after their publication, the Commentaries became the basis of legal education in England and the United States and continue to be cited by courts to this day. Orphaned by age 12, Blackstone was educated by his uncle, and then at Oxford, where he read classics, logic, and mathematics. He later became a student at Middle Temple, one of the Inns of Court, and was a barrister by 1746. After seven years of practice, he began to concentrate on teaching law, and his lectures on the common law were the first on English law ever delivered in a university. Blackstone combined his academic career with an active public life, which included membership in Parliament, the House of Commons, and a judgeship on the Court of Common Pleas.

NOTES

1. The social protection against assaults.   Does *I. de S.* give uniform protection against mental distress from the threat of assault? Should the defendant be liable for assault when he first struck the door with the hatchet if he knew that the plaintiff was inside? If he thought there was a good chance she was inside? Should it matter that the defendant struck the second blow—where? why? how?—only after he "perceived" the plaintiff?

The dangers to the social fabric from threats of force were forcefully stated in Allen v. Hannaford, 244 P. 700, 701 (Wash. 1926). The plaintiff had hired moving men to take her furniture from an apartment she had rented from the defendant. The defendant had placed a lien on the plaintiff's furniture (which gave him the right to seize the furniture, sell it, and apply the proceeds to unpaid back rent). When the defendant discovered that the furniture was being removed, she appeared with a pistol and threatened to shoot the moving men "full of holes" if they took a single piece of the plaintiff's furniture. Then, "standing only a few feet from [plaintiff], she pointed the pistol at her face and threatened to shoot her." The court rejected the defendant's argument that she could not be guilty of an assault for brandishing an unloaded gun, saying "[w]hether there is an assault in a given case depends more upon the apprehensions created in the mind of the person assaulted than upon what may be the secret intentions of the person committing the assault." The court then affirmed the $750 verdict for the plaintiff, quoting the observations from Beach v. Hancock, 27 N.H. 223 (1853):

> One of the most important objects to be attained by the enactment of laws and the institutions of civilized society is, each of us shall feel secure against unlawful

assaults. Without such security society loses most of its value. Peace and order and domestic happiness, inexpressibly more precious than mere forms of government, cannot be enjoyed without the sense of perfect security. We have a right to live in society without being put in fear of personal harm. But it must be a reasonable fear of which we complain. And it surely is not unreasonable for a person to entertain a fear of personal injury, when a pistol is pointed at him in a threatening manner, when, for aught he knows, it may be loaded, and may occasion his immediate death. The business of the world could not be carried on with comfort, if such things could be done with impunity.

If the gun was not pointed toward the plaintiff, did the defendant only make, to use Blackstone's distinction, a "mere threat," or did she commit an act of "inchoate violence"? Is there an assault if the plaintiff knows that the defendant is wielding an unloaded gun?

2. Mere words, conditional threats, and the use of force.   The time-honored common law maxim—"mere words do not amount to an assault"—applies to strong words used during argument. It has been criticized for overlooking the subtle (and not-so-subtle) ways the voice alone can convey threats of the immediate or future use of force. Undoubtedly, this formula is meant to preclude liability in common situations in which intemperate or insulting speech injures feelings or arouses apprehension. In Tuberville v. Savage, why did the court assume that the plaintiff's words gave an accurate reading of his intention, instead of being a ruse to catch the defendant off guard? What result if it had not been "assize-time," and the plaintiff had said, "If it were not for my generous nature, I would not take such language from you"?

Restatement of the Law (Second) of Torts

§21. ASSAULT

(1) An actor is subject to liability to another for assault if

(a) he acts intending to cause a harmful or offensive contact with the person of the other or a third person, or an imminent apprehension of such a contact, and

(b) the other is thereby put in such imminent apprehension.

§24. WHAT CONSTITUTES APPREHENSION

In order that the other may be put in the apprehension necessary to make the actor liable for an assault, the other must believe that the act may result in imminent contact unless prevented from so resulting by the other's self-defensive action or by his flight or by the intervention of some outside force.

> **Comment b. Distinction between apprehension and fright:** It is not necessary that the other believe that the act done by the actor will be effective in inflicting the intended contact upon him. It is enough that he believes that the act is capable of immediately inflicting the contact upon him unless something further occurs. Therefore, the mere fact that he can easily prevent the threatened contact by self-defensive measures which he feels amply capable of taking does not prevent the actor's attempt to inflict the contact upon him from being an actionable assault. So too, he may have every reason to believe that bystanders will interfere in time to prevent the blow threatened by the actor from taking effect and his belief may be justified by the event. Bystanders may intervene and prevent the actor from striking him. None the less, the actor's blow thus prevented from taking effect is an actionable assault. The apprehension which is sufficient to make the actor liable may have no relation to fear, which at least implies a doubt as to whether the actor's attempt is capable of certain frustration.

The limits of the common law action for assault are also tested when the defendant makes a threat at a distance. In Brower v. Ackerley, 943 P.2d 1141, 1145 (Wash. Ct. App. 1997), the defendants ran a billboard advertising business. The plaintiff, who was active in civic affairs, reported to the Seattle City Council that many of the defendants' billboards were operated without permits and were kept off the tax rolls. When the City did not respond, the plaintiff filed a separate lawsuit against both it and the defendants. Two days later, an anonymous male caller began a campaign of telephone harassment against the plaintiff, which included calling him a "dick" and saying, "I'm going to find out where you live and I am going to kick your ass." After the calls were traced to one of the Ackerleys' sons, the action for assault ensued, in which the plaintiff argued that even though mere words do not constitute an assault, these "spoken threats became assaultive in view of the surrounding circumstances including the fact that the calls were made to his home, at night, creating the impression that the caller was stalking him." But the court denied the action, noting the absence of an immediate threat. Which matters more, the directness of the threat or the probability that it will be carried out?

2. Offensive Battery

Alcorn v. Mitchell
63 Ill. 553 (1872)

SHELDON, J. The ground mainly relied on for the reversal of the judgment in this case is, that the damages are excessive, being $1000.

The case presented is this: There was a trial of an action of trespass between the parties, wherein the appellee was defendant, in the circuit court of Jasper county. At the close of the trial the court adjourned, and, immediately upon the adjournment, in the court room, in the presence of a large number of persons, the appellant deliberately spat in the face of the appellee.

So long as damages are allowable in any civil case, by way of punishment or for the sake of example, the present, of all cases, would seem to be a most fit one for the award of such damages.

The act in question was one of the greatest indignity, highly provocative of retaliation by force, and the law, as far as it may, should afford substantial protection against such outrages, in the way of liberal damages, that the public tranquillity may be preserved by saving the necessity of resort to personal violence as the only means of redress.

Suitors, in the assertion of their rights, should be allowed approach to the temple of justice without incurring there exposure to such disgraceful indignities, in the very presence of its ministers.

It is customary to instruct juries that they may give vindictive damages where there are circumstances of malice, wilfulness, wantonness, outrage and indignity attending the wrong complained of. The act in question was wholly made up of such qualities. It was one of pure malignity, done for the mere purpose of insult and indignity.

An exasperated suitor has indulged the gratification of his malignant feelings in this despicable mode. The act was the very refinement of malice. The defendant appears to be a man of wealth; we can not say that he has been made to pay too dearly for the indulgence. . . .

The judgment must be affirmed.

NOTE

Basis of liability for offensive battery. What result in Alcorn v. Mitchell if the appellee spat at the appellant but missed? Does it make a difference whether the appellant knew that the appellee spat at him? That others in the courtroom knew?

Restatement of the Law (Second) of Torts

§18. BATTERY: OFFENSIVE CONTACT

(1) An actor is subject to liability to another for battery if

(a) he acts intending to cause a harmful or offensive contact with the person of the other or a third person, or an imminent apprehension of such a contact, and

(b) an offensive contact with the person of the other directly or indirectly results.

(2) An act which is not done with the intention stated in Subsection (1, a) does not make the actor liable to the other for a mere offensive contact with the other's person although the act involves an unreasonable risk of inflicting it and, therefore, would be negligent or reckless if the risk threatened bodily harm.

There are many reported cases of nonharmful offensive batteries. In Respublica v. De Longchamps, 1 U.S. (1 Dall.) 111, 114 (Pa. 1784), defendant struck the cane of the French ambassador and was prosecuted under the law of nations. The court remarked: "As to the assault, this is, perhaps, one of that kind, in which the insult is more to be considered than the actual damage; for, though no great bodily pain is suffered by a blow on the palm of the hand, or the skirt of the coat, yet these are clearly within the definition of assault and battery, and among gentlemen too often induce duelling and terminate in murder." The Restatement notes that knowledge that unpermitted conduct has taken place is not necessary to establish the battery. "*A* kisses *B* while asleep but does not waken or harm her. *A* is subject to liability to *B*." RST §18, comment *d*, illus. 2.

The protection afforded against offensive battery covers not only cases of direct contact with the plaintiff's person, but also contact with "anything so closely attached [to the plaintiff's person] that it is customarily regarded as a part thereof and which is offensive to a reasonable sense of personal dignity." RST §18, comment *c*. An example is the striking of the plaintiff's cane in the *Longchamps* case, *supra*; for other such acts, see Clark v. Downing, 55 Vt. 259 (1882) (striking the horse that plaintiff was riding); Fisher v. Carrousel Motor Hotel, Inc., 424 S.W.2d 627 (Tex. 1967) (grabbing at plaintiff's plate); and Reynolds v. MacFarlane, 322 P.3d 755 (Utah 2014) (taking ten dollar bill loosely held by plaintiff employee).

3. False Imprisonment

Coblyn v. Kennedy's, Inc.
268 N.E.2d 860 (Mass. 1971)

[The plaintiff, a 70-year-old man, five feet four inches tall and dressed in a woolen shirt, topcoat, and hat, was shopping in defendant's store. Around his neck plaintiff wore an ascot he had previously purchased in Filene's, another department store. While trying on a sportscoat, the plaintiff took off his ascot and put it into his pocket. He purchased the coat, left it for alterations, and, as he was leaving the store, took the ascot out of his pocket and put it on again. At that moment the defendant Goss, an employee of Kennedy's, "loomed up" in front of the plaintiff and demanded that he stop and explain where he had gotten the ascot. As approximately eight to ten people looked on, the plaintiff agreed to return with Goss to the store. On the way up the stairs, the plaintiff experienced chest and back pains and had to stop several times. When they reached the second floor, the salesman who had sold plaintiff the sportscoat told Goss that the ascot was indeed the plaintiff's. The plaintiff was so upset by the incident that he required the attention of the store's nurse and was consequently hospitalized and treated for a "myocardial infarct." The jury awarded plaintiff $12,500 for false imprisonment. The defendant appealed.]

SPIEGEL, J. Initially, the defendants contend that as a matter of law the plaintiff was not falsely imprisoned. They argue that no unlawful restraint was imposed by either force or threat upon the plaintiff's freedom of movement. However, "[t]he law is well settled that '[a]ny general restraint is sufficient to constitute an imprisonment . . .' and '[a]ny demonstration of physical power which, to all appearances, can be avoided only by submission, operates as effectually to constitute an imprisonment, if submitted to, as if any amount of force had been exercised.' 'If a man is restrained of his personal liberty by fear of a personal difficulty, that amounts to a false imprisonment' within the legal meaning of such term."

We think it is clear that there was sufficient evidence of unlawful restraint to submit this question to the jury. Just as the plaintiff had stepped out of the door of the store, the defendant Goss stopped him, firmly grasped his arm and told him that he had "better go back and see the manager." There was another employee at his side. The plaintiff was an elderly man and there were other people standing around staring at him. Considering the plaintiff's age and his heart condition, it is hardly to be expected that with one employee in front of him firmly grasping his arm and another at his side the plaintiff could do other than comply with Goss's "request" that he go back and see the manager. . . .

The defendants next contend that the detention of the plaintiff was sanctioned by G. L. c. 231, §94B, inserted by St. 1958, c. 337. This statute provides as follows: "In an action for false arrest or false imprisonment brought by any person by reason of having been detained for questioning on or in the immediate vicinity of the premises of a merchant, if such person was detained in a reasonable manner and for not more than a reasonable length of time by a person authorized to make arrests or by the merchant or his agent or servant authorized for such purpose and if there were reasonable grounds to believe that the person so detained was committing or attempting to commit larceny of goods for sale on such premises, it shall be a defence to such action. If such goods had not been purchased and were concealed on or amongst the belongings of a person so detained it shall be presumed that there were reasonable grounds for such belief."

The defendants argue in accordance with the conditions imposed in the statute that the plaintiff was detained in a reasonable manner for a reasonable length of time and that Goss had reasonable grounds for believing that the plaintiff was attempting to commit larceny of goods held for sale.

It is conceded that the detention was for a reasonable length of time. We need not decide whether the detention was effected in a reasonable manner for we are of opinion that there were no reasonable grounds for believing that the plaintiff was committing larceny and, therefore, he should not have been detained at all. However, we observe that Goss's failure to identify himself as an employee of Kennedy's and to disclose the reasons for his inquiry and actions, coupled with the physical restraint in a public place imposed upon the plaintiff, an elderly man, who had exhibited no aggressive intention to depart, could be said to constitute an unreasonable method by which to effect detention. . . .

The defendants assert that the judge improperly instructed the jury in stating that "grounds are reasonable when there is a basis which would appear to the reasonably prudent, cautious, intelligent person." In their brief, they argue that the "prudent and cautious man rule" is an objective standard and requires a more rigorous and restrictive standard of conduct than is contemplated by G. L. c. 231, §94B. The defendants' requests for instructions, in effect, state that the proper test is a subjective one, viz., whether the defendant Goss had an honest and strong suspicion that the plaintiff was committing or attempting to commit larceny. . . .

If we adopt the subjective test as suggested by the defendants, the individual's right to liberty and freedom of movement would become subject to the "honest . . . suspicion" of a shopkeeper based on his own "inarticulate hunches" without regard to any discernible facts. In effect, the result would be to afford the merchant even greater authority than that given to a police officer. In view of the well established meaning of the words "reasonable grounds" we believe that the Legislature intended to give these words their traditional meaning. This seems to us a valid conclusion since the Legislature has permitted an individual to be detained for a "reasonable length of time."

We also note that an objective standard is the criterion for determining probable cause or reasonable grounds in malicious prosecution and false arrest cases. . . .

Exceptions overruled.

NOTES

1. Origins of false imprisonment.   In Bird v. Jones, 115 Eng. Rep. 688 (K.B. 1845), the plaintiff desired to make his way down a public street in order to watch a boat race, for which customers had paid for their seats. The defendant blocked his passage, but allowed him to retreat in the direction from which he had come. Coleridge, J., held that so long as the plaintiff was free to go false imprisonment could not be brought, even if the plaintiff could sue under a different writ for the interference with his right of way. "Some confusion seems to me to arise from confounding imprisonment of the body with mere loss of freedom: it is one part of the definition of freedom to be able to go whithersoever one pleases; but imprisonment is something more than the mere loss of this power; it includes the notion of restraint within some limits defined by a will or power exterior to our own."

Lord Denman, C.J., dissented. "As long as I am prevented from doing what I have a right to do, of what importance is it that I am permitted to do something else? How does the imposition of an unlawful condition show that I am not restrained? If I am locked in a room, am I not imprisoned because I might effect my escape through a window, or because I might find an exit dangerous or inconvenient to myself, as by wading through water or by taking a route so circuitous that my necessary affairs would suffer by delay?" He then reverted to the procedural issue: "Must I then sue out a new writ stating that the defendant employed direct force to prevent my going where my business called me, whereby I sustained loss?"

The same theme of partial restriction was evident in Whittaker v. Sandford, 85 A. 399, 403 (Me. 1912), where a woman was given complete freedom of movement on defendant's palatial yacht, but when she was occasionally allowed on shore, she was not given liberty to roam or to remain there. She was held to have been imprisoned while on the yacht so long as she was denied access to shore by a boat, but damages were reduced to take into account her relative freedom of movement.

Section 36, comment *b*, of the Second Restatement reads: "The area within which another is completely confined may be large and need not be stationary. Whether the area from which the actor prevents the other from going is so large that it ceases to be a confinement within the area and becomes an exclusion from some other area may depend upon the circumstances of the particular case and be a matter for the judgment of the court and jury." Illustration 6 under comment *b* elaborates: "*A* by an invalid process restrains *B* within prison limits which are coterminous with the boundaries of a considerable town. *A* has confined *B*." The Restatement further suggests that wrongfully excluding the plaintiff from the United States would not amount to false imprisonment even though, in a sense, the plaintiff "may be said to be confined within the residue of the habitable world."

2. *Protection of person and property.* In cases of false arrest, why should an innocent patron bear the costs of the merchant's *reasonable* mistakes? These shoplifting cases continue to make their way into court with startling regularity, where the pattern is usually similar to that found in *Coblyn*: Customer returns to a shop to exchange goods and is seen leaving without paying for the replacement goods, e.g., Forgie-Buccioni v. Hannaford Bros., Inc., 413 F.3d 175 (1st Cir. 2005), or, owing to a medical condition, engages in odd conduct that excites suspicion, e.g., Dolgencorp, Inc. v. Pounders, 912 So. 2d 523 (Ala. Civ. App. 2005).

In Taylor v. Johnson, 796 So. 2d 11, 13-14 (La. Ct. App. 2001), the defendant, a clerk at Wal-Mart, suspected that the plaintiff had submitted a false prescription, which it delayed in filling while the plaintiff continued to shop. During the interim, the police arrived and, based on the defendant's report, arrested the plaintiff, who in fact had a lawful prescription. A $40,000 verdict for false imprisonment against the various defendants was overturned for want of any detention.

> An essential element of the tort of false imprisonment is detention of the person. The record is void of any evidence that [any] Wal-Mart employee detained Ms. Taylor, restricted her movement in the store, advised her she could not leave, or caused her to be arrested. Ms. Taylor did other shopping while she waited. She testified that at one point she had grown so tired of waiting she nearly left the store.

Should that result hold if the defendants had lied as to the reasons for the delay?

Nonetheless, other false imprisonment cases raise the more difficult question of whether the defendant's actions are justified as necessary to protect defendant's person and property, even when the plaintiff suffers serious harm. In Sindle v. New York City Transit Authority, 307 N.E.2d 245, 248 (N.Y. 1973), the defendant operated a school bus carrying between 65 and 70 junior high school students, including the plaintiff. Some of the other students became rowdy, committed acts of vandalism, and remained abusive even when warned by the driver. The driver abandoned his ordinary route, passed several stops, and drove to the police station. On the way, the plaintiff, who had not behaved improperly, jumped out of a side window, only to be run over by the bus's back wheels. The plaintiff abandoned his action for negligence (why?) and pitched the case solely on false imprisonment. The trial judge refused to allow the defendants to introduce any evidence that the imprisonment was reasonable, both in time and manner. The Court of Appeals reversed:

> In view of our determination, it would be well to outline some of the considerations relevant to the issue of justification. In this regard, we note that, generally, restraint or detention, reasonable under the circumstances and in time and manner, imposed for the purpose of preventing another from inflicting personal injuries or interfering with or damaging real or personal property in one's lawful possession or custody is not unlawful. . . . Also, a parent, guardian or teacher entrusted with the care or supervision of a child may use physical force reasonably necessary to maintain discipline or promote the welfare of the child. (Penal Law, §35.10)
>
> Similarly, a school bus driver, entrusted with the care of his student-passengers and the custody of public property, has the duty to take reasonable measures for the safety and protection of both — the passengers and the property. In this regard, the reasonableness of his actions — as bearing on the defense of justification — is to be determined from a consideration of all the circumstances. At a minimum, this would seem to import, a consideration of the need to protect the persons and property in his charge, the duty to aid the investigation and apprehension of those inflicting damage, the manner and place of the occurrence, and the feasibility and practicality of other alternative courses of action.

3. Consent.   Consent is another defense to an action for false imprisonment. Its scope may be difficult to determine, however, when the plaintiff seeks to retract the consent to confinement that was previously given. In Herd v. Weardale Steel, Coal & Coke Co., [1915] A.C. 67, the plaintiff, a miner, entered the defendant's mine for a shift that normally ended at 4:00 P.M. At 11:00 A.M. plaintiff, with 29 coworkers, asked to be taken to the surface, claiming that unsafe working conditions violated his employment contract and the applicable statutory provisions. An empty elevator was available to take the men up at 1:00 P.M., but was not offered to them until 1:30 P.M. The House of Lords found that the 30-minute delay did not constitute false imprisonment. Haldane, L.C., said: "The man chose to go to the bottom of the mine under these conditions, — conditions which he accepted. He had no right to call upon the employers to make use of special machinery put there at their cost, and involving cost in its working, to bring him to the surface just when he pleased." Was there a false imprisonment if the plaintiff had a legitimate safety grievance? What if the delay was not 30 minutes, but until the end of plaintiff's shift?

4. Modern false imprisonment cases.   Litigation in false imprisonment has increased in recent years as a common law addition to complex federal claims. For example, in Chellen v. John Pickle Co., 446 F. Supp. 2d 1247, 1274 (N.D. Okla. 2006), the plaintiffs, who were workers brought over from India to work for the defendant, sued for violations of the Fair Labor Standards Act (dealing with minimum wages and working conditions), and for violations of Title VII of the Civil Rights Act of 1964, which protects persons against discrimination on grounds of race, ethnicity, or national origin. The plaintiffs also added a count for false imprisonment insisting that the defendants restricted their mobility away from the worksite. Eagan, J., allowed these actions, saying:

> [D]efendants restricted the Chellen plaintiffs' movement, communications, privacy, worship, and access to health care. The evidence demonstrates that defendants kept the Chellen plaintiffs' travel documents. . . . [D]efendants unlawfully restrained the Chellen plaintiff's ability to move about as they wished. Although initially defendants permitted the Chellen plaintiffs some ability to leave the JPC plant for shopping, worship, visiting friends and relatives on their own, or other activities, defendants discouraged the plaintiffs from leaving by telling them of unfounded dangers outside the gates. Later, defendants required the Chellen plaintiffs to obtain permission before leaving the premises, locked the main gates, employed an armed security guard to watch them, hired four "leadmen" from among the Chellen plaintiffs to report on the activities of the others, threatened the Chellen plaintiffs with arrest and deportation, and attempted to deport several of them back to India. Defendants assert no valid justification for these actions. . . . Defendants' actions constitute unlawful restraint, detention, or confinement.

The opposite result in a similar work-related false imprisonment class action was handed down in Zavala v. Wal-Mart, 691 F.3d 527, 545-547 (3d Cir. 2012), in which the plaintiffs alleged that their minimal command of English made it hard for them to leave the defendant's stores. The court awarded the defendant a summary judgment on evidence that its doors were locked for security purposes to protect staff and merchandise, that the store had accessible emergency exits that met state and federal law standards, and that managers were "often available to open locked doors." "[F]alse imprisonment cannot occur where there is a safe alternative exit." Could there be occasional instances of false imprisonment given that managers were not always available? Are those claims tenable in a class action context?

4. The Intentional Infliction of Emotional Distress: Extreme and Outrageous Conduct

Wilkinson v. Downton
[1897] 2 Q.B. 57

[The facts are set forth in the court's opinion. The jury gave a verdict of £100 1*s.* 10½*d.* for transportation money given by plaintiff to friends to fetch her husband home and £100 for injuries caused by nervous shock. Defendant contended that no recovery should be allowed for the damage caused by nervous shock.]

WRIGHT, J. In this case the defendant, in the execution of what he seems to have regarded as a practical joke, represented to the plaintiff that he was charged by her husband with a message to her to the effect that her husband was smashed up in an accident, and was lying at The Elms at Leytonstone with both legs broken, and that she was to go at once in a cab with two pillows to fetch him home. All this was false. The effect of the statement on the plaintiff was a violent shock to her nervous system, producing vomiting and other more serious and permanent physical consequences at one time threatening her reason, and entailing weeks of suffering and incapacity to her as well as expense to her husband for medical attendance. These consequences were not in any way the result of previous ill-health or weakness of constitution; nor was there any evidence of predisposition to nervous shock or any other idiosyncrasy. . . .

[The court then stated that while the 1s. 10d. was recoverable in fraud and deceit, £100 for mental distress were not "parasitic" upon that action.]

I think, however, that the verdict may be supported upon another ground. The defendant has, as I assume for the moment, wilfully done an act calculated to cause physical harm to the plaintiff—that is to say, to infringe her legal right to personal safety, and has in fact thereby caused physical harm to her. That proposition without more appears to me to state a good cause of action, there being no justification alleged for the act. This wilful injuria is in law malicious, although no malicious purpose to cause the harm which was caused nor any motive of spite is imputed to the defendant.

It remains to consider whether the assumptions involved in the proposition are made out. One question is whether the defendant's act was so plainly calculated to produce some effect of the kind which was produced that an intention to produce it ought to be imputed to the defendant, regard being had to the fact that the effect was produced on a person proved to be in an ordinary state of health and mind. I think that it was. It is difficult to imagine that such a statement, made suddenly and with apparent seriousness, could fail to produce grave effects under the circumstances upon any but an exceptionally indifferent person, and therefore an intention to produce such an effect must be imputed, and it is no answer in law to say that more harm was done than was anticipated, for that is commonly the case with all wrongs. The other question is whether the effect was, to use the ordinary phrase, too remote to be in law regarded as a consequence for which the defendant is answerable. Apart from authority, I should give the same answer and on the same ground as the last question, and say that it was not too remote. . . .

Suppose that a person is in a precarious and dangerous condition, and another person tells him that his physician has said that he has but a day to live. In such a case, if death ensued from the shock caused by the false statement, I cannot doubt that at this day the case might be one of criminal homicide, or that if a serious aggravation of illness ensued damages might be recovered. I think, however, that it must be admitted that the present case is without precedent. . . .

There must be judgment for plaintiff for £100 1s. 10½d.

NOTES

1. Nervous shock and parasitic damages.   Why does Wright, J., treat this case as one of physical damages when there has been no physical invasion? With *Wilkinson*, contrast Bouillon v. Laclede Gaslight Co., 129 S.W. 401, 402 (Mo. Ct. App. 1910). The defendant's meter reader tried to force his way in through the front door of the plaintiff's apartment while the plaintiff was pregnant and at risk for a miscarriage. He had several nasty exchanges with the plaintiff's nurse that the plaintiff overheard through the open front door, which also let in the cold air. That evening the plaintiff suffered chills, and the next day had a miscarriage that her physician attributed to the events of the prior day. The plaintiff was sick for an extended period of time after the incident, and suffered permanent impairments to her health. Nortoni, J., allowed plaintiff's cause of action.

> No one can doubt that the case fails to disclose an assault on plaintiff as the controversy was principally had with, and all the insulting language directed against, another, the nurse. However this may be, the facts reveal a valid ground of liability on the score of trespass, and this is true notwithstanding the damages laid are not for the commission of the initial act of trespass, but relate instead to its consequence alone. Although defendant's agent had a right to enter the basement beneath plaintiff's apartment for the purpose of reading the gas meter, it is entirely clear that he had no authority to enter or pass through plaintiff's flat for that purpose. She was not a consumer of gas and the gas meter was in no sense connected with her household. Plaintiff is assured peaceful repose of her home against unwarranted intrusion from others. A trespasser is liable to respond in damages for such injuries as may result naturally, necessarily, directly, and proximately in consequence of his wrong. This is true for the reason the original act involved in the trespass is unlawful. . . . The doctrine is that though a mere mental disturbance of itself may not be a cause of action in the first instance, fright and mental anguish are competent elements of damage if they arise out of a trespass upon the plaintiff's person or possession and may be included in a suit for the trespass if plaintiff chooses so to do, or, if a physical injury results from such fright, a cause of action accrues from the trespass for compensation as to the physical injury and its consequences alone, which may be pursued even though plaintiff seeks no compensation for the original wrong.

In both *Wilkinson* and *Bouillon*, the defendant committed independent torts, namely, deceit and trespass. Is there any need for a new independent tort when emotional damages are typically "parasitic" on an existing wrong? In 1 Street, Foundations of Legal Liability 466, 470 (1906), the author, in commenting on legal protection against mental distress, observes that "[a] factor which is today recognized as parasitic will, forsooth, tomorrow be recognized as an independent basis of liability."

2. The birth of intentional infliction of emotional distress.   The Restatement formulation of liability turns solely on the defendant's course of conduct, without proof of any other tort such as trespass or deceit. Modern cases place heavy reliance on the Restatement formulation in a wide number of different contexts.

Exhibit 1.4   William Prosser

Source: Law School Archives, University of California, Berkeley

William Prosser (1898-1972): As Ken Abraham and G. Edward White point out in Prosser and His Influence, 6 J. Tort L. 27, 28 (2013), William Prosser, in his Handbook on Torts, "discover[ed] the ['new'] tort[] of Intentional Infliction of Emotional Distress." He did so by "identifying the principles that he sees as linking the cases together" in a not previously understood way. *Id.* at 49-50. When his initial Handbook was published in 1941, Prosser observed that "in recent years the courts have tended to recognize the intentional causing of mental or emotional disturbance as a tort." *Id.* at 51-52. He acknowledged that the law in this area was "in a process of growth," given "tort law's traditional reluctance to redress mental injuries [on account of] difficulties of proof, the evanescence of mental consequences, and the risk of fictitious claims. *Id.* at 52. After an ostensible assessment of the relatively minimal case law in this "growing" field, Prosser concludes that ". . . the rule that seems to be emerging is that there is liability only for conduct exceeding all bounds usually tolerated by society, of a nature which is especially calculated to cause and does cause mental damage of a very serious kind." *Id.* at 54.

Restatement of the Law (Second) of Torts

§46. OUTRAGEOUS CONDUCT CAUSING SEVERE EMOTIONAL DISTRESS

(1) One who by extreme and outrageous conduct intentionally or recklessly causes severe emotional distress to another is subject to liability for such emotional distress, and if bodily harm to the other results from it, for such bodily harm.

(2) Where such conduct is directed at a third person, the actor is subject to liability if he intentionally or recklessly causes severe emotional distress

(a) to a member of such person's immediate family who is present at the time, whether or not such distress results in bodily harm, or

(b) to any other person who is present at the time, if such distress results in bodily harm.

Caveat: The Institute expresses no opinion as to whether there may not be other circumstances under which the actor may be subject to liability for the intentional or reckless infliction of emotional distress.

Comment d. Extreme and outrageous conduct: The cases thus far decided have found liability only where the defendant's conduct has been extreme and outrageous. It has not been enough that the defendant has acted with an intent which is tortious or even criminal, or that he has intended to inflict emotional distress, or even that his conduct has been characterized by "malice," or a degree of aggravation which would entitle the plaintiff to punitive damages for another tort. Liability has been found only where the conduct has been so outrageous in character, and so extreme in degree, as to go beyond all possible bounds of decency, and to be regarded as atrocious, and utterly intolerable in a civilized community. Generally, the case is one in which the recitation of the facts to an average member of the community would arouse his resentment against the actor, and lead him to exclaim, "Outrageous!"

The liability clearly does not extend to mere insults, indignities, threats, annoyances, petty oppressions, or other trivialities. The rough edges of our society are still in need of a good deal of filing down, and in the meantime plaintiffs must necessarily be expected and required to be hardened to a certain amount of rough language, and to occasional acts that are definitely inconsiderate and unkind. There is no occasion for the law to intervene in every case where some one's feelings are hurt. There must still be freedom to express an unflattering opinion, and some safety valve must be left through which irascible tempers may blow off relatively harmless steam. . . .

Comment f: The extreme and outrageous character of the conduct may arise from the actor's knowledge that the other is peculiarly susceptible to emotional distress, by reason of some physical or mental condition or peculiarity. The conduct may become heartless, flagrant, and outrageous when the actor proceeds in the face of such knowledge, where it would not be so if he did not know. . . .

a. Strong-arm tactics. In State Rubbish Collectors Ass'n v. Siliznoff, 240 P.2d 282, 284-285 (Cal. 1952), the Acme Brewing Company switched its account for the collection of garbage from Abramoff to Kosoff, who in turn assigned the account to Siliznoff. At a stormy meeting representatives of the State Rubbish Collectors Association threatened to beat up Siliznoff, destroy his property, and put him out of business unless he agreed to pay the association part of the proceeds from the Acme account. Siliznoff then promised to pay Abramoff $1,850 for the contract and gave the association a series of notes for that sum.

The association sued on the notes a year later. Siliznoff demanded that the notes be canceled because of duress and lack of consideration. He also filed a cross-complaint praying for "general and exemplary damages because of assaults made by plaintiff and its agents to compel him to join the association and pay Abramoff for the Acme account." Siliznoff recovered $1,250 general and special damages and $4,000 exemplary damages. On appeal the association contended that "the evidence does not establish an assault against defendant because the threats made all related to action that might take place in the future," and that there was no threat of "immediate physical harm." But the unanimous court, through Traynor, J., concluded that a cause of action was established "when it is shown that one, in the absence of any privilege, intentionally subjects another to mental suffering incident to serious threats to his physical well-being, whether or not the threats are made under such circumstances as to constitute a technical assault."

b. Bill collection.   In George v. Jordan Marsh Co., 268 N.E.2d 915, 921 (Mass. 1971), the plaintiff alleged that the defendant's bill collectors badgered her with phone calls during the late evening hours, sent her letters marked "account referred to law and collection department," wrote her that her credit was revoked and that she was liable for late charges, and engaged in other dunning tactics. The plaintiff further claimed that she did not owe the disputed sums because she had never guaranteed her son's unpaid debts. As a result of the calls, the plaintiff suffered a heart attack. Her attorney then protested defendant's "harassing" tactics, but the onslaught continued until the plaintiff suffered a second heart attack. After an exhaustive review of the earlier Massachusetts precedent, the court upheld the sufficiency of her claim for emotional distress under section 46 of the Restatement.

c. Outrageous professional conduct.   In Rockhill v. Pollard, 485 P.2d 28, 32 (Or. 1971), the plaintiff, her mother-in-law, and her ten-month-old daughter, Marla, were all seriously injured in an automobile accident. Both women had serious cuts and bruises, and the daughter was apparently lifeless, with a ghostly pallor to her skin. A passing motorist took them to the office of the defendant physician, who, when summoned, did not examine either woman and gave Marla only a brief examination. When Marla started vomiting, the defendant said it was a result of overeating. He then ordered the women to wait outside in the freezing rain until the plaintiff's husband arrived. The three were then taken to a hospital, where Marla was successfully operated on for a depressed skull fracture.

McAllister, J., found that the evidence supported a finding of conduct outrageous in the extreme, stressing the special duties that physicians owed their patients: "Certainly a physician who is consulted in an emergency has a duty to respect that interest, at least to the extent of making a good-faith attempt to provide adequate treatment or advice. We think a jury could infer from the evidence that defendant wilfully or recklessly failed to perform that duty."

Why does plaintiff have no action for medical malpractice or breach of contract?

d. Dead bodies.   In Estate of Trentadue v. United States, 397 F.3d 840, 857-858 (10th Cir. 2005), the Bureau of Prisons (BOP) was responsible for returning the body of Kenneth Trentadue to his next of kin after he had been found dead in his cell, which it failed to do in a proper manner. Tymkovich, J., accepted the plaintiffs' claim for the following reasons:

We agree with the district court that the government acted in deliberate disregard of a high probability that its actions would cause the Trentadues emotional distress. The Trentadues were a grieving family searching for answers in the wake of Kenneth Trentadue's untimely death. BOP's overall treatment of the Trentadue family, including its initial nondisclosure of the unusual circumstances of death, its obstinance concerning authorization for an autopsy, and its failure to inform the Trentadues of the body's battered condition amounted to outrageous conduct that "needlessly and recklessly" intensified the family's emotional distress. Thus the district court properly determined that plaintiffs proved the first, second, and third elements of the tort of emotional distress, intentional or reckless conduct, outrageousness, and causation.

However, because the district court did not make explicit findings as to the severity of each individual plaintiff's emotional distress, we are unable to determine from the district court's order whether . . . the emotional distress suffered by each plaintiff was severe under Oklahoma law.

He therefore remanded the case for further findings.

e. Harassment. Various forms of racial insults have been treated as forms of extreme and outrageous conduct. In Patterson v. McLean Credit Union, 805 F.2d 1143, 1146 (4th Cir. 1986), the African American plaintiff alleged that her supervisor engaged in racially motivated harassment by "staring" at her for several minutes at a time, by assigning her too many tasks, by making her do sweeping and dusting jobs not assigned to whites, and by telling her that blacks were known to work "slower than" whites. Phillips, J., rejected the tort suit, noting that the allegations fell "far short" of the stringent requirements of North Carolina law. The plaintiff also raised civil rights claims that were rebuffed by the Supreme Court in Patterson v. McLean Credit Union, 491 U.S. 164 (1989), which gave a relatively narrow construction of the scope of the protection afforded the plaintiff under 42 U.S.C. §1981. Plaintiffs have had more success in bypassing the stringent requirements of the tort by arguing sexual harassment. The Supreme Court has held that "Title VII comes into play before the harassing conduct leads to a nervous breakdown. . . . So long as the environment would reasonably be perceived, and is perceived, as hostile or abusive, there is no need for it also to be psychologically injurious." Harris v. Forklift Systems, Inc., 510 U.S. 17, 22 (1993). These cases are typically judged by a "reasonable woman standard." See Ellison v. Brady, 924 F.2d 872, 879 (9th Cir. 1991).

3. Constitutional overtones. In other settings, the Supreme Court uses constitutional arguments to limit the scope of the common law tort of intentional infliction of emotional distress in order to protect freedom of speech. Thus, in Hustler Magazine v. Falwell, 485 U.S. 46, 53-54 (1988), Hustler parodied Jerry Falwell by having him state in a mock "interview" that his "first time" was during a drunken incestuous rendezvous with his mother in an outhouse. In small print at the bottom of the page, the ad contains the disclaimer, "ad parody — not to be taken seriously." Rehnquist, C.J., overturned a jury verdict for Falwell of $100,000 in actual damages and $50,000 in punitive damages against both Hustler and its publisher,

Larry Flynt, on constitutional grounds. The Court stressed the press's need for "breathing room" under the First Amendment:

> Generally speaking the law does not regard the intent to inflict emotional distress as one which should receive much solicitude, and it is quite understandable that most if not all jurisdictions have chosen to make it civilly culpable where the conduct in question is sufficiently "outrageous." But in the world of debate about public affairs, many things done with motives that are less than admirable are protected by the First Amendment. . . .

Rehnquist, C.J., then noted that cartoonists such as Thomas Nast, who took on the Tweed Ring, which ran New York City in the late nineteenth century, would be at risk under the alternative rule. Is there a slippery slope from Nast to Flynt? Why no action for defamation?

The Court upheld a defense based on the First Amendment against a claim of intentional infliction of emotional distress in Snyder v. Phelps, 562 U.S. 443, 458 (2011). The so-called Westboro Baptist Church, based in Topeka, Kansas, systematically pickets funerals of fallen soldiers to protest the military's tolerance of homosexuality. Phelps and six members of his congregation picketed Lance Corporal Snyder's funeral with signs (among others) reading "God Hates the USA/Thank God for 9/11," "Thank God for Dead Soldiers," and "You're Going to Hell." Snyder's father did not see the slogans on the picket signs at the time of the funeral, but when he saw them broadcast on the news later that evening he became extremely distressed and sued Phelps and Westboro. A jury awarded Snyder's father $2.9 million in compensatory damages and $8 million in punitive damages. The Fourth Circuit Court of Appeals overturned the jury's verdict, and the Supreme Court affirmed:

> The jury here was instructed that it could hold Westboro liable for intentional infliction of emotional distress based on a finding that Westboro's picketing was "outrageous." "Outrageousness," however, is a highly malleable standard with "an inherent subjectiveness about it which would allow a jury to impose liability on the basis of the jurors' tastes or views, or perhaps on the basis of their dislike of a particular expression."

CHAPTER 2

STRICT LIABILITY AND NEGLIGENCE: HISTORIC AND ANALYTIC FOUNDATIONS

SECTION A. INTRODUCTION

We now turn to the central issue of tort theory: When is a defendant liable for the physical harm he accidentally or inadvertently causes to the plaintiff? Historically, this apparently simple question has generated much debate but little consensus. One approach—traditional strict liability—holds the defendant prima facie liable for any harm that he causes to the plaintiff's person or property. The opposing negligence position allows the plaintiff to recover only if, intentional harms aside, the defendant acted with insufficient care. Both approaches allow for affirmative defenses, especially those based on plaintiff's conduct.

The juxtaposition of these two approaches raises several thorny issues. Must one theory be accepted completely to the exclusion of the other, or is it possible to define appropriate areas for each? If the latter, has the law drawn the lines in the proper places? Note, too, causation forms a common bond between the two theories. But how should "causation" be interpreted? Does its meaning shift as we move from strict liability to negligence and, if so, how? What is meant by "negligence"? Is it a technical term or one of ordinary language? Is it enough that the defendant was careless, or must he also owe the plaintiff some duty of care to render his carelessness not only morally blameworthy but also legally culpable? Finally, the differences found in the two respective prima face cases may be narrowed as the theories are elaborated. For example, a court in a negligence case may impose the burden of proving due care on the defendant under the rule of res ipsa loquitur. How wide, then, is the gulf between the two systems in their day-to-day operation?

This chapter retraces the long dialogue among judges over these recurrent issues. Section B examines the tension between negligence and strict liability in

71

the formative English cases. Section C traces the influence of the forms of action on the choice of liability rules. Section D follows the nineteenth-century debate over liability rules both in England and the United States after the abolition of the forms of action. Section E examines the same conflict in the twentieth century. The law in each period builds heavily on what came before, as previous precedents are followed, reshaped, expanded, or abandoned in litigation.

SECTION B. THE FORMATIVE CASES

The Thorns Case (Hull v. Orange)
Y.B. Mich. 6 Ed. 4, f. 7, pl. 18 (1466)

A man brought a writ of Trespass quare vi et armis clausum fregit, etc. et herbam suam pedibus conculcando consumpsit, [Roughly: wherefore by force and arms he broke into the plaintiff's close, and consumed his crops by trampling them with his feet] and alleged the trespass in 5 acres and the defendant said, as to the coming, etc. and as to the trespass in the 5 acres, not guilty and, as to the trespass in the 5 acres, that the plaintiff ought not to have an action for he says that he [the defendant] has an acre of land on which a thorn hedge grows, adjoining the said 5 acres, and that he [the defendant], at the time of the supposed trespass, came and cut the thorns, and that they, against his will, fell on the said acres of the plaintiff, and that he [the defendant] came freshly on to the said acres and took them, which is the same trespass for which he has conceived this action. And on this they demurred and it was well argued, and was adjourned.

And now Catesby says: Sir, it has been said that, if a man does some act, even if it be lawful, and by this act tort and damage are done to another against his will, yet, if he could by any means have eschewed the damage, he shall be punished for this act. Sir, it seems to me that the contrary is true, and, as I understand, if a man does a lawful act and thereby damage comes to another against his will, he shall not be punished. Thus, I put the case that I drive my cattle along the highway, and you have an acre of land lying next the highway, and my beasts enter your land and eat your grass, and I come freshly and chase them out of your land; now here, because the chasing out was lawful and the entry on the land was against my will, you shall not have an action against me. No more shall you have an action here, for the cutting was lawful and the falling on your land was against my will, and so the re-taking was good and lawful. And, Sir, I put the case that I cut my trees and the boughs fall on a man and kill him; in this case I shall not be attainted as of felony, for my cutting was lawful and the falling on the man was against my will. No more here, therefore, etc.

Fairfax: It seems to me that the contrary is true and I say that there is a difference where a man does a thing from which felony ensues and one from which trespass ensues; for in the case which Catesby puts there was no felony, since felony is of malice prepense and, as the act was against his will, it was not animo felonico. But if one cuts his trees and the boughs fall on a man and hurt him, in

One of the earliest known illustrations of the English Court of Common
Pleas, c. 1460
Source: The Inner Temple Library

this case he shall have an action of Trespass. So, too, Sir, if a man shoots at the butts and his bow trembles in his hands and he kills a man ipso invito [against his will], this is no felony, as has been said. But if he wounds a man by his shooting, he shall have a good action of Trespass against him, and yet the shooting was lawful and the tort that the other had was against his will. And so here.

Pigot: To the same intent. I put the case that I have a mill and the water which comes to my mill runs past your land, and you have willows growing by the water, and you cut your willows and against your will they fall in the water and stop the water so that I have not sufficient water for my mill, in this case I shall have an action of Trespass, and yet the cutting was lawful and the falling was against my will. And so if a man has a fish-pond in his manor and he empties the water out of the pond to take the fishes and the water floods my land, I shall have a good action, and yet the act was lawful.

Yonge: The contrary seems to me to be true; and in such a case, where a man has dampnum absque injuria [harm without legal injury], he shall have no action, for if he has no tort he has no reason to recover damages. So in this case, when he came on to his close to take the thorns which had fallen on to it, this entry was not tortious, for when he cut them and they fell on his close ipso invito, the property in them was in him and thus it was lawful for him to take them out of his close; wherefore, notwithstanding that he has done damage, he has done no tort.

Brian: I think the contrary. To my intent, when any man does an act, he is bound to do it in such manner that by his act no prejudice or damage is done to others. Thus, in a case where I am building a house and, while the timber is being put up, a piece of it falls on my neighbour's house and damages it, he shall have a good action, and yet the building of the house was lawful and the timber fell me invito [against my will]. So, too, if a man makes an assault upon me and I cannot avoid him, and in my own defence I raise my stick to strike him, and a man is behind me and in raising my stick I wound him, in this case he shall have an action against me, and yet the raising of my stick to defend myself was lawful and I wounded him me invito. So in this case.

LITTLETON, J. To the same intent. If a man suffers damage, it is right that he be recompensed; and to my intent the case which Catesby has put is not law; for if your cattle come on to my land and eat my grass, notwithstanding you come freshly and drive them out, it is proper for you to make amends for what your cattle have done, be it more or less. . . . And, Sir, if it were law that he could enter and take the thorns, by the same reasoning, if he cut a great tree, he could come with his carts and horses to carry off the tree, which is not reason, for peradventure he has corn or other crops growing, etc. No more here may he do it, for the law is all one in great things and in small and so, according to the amount of the trespass, it is proper that he should make amends.

CHOKE, C.J. I think the same; for when the principal thing is not lawful, then the thing which depends upon it is not lawful. For when he cut the thorns and they fell on to my land, this falling was not lawful, and then his coming to take them away was not lawful. As to what has been said that they fell ipso invito, this is not a good plea; but he should have said that he could not do it in any other manner or that he did all that was in his power to keep them out; otherwise he shall pay damages. And, Sir, if the thorns or a great tree had fallen on his land by the blowing of the wind, in this case he might have come on to the land to take them, since the falling had then been not his act, but that of the wind.

NOTES

1. Basis for liability in tort.   The *Thorns Case* is one of the earliest English cases to discuss in general terms the basis for liability in tort. Two judges, Littleton and Choke, offer their opinions after a spirited debate among five lawyers. Note that Catesby, for the defendant, tries to persuade the court that the defendant can be liable in tort only if he has committed a crime. Does Fairfax, for the plaintiff, adequately respond to that contention or give any explanation why it is generally false?

One puzzle about the *Thorns Case* is why the plaintiff sued for these trifling damages. One explanation is that the dispute over the thorns was a cover for the larger issue, which was whether the plaintiff owned the property on which the thorns fell. Further legal research has revealed that "the *Case of Thorns* was likely a boundary dispute, where the trespasser was nibbling into his neighbour's territory, acting as if the land was his to use." Getzler, Richard Epstein, Strict Liability and the History of Torts, 3 J. Tort L. (Iss. 1, Art. 3) 9 (2010). The court records show that the plaintiff released the defendant from all damages once the legal point was established.

Doctrinally, however, the major controversy over the *Thorns Case* is whether it adopts the theory of strict liability in tort. The case's connection to the negligence/strict liability debate seems attenuated at first glance given the defendant's deliberate entry onto the plaintiff's land. The sticking point in the case, however, is reminiscent of the dispute over the necessity defense in Chapter 1, *supra* at 41, for it concerns the scope of the defendant's privilege to retake his thorns from the plaintiff's property even if he causes damage thereby. The judges and lawyers accept that outcome so long as the defendant's original cutting was not tortious. The choice between strict liability and negligence is used to set the appropriate boundaries for the plaintiff's privilege. What passages in the *Thorns Case* point to the strict liability rule? To some alternative rule? To negligence? Could trespass be used to settle title under a negligence theory?

The historical basis of tort liability was reviewed in Arnold, Accident, Mistake, and Rules of Liability in the Fourteenth Century Law of Torts, 128 U. Pa. L. Rev. 361, 374-375 (1979). Arnold concludes that "the inference to be drawn from all the available evidence is that in fourteenth-century tort actions civil liability was strict." He then identifies a number of grounds that allowed a defendant to escape liability. He points to "a familiar principle in the law of torts that no one was liable to make compensation for injuries that were attributable to some entirely providential cause," such as harms brought about by tempests, earthquakes, or fires of spontaneous origin, which are commonly grouped as acts of

God. Likewise, the plaintiff's own contributory negligence was regarded a good defense because "it is the plaintiff, not the defendant, who is perceived as having 'done' the act resulting in injury." Within these settled principles, Arnold found only a few cases in which the plaintiff alleged the defendant's negligence in his complaint, and fewer still in which the defendant sought to raise his own lack of negligence as a defense. For Arnold, the clue to the substantive issue lies in the logic of pleading:

> The most telling difficulty is that the absence of pleas of this sort may simply be attributable not to any abstract liability rule but rather to a pleading rule that barred the defendant from asserting such facts purely as a technical matter. To simplify somewhat, a defendant in a writ of trespass was obligated to choose between two kinds of answer: He either had to deny the physical acts he was alleged to have done, or he had to admit them and assign a cause for them. In the case of an assault and battery, for instance, an acceptable "cause" would have been self-defense. Now if a defendant wanted to say that he had hit the plaintiff accidentally (that is, nonnegligently), his story would not technically have fit either of the two modes of responding to complaints. He had, in fact, hit the plaintiff, so a denial was obviously of no use; moreover, he had had no cause, no justification, for hitting him because "cause," as we have seen, was thought of in motivational terms. Here, the defendant's case was that he had had no motive at all in hitting the plaintiff, for the act of hitting him had been unintentional.

2. "Best efforts" as a means to avoid liability.   In Millen v. Fandrye, 79 Eng. Rep. 1259 (K.B. 1626), the plaintiff sued for damage to his sheep when the defendant's dog chased the sheep off the defendant's land, where they had been trespassing. The dog, moreover, continued the chase even after the sheep had entered a neighbor's land. In giving judgment for the defendant on the plaintiff's demurrer to his plea, Crew, C.J., noted:

> It seems to me that he might drive the sheep out with the dog, and he could not withdraw his dog when he would in an instant. . . . [A] man cuts thorns and they fall into another man's land, and in trespass he justified for it; and the opinion was, that notwithstanding this justification trespass lies, because he did not plead that he did his best endeavour to hinder their falling there, yet this was a hard case; but this case is not like to [the instant case], for here it was lawful to chase them [the sheep] out of his own land, and he did his best endeavour to recall the dog, and therefore trespass does not lie.

Millen endorses Choke's view in the *Thorns Case*, but the result in *Millen* can also be reconciled with Littleton's purer version of strict liability. In *Millen*, the "best efforts" defense arose from the defendant's defense of his property against the wrongful incursions of the plaintiff's sheep. The law in these cases tolerates the use of excessive force when the defendant tries in good faith to minimize the damage to the plaintiff's property. The rule is a variation on the familiar theme that the aggressor takes his victim as he finds him (Vosburg v. Putney, *supra* Chapter 1, at 4). In contrast, the defendant's cutting in the *Thorns Case* was in no sense justified or excused by any prior wrong of the plaintiff, so that defendant did not have the latitude afforded by the self-defense privilege. Under *Millen*, what result if a third person sues after the defendant's dog drives the sheep onto her property, even though the dog's owner tried to call him off? Should the landowner have a "best efforts" defense in that third-party suit? See Morris v. Platt, *supra* Chapter 1, at 34.

3. Justification in trespass. In the *Tithe Case*, Y.B. Trin., 21 Hen. 7, f. 26, 27, 28, pl. 5 (1506), the plaintiff, a local parson, sued for the loss of corn tithed to him. The corn in question had been cut by a local farmer, who had placed it in a separate part of his field for the parson. The defendant removed the corn to the plaintiff's barn, where it perished from causes not specified in the opinion. The defendant justified his conduct on the ground that the plaintiff was in danger of losing the corn to beasts that were straying in the field. The courts disallowed the justification:

KINGSMILL, J.: Where the goods of another are taken against his will, it must be justified either as a thing necessary for the Commonwealth or through a condition recognized by the law. First, as a thing concerning the Commonwealth, one may justify for goods taken out of a house when it is purely to safeguard the goods, or for breaking down a house to safeguard others; and so in time of war one may justify the entry into another's land to make a bulwark in defence of King and Country; and these things are justifiable and lawful for the maintenance of the Commonwealth. The other cause of justification is where one distrains [i.e., seizes to hold as security] my horse for his rent, and that is justifiable because the land was bound by such a condition of distress; and so in the case of other such conditions. Thus for these two reasons one may justify the taking of a thing against the will of its owner. But in this case here we are outside these reasons, for we are not within the cases of the Commonwealth nor in those of a condition; and, although it is pleaded that this corn was in danger of being lost, yet it was not in such danger but that the party could have had his remedy. Thus, if I have beasts damage feasant, [causing damage] I shall not justify my entry to chase them out unless I first tender all amends. So here, when the defendant took the plaintiff's corn that it might not be destroyed, yet this is not justifiable. For if it had been destroyed, the plaintiff would have his remedy against those who destroyed it. And as for his having put it into the plaintiff's barn, yet he must keep it safe against any other mischance; and so no advantage thereby comes to the plaintiff. So this plea is not good.

REDE, C.J.: Although the defendant's intent here was good, yet the intent is not to be construed, though in felony it shall be; as where one shoots at the butts and kills a man, this is not felony, since he had no intent to kill him; and so of a tiler on a house where against his knowledge a stone kills a man, it is not felony. But where one shoots at the butts and wounds a man, although it be against his will, yet he shall be called a trespasser against his will. So it is necessary always to have a good case to justify; as in Trespass, a license is good justification. . . . But, to return to the case here, when he took the corn, although this was a good deed as regards the damage which cattle or a stranger might do to it, yet this is not a good deed and no manner of justification as regards the owner of the corn; for the latter would have his remedy by action against him who destroyed the corn, if it had been destroyed. Thus, if my beasts are damage feasant in another's land, I cannot enter to chase them out; and yet it would be a good deed to chase them out, to save them doing more damage. But it is otherwise where a stranger drives my horses into another's land, where they do damage; for here I may justify my entry to drive them out, since this tort has its beginning in the tort of another. But here, because the plaintiff could have his remedy if the corn had been destroyed, it was not lawful to take them; and it is not like the cases where things are in jeopardy of loss through water or fire and the like, for there the plaintiff has no remedy for the destruction against anyone. So the plea is not good.

The *Tithe Case* raises a variation on the necessity issue already encountered in *Vincent*, *supra* Chapter 1, at 44. However, the defendant in *Vincent* acted to preserve his own property, whereas the defendant in the *Tithe Case* acted to preserve the plaintiff's property. Both Kingsmill and Rede allow the necessity defense when corn is moved to protect it against natural losses, but neither allow it when third parties threaten its destruction, on the unrealistic assumption that the owner faces no loss because he has a valid cause of action against the third party. With third-party threats, therefore, the *Tithe Case* raises the same problem of asymmetrical incentives encountered in the public necessity cases, *supra* at 48-50. Why should anyone act to benefit a stranger if he must bear the risk of loss? One way to offset that risk is to allow the defendant to sue the plaintiff in restitution should he save the corn; but that remedy is limited to a recovery of plaintiff's out-of-pocket expenses, which includes neither the plaintiff's labor nor her risk of loss. Should this necessity privilege cover the risk of loss from third parties as well as from natural events? Should a system of rewards be introduced? For discussion, see Epstein, Holdouts, Externalities and the Single Owner: One More Salute to Ronald Coase, 36 J.L. & Econ. 553, 579-581 (1993).

Weaver v. Ward
80 Eng. Rep. 284 (K.B. 1616)

Weaver brought an action of trespass of assault and battery against Ward. The defendant pleaded, that he was amongst others by the commandment of the Lords of the Council a trained soldier in London, of the band of one Andrews captain; and so was the plaintiff, and that they were skirmishing with their musquets charged with powder for their exercise in re militari, [on military matters] against another captain and his band; and as they were so skirmishing, the defendant casualiter & per infortunium & contra voluntatem suam, [accidentally, and by misfortune, and against his own will] in discharging of his piece did hurt and wound the plaintiff. And upon demurrer by the plaintiff, judgment was given for him; for though it were agreed, that if men tilt or turney in the presence of the King, or if two masters of defence playing their prizes kill one another, that this shall be no felony; or if a lunatick kill a man, or the like, because felony must be done animo felonico [with felonious intent]: yet in trespass, which tends only to give damages according to hurt or loss, it is not so; and therefore if a lunatick hurt a man, he shall be answerable in trespass: and therefore no man shall be excused of a trespass (for this is the nature of an excuse, and not of a justification, prout ei bene licuit) [as it well appeared to him] except it may be judged utterly without his fault.

As if a man by force take my hand and strike you, or if here the defendant had said, that the plaintiff ran cross his piece when it was discharging, or had set forth the case with the circumstances, so as it had appeared to the Court that it had been inevitable, and that the defendant had committed no negligence to give occasion to the hurt.

NOTES

1. Inevitable accident: conceptual difficulties.   In Weaver v. Ward, the court offers neither a definition of inevitable accident nor any examples of its application. Many modern cases and commentators, contra Arnold, have tended to regard "inevitable accident" as a backhanded way of saying that the defendant acted neither negligently nor with intent to harm. That position is taken by Baker, An Introduction to English Legal History 405 (4th ed. 2002), who observed that "[w]hat the judges wanted to know was whether the defendant could have taken steps to avoid the accident; in other words, whether it was 'inevitable'— not in the sense of being predestined, but in that there was no reasonable opportunity of avoidance." For other versions of that position, see also Brown v. Kendall, *infra* at 92; Holmes, The Common Law, *infra* at 114. For a somewhat different reading, see Gilles, Inevitable Accident in Classical English Tort Law, 43 Emory L.J. 575, 577 (1994), who reads such phrases as "utterly without his fault" and "unavoidable necessity" as asking "not whether the actors had behaved unreasonably—whether they *should* have avoided the accident—but whether they *could* have avoided it by greater practical care."

This common argument is, however, inconsistent with the procedural posture of the earlier cases, and seems odd on textual grounds because it renders the last clause in Weaver v. Ward (referring to antecedent negligence) wholly superfluous. In contrast, a literal reading of inevitable accident applies solely to those accidents that "had to happen," no matter what the defendant did. Within this narrower definition, the damage to the dock in *Vincent* is inevitable if it would have occurred whether or not the defendant made efforts to keep its ship fast to the dock during the storm.

Is there a case of inevitable accident in the *Thorns Case* put by Choke, J., where the defendant enters the plaintiff's lands to recover a tree blown there by a great wind?

2. Inevitable accident: historical treatment.   The full report of Smith v. Stone, 82 Eng. Rep. 533 (K.B. 1647), reads:

> Smith brought an action of trespasse against Stone pedibus ambulando [walking by his feet], the defendant pleads this speciall plea in justification, viz. that he was carried upon the land of the plaintiff by force, and violence of others, and was not there voluntarily, which is the same trespasse, for which the plaintiff brings his action. The plaintiff demurs to this plea: in this case Roll Iustice said, that it is

the trespasse of the party that carryed the defendant upon the land, and not the trespasse of the defendant: as he that drives my cattell into another mans land is the trespassor against him, and not I who am owner of the cattell.

Note that the defendant pleaded the compulsion of the third party specially because it was not a general denial as was the defense — it was not my act — in Weaver v. Ward.

With Smith v. Stone, contrast Gilbert v. Stone, 82 Eng. Rep. 539 (K.B. 1647):

Gilbert brought an action of trespasse quare clausum fregit, and taking of a gelding, against Stone. The defendant pleads that he for fear of his life, and wounding of twelve armed men, who threatened to kill him if he did not [do the act] went into the house of the plaintiff, and took the gelding. The plaintiff demurred to this plea; Roll Iustice, This is no plea to justifie the defendant; for I may not do a trespasse to one for fear of threatnings of another, for by this means the party injured shall have no satisfaction, for he cannot have it of the party that threatned. Therefore let the plaintiff have his judgement.

Dickenson v. Watson, 84 Eng. Rep. 922 1218 (K.B. 1682) also gave a narrow construction to inevitable accident. The defendant, a tax-collector of "hearth-money," discharged his firearm when no one was in view, without intending to harm anyone. Nonetheless he shot the plaintiff who was walking along the road minding his own business. The court upheld a judgment for the plaintiff, "for in trespass the defendant shall not be excused without unavoidable necessity, which is not shewn here . . . ."

In Gibbons v. Pepper, 91 Eng. Rep. 922 (K.B. 1695), the defendant was riding a horse on the highway. The horse, being frightened, bolted, carrying the defendant along until it struck and injured the plaintiff. The defendant also claimed that he called out to the plaintiff to take care, "but that notwithstanding the plaintiff did not go out of the way, but continued there." The defendant pleaded as his justification "that the accident was inevitable, and that the negligence of the defendant did not cause it." Again on demurrer, judgment was given for the plaintiff ("[o]f which opinion was the whole court"):

For if I ride upon a horse, and J. S. whips the horse so that he runs away with me and runs over any other person, he who whipped the horse is guilty of the battery, and not me. But if I by spurring was the cause of such accident, then I am guilty. In the same manner, if *A* takes the hand of *B* and with it strikes *C*, *A* is the trespasser and not *B*. And, per Curiam, the defendant might have given this justification in evidence upon the general issue pleaded. And therefore judgment was given for the plaintiff.

Should the issue of plaintiff's conduct have been considered in light of Weaver v. Ward?

Gibbons rests on the assumption that the defendant's animal should be treated as the passive instrument of any third party who incites it to hurt the plaintiff or his property. Yet this equation between animal and inanimate object is far from evident, given that animals have wills of their own. Another approach is to hold the owner (vicariously) responsible for the harms caused by his animals, but to grant him an action against any third party who rode, spurred or otherwise caused the animal to do damage. In deciding between these two approaches, it is instructive to ask who should bear the risk of insolvency of the third party, the owner of the animal or the victim? How should that question be answered if *A* picks *B*'s stick off the ground and uses it to strike *C*? For further elaboration of these examples, see Scott v. Shepherd, *infra* at 84, and Chapter 7, Section C.

3. Inevitable accident: modern response. Modern courts have uniformly rejected the plaintiff's request for an inevitable accident instruction in the few cases in which it has been requested. In Butigan v. Yellow Cab Co., 320 P.2d 500, 504 (Cal. 1958), the court repudiated its earlier flirtation with that defense in intersection collisions, noting that "an accident may be 'unavoidable or inevitable' where it is caused by a superior or irresistible force or by an absence of exceptional care which the law does not expect of the ordinary prudent man." The court held that no defendant should be held to such a high standard of care:

> In reality, the so-called defense of unavoidable accident has no legitimate place in our pleading. It appears to be an obsolete remnant from a time when damages for injuries to person or property directly caused by a voluntary act of the defendant could be recovered in an action of trespass and when strict liability would be imposed unless the defendant proved that the injury was caused through "inevitable accident."

In its place, ordinary negligence principles were held to govern so that "the defendant under a general denial may show any circumstance which militates against his negligence or its causal effect."

A similar view was advanced in McWilliams v. Masterson, 112 S.W.3d 314 (Tex. App. 2003). The plaintiff was driving his car with his family at night at 65 miles per hour through a severe snowstorm on a four-lane highway when he attempted to pass the defendant's 18-wheeler in the right lane going about 50 miles per hour. Both drivers were within the speed limit. As the plaintiff attempted to move back to the right, he suddenly saw cattle ahead. He struck one of the animals, which drove him back in front of the truck, resulting in the death of his wife and injuries to the other passengers. The defendant received an "unavoidable accident" instruction because of "the truism that some events or injuries may not be proximately caused by the negligence of anyone," but are best attributable to "fate." The defense was also held applicable to the two cattle owners, named Gabels, whose fence and gates were in good repair, on the ground that nothing could restrain their cattle in the face of the storm, according to a witness who testified about cattle's fierce survival instinct. Thus, even though the court held that human and animal actions caused the various harms, the absence of all negligence was found to negate liability. Note that a rigorous system of strict liability protects the defendant Masterson who had the right of way at all times.

But should it protect the Gabels in light of their decision to keep cattle near the road? Under *Gibbons*?

The current case law on inevitable accident was summarized in Lenards v. DeBoer, 865 N.W.2d 867 (S.D. 2015), where the court rejected the defense in a rear-end collision where the defendant claimed that he was temporarily blinded by the sun. Kern, J., concurring, first noted that the decision in *Butigan* was "unique" when made, and continued:

> Today, however, 21 States and the District of Columbia have abandoned the un-avoidable accident instruction and 15 States have severely criticized or limited it. Certainly our own precedents and this national trend are cause to question the continued use of the unavoidable accident instruction.

SECTION C. THE FORMS OF ACTION

1. The Significance of the Forms

These early historical materials show a close interplay between substantive and procedural issues. This section examines the early forms of action, which also exerted a strong, if unintended, influence upon the growth of substantive tort law. In the well-known phrase of Henry Maine, "So great is the ascendancy of the Law of Actions in the infancy of Courts of Justice, that substantive law has at first the look of being gradually secreted in the interstices of procedure." Maine, Early Law and Custom 389 (1907). The most distinctive feature of the forms of action was their jurisdictional significance. Under the forms, the plaintiff could not simply state in his complaint the facts sufficient to get relief. Compare Federal Rules of Civil Procedure, Rule 8(a). She had to further show that her cause of action fell within one of the writs (royal orders used to commence civil actions) recognized at that time.

The choice of writs mattered. As Frederic W. Maitland observed in his masterly essay, The Forms of Action at Common Law 4-5 (1936 ed.):

> [T]o a very considerable degree the substantive law administered in a given form of action has grown up independently of the law administered in other forms. Each procedural pigeon-hole contains its own rules of substantive law, and it is with great caution that we may argue from what is found in one to what will probably be found in another; each has its own precedents. It is quite possible that a litigant will find that his case will fit some two or three of these pigeon-holes. If that be so he will have a choice, which will often be a choice between the old, cumbrous, costly, on the one hand, the modern, rapid, cheap, on the other. Or again he may make a bad choice, fail in his action, and take such comfort as he can from the hints of the judges that another form of action might have been more successful. The plaintiff's choice is irrevocable; he must play the rules of the game that he has chosen. Lastly he may find that, plausible as his case may seem, it just will not fit any one of the receptacles provided by the courts and he may take to himself the lesson that where there is no remedy there is no wrong.

2. Trespass and Case

Two writs—trespass and trespass on the case (or more simply "case")—covered most of the physical harms actionable at common law. By the final stages of the writ system, it was generally settled that trespass lay for the redress of harm caused by the defendant's direct and immediate application of force against the plaintiff's person or property. Case, on the other hand, covered all those "indirect" harms, not involving the use of force, actionable at common law. The classic illustration of the difference was given by Fortescue, J., in Reynolds v. Clarke:

> [I]f a man throws a log into the highway, and in that act it hits me, I may maintain trespass, because it is an immediate wrong; but if as it lies there I tumble over it, and receive an injury, I must bring an action upon the case; because it is only prejudicial in consequence, for which originally I could have no action at all.

92 Eng. Rep. 410 (K.B. 1726). Is there an intelligible distinction between "slip and fall" cases and collision cases? If so, what is its significance?

The last sentence of Fortescue's opinion offers a view of the evolution of the substantive tort law. Under that view, royal recognition of the action of trespass came first because it offered vital protection against the direct use of force. Telltale signs of the original scope of the trespass writ are found in two of its Latin phrases: vi et armis, by force and arms, and contra pacem regis, against the peace of the king. According to the traditional view, the action on the case was a much later development, one that took place well after the Norman Conquest, toward the middle of the fourteenth century, when the royal courts completed a silent revolution by finally allowing tort actions to those plaintiffs who were not the victims of direct and immediate force. Fifoot, History and Sources of the Common Law, Tort and Contract ch. 4 (1949).

Subsequently, however, Professor Milsom effectively, indeed decisively, challenged this view by demonstrating that the emergence of trespass on the case as a distinct writ in the fourteenth century did not signal a transformation of the substantive law. Milsom, Historical Foundations of the Common Law ch. 11 (2d ed. 1981). Like the Latin "transgressio," trespass originally meant simply "wrong," and cases brought under that writ in royal courts covered not only wrongs involving the use of force, but all manner of other actionable harms as well. "If we identify trespass not with a narrow category of wrongs but with wrong generally, with the category of tort rather than a particular tort, we are a good deal closer to thinking fourteenth-century thoughts than we previously were." Arnold, Select Cases of Trespass from the King's Courts—1307-1399, at ix (Selden Society, vol. 100 (1984)). Shades of that position are evident in the *Thorns Case*, when Pigot argued that blocking water to a mill by cutting willows was a trespass, even in the absence of the direct use of force against the mill owner.

The radical change in subsequent centuries, far from altering the underlying substantive principles, came about for procedural reasons. The courts no longer required the magic words, vi et armis and contra pacem regis, in situations to which their ordinary meanings did not apply. To support his thesis, Milsom collected from the old legal records a large number of writs framed in trespass in which the phrases vi et armis and contra pacem regis were included solely as legal fiction to secure the jurisdiction of the royal courts. The writ of trespass was, for example, broad enough to encompass suits brought by lower riparians who suffered flooding because upper riparians had not made the required repairs to their river walls. Similarly, early trespass actions were used to stop unfair competition by, for example, the owner of a fair against persons who had sold goods in violation of his exclusive franchise granted by the king. In neither case did the words vi et armis or contra pacem regis describe the event for which redress was sought. Finally, an action for professional malpractice brought by the owner of a horse against the smith who cared for his horse also sounded in trespass, even though the plaintiff fictitiously pleaded that the horse had been taken by force and arms in order to be able to maintain the suit in royal court. "[W]ere it not for the chinks of a few unusual cases, there would be nothing to make us suspect the truth, except this: the defendants in many such actions for killing horses are named or described as smiths." Milsom, Historical Foundations of the Common Law 289 (2d ed. 1981).

The royal judges eventually removed these elaborate fictions, and in the Farrier's Case of 1372, they allowed the plaintiff to sue in royal court without pleading either vi et armis or contra pacem regis. The explicit emergence of a separate action on the case did not expand the scope of the tort law in the royal courts, but it did require clarification of the boundary between the two distinct writs of trespass and case for both procedural and substantive reasons. With trespass, the plaintiff could begin his suit with the stringent process of capias, whereby he could seize the defendant's personal property. With case, however, the plaintiff had to commence his action with the less coercive summons and complaint. That distinction was eliminated by statute in 1504. Yet by a statute of 1677 (16 & 17 Car. 2), a second procedural point separated the two writs. In the words of Lord Kenyon in Savignac v. Roome, 101 Eng. Rep. 470 (K.B. 1794): "[I]f in an action of trespass the plaintiff recover less than 40 s., he is entitled to no more costs than damages; whereas a verdict with nominal damages only in an action on the case carries all the costs."

The division in the writs between trespass and case raised substantive problems as well, as in the famous *Squib Case*.

Scott v. Shepherd
96 Eng. Rep. 525 (K.B. 1773)

Trespass and assault for throwing, casting, and tossing a lighted squib at and against the plaintiff, and striking him therewith on the face, and so burning one of his eyes, that he lost the sight of it, whereby, & c. On Not Guilty pleaded, the cause came on to be tried before Nares, J., last Summer Assizes, at Bridgwater, when the jury found a verdict for the plaintiff with £100 damages, subject to the opinion of the Court on this case: — On the evening of the fair-day at Milborne Port, 28th October, 1770, the defendant threw a *lighted squib*, made of gun powder, &c.

"It's my fault—I wasn't worrying enough."

from the street into the market-house, which is a covered building, supported by arches, and enclosed at one end, but open at the other and both the sides, where a large concourse of people were assembled; which lighted squib, so thrown by the defendant, fell upon the standing of one Yates, who sold gingerbread, & c. That one Willis instantly, and to prevent injury to himself and the said wares of the said Yates, took up the said lighted squib from off the said standing, and then threw it across the said market-house, when it fell upon another standing there of one Ryal, who sold the same sort of wares, who instantly, and to save his own goods from being injured, took up the said lighted squib from off the said standing, and then threw it to another part of the said market-house, and, in so throwing it, struck the plaintiff then in the said market-house in the face therewith, and the combustible matter then bursting, put out one of the plaintiff's eyes. *Qu.* If this action be maintainable? . . .

NARES, J., was of opinion, that trespass would well lie in the present case. That the natural and probable consequence of the act done by the defendant was injury to somebody, and therefore the act was illegal at common law. And the throwing of squibs has by statute W.3, been since made a nuisance. Being therefore unlawful, the defendant was liable to answer for the consequences, be the injury mediate or immediate. 21 Hen. 7, 28, is express that malus animus is not necessary to constitute a trespass. . . .

BLACKSTONE, J., was of opinion, that an action of trespass did not lie for Scott against Shepherd upon this case. He took the settled distinction to be, that where the injury is *immediate*, an action of trespass will lie; where it is only *consequential*, it must be an action on the case: Reynolds and Clarke, Lord Raym. 1401, Stra. 634; . . . The lawfulness or unlawfulness of the original act is not the criterion;

though something of that sort is put into Lord Raymond's mouth in Stra. 635, . . . [L]awful or unlawful is quite out of the case; the solid distinction is between direct or immediate injuries on the one hand, and mediate or consequential on the other. And trespass never lay for the latter. If this be so, the only question will be, whether the injury which the plaintiff suffered was immediate, or consequential only; and I hold it to be the latter. The original act was, as against Yates, a trespass; not as against Ryal, or Scott. The tortious act was complete when the squib lay at rest upon Yates's stall. He, or any bystander, had, I allow, a right to protect themselves by removing the squib, but should have taken care to do it in such a manner as not to endamage others. But Shepherd, I think, is not answerable in an action of trespass and assault for the mischief done by the squib in the new motion impressed upon it, and the new direction given it, by either Willis or Ryal; who both were free agents, and acted upon their own judgment. This differs it from the cases put of turning loose a wild beast or a madman. They are only instruments in the hand of the first agent. Nor is it like diverting the course of an enraged ox, or of a stone thrown, or an arrow glancing against a tree; because there the original motion, the vis impressa, is continued, though diverted. Here the instrument of mischief was at rest, till a new impetus and a new direction are given it, not once only, but by two successive rational agents. But it is said that the act is not complete, nor the squib at rest, till after it is spent or exploded. It certainly has a power of doing fresh mischief, and so has a stone that has been thrown against my windows, and now lies still. Yet if any person gives that stone a new motion, and does farther mischief with it, trespass will not lie for that against the original thrower. No doubt but Yates may maintain trespass against Shepherd. And, according to the doctrine contended for, so may Ryal and Scott. Three actions for one single act! nay, it may be extended in infinitum. If a man tosses a football into the street, and, after being kicked about by one hundred people, it at last breaks a tradesman's windows; shall he have trespass against the man who first produced it? Surely only against the man who gave it that mischievous direction. But it is said, if Scott has no action against Shepherd, against whom must he seek his remedy? I give no opinion whether case would lie against Shepherd for the consequential damage; though, as at present advised, I think, upon the circumstances, it would. But I think, in strictness of law, trespass would lie against Ryal, the immediate actor in this unhappy business. Both he and Willis have exceeded the bounds of self-defence, and not used sufficient circumspection in removing the danger from themselves. The throwing it across the market-house, instead of brushing it down, or throwing [it] out of the open sides into the street, (if it was not meant to continue the sport, as it is called), was at least an unnecessary and incautious act. Not even menaces from others are sufficient to justify a trespass against a third person; much less a fear of danger to either his goods or his person—nothing but inevitable necessity; Weaver and Ward, Hob. 134; Gilbert and Stone, Al. 35, Styl. 72. . . . And I admit that the defendant is answerable in trespass for all the direct and inevitable effects caused by his own immediate act.—But what is his own immediate act? The throwing the squib to Yates's stall. Had Yates's goods been burnt, or his person injured,

Shepherd must have been responsible in trespass. But he is not responsible for the acts of other men. The subsequent throwing across the market-house by Willis, is neither the act of Shepherd, nor the inevitable effect of it; much less the subsequent throwing by Ryal. . . . It is said by Lord Raymond, and very justly, in Reynolds and Clarke, "We must keep up the boundaries of actions, otherwise we shall introduce the utmost confusion." As I therefore think no immediate injury passed from the defendant to the plaintiff (and without such immediate injury no action of trespass can be maintained), I am of opinion, that in this action judgment ought to be for the defendant.

DE GREY, C.J. This case is one of those wherein the line drawn by the law between actions on the case and actions of trespass is very nice and delicate. Trespass is an injury accompanied with force, for which an action of trespass vi et armis lies against the person from whom it is received. The question here is, whether the injury received by the plaintiff arises from the force of the original act of the defendant, or from a new force by a third person. I agree with my Brother Blackstone as to the principles he has laid down, but not in his application of those principles to the present case. . . . [T]he true question is, whether the injury is the direct and immediate act of the defendant; and I am of opinion, that in this case it is. The throwing the squib was an act unlawful and tending to affright the bystanders. So far, mischief was originally intended; not any particular mischief, but mischief indiscriminate and wanton. Whatever mischief therefore follows, he is the author of it;—Egreditur personam, as the phrase is in criminal cases. And though criminal cases are no rule for civil ones, yet in trespass I think there is an analogy. Every one who does an unlawful act is considered as the doer of all that follows; if done with a deliberate intent, the consequence may amount to murder; if incautiously, to manslaughter. So too a person breaking a horse in Lincoln's Inn Fields hurt a man; held, that trespass lay: and that it need not be laid scienter. I look upon all that was done subsequent to the original throwing as a continuation of the first force and first act, which will continue till the squib was spent by bursting. And I think that any innocent person removing the danger from himself to another is justifiable; the blame lights upon the first thrower. The new direction and new force flow out of the first force, and are not a new trespass. . . . It has been urged, that the intervention of a free agent will make a difference: but I do not consider Willis ad Ryal as free agents in the present case, but acting under a compulsive necessity for their own safety and self-preservation. On these reasons I concur with Brothers Gould and Nares, that the present action is maintainable.

NOTE

Under which writ lies the cause of action? *Scott* proposes two complementary ways to determine the boundary line between trespass and case. One method held that trespass lay when the harm was direct, and case when it was consequential. The second method, championed by Nares, J., insisted that trespass also lies for all harm, direct or consequential, when the defendant's action is unlawful by statute, including one that declares the throwing of a lighted squib a public nuisance. In Reynolds v. Clarke, 92 Eng. Rep. 410 (K.B. 1726), moreover, the plaintiff's action for trespass was dismissed when the defendant fixed a spout in plaintiff's yard from which water leaked, thereby rotting the walls of plaintiff's house. When the invasion is direct and the harm is consequential, which action should prevail?

A similar dispute over the proper form of action arose in the celebrated case of Guille v. Swan, 19 Johns. (N.Y.) 381 (1822). There the defendant Guille flew in a balloon that landed in the garden of the plaintiff Swan. When the balloon landed it dragged for about 30 feet causing damage to Swan's potatoes and radishes. Given his perilous position, Guille called out to a workman in Swan's field for help in a voice that could be heard by the crowd assembled at the boundary line. About 200 people came tearing across plaintiff's land causing additional damage to his vegetables and flowers, for which Swan sued Guille in trespass. Guille sought to limit his liability to the damage that he had caused, not that of the crowd. But Spencer, C.J., upheld a jury verdict against Guille for the full $90 in damages.

> The *intent* with which an act is done, is by no means the test of liability of a party to an action of trespass. If the act causes the immediate injury, whether it was intentional or unintentional, trespass is the proper action to redress the wrong. [The court discusses Scott v. Shepherd among other cases, and continues.]
>
> I will not say that ascending in a balloon is an unlawful act, for it is not so; but, it is certain, that the *Aeronaut* has no control over its motion horizontally; he is at the sport of the winds, and is to descend when and how he can; his reach[ing] the earth is a matter of hazard. He did descend on the premises of the plaintiff below, at a short distance from the place where he ascended. Now, if his descent, under such circumstances, would, ordinarily and naturally, draw a crowd of people about him, either from curiosity, or for the purpose of rescuing him from a perilous situation; all this he ought to have foreseen, and must be responsible for. Whether the crowd heard him call for help, or not, is immaterial; he had put himself in a situation to invite help, and they rushed forward, impelled, perhaps, by the double motive of rendering aid, and gratifying a curiosity which he had excited. Can it be doubted, that if the plaintiff in error [i.e., defendant-appellant] had beckoned to the crowd to come to his assistance, that he would be liable for their trespass in entering the enclosure? I think not. In that case, they would have been co-trespassers, and we must consider the situation in which he placed himself, voluntarily and designedly, as equivalent to a direct request to the crowd to follow him. In the present case, he did call for help and may have been heard by the crowd; he is, therefore, undoubtedly, liable for all the injury sustained.

In trespass?

3. The Breakdown of the Forms of Action

The lighted squib in Scott v. Shepherd and the descending balloon in Guille v. Swan tested the uncertain line between trespass and case. Yet only rarely did

American and English courts encounter lighted squibs or falling balloons. The division between the writs, however, was critical in cases involving accidents on the highway or the high seas that reached the courts in great numbers by the 1790s. In these cases, the courts failed to make any firm or authoritative choice between trespass and case. The root problem was as much practical as theoretical. Even if courts could define conceptually the line between trespass and case, the plaintiff might not know in advance of trial whether her case fell on one side of the line or the other. If the plaintiff sued in trespass, the defendant could prevail by showing that his horse, which he had outfitted with too-weak reins, had bolted out of control. If the plaintiff sued in case, the defendant might still prevail if he had indeed run right over the plaintiff. Collisions at sea were even more complicated. It was always a delicate judgment whether a captain had rammed his ship into another ship, or whether the wind or the sea (an act of God) had carried his disabled ship into the other craft. See, e.g., Ogle v. Barnes, 101 Eng. Reg. 1338 (K.B. 1799).

The situation was further complicated by the twin problems of vicarious liability and joinder of actions. If the plaintiff was run down by a carriage owned by the defendant, it was settled that trespass did not lie against the master, who could only be vicariously liable, even if trespass lay against his servant. McManus v. Crickett, 102 Eng. Rep. 580 (K.B. 1800); Sharrod v. London & N.W. Ry., 154 Eng. Rep. 1345 (Ex. 1849). Yet, if the original action was brought in case, to cover the possibility that the coach had been driven by a servant in the defendant's employ, plaintiff now ran the risk of nonsuit (that is, dismissal) if the defendant personally had driven the coach. Equally important, the rules governing the joinder of actions prohibited the plaintiff in an accident involving direct harm from suing both the owner and his servant-driver under the same writ: Direct harm required trespass and indirect harms required case. The limitations on the two writs forced the plaintiffs and courts to play an uncertain shell game for the defendant's benefit, as several separate and expensive actions were needed to guard against all the unhappy possibilities that might emerge at trial.

How could the courts break the logjam? The most obvious proposal was to disregard tradition by allowing a plaintiff to include separate counts of trespass and case within a single writ. That result was achieved by statute by the middle of the nineteenth century under the Common Law Procedure Act 15 & 16 Vict., c. 76, §41 (1852), after the early nineteenth-century English judges refused to introduce so bold a reform on their own initiative. A second possibility was to bend the rules by allowing the plaintiff to use trespass against the master when the servant caused immediate and direct harm, a proposal that would have eliminated the gamesmanship involved in the joinder of actions. Yet, here too, the writ tradition resisted judicial innovation.

In the end, the courts adopted a third solution. In the watershed case of Williams v. Holland, 131 Eng. Rep. 848 (C.P. 1833), the Court of Common Pleas held that the plaintiff could sue in case, no matter whether the harm was immediate or consequential, as long as the plaintiff could show that the harm occurred as a result of the defendant's negligence. The writ of trespass was still available for

COURT OF COMMON PLEAS,
WESTMINSTER HALL.

London Pub. 1.st June 1808 at R Ackermann's Repository of Arts 101 Strand.

Illustration of the Court of Common Pleas in Westminster Hall, c. 1808-1810
Source: The British Library

all immediate harms, whether willful or negligent, and only trespass would lie in cases of willful and immediate harm. Harms directly and negligently caused could under this rule be remedied in either trespass or case. Under the rule in Williams v. Holland, the plaintiff in virtually all running-down cases would prefer case to trespass because case allowed him, first, to avoid having to guess whether harm was immediate or consequential and, second, to join both master and servant in a single suit. Joinder of claims was unavailable under Williams v. Holland when the injury inflicted by the servant was both willful and direct, but that limitation hardly mattered for most road accidents. Moreover, when these cases did occur, the master was probably not liable. He could defend himself under an early version of the "frolic and detour" doctrine, an exception to the general rule of vicarious liability, applicable to the willful wrongs that servants committed outside the course of their employment. See *infra* Chapter 7, Section F, at 629-630.

Williams v. Holland did more than usher in a procedural revolution; it also shifted the terms of debate in the strict liability/negligence controversy. The earlier cases, such as Scott v. Shepherd, contained many hints that trespass would lie for direct harm caused by the defendant even in the absence of negligence or intent. The law invited actions under a causal theory of strict liability: You struck my wagon. After Williams v. Holland, negligence became more prominent as an essential element for recovery in all highway accident cases for either direct or consequential damages. The English position was summed up by Bramwell, B., in Holmes v. Mather, L.R. 10 Ex. 261, 268-269 (1875), in giving judgment for the defendant:

> As to the cases cited, most of them are really decisions on the form of action, whether case or trespass. The result of them is this, and it is intelligible enough: if the act that does an injury is an act of direct force *vi et armis*, trespass is the proper remedy (if there is any remedy) where the act is wrongful, either as being wilful or as being the result of negligence. Where the act is not wrongful for either of these reasons, no action is maintainable, though trespass would be the proper form of action if it were wrongful.

Even after the English courts settled the substantive issue, some procedural issues surrounded the affirmative defense of "inevitable accident." Even though the plaintiff had to plead and prove negligence in actions on the case, a defendant had to show himself free from fault in cases of direct harm. Stanley v. Powell, [1891] 1 Q.B. 86. Indeed, in England it took until 1959 for the law to require the plaintiff to both plead and prove negligence in all claims for unintended personal injury. Fowler v. Lanning, [1959] 1 Q.B. 426. The procedural problems created by the division between the two writs also carried over to other areas. To give but one example, it took until 1965 to hold that the same three-year statute of limitations applied to all personal injury actions, whether framed in trespass or negligence. Letang v. Cooper, [1965] 1 Q.B. 232.

The history of trespass and case in England is given here in much abbreviated form. For further materials see Arnold, Select Cases of Trespass from the King's Courts: 1307-1399 (Seldon Society, vol. 100, 1984); Fifoot, History and Sources of the Common Law, Tort and Contract ch. 9 (1949); Milsom, Historical Foundations of the Common Law chs. 11, 13 (2d ed. 1981); Epstein, Assumption of Risk in a System of Strict Liability: Conceptual Tangles and Social Consequences 265 (Goudkamp, Wilmot-Smith & Dyson eds., 2015); and Prichard, Trespass, Case and the Rule in Williams v. Holland, 22 Cambridge L.J. 234 (1964) (an excellent article from which much of the account given here is drawn).

SECTION D. STRICT LIABILITY AND NEGLIGENCE IN THE SECOND HALF OF THE NINETEENTH CENTURY

Toward the middle of the nineteenth century, the forms of action fell by the wayside in both England and the United States. Just before the English Common Law Procedure Acts of 1852 removed the last vestiges of the forms of action from English law, the widespread adoption of the so-called Field Codes—named after the reformer David Dudley Field, who championed the adoption of "code pleading" in New York—did the same thing in the United States. See First Report of Commissioners on Practice and Pleading (N.Y. 1848). The purpose of these reforms was simply to abolish the forms of action as procedural devices. "No rule of law, by which rights and wrongs are measured, will be touched, the object and effect of the change being only the removal of old obstructions, in the way of enforcing the rights, and redressing the wrongs." *Id.* at 146-147. Therefore, the legal precedents in tort, both in England and the United States, survived the procedural reforms. With the removal of the forms, the choice between negligence and strict liability was inescapably presented in its most general form. See generally Clark, Code Pleading (2d ed. 1947).

The emergence of negligence as the dominant standard of civil liability in American tort law during the first half of the nineteenth century parallels the English experience. At the beginning of the nineteenth century, negligence was a shadowy concept, with a subordinate role in the tort law. In its primary sense, the negligence concept applied to the *nonfeasance* of individuals charged either by contract or statute with a duty of care. Smiths and surgeons were, for example, bound by contract to conduct their professions carefully, while jailors and those charged with the maintenance of the public highways were persons on whom statutes placed the duty of care. Negligence, in the sense of carelessness in the performance of some affirmative act that causes harm to a stranger, was not the prevalent conception.

Yet by 1830, the increase in collision cases slowly brought this second sense of negligence to the fore. See Harvey v. Dunlop, (Hill & Denio) 193 (N.Y. 1843); Bridge Co. v. Lehigh Coal & Navigation Co., 4 Rawle 8 (Pa. 1833); Sullivan v. Murphy, 2 Miles 298, 2 Law Rep. 246 (1839). See generally Horwitz, The Transformation of American Law: 1780 to 1860, 89-94 (1977).

Brown v. Kendall
60 Mass. 292 (1850)

It appeared in evidence, on the trial, which was before Wells, C.J., in the court of common pleas, that two dogs, belonging to the plaintiff and the defendant, respectively, were fighting in the presence of their masters; that the defendant took a stick about four feet long, and commenced beating the dogs in order to separate them; that the plaintiff was looking on, at the distance of about a rod [= 16.5 feet], and that he advanced a step or two towards the dogs. In their struggle, the dogs approached the place where the plaintiff was standing. The defendant retreated backwards from the dogs, striking them as he retreated; and as he approached the plaintiff, with his back towards him, in raising his stick over his shoulder, in order to strike the dogs, he accidentally hit the plaintiff in the eye, inflicting upon him a severe injury. . . .

SHAW, C.J. This is an action of trespass, vi et armis, brought by George Brown against George K. Kendall, for an assault and battery; and the original defendant having died pending the action, his executrix has been summoned in. The rule of the common law, by which this action would abate by the death of either party, is reversed in this commonwealth by statute, which provides that actions of trespass for assault and battery shall survive. Rev. Sts. c. 93, §7.

Exhibit 2.1   Lemuel Shaw

Lemuel Shaw (1781-1861) was chief justice of the Supreme Judicial Court of Massachusetts from 1830 to 1860. After studying at Harvard and reading law privately, he became a successful lawyer in Boston, working on corporate matters in the commercializing Northeast. Before being named to the Massachusetts high court, he served as a justice of the peace and a legislator in both the state house and senate. Once on the bench as chief justice of the Supreme Judicial Court, he penned (quite literally by hand) more than 2,000 opinions.

Much of his jurisprudence is thought to favor the bustling industrial development of the country at the time, while still deferring to the legislature's action intervening in economic matters. His harsh (by today's standards) decision in Farwell v. Boston & Worcester R.R. Corp., 45 Mass. 49, 58-59 (1842) (see Chapter 4, *infra*) established the "fellow servant rule" and became a template for accident law across the country. Besides industrialization, Shaw is also known for his legal analysis of slavery, the predominant social topic of the day. While he repudiated the practice of slavery, even holding that slaves brought into Massachusetts were automatically free, see Commonwealth v. Aves, 18 Pick. 193 (Mass. 1836), he was less forgiving when it came to enforcing fugitive slave laws, and upheld the rights of businesses to discriminate against blacks. See McCrea v. Marsh, 12 Gray 211 (Mass. 1858).

Bio source: Paul Finkelman, Lemuel Shaw: The Shaping of State Law, in Noble Purposes: Nine Champions of the Rule of Law 33-46 (Gross ed., 2007) Image source: Wikimedia Commons

The facts set forth in the bill of exceptions preclude the supposition, that the blow, inflicted by the hand of the defendant upon the person of the plaintiff, was intentional. The whole case proceeds on the assumption, that the damage sustained by the plaintiff, from the stick held by the defendant, was inadvertent and unintentional; and the case involves the question how far, and under what qualifications, the party by whose unconscious act the damage was done is responsible for it. We use the term "unintentional" rather than involuntary, because in some of the cases, it is stated, that the act of holding and using a weapon or instrument, the movement of which is the immediate cause of hurt to another, is a voluntary act, although its particular effect in hitting and hurting another is not within the purpose or intention of the party doing the act.

It appears to us, that some of the confusion in the cases on this subject has grown out of the long-vexed question, under the rule of the common law, whether a party's remedy, where he has one, should be sought in an action of the case, or of trespass. This is very distinguishable from the question, whether in a given case, any action will lie. The result of these cases is, that if the damage complained of is the immediate effect of the act of the defendant, trespass vi et armis lies; if consequential only, and not immediate, case is the proper remedy. . . .

In these discussions, it is frequently stated by judges, that when one receives injury from the direct act of another, trespass will lie. But we think this is said in reference to the question, whether trespass and not case will lie, assuming that the facts are such, that some action will lie. These dicta are no authority, we think, for holding, that damage received by a direct act of force from another will be sufficient to maintain an action of trespass, whether the act was lawful or unlawful, and neither wilful, intentional, nor careless. . . .

We think, as the result of all the authorities, the rule is correctly stated by Mr. Greenleaf, that the plaintiff must come prepared with evidence to show either that the *intention* was unlawful, or that the defendant was *in fault*; for if the injury was unavoidable, and the conduct of the defendant was free from blame, he will not be liable. 2 Greenl. Ev. §§85 to 92. If, in the prosecution of a lawful act, a casualty purely accidental arises, no action can be supported for an injury arising therefrom. . . . In applying these rules to the present case, we can perceive no reason why the instructions asked for by the defendant ought not to have been given; to this effect, that if both plaintiff and defendant at the time of the blow were using ordinary care, or if at that time the defendant was using ordinary care, and the plaintiff was not, or if at that time, both the plaintiff and defendant were not using ordinary care, then the plaintiff could not recover.

In using this term, ordinary care, it may be proper to state, that what constitutes ordinary care will vary with the circumstances of cases. In general, it means that kind and degree of care, which prudent and cautious men would use, such as is required by the exigency of the case, and such as is necessary to guard against probable danger. A man, who should have occasion to discharge a gun, on an open and extensive marsh, or in a forest, would be required to use less circumspection and care, than if he were to do the same thing in an inhabited town, village, or city. To make an accident, or casualty, or as the law sometimes states it, inevitable accident, it must be such an accident as the defendant could not have avoided by the use of the kind and degree of care necessary to the exigency, and in the circumstances in which he was placed.

We are not aware of any circumstances in this case, requiring a distinction between acts which it was lawful and proper to do, and acts of legal duty. There are cases, undoubtedly, in which officers are bound to act under process, for the legality of which they are not responsible, and perhaps some others in which this distinction would be important. We can have no doubt that the act of the defendant in attempting to part the fighting dogs, one of which was his own, and for the injurious acts of which he might be responsible, was a lawful and proper act, which he might do by proper and safe means. If, then, in doing this act, using due care and all proper precautions necessary to the exigency of the case, to avoid hurt to others, in raising his stick for that purpose, he accidentally hit the plaintiff in his eye, and wounded him, this was the result of pure accident, or was involuntary and unavoidable, and therefore the action would not lie. Or if the defendant was chargeable with some negligence, and if the plaintiff was also chargeable with negligence, we think the plaintiff cannot recover without showing that the damage was caused wholly by the act of the defendant, and that the plaintiff's own negligence did not contribute as an efficient cause to produce it.

The court instructed the jury, that if it was not a necessary act, and the defendant was not in duty bound to part the dogs, but might with propriety interfere or not as he chose, the defendant was responsible for the consequences of the blow, unless it appeared that he was in the exercise of extraordinary care, so that the accident was inevitable, using the word not in a strict but a popular sense. This is to be taken in connection with the charge afterwards given, that if the jury believed, that the act of interference in the fight was unnecessary, (that is, as before explained, not a duty incumbent on the defendant), then the burden of proving extraordinary care on the part of the defendant, or want of ordinary care on the part of plaintiff, was on the defendant.

The court is of opinion that these directions were not conformable to law. If the act of hitting the plaintiff was unintentional, on the part of the defendant, and done in the doing of a lawful act, then the defendant was not liable, unless it was done in the want of exercise of due care, adapted to the exigency of the case, and therefore such want of due care became part of the plaintiff's case, and the burden of proof was on the plaintiff to establish it. . . .

Perhaps the learned judge, by the use of the term extraordinary care, in the above charge, explained as it is by the context, may have intended nothing more than that increased degree of care and diligence, which the exigency of particular circumstances might require, and which men of ordinary care and prudence would use under like circumstances, to guard against danger. If such was the meaning of this part of the charge, then it does not differ from our views, as above explained. But we are of opinion, that the other part of the charge, that the burden of proof was on the defendant, was incorrect. Those facts which are essential to enable the plaintiff to recover, he takes the burden of proving. The evidence may be offered by the plaintiff or by the defendant; the question of due care, or want of care, may be essentially connected with the main facts, and arise from the same proof; but the effect of the rule, as to the burden of proof, is this, that when the proof is all in, and before the jury, from whatever side it comes, and whether directly proved, or inferred from circumstances, if it appears that the defendant was doing a lawful act, and unintentionally hit and hurt the plaintiff, then unless it also appears to the satisfaction of the jury, that the defendant is chargeable with some fault, negligence, carelessness, or want of prudence, the plaintiff fails to sustain the burden of proof, and is not entitled to recover.

New trial ordered.

NOTE

Negligence and economic growth.   The rise of negligence in American tort law has been often viewed as a subsidy for the protection of infant industries. See, e.g., Gregory, Trespass, to Negligence, to Absolute Liability, 37 Va. L. Rev. 359 (1951). Subsequently, the thesis was advanced by Professor Morton Horwitz in his influential work, The Transformation of American Law, 1780-1860, 99-101 (1977): "One of the most striking aspects of legal change during the antebellum period is the extent to which common law doctrines were transformed to create immunities from legal liability and thereby to provide substantial subsidies for those who undertook schemes of economic development." In his view the effort to obtain subsidies through common law rule instead of through the tax system was designed to "more easily disguise underlying political choices. Subsidy through the tax system, by contrast, inevitably involves greater danger of political conflict." In Horwitz's view, more empirical research is needed to compare the effects of taxation (typically low in the nineteenth century) with those attributable to changes in common law rules. "Nevertheless, it does seem fairly clear that the tendency of subsidy through legal change during this period was dramatically to throw the burden of economic development on the weakest and least active elements in the population."

The subsidy thesis itself has been challenged on several counts. First, it has been observed that "Brown [v. Kendall] itself, after all, did not involve industry; it involved private persons and a dog fight. Rather than simply promoting 'General Motors,' is it not more accurate to say that Chief Judge Shaw saw the change in moral terms as well, as a sound social policy not only for business but for every man?" Roberts, Negligence: Blackstone to Shaw to ?: An Intellectual Escapade in a Tory Vein, 50 Cornell L.Q. 191, 205 (1965). Is it a fair reply to say that Shaw well understood the implications of his decision upon the growth of industry and trade?

The Horwitz thesis was in turn challenged by Gary Schwartz, Tort Law and the Economy in Nineteenth-Century America: A Reinterpretation, 90 Yale L.J. 1717 (1981). Schwartz's reading of the earlier English cases, and particularly the American cases around 1800, indicates that the negligence principle was already operative in many, if not most, instances. Schwartz also read and analyzed every nineteenth-century tort case decided in both California and New Hampshire, and found no support for the subsidy thesis and no effort by the courts to engage in the "dynamic, utilitarian" calculations that Horwitz attributes to them. Schwartz also noted that it was unlikely that the subsidy question could be kept underground in the face of explicit legislative debate over subsidies to both railroads and canals.

The Horwitz thesis has also been challenged on theoretical grounds. Most accident cases come out the same way under both negligence and strict liability, meaning that manipulating common law tort rules is a poor way to create interest group subsidies, especially since many large industries often found themselves as plaintiffs as well as defendants. See Epstein, The Social Consequences of Common Law Rules, 95 Harv. L. Rev. 1717 (1982). One more limited explanation for the rise of negligence law ties it to the slow abolition of the now-disregarded common law rule of evidence that prevented either party to a dispute from testifying in the case. Thus Professor Abraham claims that the lower evidentiary requirements of trespass rules lost much of their advantage once the parties to the dispute were able to testify on their own behalf. See Abraham, The Common Law Prohibition on Party Testimony and the Development of Tort Liability, 95 Va. L. Rev. 489 (2009). Do the strict liability rules retain an evidentiary advantage even when both parties can testify? Is the evidentiary change likely to prove more important than the abolition of the common law rule that barred any action for wrongful death? In any event, the same debate over negligence and strict liability also surfaced in the English cases shortly after *Brown*, with dramatically different results.

Fletcher v. Rylands
159 Eng. Rep. 737 (Ex. 1865)

[The following statement of facts is taken from the opinion of Blackburn, J., in the intermediate appellate court:

"It appears from the statement in the case, that the plaintiff was damaged by his property being flooded by water, which, without any fault on his part, broke out of a reservoir constructed on the defendants' land by the defendants' orders, and maintained by the defendants.

It appears from the statement in the case, that the coal under the defendants' land had, at some remote period, been worked out; but this was unknown at the time when the defendants gave directions to erect the reservoir, and the water in the reservoir would not have escaped from the defendants' land, and no mischief would have been done to the plaintiff, but for this latent defect in the defendants' subsoil. And it further appears, that the defendants selected competent engineers and contractors to make their reservoir, and themselves personally continued in total ignorance of what we have called the latent defect in the subsoil; but that these persons employed by them in the course of the work became aware of the existence of the ancient shafts filled up with soil, though they did not know or suspect that they were shafts communicating with old workings.

It is found that the defendants, personally, were free from all blame, but that in fact proper care and skill was not used by the persons employed by them, to provide for the sufficiency of the reservoir with reference to these shafts. The consequence was, that the reservoir when filled with water burst into the shafts, the water flowed down through them into the old workings, and thence into the plaintiff's mine, and there did the mischief."

The above statement of facts should be supplemented by a few additional facts drawn from Lord Cairns' opinion in the House of Lords. (1) the plaintiff had leased his coal mines from the Earl of Wilton; (2) the defendants had constructed their new reservoir upon other land of the Earl of Wilton, with his permission; (3) the reservoir in question was to be used to collect water for the defendants' mill; (4) the defendants had already placed, on their own nearby land, a small reservoir and a mill; (5) the plaintiff in the course of working his mines came across some abandoned shafts and mine passages of unknown origin; and (6) the reservoir burst when it was partially filled with water after one of the vertical shafts beneath it gave way.]

BRAMWELL, B. . . . Now, what is the plaintiff's right? He had the right to work his mines to their extent, leaving no boundary between himself and the next owner. By so doing he subjected himself to all consequences resulting from natural causes, among others, to the influx of all water naturally flowing in. But he had a right to be free from what has been called "foreign" water, that is, water artificially brought or sent to him directly, or indirectly by its being sent to where it would flow to him. The defendants had no right to pour or send water onto the plaintiff's works. Had they done so knowingly it is admitted an action would lie; and that it would if they did it again. . . . The plaintiff's right then has been infringed; the defendants in causing water to flow to the plaintiff have done that which they had no right to do; what difference in point of law does it make that they have done it unwittingly? I think none, and consequently that the action is maintainable. . . . As a rule the knowledge or ignorance of the damage done is immaterial. The burden of proof of this proposition is not on the plaintiff.

Exhibit 2.2   George William Wilshere Bramwell

George William Wilshere Bramwell, 1st Baron Bramwell (1808-1892), was an English judge who decided Blyth v. Birmingham Water Works, 156 Eng. Rep. 1047 (Ex. 1856), during his first year as a baron of the Court of Exchequer. Beginning his career as a clerk in his father's banking business, Bramwell turned to the law and quickly established his legal and procedural acumen. His work on the Common Law Procedure Commission led to an 1852 act of Parliament, which prescribed rules of procedure for common law courts. He was also influential in the creation of limited liability for corporate entities in Britain.

Bio source: Herbert Stephen, Bramwell, George William Wilshere, Dictionary of National Biographies 256-257 (1901 supp.)
Image source: Wikimedia Commons

I proceed to deal with the arguments the other way. It is said there must be a trespass, a nuisance or negligence. I do not agree. . . . But why is this not a trespass? Wilfulness is not material. . . . Why is it not a nuisance? The nuisance is not in the reservoir, but in the water escaping. . . . [T]he act was lawful, the mischievous consequence is a wrong. Where two carriages come in collision, if there is no negligence in either it is as much the act of the one driver as of the other that they meet. The cases of carriers and innkeepers are really cases of contract, and, though exceptional, furnish no evidence that the general law in matters wholly independent of contract is not what I have stated. The old common law liability for fire, created a liability beyond what I contend for here. . . .

I think, therefore, on the plain ground that the defendants have caused water to flow into the plaintiff's mines which but for their, the defendants', act would not have gone there, this action is maintainable. I think that the defendants' innocence, whatever may be its moral bearing on the case, is immaterial in point of law. But I may as well add, that if the defendants did not know what would happen their agents knew that there were old shafts on their land—knew therefore that they must lead to old workings—knew that those old workings *might* extend in any direction, and consequently knew damage might happen. The defendants surely are as liable as their agents would be—why should not they and the defendants be held to act at their peril? But I own this seems to me rather to enforce the rule, that knowledge and wilfulness are not necessary to make the defendants liable, than to give the plaintiff a separate ground of action.

MARTIN, B. . . . First, I think there was no trespass. In the judgment of my brother Bramwell, to which I shall hereafter refer, he seems to think the act of the defendants was a trespass, but I cannot concur, and I own it seems to me that the cases cited by him, viz., Leame v. Bray[, 102 Eng. Rep. 724 (K.B. 1803)], and Gregory v. Piper, 9 B. & C. 591 (E.C.L.R. vol. 17) [, 109 Eng. Rep. 220 (K.B. 1829)], prove the contrary. I think the true criterion of trespass is laid down in the judgments in the former case, viz., that to constitute trespass the act doing the damage must be immediate, and that if the damage be mediate or consequential (which I think the present was) it is not a trespass. Secondly, I think there was no nuisance in the ordinary and generally understood meaning of that word, that is to say, something hurtful or injurious to the senses. The making a pond for holding water is a nuisance to no one. The digging a reservoir in a man's own land is a lawful act. It does not appear that there was any embankment, or that the water in the reservoir was ever above the level of the natural surface of the land, and the water escaped from the bottom of the reservoir, and in ordinary course would descend by gravitation into the defendants' own land, and they did not know of the existence of the old workings. To hold the defendants liable would therefore make them insurers against the consequence of a lawful act upon their own land when they had no reason to believe or suspect that any damage was likely to ensue.

No case was cited in which the question has arisen as to real property; but as to personal property the question arises every day, and there is no better established rule of law than that when damage is done to personal property, and even to the person, by collision either upon the road or at sea, there must be negligence in the party doing the damage to render him legally responsible, and if there be no negligence the party sustaining the damage must bear with it. The existence of this rule is proved by the exceptions to it, viz., the cases of the innkeeper and common carrier of goods for hire, who are quasi insurers. These cases are said to be by the custom of the realm, treating them as exceptions from the ordinary rule of law. In the absence of authority to the contrary, I can see no reason why damage to real property should be governed by a different rule or principle than damage to personal property. There is an instance also of damage to real property, when the party causing it was at common law liable upon the custom of the realm as a quasi insurer, viz., the master of a house if a fire had kindled there and consumed the house of another. In such case the master of the house was liable at common law without proof of negligence on his part. This seems to be an exception from the ordinary rule of law, and in my opinion affords an argument that in other cases such as the present there must be negligence to create a liability. For these reasons I think the first question ought to be answered in favour of the defendants. . . .

I have already referred to the judgment of my brother Bramwell, which I have carefully read and considered, but cannot concur in it. I entertain no doubt that if the defendants directly and by their immediate act cast water upon the plaintiff's land it would have been a trespass, and that they would be liable to an action for it. But this they did not do. What they did was this, they dug a reservoir in their own land and put water in it, which, by underground openings of which they were ignorant, escaped into the plaintiff's land. I think this a very different thing from a direct casting of water upon the land, and that the legal liabilities consequent upon it are governed by a different principle. . . .

I still retain the opinion I originally formed. I think . . . that to hold the defendant liable without negligence would be to constitute him an insurer, which, in my opinion, would be contrary to legal analogy and principle.

[Pollock, C.B., after stating that the issue was "one of great difficulty, and therefore of much doubt," wrote a brief opinion agreeing with Martin, B.]

Fletcher v. Rylands
L.R. 1 Ex. 265 (1866)

BLACKBURN, J. . . . The plaintiff, though free from all blame on his part, must bear the loss, unless he can establish that it was the consequence of some default for which the defendants are responsible. The question of law therefore arises, what is the obligation which the law casts on a person who, like the defendants, lawfully brings on his land something which, though harmless whilst it remains there, will naturally do mischief if it escape out of his land. It is agreed on all hands that he must take care to keep in that which he has brought on the land and keeps there, in order that it may not escape and damage his neighbours, but the question arises whether the duty which the law casts upon him, under such circumstances, is an absolute duty to keep it in at his peril, or is, as the majority of the Court of Exchequer have thought, merely a duty to take all reasonable and prudent precautions, in order to keep it in, but no more. If the first be the law, the person who has brought on his land and kept there something dangerous, and failed to keep it in, is responsible for all the natural consequences of its escape. If the second be the limit of his duty, he would not be answerable except on proof of negligence, and consequently would not be answerable for escape arising from any latent defect which ordinary prudence and skill could not detect.

Exhibit 2.3   Colin Blackburn

Colin Blackburn, Baron Blackburn (1813-1896), a Scottish judge who served in English courts and delivered the leading opinion in Rylands v. Fletcher, earned a reputation throughout his judicial career as a marvel of common law wisdom. Upon his death, a remembrance in the Harvard Law Review mourned the loss of the "greatest English common law judge of recent years." The piece remarked that in his absence, "one hardly knows yet where to turn for that combination of sound thinking, exact and instructive discrimination, and large, rational, and just exposition by which the law of all English-speaking countries has profited for these many years." Note, 9 Harv. L. Rev. 420-421 (1896).

Source: Wikimedia Commons

Supposing the second to be the correct view of the law, a further question arises subsidiary to the first, viz., whether the defendants are not so far identified with the contractors whom they employed, as to be responsible for the consequences of their want of care and skill in making the reservoir in fact insufficient with reference to the old shafts, of the existence of which they were aware, though they had not ascertained where the shafts went to.

We think that the true rule of law is, that the person who for his own purposes brings on his lands and collects and keeps there anything likely to do mischief if it escapes, must keep it in at his peril, and, if he does not do so, is prima facie answerable for all the damage which is the natural consequence of its escape. He can excuse himself by shewing that the escape was owing to the plaintiff's default; or perhaps that the escape was the consequence of vis major, or the act of God; but as nothing of this sort exists here, it is unnecessary to inquire what excuse would be sufficient. The general rule, as above stated, seems on principle just. The person whose grass or corn is eaten down by the escaping cattle of his neighbour, or whose mine is flooded by the water from his neighbour's reservoir, or whose cellar is invaded by the filth of his neighbour's privy, or whose habitation is made unhealthy by the fumes and noisome vapours of his neighbour's alkali works, is damnified without any fault of his own; and it seems but reasonable and just that the neighbour, who has brought something on his own property which was not naturally there, harmless to others so long as it is confined to his own property, but which he knows to be mischievous if it gets on his neighbour's, should be obliged to make good the damage which ensues if he does not succeed in confining it to his own property. But for his act in bringing it there no mischief could have accrued, and it seems but just that he should at his peril keep it there so that no mischief may accrue, or answer for the natural and anticipated consequences. And upon authority, this we think is established to be the law whether the things so brought be beasts, or water, or filth, or stenches.

The case that has most commonly occurred, and which is most frequently to be found in the books, is as to the obligation of the owner of cattle which he has brought on his land, to prevent their escaping and doing mischief. The law as to them seems to be perfectly settled from early times; the owner must keep them in at his peril, or he will be answerable for the natural consequences of their escape; that is with regard to tame beasts, for the grass they eat and trample upon, though not for any injury to the person of others, for our ancestors have settled that it is not the general nature of horses to kick, or bulls to gore; but if the owner knows that the beast has a vicious propensity to attack man, he will be answerable for that too. [The opinion then exhaustively examines the earlier cases in support of the general proposition, and continues:]

. . . But it was further said by Martin, B., that when damage is done to personal property, or even to the person, by collision, either upon land or at sea, there must be negligence in the party doing the damage to render him legally responsible; and this is no doubt true, and as was pointed out by Mr. Mellish during his argument before us, this is not confined to cases of collision, for there are many cases in which proof of negligence is essential, as for instance, where an unruly horse gets on the footpath of a public street and kills a passenger . . . ; or where a person in a dock is struck by the falling of a bale of cotton which the defendant's servants are lowering . . . ; and many other similar cases may be found. But we think these cases distinguishable from the present. Traffic on the highways, whether by land or sea, cannot be conducted without exposing those whose persons or property are near it to some inevitable risk; and that being so, those who go on the highway, or have their property adjacent to it, may well be held to do so subject to their taking upon themselves the risk of injury from that inevitable danger; and persons who by the licence of the owner pass near the warehouses where goods are being raised or lowered, certainly do so subject to the inevitable risk of accident. In neither case, therefore, can they recover without proof of want of care or skill occasioning the accident; and it is believed that all the cases in which inevitable accident has been held an excuse for what prima facie was a trespass, can be explained on the same principle, viz., that the circumstances were such as to shew that the plaintiff had taken that risk upon himself. But there is no ground for saying that the plaintiff here took upon himself any risk arising from the uses to which the defendants should choose to apply their land. He neither knew what these might be, nor could he in any way control the defendants, or hinder their building what reservoirs they liked, and storing up in them what water they pleased, so long as the defendants succeeded in preventing the water which they there brought from interfering with the plaintiff's property.

The view which we take of the first point renders it unnecessary to consider whether the defendants would or would not be responsible for the want of care and skill in the persons employed by them, under the circumstances stated in the case.

Rylands v. Fletcher
L.R. 3 H.L. 330 (1868)

CAIRNS, L. C. . . . My Lords, the principles on which this case must be determined appear to me to be extremely simple. The Defendants, treating them as the owners or occupiers of the close on which the reservoir was constructed, might lawfully have used that close for any purpose for which it might in the ordinary course of the enjoyment of land be used, and if, in what I may term the natural use of that land, there had been any accumulation of water, either on the surface or underground, and if, by the operation of the laws of nature, that accumulation of water had passed off into the close occupied by the Plaintiff, the Plaintiff could not have complained that that result had taken place. If he had desired to guard himself against it, it would have lain upon him to have done so, by leaving, or by interposing, some barrier between his close and the close of the Defendants in order to have prevented the operation of the law of nature. . . .

On the other hand if the Defendants, not stopping at the natural use of their close, had desired to use it for any purpose which I may term a non-natural use, for the purpose of introducing into the close that which in its natural condition was not in or upon it, for the purpose of introducing water either above or below ground in quantities and in a manner not the result of any work or operation on or under the land,—and if in consequence of their doing so, or in consequence of any imperfection in the mode of their doing so, the water came to escape and to pass off into the close of the Plaintiff, then it appears to me that that which the Defendants were doing they were doing at their own peril and, if in the course of their doing it, the evil arose to which I have referred, the evil, namely, of the escape of the water and its passing away to the close of the Plaintiff and injuring the Plaintiff, then for the consequence of that, in my opinion, the Defendants would be liable. . . .

LORD CRANWORTH. My Lords, I concur with my noble and learned friend in thinking that the rule of law was correctly stated by Mr. Justice Blackburn in delivering the opinion of the Exchequer Chamber. If a person brings, or accumulates, on his land anything which, if it should escape, may cause damage to his neighbour, he does so at his peril. If it does escape, and cause damage, he is responsible, however careful he may have been, and whatever precautions he may have taken to prevent the damage.

In considering whether a Defendant is liable to a Plaintiff for damage which the Plaintiff may have sustained, the question in general is not whether the Defendant has acted with due care and caution, but whether his acts have occasioned the damage. . . . And the doctrine is founded on good sense. For when one person, in managing his own affairs, causes, however innocently, damage to another, it is obviously only just that he should be the party to suffer. He is bound sic uti suo ut non laedat alienum. [He is bound to use his own property not to harm another.] This is the principle of law applicable to cases like the present, and I do not discover in the authorities which were cited anything conflicting with it.

The doctrine appears to me to be well illustrated by the two modern cases in the Court of Common Pleas. . . . I allude to the two cases of Smith v. Kenrick[, 137 Eng. Rep. 205 (C.P. 1849)], and Baird v. Williamson[, 143 Eng. Rep. 831 (C.P. 1863)]. In the former the owner of a coal mine on the higher level worked out the whole of his coal, leaving no barrier between his mine and the mine on the lower level, so that the water percolating through the upper mine flowed into the lower mine, and obstructed the owner of it in getting his coal. It was held that the owner of the lower mine had no ground of complaint. The Defendant, the owner of the upper mine, had a right to remove all his coal. The damage sustained by the Plaintiff was occasioned by the natural flow or percolation of water from the upper strata. There was no obligation on the Defendant to protect the Plaintiff against this. It was his business to erect or leave a sufficient barrier to keep out the water, or to adopt proper means for so conducting the water as that it should not impede him in his workings. The water, in that case, was only left by the Defendant to flow in its natural course.

But in the later case of Baird v. Williamson the Defendant, the owner of the upper mine, did not merely suffer the water to flow through his mine without leaving a barrier between it and the mine below, but in order to work his own mine beneficially he pumped up quantities of water which passed into the Plaintiff's mine in addition to that which would have naturally reached it, and so occasioned him damage. Though this was done without negligence, and in the due working of his own mine, yet he was held to be responsible for the damage so occasioned. It was in consequence of his act, whether skilfully or unskilfully performed, that the Plaintiff had been damaged, and he was therefore held liable for the consequences. The damage in the former case may be treated as having arisen from the act of God; in the latter, from the act of the Defendant.

Applying the principle of these decisions to the case now before the House, I come without hesitation to the conclusion that the judgment of the Exchequer Chamber was right. . . . The Defendants, in order to effect an object of their own, brought on to their land, or on to land which for this purpose may be treated as being theirs, a large accumulated mass of water, and stored it up in a reservoir. The consequence of this was damage to the Plaintiff, and for that damage, however skilfully and carefully the accumulation was made, the Defendants, according to the principles and authorities to which I have adverted, were certainly responsible.

Judgment of the Court of Exchequer Chamber affirmed.

NOTES

1. Rylands v. Fletcher, the forms of action, and common law precedent.   The initial debate between Martin and Bramwell harkens back to the forms of action by asking whether the harm was immediate or consequential, where proof of negligence was required only in the latter case. On this question, does it make a difference that the reservoir was not in fact completely filled when its floor gave way? Blackburn, J., sidesteps the disagreement below, first by treating the harm as consequential, and then by applying a strict liability rule. Do the earlier precedents on cattle trespass, fire, nuisance, and filth escaping from privies support his decision, or were these all instances of "direct harm"?

The extent to which *Rylands* marks a departure from the earlier law has given rise to a spirited debate. Wigmore's view was that the case was soundly reasoned from its precedents: "Briefly, the [scattered classes of cases] wandered about, unhoused and unshepherded, except for casual attention, in the pathless fields of jurisprudence, until they were met, some thirty years ago, by the master-mind of Mr. Justice Blackburn, who guided them to the safe fold where they have since rested." Wigmore, Responsibility for Tortious Acts: Its History—III, 7 Harv. L. Rev. 441, 454 (1894). In contrast, the noted English torts scholar Frederick Pollock wrote of *Rylands* that "carefully prepared as it evidently was, [it] hardly seems to make such grounds clear enough for universal acceptance." See Pollock, Torts 398-399 (1st ed. 1887). He concluded that "the policy of the law might not have been satisfied by requiring the defendant to insure diligence in proportion to the manifest risk." Pollock subsequently adopted the suggestion proposed in Thayer, Liability Without Fault, 29 Harv. L. Rev. 801 (1916), that the principle of res ipsa loquitur (*infra* at Chapter 3, Section G.2) "which was hardly developed at the date of Rylands v. Fletcher, would suffice to cover the ground for all useful purposes in a simpler and more rational manner." See Pollock, Torts 507 (13th ed. 1929). Holmes, for his part, devoted relatively little attention to Rylands v. Fletcher, which he treated gingerly:

> It may even be very much for the public good that the dangerous accumulation should be made (a consideration which might influence the decision in some instances, and differently in others): but as there is a limit to the nicety of an inquiry which is possible in a trial, it may be considered that the safest way to secure care is to throw the risk upon the person who decides what precautions shall be taken.

Holmes, The Common Law 117 (1881). Is this point universally true in all negligence cases?

2. Scope of Rylands v. Fletcher?   Should *Rylands* apply to personal injury cases, or only property damages? See Transco plc v. Stockport Metropolitan Borough Council, [2003] U.K. H. L. 61, where Lord Bingham observed:

> The rule in Rylands v. Fletcher is a sub-species of nuisance, which is itself a tort based on the interference by one occupier of the land with the right in or enjoyment of land by another occupier of land as such. From this simple proposition two consequences at once flow. First, as very clearly decided by the House in Read v. J. Lyons & Co., Ltd. [1947] A.C. 156, no claim in nuisance under the rule can arise if the events complained of take place wholly on the land of a single occupier. There must, in other words, be an escape from one tenement to another. Second, the claim cannot include a claim for death or personal injury, since such a claim does not relate to any right in or enjoyment of land.

Would Blackburn, J., have denied recovery if a workman had been killed by flooding? See, for a contemporary analysis of *Rylands*, Ripstein, Tort Law in a Liberal State, 1 J. Tort Law (Iss. 2, Art. 3) 27-30 (2007), treating *Rylands* as a fault-based case.

3. Rylands v. Fletcher in historical context.   For an exhaustive account of the historical setting of *Rylands*, see Simpson, Legal Liability for Bursting Reservoirs, 13 J. Legal Stud. 209, 244 (1984). Simpson notes that during the nineteenth century dam failures were regarded as major disasters, much as airplane crashes are today. *Rylands* itself followed several major dam failures in England, each of which resulted in a massive loss of life and property and prompted major campaigns of private relief to aid accident victims. Simpson also observed the following about nineteenth-century England: "Most large reservoirs (indeed, almost all) had been constructed under special statutory powers, conferred by private and local acts, and it would have been normal to turn to the legislation to determine what Parliament had laid down as to the legal liability of those responsible for them."

4. "Non-natural use" and acts of third parties.   What importance should be attached to the qualification of "non-natural use" mentioned by Lord Cairns, but not by the other judges? One way to read the term "natural" is in opposition to "artificial" or "man-made." A second way is to read it in opposition to "unreasonable or inappropriate." The second reading appears to have been adopted in Rickards v. Lothian, [1913] A.C. 263, in which the defendant owned a business

Hugh McCalmont Cairns, 1st Earl
Cairns, c. 1860
Source: John Watkins / National Portrait Gallery, London

building with a lavatory on the fourth floor. One night, after the defendant's caretaker had made his usual tour of inspection, an unknown person entered the building, stuffed the lavatory with "various articles such as nails, penholders, string and soap," and turned the faucet on all the way. The next morning, the plaintiff discovered that his stock in trade had been damaged, and sued the defendant for his losses. The House of Lords held for the defendant, on the ground that the case fell outside the scope of Rylands v. Fletcher because "the provision of a proper supply of water to the various parts of a house is not only reasonable, but has become, in accordance with modern sanitary views, an almost necessary feature of town life. . . . It would be unreasonable for the law to regard those who install and maintain such a system of supply as doing so at their own peril." Given the stable condition of the privy before the act of the third party, could the defendant have prevailed on causal grounds—the independent act of a third party—even if the lavatory, however common, was in Lord Cairns' sense a non-natural use? If water had leaked into the plaintiff's premises when the lavatory had been used in an ordinary manner, is the defendant liable under *Rylands*? As interpreted in *Rickards*? What if the defendant had hired competent plumbers to repair the lavatory before the flooding took place?

The House of Lords reevaluated the phrase "non-natural use" in Cambridge Water Co. v. Eastern Counties Leather PLC, [1994] 2 A.C. 264, 309 in which toxic perchloroethenes (P.C.E.s) escaped from the defendant E.C.L.'s tannery and slowly worked their way through an aquifer to the plaintiff's borehole, located some 1.3 miles away in Sawton. Lord Goff rejected defendant's attempt to expand the definition of natural use to do away with the strict liability rule in *Rylands*.

> I am satisfied that the storage of chemicals in substantial quantities, and their use in the manner employed at E.C.L.'s premises, cannot fall within the exception [of natural and ordinary use]. For the purpose of testing the point, let it be assumed that E.C.L. was well aware of the possibility that P.C.E., if it escaped, could indeed cause damage, for example by contaminating any water with which it became mixed so as to render that water undrinkable by human beings. I cannot think that it would be right in such circumstances to exempt E.C.L. from liability under the rule of Rylands v. Fletcher on the ground that the use was natural or ordinary. The mere fact that the use is common in the tanning industry cannot, in my opinion, be enough to bring the use within the exception, nor the fact that Sawston contains a small industrial community which is worthy of encouragement or support. Indeed I feel bound to say that the storage of substantial quantities of chemicals on industrial premises should be regarded as an almost classic case of non-natural

use; and I find it very difficult to think that it should be thought objectionable to impose strict liability for damage caused in the event of their escape.

Nonetheless, the defendant prevailed on its appeal. The trial judge had found that "a reasonable supervisor at E.C.L. would not have foreseen, in or before 1976, that such repeated spillages of small quantities of solvent would lead to any environmental hazard or danger." Lord Goff then held that the rule in *Rylands* should not be exempt from the general test of reasonable foresight that in England applies in both nuisance and negligence cases. See *The Wagon Mound, infra* Chapter 5, at 423. On a more functional level, he noted that the solution to the pressing environmental issues rested more on "informed and carefully structured legislation" than the revision of a common law rule. How would the foresight limitation apply to the facts of *Rylands*?

For an excellent critique of the non-natural use requirement of Rylands v. Fletcher, see Harari, The Place of Negligence in the Law of Torts 157-167 (1962). For an evaluation of the recent developments, see Schwartz, Rylands v. Fletcher, Negligence, and Strict Liability, *in* The Law of Obligations 209 (Cane & Stapleton eds., 1998).

5. Acts of God under Rylands v. Fletcher.   What distinguishes a mere "escape" from an act of God in *Rylands*? In Nichols v. Marsland, 2 Ex. D. 1 (1876), the plaintiff's land was flooded when the defendant's "ornamental pools" containing large amounts of water broke their banks during an extraordinary rainfall of unanticipated severity. Bramwell, B., found this storm to be an act of God, thus within the exception to Rylands v. Fletcher, and accordingly he affirmed a judgment for the defendant. The court also found no negligence in the construction or maintenance of the pools. Further, in Carstairs v. Taylor, L.R. 6 Ex. 217 (1871), the plaintiff, a tenant in the defendant's building, was unable to recover when rats ate through a box containing water that was collected by gutters from the roof of the building. Bramwell, B., noted that the box and gutters had been installed for the mutual benefit of both parties. Hence, the rule in Rylands v. Fletcher did not apply because the defendant did not bring the water into the structure for his purposes alone.

The act of God issue continues to play a powerful role in modern tort litigation. In In re Flood Litigation, 607 S.E.2d 863, 879 (W. Va. 2004), large numbers of property owners filed tort actions against a group of defendant coal companies, railroads, landowners, and gas companies, claiming that the defendants' joint alteration of the landscape was responsible for flooding damage under *Rylands*. Maynard, C.J., refused to apply *Rylands* on the ground that the defendants had not engaged in abnormally dangerous activities. In addressing the act of God defense, he first noted the difficulties in apportioning loss between natural forces and a defendant's activities, and continued:

> Accordingly, we hold that where a rainfall event of an unusual and unforeseeable nature combines with a defendant's actionable conduct to cause flood damage, and where it is shown that a discrete portion of the damage complained of was unforeseeable and solely the result of such event and in no way fairly attributable

to the defendant's conduct, the defendant is liable only for the damages that are fairly attributable to the defendant's conduct. However, in such a case, a defendant has the burden to show by clear and convincing evidence the character and measure of damages that are not the defendant's responsibility; and if the defendant cannot do so, then the defendant bears the entire liability.

Would this rule require liability in *Nichols* if any water in the ornamental pool escaped in the midst of the storm?

6. Default of plaintiff.   What sorts of conduct might constitute "a default of the plaintiff" to which Blackburn, B., referred? Note that under Smith v. Kenrick, a plaintiff who removes all the coal up to the boundary of his mine is not in default under *Rylands*, even if the coal removed served as a barrier between the plaintiff's and the defendant's properties. In Holgate v. Bleazard, [1917] 1 K.B. 443, the court held that the plaintiff was not in default in a case of horse trespass when he had not repaired the fence around his own land as required by the covenant with his landlord. How would the case be decided if the covenant to fence had been made with the defendant?

Brown v. Collins
53 N.H. 442 (1873)

Trespass. . . . [The plaintiff owned a stone post with street lamp. The defendant was waiting by a railroad crossing on his wagon loaded with grain and drawn by two horses.] The horses became frightened by an engine on the railroad near the crossing, and by reason thereof became unmanageable, and ran, striking the post. . . . The shock produced by the collision with the post threw the defendant from his seat in the wagon, and he struck on the ground between horses, but suffered no injury except a slight concussion. The defendant was in the use of ordinary care and skill in managing his team, until they became frightened. . . .

DOE, J. . . . We take the case as one where, without actual fault in the defendant, his horses broke from his control, ran away with him, went upon the plaintiff's land, and did damage there, against the will, intent, and desire of the defendant. [The court then discusses the rule in Rylands v. Fletcher, continuing:]

. . . The rule of such cases is applied, by Blackburn, to everything which a man brings on his land, which will, if it escapes, naturally do damage. One result of such a doctrine is, that every one building a fire on his own hearth, for necessary purposes, with the utmost care, does so at the peril, not only of losing his own house, but of being irretrievably ruined if a spark from his chimney starts a conflagration which lays waste the neighborhood. "In conflict with the rule, as laid down in the English cases, is a class of cases in reference to damage from fire communicated from the adjoining premises. Fire, like water or steam, is likely to produce mischief if it escapes and goes beyond control; and yet it has never been held in this country that one building a fire upon his own premises can be made liable if it escapes upon his neighbor's premises, and does him damage without proof of negligence." Losee v. Buchanan, 51 N.Y. 476, 487 (1873).

Everything that a man can bring on his land is capable of escaping, — against his will, and without his fault, with or without assistance, in some form, solid, liquid, or gaseous, changed or unchanged by the transforming processes of nature or art, — and of doing damage after its escape. Moreover, if there is a legal principle that makes a man liable for the natural consequences of the escape of things which he brings on his land, the application of such a principle cannot be limited to those things: it must be applied to all his acts that disturb the original order of creation or, at least, to all things which he undertakes to possess or control anywhere, and which were not used and enjoyed in what is called the natural or primitive condition of mankind, whatever that may have been. This is going back a long way for a standard of legal rights, and adopting an arbitrary test of responsibility that confounds all degrees of danger, pays no heed to the essential elements of actual fault, puts a clog upon natural and reasonably necessary uses of matter, and tends to embarrass and obstruct much of the work which it seems to be man's duty carefully to do. The distinction made by Lord Cairns — Rylands v. Fletcher, L.R. 3 H.L. 330 — between a natural and non-natural use of land, if he meant anything more than the difference between a reasonable use and an unreasonable one, is not established in the law. Even if the arbitrary test were applied only to things which a man brings on his land, it would still recognize the peculiar rights of savage life in a wilderness, ignore the rights growing out of a civilized state of society, and make a distinction not warranted by the enlightened spirit of the common law: it would impose a penalty upon efforts, made in a reasonable, skillful, and careful manner, to rise above a condition of barbarism. It is impossible that legal principle can throw so serious an obstacle in the way of progress and improvement. Natural rights are, in general, legal rights; and the rights of civilization are, in a legal sense, as natural as any others. "Most of the rights of property, as well as of person, in the social state, are not absolute but relative" — Losee v. Buchanan, 51 N.Y. 485; and, if men ever were in any other than the social state, it is neither necessary nor expedient that they should now govern themselves on the theory that they ought to live in some other state. The common law does not usually establish tests of responsibility on any other basis than the propriety of their living in the social state, and the relative and qualified character of the rights incident to that state. . . .

It is not improbable that the rules of liability for damage done by brutes or by fire, found in the early English cases, were introduced, by sacerdotal influence, from what was supposed to be the Roman or the Hebrew law. 7 Am. L. Rev. 652, note; 1 Domat Civil Law (Strahan's translation, 2d ed.) 304, 305, 306, 312, 313; Exodus xxi:28-32, 36; xxii:5, 6, 9. It would not be singular if these rules should be spontaneously produced at a certain period in the life of any community. Where they first appeared is of little consequence in the present inquiry. They were certainly introduced in England at an immature stage of English jurisprudence, and an undeveloped state of agriculture, manufactures, and commerce, when the nation had not settled down to these modern, progressive, industrial pursuits which the spirit of the common law, adapted to all conditions of society, encourages and defends. They were introduced when the development of many of the rational rules now universally recognized as principles of the common law had not been demanded by the growth of intelligence, trade, and productive enterprise,—when the common law had not been set forth in the precedents, as a coherent and logical system on many subjects other than the tenures of real estate. At all events, whatever may be said of the origin of those rules, to extend them, as they were extended in Rylands v. Fletcher, seems to us contrary to the analogies and the general principles of the common law, as now established. To extend them to the present case would be contrary to American authority, as well as to our understanding of legal principles. . . .

Upon the facts stated, taken in the sense in which we understand them, the defendant is entitled to judgment.

NOTES

1. The reception of Rylands v. Fletcher into American common law.   Initially *Rylands* received a frosty reception in the United States, as it was explicitly repudiated not only in Brown v. Collins but also in Losee v. Buchanan, 51 N.Y. 483, 484-485 (1873). In *Losee*, the plaintiff sued for damages that resulted when the defendant's boiler, while being operated with all care and skill, exploded and "was projected and thrown onto the plaintiff's premises," causing damage to the buildings located thereon. The action was denied for the following reasons:

> By becoming a member of civilized society, I am compelled to give up many of my natural rights, but I receive more than a compensation from the surrender by every other man of the same rights, and the security, advantage and protection which the laws give me. So, too, the general rules that I may have the exclusive and undisturbed use and possession of my real estate, and that I must so use my real estate as not to injure my neighbor, are much modified by the exigencies of the social state. We must have factories, machinery, dams, canals and railroads. They are demanded by the manifold wants of mankind, and lay at the basis of all our civilization. If I have any of these upon my lands, and they are not a nuisance and are not so managed as to become such, I am not responsible for any damage they accidentally and unavoidably do my neighbor. He receives his compensation for such damage by the general good, in which he shares, and the right which he has to place the same things upon his lands.

Why does the argument of implicit compensation work only in one direction? Does the greater security obtained under a uniform rule of strict liability supply the compensation to the defendant that justifies imposing liability in the instant case? Note that no matter which starting point or "baseline" is used, a sound decision protocol only displaces it if the new rule generates greater gains across the board than the old one. Can this system work if all people are not situated the same way in some original position? For a further expansion of this theme of "reciprocity," see Fletcher, Fairness and Utility in Tort Law, 85 Harv. L. Rev. 537 (1972), *infra* Chapter 7, at 580. The test of reciprocity only shows a need for consistency of treatment between cases. How should one choose between a blanket rule of negligence or strict liability in disputes between neighbors? On the fate of *Losee*, see Spano v. Perini, *infra* at 572.

2. Damages versus injunction?   In Turner v. Big Lake Oil Co., 96 S.W.2d 221, 226 (Tex. 1936), the court rejected Rylands v. Fletcher as inapplicable to Texas, where the storage of water in large cisterns was a "natural" use of the land:

> In Texas we have conditions very different from those which obtain in England. A large portion of Texas is an arid or semi-arid region. West of the 98th meridian of longitude, where the rainfall is approximately 30 inches, the rainfall decreases until finally, in the extreme western part of the State, it is only about 10 inches. This land of decreasing rainfall is the great ranch or livestock region of the state, water for which is stored in thousands of ponds, tanks, and lakes on the surface of the ground. The country is almost without streams and without the storage of water from rainfall in basins constructed for the purpose, or to hold waters pumped from the earth, the great livestock industry of West Texas must perish. No such condition obtains in England. With us the storage of water is a natural or necessary and common use of the land, necessarily within the contemplation of the State and its grantees when grants were made, and obviously the rule announced in Rylands v. Fletcher, predicated upon different conditions, can have no application here.
>
> Again, in England there are no oil wells, no necessity for using surface storage facilities for impounding and evaporating salt waters therefrom. In Texas the situation is different. Texas has many great oil fields, tens of thousands of wells in almost every part of the State. Producing oil is one of our major industries. One of the by-products of oil production is salt water, which must be disposed of without injury to property or the pollution of streams. The construction of basins or ponds to hold this salt water is a necessary part of the oil business.

Does the need for water in Texas go to the issue of liability for the damage caused by water or to regulating its use by statute or private injunction? It would be disastrous to shut down the entire oil industry, but would the industry suffer any major dislocations if losses from the storage of water were governed by a strict liability scheme, so long as the operators of oil rigs may store water as they please? See the discussion in Powell v. Fall, *infra*.

In spite of the judicial concerns with the reach of *Rylands*, the case made substantial inroads in the United States in the first half of the twentieth century. In 1984, Prosser and Keeton (Torts at 549) reported that only seven states reject the *Rylands* principle and 30 now accept it; that balance continues to swing in favor of the decision. Similar results are reported in 3 Harper, James & Gray §14.4. Representative of the modern trend is Clark-Aiken Co. v. Cromwell-Wright Co., 323 N.E.2d 876 (Mass. 1975), in which the Supreme Judicial Court of Massachusetts, after exhaustive discussion, unanimously applied *Rylands* when the plaintiff's land was flooded by waters that the defendant had stored behind an upstream dam that failed.

Powell v. Fall
5 Q.B. 597 (1880)

MELLOR, J. This was an action tried before me at Devizes without a jury. It was brought by the plaintiffs to recover a sum of £53 6s. 8d., in respect of injury done to a rick of hay upon a farm of the plaintiff, John Thomas Powell, adjoining a public highway, and which injury was caused by sparks escaping from the fire of a traction engine belonging to the defendant, which was then being propelled by steam power along the highway. The engine was constructed in conformity with the provisions of 24 & 25 Vict. c.70, and of 28 & 29 Vict. c.83, being the Acts then in force for regulating the use of locomotives on turnpike and other roads.

At the time when the injury was occasioned to the hay stack by the sparks of fire issuing from the defendant's engine, it was not travelling at a greater speed than that prescribed by the Acts referred to, nor was the injury occasioned by any negligence on the part of the defendant's servants conducting or managing the same. . . .

The 13th section of 24 & 25 Vict. c.70, is as follows: "Nothing in this Act contained shall authorize any person to use upon a highway a locomotive engine, which shall be so constructed or used as to cause a public or private nuisance, and every such person so using such engine shall notwithstanding this Act be liable to an indictment or action as the case may be, for such use where, but for the passing of this Act, such indictment or action could be maintained:" and by s.12 of 28 & 29 Vict. c.83, it is enacted that "Nothing in this Act contained shall authorize any person to use a locomotive which may be so constructed or used as to be a public nuisance at common law, and nothing herein contained shall affect the right of any person to recover damages in respect of any injury he may have sustained in consequence of the use of a locomotive." And it was further contended on the part of the plaintiffs that whilst the Acts entitled the defendant to use a locomotive properly constructed on the public highway, yet it never was intended by the legislature to exempt him from liability to damages in respect of any injury sustained by third persons in consequence of the use by him of a locomotive, and that it was wholly immaterial to the result that such injury arose from no want of care or negligence on the part of the defendant's servants in the management and use of the same. On the part of the defendant it was contended that the effect of the several statutes being to authorize the use of locomotives on public highways, if constructed and managed according to the provisions of such statutes, was to exempt the owners from liability to make good any injury arising from the use of locomotives, unless some improper construction of the engine, or some act of negligence in the use of it, could be imputed to such owners or their servants. I am of opinion that the contention on the part of the plaintiffs must prevail.

The principle which governs this case is that established by Fletcher v. Rylands, and affirmed in the House of Lords: Rylands v. Fletcher. . . .

The defendant appealed. . . .

BRAMWELL, L.J. I think that the judgment of Mellor, J., ought to be affirmed. The passing of the engine along the road is confessedly dangerous, inasmuch as sparks cannot be prevented from flying from it. It is conceded that at common law an action may be maintained for the injury suffered by the plaintiffs. The Locomotive Acts are relied upon as affording a defence, but instead of helping the defendant they shew not only that an action would have been maintainable at common law, but also that the right to sue for an injury is carefully preserved. It is just and reasonable that if a person uses a dangerous machine, he should pay for the damage which it occasions; if the reward which he gains for the use of the machine will not pay for the damage, it is mischievous to the public and ought to be suppressed, for the loss ought not to be borne by the community or the injured person. If the use of the machine is profitable, the owner ought to pay compensation for the damage. The plaintiffs are protected by the common law, and nothing adverse to their right to sue can be drawn from the statutes: the statutes do not make it lawful to damage property without paying for the injury. A great deal has been said about the liability of persons who have stored water which has subsequently escaped and done injury, and it has been urged that the emission of sparks from an engine is not so mischievous as the overflow of a large body of water. The arguments which we have heard are ingenious; but I need only say in reply to them that they have hardened my conviction that Rex v. Pease [168 Eng. Rep. 216 (K.B. 1832)] and Vaughan v. Taff Vale Ry. Co. (5 H. & N. 679 29 L. J. (Ex.) 247) were wrongly decided.

NOTES

1. The impact of statute on common law liability.   In Vaughn v. Taff Vale Ry., 157 Eng. Rep. 1351, 1354 (Ex. 1860), disapproved by Bramwell, J., Cockburn, C.J., held that because the defendant operated the railroad under statutory authorization, the plaintiff had to show negligence to hold it liable for damages:

> Although it may be true, that if a person keeps an animal of known dangerous propensities, or a dangerous instrument, he will be responsible to those who are thereby injured, independently of any negligence in the mode of dealing with the animal or using the instrument; yet when the legislature has sanctioned and authorized the use of a particular thing, and it is used for the purpose for which it was authorized, and every precaution has been observed to prevent injury, the sanction of the legislature carries with it this consequence, that if damage results from the use of such thing independently of negligence, the party using it is not responsible. . . . It is admitted that the defendants used fire for the purpose of propelling locomotive engines, and no doubt they were bound to take proper precaution to prevent injury to persons through whose lands they passed; but the mere use of fire in such engines does not make them liable for injury resulting from such use without any negligence on their part.

The effect of a statute upon a private cause of action was also raised in River Wear Commissioners v. Adamson, L.R. 2 App. Cas. 743, 767 (H.L. (E.) 1877), when the applicable statute provided that "the owner of every vessel . . . shall be answerable to the undertakers [plaintiffs] for any damage done by such vessel . . . and the master or person having charge of such vessel through whose wilful act or negligence any such damage is done, shall also be liable to make good the same." In *Adamson*, the defendant's boat was wrecked in a storm. After the crew abandoned it, the boat crashed into the plaintiff's dock. The owners of the ship were sued under the statute. Lord Blackburn, who wrote Rylands v. Fletcher, concurred in the judgment that the owners were not liable without proof of negligence:

> My Lords, the Common Law is, I think, as follows:—Property adjoining to a spot on which the public have a right to carry on traffic is liable to be injured by that traffic. In this respect there is no difference between a shop, the railings or windows of which may be broken by a carriage on the road, and a pier adjoining to a harbour or a navigable river or the sea, which is liable to be injured by a ship. In either case the owner of the injured property must bear his own loss, unless he can establish that some other person is in fault, and liable to make it good. And he does not establish this against a person merely by shewing that he is owner of the carriage or ship which did the mischief, for the owner incurs no liability merely because he is owner.
>
> But he does establish such a liability against any person who either wilfully did the damage, or neglected that duty which the law casts upon those in charge of a carriage on land, and a ship or a float of timber on water, to take reasonable care and use reasonable skill to prevent it from doing injury, and that this wilfulness or neglect caused the damage.

Is the result consistent with the statute? At common law would the act of God exception under Rylands v. Fletcher apply?

2. The subsequent history of Powell v. Fall. "Over the next forty years, Powell v. Fall was repeatedly followed in cases involving traction-engines and steam-rollers which, though driven with due care, had scared horses, crushed water-mains, or started fires." Spencer, Motor-Cars and the Rule in Rylands v. Fletcher: A Chapter of Accidents in the History of Law and Motoring, [1983] Cambridge L.J. 65, 70. Spencer nonetheless reports that *Powell* could not exert enough influence to make strict liability the norm in ordinary highway accidents, even though buses and cars were dangerous, with hard rubber tires and thin wheels prone to skidding. See Wing v. L.G.O.C., [1908] 25 Times L. Rep. 14, for skidding buses, and for ordinary cars, see Park v. L.G.O.C., [1909] 73 J.P. 283. Note that the early buses and autos were greeted with much public hostility. In part, the justification for these later cases was that cars (but not buses) are not run for profit within the rationale of *Powell*. Spencer, *supra*, at 76-77.

Oliver Wendell Holmes, The Common Law
77-84, 88-96 (1881)

The object of the next two Lectures is to discover whether there is any common ground at the bottom of all liability in tort, and if so, what that ground is. Supposing the attempt to succeed, it will reveal the general principle of civil liability at common law. The liabilities incurred by way of contract are more or less expressly fixed by the agreement of the parties concerned, but those arising from a tort are independent of any previous consent of the wrong-doer to bear the loss occasioned by his act. If *A* fails to pay a certain sum on a certain day, or to deliver a lecture on a certain night, after having made a binding promise to do so, the damages which he has to pay are recovered in accordance with his consent that some or all of the harms which may be caused by his failure shall fall upon him. But when *A* assaults or slanders his neighbor, or converts his neighbor's property, he does a harm which he has never consented to bear, and if the law makes him pay for it, the reason for doing so must be found in some general view of the conduct which every one may fairly expect and demand from every other, whether that other has agreed to it or not.

Such a general view is very hard to find. The law did not begin with a theory. It has never worked one out. The point from which it started and that at which I shall try to show that it has arrived, are on different planes. In the progress from one to the other, it is to be expected that its course should not be straight and its direction not always visible. All that can be done is to point out a tendency, and to justify it. The tendency, which

Cover of the first edition of *The Common Law,* one of the most influential texts in American law. Beyond his exposition on the rule of negligence, Holmes set out on the first page an enduring legal aphorism: "The life of the law has not been logic: it has been experience."
Source: Wikimedia Commons

is our main concern, is a matter of fact to be gathered from the cases. But the difficulty of showing it is much enhanced by the circumstances that, until lately, the substantive law has been approached only through the categories of the forms of action. Discussions of legislative principle have been darkened by arguments on the limits between trespass and case, or on the scope of a general issue. In place of a theory of tort, we have a theory of trespass. And even within that narrower limit, precedents of the time of the assize and jurata have been applied without a thought of their connection with a long forgotten procedure.

Since the ancient forms of action have disappeared, a broader treatment of the subject ought to be possible. Ignorance is the best of law reformers. People are glad to discuss a question on general principles, when they have forgotten the special knowledge necessary for technical reasoning. But the present willingness to generalize is founded on more than merely negative grounds. The philosophical habit of the day, the frequency of legislation, and the ease with which the law may be changed to meet the opinions and wishes of the public, all make it natural and unavoidable that judges as well as others should openly discuss the legislative principles upon which their decisions must always rest in the end, and should base their judgments upon broad considerations of policy to which the traditions of the bench would hardly have tolerated a reference fifty years ago.

The business of the law of torts is to fix the dividing lines between those cases in which a man is liable for harm which he has done, and those in which he is not. But it cannot enable him to predict with certainty whether a given act under given circumstances will make him liable, because an act will rarely have that effect unless followed by damage, and for the most part, if not always, the consequences of an act are not known, but only guessed at as more or less probable. All the rules that the law can lay down beforehand are rules for determining the conduct which will be followed by liability if it is followed by harm,—that is, the conduct which a man pursues at his peril. The only guide for the future to be drawn from a decision against a defendant in an action of tort is that similar acts, under circumstances which cannot be distinguished except by the result from those of the defendant, are done at the peril of the actor; that if he escapes liability, it is simply because by good fortune no harm comes of his conduct in the particular event.

If, therefore, there is any common ground for all liability in tort, we shall best find it by eliminating the event as it actually turns out, and by considering only the principles on which the peril of his conduct is thrown upon the actor. We are to ask what are the elements, on the defendant's side, which must all be present before liability is possible, and the presence of which will commonly make him liable if damage follows.

The law of torts abounds in moral phraseology. It has much to say of wrongs, of malice, fraud, intent, and negligence. Hence it may naturally be supposed that the risk of a man's conduct is thrown upon him as the result of some moral shortcoming. But while this notion has been entertained, the extreme opposite will be found to have been a far more popular opinion—I mean the notion that a man is answerable for all the consequences of his acts, or, in other words, that he acts at his peril always, and wholly irrespective of the state of his consciousness upon the matter. . . .

As has just been hinted, there are two theories of the common-law liability for unintentional harm. Both of them seem to receive the implied assent of popular textbooks, and neither of them is wanting in plausibility and the semblance of authority.

The first is that of Austin, which is essentially the theory of a criminalist. According to him, the characteristic feature of law, properly so called, is a sanction or detriment threatened and imposed by the sovereign for disobedience to the sovereign's commands. As the greater part of the law only makes a man civilly answerable for breaking it, Austin is compelled to regard the liability to an action as a sanction, or, in other words, as a penalty for disobedience. It follows from this, according to the prevailing views of penal law, that such liability ought only to be based upon personal fault; and Austin accepts that conclusion, with its corollaries, one of which is that negligence means a state of the party's mind. These doctrines will be referred to later, so far as necessary.

The other theory is directly opposed to the foregoing. It seems to be adopted by some of the greatest common-law authorities, and requires serious discussion before it can be set aside in favor of any third opinion which may be maintained. According to this view, broadly stated, under the common law a man *acts* at his peril. It may be held as a sort of setoff, that he is never liable for omissions except in consequence of some duty voluntarily undertaken. But the whole and sufficient ground for such liabilities as he does incur outside the last class is supposed to be that he has voluntarily acted, and that damage has ensued. If the act was voluntary, it is totally immaterial that the detriment which followed from it was neither intended nor due to the negligence of the actor.

In order to do justice to this way of looking at the subject, we must remember that the abolition of the common-law forms of pleading has not changed the rules of substantive law. Hence, although pleaders now generally allege intent or negligence, anything which would formerly have been sufficient to charge a defendant in trespass is still sufficient, notwithstanding the fact that the ancient form of action and declaration has disappeared.

In the first place, it is said, consider generally the protection given by the law to property, both within and outside the limits of the last-named action. If a man crosses his neighbor's boundary by however innocent a mistake, or if his cattle escape into his neighbor's field, he is said to be liable in trespass quare clausum fregit. . . . [wherefore he broke into the [plaintiff's] close, i.e., land].

Now suppose that, instead of a dealing with the plaintiff's property, the case is that force has proceeded directly from the defendant's body to the plaintiff's body, it is urged that, as the law cannot be less careful of the persons than of the property of its subjects, the only defences possible are similar to those which would have been open to an alleged trespass on land. You may show that there was no trespass by showing that the defendant did no act; as where he was thrown from his horse upon the plaintiff, or where a third person took his hand and struck the plaintiff with it. In such cases the defendant's body is the passive instrument of an external force, and the bodily motion relied on by the plaintiff is not his act at all. So you may show a justification or excuse in the conduct of the plaintiff himself. But if no such excuse is shown, and the defendant has voluntarily acted, he must answer for the consequences, however little intended and however unforeseen. If, for instance, being assaulted by a third person, the defendant lifted his stick and accidentally hit the plaintiff, who was standing behind him, according to this view he is liable, irrespective of any negligence toward the party injured.

The arguments for the doctrine under consideration are, for the most part, drawn precedent, but it is sometimes supposed to be defensible as theoretically sound. Every man, it is said, has an absolute right to his person, and so forth, free from detriment at the hands of his neighbors. In the cases put, the plaintiff has done nothing; the defendant, on the other hand, has chosen to act. As between the two, the party whose voluntary conduct has caused the damage should suffer, rather than one who has had no share in producing it. . . .

[Holmes then reviews the historical precedents set out in Section A and continues.]

In spite, however, of all the arguments which may be urged for the rule that a man acts at his peril, it has been rejected by very eminent courts, even under the old forms of action. . . . But we may go further with profit, and inquire whether there are not strong grounds for thinking that the common law has never known such a rule, unless in that period of dry precedent which is so often to be found midway between a creative epoch and a period of solvent philosophical reaction. Conciliating the attention of those who, contrary to most modern practitioners, still adhere to the strict doctrine, by reminding them once more that there are weighty decisions to be cited adverse to it, and that, if they have involved an innovation, the fact that it has been made by such magistrates as Chief Justice Shaw goes far to prove that the change was politic, I think I may assert that a little reflection will show that it was required not only by policy, but by consistency. I will begin with the latter.

The same reasoning which would make a man answerable in trespass for all damage to another by force directly resulting from his own act, irrespective of negligence or intent, would make him answerable in case for the like damage similarly resulting from the act of his servant, in the course of the latter's employment. The discussions of the company's negligence in many railway cases would therefore be wholly out of place, for although, to be sure, there is a contract which would make the company liable for negligence, that contract cannot be taken to diminish any liability which would otherwise exist for a trespass on the part of its employees.

More than this, the same reasoning would make a defendant responsible for all damage, however remote, of which his act could be called the cause. So long, at least, as only physical or irresponsible agencies, however unforeseen, cooperated with the act complained of to produce the result, the argument which would resolve the case of accidentally striking the plaintiff, when lifting a stick in necessary self-defence, adversely to the defendant, would require a decision against him in every case where his act was a factor in the result complained of. The distinction between a direct application of force, and causing damage indirectly, or as a more remote consequence of one's act, although it may determine whether the form of action should be trespass or case, does not touch the theory of responsibility, if that theory be that a man acts at his peril. As was said at the outset, if the strict liability is to be maintained at all, it must be maintained throughout. A principle cannot be stated which would retain the strict liability in trespass while abandoning it in case. It cannot be said that trespass is for acts alone, and case for consequences of those acts. All actions of trespass are for consequences of acts, not for the acts themselves. And some actions of trespass are for consequences more remote from the defendant's act than in other instances where the remedy would be case.

An act is always a voluntary muscular contraction, and nothing else. The chain of physical sequences which it sets in motion or directs to the plaintiff's harm is no part of it, and very generally a long train of such sequences intervenes. An example or two will make this extremely clear.

When a man commits an assault and battery with a pistol, his only act is to contract the muscles of his arm and forefinger in a certain way, but it is the delight of elementary writers to point out what a vast series of physical changes must take place before the harm is done. Suppose that, instead of firing a pistol, he takes up a hose which is discharging water on the sidewalk, and directs it at the plaintiff, he does not even set in motion the physical causes which must cooperate with his act to make a battery. Not only natural causes, but a living being, may intervene between the act and its effect. Gibbons v. Pepper [91 Eng. Rep. 922 (K.B. 1695)], which decided that there was no battery when a man's horse was frightened by accident or a third person and ran away with him, and ran over the plaintiff, takes the distinction that, if the rider by spurring is the cause of the accident, then he is guilty. In Scott v. Shepherd[, 96 Eng. Rep. 525 (K.B. 1773)], already mentioned, trespass was maintained against one who had thrown a squib into a crowd, where it was tossed from hand to hand in self-defence until it burst and injured the plaintiff. Here even human agencies were a part of the chain between the defendant's act and the result, although they were treated as more or less nearly automatic, in order to arrive at the decision.

Now I repeat, that, if principle requires us to charge a man in trespass when his act has brought force to bear on another through a comparatively short train of intervening causes, in spite of his having used all possible care, it requires the same liability, however numerous and unexpected the events between the act and the result. If running a man down is a trespass when the accident can be referred to the rider's act of spurring, why is it not a tort in every case, as was argued in Vincent v. Stinehour [7 Vt. 62 (1835)], seeing that it can always be referred more remotely to his act of mounting and taking the horse out?

Why is a man not responsible for the consequences of an act innocent in its direct and obvious effects, when those consequences would not have followed but for the intervention of a series of extraordinary, although natural, events? The reason is, that, if the intervening events are of such a kind that no foresight could have been expected to look out for them, the defendant is not to blame for having failed to do so. . . .

But there is no difference in principle between the case where a natural cause or physical factor intervenes after the act in some way not to be foreseen, and turns what seemed innocent to harm, and the case where such a cause or factor intervenes, unknown, at the time; as for the matter of that, it did in the English cases cited. If a man is excused in the one case because he is not to blame, he must be in the other. The difference taken in Gibbons v. Pepper, cited above, is not between results which are and those which are not the consequences of the defendant's acts: it is between consequences which he was bound as a reasonable man to contemplate, and those which he was not. Hard spurring is just so much more likely to lead to harm than merely riding a horse in the street, that the court thought that the defendant would be bound to look out for the consequences of the one, while it would not hold him liable for those resulting merely from the other; because the possibility of being run away with when riding quietly, though familiar, is comparatively slight. If, however, the horse had been unruly, and had been taken into a frequented place for the purpose of being broken, the owner might have been liable, because "it was his fault to bring a wild horse into a place where mischief might probably be done."

To return to the example of the accidental blow with a stick lifted in self-defence, there is no difference between hitting a person standing in one's rear and hitting one who was pushed by a horse within range of the stick just as it was lifted, provided that it was not possible, under the circumstances, in the one case to have known, in the other to have anticipated, the proximity. In either case there is wanting the only element which distinguishes voluntary acts from spasmodic muscular contractions as a ground of liability. In neither of them, that is to say, has there been an opportunity of choice with reference to the consequence complained of,—a chance to guard against the result which has come to pass. A choice which entails a concealed consequence is as to that consequence no choice.

The general principle of our law is that loss from accident must lie where it falls, and this principle is not affected by the fact that a human being is the instrument of misfortune. But relatively to a given human being anything is accident which he could not fairly have been expected to contemplate as possible, and therefore to avoid. In the language of the late Chief Justice Nelson of New York: "No case or principle can be found, or if found can be maintained, subjecting an individual to liability for an act done without fault on his part. . . . All the cases concede that an injury arising from inevitable accident, or, which in law or reason is the same thing, from an act that ordinary human care and foresight are unable to guard against, is but the misfortune of the sufferer, and lays no foundation for legal responsibility." [Harvey v. Dunlop, Lalor 193 (N.Y. Sup. Ct. 1843).] If this were not so, any act would be sufficient, however remote, which set in motion or opened the door for a series of physical sequences ending in damage such as riding the horse, in the case of the runaway, or even coming to a place where one is seized with a fit and strikes the plaintiff in an unconscious spasm. Nay, why need the defendant have acted at all, and why is it not enough that his existence has been at the expense of the plaintiff? The requirement of an act is the requirement that the defendant should have made a choice. But the only possible purpose of introducing this moral element is to make the power of avoiding the evil complained of a condition of liability. There is no such power where the evil cannot be foreseen. . . .

A man need not, it is true, do this or that act,—the term *act* implies a choice,—but he must act somehow. Furthermore, the public generally profits by individual activity. As action cannot be avoided, and tends to the public good, there is obviously no policy in throwing the hazard of what is at once desirable and inevitable upon the actor.

The state might conceivably make itself a mutual insurance company against accidents, and distribute the burden of its citizens' mishaps among all its members. There might be a pension for paralytics, and state aid for those who suffered in person or estate from tempest or wild beasts. As between individuals it might adopt the mutual insurance principle *pro tanto*, and divide damages when both were in fault, as in the *rusticum judicium* of the admiralty, or it might throw all loss upon the actor irrespective of fault. The state does none of those things, however, and the prevailing view is that its cumbrous and expensive machinery ought not to be set in motion unless some clear benefit is to be derived from disturbing the status quo. State interference is an evil, where it cannot be shown to be a good. Universal insurance, if desired, can be better and more cheaply accomplished by private enterprise. The undertaking to redistribute losses simply on the ground that they resulted from the defendant's act would not only be open to these objections, but, as it is hoped the preceding discussion has shown, to the still graver one of offending the sense of justice. Unless my act is of a nature to threaten others, unless under the circumstances a prudent man would have foreseen the possibility of harm, it is no more justifiable to make me indemnify my neighbor against the consequences, than to make me do the same thing if I had fallen upon him in a fit, or to compel me to insure him against lightning.

NOTE

Liability ex ante or ex post.   The Holmes excerpt above represents the most influential theoretical argument on behalf of a negligence rule tied to the principle of reasonable foresight. One key to his argument is that standards of conduct must be known in advance, which is not possible if liability is made to turn exclusively on the outcome of the event. Hence his emphasis on the reasonableness of the defendant's conduct, irrespective of the outcome. Yet why should that be so? The contrary argument for strict liability starts with the premise that no party can take comfort in a standard that speaks only of reasonable care under the circumstances. But any party is able to choose some desired level of precautions if instructed from the outset that he or she is responsible for the harms that are caused either by the direct application of force on the one hand or the creation of dangerous conditions (e.g., traps) on the other. Those rules could be extended to hold owners of animals strictly responsible for the damage their animals cause, wholly irrespective of the level of precautions taken. No longer is it necessary to distinguish between ordinary riding and hard spurring. This system, moreover, does not discourage taking precautions. To be sure, the defendant pays the full price for all harms caused. Yet by the same token, the defendant gets the benefit of the reduced level of accidents for which liability should be imposed. The defendant who knows the standard can then choose the appropriate level of care without having to guess in advance what rules of conduct the law might require after the fact.

SECTION E. STRICT LIABILITY AND NEGLIGENCE IN MODERN TIMES

Stone v. Bolton
[1950] 1 K.B. 201 (C.A.)

[The plaintiff, Bessie Stone, lived on Beckenham Road, a side street next to a cricket ground. One day, as she had just walked onto the road through the gate in front of her house, she was struck on the head by a cricket ball that had been hit out of the grounds. The ball was hit by a visiting player, and by all accounts, was one of the longest balls—travelling about 100 yards before it struck the plaintiff—that had ever been hit at the grounds during the previous 40 years. The cricket ground was found at trial to be "quite large enough for all practical purposes," even after it was remodeled in 1910 or 1911 to allow for construction of Beckenham Road. The field itself was surrounded by a 12-foot-high fence or hoarding which, owing to a rise in the ground, was about 17 feet above the street on the Beckenham Road side. The southern wicket from which the ball was struck was about 78 yards from Beckenham Road fence. Witnesses testified that over a 30-year period about six to ten balls had been hit onto Beckenham Road, and that several others had landed in the garden of one Brownson, the nearest neighboring house to the cricket grounds. The plaintiff did not sue the batsman or his club but she did sue the home cricket club and all of its members. She first alleged that the grounds constituted a public nuisance. She separately alleged common law negligence, claiming that the defendants had placed the cricket pitch too close to Beckenham Road, that they had failed to erect a fence of sufficient height to prevent balls from being hit onto the road, and that they had otherwise failed to insure that cricket balls would not be hit into the road. At trial, Oliver, J., gave judgment to the defendants on both the public nuisance and negligence counts. The Court of Appeal reversed the judgment on the negligence claim by a two-to-one vote.]

JENKINS, L.J. . . . The case as regards negligence, therefore, seems to me to resolve itself into the question whether, with the wickets sited as they were, and the fence at the Beckenham Road end as it was, on August 9, 1947, the hitting into Beckenham Road of the ball which struck and injured the plaintiff was the realization of a reasonably foreseeable risk, or was in the nature of an unprecedented occurrence which the defendants could not reasonably have foreseen.

On the evidence this question seems to me to admit of only one answer. Balls had been hit into Beckenham Road before. It is true this had happened only at rare intervals, perhaps no more than six times in thirty seasons. But it was known from practical experience to be an actual possibility in the conditions in which matches were customarily played on the ground from about 1910 onwards, that is to say, with the wickets sited substantially as they were, and the fence at the Beckenham Road end, I gather, exactly as it was as regards height and position on August 9, 1947. What had happened several times before could, as it seems to me, reasonably be expected to happen again sooner or later. It was not likely to happen often, but it was certainly likely to happen again in time. When or how often it would happen again no one could tell, as this would depend on the strength of the batsmen playing on the ground (including visitors about whose capacity the defendants might know nothing) and the efficiency or otherwise of the bowlers. In my opinion, therefore, the hitting out of the ground of the ball which struck and injured the plaintiff was a realization of a reasonably foreseeable risk, which because it could reasonably be foreseen, the defendants were under a duty to prevent.

The defendants had, in fact, done nothing since the rearrangement of the ground on the making of Beckenham Road in or about 1910, whether by heightening the fence (e.g., by means of a screen of wire netting on poles) or by altering the position of the pitch, to guard against the known possibility of balls being hit into Beckenham Road. It follows that, if I have rightly defined the extent of the defendants' duty in this matter, the hitting out of the ground of the ball which injured the plaintiff did involve a breach of that duty for the consequences of which the defendants must be held liable to the plaintiff in damages. . . .

It was also, I think, suggested that no possible precaution would have arrested the flight of this particular ball, so high did it pass over the fence. This seems to me an irrelevant consideration. If cricket cannot be played on a given ground without foreseeable risk of injury to persons outside it, then it is always possible in the last resort to stop using that ground for cricket. The plaintiff in this case might, I apprehend, quite possibly have been killed. I ask myself whether in that event the defendants would have claimed the right to go on as before, because such a thing was unlikely to happen again for several years, though it might happen again on any day on which one of the teams in the match included a strong hitter. No doubt as a practical matter the defendants might decide that the double chance of a ball being hit into the road and finding a human target there was so remote that, rather than go to expense in the way of a wire screen or the like, or worse still abandon the ground, they would run the risk of such an occurrence and meet any ensuing claim for damages if and when it arose. But I fail to see on what principle they can be entitled to require people in Beckenham Road to accept the risk, and, if hit by a ball, put up with the possibly very serious harm done to them as *damnum sine injuria*, unless able to identify, trace, and successfully sue the particular batsman who made the hit.

Bolton v. Stone
[1951] A.C. 850

[The defendants then appealed to the House of Lords, which unanimously ruled in their favor.]

LORD REID. . . . This case, therefore raises sharply the question what is the nature and extent of the duty of a person who promotes on his land operations which may cause damage to persons on an adjoining highway. Is it that he must not carry out or permit an operation which he knows or ought to know clearly can cause such damage, however improbable that result may be, or is it that he is only bound to take into account the possibility of such damage if such damage is a likely or probable consequence of what he does or permits, or if the risk of damage is such that a reasonable man, careful of the safety of his neighbor, would regard that risk as material? . . .

Counsel for the respondent in this case had to put his case so high as to say that, at least as soon as one ball had been driven into the road in the ordinary course of a match, the appellants could and should have realized that that might happen again and that, if it did, someone might be injured; and that that was enough to put on the appellants a duty to take steps to prevent such an occurrence. If the true test is foreseeability alone I think that must be so. Once a ball has been driven on to a road without there being anything extraordinary to account for the fact, there is clearly a risk that another will follow, and if it does there is clearly a chance, small though it may be, that someone may be injured. On the theory that it is foreseeability alone that matters it would be irrelevant to consider how often a ball might be expected to land in the road and it would not matter whether the road was the busiest street, or the quietest country lane; the only difference between these cases is in the degree of risk.

It would take a good deal to make me believe that the law has departed so far from the standards which guide ordinary careful people in ordinary life. In the crowded conditions of modern life even the most careful person cannot avoid creating some risks and accepting others. What a man must not do, and what I think a careful man tries not to do, is to create a risk which is substantial. Of course there are numerous cases where special circumstances require that a higher standard shall be observed and where that is recognized by the law. But I do not think that this case comes within any such special category. It was argued that this case comes within the principle in Rylands v. Fletcher, but I agree with your Lordships that there is no substance in this argument. In my judgment the test to be applied here is whether the risk of damage to a person on the road was so small that a reasonable man in the position of the appellants, considering the matter from the point of view of safety, would have thought it right to refrain from taking steps to prevent the danger.

In considering that matter I think that it would be right to take into account not only how remote is the chance that a person might be struck but also how serious the consequences are likely to be if a person is struck; but I do not think that it would be right to take into account the difficulty of remedial measures. If cricket cannot be played on a ground without creating a substantial risk, then it should not be played there *at all.* I think that this is in substance the test which Oliver, J., applied in this case. He considered whether the appellants' ground was large enough to be safe for all practical purposes and held that it was. This is a question not of law but of fact and degree. It is not an easy question and it is one on which opinions may well differ. I can only say that having given the whole matter repeated and anxious consideration I find myself unable to decide this question in favour of the respondent. But I think that this case is not far from the borderline. If this appeal is allowed, that does not in my judgment mean that in every case where cricket has been played on a ground for a number of years without accident or complaint those who organize matches there are safe to go on in reliance on past immunity. I would have reached a different conclusion if I had thought that the risk here had been other than extremely small, because I do not think that a reasonable man considering the matter from the point of view of safety would or should disregard any risk unless it is extremely small.

LORD RADCLIFFE. My Lords, I agree that this appeal must be allowed. I agree with regret, because I have much sympathy with the decision that commended itself to the majority of the members of the Court of Appeal. I can see nothing unfair in the appellants being required to compensate the respondent for the serious injury that she has received as a result of the sport that they have organized on their cricket ground at Cheetham Hill. But the law of negligence is concerned less with what is fair than with what is culpable, and I cannot persuade myself that the appellants have been guilty of any culpable act or omission in this case.

. . . [A] breach of duty has taken place if they show the appellants guilty of a failure to take reasonable care to prevent the accident. One may phrase it as "reasonable care" or "ordinary care" or "proper care"—all these phrases are to be found in decisions of authority—but the fact remains that, unless there has been something which a reasonable man would blame as falling beneath the standard of conduct that he would set for himself and require of his neighbour, there has been no breach of legal duty. And here, I think, the respondent's case breaks down. It seems to me that a reasonable man, taking account of the chances against an accident happening, would not have felt himself called upon either to abandon the use of the ground for cricket or to increase the height of his surrounding fences. He would have done what the appellants did: in other words, he would have done nothing. Whether, if the unlikely event of an accident did occur and his play turn to another's hurt, he would have thought it equally proper to offer no more consolation to his victim than the reflection that a social being is not immune from social risks, I do not say, for I do not think that that is a consideration which is relevant to legal liability.

NOTES

1. Negligence, strict and vicarious liability in Bolton v. Stone.   The plaintiff in Bolton v. Stone might have sued any of three possible defendants: the batsman from the visiting team, the visiting team, or the owner of the home team. Should an action lie against the batsman on a theory of strict liability—he hit Bessie Stone? If so, is the visiting team vicariously liable for the torts of its servant? See *infra* Chapter 8, Section F. Could vicarious liability also be imposed on the owners of the cricket field, or is it limited to employers? Note that at common law, the owner of property was held responsible for fires set on his land by his guests, but not those set by strangers. See the opinion of Markham, J., in Beaulieu v. Finglam, *infra* at 405.

Alternatively, how should the negligence action against the defendant be evaluated? What would be the relevance of the location of the cricket field? The shape of the pitch? The efforts of the home team to get the batsman out? The balls that landed in Brownson's garden? In dealing with the negligence issue, note that the dominant offensive strategy in cricket, a game in which, unlike baseball, runs are plentiful (a batsman hitting for a century is not uncommon) while outs (of which there are ten per inning) represent major setbacks for the batting team. The astute batsman therefore will normally try to keep the ball on the ground, knowing that if it crosses the boundary at the edge of the field, he will get four runs. Hitting the ball out of the field on a fly is worth six runs, but carries with it a substantial risk of being caught. Hence the infrequency of long hits.

Bolton had an uneasy public reception. Professor Goodhart's note on the case, for example, was entitled "Is It Cricket?" 67 Law Q. Rev. 460 (1951). In order to soften the public criticism, the Cricket Clubs in England that supported the defendants' appeal to the House of Lords wrote to the editor of the Law Quarterly Review that they "have done everything that they can to see that Stone does not suffer financially. In fact, so far as they are concerned, she has been left in possession of the damages originally awarded." Note, 68 Law Q. Rev. 1, 3 (1952). Defendants also waived costs of £3,000, to which they were entitled under the English winner-take-all system. Glanville Williams developed the notion of "ethical compensation" to defend this peculiar turn of events in The Aims of the Law of Tort, 4 Current Legal Probs. 137 (1951). Salmond on Torts 30 (13th ed. 1961) notes that "one who is under no legal liability for damage caused to another may yet think it right and proper to offer some measure of compensation." Is the principle of ethical compensation needed in a strict liability system? Does it account for the divergence between the legal and the moral duty? For criticism of Bolton v. Stone, see Harari, The Place of Negligence in the Law of Torts 170-179 (1962).

2. Cricket versus golf?   With *Bolton*, contrast Rinaldo v. McGovern, 587 N.E.2d 264, 267 (N.Y. 1991). There one of two defendants—it was not clear who—sliced a golf ball that "soared" off the course and shattered the plaintiff's windshield as she "happened" to drive her car down a public street. In rejecting the plaintiff's negligence claim, Titone, J., held that neither defendant could be held liable for "what amounted to no more than his poorly hit tee shot" because the defendants had no duty to warn persons who were not in the intended line of flight and who, in any event, could not have responded to the warning even if they had heard it. The court also rejected any distinction between individuals who chose to live next to the fairway on golf course grounds and strangers who drove along the public street. Titone, J., then continued:

> Plaintiffs' cause of action based on the claimed negligence of the defendant golfer is similarly untenable. Although the object of the game of golf is to drive the ball as cleanly and directly as possible toward its ultimate intended goal (the hole), the possibility that the ball will fly off in another direction is a risk inherent in the game. Contrary to the view of the dissenters below, the presence of such a risk does not, by itself, import tort liability. The essence of tort liability is the failure to take reasonable steps, where possible, to minimize the chance of harm. Thus, to establish liability in tort, there must be both the existence of a recognizable risk

"If you're so enlightened, how come you can't lick that slice?"

Source: Sam Gross / The New Yorker Collection / The Cartoon Bank

and some basis for concluding that the harm flowing from the consummation of that risk was reasonably preventable.

Since "even the best professional golfers cannot avoid an occasional 'hook' or 'slice,'" it cannot be said that the risk of a mishit golf ball is a fully preventable occurrence. To the contrary, even with the utmost concentration and the "tedious preparation" that often accompanies a golfer's shot, there is no guarantee that the ball will be lofted onto the correct path. For that reason, we have held that the mere fact that a golf ball did not travel in the intended direction does not establish a viable negligence claim. To provide an actionable theory of liability, a person injured by a mishit golf ball must affirmatively show that the golfer failed to exercise due care by adducing proof, for example, that the golfer "aimed so inaccurately as to unreasonably increase the risk of harm."

What result under *Bolton* in a suit against the golf club? Should the club stop its operations altogether? What difference would it make if the plaintiff were speeding toward the golf ball when her car was struck? Driving away from it?

A different approach to this question was taken in Hennessey v. Pyne, 694 A.2d 691 (R.I. 1997), when the defendant's errant shot hit the plaintiff while she was on her condominium grounds. Flanders, J., parted company with *Rinaldo*. He first rejected that the plaintiff could bring either a nuisance or assault and battery claim against the defendant, but held that negligence claims for a poor shot and an insufficient warning could both go to the jury, referring to

Pyne's awareness of the existence and the proximity of Hennessey's condominium as being within striking distance of his tee shot (midway down the fairway in the crook of a slight dogleg left); his knowledge that the condominiums where Hennessey lived were regularly hit by golf balls; his consciousness of Hennessey's apparently ubiquitous and complaining presence on or near the course and his appreciation of the golfing advantage to be gained on this dogleg hole if he drove the ball off the tee as closely as possible past Hennessey's condominium (without striking it), thereby maximizing the distance of his shot and the lie of his ball down the fairway.

How should a jury distinguish between the shooting and the warning claims?

3. Corrective justice and Bolton v. Stone.   Bolton v. Stone raises important questions about the proper theoretical orientation of tort law. A *corrective justice* approach sees the law as providing *rectification* or *redress* for an invasion of a legal right. Dating back to Aristotle's Nicomachean Ethics, Book IV (R.W. Browne, translation, 1853), the initial statement of the principle read:

> [I]t matters not whether a good man has robbed a bad man, or a bad man a good man, nor whether a good or bad man has committed adultery; the law looks to the difference of the hurt alone, and treats persons, if one commits and the other suffers injury, as equal, and also if one has done and the other suffered hurt.

More modern formulations stress the view that the purpose of law, solely as a matter of fairness between the parties to a dispute, undoes the imbalance created by the violation of a preexisting right, most notably the right to exclusive control over one's body and property. Violations of these rights are usually (but not exclusively) understood in terms of physical invasions. Explicit concern with long-term incentive effects on either the wrongdoer or victim are not part of the basic equation, and are often thought extrinsic to the basic purpose of the law or, as is sometimes said, that corrective justice "provides the immanent critical standpoint informing the law's effort to work itself pure." Weinrib, Corrective Justice in a Nutshell, 52 U. Toronto L.J. 349, 356 (2002).

In Bolton v. Stone, the prima facie causal case against the batsman is simply "he hit me." This causal paradigm has been defended in Epstein, A Theory of Strict Liability, 2 J. Legal Stud. 151, 168-169 (1973):

> Once this simple causal paradigm is accepted, its relationship to the question of responsibility for the harm so caused must be clarified. Briefly put, the argument is that proof of the proposition *A* hit *B* should be sufficient to establish a prima facie case of liability. I do not argue that proof of causation is equivalent to a conclusive demonstration of responsibility. Both the modern and classical systems of law are based upon the development of prima facie cases and defenses thereto. They differ not in their use of presumptions but in the elements needed to create the initial presumption in favor of the plaintiff. The doctrine of strict liability holds that proof that the defendant caused harm creates that presumption because proof of the non-reciprocal source of the harm is sufficient to upset the balance

where one person must win and the other must lose. There is no room to consider, as part of the prima facie case, allegations that the defendant intended to harm the plaintiff, or could have avoided the harm he caused by the use of reasonable care. The choice is plaintiff or defendant, and the analysis of causation is the tool which, prima facie, fastens responsibility upon the defendant. Indeed for most persons, the difficult question is often not whether these causal assertions create the presumption, but whether there are in fact any means to distinguish between causation and responsibility, so close is the connection between what a man does and what he is answerable for.

The corrective justice principle has also been invoked on defense of a negligence rule on the ground that the defendant's standard of conduct should be set no higher than the standard the plaintiff could demand from herself. If, therefore, the plaintiff cannot identify any flaw in the defendant's conduct, she cannot characterize his conduct as *wrongful.* Thus it is said that "corrective justice requires annulling a departure from the preexisting distribution of money or honors in accordance with merit, but only when the departure is the result of *an act of injustice,* causing injury." Posner, The Concept of Corrective Justice in Recent Theories of Tort Law, 10 J. Legal Stud. 187, 200 (1981). The same idea is expressed by Glanville Williams in The Aims of the Law of Tort, 4 Current Legal Probs. 137, 151 (1951):

> Finally there is the compensatory or reparative theory, according to which one who has caused injury to another must make good the damage whether he was at fault or not. This is the same as the theory of ethical compensation except that it does not require culpability on the part of the defendant. If valid, it justifies strict liability, which the theory of ethical compensation does not. The difficulty is, however, to state it in such a form as to make it acceptable. If it is said that a person who has been damaged by another ought to be compensated, we readily assent, moved as we are by sympathy for the victim's loss. But what has to be shown is not merely that the sufferer ought to be compensated, but that he ought to be compensated by the defendant. In the absence of any moral blame of the defendant, how is this demonstration possible?

More recently the insistence on wrongfulness has been stressed in Goldberg & Zipursky, Torts as Wrongs, 88 Tex. L. Rev. 917, 937 (2010), who write:

> Tortious wrongdoing always involves an interference with one of a set of individual interests that are significant enough aspects of a person's well-being to warrant the imposition of a duty on others not to interfere with the interest in certain ways, notwithstanding the liberty restriction inherent in such a duty imposition.

According to Epstein, Toward a General Theory of Tort Law: Strict Liability, 3 J. Tort L. (Iss. 1, Art. 6) 7-8 (2010):

> [Goldberg and Zipursky] are quite correct to insist that there is no way to understand the distinctive role of tort law without building the notion of wrongfulness

into the ground floor of the system. But that objective cannot be achieved by offering a simple definition of the notion of wrong. It does little to advance the ball to observe that wrongful conduct is conduct which is unlawful, illegal, or improper. Synonyms are not the same as analysis.

This alternative account of wrongful conduct ties into the system of pleadings outlined by Arnold, *supra* at 75, by stressing that a strict liability system (unlike a system of absolute liability) still allows for many defenses based, for example, on the plaintiff's misconduct or inevitable accident, narrowly construed. Accordingly strict liability explicates the idea of wrongfulness, not in terms of the lack of negligence or intention, but in terms of these other substantive defenses.

4. Economic efficiency as an alternative to corrective justice.   Not all accounts of modern tort law regard corrective justice as the touchstone of liability, and much of modern tort scholarship has sought to develop alternative economic accounts of the tort system. One early notable explication of an economic approach is contained in Calabresi & Melamed, Property Rules, Liability Rules and Inalienability: One View of the Cathedral, 85 Harv. L. Rev. 1089, 1093-1094 (1972):

> Perhaps the simplest reason for a particular entitlement is to minimize the administrative costs of enforcement. This was the reason Holmes gave for letting the costs lie where they fall in accidents unless some clear societal benefit is achieved by shifting them. By itself this reason will never justify any result except that of letting the stronger win, for obviously that result minimizes enforcement costs. Nevertheless, administrative efficiency may be relevant to choosing entitlements when other reasons are taken into account. This may occur when the reasons accepted are indifferent between conflicting entitlements and one entitlement is cheaper to enforce than the others. It may also occur when the reasons are not indifferent but lead us only slightly to prefer one over another and the first is considerably more expensive to enforce than the second.
>
> But administrative efficiency is just one aspect of the broader concept of economic efficiency. Economic efficiency asks that we choose the set of entitlements which would lead to that allocation of resources which could not be improved in the sense that a further change would not so improve the condition of those who gained by it that they could compensate those who lost from it and still be better off than before. This is often called Pareto optimality. To give two examples, economic efficiency asks for that combination of entitlements to engage in risky activities and to be free from harm from risky activities which will most likely lead to the lowest sum of accident costs and of costs of avoiding accidents. It asks for that form of property, private or communal, which leads to the highest product for the effort of producing.

Technically speaking, what Calabresi and Melamed called Pareto efficiency is known as Kaldor-Hicks efficiency. Pareto efficiency requires that the winners *actually* compensate the losers so that at least some one is better off and no one is worse off than before. Kaldor-Hicks efficiency is satisfied with a demonstration that *hypothetical* compensation was possible. Stated otherwise, it allows the move to go forward so long as the gains to the winner are sufficient to compensate the losers, even if such compensation is not paid. The Pareto standard is less problematic but more demanding; the Kaldor-Hicks standard is the opposite. Note that both standards preclude social changes that yield systematic losses. Is there a fair distribution of the gains under the Pareto standard if one person gains huge amounts and everyone else is left indifferent? For one retrospective on the Calabresi/Melamed paper, see Symposium, Property Rules, Liability Rules, and Inalienability: A Twenty-Five Year Retrospective, 106 Yale L.J. 2081-2213 (1997), with articles by, among others, Epstein, Krier and Schwab, Levmore, and Rose. See also Schwab, Property Rules and Liability Rules: The Cathedral in Another Light, 70 N.Y.U. L. Rev. 440 (1995).

Transaction costs, i.e., the costs involved in establishing and enforcing both property rights and contractual arrangements, are critical to the economic analysis. If these could be held to zero, the initial distribution of rights would be of little economic consequence, as private parties could, through repeated, costless, and instantaneous transactions, move all resources to their highest valued use. The end use of any resource would be the same regardless of who was its original owner. Thus the decisions about property rights would only affect their initial distribution, but not their final allocation. See Coase, The Problem of Social Cost, 3 J.L. & Econ. 1 (1960), for the initial elaboration of what is today known as the Coase theorem. In all real world situations, however, transaction costs are positive, if not prohibitive. In contractual situations, the high costs of transacting can be reduced when either courts or legislatures announce standard "gap-filling" terms for matters on which the parties are silent. In tort cases between strangers, however, antecedent voluntary transactions are typically unattainable. The tort rule, therefore, cannot be displaced before harm occurs, and must govern liability afterward. What factors should be considered in fashioning the ideal liability rule where there are high transaction costs? Drawing heavily on Calabresi's book, The Cost of Accidents, Calabresi and Melamed, *supra* at 1096-1097, tackled this problem as follows:

> (1) that economic efficiency standing alone would dictate that set of entitlements which favors knowledgeable choices between social benefits and the social costs of obtaining them, and between social costs and the social costs of avoiding them; (2) that this implies, in the absence of certainty as to whether a benefit is worth its costs to society, that the cost should be put on the party or activity best located to make such a cost-benefit analysis; (3) that in particular contexts like accidents or pollution this suggests putting costs on the party or activity which can most cheaply avoid them; (4) that in the absence of certainty as to who that party or activity is, the costs should be put on the party or activity which can with the lowest transaction costs act in the market to correct an error in entitlements by inducing the party who can avoid social costs most cheaply to do so; and (5) that since we are in an area where by hypothesis markets do not work perfectly — there are transaction costs — a decision will often have to be made on whether market transactions or collective fiat is most likely to bring us closer to the Pareto optimal result the "perfect" market would reach.

How does a judge or jury determine which party is "best located to make a cost-benefit analysis" if the parties to the accident are not known to each other before the accident occurs? What should be done if the defendant knows more about the probability of harm to another, but the plaintiff knows more about its likely extent? How does this analysis apply to Bolton v. Stone? To the other cases in this chapter?

For a recent effort to link together the various claims of corrective justice and efficiency, see Shmueli, Legal Pluralism in Tort Law Theory: Balancing Instrumental Theories and Corrective Justice, 48 U. Mich. J.L. Reform 745 (2015).

Hammontree v. Jenner
97 Cal. Rptr. 739 (Cal. App. 1971)

LILLIE, J. Plaintiffs Maxine Hammontree and her husband sued defendant for personal injuries and property damage arising out of an automobile accident. The cause was tried to a jury. Plaintiffs appeal from judgment entered on a jury verdict returned against them and in favor of defendant.

The evidence shows that on the afternoon of April 25, 1967, defendant was driving his 1959 Chevrolet home from work; at the same time plaintiff Maxine Hammontree was working in a bicycle shop owned and operated by her and her husband; without warning defendant's car crashed through the wall of the shop, struck Maxine and caused personal injuries and damage to the shop.

Defendant claimed he became unconscious during an epileptic seizure, losing control of his car. He did not recall the accident, but his last recollection before it was leaving a stop light after his last stop, and his first recollection after the accident was being taken out of his car in plaintiffs' shop. Defendant testified he has a medical history of epilepsy and knows of no other reason for his loss of consciousness except an epileptic seizure. [The defendant first learned of his epileptic condition in 1952 and from that time until his accident, he was under the constant care of a neurologist who treated him first with dilantin and then with phelantin. The defendant's last seizure was in 1953, and thereafter he had no trouble at all. His physician testified that he had seen the defendant on a regular basis over the years and that at all times he was "doing normally." He further testified that he believed that it was "safe" for the defendant to drive with the medication, even though it was impossible for the defendant to drive during a seizure.]

In 1955 or 1956 the Department of Motor Vehicles was advised that defendant was an epileptic and placed him on probation under which every six months he had to report to the doctor who was required to advise it in writing of defendant's condition. In 1960 his probation was changed to a once-a-year report. . . .

[The plaintiffs withdrew their negligence count during trial, "electing to stand solely on the theory of absolute liability." But the trial judge nonetheless instructed the jury on negligence and res ipsa loquitur. The jury found for the defendant. The plaintiff then appealed the refusal of the trial judge to grant summary judgment in their favor by failing to give an instruction on absolute liability.][1]

Under the present state of the law found in appellate authorities beginning with Waters v. Pacific Coast Dairy, Inc., [131 P.2d 588 (Cal. App. 1942)] (driver rendered unconscious from sharp pain in left arm and shoulder) through Ford v. Carew & English, [200 P.2d 828 (Cal. App. 1948)] (fainting spells from strained heart muscles), Zabunoff v. Walker, [13 Cal. Rptr. 463 (Cal. App. 1961)] (sudden sneeze), and Tannyhill v. Pacific Motor Trans. Co., [38 Cal. Rptr. 774 (Cal. App. 1964)] (heart attack), the trial judge properly refused the instruction. The foregoing cases generally hold that liability of a driver, suddenly stricken by an illness rendering him unconscious, for injury resulting from an accident occurring during that time rests on principles of negligence. . . .

Appellants seek to have this court override the established law of this state which is dispositive of the issue before us as outmoded in today's social and economic structure, particularly in the light of the now recognized principles imposing liability upon the manufacturer, retailer and all distributive and vending elements and activities which bring a product to the consumer to his injury, on the basis of strict liability in tort expressed first in Justice Traynor's concurring opinion in Escola v. Coca Cola Bottling Co., [150 P.2d 436 (Cal. 1944)]; and then in Greenman v. Yuba Power Products, Inc., [377 P.2d 897 (Cal. 1963)]; Vandermark v. Ford Motor Co., [391 P.2d 168 (Cal. 1964)]; and Elmore v. American Motors Corp., [451 P.2d 84 (Cal. 1969)]. These authorities hold that "A manufacturer [or retailer] is strictly liable in tort when an article he places on the market, knowing that it is to be used without inspection for defects, proves to have a defect that causes injury to a human being." (*Greenman* supra.) Drawing a parallel with these products liability cases, appellants argue, with some degree of logic, that only the driver affected by a physical condition which could suddenly render him unconscious and who is aware of that condition can anticipate the hazards and foresee the dangers involved in his operation of a motor vehicle, and that the liability of those who by reason of seizure or heart failure or some other physical condition lose the ability to safely operate and control a motor vehicle resulting in injury to an innocent person should be predicated on strict liability.

We decline to superimpose the absolute liability of products liability cases upon drivers under the circumstances here. The theory on which those cases are predicated is that manufacturers, retailers and distributors of products are engaged in the business of distributing goods to the public and are an integral part of the over-all producing and marketing enterprise that should bear the cost of injuries from defective parts. . . . This policy hardly applies here and it is not enough to simply say, as do appellants, that the insurance carriers should be the ones to

---

1. "When the evidence shows that a driver of a motor vehicle on a public street or highway loses his ability to safely operate and control such vehicle because of some seizure or health failure, that driver is nevertheless legally liable for all injuries and property damage which an innocent person may suffer as a proximate result of the defendant's inability to so control or operate his motor vehicle.

"This is true even if you find the defendant driver had no warning of any such impending seizure or health failure."

bear the cost of injuries to innocent victims on a strict liability basis. In Maloney v. Rath, [445 P.2d 513 (Cal. 1968)], followed by Clark v. Dziabas, [445 P.2d 517 (Cal. 1968)], appellant urged that defendant's violation of a safety provision (defective brakes) of the Vehicle Code makes the violator strictly liable for damages caused by the violation. While reversing the judgment for defendant upon another ground, the California Supreme Court refused to apply the doctrine of strict liability to automobile drivers. The situation involved two users of the highway but the problems of fixing responsibility under a system of strict liability are as complicated in the instant case as those in Maloney v. Rath, and could only create uncertainty in the area of its concern. As stated in *Maloney*, at page 446: "To invoke a rule of strict liability on users of the streets and highways, however, without also establishing in substantial detail how the new rule should operate would only contribute confusion to the automobile accident problem. Settlement and claims adjustment procedures would become chaotic until the new rules were worked out on a case-by-case basis, and the hardships of delayed compensation would be seriously intensified. Only the Legislature, if it deems it wise to do so, can avoid such difficulties by enacting a comprehensive plan for the compensation of automobile accident victims in place of or in addition to the law of negligence."

The instruction tendered by appellants was properly refused for still another reason. Even assuming the merit of appellants' position under the facts of this case in which defendant knew he had a history of epilepsy, previously had suffered seizures and at the time of the accident was attempting to control the condition by medication, the instruction does not except from its ambit the driver who suddenly is stricken by an illness or physical condition which he had no reason whatever to anticipate and of which he had no prior knowledge.

The judgment is affirmed.

WOOD, P.J., and THOMPSON, J., concurred.

Appellants' petition for a hearing by the Supreme Court was denied December 16, 1971.

NOTES

1. Physician liability.   Should the treating physician of an epileptic driver be held responsible to an injured third party if he fails to warn his patients of the relevant risk and erroneously supplies favorable documentation to the Department of Transportation that allows her to obtain a driver's license? In Schmidt v. Mahoney, 659 N.W.2d 552, 555 (Iowa 2003), Carter, J., answered that question in the negative, noting:

> [I]t is highly likely that a consequence of recognizing liability to members of the general public . . . will be that physicians treating patients with seizure disorders will become reluctant to allow them to drive or engage in any other activity in which a seizure could possibly harm a third party. In order to curtail liability, physicians may become prone to make overly restrictive recommendations concerning the activities of their patients and will exercise their role as reporters to the department of transportation in an inflexible manner not in their patient's best interest.

Does the insulation of the physician from liability strengthen or weaken the case for strict liability against the driver?

2. Why the choice between negligence and strict liability is so difficult. For over 200 years courts have vacillated over the key choice between negligence and strict liability. Why, then, is it likely that this tension is not likely to resolve itself quickly? Courts seek to identify some social gain to justify the manifest social costs of litigation. Compensation of the plaintiff, taken alone, fails to justify this expense as long as first-party insurance is available. That insurance allows each person to choose the type of coverage desired based upon an intimate knowledge of her personal needs and circumstances that no tort defendant could ever obtain. What overcomes the initial bias for first-party coverage?

Since compensation alone does not supply the missing justification, the case for tort liability rests on the need to fashion incentives that reduce the costs of accidents and their prevention. Imposing liability for negligence thus seems unproblematic because the tort rule unambiguously provides incentives to avoid costs that exceed the benefits generated by a particular activity. To see why, think of the optimal level of care as the same amount of care that a single person would take if he himself were the only person at risk for property damage or bodily injury. That individual would prefer suffering the consequences of some accidents to bearing the greater costs of avoiding them.

Tort litigation arises only because the victim and injurer are separate parties. At this point intuitions cut in two contrary directions. One impulse imposes liability to force the defendant-injurer to internalize the costs that his conduct would otherwise impose on others. The law makes the actor bear the same costs he would incur if he were the sole owner. The rival impulse is to dismiss the plaintiff's suit because the defendant acted just as the plaintiff would (and should) have acted under the same circumstances: He took the optimal level of precautions by treating the plaintiff's loss as if it were his own. There is no occasion for the law to intervene because there is no defect in conduct to fix. The strict liability theory makes a defendant bear the plaintiff's loss; the negligence theory imposes liability only when it spots a shortfall in the defendant's basic behavior. How then to choose between them?

One possible way to choose invokes the considerations of reciprocity encountered in *Losee, supra* at 110. Unfortunately, the norm of reciprocity is consistent with either negligence or strict liability. The incentive effects of the two rules are the same when viewed from the "ex ante" perspective (that is, before the harm), and it is difficult to identify any systematic distributional consequences that flow from the choice of liability rules. This stalemate tends to make administrative costs the deciding factor in the debate. Yet again, the relevant considerations tug in both directions. The strict liability rule eliminates the need to make a nice determination of the standard of care; it also eliminates the need to ask whether the defendant complied with that standard. But the negligence rule cuts out some expensive lawsuits (since plaintiff must do more to win), although the ones that remain are of greater complexity. The tradeoff between these two effects rests on empirical judgments about their relative magnitude: Do we worry more about the cost per suit, or the number of suits?

This inquiry takes us a long way from the principles of fundamental fairness or immanence traditionally and plausibly invoked on *both* sides of the controversy. Yet, if this tradeoff shapes the strict liability/negligence debate, it is easy to see why a consensus has been so slow in developing. While the choice of liability rule has an enormous impact in deciding specific cases, the overall social consequences are less dramatic than first meet the eye. Since both rules create the same basic incentives and have, roughly speaking, the same administrative costs, either rule can provide a workable foundation for tort law. Indeed, so great are the similarities between them that the vast majority of cases come out the same way under either rule. It is only when these tort rules are contrasted with radical system-wide changes such as no-fault automobile insurance or workers' compensation that major differences emerge. At this point, therefore, it is best to leave the grand question and turn to the more detailed operation of the dominant negligence system.

CHAPTER 3

NEGLIGENCE

Ezra Ripley Thayer, Public Wrong and Private Action
27 Harv. L. Rev. 317, 318 (1914)

In the law of negligence no doctrine is useful or appropriate which cannot be plainly and simply stated, and which, when so stated, does not respond to the test of common sense.

Leon Green, Judge and Jury
185 (1930)

In other words, we may have a process for passing judgment in negligence cases, but practically no "law of negligence" beyond the process itself.

SECTION A.   INTRODUCTION

The inconclusive debate between negligence and strict liability theories, which was the subject of the last chapter, only affirms the critical—many would say dominant—role of negligence in the law of unintentional harms. This chapter explores how negligence principles, both in theory and practice, determine the scope of a defendant's liability for accidental harms. In dealing with these issues, it is important to draw a preliminary distinction between negligence as a form of subpar conduct and negligence as a separate and distinct tort. The former is an element of the tort of negligence, which in its modern elaboration contains four distinct elements: duty, breach, causation, and damage. A plaintiff must meet all four requirements to establish the prima facie case (which, in turn, is subject to the various defenses discussed *infra* in Chapter 4). These four elements are:

First, **duty**: Did the defendant owe the plaintiff a duty to conform his conduct to a standard necessary to avoid an unreasonable risk of harm to others?

Second, **breach**: Did the defendant's conduct, whether by way of act or omission, fall below the applicable standard of care?

Third, **causation**: Was the defendant's failure to meet the applicable standard of care causally connected to the plaintiff's harm? Often this inquiry is divided into two parts: causation in fact and proximate causation.

Fourth, **damages**: Did the plaintiff suffer harm?

This chapter concentrates on the first two elements—whether the defendant breached a duty of care owed to the plaintiff. The issue of causation is addressed in Chapter 5, and that of affirmative duties is the topic of Chapter 6. Damages are discussed in Chapter 9.

The question of negligence spans all of tort law. Its dictates apply not only to ordinary individuals, with the full range of human strengths and frailties, but also to small businesses, large corporations, government entities, unions, and nonprofit associations. This chapter is designed to give some sense of the reach and application of the negligence principle in its various institutional settings. Accordingly, Section B develops the common sense approach to negligence determinations and the efforts to breathe life into the abstract concept of the reasonable person. The key inquiry asks what allowances, if any, the law should make for the weaknesses of those individuals who are not blessed with the knowledge, skill, or ability of that durable but hypothetical construct of negligence—the reasonable person.

Section C traces the evolution of the reasonable person standard by examining the "balancing of interests" needed to determine whether the risks taken by the defendant are justified by the ends sought. The Restatement (Third) of Torts on Liability for Physical and Emotional Harm simply states that "[c]onduct is negligent if its disadvantages outweigh its advantages, while conduct is not negligent if its advantages outweigh its disadvantages." RTT:LPEH §3, comment *e.* This inquiry delves into the uses and limitations of the various economic interpretations of the negligence principle, which are often couched in "risk-benefit" or "cost-benefit" terms. The term "risk" stresses the probability of harm, without regard to its severity. Cost takes into account both the probability of harm and its expected severity. *Id.* Which measure is more accurate from an economic point of view? Often both tests work at too high a level of abstraction, so skillful lawyers typically supplement that basic approach by pointing to some specific "untaken precaution" that, if taken, could have prevented the accident that actually occurred. See Grady, Untaken Precautions, 18 J. Legal Stud. 139 (1989). At trial, the plaintiff tries to show that some inexpensive precaution (such as a railing, a warning, or an inspection) could have prevented some likely serious injury. In contrast, the defendant tries to show that the precaution was excessively costly, redundant, ineffective, or downright dangerous. In hotly contested cases, there is no shortcut for a complete mastery of a case's relevant social and technical facts. Of necessity, skilled negligence lawyers become experts on everything from printing presses to toxic chemicals, from product warnings to complex surgery. Indeed, within law firms, personal injury law is often broken down by subject matter, such as highway accidents, medical malpractice, machine tools, chemicals, athletic injuries, or hunting accidents.

Sometimes, however, the law supplies more concrete guideposts in the featureless landscape created by the concept of an unreasonable risk. Our general analysis of negligence is accordingly supplemented in Section D by looking at the relationship between customary practice relevant to the defendant's actions and negligence determinations. Section D also addresses the central role that professional custom plays in setting the standard of care in medical malpractice cases, introduces the heated debate about the efficacy of the medical malpractice system and various reform proposals, and explores the role and scope of the doctrine of informed consent. Section E extends the inquiry to criminal statutes and examines the role of safety regulations in determining whether the parties acted negligently.

"Why carry malpractice insurance if you don't malpractice once in a while?"

Source: Peter Steiner / The New Yorker Collection / The Cartoon Bank

The last two sections of the chapter deal with how trials are conducted in negligence cases. Section F examines the allocation of responsibility between judge and jury and explores some aspects of the ongoing debate about the efficacy of the civil jury. Section G then examines the principles governing the proof of negligence at trial, especially the doctrine of res ipsa loquitur — "the thing speaks for itself" (but usually not as clearly as we would like).

SECTION B. THE REASONABLE PERSON

Harry Kalven, Jr.

It is sometimes said that the study of negligence is the study of the mistakes a reasonable man might make.

Vaughan v. Menlove
132 Eng. Rep. 490 (C.P. 1837)

[The plaintiff owned two cottages in the County of Salop. The defendant was a neighbor who had placed a haystack, or rick, on his own property, near the plaintiff's two cottages. The rick caught fire, which spread first to the defendant's nearby wood and thatch buildings, and then destroyed the plaintiff's cottages. The plaintiff brought suit, alleging that the defendant negligently constructed and maintained the rick.]

At the trial it appeared that the rick in question had been made by the Defendant near the boundary of his own premises; that the hay was in such a state when put together, as to give rise to discussions on the probability of fire: that though there were conflicting opinions on the subject, yet during a period of five weeks, the Defendant was repeatedly warned of his peril; that his stock was insured; and that upon one occasion, being advised to take the rick down to avoid all danger, he said "he would chance it." He made an aperture or chimney through the rick; but in spite, or perhaps in consequence of this precaution, the rick at length burst into flames from the spontaneous heating of its materials; the flames communicated to the Defendant's barn and stables, and thence to the Plaintiff's cottages, which were entirely destroyed.

PATTESON, J., before whom the cause was tried, told the jury that the question for them to consider, was, whether the fire had been occasioned by gross negligence on the part of the Defendant; adding, that he was bound to proceed with such reasonable caution as a prudent man would have exercised under such circumstances.

A verdict having been found for the Plaintiff, a rule nisi for a new trial was obtained [i.e., defendant appealed], on the ground that the jury should have been directed to consider, not, whether the Defendant had been guilty of gross negligence with reference to the standard of ordinary prudence, a standard too uncertain to afford any criterion; but whether he had acted bona fide to the best of his judgment; if he had, he ought not to be responsible for the misfortune of not possessing the highest order of intelligence. The action under such circumstances, was of the first impression. . . .

TALFOURD SERJT. and WHATELY, shewed cause [for plaintiff].

The pleas having expressly raised issues on the negligence of the Defendant, the learned Judge could not do otherwise than leave that question to the jury. . . . And the action, though new in specie, is founded on a principle fully established, that a man must so use his own property as not to injure that of others. On the same circuit a defendant was sued a few years ago, for burning weeds so near the extremity of his own land as to set fire to and destroy his neighbours' wood. The plaintiff recovered damages, and no motion was made to set aside the verdict. Then, there were no means of estimating the defendant's negligence, except by taking as a standard, the conduct of a man of ordinary prudence: that has been the rule always laid down, and there is no other that would not be open to much greater uncertainties.

R. V. RICHARDS, in support of the rule [for defendant].

First, there was no duty imposed on the Defendant, as there is on carriers or other bailees, under an implied contract, to be responsible for the exercise of any given degree of prudence: the Defendant had a right to place his stack as near to the extremity of his own land as he pleased . . . : under that right, and subject to no contract, he can only be called on to act bona fide to the best of his judgment: if he has done that, it is a contradiction in terms, to inquire whether or not he has been guilty of gross negligence. At all events what would have been gross negligence ought to be estimated by the faculties of the individual, and not by those of other men. The measure of prudence varies so with the varying faculties of men, that it is impossible to say what is gross negligence with reference to the standard of what is called ordinary prudence. . . .

TINDAL, C.J. I agree that this is a case primae impressionis [of first impression]; but I feel no difficulty in applying to it the principles of law as laid down in other cases of a similar kind. Undoubtedly this is not a case of contract, such as a bailment or the like where the bailee is responsible in consequence of the remuneration he is to receive: but there is a rule of law which says you must so enjoy your own property as not to injure that of another; and according to that rule the Defendant is liable for the consequence of his own neglect: and though the Defendant did not himself light the fire, yet mediately, he is as much the cause of it as if he had himself put a candle to the rick; for it is well known that hay will ferment and take fire if it be not carefully stacked. It has been decided that if an occupier burns weeds so near the boundary of his own land that damage ensues to the property of his neighbour, he is liable to an action for the amount of injury done, unless the accident were occasioned by a sudden blast which he could not foresee: Tuberville v. Stamp (1 Salk. 13 [1697]). But put the case of a chemist making experiments with ingredients, singly innocent, but when combined, liable to ignite if he leaves them together, and injury is thereby occasioned to the property of his neighbour, can any one doubt that an action on the case would lie?

Exhibit 3.1   Sir Nicholas Conyngham Tindal

Sir Nicholas Conyngham Tindal (1776-1846) served as Chief Justice of Common Pleas from 1829 until his death, and won great respect from the British public. An obituary of Chief Justice Tindal reported: "As to the merits of Chief Justice Tindal, the bar may be divided, but the public are unanimous. They looked at his summings up as among the most masterly exhibitions of judicial sagacity, and they regarded his calm, thoughtful, and tranquil inflexibility as the impersonation of British justice." Obituary—Lord Chief Justice Tindal, 26 Gentleman's Mag. 199, 200 (1846).

Bio source: Obituary—Lord Chief Justice Tindal, 26 Gentleman's Mag. 199, 200 (1846)
Image source: Thomas Philips / National Portrait Gallery, London

It is contended, however, that the learned Judge was wrong in leaving this to the jury as a case of gross negligence, and that the question of negligence was so mixed up with reference to what would be the conduct of a man of ordinary prudence that the jury might have thought the latter the rule by which they were to decide; that such a rule would be too uncertain to act upon; and that the question ought to have been whether the Defendant had acted honestly and bona fide to the best of his own judgment. That, however, would leave so vague a line as to afford no rule at all, the degree of judgment belonging to each individual being infinitely various: and though it has been urged that the care which a prudent man would take, is not an intelligible proposition as a rule of law . . . yet such has always been the rule adopted in cases of bailment, as laid down in Coggs v. Bernard (2 Ld. Raym. 909 [1703]). Though in some cases a greater degree of care is exacted than in others, yet in "the second sort of bailment, viz. commodatum or lending gratis, the borrower is bound to the strictest care and diligence to keep the goods so as to restore them back again to the lender; because the bailee has a benefit by the use of them, so as if the bailee be guilty of the least neglect he will be answerable; as if a man should lend another a horse to go westward, or for a month; if the bailee put this horse in his stable, and he were stolen from thence, the bailee shall not be answerable for him: but if he or his servant leave the house or stable doors open, and the thieves take the opportunity of that, and steal the horse, he will be chargeable, because the neglect gave the thieves the occasion to steal the horse." The care taken by a prudent man has always been the rule laid down; and as to the supposed difficulty of applying it, a jury has always been able to say, whether, taking that rule as their guide, there has been negligence on the occasion in question.

Instead, therefore, of saying that the liability for negligence should be co-extensive with the judgment of each individual, which would be as variable as the length of the foot of each individual, we ought rather to adhere to the rule which requires in all cases a regard to caution such as a man of ordinary prudence would observe. That was in substance the criterion presented to the jury in this case, and therefore the present rule must be discharged.

PARK, J. I entirely concur in what has fallen from his lordship. Although the facts in this case are new in specie, they fall within a principle long established, that a man must so use his own property as not to injure that of others. [Park, J., then recited extensively from Tuberville v. Stamp and concluded:]

As to the direction of the learned judge, it was perfectly correct. Under the circumstances of the case it was proper to leave it to the jury whether with reference to the caution which would have been observed by a man of ordinary prudence, the Defendant had not been guilty of gross negligence. After he had been warned repeatedly during the five weeks as to the consequences likely to happen, there is no colour for altering the verdict, unless it were to increase the damages.

VAUGHAN, J. The principle on which this action proceeds, is by no means new. It has been urged that the Defendant in such a case takes no duty on himself; but I do not agree in that position: every one takes upon himself the duty of so dealing with his own property as not to injure the property of others. It was, if any thing, too favourable to the Defendant to leave it to the jury whether he had been guilty of gross negligence; for when the Defendant upon being warned as to the consequences likely to ensue from the condition of the rick, said, "he would chance it," it was manifest he adverted to his interest in the insurance office. The conduct of a prudent man has always been the criterion for the jury in such cases: but it is by no means confined to them. . . . Here, there was not a single witness whose testimony did not go to establish gross negligence in the Defendant. He had repeated warnings of what was likely to occur, and the whole calamity was occasioned by his procrastination.

Rule discharged. [Appeal denied.]

NOTES

1. Standard of ordinary prudence.   Vaughan v. Menlove speaks not only of the defendant's duty to exercise "ordinary care," but also his "gross negligence" in conducting his own affairs. Does the distinction between ordinary and gross negligence matter? See, in this regard, the famous bon mot of Baron Rolfe, who described gross negligence as the same thing as ordinary negligence "with the addition of a vituperative epithet." Wilson v. Brett, 152 Eng. Rep. 737 (Ex. 1843). Most of the 48 states that have pattern jury instructions use the concept of the objective "reasonable person," or a variant of the same, to define the duty of ordinary care. Kelley & Wendt, What Judges Tell Juries About Negligence: A Review of Pattern Jury Instructions, 77 Chi.-Kent L. Rev. 587, 594-597 (2002). The common feature of the variously worded pattern instructions "is the device of defining the negligence standard by reference to the conduct of a hypothesized person"—a construct traced to *Vaughan.*

2. Conscience of the community.   Abraham, The Trouble with Negligence, 54 Vand. L. Rev. 1187, 1196 (2001), disputes the conventional view that in simple negligence cases, such as slip-and-fall or motor vehicle accidents, the finder of fact, given his familiarity with the activity, can simply invoke his conscience and thereby accurately enforce a community norm of appropriate behavior. According to Professor Abraham, *Vaughan*, the classic paradigmatic example, defies this notion:

> The principal issue was whether an aperture should or should not have been built in the stack. One would think that if there were such a thing as a community norm regarding haystack construction, it would encompass whether and when to build apertures. But right at this seminal moment in the development of negligence law, the report of the decision in *Vaughan*—apparently recounting the evidence—makes a deeply revealing statement. The defendant ". . . made an aperture or chimney through the rick; but in spite, or perhaps in consequence of this precaution, the rick at length burst into flames. . . ." Just as in my hypothetical slip-and-fall case, the community norm in *Vaughan*, if there was one, did not come all the way down to the ground. The conscience of the community in *Vaughan* apparently was divided about apertures.

3. The standard of care for bailments.   Epstein, The Many Faces of Fault in Contract Law: Or How to Do Economics Right, Without Really Trying, 107 Mich. L. Rev. 1461, 1464 (2009), notes the irony that

> Vaughan v. Menlove is generally credited with introducing the objective standard of care in negligence cases. Yet most suggestively, the defendant in *Vaughan* insisted that the appropriate rules for liability should be drawn from the law of bailments—cases where one party delivers a chattel with a promise for its return at some future date. The unavoidable element of divided control in bailment cases makes the simple boundary-crossing rules used in boundary disputes and highway accidents a poor guide for the ultimate decision.

In the leading case of Coggs v. Bernard, 92 Eng. Rep. 107 (Q.B. 1704), Holt, C.J., explicitly adopted the six types of bailments (i.e., consensual arrangements under which goods are delivered to another with the intention that they be redelivered at some future time) in Roman law, each with its distinct standard of care.

He categorized them as: (1) gratuitous bailment for safekeeping (depositum); (2) bailment for the bailee's use (commodatum); (3) a simple pawn (vadium); (4) bailment for hire (locatio rei); (5) bailment whereby the bailee agrees for a fee to operate or manage the thing bailed (locatio operis faciendi); and (6) bailment of a thing to be managed (not merely stored) by the bailee without compensation (mandatum). The underlying principle ties the bailee's standard of care to the benefit that he derives from the bailment. He is held liable for the "slightest negligence" where the loan is for his own benefit or use, but for only gross neglect when he undertakes safekeeping for the bailor. If both parties benefit, the usual standard is that of ordinary care. In all cases it is, of course, possible to vary the standard of care by private agreement. How successful is defendant's implicit argument that the law of bailment authorizes the use of a good-faith standard in disputes between neighbors? If both the good-faith and reasonable care standards are used consensually, how can either be too uncertain to be serviceable? Which standard should be used when?

Oliver Wendell Holmes, The Common Law
107-109 (1881)

Supposing it now to be conceded that the general notion upon which liability to an action is founded is fault or blameworthiness in some sense, the question arises, whether it is so in the sense of personal moral shortcoming, . . . Suppose that a defendant were allowed to testify that, before acting, he considered carefully what would be the conduct of a prudent man under the circumstances, and, having formed the best judgment he could, acted accordingly. If the story was believed, it would be conclusive against the defendant's negligence judged by a moral standard which would take his personal characteristics into account. But supposing any such evidence to have got before the jury, it is very clear that the court would say, Gentlemen, the question is not whether the defendant thought his conduct was that of a prudent man, but whether you think it was.

Exhibit 3.2   Oliver Wendell Holmes, Jr.

Oliver Wendell Holmes, Jr. (1841-1935) was a lawyer, scholar, and judge. Before attending Harvard Law School, he fought in the Civil War. He served as a Justice of the United States Supreme Court from 1902 to 1932, and for 20 years before that, sat on the Massachusetts Supreme Judicial Court. The Common Law, one of his most enduring works, resulted from a series of lectures delivered at Boston's Lowell Institute in 1880 and 1881, in which he declared, "The life of the law has not been logic; it has been experience."

Bio source: Edmund Fuller, Oliver Wendell Holmes, Jr.: The Great Dissenter, Encyclopaedia Britannica (2014)
Image source: Library of Congress

Some middle point must be found between the horns of this dilemma.

The standards of the law are standards of general application. The law takes no account of the infinite varieties of temperament, intellect, and education which make the internal character of a given act so different in different men. It does not attempt to see men as God sees them, for more than one sufficient reason. In the first place, the impossibility of nicely measuring a man's powers and limitations is far clearer than that of ascertaining his knowledge of law, which has been thought to account for what is called the presumption that every man knows the law. But a more satisfactory explanation is, that, when men live in society, a certain average of conduct, a sacrifice of individual peculiarities going beyond a certain point, is necessary to the general welfare. If, for instance, a man is born hasty and awkward, is always having accidents and hurting himself or his neighbors, no doubt his congenital defects will be allowed for in the courts of Heaven, but his slips are no less troublesome to his neighbors than if they sprang from guilty neglect. His neighbors accordingly require him, at his proper peril, to come up to their standard, and the courts which they establish decline to take his personal equation into account.

The rule that the law does, in general, determine liability by blameworthiness, is subject to the limitation that minute differences of character are not allowed for. The law considers, in other words, what would be blameworthy in the average man, the man of ordinary intelligence and prudence, and determines liability by that. If we fall below the level in those gifts, it is our misfortune so much as that we must have at our peril, for the reasons just given. But he who is intelligent and prudent does not act at his peril, in theory of law. On the contrary, it is only when he fails to exercise the foresight of which he is capable, or exercises it with evil intent, that he is answerable for the consequences.

There are exceptions to the principle that every man is presumed to possess ordinary capacity to avoid harm to his neighbors, which illustrate the rule, and also the moral basis of liability in general. When a man has a distinct defect of such a nature that all can recognize it as making certain precautions impossible, he will not be held answerable for not taking them. A blind man is not required to see at his peril; and although he is, no doubt, bound to consider his infirmity in regulating his actions, yet if he properly finds himself in a certain situation, the neglect of precautions requiring eyesight would not prevent his recovering for an injury to himself, and, it may be presumed, would not make him liable for injuring another. So it is held that, in cases where he is the plaintiff, an infant of very tender years is only bound to take the precautions of which an infant is capable; the same principle may be cautiously applied where he is defendant. Insanity is a more difficult matter to deal with, and no general rule can be laid down about it. There is no doubt that in many cases a man may be insane, and yet perfectly capable of taking the precautions, and of being influenced by the motives, which the circumstances demand. But if insanity of a pronounced type exists, manifestly incapacitating the sufferer from complying with the rule which he has broken, good sense would require it to be admitted as an excuse.

Roberts v. Ring
173 N.W. 437 (Minn. 1919)

HALLAM, J. Plaintiff brings this action on behalf of his minor son, John B. Roberts, seven years old, to recover damages for injury from collision with defendant's automobile. The jury found for defendant. Plaintiff appeals. Plaintiff assigns as error certain portions of the charge. Defendant contends that the charge was without error and further contends that as a matter of law, defendant was without negligence and that the boy was negligent.

1. Defendant was driving south on a much traveled street in Owatonna. He was seventy-seven years old. His sight and hearing were defective. A buggy was approaching him from the south. There were other conveyances on the street. The travel was practically blocked. The boy ran from behind the buggy across the street to the west and in front of defendant's automobile. There is evidence that he had been riding on the rear of the buggy. He himself testified that he was crossing the street. As he passed in front of defendant's automobile he was struck and injured.

The question of defendant's negligence was a proper one to be submitted to the jury. Defendant was driving from four to five miles an hour, not a negligent rate of speed. If he was negligent, it was in failing to keep a proper lookout and in failing to promptly stop his car. He testified that he saw the boy when he was four or five feet from the automobile. It is a matter of common knowledge that an automobile traveling four or five miles an hour can be stopped within a very few feet, yet defendant knocked the boy down and his car passed clear over him. If defendant saw the boy, as he now claims, he was not alert in stopping his car. If he did not see him as he is alleged to have stated to others he was not keeping a sharp lookout in this crowded street. We are of the opinion that the evidence was such as to raise an issue of fact as to his negligence.

2. The question of the boy's negligence was likewise for the jury. Had a mature man acted as did this boy he might have been chargeable with negligence as a matter of law. But a boy of seven is not held to the same standard of care in self-protection. In considering his contributory negligence the standard is the degree of care commonly exercised by the ordinary boy of his age and maturity. It would be different if he had caused injury to another. In such a case he could not take advantage of his age or infirmities.

As to the negligence of defendant the court charged:

In determining whether the defendant was guilty of negligence you may take into consideration . . . the age of the defendant . . . and whether or not the defendant had any physical infirmities.

. . . As above indicated, defendant's infirmities did not tend to relieve him from the charge of negligence. On the contrary they weighed against him. Such infirmities, to the extent that they were proper to be considered at all, presented only a reason why defendant should refrain from operating an automobile on a crowded street where care was required to avoid injuring other travelers. When one, by his acts or omissions causes injury to others, his negligence is to be judged by the standard of care usually exercised by the ordinarily prudent normal man.

Order reversed.

NOTES

1. Old age. The Third Restatement follows *Roberts* by refusing to take old age, as such, into account, although it takes into account such infirmities associated with old age by using the standard of a reasonably careful person with the same physical condition. RTT:LPEH §11, comment *c*. In Estate of Burgess v. Peterson, 537 N.W.2d 115, 119 (Wis. Ct. App. 1995), Cane, J., explained the logic behind this rule: "[W]hile it is impossible to quantify or measure the degree to which age slows thought processes, physical infirmities (e.g., arthritis, osteoporosis, etc.) have physical manifestations that can be objectively observed and measured."

2. Beginners and experts. The question of variable standards of care also arises with different levels of performance that are expected from beginners and experts in certain endeavors. The use of a lower standard of care for beginners encourages them to undertake activities that they might not otherwise attempt, which is often a socially desirable outcome; but it also exacts a subsidy from the people they may hurt in the process, and not from the public at large. To avoid that risk, the general rule holds beginners to the standard of care expected of those who are reasonably skilled and practiced in the art. See, for example, Stevens v. Veenstra, 573 N.W.2d 341 (Mich. App. 1997) ("[S]ome activities are so dangerous that the risk must be borne by the beginner rather than the innocent victims, and lack of competence is no excuse."). Under the Third Restatement, below-average skills and judgment are "generally ignored" in order to discourage excessive risk taking by those with below-average skills, encourage the acquisition of a skill, prevent the multiplication of separate standards, and forestall the risk of fraud. RTT:LPEH §12, comment *b*. One critical exception covers cases in which the plaintiff has assumed the risk that the defendant will exercise a lower standard of care, as happens when an experienced driver agrees to teach a novice how to drive. Holland v. Pitocchelli, 13 N.E.2d 390 (Mass. 1938). The inexperienced driver gets the benefit of the lower standard against her driving instructor (with whom she has a special relationship), but not against an injured pedestrian (a stranger) who did not assume the risk. *Id.*

The converse problem arises when a defendant has greater skills than most people in a particular activity. The Second Restatement provides that a defendant who provides services is "required to exercise the skill and knowledge normally possessed by members of that profession or trade in good standing in similar communities," but that standard is subject to an important caveat: "unless he represents that he has greater or less skill" than the average. RST §299A, comment *d*. Second Restatement section 289 also provides that "[t]he actor is required to recognize that his conduct involves a risk of causing an invasion of another's interest if a reasonable man would do so while exercising . . . (b) such superior attention, perception, memory, knowledge, intelligence, and judgment as the actor himself has."

The Third Restatement similarly holds that the case for applying a higher standard is strongest when the two parties have agreed to it, or when the defendant is engaged in dangerous activities. RTT:LPEH §12. But the Third Restatement does not issue any categorical rule, noting that "skills or knowledge are circumstances to be taken into account in determining whether the actor has behaved as a reasonably careful person." Expert testimony may be necessary to determine the standard of care when specialized knowledge, skill, or training is involved. The Third Restatement also expresses some doubt as to whether the skilled skier or skilled driver should be held to a higher standard if sued for a skiing accident or a highway collision, respectively. *Id.*, comment *a.*

In Dakter v. Cavallino, 866 N.W.2d 656, 663, 675 (Wis. 2015), the plaintiff automobile driver, heading north, turned left (west) at an intersection when the defendant, the professional driver of an empty 65-foot-long semi tractor-trailer, heading south, came through the intersection behind another car that was either waiting or had just turned left (east), leaving the plaintiff seriously injured in the ensuing collision. The jury instruction held the defendant "to use the degree of care, skill, and judgment which reasonable semi truck drivers would exercise in the same or similar circumstances, having due regard for the state of learning, education, experience, and knowledge possessed by semi truck drivers holding Commercial Driver's Licenses." The plaintiff's expert testified that the defendant should have reduced speed by a third on a wet and slick road, which he did not do. Abrahamson, C.J., held that it was proper for the jury to take into account both "the superior knowledge rule, which requires an actor with special knowledge or skill to act commensurate with that knowledge or skill, and the profession or trade principle, which requires an actor engaged in a profession or trade to act as a reasonable member of such profession or trade would act under the same or similar circumstances," following both Restatements.

Daniels v. Evans
224 A.2d 63 (N.H. 1966)

[Plaintiff's decedent, a 19-year-old youth, was killed when his motorcycle collided with defendant's automobile. A trial by jury resulted in a verdict for plaintiff, and the only alleged error argued on appeal was the trial court's charge pertaining to the standard of care required of the decedent.]

LAMPRON, J. As to the standard of care to be applied to the conduct of the decedent Robert E. Daniels, 19 years of age, the Trial Court charged the jury in part as follows:

"Now, he is considered a minor, being under the age of twenty-one, and a minor child must exercise the care of the average child of his or her age, experience and stage of mental development. In other words, he is not held to the same degree of care as an adult."

Concededly these instructions substantially reflect the rule by which the care of a minor has been judged heretofore in the courts of our State. Charbonneau v. MacRury[, 153 A. 457 (N.H. 1931)]. However an examination of the cases will reveal that in most the minors therein were engaged in activities appropriate to their age, experience and wisdom. These included being a pedestrian, riding a bicycle, riding a horse, [and] coasting.

We agree that minors are entitled to be judged by standards commensurate with their age, experience, and wisdom when engaged in activities appropriate to their age, experience, and wisdom. Hence when children are walking, running, playing with toys, throwing balls, operating bicycles, sliding or engaged in other childhood activities their conduct should be judged by the rule of what is reasonable conduct under the circumstances among which are the age, experience, and stage of mental development of the minor involved.

However, the question is raised by the defendant in this case whether the standard of care applied to minors in such cases should prevail when the minor is engaged in activities normally undertaken by adults. In other words, when a minor undertakes an adult activity which can result in grave danger to others and to the minor himself if the care used in the course of the activity drops below that care which the reasonable and prudent adult would use, the defendant maintains that the minor's conduct in that instance should meet the same standards as that of an adult.

Many recent cases have held that "when a minor assumes responsibility for the operation of so potentially dangerous an instrument as an automobile, he should . . . assume responsibility for its careful and safe operation in the light of adult standards." 2 Idaho L. Rev., 103, 111 (1965); Dellwo v. Pearson, 107 N.W.2d 859 (Minn. 1961). The rule has been recognized in Restatement (Second), Torts, §283A, comment *c*. . . . In an annotation in 97 A.L.R.2d 872 at page 875 it is said that recent decisions "hold that when a minor engages in such activities as the operation of an automobile or similar power driven device, he forfeits his rights to have the reasonableness of his conduct measured by a standard commensurate with his age and is thenceforth held to the same standard as all other persons."

One of the reasons for such a rule has been stated thusly in Dellwo v. Pearson, supra: "To give legal sanction to the operation of automobiles by teen-agers with less than ordinary care for the safety of others is impractical today, to say the least. We may take judicial notice of the hazards of automobile traffic, the frequency of accidents, the often catastrophic results of accidents, and the fact that immature individuals are no less prone to accidents than adults. . . . [I]t would be unfair to the public to permit a minor in the operation of a motor vehicle to observe any other standards of care and conduct than those expected of all others. A person observing children at play . . . may anticipate conduct that does not reach an adult standard of care or prudence. However, one cannot know whether the operator of an approaching automobile . . . is a minor or an adult, and usually cannot protect himself against youthful imprudence even if warned." . . .

RSA 262-A:2 which establishes rules of the road for the operation of motor vehicles on our highways reads as follows: "Required Obedience to Traffic Laws. It is unlawful and . . . a misdemeanor for *any person* to do any act forbidden or fail to perform any act required in this chapter." (Emphasis supplied.) This is some indication of an intent on the part of our Legislature that all drivers must, and have the right to expect that others using the highways, regardless of their age and experience, will, obey the traffic laws and thus exercise the adult standard of ordinary care. . . .

The rule charged by the Trial Court pertaining to the standard of care to be applied by the jury to the conduct of the minor plaintiff Robert E. Daniels in the operation of the motorcycle was proper in "the bygone days" when children were using relatively innocent contrivances. However in the circumstances of today's modern life, where vehicles moved by powerful motors are readily available and used by many minors, we question the propriety of a rule which would allow such vehicles to be operated to the hazard of the public, and to the driver himself, with less than the degree of care required of an adult.

We are of the opinion that to apply to minors a more lenient standard in the operation of motor vehicles, whether an automobile or a motorcycle, than that applied to adults is unrealistic, contrary to the expressed legislative policy, and inimical to public safety. Furthermore when a minor is operating a motor vehicle there is no reason for making a distinction based on whether he is charged with primary negligence, contributory negligence, or a causal violation of a statute and we so hold.

We hold therefore that a minor operating a motor vehicle, whether an automobile or a motorcycle, must be judged by the same standard of care as an adult and the defendant's objection to the Trial Court's charge applying a different standard to the conduct of plaintiff's intestate was valid. . . .

Exception sustained.

NOTES

1. Infancy and childhood.   All U.S. jurisdictions take account of childhood in determinations of negligence. The Third Restatement adheres to the general rule, holding a child to the standard of "a reasonably careful person of the same age, intelligence, and experience." RTT:LPEH §10(a). What explains the differential standard applied to children but not the elderly?

In addition to the exception for dangerous, adult-like activities, the Third Restatement provides that a child under five years of age is incapable of negligence. RTT:LPEH §10(b). Does this confer additional duties on the child's guardian?

2. Adult and child activities.   In Charbonneau v. MacRury, 153 A. 457, 462-463 (N.H. 1931), overruled by Daniels v. Evans, the court justified its use of a variable standard of care for infants as follows:

> Unless infants are to be denied the environment and association of their elders until they have acquired maturity, there must be a living relationship between them on terms which permit the child to act as a child in his stage of development. As well expect a boy to learn to swim without experience in the water as to expect him to learn to function as an adult without contact with his superiors. For the law to hold children to the exercise of the care of adults "would be to shut its eyes, ostrich-like to the facts of life and to burden unduly the child's growth to majority." [Shulman, The Standard of Care Required of Children, 37 Yale L.J. 618 (1928)]. During the period of his development he must participate in human activities on some basis of reason. Reason requires that indulgence be shown him

commensurate with his want of development as indicated by his age and experience. Id. 621. Though strictly speaking it is the resultant qualities reasonably attributable to these factors that measure his capacity, it is sufficient, as a practical matter, to speak of age and experience as inclusive of these qualities. . . .

In Hudson-Connor v. Putney, 86 P.3d 106, 111 (Or. App. 2004), Brewer, J., held first that it was not an adult activity for a 14-year-old child to entrust a golf cart to an 11-year-old plaintiff, and further, that driving a golf cart on private property was not an adult activity:

> To obtain a license to operate an automobile on the highways, a driver must demonstrate mastery of those skills by passing a knowledge test, a driving skills test, and, if the driver is under the age of 18, a safe driving practices test. No such license is required to operate a motorized golf cart on premises that are not open to the public. Significantly, there is no evidence in the record that the operation of golf carts on private premises and automobiles on premises open to the public requires similar driving skills beyond the most rudimentary level. In short, on the factual record before us, we conclude that the operation of a motorized golf cart on private premises does not require adult qualifications.

In Dellwo v. Pearson, 107 N.W.2d 859 (Minn. 1961), cited in *Daniels*, a 12-year-old defendant was held to the adult standard of care in the operation of a speed boat, even though there was apparently no licensing statute for such boats. In Harrelson v. Whitehead, 365 S.W.2d 868 (Ark. 1963), a 15-year-old plaintiff operating a motorcycle was held to the adult standard of care on the issue of contributory negligence. Jackson v. McCuiston, 448 S.W.2d 33 (Ark. 1969), held that a 13-year-old farm boy should be judged by the adult standard of care in operating a tractor-propelled stalk cutter, a large piece of machinery with a dangerous cutting blade.

The use of firearms presents a particularly vexing application. In Purtle v. Shelton, 474 S.W.2d 123 (Ark. 1971), the Arkansas Supreme Court cut back on *Jackson,* refusing to hold a 17-year-old boy to the adult standard of care in using dangerous firearms. It applied a lower standard for minors because deer hunting was not exclusively an adult activity. One dissenting justice protested: "Because a bullet fired from the gun by a minor is just as deadly as a bullet fired by an adult, I'm at a loss to understand why one with 'buck fever' because of his minority is entitled to exercise any less care than any one else deer hunting. One killed by a bullet so fired would be just as dead in one instance as the other and without any more warning." The Third Restatement holds that "[h]andling firearms is best regarded as a dangerous adult activity. The dangers involved in firearm use are obvious and dramatic." RTT:LPEH §10, comment *f.* But most courts refuse to apply an adult standard of care when a juvenile injures another with a firearm. Is hunting more or less of an inherently adult activity than driving? More or less of a distinctly dangerous activity? Should regional differences be relevant? See Thomas v. Inman, 578 P.2d 399, 403 (Or. 1978) ("In the rural districts of this state, children, or those who have not been licensed to drive automobiles, have always used guns both for target practice and hunting under differing circumstances.").

3. Parental supervision of children's activities.   In Becker v. Litenberger, 989 N.Y.S.2d 823, 825 (N.Y. Sup. Ct. 2014), the plaintiff, a 15-year-old girl, was warming up before her lacrosse team practice when she was struck in the mouth by the nine-year-old son of the assistant coach, himself an experienced lacrosse player, causing the loss of several teeth. The court did not ask whether the activity in question was adult or infant, but followed the New York rule that provides that a "parent owes a duty to protect third parties from harm that is clearly foreseeable from the child's improvident use or operation of a dangerous instrument, where such use is found to be subject to the parent's control," and held as a matter of law that the stick, like a baseball bat, was not a dangerous instrument in light of the "age, maturity, intelligence, and physical characteristics" of the boy. Should the case be resolved on the view that recovery for athletic injuries is governed by a standard of recklessness, wholly without regard to age? What result if the boy had thrown a ball that had hit and injured a bystander?

4. Reasonable plaintiff versus reasonable defendant.   In Daniels v. Evans, the court held both child plaintiffs and child defendants to the same standard of care in highway accidents, a view that is widely followed today. See RTT:LPEH §10, comment *e*. While the case law has moved toward the unitary standard of care for all youthful drivers, the case for a general dual standard was advanced in James, The Qualities of the Reasonable Man in Negligence Cases, 16 Mo. L. Rev. 1, 1-2 (1951):

> By and large the law has chosen external, objective standards of conduct. The reasonably prudent man is, to be sure, endowed with some of the qualities of the person whose conduct is being judged, especially where the latter has greater knowledge, skill, or the like, than people generally. But many of the actor's shortcomings such as awkwardness, faulty perception, or poor judgment, are not taken into account if they fall below the general level of the community. This means that individuals are often held guilty of legal fault for failing to live up to a standard which as a matter of fact they cannot meet. Such a result shocks people who believe in refining the fault principle so as to make legal liability correspond more closely to personal moral shortcoming. There has, therefore, been some pressure towards the adoption of a more subjective test. But if the standard of conduct is relaxed for *defendants* who cannot meet a normal standard, then the burden of accident loss resulting from the extra hazards created by society's most dangerous groups (e.g. the young, the novice, the accident prone) will be thrown on the innocent victims of substandard behavior. Such a conclusion shocks people who believe that the compensation of accident victims is a more important objective of modern tort law than a further refinement of the tort principle, and that compensation should prevail when the two objectives conflict. The application of a relaxed subjective standard to the issue of *plaintiff's* contributory negligence, however, involves no such conflict. On this issue the forces of the two objectives combine to demand a subjective test: the refinement of the fault principle furthers the compensation of accident victims by cutting down a defense that would stand in its way. For this reason the writer has elsewhere developed the thesis that there should be an explicit double standard of conduct, namely, an external standard for a defendant's negligence, and a (relaxed) subjective standard for contributory negligence. Even

Section B. The Reasonable Person

if this thesis is rejected, the same result probably prevails anyhow, because the application of the legal standard is largely left to the jury, and juries, by and large, tend to resolve doubts on both issues in favor of plaintiffs.

Using different standards for negligence and contributory negligence leaves the outcome unclear when both parties are children and both are injured. Should the result depend on whether either or both are insured? Note that the double standard necessarily increases the administrative costs of both settlement and litigation.

Breunig v. American Family Insurance Co.
173 N.W.2d 619 (Wis. 1970)

[Plaintiff brought this action for personal injuries sustained when his car was struck by a car driven by Erma Veith, an insured of the defendant. The accident occurred when Mrs. Veith's car veered across the center of the road into the lane in which plaintiff was traveling. Defendant argued that Mrs. Veith "was not negligent because just prior to the collision she suddenly and without warning was seized with a mental aberration or delusion which rendered her unable to operate the automobile with her conscious mind." The jury returned a verdict finding her causally negligent on the theory she "had knowledge or forewarning of her mental delusions or disability." From the award of $7,000 damages, the defendant insurance company—which under Wisconsin law could be directly sued for the torts of its insured—appeals.]

HALLOWS, C.J. There is no question that Erma Veith was subject at the time of the accident to an insane delusion which directly affected her ability to operate her car in an ordinarily prudent manner and caused the accident. The specific question considered by the jury under the negligence inquiry was whether she had such foreknowledge of her susceptibility to such a mental aberration, delusion or hallucination as to make her negligent in driving a car at all under such conditions.

. . . The evidence established that Mrs. Veith, while returning home after taking her husband to work, saw a white light on the back of a car ahead of her. She followed this light for three or four blocks. Mrs. Veith did not remember anything else except landing in a field, lying in the side of the road and people talking. She recalled awaking in the hospital.

The psychiatrist testified Mrs. Veith told him she was driving on a road when she believed that God was taking ahold of the steering wheel and was directing her car. She saw the truck coming and stepped on the gas in order to become airborne because she knew she could fly because Batman does it. To her surprise she was not airborne before striking the truck but after the impact she was flying. . . .

The insurance company argues Erma Veith was not negligent as a matter of law because there is no evidence upon which the jury could find that she had knowledge or warning or should have reasonably foreseen that she might be subject to a mental delusion which would suddenly cause her to lose control of the car. Plaintiff argues there was such evidence of forewarning and also suggests Erma Veith should be liable because insanity should not be a defense in negligence cases.

The case was tried on the theory that some forms of insanity are a defense to and preclude liability for negligence under the doctrine of Theisen v. Milwaukee Automobile Mut. Ins. Co.[, 19 N.W.2d 393 (Wis. 1963)]. We agree. Not all types of insanity vitiate responsibility for a negligent tort. The question of liability in every case must depend upon the kind and nature of the insanity. The effect of the mental illness or mental hallucinations or disorder must be such as to affect the person's ability to understand and appreciate the duty which rests upon him to drive his car with ordinary care, or if the insanity does not affect such understanding and appreciation, it must affect his ability to control his car in an ordinarily prudent manner. And in addition, there must be an absence of notice or forewarning to the person that he may be suddenly subject to such a type of insanity or mental illness.

In *Theisen* we recognized one was not negligent if he was unable to conform his conduct through no fault of his own but held a sleeping driver negligent as a matter of law because one is always given conscious warnings of drowsiness and if a person does not heed such warnings and continues to drive his car, he is negligent for continuing to drive under such conditions. But we distinguished those exceptional cases of loss of consciousness resulting from injury inflicted by an outside force, or fainting, or heart attack, or epileptic seizure, or other illness which suddenly incapacitates the driver of an automobile when the occurrence of such disability is not attended with sufficient warning or should not have been reasonably foreseen. . . .

There are authorities which generally hold insanity is not a defense in tort cases except for intentional torts. Restatement, 2 Torts, 2d, p. 16, sec. 283 B, and appendix (1966) and cases cited therein. These cases rest on the historical view of strict liability without regard to the fault of the individual. Prosser, in his Law of Torts (3d ed.), p. 1028, states this view is a historical survival which originated in the dictum in Weaver v. Ward (1616), Hob. 134, 80 English Reports 284, when the action of trespass still rested upon strict liability. He points out that when the modern law developed to the point of holding the defendant liable for negligence, the dictum was repeated in some cases.

The policy basis of holding a permanently insane person liable for his tort is: (1) Where one of two innocent persons must suffer a loss it should be borne by the one who occasioned it; (2) to induce those interested in the estate of the insane person (if he has one) to restrain and control him and; (3) the fear an insanity defense would lead to false claims of insanity to avoid liability. . . .

We think the statement that insanity is no defense is too broad when it is applied to a negligence case where the driver is suddenly overcome without forewarning by a mental disability or disorder which incapacitates him from conforming his conduct to the standards of a reasonable man under like circumstances. These are rare cases indeed, but their rarity is no reason for overlooking their existence and the justification which is the basis of the whole doctrine of liability for negligence, i.e., that it is unjust to hold a man responsible for his conduct which he is incapable of avoiding and which incapability was unknown to him prior to the accident.

We need not reach the question of contributory negligence of an insane person or the question of comparative negligence as those problems are not now presented. All we hold is that a sudden mental incapacity equivalent in its effect to such physical causes as a sudden heart attack, epileptic seizure, stroke, or fainting should be treated alike and not under the general rule of insanity. . . .

The insurance company argues that since the psychiatrist was the only expert witness who testified concerning the mental disability of Mrs. Veith and the lack of forewarning that as a matter of law there was no forewarning and she could not be held negligent and the trial court should have so held. While there was testimony of friends indicating she was normal for some months prior to the accident, the psychiatrist testified the origin of her mental illness appeared in August, 1965, prior to the accident. In that month Mrs. Veith visited the Necedah Shrine where she was told the Blessed Virgin had sent her to the shrine. She was told to pray for survival. Since that time she felt it had been revealed to her the end of the world was coming and that she was picked by God to survive. Later she had visions of God judging people and sentencing them to Heaven or Hell; she thought Batman was good and was trying to help save the world and her husband was possessed of the devil. Mrs. Veith told her daughter about her visions.

The question is whether she had warning or knowledge which would reasonably lead her to believe that hallucinations would occur and be such as to affect her driving an automobile. Even though the doctor's testimony is uncontradicted, it need not be accepted by the jury. It is an expert's opinion but it is not conclusive. It is for the jury to decide whether the facts underpinning an expert opinion are true. . . . The jury could find that a woman, who believed she had a special relationship to God and was the chosen one to survive the end of the world, could believe that God would take over the direction of her life to the extent of driving her car. Since these mental aberrations were not constant, the jury could infer she had knowledge of her condition and the likelihood of a hallucination just as one who has knowledge of a heart condition knows the possibility of an attack. While the evidence may not be strong upon which to base an inference, especially in view of the fact that two jurors dissented on this verdict and expressly stated they could find no evidence of forewarning, nevertheless, the evidence to sustain the verdict of the jury need not constitute the great weight and clear preponderance.

The insurance company claims the jury was perverse because the verdict is contrary both to the evidence and to the law. We think this argument is without merit.

[Judgment affirmed.]

NOTES

1. Mental and emotional disabilities. According to the Third Restatement, an adult defendant's mental and emotional disability is generally not considered in negligence determinations. RTT:LPEH §11(c). Notwithstanding the fact that "modern society is increasingly inclined to treat physical disabilities and mental disabilities similarly," courts tend to exonerate defendants for injuries resulting from "a sudden incapacitation or loss of consciousness resulting from *physical* injury" (unless the incapacitating event was foreseeable), but hold them liable if the sudden and unforeseen incapacitation is due to *mental* illness. RTT:LPEH §11(b) & comment *e*. Conversely, many courts do consider a *plaintiff's* mental illness in contributory negligence determinations. *Id.*, comment *e*. Is the distinction between physical and mental infirmities justified on administrative grounds? If so, is this rationale undercut by courts' consideration of plaintiff's mental illness?

2. *The* Breunig *approach.*   Several courts deviate from the Third Restatement and continue to recognize the *Breunig* exception for sudden and unforeseeable mental incapacity. In Ramey v. Knorr, 124 P.3d 314, 319-320 (Wash. Ct. App. 2005), the defendant Knorr turned her car around on I-405 and rammed headlong into the plaintiff in an attempt to commit suicide. Her defense of sudden mental incapacity was rejected because the record showed "that in 1994, Knorr had a mental breakdown and was hospitalized for ten days. During that period, Knorr believed the person she worked for was conspiring to steal her and her husband's assets, was going to kill them, and was poisoning her. She also had concerns about her brother being a murderer. . . . Knorr was diagnosed with possible delusional disorder, was put on medication, and was advised to see a psychiatrist. . . . [B]eginning in March 2001, Knorr's delusional thoughts about her brother being a murderer came back. . . . [B]y November 2001, her thoughts escalated and [her husband] tried to get her to agree to go to the hospital. Knorr wanted to wait until after the holidays to go to the hospital and had an appointment scheduled for two days after the accident."

3. *Institutionalized insane persons.*   *Breunig* has been narrowed in custodial settings. In Gould v. American Family Mutual Insurance, 543 N.W.2d 282 (Wis. 1996), the defendant, an institutionalized patient with Alzheimer's disease, injured his paid caregiver. The court refused to apply *Breunig*.

> In sum, we agree with the Goulds that ordinarily a mentally disabled person is responsible for his or her torts. However, we conclude that this rule does not apply in this case because the circumstances totally negate the rationale [in *Breunig*] behind the rule and would place an unreasonable burden on the negligent institutionalized mentally disabled. When a mentally disabled person injures an employed caretaker, the injured party can reasonably foresee the danger and is not "innocent" of the risk involved. By placing a mentally disabled person in an institution or similar restrictive setting, "those interested in the estate" of that person are not likely to be in need of an inducement for greater restraint. It is incredible to assert that a tortfeasor would "simulate or pretend insanity" over a prolonged period of time and even be institutionalized in order to avoid being held liable for damages for some future civil act. Therefore, we hold that a person institutionalized, as here, with a mental disability, and who does not have the capacity to control or appreciate his or her conduct cannot be liable for injuries caused to caretakers who are employed for financial compensation.

Thereafter, in Jankee v. Clark County, 612 N.W.2d 297, 316 (Wis. 2000), the Wisconsin Supreme Court refused to impose liability on an institution that had not restrained the plaintiff, a mental health patient, who had injured himself while trying to escape by jumping through a window that he had pried open in the county psychiatric hospital. Following *Breunig*, Prosser, J., held the insane *plaintiff* to an objective standard of care, again to minimize the level of institutionalization required of insane people. Prosser, J., distinguished *Gould*, noting the perverse incentive on the psychiatric hospital "to intensify security considerations for the mentally disabled, not to protect the disabled but rather to protect themselves from liability," for example, by "restor[ing] bars to all windows in the facility." How do these cases square up with James' rationale (*supra* at 152, Note 4) for a lower standard for contributory negligence? Why not resolve these cases (and *McGuire, supra* at 28) with a no-duty rule, leaving the plaintiff with workers' compensation coverage? See generally Light, Note, Rejecting the Logic of Confinement: Care Relationships and the Mentally Disabled Under Tort Law, 109 Yale L.J. 381 (1999).

Fletcher v. City of Aberdeen
338 P.2d 743 (Wash. 1959)

FOSTER, J. . . . For the purpose of placing electric wires underground, the city dug a ditch in the parking strip adjacent to the sidewalk at the intersection of Broadway and Fourth streets in the city of Aberdeen. Suitable barricades were erected to protect pedestrians from falling into the excavation, but, unfortunately, at the time of the mishap in question, one of the city's employees had removed the barriers to facilitate his work in the excavation. When he went elsewhere to work, he negligently failed to replace the barricades, which left the excavation unprotected. In approaching the intersection, the respondent husband, who had been blind since his eighth year, had his kit of piano-tuning tools in his left hand and his cane in his right. With the cane he was cautiously feeling his way. Because the protective barriers had been removed, the existence of the excavation was unknown to the respondent. By the use of the cane, the barriers would have protected the respondent if they had been in place. The jury was entitled to find that the city was negligent in removing the barriers without providing other warning.

. . . The city's argument is that it had discharged its duty by the erection of barricades. It may be assumed for present purposes, that the barriers originally erected were sufficient to discharge the city's duty of maintaining its streets and adjacent parking strips in a reasonably safe condition for pedestrian use. However, the city's argument completely ignores the undisputed evidence that its workman had removed the barricades and that the accident in question occurred during this interval. The duty of maintaining the sidewalks and adjacent parking strips is a continuing one. . . .

The city assigns error upon the refusal to instruct as requested that "[t]he fact that the plaintiff is blind does not impose on the City any higher degree of care." . . . The supreme court of Oregon recently commented:

"... Public thoroughfares are for the beggar on his crutches as well as the millionaire in his limousine. Neither is it the policy of the law to discriminate against those who suffer physical infirmity. The blind and the halt may use the streets without being guilty of negligence if, in so doing, they exercise that degree of care which an ordinarily prudent person similarly afflicted would exercise under the same circumstances. . . ." Weinstein v. Wheeler, 127 Or. 406 (1928). . . .

The city is charged with knowledge that its streets will be used by those who are physically infirm as well as those in perfect physical condition. . . . The obligations are correlative. The person under a physical disability is obliged to use the care which a reasonable person under the same or similar disability would exercise under the circumstances. The city, on the other hand, is obliged to afford that degree of protection which would bring to the notice of the person so afflicted the danger to be encountered. There was no error, therefore, in the denial of the appellant's requested instruction. . . .

The judgment is, therefore, affirmed.

WEAVER, C.J., and DONWORTH, OTT and HUNTER, JJ., concur.

NOTES

1. Heightened duty of care. A city is obliged to provide use of its streets to the physically disabled. In similar fashion, drivers on the roads should anticipate disabled pedestrians (as well as children) and adjust their level of care accordingly. How do such heightened duties affect the standard of reasonable self-care demanded of these classes of persons?

2. Legal blindness. Under the Third Restatement, "the conduct of an actor with a ['significant and objectively verifiable'] physical disability is negligent only if the conduct does not conform to that of a reasonably careful person with the same disability." RTT:LPEH §11(a) & comment *a*. In Kent v. Crocker, 562 N.W.2d 833 (Neb. 1997), a driver with failing eyesight struck and killed a pedestrian. The court found that the defendant's choice to drive with failing eyesight did not conclusively establish negligence, given that medical evidence suggested her eyesight was sufficient for driving. By contrast, in Poyner v. Loftus, 694 A.2d 69 (D.C. 1997), a legally blind plaintiff, capable of seeing about six to eight feet in front of him, was injured as he fell from an incline leading to the defendant's cleaners about four feet above street level. A bush had been removed from the end of the incline, which the plaintiff would have seen had he not been distracted by a call from down the street. The court affirmed summary judgment for the defendant, noting that the plaintiff's testimony conclusively showed his own negligence when "he turned his head, but continued to walk forward," and reasoning that those with poor eyesight must take keener watchfulness in conducting their own affairs. What result if the plaintiff had been totally blind?

3. Incentive effects. In Arroyo v. United States, 656 F.3d 663, 673-674 (7th Cir. 2011), Posner, C.J., commented on *Fletcher* as follows:

A blind person who, while using the blind person's white cane, is hit at an intersection, when a sighted person would easily have dodged the vehicle hurtling toward him driven by the defendant, is not deemed negligent if he was being as careful as it is reasonable to expect a blind person to be, bearing in mind the cost to the blind of holding them to the same standard of care in crossing streets as sighted persons. Otherwise a blind person would lose the protection of tort law when he ventured to cross a street.

The goal of the average-person rule . . . , in instrumental terms, is to provide an additional incentive, beyond that of moral duty or concern with personal safety, to avoid injuring people (or being injured). A driver who falls below the average of care, and as a result injures someone, is subject to tort liability; it is hoped that the threat will motivate drivers to be careful to avoid injuring others (or themselves).

What result if the blind person crossed against the light?

Denver & Rio Grande R.R. v. Peterson
69 P. 578 (Colo. 1902)

CAMPBELL, C.J. The care required of a warehouseman is the same, whether he be rich or poor. For, if the fact that he is rich requires of him greater care than if he possessed only moderate means or is poor, then, if he were extremely poor, the care required might be such as practically to amount to nothing; and no one would claim that such an uncertain and sliding rule should be the measure of his liability. . . .

NOTE

The relevance of wealth to negligence liability. *Peterson* suggests that the level of care required of a defendant is constant regardless of his wealth. In Should Legal Rules Favor the Poor? Clarifying the Role of Legal Rules and the Income Tax in Redistributing Income, 20 J. Legal Stud. 821, 823 (2000), Kaplow and Shavell defend the proposition that substantive legal rules should not offer special preference to the poor because

> the income tax system possesses several clear advantages over legal rules as a means of redistribution. Notably, the income tax system affects the entire population and, by its nature treats individuals on the basis of their income. By contrast, the influence of legal rules often is confined to the small fraction of individuals who find themselves involved in legal disputes. Also, legal rules often are very imprecise tools for redistribution because there tends to be substantial income variation within groups of plaintiffs and defendants (so that much of the redistribution will be in the wrong direction). Additionally, many legal rules—such as those of contract, corporate, and commercial law—often leave the distribution of income essentially unchanged because price adjustments negate the distributive effects of the legal rules.

Generally, evidence of a defendant's wealth is not admissible at trial in a tort case, nor is it subject to disclosure during discovery. Evidence regarding insurance is likewise not admissible, but is discoverable in most states and under Fed. R. Civ. P. 26(a)(1)(A)(iv) and Fed. R. Evid. 411. The relevance of a defendant's wealth to the determination of punitive damages is the subject of current debate; see *infra* Chapter 9, Section D.

SECTION C. CALCULUS OF RISK

This section turns to the judicial efforts to fashion and apply a standard of reasonable care. Our discussion proceeds on two levels. The first deals with the common sense, intuitive meaning of negligence as it applies to ordinary individuals and corporate or business entities. The second addresses the judicial effort to impart a more precise economic meaning to the term, adopting the language of costs and benefits—the "calculus" of risk. Both approaches have uneasily coexisted throughout the history of the common law.

Blyth v. Birmingham Water Works
156 Eng. Rep. 1047 (Ex. 1856)

[The defendants owned a nonprofit waterworks charged by statute with the laying of water mains and fire plugs in the city streets. The pipes were to be buried 18 inches under ground. The fireplug in the instant case was built "according to the best known system, and the materials of it were at the time of the accident sound and in good order."]

On the 24th of February, a large quantity of water, escaping from the neck of the main, forced its way through the ground into the plaintiff's house. The apparatus had been laid down 25 years, and had worked well during that time. The defendants' engineer stated, that the water might have forced its way through the brickwork round the neck of the main, and that the accident might have been caused by the frost, inasmuch as the expansion of the water would force up the plug out of the neck, and the stopper being encrusted with ice would not suffer the plug to ascend. One of the severest frosts on record set in on the 15th of January, 1855, and continued until after the accident in question. An incrustation of ice and snow had gathered about the stopper, and in the street all round, and also for some inches between the stopper and the plug. The ice had been observed on the surface of the ground for a considerable time before the accident. A short time after the accident, the company's turncock removed the ice from the stopper, took out the plug, and replaced it.

The judge left it to the jury to consider whether the company had used proper care to prevent the accident. He thought that, if the defendants had taken out the ice adhering to the plug, the accident would not have happened, and left it to the jury to say whether they ought to have removed the ice. The jury found a verdict for the plaintiff for the sum claimed. . . .

ALDERSON, B. I am of opinion that there was no evidence to be left to the jury. The case turns upon the question, whether the facts proved shew that the defendants were guilty of negligence. Negligence is the omission to do something which a reasonable man, guided upon those considerations which ordinarily regulate the conduct of human affairs, would do, or doing something which a prudent and reasonable man would not do. The defendants might have been liable for negligence, if, unintentionally, they omitted to do that which a reasonable person would have done, or did that which a person taking reasonable precautions would not have done. A reasonable man would act with reference to the average circumstances of the temperature in ordinary years. The defendants had provided against such frosts as experience would have led men, acting prudently, to provide against; and they are not guilty of negligence, because their precautions proved insufficient against the effects of the extreme severity of the frost of 1855, which penetrated to a greater depth than any which ordinarily occurs south of the polar regions. Such a state of circumstances constitutes a contingency against which no reasonable man can provide. The result was an accident, for which the defendants cannot be held liable.

BRAMWELL, B. The Act of Parliament directed the defendants to lay down pipes, with plugs in them, as safety-valves, to prevent the bursting of the pipes. The plugs were properly made, and of proper material; but there was an accumulation of ice about this plug, which prevented it from acting properly. The defendants were not bound to keep the plugs clear. It appears to me that the plaintiff was under quite as much obligation to remove the ice and snow which had accumulated, as the defendants. However that may be, it appears to me that it would be monstrous to hold the defendants responsible because they did not foresee and prevent an accident, the cause of which was so obscure, that it was not discovered until many months after the accident had happened.

Verdict to be entered for the defendants.

NOTE

The influence of Blyth. Baron Alderson's definition of negligence continues to exert enormous influence on modern tort litigation. Section 2:10 of the New York Pattern Jury Instructions—Civil (West 2009) reads:

> Negligence is lack of ordinary care. It is a failure to use that degree of care that a reasonably prudent person would have used under the same circumstances. Negligence may arise from doing an act that a reasonably prudent person would not have done under the circumstances, or, on the other hand, from failing to do an act that a reasonably prudent person would have done under the same circumstances.

In applying this formula in *Blyth,* should the focus be on the design of the original system or on the removal of the ice after the storm? If the former, is it sufficient if the pipes withstand the frost found in "ordinary years"? If the latter, does the formula indicate who has the duty to remove the ice, and why?

Henry Terry, Negligence
29 Harv. L. Rev. 40, 42-44 (1915)

To make conduct negligent the risk involved in it must be unreasonably great; some injurious consequences of it must be not only possible or in a sense probable, but unreasonably probable. It is quite impossible in the business of life to avoid taking risks of injury to one's self or others, and the law does not forbid doing so; what it requires is that the risk be not unreasonably great. The essence of negligence is unreasonableness; due care is simply reasonable conduct. There is no mathematical rule of percentage of probabilities to be followed here. A risk is not necessarily unreasonable because the harmful consequence is more likely than not to follow the conduct, nor reasonable because the chances are against that. A very large risk may be reasonable in some circumstances, and a small risk unreasonable in other circumstances. When due care consists in taking precautions against harm, only reasonable precautions need be taken, not every conceivable or possible precaution. And precautions need not be taken against every conceivable or foreseeable danger, but only against probable dangers. The books are full of cases where persons have been held not negligent for not guarding against a certain harmful event, on the ground that they need not reasonably have expected it to happen. . . .

The reasonableness of a given risk may depend upon the following five factors:

(1) The magnitude of the risk. A risk is more likely to be unreasonable the greater it is.

(2) The value or importance of that which is exposed to the risk, which is the object that the law desires to protect, and may be called the principal object. The reasonableness of a risk means its reasonableness with respect to the principal object.

(3) A person who takes a risk of injuring the principal object usually does so because he has some reason of his own for such conduct, — is pursuing some object of his own. This may be called the collateral object. In some cases, at least, the value or importance of the collateral object is properly to be considered in deciding upon the reasonableness of the risk.

(4) The probability that the collateral object will be attained by the conduct which involves risk to the principal; the utility of the risk.

(5) The probability that the collateral object would not have been attained without taking the risk; the necessity of the risk. The following case will serve as an illustration.

[In Eckert v. Long Island R.R., 43 N.Y. 502 (1871),] [t]he plaintiff's intestate, seeing a child on a railroad track just in front of a rapidly approaching train, went upon the track to save him. He did save him, but was himself killed by the train. The jury were allowed to find that he had not been guilty of contributory negligence. The question was of course whether he had exposed himself to an unreasonably great risk. Here the above-mentioned elements of reasonableness were as follows:

(1) The magnitude of the risk was the probability that he would be killed or hurt. That was very great.
(2) The principal object was his own life, which was very valuable.
(3) The collateral object was the child's life, which was also very valuable.
(4) The utility of the risk was the probability that he could save the child. That must have been fairly great, since he in fact succeeded. Had there been no fair chance of saving the child, the conduct would have been unreasonable and negligent.
(5) The necessity of the risk was the probability that the child would not have saved himself by getting off the track in time.

Here, although the magnitude of the risk was very great and the principal object very valuable, yet the value of the collateral object and the great utility and necessity of the risk counterbalanced those considerations, and made the risk reasonable. The same risk would have been unreasonable, had the creature on the track been a kitten, because the value of the collateral object would have been small. There is no general rule that human life may not be put at risk in order to save property; but since life is more valuable than property, such a risk has often been held unreasonable in particular cases, which has given rise to dicta to the effect that it is always so. But in the circumstances of other cases a risk of that sort has been held reasonable.

Warren Abner Seavey, Negligence — Subjective or Objective?
41 Harv. L. Rev. 1, 8 n.7 (1927)

We must not assume that we can rely upon any formula in regard to "balancing interests" to solve negligence cases. The phrase is only a convenient one to indicate factors which may be considered and should not connote any mathematical correspondence. Thus I would assume that an actor is liable if, to save his own horse of equal value with the plaintiff's, he were to take a fifty per cent chance of killing the plaintiff's horse, while it would at least be more doubtful whether he might not take a fifty per cent chance of killing another to save his own life. In either event, if the plaintiff's and the defendant's interests are considered of equal value, the defendant would not be liable upon the theory of balancing interests. Upon the same theory one doing an unlawful act or an act in preparation for one, would be liable to any one injured as a consequence, since, by hypothesis, his act has no social value. In the field of negligence, interests are balanced only in the sense that the purposes of the actor, the nature of his act and the harm that may result from action or inaction are elements to be considered. Some of these elements are not considered when the actor knows or desires that his conduct will result in interference with the plaintiff or his property. Thus if, to save his life, *A* intentionally destroys ten cents worth of *B*'s property, *A* must pay; if, however, he takes a ten per cent chance of killing *B* in an effort to save his own life, his conduct might not be found to be wrongful, although obviously *B* would much prefer, antecedently, to lose ten cents worth of property than to submit to a ten per cent chance of being killed.

NOTE

An economic or moral calculus.   The two opinions in *Eckert* reveal more complexity than is found in Terry's brief summary of the case. At the time, the defendant's train was running at a "very moderate speed of seven or eight miles per hour," and the evidence suggested that the boy was not located on the tracks over which the train had run. Does that influence any judgment of the reasonableness of the plaintiff's conduct? In addition, the court stressed the predicament in which the defendant found himself. "He had no time for deliberation. He must act instantly, if at all, as a moment's delay would have been fatal to the child. The law has so high a regard for human life that it will not impute negligence to an effort to preserve it, unless made under such circumstances as to constitute rashness in the judgment of prudent persons." Does that necessity alter the level of care required? Make "rashness" the appropriate standard of care? Was the dissent correct to accept the defense of voluntary assumption of the risk, given that "[h]e was not compelled, or apparently compelled, to take any action to avoid a peril, and harm to himself, from the negligent or wrongful act of the defendant, or the agents in charge of the train"?

Putting these complexities aside, it is perhaps useful to formalize the intuitions that are present in Terry and Seavey. The Terry calculus is as follows: The magnitude of the risk multiplied by the value of the exposed object equals the expected loss from the relevant conduct. The value of the desired, or principal, object multiplied by the *difference* between the probability of success *with* the risk and the probability of success *without* the risk is the expected gain. The action is negligent if the expected loss exceeds the expected gain. Seavey takes a different view, treating the deliberate destruction of ten cents worth of property as a compensable event, no matter how great the gain, but treating the 50 percent loss of another life as noncompensable, because the expected gain exceeds the expected loss. Why balance in the one case but not in the other?

Osborne v. Montgomery
234 N.W. 372 (Wis. 1931)

On August 30, 1928, the plaintiff Lester Osborne, then a boy of thirteen years of age, was employed by the Wisconsin State Journal in running errands. He was returning to his place of employment on a bicycle. Traveling westerly on East Washington avenue, he turned northerly on Pinckney street and as he proceeded north on Pinckney street he followed a car driven by the defendant. The defendant stopped his car for the purpose of leaving some clothing at a cleaner's. The defendant opened the door to his car intending to step from it on the left-hand side. The defendant's car at the time of the accident stood between a line of cars parked at the curb and the easterly rail of the street car tracks. As the defendant's car stopped and the door opened, and the plaintiff endeavored to pass, the right handle bar of his bicycle came in contact with the outside edge of the door, tipping the bicycle and throwing the plaintiff to the ground, causing the injuries complained of.

There was a jury trial, the jury found the defendant negligent as to lookout and the opening of his car door, but that he was not negligent in stopping his car where he did; that defendant's negligence was the cause of the injury; that the plaintiff was not guilty of contributory negligence; and assessed plaintiff's damages at $2,500, which covered plaintiff's pain and suffering, and the loss of earning capacity he would experience after he turned 21. . . . [The instruction of the trial judge on the definition of negligence read as follows: "1. By ordinary care is meant that degree of care which the great mass of mankind, or the type of that mass, the ordinarily prudent man, exercises under like or similar circumstances. 2. Negligence is the want of ordinary care. 3. Every person is negligent when . . . he does such an act, or omits to take such a precaution, that, under the circumstances present, he ought reasonably to foresee that some injury or damage might probably result from his conduct. He is in duty bound to foresee all such natural consequences of his conduct as an ordinarily prudent and intelligent person would ordinarily foresee under the then present circumstances."]

ROSENBERRY, C.J. Manifestly, not every want of care results in liability. In order to measure care some standards must be adopted. Human beings must live in association with each other, as a consequence of which their rights, duties, and obligations are relative, not absolute. We apply the standards which guide the great mass of mankind in determining what is proper conduct of an individual under all the circumstances and say that he was or was not justified in doing the act in question. While it is true that the standard thus set up is varying and indefinite, it is nevertheless one which may be fairly and justly applied to human

Staff at the *Wisconsin State Journal* in 1924, in Madison, Wisconsin
Source: Wisconsin State Journal Archive

conduct. Such a standard is usually spoken of as ordinary care, being that degree of care which under the same or similar circumstances the great mass of mankind would ordinarily exercise.

In a consideration of this subject it is easy to get lost in a maze of metaphysical distinctions, or perhaps it may better be said it is difficult not to be so lost. The defect in the instruction [in paragraph 3] is that it indicates no standard by which the conduct of the defendant is to be measured. In support of the instruction it is argued that the great mass of mankind do not indulge in conduct which results in harm to others; and therefore it must follow that if one does an act which results in injury to another, he departs from the standards which are followed by the great mass of mankind. The argument is based upon an inference not readily drawn, and, in addition to that, the premise is not sound. We are constantly doing acts which result in injury to others which are not negligent and do not result in liability. Many of the cases classified as those damnum absque injuria [harm without legal injury] and cases where the damages are said to be consequential and remote are illustrations of this. While the acts result in injury to others, they are held to be not negligent because they are in conformity to what the great mass of mankind would do under the same or similar circumstances. The statement is true in all situations where liability exists, but it does not exclude situations where liability does not exist.

The fundamental idea of liability for wrongful acts is that upon a balancing of the social interests involved in each case, the law determines that under the circumstances of a particular case an actor should or should not become liable for the natural consequences of his conduct. One driving a car in a thickly populated district on a rainy day, slowly and in the most careful manner, may do injury to the person of another by throwing muddy or infected water upon that person. Society does not hold the actor responsible because the benefit of allowing people to travel under such circumstances so far outweighs the probable injury to bystanders that such conduct is not disapproved. Circumstances may require the driver of a fire truck to take his truck through a thickly populated district at a high rate of speed, but if he exercises that degree of care which such drivers ordinarily exercise under the same or similar circumstances, society, weighing the benefits against the probabilities of damage, in spite of the fact that as a reasonably prudent and intelligent man he should foresee that harm may result, justifies the risk and holds him not liable.

The instruction [in paragraph 3] indicates no standard, but in the present case the court included that element in the instruction in paragraphs 1 and 2.

[Reversed and remanded on the question of damages only.]

Cooley v. Public Service Co.
10 A.2d 673 (N.H. 1940)

PAGE, J. On November 29, 1935, the telephone company maintained a cable on Taylor Street, Manchester, running north and south. This cable consisted of a lead sheath, inside which were carried a large number of wires connected with the service stations of its subscribers. The cable was supported by rings from a messenger wire strung on the telephone company poles. The construction conformed to standard practices, and the messenger wire was grounded every thousand feet. The sheath of the cable also was grounded. The telephone company further maintained at the station which the plaintiff was using when she received her injuries, two protective devices for grounding foreign currents in order to prevent their entrance to the house and to the subscriber's instrument. There is no evidence that these devices did not operate perfectly.

At a point about a mile distant from the plaintiff's house, the Public Service Company's lines, east and west along Valley Street, crossed the telephone cable at right angles and some eight or ten feet above it. These lines were not insulated.

Shortly after midnight, during a heavy storm, several of the Public Service wires over the intersection of Valley and Taylor Streets broke and fell to the ground. One of them came into contact with the telephone messenger. This particular wire of the defendant carried a voltage of about 2300. Consequently an arc was created, which burned through the messenger and nearly half through the cable before the current was shut off. . . .

When the contact of the wires occurred, the plaintiff was standing at the telephone, engaged in a long-distance conversation. The contact created a violent agitation in the diaphragm of the receiver and a loud explosive noise. The plaintiff fell to the floor. She has since suffered from what her physicians describe as traumatic neurosis, accompanied by loss of sensation on the left side.

[Plaintiff sued the power company and the telephone company. At the trial the jury found for the telephone company but against the power company. The power company appealed, and the judgment was reversed.]

Apparently there is no claim that the negligence of the defendant caused the wires to fall. The plaintiff's sole claim is that the defendant could have anticipated (1) that its wire might fall for a variety of reasons, which is true; (2) that a telephone subscriber in such case might hear a great noise, which also is true; (3) that as a result of fright thereby induced the user of the telephone would suffer physical injuries, which, as we have seen, is a rare contingency, though it may be anticipated. It is urged that the defendant's consequent duty was to maintain such devices at cross-overs as would prevent one of its falling wires from coming into contact with a telephone wire.

The devices suggested are two. The first is a wire-mesh basket suspended from the poles of the defendant at the point of cross-over, above the cable and below the defendant's wires. Two forms were suggested. One would be about six by eight feet. The other would be of an unassigned width and would stretch the full distance between defendant's poles. In either case the basket would be insulated. The theory is that falling wires, though alive, would remain harmless in the basket.

[The court, after detailed examination of these proposals, concluded that each of these suggested devices would have entailed a greater risk of electrocution to people passing on the street, even assuming that they might have reduced the risk of loud noises to those using the telephone. The court then continued, in part:]

There was evidence that baskets and similar devices were used by the telephone company, some years ago, for the protection of their wires at cross-overs. But the verdict establishes its lack of duty thus to protect its customers in this particular instance. There was no evidence that electric light companies ever erected baskets or insulated wires in such situations, and there was positive evidence that standard construction practices do not require either. The plaintiff cannot claim that the defendant maintained a system less carefully devised than one conforming to accepted practice. It is conceded, however, that due care might require some device better than the usual one. If the plaintiff and persons in her situation could be isolated, and duties to others ignored, due care might require the use of such devices as are here urged.

But the same reasoning that would establish a duty to do so raises another duty to the people in the street, not to lessen the protective effect of their circuit-breaking device. . . .

In the case before us, there was danger of electrocution in the street. As long as the telephone company's safety devices are properly installed and maintained, there is no danger of electrocution in the house. The only foreseeable danger to the telephone subscriber is from noise—fright and neuroses. Balancing the two, the danger to those such as the plaintiff is remote, that to those on the ground near the broken wires is obvious and immediate. The balance would not be improved by taking a chance to avoid traumatic neurosis of the plaintiff at the expense of greater risk to the lives of others. To the extent that the duty to use care depends upon relationship, the defendant's duty of care towards the plaintiff is obviously weaker than that towards the man in the street.

The defendant's duty cannot, in the circumstances, be to both. If that were so, performance of one duty would mean non-performance of the other. If it be negligent to save the life of the highway traveler at the expense of bodily injury resulting from the fright and neurosis of a telephone subscriber, it must be equally negligent to avoid the fright at the risk of another's life. The law could tolerate no such theory of "be liable if you do and liable if you don't." The law does not contemplate a shifting duty that requires care towards *A* and then discovers a duty to avoid injury incidentally suffered by *B* because there was due care with respect to *A*. Such a shifting is entirely inconsistent with the fundamental conception that the duty of due care requires precisely the measure of care that is reasonable under all the circumstances. 2 Restatement Torts, §§291-295. . . .

It is not doubted that due care might require the defendant to adopt some device that would afford protection against emotional disturbances in telephone-users without depriving the traveling public of reasonable protection from live wires immediately dangerous to life. Such a device, if it exists, is not disclosed by the record. The burden was upon the plaintiff to show its practicability. Since the burden was not sustained a verdict should have been directed for the defendant.

Other exceptions therefore require no consideration.

Judgment for the defendant. All concurred.

NOTE

Activity level versus care level. The plaintiff in *Cooley* tried to find fault with how the power company maintained its wires above ground. Accordingly, Page, J., never had to ask whether the power company made a sound decision to place the wires above ground in the first place. If that claim were asserted, should courts and juries examine only the level of care once the defendant has decided to undertake a given activity, or should they also examine the type or level of the defendant's activity?

The theoretical point is raised in Shavell, Strict Liability Versus Negligence, 9 J. Legal Stud. 1, 2-3 (1980). There Shavell discusses the "unilateral case," "by which it is meant the actions of injurers but not of victims are assumed to affect the probability or severity of losses."

> By definition, under the negligence rule all that an injurer needs to do to avoid the possibility of liability is to make sure to exercise due care if he engages in his activity. Consequently *he will not be motivated to consider the effect on accident losses of his choice of whether to engage in his activity or, more generally, of the level at which to engage in his activity;* he will choose his level of activity in accordance only with the personal benefits so derived. But surely any increase in his level of activity will typically raise expected accident losses (holding constant the level of care). Thus he will be led to choose too high a level of activity; the negligence rule is not "efficient."
>
> Consider by way of illustration the problem of pedestrian-automobile accidents (and, as we are now discussing the unilateral case, let us imagine the behavior of pedestrians to be fixed). Suppose that drivers of automobiles find it in their interest to adhere to the standard of due care but that the possibility of accidents is not thereby eliminated. Then, in deciding how much to drive, they will contemplate only the enjoyment they get from doing so. Because (as they exercise due care) they will not be liable for harm suffered by pedestrians, drivers will not take into account that going more miles will mean a higher expected number of accidents. Hence, there will be too much driving; an individual will, for example, decide to go for a drive on a mere whim despite the imposition of a positive expected cost to pedestrians.

However, under a rule of strict liability, the situation is different. Because an injurer must pay for losses whenever he is involved in an accident, he will be induced to consider the effect on accident losses of both his level of care *and* his level of activity. His decisions will therefore be efficient. Because drivers will be liable for losses sustained by pedestrians, they will decide not only to exercise due care in driving but also to drive only when the utility gained from it outweighs expected liability payments to pedestrians.

Does it follow as a matter of definition that choices of activity level are outside judicial review under a negligence standard? Recall in this context the suggestion made in Bolton v. Stone, *supra* at 123, that it might have been negligent to play cricket *at all* if the field could not be made safe. Is a jury as competent in making decisions on activity levels as it is on care levels? For an updated version of the activity level point, see Shavell, Liability for Accidents ch. 2 (2007).

United States v. Carroll Towing Co.
159 F.2d 169 (2d Cir. 1947)

L. HAND, J. These appeals concern the sinking of the barge, "*Anna C*," on January 4, 1944, off Pier 51, North River. [The accident occurred when the tug *Carroll* (owned by Carroll Towing Company) attempted a tricky maneuver to move a barge that had been tied up in a tier of barges on the so-called Public Pier just to the north of Pier 52, where the *Anna C* (owned by the Conners Company) was berthed. During the attempt, the fasts directly connecting the *Anna C* to Pier 52 broke. Tides and wind carried the *Anna C* (and the five other barges tied to her) down the Hudson River. The drifting *Anna C* collided with a tanker, and the tanker's propeller punctured a hole near the bottom of the *Anna C*. The barge began to leak, and shortly thereafter "careened," dumped her cargo of flour, and sank. In the admiralty proceeding below, two suits were brought. In the first, the United States sued Carroll Towing Company for the loss of its cargo of flour. In the second, Conners recovered one-half of the damages for the loss of the barge from Carroll Towing. The record revealed that the Conners Company had chartered the *Anna C* to the Pennsylvania Railroad "at a stated hire per diem, by a charter of the kind usual in the Harbor, which included the services of a bargee, apparently limited to the hours 8 A.M. to 4 P.M." In the second suit, the contributory negligence of Conners was raised as a partial defense, as was then allowed in admiralty cases. The gist of the claim of contributory negligence was that "if the bargee had been on board, and had done his duty to his employer, he would have gone below at once, examined the injury, and called for help from the 'Carroll' and [another tug.] . . . [T]he question arises whether a barge owner is slack in the care of his barge if the bargee is absent."]

Exhibit 3.3 Learned Hand

Learned Hand (1872-1961) served as a federal judge for 52 years, including 37 years on the Court of Appeals for the Second Circuit, covering New York, Connecticut, and Vermont. He is considered by many legal scholars to be among the greatest judges in United States history. His influence extended through myriad areas of the law, including copyright, antitrust, tax, criminal law, and torts. The principle for negligence he announced in *Carroll Towing*, known universally by law students as the "Hand Formula," played a central role in the development of economic frameworks to describe legal rules. His opinion in the famous *Alcoa* case, United States v. Aluminum Co. of Am., 148 F.2d 416 (2d Cir. 1945), became a landmark in antitrust law, finding that monopoly was illegal whether or not those involved in the enterprise pursued otherwise nefarious business dealings. He was also known to be tough on the bench, even turning his back on attorneys who appeared before him with weak arguments.

Bio sources: Richard A. Posner, The Learned Hand Biography and the Question of Judicial Greatness, 104 Yale L.J. 511 (1994); *Learned Hand,* Encyclopaedia Britannica
Image Source: Wikimedia Commons

It appears from the foregoing review [of prior case law] that there is no general rule to determine when the absence of a bargee or other attendant will make the owner of the barge liable for injuries to other vessels if she breaks away from her moorings. However, in any cases where he would be so liable for injuries to others, obviously he must reduce his damages proportionately, if the injury is to his own barge. It becomes apparent why there can be no such general rule, when we consider the grounds for such a liability. Since there are occasions when every vessel will break from her moorings, and since, if she does, she becomes a menace to those about her; the owner's duty, as in other similar situations, to provide against resulting injuries is a function of three variables: (1) The probability that she will break away; (2) the gravity of the resulting injury, if she does; (3) the burden of adequate precautions. Possibly it serves to bring this notion into relief to state it in algebraic terms: if the probability be called P; the injury, L; and the burden, B; liability depends upon whether B is less than L multiplied by P: i.e., whether B is less than PL. Applied to the situation at bar, the likelihood that a barge will break from her fasts and the damage she will do, vary with the place and time; for example, if a storm threatens, the danger is greater; so it is, if she is in a crowded harbor where moored barges are constantly being shifted about. On the other hand, the barge must not be the bargee's prison, even though he lives aboard; he must go ashore at times. We need not say whether, even in such crowded waters as New York Harbor a bargee must be aboard at night at all; it may be that the custom is otherwise, as Ward, J., supposed in "The Kathryn B. Guinan," [176 F. 301 (2d Cir. 1910)]; and that, if so, the situation is one where custom should control. We leave that question open; but we hold that it is not in all cases a sufficient answer to a bargee's absence without excuse, during working hours, that he has properly made fast his barge to a pier, when he leaves her. In the case at bar the bargee left at five o'clock in the afternoon of January 3rd, and the flotilla broke away at about two o'clock in the afternoon of the following day, twenty-one hours afterwards. The bargee had been away all the time, and we hold that his fabricated story was affirmative evidence that he had no excuse for his absence. At the locus in quo—especially during the short January days and in the full tide of war activity—barges were being constantly "drilled" in and out. Certainly it was not beyond reasonable expectation that, with the inevitable haste and bustle, the work might not be done with adequate care. In such circumstances we hold—and it is all that we do hold—that it was a fair requirement that the Conners Company should have a bargee aboard (unless he had some excuse for his absence), during the working hours of daylight.

NOTES

1. The parties and claims in Carroll Towing.   The sinking of the *Anna C* gave rise to a separate claim brought by the United States against Carroll Towing and Conners for the loss of a load of flour that it was shipping on the *Anna C*. In light of the terms of Conners's charter to the Pennsylvania Railroad, could the United States take advantage of the bargee's absence by claiming to be a third-party beneficiary to the contract between Conners and the Pennsylvania Railroad? Why would either party wish to create any benefit for a stranger to their own contract? For further details on the complex parties and claims, see Gilles, United States v. Carroll Towing Co.: The Hand Formula's Home Port, *in* Torts Stories 11 (Rabin & Sugarman eds., 2003).

Exhibit 3.3   Progenitors of Law and Economics

The application of economic analysis to legal rules has a long history, but its influential modern incarnation was largely developed in the latter half of the twentieth century by two noted jurists, Judge Richard A. Posner, left, now of the Seventh Circuit Court of Appeals, and Judge Guido Calabresi, right, of the Second Circuit Court of Appeals.
Sources: Posner – University of Chicago Law School; Calabresi – Robert Benson Photography

   2. An economic interpretation of negligence?   Hand's use of the formula— whether *PL* is less than *B*— spawned a burgeoning academic literature on the economic interpretation of negligence and, by implication, the entire tort law. Judge Posner, A Theory of Negligence, 1 J. Legal Stud. 29, 32-33 (1972), opened the debate by arguing that the Hand formula provides an operational definition of unreasonable risk under the negligence law:

   Hand was adumbrating, perhaps unwittingly, an economic meaning of negligence. Discounting (multiplying) the cost of an accident if it occurs by the probability of occurrence yields a measure of the economic benefit to be anticipated from incurring the costs necessary to prevent the accident. The cost of prevention is what Hand meant by the burden of taking precautions against the accident. It may be the cost of installing safety equipment or otherwise making the activity safer, or the benefit forgone by curtailing or eliminating the activity. If the cost of safety measures or of curtailment—whichever cost is lower—exceeds the benefit in accident avoidance to be gained by incurring that cost, society would be better off, in economic terms, to forgo accident prevention. A rule making the enterprise liable for the accidents that occur in such cases cannot be justified on the ground that it will induce the enterprise to increase the safety of its operations. When the cost of accidents is less than the cost of prevention, a rational profit-maximizing enterprise will pay tort judgments to the accident victims rather than incur the larger cost of avoiding liability. Furthermore, overall economic value or welfare would be diminished rather than increased by incurring a higher accident-prevention cost in order to avoid a lower accident cost. If, on the other hand, the benefits in accident avoidance exceed the costs of prevention, society is better off if those costs are incurred and the accident averted, and so in this case the enterprise is made liable, in the expectation that self-interest will lead it to adopt the precautions in order to avoid a greater cost in tort judgments.

The Third Restatement also takes a "balancing approach" to negligence. The effort to reduce negligence to the three elements in the Hand formula has been subject to wholesale attacks. Thus Wright, in Hand, Posner, and the Myth of the "Hand Formula," 4 Theoretical Inquiries in Law 145, 273 (2003), examines all of Hand's opinions on negligence, and concludes that only a small fraction of these cases make reference to or rely upon his cost benefit formula. Wright concludes:

> If one then follows the legal realists' advice and looks carefully, in those cases in which the aggregate-risk-utility test is mentioned, at what the courts are actually doing rather than (merely) at what they are saying, one finds that the courts almost never attempt to apply the test; instead, the test is merely trotted out as *dicta* or boilerplate separate from the real analysis. The very few judges who actually try to apply the test either fail in the attempt to do so or end up using the test as window-dressing for results reached on other (justice-based) grounds.

This observation leads Zipursky, Sleight of Hand, 48 Wm. & Mary L. Rev. 1999, 2040 (2007), to suggest that "[n]egligence law is not best understood . . . as a device for deterrence and compensation," but rather as a theory of "civic competency," or an institutionalized set of norms about reasonable and socialized behavior that builds on rights-based and virtue-based theories. Are the two approaches mutually exclusive? Inconsistent? Within the negligence framework, could any system of justice afford to ignore the diminishing marginal value of additional precautions?

Restatement of the Law (Third) of Torts: Liability for Physical and Emotional Harm

§3. NEGLIGENCE

A person acts negligently if the person does not exercise reasonable care under all the circumstances. Primary factors to consider in ascertaining whether the person's conduct lacks reasonable care are the foreseeable likelihood that the person's conduct will result in harm, the foreseeable severity of any harm that may ensue, and the burden of precautions to eliminate or reduce the risk of harm.

Compare to the Hand formula:

$$B < PL$$

Where "the probability [of injury] be called P; the injury, L; and the burden, B; liability depends upon whether B is less than L multiplied by P. i.e., whether B is less than PL." *Carroll Towing, supra.*

Does the Restatement's definition embody the Hand formula? Are the two uses of the term "foreseeable" redundant? If the three elements are only "primary factors," what other elements could be considered? What is the relationship between the Hand formula and the customary account of "ordinary care" or the "reasonably prudent person"?

For yet another criticism of the Posner approach, see Cunningham, Traditional Versus Economic Analysis: Evidence from Cardozo and Posner Torts Opinions, 62 Fla. L. Rev. 667 (2010), taking the view that "traditional legal analysis [Cardozo style] is a more capacious basis of justification than contemporary economic analysis of law and that this feature, though suffering from some indeterminacy, yields more persuasive justification in a wider range of cases." How can this proposition be tested?

3. Measurement problems under the Hand formula. How does a court or jury find the information needed to apply the Hand formula? Hand himself was sensitive to the problem. In Moisan v. Loftus, 178 F.2d 148, 149 (2d Cir. 1949), he wrote:

The difficulties are in applying the rule. . . . [T]hey arise from the necessity of applying a quantitative test to an incommensurable subject-matter and the same difficulties inhere in the concept of "ordinary" negligence. [Of the three factors, B, P, and L,] care is the only one ever susceptible of quantitative estimate, and often that is not. The injuries are always a variable within limits, which do not admit of even approximate ascertainment and, although probability might theoretically be estimated, if any statistics were available, they never are and, besides, probability varies with the severity of the injuries. It follows that all such attempts are illusory, and, if serviceable at all, are so only to center attention upon which one of the factors may be determinative in any given situation.

What should be done if the estimates of *B*, *P*, and *L* can each vary independently by a factor of 10? If human life (unlike property damage) has no estimable market value? Does the ordinary care formulation eliminate or conceal this problem?

4. Marginal precautions and the Hand formula. One conceptual problem under the Hand formula involves choosing the correct interval for assessing defendant's conduct. Suppose the defendant could take an extra $100 in precautions that would yield $150 in additional benefits. At first blush, the defendant should take these precautions given that *in aggregate* the expected benefits exceed the expected costs. Nonetheless, a closer analysis reveals that this action could lead to excessive care. The key point is that in economic terms additional precautions should be tested *at the margin* and only taken so long as an additional dollar of precautions reduces the expected costs of injury by at least a dollar. Thus, in the example above, suppose that the first $60 in precautions yield $120 in benefits, while the next $40 in precautions yield only $30 in benefits. In principle the lesser precaution is more desirable because it generates $60 in *net* benefits ($120 − $60), while the next $40 in precautions generates *minus* $10 in net benefits ($30 − $40). The lesser precaution therefore generates the greater social benefit. On this analysis, therefore, the plaintiff conclusively establishes negligence by showing only a net social gain from taking the proposed precautions. In principle, the defendant should be allowed to show that some lower level of precaution would have generated a higher net social return. Assuming this issue can be litigated, how should the burdens of proof be distributed on the question of marginal precautions?

This analysis has important implications for applying the Hand formula in cases of self-risk. As a theoretical matter, the Hand formula is capacious enough to take into account any potential losses that a bargee has either as a potential plaintiff or potential defendant. Thus, if the expected loss of a bargee's conduct to some third party (such as the United States for its flour) were $100 and the additional "sinking" damages to the barge itself were $50, then the defendant should be regarded as negligent if the costs of its precautions were less than $150, not $100. Stated otherwise, the avoidance of harm to self reduces the incremental cost in preventing harms to others. See Cooter & Porat, Does Risk to Oneself Increase the Care Owed to Others? Law and Economics in Conflict, 29 J. Legal Stud. 19 (2000), concluding that "omitting the injurer's possible harm to himself causes courts to set the legal standard of care too low." Compare this with the argument in Cooter & Porat, Lapses of Attention in Medical Malpractice and Road Accidents, 15 Theoretical Inquiries in Law 329, 331 (2014), which argues: "If the person lapses and harms someone, the injurer is arguably no worse morally than other reasonable people who did not lapse. The injurer, consequently, does not deserve a sanction in the form of tort liability: his bad luck should not count against him." Are the conclusions of these two pieces in tension? Should the defendant's bad luck count as against the injured plaintiff? Are lapses equally forgivable in driving as in medical malpractice? How frequent do lapses have to be before they become negligence?

5. *Risk neutrality.*   On its face, the Hand formula treats all individuals as risk neutral. A risk-neutral actor responds to the expected gains or losses of a future uncertain event by simply multiplying the probability of its occurrence by its magnitude, as in the Hand formula itself. In practice, however, sometimes people prefer risk and sometimes they are averse to it. These tastes can vary across persons. In essence, people who prefer risk gain positive satisfaction from taking chances, while people who are averse to risk are prepared to pay to avoid confronting it. Thus a person who prefers risk would prefer a 10 percent chance of losing $100 to a certainty of losing $10. Conversely, the risk-averse person prefers the certainty of losing $10 to a 10 percent chance of losing $100. Risk preference and risk aversion are both matters of degree; it is quite possible that some would pay only $11 to avoid the 10 percent chance of a $100 loss while others might pay as much as $20. For a defense of the risk neutrality assumption in the Hand formula, see Landes & Posner, The Economic Structure of Tort Law 55-57 (1987). Should neutrality be presumed if most individuals and most corporations are risk averse? Note that some modern literature in the field of cognitive biases suggests that individuals may be risk preferrers in the domain of losses and risk averse in the domain of gains. See, e.g., Plous, The Psychology of Judgment and Decision Making 96 (1993). Why do people both gamble and buy liability insurance?

6. *Does efficiency require negligence?*   Under the orthodox economic accounts of tort law, the Hand formula is not the only road to social efficiency. Strict liability with contributory negligence, or even a system of negligence without contributory negligence, should also induce (as a first approximation) optimal behavior by both parties. The proposition was demonstrated in Brown, Toward an Economic Theory of Liability, 2 J. Legal Stud. 323 (1973), and more complete expositions can be found in Landes & Posner, The Economic Structure of Tort Law ch. 3 (1987), and Shavell, Economic Analysis of Accident Law 26-46 (1987).

The basic intuition behind the position is as follows. Let us assume that each (rationally self-interested) party wishes to minimize the sum of its precaution and accident costs. When liability is predicated on proof of defendant's negligence alone, the defendant will take care, even *without* the defense of contributory negligence: The cost of precautions is below that of the anticipated liability. Once the plaintiff knows that the defendant will take care, the plaintiff also knows that all prospect of recovery is thereby precluded. The plaintiff therefore now has (wholly without regard to the contributory negligence defense) an incentive to take the optimal level of care as well. Both parties will behave optimally, even without the contributory negligence defense.

Similarly, under strict liability, the plaintiff will recover unless barred by contributory negligence. Yet so long as precautions are cheaper than expected accidents, the rational plaintiff will take care in order to preserve the right of action.

Andrews v. United Airlines
24 F.3d 39 (9th Cir. 1994)

KOZINSKI, J.

We are called upon to determine whether United Airlines took adequate measures to deal with that elementary notion of physics—what goes up, must come down. For, while the skies are friendly enough, the ground can be a mighty dangerous place when heavy objects tumble from overhead compartments.

I

During the mad scramble that usually follows hard upon an airplane's arrival at the gate, a briefcase fell from an overhead compartment and seriously injured plaintiff Billie Jean Andrews. No one knows who opened the compartment or what caused the briefcase to fall, and Andrews doesn't claim that airline personnel were involved in stowing the object or opening the bin. Her claim, rather, is that the injury was foreseeable and the airline didn't prevent it.

The district court dismissed the suit on summary judgment, and we review de novo. This is a diversity action brought in California, whose tort law applies.

II

The parties agree that United Airlines is a common carrier and as such "owe[s] both a duty of utmost care and the vigilance of a very cautious person towards [its] passengers." Acosta v. Southern Cal. Rapid Transit Dist., 465 P.2d 72 (1970). Though United is "responsible for any, even the slightest, negligence and [is] required to do all that human care, vigilance, and foresight reasonably can do under all the circumstances," *Acosta*, 465 P.2d at 72, it is not an insurer of its passengers' safety, Lopez v. Southern Cal. Rapid Transit Dist., 710 P.2d 907 (1985). "[T]he degree of care and diligence which [it] must exercise is only such as can reasonably be exercised consistent with the character and mode of conveyance adopted and the practical operation of [its] business. . . ." Id.

To show that United did not satisfy its duty of care toward its passengers, Ms. Andrews presented the testimony of two witnesses. The first was Janice Northcott, United's Manager of Inflight Safety, who disclosed that in 1987 the airline had received 135 reports of items falling from overhead bins. As a result of these incidents, Ms. Northcott testified, United decided to add a warning to its arrival announcements, to wit, that items stored overhead might have shifted during flight and passengers should use caution in opening the bins. This announcement later became the industry standard.

Ms. Andrews's second witness was safety and human factors expert Dr. David Thompson, who testified that United's announcement was ineffective because passengers opening overhead bins couldn't see objects poised to fall until the bins were opened, by which time it was too late. Dr. Thompson also testified that United could have taken additional steps to prevent the hazard, such as retrofitting its overhead bins with baggage nets, as some airlines had already done, or by requiring passengers to store only lightweight items overhead.

United argues that Andrews presented too little proof to satisfy her burden [to withstand summary judgment]. One hundred thirty-five reported incidents, United points out, are trivial when spread over the millions of passengers travelling on its 175,000 flights every year. Even that number overstates the problem, according to United, because it includes events where passengers merely observed items falling from overhead bins but no one was struck or injured. Indeed, United sees the low incidence of injuries as incontrovertible proof that the safety measures suggested by plaintiff's expert would not merit the additional cost and inconvenience to airline passengers.

III

It is a close question, but we conclude that plaintiff has made a sufficient case to overcome summary judgment. United is hard-pressed to dispute that its passengers are subject to a hazard from objects falling out of overhead bins, considering the warning its flight crews give hundreds of times each day. The case then turns on whether the hazard is serious enough to warrant more than a warning. Given the heightened duty of a common carrier, even a small risk of serious injury to passengers may form the basis of liability if that risk could be eliminated "consistent with the character and mode of [airline travel] and the practical operation of [that] business. . . ." *Lopez*, 710 P.2d at 907. United has demonstrated neither that retrofitting overhead bins with netting (or other means) would be prohibitively expensive, nor that such steps would grossly interfere with the convenience of its passengers. Thus, a jury could find United has failed to do "all that human care, vigilance, and foresight reasonably can do under all the circumstances." *Acosta*, 465 P.2d at 72.

The reality, with which airline passengers are only too familiar, is that airline travel has changed significantly in recent years. As harried travelers try to avoid the agonizing ritual of checked baggage, they hand-carry more and larger items — computers, musical instruments, an occasional deceased relative. The airlines have coped with this trend, but perhaps not well enough. Given its awareness of the hazard, United may not have done everything technology permits and prudence dictates to eliminate it. . . .

Jurors, many of whom will have been airline passengers, will be well equipped to decide whether United had a duty to do more than warn passengers about the possibility of falling baggage. A reasonable jury might conclude United should have done more; it might also find that United did enough. Either decision would be rational on the record presented to the district court which, of course, means summary judgment was not appropriate.

Reversed and remanded.

NOTE

Negligence and the common carrier. *Andrews* settled shortly after remand—a reminder of the powerful effect, in terms of inducing private settlement, of a legal decision that plaintiff's evidence withstands summary judgment (or motion to dismiss). Is its utmost care standard consistent with the Hand formula? If not, how would *Andrews* come out under that test? Historically the utmost care standard has had an uneven reception in common carrier cases. In Kelly v. Manhattan Ry., 20 N.E. 383, 385 (N.Y. 1889), the plaintiff slipped on heavy snow that had accumulated during the night on the stairs leading to the train station. Peckham, J., rejected the utmost care standard in this context, reserving it for those distinctive railroad operations in which the passenger had no control over the operation of the train, as when injury "occurs from a defect in the road-bed, machinery, or in the construction of the cars." He observed that the level of serious injury or death from those "compelled" to use the rails was far higher than those associated with ancillary facilities, such as "platforms, halls, stairways, and the like." In principle, the Hand formula could accommodate these differences, by insisting that greater peril requires greater precaution independent of the utmost care standard.

In light of that observation, *Kelly* was overturned in Bethel v. New York City Transit Authority, 703 N.E.2d 1214, 1216-1217 (N.Y. 1998). The plaintiff was injured when a movable bus seat collapsed as she attempted to sit down. *Bethel* treated *Kelly* as a bygone response to "the advent of the age of steam railroads in 19th century America. Their primitive safety features resulted in a phenomenal growth in railroad accident injuries and with them, an explosion in personal injury litigation, significantly affecting the American tort system." Levine, J., observed that the earlier development represented a needless departure from the fundamental doctrine of negligence, which relies on a "sliding scale" that makes the level of care commensurate with the level of danger involved in a particular activity. In his view, contemporary negligence jurisprudence has undermined "both of the main policy justifications for exacting of common carriers a duty of extraordinary care. The two most often expressed rationales for the duty of highest care were (1) the perceived ultrahazardous nature of the instrumentalities of public rapid transit, and (2) the status of passengers and their relationship to the carrier, notably their total dependency upon the latter for safety precautions."

Why should a broken seat generate one consequence on a bus and another in the station? What is wrong with a strict duty to keep seats safe, subject to a defense of assumption of risk when passengers know of the defect before they sit down? How should *Andrews* be decided under *Bethel?* Under *Kelly?*

SECTION D. CUSTOM

The general principles of negligence law leave judges and juries a great deal of latitude in setting the appropriate standard of care. Sometimes that latitude is a sign of the strength of the system, for it supplies the flexibility necessary to apply traditional standards to new situations without having to fundamentally remake the substantive law. Unfortunately, the "featureless generality" of reasonable care also introduces a large element of uncertainty even into ostensibly routine cases. Using custom to set the standard of care helps reduce this uncertainty. Custom lacks the generality of the basic reasonable care standard, but within its specific area of application it promises greater direction than any broader standard can provide.

This section addresses the role of custom in negligence cases. Does local custom or industry practice provide a decent proxy for a standard of reasonable care? What factors make that more or less likely? Should custom be given the same deference in actions between strangers as in actions arising out of long-term consensual relationships (such as employer-employee, physician-patient)? Should custom carry the same weight when used as a shield (defendant argues that he is not negligent because his conduct conforms to custom), as when used as a sword (plaintiff argues that defendant is negligent because his conduct fails to conform to custom)?

This section also examines the unique role that custom plays in medical malpractice cases, aspects of the modern debate about medical malpractice liability in the health care system, and proposals for reforming it. Finally, the section addresses a subset of malpractice liability, "informed consent" cases, and the relevance of custom in determining the scope of a physician's duty to disclose information to an individual patient.

Titus v. Bradford, B. & K. R. Co.
20 A. 517 (Pa. 1890)

[The defendant railroad operated a narrow gauge railroad track between Bradford and Smethport. This line was connected with the standard-gauge tracks of major lines, and part of the defendant's business was to transfer over its tracks the loaded and unloaded freight cars of major carriers. The transfers were accomplished by means of a "hoist" which lifted car bodies from the standard trucks (bases) used on the major lines and set them down on the narrow trucks used on the defendant's lines. Most of the car bodies from the major lines were designed with flat bottoms, which could be set down relatively easily on the flat trucks in use on the narrow-gauge rails. A substantial portion of the defendant's business, however, involved the transfer of cars from the New York, Pennsylvania and Ohio Railroad. These "Nypano" cars had slightly rounded bottoms, "shaped somewhat like the bottom of a common saucer," which fit into correspondingly shaped trucks when in use on the Nypano lines. When transferred to the defendant's tracks, however, this car body did not sit securely on its truck, since its bottom was about three inches higher at its edges than at its center. In order to prevent the car bodies from wobbling and toppling when the defendant's train was in motion, the defendant's employees routinely secured them with blocks of hard wood, which were either bolted in place or tied down with telegraph wire.

The decedent had worked on the defendant's railroad with the Nypano cars for nearly two years and was quite familiar with the methods used to secure them to the flat trucks. In the spring of 1888, he became a brakeman on the line. On June 7, 1888, in that capacity, he was riding atop a loaded Nypano freight car. Before setting off, the train's conductor had visually inspected the blocks and believed that they had been properly tied in place with telegraph wire. As the train rounded a curve at a speed of between 7 and 10 miles per hour, it started to sway from side to side. The decedent, who was sitting by the brake wheel on the top rear of the car, tried to run forward over the load to the car in front of him, but could not reach the safety of the next car before his car tipped over. He jumped off onto the track and was killed when struck by the car immediately behind him. A subsequent investigation showed that some of the wire fastening around the blocks of his car had come loose, which allowed the block to become dislodged and the car to wobble and tumble.

"The contention of the plaintiff in this case is, that the company was negligent in using on this narrow-gauge road these standard car bodies," this "on account of the ill-adoption of this car body to the truck." The jury returned a verdict for the plaintiff in the amount of $5,325, and the defendant appealed.]

MITCHELL, J. We have examined all the testimony carefully, and fail to find any evidence of defendant's negligence. The negligence declared upon is the placing of a broad-gauge car upon a narrow-gauge truck, and the use of "an unsafe, and not the best appliance, to wit, the flat centre plate"; or, as expressed by the learned judge in his charge, in using on the narrow-gauge road the standard car bodies, and particularly the New York, Pennsylvania & Ohio car body described by the witnesses. But the whole evidence, of plaintiff's witnesses as well as of defendant's, shows that the shifting of broad-gauge or standard car bodies on to narrow-gauge trucks for transportation, is a regular part of the business of narrow-gauge railroads, and the plaintiff's evidence makes no attempt to show that the way in which it was done here was either dangerous or unusual. . . . Cazely and Richmond say it was the custom to haul these broad-gauge cars on the narrow-gauge trucks, though most of the broad-gauge were Erie cars, of a somewhat different construction; and Morris says the car in question was put on a Hays truck, fitted for carrying standard-gauge cars on a narrow-gauge road, and that this particular kind of "Nypano" car was so hauled quite often. These are plaintiff's own witnesses, and none of them say the practice was dangerous. The nearest approach to such testimony is by Morris, who says he "had his doubts."

But, even if the practice had been shown to be dangerous, that would not show it to be negligent. Some employments are essentially hazardous, as said by our Brother Green, in North C. Ry. Co. v. Husson, 101 Pa. 1 [(1882)], of coupling railway cars; and it by no means follows that an employer is liable "because a particular accident might have been prevented by some special device or precaution not in common use." All the cases agree that the master is not bound to use the newest and best appliances. He performs his duty when he furnishes those of ordinary character and reasonable safety, and the former is the test of the latter; for, in regard to the style of implement or nature of the mode of performance of any work, "reasonably safe" means safe according to the usages, habits, and ordinary risks of the business. Absolute safety is unattainable, and employers are not insurers. They are liable for the consequences, not of danger but of negligence; and the unbending test of negligence in methods, machinery, and appliances is the ordinary usage of the business. No man is held by law to a higher degree of skill than the fair average of his profession or trade, and the standard of due care is the conduct of the average prudent man. The test of negligence in employers is the same, and however strongly they may be convinced that there is a better or less dangerous way, no jury can be permitted to say that the usual and ordinary way, commonly adopted by those in the same business, is a negligent way for which liability shall be imposed. Juries must necessarily determine the responsibility of individual conduct, but they cannot be allowed to set up a standard which shall, in effect, dictate the customs or control the business of the community. . . .

It is also entirely clear that defendant's third point should have been affirmed. The deceased had been a brakeman on this train for five or six months, during which this mode of carrying broad-gauge cars had been used; cars similar to the one on which the accident occurred had been frequently carried, and that very car at least once, about ten days before. He not only thus had ample opportunity to know the risks of such trains, but he had his attention specially called to the alleged source of the accident, by having worked, just before becoming a brakeman, on the hoist by which the car bodies were transferred to the trucks. It was a perfectly plain case of acceptance of an employment, with full knowledge of the risks.

Judgment reversed.

Mayhew v. Sullivan Mining Co.
76 Me. 100 (1884)

[The plaintiff, an independent contractor, had been hired by the defendant to trace veins of new ore. During the course of his duties, the plaintiff worked on a platform in a mine shaft some 270 feet below ground. Near one corner of the platform was a "bucket-hole," which the plaintiff used in his work. The plaintiff alleged that on the day of the accident the defendant "carelessly and negligently caused a hole three feet in length by twenty-six inches in breadth to be cut for a ladder-hole in the platform near the centre of it directly back of the bucket-hole and twenty inches distant therefrom, without placing any rail or barrier about it, or any light or other warning there, and without giving plaintiff notice that any such dangerous change had been made in the platform; and that without any knowledge of its existence or fault on his part, the plaintiff, in the ordinary course of his business having occasion to go upon the platform fell through this new hole a distance of thirty-five feet, and received serious injury." The ladder-hole was made by one Stanley under the direction of the superintendent. The defendant sought to ask Stanley at trial whether he had "ever known ladder holes at a low level to be railed or fenced around," whether "as a miner" he thought it was "feasible" to use a ladder-hole with a railing around it, or whether he had "ever seen a ladder-hole in a mine, below the surface, with a railing around it." The court refused to allow the questions to be asked. Thereafter the jury found negligence and returned a verdict for the plaintiff of $2,500.]

BARROWS, J. Defendants' counsel claim that the favorable answers to these questions which they had a right to expect would have tended to show that there was no want of "average ordinary care" on the part of the defendants. We think the questions were properly excluded. The nature of the act in which the defendants'

Maine Mining Journal.

DEVOTED TO THE MINING INTERESTS OF THE STATE OF MAINE.

Vol. I. No. 10.   BANGOR, MAINE, MARCH 5, 1880.

C. B. AYER, Mining Stock Broker,

J. A. STROUT, Broker, For Maine and N.H. Mining Stocks.

93 Exchange Street, Portland, Maine.

N. S. GARDINER, MINING STOCK BROKER, 93 Exchange St., Portland.

MAINE AND NEW HAMPSHIRE MINING STOCK
BOUGHT AND SOLD BY

T. H. MANSFIELD & CO., Brokers, - Portland Mining Exchange.

67 Exchange Street, Portland, Maine.

CLUB STOCKS IN THE LEADING MINES.   AUCTION SALES EVERY SATURDAY AT 10 O'CLOCK A. M.

Maine Mining Exchange.

For full and reliable information regarding the value of Maine Mines and Maine Mining Stocks, application should be made to ISAIAH S. EMERY, at the MAINE MINING EXCHANGE, No. 33 West Market Square, or at the branch office, No. 28 Congress Street, corner Exchange Place, Boston.

Capitalists who desire good investments at low prices, either in the mines themselves, or in the companies in process of organization, will find it greatly to their advantage to apply directly to the

MAINE MINING EXCHANGE,
ISAIAH S. EMERY.

Front page of a weekly mining newspaper during a notorious metal mining rush that overtook parts of Maine from 1879 to 1882. The accident in *Mayhew* took place in December 1881.

Source: Maine Department of Agriculture, Conservation and Forestry

negligence was asserted to consist, with all the circumstances of time and place, whether of commission or omission, and its connection with the plaintiff's injury, presented a case as to which the jury were as well qualified to judge as any expert could be. It was not a case where the opinion of experts could be necessary or useful. . . . If the defendants had proved that in every mining establishment that has existed since the days of Tubal-Cain, it has been the practice to cut ladder-holes in their platforms, situated as this was while in daily use for mining operations, without guarding or lighting them, and without notice to contractors or workmen, it would have no tendency to show that the act was consistent with ordinary prudence or a due regard for the safety of those who were using their premises by their invitation. The gross carelessness of the act appears conclusively upon its recital. Defendants' counsel argue that "if it should appear that they rarely had railings, then it tends to show no want of ordinary care in that respect," that "if one conforms to custom he is so far exercising average ordinary care." The argument proceeds upon an erroneous idea of what constitutes ordinary care. "Custom" and "average" have no proper place in its definition.

It would be no excuse for a want of ordinary care that carelessness was universal about the matter involved, or at the place of the accident, or in the business generally. . . .

The T.J. Hooper
53 F.2d 107 (S.D.N.Y. 1931)

[The operator of the tugboats *The T.J. Hooper* and the *Montrose* was sued under a towing contract when two barges and their cargo of coal were lost in a gale off the New Jersey coast while in transit from Virginia to New York. The gist of the negligence claim was that neither tug was equipped with reliable radios that would have allowed them to receive the storm warnings broadcast in both the morning and the afternoon of March 8, 1928, by the naval station at Arlington. Four other tugs, the *Mars*, the *Menominee*, *The A.L. Walker*, and the *Waltham*, were on the same northbound route as *The T.J. Hooper*. They had received the messages and put safely into the Delaware breakwater.]

COXE, DISTRICT JUDGE: This raises the question whether the *Hooper* and *Montrose* were required to have effective radio sets to pick up weather reports broadcast along the coast. Concededly, there is no statutory law on the subject applicable to tugs of that type, the radio statute applying only to steamers "licensed to carry, or carrying, fifty or more persons"; and excepting by its terms "steamers plying between ports, or places, less than two hundred miles apart." U.S. Code Annotated, title 46, §484. The standard of seaworthiness is not, however, dependent on statutory enactment, or condemned to inertia or rigidity, but changes "with advancing knowledge, experience, and the changed appliances of navigation." It is particularly affected by new devices of demonstrated worth, which have become recognized as regular equipment by common usage.

Radio broadcasting was no new or untried thing in March, 1928. Everywhere, and in almost every field of activity, it was being utilized as an aid to

.munication, and for the dissemination of information. And that radio sets .ere in widespread use on vessels of all kinds is clearly indicated by the testimony in this case. Twice a day the government broadcast from Arlington weather reports forecasting weather conditions. Clearly this was important information which navigators could not afford to ignore.

Captain Powell, master of the *Menominee,* who was a witness for the tugs, testified that prior to March, 1928, his tug, and all other seagoing tugs of his company, were equipped by the owner with efficient radio sets, and that he regarded a radio as part "of the necessary equipment" of every reasonably well-equipped tug in the coastwise service. He further testified that 90 per cent of the coastwise tugs operating along the coast were so equipped. It is, of course, true that many of these radio sets were the personal property of the tug master, and not supplied by the owner. This was so with the *Mars, Waltham,* and *Menominee;* but, notwithstanding that fact, the use of the radio was shown to be so extensive as to amount almost to a universal practice in the navigation of coastwise tugs along the coast. I think therefore there was a duty on the part of the tug owner to supply effective receiving sets.

How have the tugs met this requirement? The *Hooper* had a radio set which belonged to her master, but was practically useless even before the tug left Hampton Roads, and was generally out of order. . . .

I hold therefore . . . (2) that the tugs *T.J. Hooper* and *Montrose* were unseaworthy in failing to have effective radio sets, capable of receiving weather reports on March 8th, . . . [and] (3) that the claims of the cargo owners against the tugs should be allowed. . . .

The T.J. Hooper
60 F.2d 737 (2d Cir. 1932)

[On appeal from the lower court. The court first noted that the evidence supported the claim that *The T.J. Hooper* would have taken shelter if its captain had received the naval broadcasts.]

L. HAND, J. They did not, because their private radio receiving sets, which were on board, were not in working order. These belonged to them personally, and were partly a toy, partly a part of the equipment, but neither furnished by the owner, nor supervised by it. It is not fair to say that there was a general custom among coastwise carriers so to equip their tugs. One line alone did it; as for the rest, they relied upon their crews, so far as they can be said to have relied at all. An adequate receiving set suitable for a coastwise tug can now be got at small cost and is reasonably reliable if kept up; obviously it is a source of great protection to their tows. Twice every day they can receive these predictions, based upon the widest possible information, available to every vessel within two or three hundred miles and more. Such a set is the ears of the tug to catch the spoken word, just as the master's binoculars are her eyes to see a storm signal ashore. Whatever may be said as to other vessels, tugs towing heavy coal laden barges, strung out for half a mile, have little power to manoeuvre, and do not, as this case proves, expose themselves to weather which would not turn back stauncher craft. They can have at hand protection against dangers of which they can learn in no other way.

Is it then a final answer that the business had not yet generally adopted receiving sets? There are, no doubt, cases where courts seem to make the general practice of the calling the standard of proper diligence; we have indeed given some currency to the notion ourselves. Indeed in most cases reasonable prudence is in fact common prudence; but strictly it is never its measure; a whole calling may have unduly lagged in the adoption of new and available devices. It never may set its own tests, however persuasive be its usages. Courts must in the end say what is required; there are precautions so imperative that even their universal disregard will not excuse their omission. But here there was no custom at all as to receiving sets; some had them, some did not; the most that can be urged is that they had not yet become general. Certainly in such a case we need not pause; when some have thought a device necessary, at least we may say that they were right, and the others too slack. The statute [46 U.S.C.A. §484] does not bear on this situation at all. It prescribes not a receiving, but a transmitting set, and for a very different purpose; to call for help, not to get news. We hold the tugs therefore because had they been properly equipped, they would have got the Arlington reports. The injury was a direct consequence of this unseaworthiness.

Decree affirmed.

NOTES

1. *The relationship between custom and negligence.* The four opinions in the three previous cases express different views on the relationship between custom and negligence. *Mayhew* has gained little following, either in its own time or today. *Titus* once enjoyed a considerable following, especially in the context of industrial accidents, although the balance of authority was probably against it even during the nineteenth century. See, e.g., Maynard v. Buck, 100 Mass. 40 (1868), and Wabash Railway v. McDaniels, 107 U.S. 454 (1883). The unrelenting attack on *Titus* often took a strong theoretical turn. Thus, Miller, The So-Called Unbending Test of Negligence, 3 Va. L. Rev. 537, 543 (1916), argued that the *Titus* rule would deter new innovations by firms that might otherwise be prepared to make them, because "the rule of the 'unbending test' constrains him to adopt the unsafe method in order to bring himself within the rule and escape the charge of negligence." Parchomovksy and Stein carry forward the argument that the "custom-based design of our tort law . . . subsidizes producers and users of conventional technologies while taxing innovators," in Torts and Innovation, 107 Mich. L. Rev. 285, 288 (2008). Is this sound? Do firms in a competitive industry have an incentive to improve methods of ensuring worker safety in order to lower wage levels? In a monopolistic industry?

The *T.J. Hooper* did not therefore mark a radical break from tradition, although its allusion that "a whole calling may have unduly lagged in the adoption of new and available devices" has allowed wholesale attacks on standard industry policy, not only in admiralty cases but also for industrial accidents and product cases. Some sense of this approach is found in Bimberg v. Northern Pacific Ry., 14 N.W.2d 410, 413 (Minn. 1944), a wrongful death action brought under the Federal Employers' Liability Act. The defendant argued that designing a trestle was "an engineering problem for solution by the railroads and not by the courts," but the court took a different view of the subject:

> Local usage and general custom, either singly or in combination, will not justify or excuse negligence. They are merely foxholes in one of the battlefields of law, providing shelter, but not complete protection against charges of negligence. The generality of its plan of construction for trestles or bridges cannot excuse a railroad company from responsibility for negligence in its construction. Such plan of construction, commonly followed and "fortified," as defendant insists, "by many years of successful railroad operation," may be evidence of due care, but it cannot avail to establish as safe in law that which is dangerous in fact.

Even after these decisions, the precise relationship between custom and negligence remains controversial. Should compliance with custom establish a prima facie case of due care? Or should it only be evidence tending to show that the defendant did not take unreasonable risks of harm to others? On this question, the Third Restatement downgrades the role of custom. New York's Pattern Jury Instruction on Customary Business Practices is typical.

Restatement of the Law (Third) of Torts: Liability for Physical and Emotional Harm

§13. CUSTOM

(a) An actor's compliance with the custom of the community, or of others in like circumstances, is evidence that the actor's conduct is not negligent but does not preclude a finding of negligence.

(b) An actor's departure from the custom of the community, or of others in like circumstances, in a way that increases risk is evidence of the actor's negligence but does not require a finding of negligence.

Comment b. Compliance with custom: rationale: . . . Possibly, the entire community or industry has lagged: all members of the group to which the actor belongs may have been inattentive to new developments or may have been pursuing self-interest in a way that has encouraged the neglect of a reasonable precaution. . . .

Comment c. Departure from custom: rationale: . . . While proof of deviation from custom is only evidence of negligence, this evidence often has significant weight. As a practical matter, the party who has departed from custom can counter the effect of this evidence by questioning the intelligence of the custom, by showing that its operation poses different or less serious risks than those occasioned by others engaging in seemingly similar activities, or by showing that it has adopted an alternative method for reducing or controlling risks that is at least as effective as the customary method. . . .

New York Pattern Jury Instruction on Customary Business Practices

Civil 2:16. COMMON LAW STANDARD OF CARE—CUSTOMARY BUSINESS PRACTICES

. . . Defendant's conduct is not to be considered unreasonable simply because someone else may have used a better [or safer] practice. On the other hand, a general custom, use, or practice by those in the same business or trade may be considered some evidence of what constitutes reasonable conduct in that trade or business . . . . If you find that there is a custom or practice, you may take that general custom or practice into account in considering the care used by defendant in this case. However, a general custom or practice is not the only test; what you must decide is whether, taking all the facts and circumstances into account, defendant acted with reasonable care.

    2. Custom and cost-benefit analysis.   Hand's decision in *The T.J. Hooper* complements his analysis in *Carroll Towing, supra* at 170. While *Carroll Towing* articulates Hand's use of a cost-benefit formula, *The T.J. Hooper* denies any conclusive weight to custom—its major rival in setting the standard of care. Hand's view has received overwhelming acceptance in the courts and among commentators. What should the jury do when custom conflicts with the cost-benefit standard? See Abraham, Custom, Noncustomary Practice, and Negligence, 109 Colum. L. Rev. 1784, 1818-1820 (2009), insisting that when they conflict, "the jury can make its own informed choice between the outcomes dictated by the competing conceptions." Was there such a conflict in The T.J Hooper?

    A greater respect for custom is found in Epstein, The Path to *The T.J. Hooper:* The Theory and History of Custom in the Law of Tort, 21 J. Legal Stud. 1, 4-5 (1992), which argues:

[G]iven the imperfections of the legal system, the conventional wisdom that places cost-benefit analysis first and custom second is incorrect in at least two ways. First, in cases that arise out of a consensual arrangement, negligence is often the appropriate standard for liability, and, where it is so, custom should be regarded as conclusive evidence of due care in the absence of any contractual stipulation to the contrary. It is quite possible in some consensual settings no custom will emerge, at which point the negligence inquiry will be inescapably ad hoc. But where consistent custom emerges, regardless of its origins, it should be followed. Second, in stranger cases—that is, those where the harm does not fall on a contracting party or someone with whom the defendant has a special relationship—negligence should normally not be the appropriate standard of care, so that reliance on custom is as irrelevant as the negligence issue to which custom alone is properly directed. But where negligence is adopted in these stranger cases, then custom is normally *not* the appropriate standard because it registers the preferences of the parties to the custom, not those who are victimized by it. It should be taken into account, but given no dispositive weight. . . .

Note that *The T.J. Hooper* arose out of a consensual situation, as does most of the litigation that implicates questions of custom. Accordingly, the choice between the customary and cost-benefit approaches lies at the heart of understanding the distribution of power between the market and the courts in setting the standards of conduct for defendants across many lines of business and endeavors. Here the Hand formula turns out in practice to be far more interventionist than any standard of care based on custom. These cost-benefit tests are used to challenge the rationality of markets, while formulas based on custom accept and rely on some level of implicit rationality in market behavior.

How do customs emerge? Should it make any difference whether we are dealing with customs in a closely knit industry or with those that reach a broad commercial market? Whether we are dealing with parties who have overlapping roles (i.e., transactions between merchants in the same line of business) or with parties having specialized distinctive relationships (e.g., physician/patient or landlord/tenant)? Is it possible to have an accurate picture of the soundness of industry practices if customary evidence is ruled inadmissible, as in *Mayhew*? For a negative answer, see Abraham, *supra* at 1803-1804.

3. Custom and private rules of conduct. Can the plaintiff use the defendant's established rules that govern the conduct of his employees as evidence of negligence? In Fonda v. St. Paul City Ry., 74 N.W. 166, 169 (Minn. 1898), the plaintiff, an injured pedestrian, sued the defendant for the negligence of its servant in the operation of its train. The plaintiff was "a stranger to and not an employee of" the defendant, so that his "conduct could not have been in any way affected or influenced" by rules of which he had no knowledge. Mitchell, J., differentiated these internal house rules from statutes and municipal ordinances because of the perverse incentives created. "The effect of it is that, the more cautious and careful a man is in the adoption of rules in the management of his business in order to protect others, the worse he is off, and the higher the degree of care he is bound to exercise. A person may, out of abundant caution, adopt rules requiring of his employees a much higher degree of care than the law imposes. This is a practice that ought to be encouraged, and not discouraged. But, if the adoption of such a course is to be used against him as an admission, he would naturally find it to his interest not to adopt any rules at all." Is that the case if the proprietor can advertise his compliance with higher standards? Does this issue arise in stranger cases brought under a strict liability theory?

In any event, more recent cases have shown a willingness to allow the plaintiff to introduce the defendant's own internal rules on the standard of care question. In Lucy Webb Hayes National Training School v. Perotti, 419 F.2d 704, 710 (D.C. Cir. 1969), the plaintiff's decedent had been admitted into the defendant's psychiatric hospital as a mental patient for observation and treatment. Shortly after being admitted, the decedent slipped past the nurses' station that separated the secured portion of the floor, Ward 7-W, into the unsecured area on the same floor. While the defendant's attendant was leading the decedent back to Ward 7-W, he bolted away, jumped through a window, and plunged to his death. The plaintiff argued that the hospital fell short of its own internal standard by allowing the decedent to wander from the closed to the open ward. The court held:

> We think the jury could find negligence upon the part of the hospital from this evidence without the assistance of expert testimony. The jurors might not be able to determine the necessity for a closed ward for mental patients of the type admitted to Ward 7-W, nor to evaluate the need for restrictions upon the movement of patients into and out of the closed ward. But the hospital itself had made these decisions. It could, of course, have presented evidence that the limitations upon patient movement constituted more than due care, or were unrelated to patient safety. Indeed, witnesses did testify for the hospital that the open and closed wards were separated by a locked door chiefly, or only, to isolate the more disturbed patients from those not so acutely ill. On the basis of all the evidence, however, the jury could reasonably conclude that the hospital's failure to observe the standards it had itself established represented negligence.

For the modern equivocation on the question of private standards, see RTT:LPEH §13, comment *f,* which first notes that "allowing the defendant's departure from its own standard to be used against the defendant might seem unfair, since it penalizes the defendant who has voluntarily provided an extra measure of safety." On the other hand, "the plaintiff may well have relied on the defendant's standard (or the defendant's general reputation for safety) in choosing to deal with the defendant; furthermore, the plaintiff may well be paying for at least the general costs of compliance that the standard imposes on the defendant." Should general reputation play the same role as an internal directive?

4. Updating custom.   In Trimarco v. Klein, 436 N.E.2d 502 (N.Y. 1982), the plaintiff was injured in 1976 when he slipped in his bathroom and received serious lacerations from crashing against a shower door made of ordinary glass estimated to be between $\frac{1}{16}$ and $\frac{1}{4}$ of an inch thick. The shower door had been installed in the 1950s, when the use of ordinary glass was standard practice. Since the mid-1960s, the common practice in New York City had been to use safer tempered glass "whether to replace broken glass or to comply with the request of a tenant." The plaintiff in this instance did not know that ordinary glass was used in his shower door. Reversing a decision of the Appellate Division, the New York Court of Appeals allowed the plaintiff to reach the jury. Fuchsberg, J., first noted that evidence of custom was admissible because "it reflects the judgment and experience and conduct of many," and because "its relevancy and reliability comes too from the direct bearing it has on feasibility, for its focusing is on the practicability of a precaution in actual operation and the readiness with which it can be employed." Nonetheless, the court refused to give the custom conclusive weight, noting that "[a]fter all, customs and usages run the gamut of merit like anything else." The court then concluded that "it was also for the jury to decide whether, at the point in time when the accident occurred, the modest cost and ready availability of safety glass and the dynamics of the growing custom to use it for shower enclosures had transformed what once may have been considered a reasonably safe part of the apartment into one which, in light of later developments, no longer could be so regarded." Nonetheless, Fuchsberg, J., ordered a new trial holding that it was improper to admit the applicable statutory provisions, which "protected only those tenants for whom shower glazing was installed after the statutory effective date." For the contrary result, see Considine v. City of Waterbury, 905 A.2d 70, 90 (Conn. 2006). On either view, must all old shower doors be replaced? Sprinklers and burglar alarms be retrofitted in old buildings?

Lama v. Borras
16 F.3d 473 (1st Cir. 1994)

STAHL, J. Defendants-appellants Dr. Pedro Borras and Asociación Hospital del Maestro, Inc. (Hospital) appeal from a jury verdict finding them liable for medical malpractice to plaintiffs Roberto Romero Lama (Romero) and his wife, Norma. . . . Finding no error, we affirm.

I. BACKGROUND

Since the jury found defendants liable, we recount the facts in the light most favorable to plaintiffs, drawing all reasonable inferences in their favor; we do not evaluate the credibility of witnesses or the weight of the evidence. . . .

In 1985, Romero was suffering from back pain and searching for solutions. Dr. Nancy Alfonso, Romero's family physician, provided some treatment but then referred him to Dr. Borras, a neurosurgeon. Dr. Borras concluded that Romero had a herniated disc and scheduled surgery. Prior to surgery, Dr. Borras neither prescribed nor enforced a regime of absolute bed rest, nor did he offer other key components of "conservative treatment." Although Dr. Borras instructed Romero, a heavy smoker, to enter the hospital one week before surgery in order to "clean out" his lungs and strengthen his heart, Romero was still not subjected to standard conservative treatment.

While operating on April 9, 1986, Dr. Borras discovered that Romero had an "extruded" disc and attempted to remove the extruding material. Either because Dr. Borras failed to remove the offending material or because he operated at the wrong level, Romero's original symptoms returned in full force several days after the operation. Dr. Borras concluded that a second operation was necessary to remedy the "recurrence."

Dr. Borras operated again on May 15, 1986. Dr. Borras did not order pre- or post-operative antibiotics. It is unclear whether the second operation was successful in curing the herniated disc. In any event, as early as May 17, a nurse's note indicates that the bandage covering Romero's surgical wound was "very bloody," a symptom which, according to expert testimony, indicates the possibility of infection. On May 18, Romero was experiencing local pain at the site of the incision, another symptom consistent with an infection. On May 19, the bandage was "soiled again." A more complete account of Romero's evolving condition is not available because the Hospital instructed nurses to engage in "charting by exception," a system whereby nurses did not record qualitative observations for each of the day's three shifts, but instead made such notes only when necessary to chronicle important changes in a patient's condition.

On the night of May 20, Romero began to experience severe discomfort in his back. He passed the night screaming in pain. At some point on May 21, Dr. Edwin Lugo Piazza, an attending physician, diagnosed the problem as discitis—an infection of the space between discs—and responded by initiating antibiotic treatment. Discitis is extremely painful and, since it occurs in a location with little blood circulation, very slow to cure. Romero was hospitalized for several additional months while undergoing treatment for the infection.

After moving from Puerto Rico to Florida, the Romeros filed this diversity tort action in United States District Court for the District of Puerto Rico. Plaintiffs alleged that Dr. Borras was negligent in four general areas: (1) failure to provide proper conservative medical treatment; (2) premature and otherwise improper discharge after surgery; (3) negligent performance of surgery; and (4) failure to provide proper management for the infection. While plaintiffs did not claim that the Hospital was vicariously liable for any negligence on the part of Dr. Borras, they alleged that the Hospital was itself negligent in [its] failure to prepare, use, and monitor proper medical records. . . .

[At trial the jury awarded plaintiffs $600,000, and the district court rejected defendant's motion for a judgment as a matter of law under Fed. R. Civ. P. 50(b), as well as defendant's motion for a new trial under Fed. R. Civ. P. 59. The district court concluded that had Dr. Borras used conservative treatment, he might have obviated all the risks of a complex laminectomy, and that better record keeping could have allowed hospital personnel to detect the infection at an earlier stage, and finally that the hospital staff could have been negligent in handling the dressings and bandages.]

We find the reasoning of the district court to be substantially sound and therefore affirm the result. . . .

III. DISCUSSION

A.   MEDICAL MALPRACTICE UNDER PUERTO RICO LAW

We begin our analysis by laying out the substantive law of Puerto Rico governing this diversity suit. To establish a prima facie case of medical malpractice in Puerto Rico, a plaintiff must demonstrate: (1) the basic norms of knowledge and medical care applicable to general practitioners or specialists; (2) proof that the medical personnel failed to follow these basic norms in the treatment of the patient; and (3) a causal relation between the act or omission of the physician and the injury suffered by the patient.

The burden of a medical malpractice plaintiff in establishing the physician's duty is more complicated than that of an ordinary tort plaintiff. Instead of simply appealing to the jury's view of what is reasonable under the circumstances, a medical malpractice plaintiff must establish the relevant national standard of care. . . .

Naturally, the trier of fact can rarely determine the applicable standard of care without the assistance of expert testimony. The predictable battle of the experts then creates a curious predicament for the fact-finder, because an error of judgment regarding diagnosis or treatment does not lead to liability when expert opinion suggests that the physician's conduct fell within a range of acceptable alternatives. While not allowed to speculate, the fact-finder is of course free to find some experts more credible than others.

Proof of causation is also more difficult in a medical malpractice case than in a routine tort case because a jury must often grapple with scientific processes that are unfamiliar and involve inherent uncertainty. A plaintiff must prove, by a preponderance of the evidence, that the physician's negligent conduct was the factor that "most probably" caused harm to the plaintiff. As in the case of duty, however, a jury normally cannot find causation based on mere speculation and conjecture; expert testimony is generally essential. . . .

B. NEGLIGENCE OF DR. BORRAS

The Borras Defendants claim that plaintiffs failed to introduce any evidence sufficient to prove either (1) the relevant standards of acceptable medical practice or (2) the causal link between Dr. Borras' conduct and harm to the plaintiffs. While plaintiffs may not have been able to substantiate the broad attack outlined in their complaint, we focus here on only one allegation of negligence: Dr. Borras' failure to provide conservative treatment prior to the first operation.

Defendants argue that plaintiffs failed to prove a general medical standard governing the need for conservative treatment in a case like that of Romero. We disagree. Plaintiffs' chief expert witness, Dr. George Udvarhelyi, testified that, absent an indication of neurological impairment, the standard practice is for a neurosurgeon to postpone lumbar disc surgery while the patient undergoes conservative treatment, with a period of absolute bed rest as the prime ingredient. In these respects, the views of defendants' neurosurgery experts did not diverge from those of Dr. Udvarhelyi. For example, Dr. Luis Guzman Lopez testified that, in the absence of extraordinary factors, "all neurosurgeons go for [conservative treatment] before they finally decide on [an] operation." Indeed, when called by plaintiffs, Dr. Borras (who also testified as a neurosurgery expert) agreed on cross-examination with the statement that "bed rest is normally recommended before surgery is decided in a patient like Mr. Romero," and claimed that he *did* give conservative treatment to Romero.

In spite of Dr. Borras' testimony to the contrary, there was also sufficient evidence for the jury to find that Dr. Borras failed to provide the customary conservative treatment. Dr. Alfonso, Romero's family physician, testified that Dr. Borras, while aware that Romero had not followed a program of absolute bed rest, proceeded with surgery anyway. Although Romero was admitted to the hospital one week before surgery, there was evidence that Dr. Borras neither prescribed nor attempted to enforce a conservative treatment regime. In fact, there was evidence that Dr. Borras' main goal was simply to admit Romero for a week of smoke-free relaxation, not absolute bed rest, because Romero's heavy smoking and mild hypertension made him a high-risk surgery patient. In short, we agree with the district court that the jury could reasonably have concluded that Dr. Borras failed to institute and manage a proper conservative treatment plan.

The issue of causation is somewhat more problematic. There are two potential snags in the chain of causation. First, it is uncertain that premature surgery was the cause of Romero's infection. Second, it is uncertain whether conservative treatment would have made surgery unnecessary. With respect to the first problem, the Puerto Rico Supreme Court has suggested that, when a physician negligently exposes a patient to risk-prone surgery, the physician is liable for the harm associated with a foreseeable risk. In this case, it is undisputed that discitis was a foreseeable risk of lumbar disc surgery.

Turning to the second area of uncertainty, we observe that nearly all of the experts who testified on the subject for both plaintiffs and defendants were of the opinion that conservative treatment would eliminate the need for surgery in the overwhelming majority of cases. Nonetheless, defendants introduced expert testimony that, because Romero suffered from an "extruded" disc, conservative treatment would not have helped. Dr. Udvarhelyi testified, however, that an extruded disc is indeed amenable to conservative treatment. With competent expert testimony in the record, the jury was not left to conjure up its own theories of causation. And certainly, the jury was free to credit some witnesses more than others. The question is admittedly close, but the jury could have reasonably found that Dr. Borras' failure to administer conservative treatment was the "most probable cause" of the first operation.

We conclude that plaintiffs introduced legally sufficient evidence to support each element of at least one major allegation of negligence on the part of Dr. Borras. We therefore hold that the district court properly denied the Borras Defendants' Rule 50 and 59 motions.

C.   NEGLIGENCE OF ASOCIACIÓN HOSPITAL DEL MAESTRO

While plaintiffs made a number of allegations against the Hospital, we focus on the allegation that the failure of hospital nurses to report on each nursing shift was a negligent cause of the late detection of Romero's infection.

The Hospital cannot seriously dispute that plaintiffs introduced sufficient evidence on the elements of duty and breach. [The court then held that the jury could properly find that the nursing staff's failure to keep qualitative notes of each nursing shift, as required by regulation, could count as the proximate cause of the harm. It first noted that the sketchy notes could have delayed the diagnosis of plaintiff's excessive bleeding at the site of the wound, which in turn "could have prevented the infection from reaching the disc interspace in the critical period prior to May 20."]

Affirmed.

NOTES

1. Unique role of custom in medical malpractice.   Custom occupies a privileged position in medical malpractice cases: "Health care professionals must exercise the same care that other professionals customarily exercise. Thus, the duty applied to medical professionals is a purely factual one, unlike the normative 'reasonable care' standard invoked for non-professionals." Cramm & Hartz, Ascertaining Customary Care in Malpractice Cases: Asking Those Who Know, 37 Wake Forest L. Rev. 699, 699-700 (2002).

Why reject *The T.J. Hooper* in medical malpractice cases in favor of deference to custom? One influential explanation is offered in Morris, Custom and Negligence, 42 Colum. L. Rev. 1147, 1164-1165 (1942):

> Why should conformity to the practice protect a physician from liability? Drovers [cattle drivers], railroads, merchants, etc., are not so protected. The doctor escapes liability even though he conforms only to the practice in his locality or the practice in similar localities. And treatment need not conform to a general usage, it need only be like that used by some reputable doctors. If all doctors reasonably developed and applied their skill and knowledge, the conformity test might be the equivalent of reasonable care under the circumstances. Doctors as a class may be more likely to exert their best efforts than drovers, railroads, and merchants but they are human and subject to the temptations of laziness and unthinking acceptance of traditions. The rationale is: no other standard is practical. Our judges and juries are usually not competent to judge whether or not a doctor has acted reasonably. The conformity test is probably the only workable test available. . . .
>
> The patient who has endured suffering is an appealing plaintiff. Juries are likely to favor him. And it is widely known that doctors usually carry liability insurance. But a doctor who loses a malpractice case stands to lose more than the amount of the judgment—he may also lose his professional reputation and his livelihood. These considerations heighten the need for a test of malpractice that will protect doctors against undeserved liability. The law may be academically deficient in countenancing an excuse that may occasionally be based on the negligence of the other doctors. But the grossly incompetent practitioner will find little comfort in the tests of malpractice. A few negligent doctors may escape, but the quack will not. The reasonably prudent man "test" would enable the ambulance chaser to make a law suit out of any protracted illness.

See also Epstein, Medical Malpractice: The Case for Contract, 1 Am. B. Found. Res. J. 87, 108-113 (1976). For a modern critique of Morris' account, see Hetcher, Creating Safe Social Norms in a Dangerous World, 73 S. Cal. L. Rev. 1, 19-22 (1999).

2. The standard of care in medical malpractice cases.   Although *Lama* was decided under Puerto Rican law, its basic principles are indistinguishable from those applicable in virtually all common law jurisdictions. Thus, in Fay v. Grand Strand Regional Medical Center, 771 S.E.2d 639, 644 (S.C. 2015), the standard was put as follows:

> A plaintiff in a medical malpractice case must present (1) evidence of the generally recognized practices and procedures that would be exercised by competent

practitioners in a defendant doctor's field of medicine under the same or similar circumstances, (2) evidence that the defendant doctor departed from the recognized and generally accepted standards, practices, and procedures in the manner alleged by the plaintiff, and (3) evidence that the defendant's departure from the generally accepted standards and practices was the proximate cause of the plaintiff's injuries and damages.

Often, no single custom covers a given medical question. In Jones v. Chidester, 610 A.2d 964, 965, 969 (Pa. 1992), the court described the "two schools" problem as follows:

A medical practitioner has an absolute defense to a claim of negligence when it is determined that the prescribed treatment or procedure has been approved by one group of medical experts even though an alternate school of thought recommends another approach, or it is agreed among experts that alternative treatments and practices are acceptable. The doctrine is applicable only where there is more than one method of accepted treatment or procedure. In specific terms, however, we are called upon in this case to decide once again whether a school of thought qualifies as such when it is advocated by a "considerable number" of medical experts or when it commands acceptance by "respective, reputable and reasonable" practitioners. The former test calls for a quantitative analysis, while the latter is premised on qualitative grounds.

The court then noted that the precedents left the question unresolved, and continued:

It is incumbent upon us to settle this confusion. The "two schools of thought doctrine" provides a complete defense to malpractice. It is therefore insufficient to show that there exists a "small minority" of physicians who agree with the defendant's questioned practice. Thus, the Superior Court's "reputable and respected by reasonable medical experts" test is improper. Rather, there must be a considerable number of physicians, recognized and respected in their field, sufficient to create another "school of thought."

On the two schools test generally, see Bradford, The "Respectable Minority" Doctrine in Missouri Medical Negligence Law, 56 J. Mo. B. 326 (2000).

3. Setting the customary standard.   Expert testimony is generally required to determine the applicable standard of care in medical malpractice cases. "[A] universal corollary to the professional-standards-based regime of medical negligence law is that testimony by a legally competent medical expert is . . . essential for the plaintiff to make out a prima facie case of professional medical liability. . . . [T]he plaintiff must present [expert] testimony that both identifies the relevant professional standard and also establishes its violation." King, The Common Knowledge Exception to the Expert Testimony Requirement for Establishing the Standard of Care in Medical Malpractice, 59 Ala. L. Rev. 51, 59 (2007). The "common knowledge rule" is a widely accepted (albeit narrow) exception; when a court determines that the allegedly negligent conduct in a medical malpractice case is "within the understanding of lay members of the public," it generally does not require expert testimony to determine the applicable standard of care. *Id.* at 63.

Other sources are sometimes available but are rarely dispositive. In Morlino v. Medical Center of Ocean County, 706 A.2d 721, 729-730 (N.J. 1998), the defendant emergency room physician, Dr. Dugenio, prescribed Ciprofloxacin to the plaintiff, then eight and one-half months pregnant, when she complained of a serious sore throat. Her fetus was dead the next day. Before prescribing the drug the defendant consulted the Physician's Desk Reference, "a compilation of information about prescription drugs that is published annually and distributed to the medical professional free of charge." The PDR contains a list of indications and contraindications for the use of various drugs, alone and in combination, for treating various conditions. It contained the following warning: CIPROFLOXA-CIN SHOULD NOT BE USED IN CHILDREN OR PREGNANT WOMEN, noting that animal studies indicated some fetal risk. Having read this warning, Dr. Dugenio nonetheless prescribed the drug because he was concerned that an influenza bacteria, if untreated, could lead to greater patient illness, which in turn could jeopardize the fetus's own welfare. In affirming a jury verdict for the defendants, Pollock, J., had allowed evidence of PDR warnings to establish the applicable standard of care for prescribing medicine, but cautioned:

> Nevertheless, drug manufacturers do not design package inserts and PDR entries to establish a standard of medical care. Manufacturers write drug package inserts and PDR warnings for many reasons including compliance with FDA requirements, advertisement, the provision of useful information to physicians, and an attempt to limit the manufacturer's liability. After a drug has been on the market for a sufficient period of time, moreover, physicians may rely more on their own experience and the professional publications of others than on a drug manufacturer's advertisements, inserts, or PDR entries. . . .
>
> Accordingly, we hold that the package inserts and PDR references alone do not establish the standard of care. It follows that a physician's failure to adhere to PDR warnings does not by itself constitute negligence. Reliance on the PDR alone to establish negligence would both obviate expert testimony on an issue where it is needed and could mislead the jury about the appropriate standard of care.

4. The locality rule. If the customary standard has survived, the locality rule, as defended by Morris, has taken a beating in the modern age of national medical standards and accreditation, complete with board-certified physicians. One key transitional decision is Brune v. Belinkoff, 235 N.E.2d 793 (Mass. 1968). There, the plaintiff claimed that the defendant anesthesiologist negligently administered a spinal anesthetic during the delivery of plaintiff's baby in October 1958. The defendant, practicing in New Bedford, Massachusetts, gave plaintiff an eight-milligram dosage of pontocaine. Eleven hours later plaintiff attempted to climb out of bed, but slipped and fell, suffering persistent injuries, due to an excessive dosage of pontocaine. Some medical evidence was introduced to show that good medical practice required a dosage of less than five milligrams. Other evidence, including that of defendant, tended to show that the dosage given was customary in New Bedford, and that the smaller dosages given in New York and Boston were appropriate because of the different obstetrical procedures used in those two cities. "The New Bedford obstetricians use supra fundi pressure (pressure applied to the uterus during delivery) which 'requires a higher level of anesthesia.'"

On appeal from judgment for the defendant, Spaulding, J., upheld the plaintiff's exception to that charge. He agreed that the traditional locality rule announced in Small v. Howard, 128 Mass. 131 (1880), rightly protected a jack-of-all-trades general practitioner performing difficult surgery in a small country village. But for today's high-powered specialists he opted for a national standard:

> The time has come when the medical profession should no longer be Balkanized by the application of varying geographic standards in malpractice cases. Accordingly, Small v. Howard is hereby overruled. The present case affords a good illustration of the inappropriateness of the "locality" rule to existing conditions. The defendant was a specialist practising in New Bedford, a city of 100,000, which is slightly more than fifty miles from Boston, one of the medical centers of the nation, if not the world. This is a far cry from the country doctor in Small v. Howard, who ninety years ago was called upon to perform difficult surgery. Yet the trial judge told the jury that if the skill and ability of New Bedford physicians were "fifty percent inferior" to those obtaining in Boston the defendant should be judged by New Bedford standards, "having regard to the current state of advance of the profession." This may well be carrying the rule of Small v. Howard to its logical conclusion, but it is, we submit, a reductio ad absurdum of the rule.
>
> The proper standard is whether the physician, if a general practitioner, has exercised the degree of care and skill of the average qualified practitioner, taking into account the advances in the profession. In applying this standard it is permissible to consider the medical resources available to the physician as *one* circumstance in determining the skill and care required. Under this standard some allowance is thus made for the type of community in which the physician carries on his practice. . . .

Under the modern rule, should a rural clinic be required to have the s equipment as a state-of-the-art university hospital? Take costs in general account? Should the standard of care vary for residents and fellows who a in training? For a negative response, see Clark v. University Hospital-UMDI A.2d 838, 843 (N.J. Super. 2006): "Defendants held themselves out as doct should be held to the standard of care they claimed to profess." What if th themselves out as residents in training?

Murray v. UNMC Physicians
806 N.W.2d 118 (Neb. 2011)

GERRARD, J.: [The decedent, Mary Murray, suffered from pulmo hypertension, which can lead to a constriction of blood vessels in the in turn leads to heart failure. Flolan vasodilator, if administered day, can extend life at a cost of about $100,000 per year for the

The decedent's physician had written the order for Flolan, "before the catheterization, pending the results of the catheterization and insurance approval." But before the paperwork could be cleared, the decedent returned to the emergency room where she died of cardiac arrest. There was sharply conflicting expert evidence as to the cause of death—was it arterial hypertension, or myocarditis, a heart inflammation caused by bacteria—and whether, if it was cardiac arrest, it could have been prevented by the earlier use of Flolan. The defendant's experts also testified that it would be "devastating" to the patient to discontinue treatment once it had started.]

Robert [Mary's husband] moved for a directed verdict on the standard of care, arguing that as a matter of law, insurance coverage cannot dictate what doctors do. UNMC replied that according to its experts, a continuing source for treatment is something that doctors should consider in determining how treatment is to be administered. Robert's motion was overruled. Robert also asked that the jury be instructed that if the standard of care requires prescription of a drug, it is not a defense to a claim the standard of care has been violated that the drug would not be provided until approved by an insurance carrier. That instruction was refused.

[After the jury entered a verdict for the defendants, the trial judge announced]

> . . . that, as a matter of law, a medical standard of care cannot be tied to or controlled by an insurance company or the need for payment. The "bean counters" in an insurance office are not physicians. Medicine cannot reach the point where an insurance company determines the medical standard of care for the treatment of a patient. Nor, can we live in a society where the medical care required is not controlled by the physicians treating the patient. The position advanced by [UNMC's] expert tells us that the standard of care is different for those with money than for those without. This is neither moral nor just. It is wrong. . . .

[On appeal, Gerrard, J., noted that the standard articulation of the customary standard of care is both unitary and wealth-blind. He then noted that it] has been suggested that at a fundamental level, a unitary, wealth-blind standard of care cannot be reconciled with the growth of technology and the stratification of available health care. Custom is increasingly difficult to identify in today's medical marketplace, as resource distinctions produce fragmentation and disintegration. It has also been suggested that maintaining a unitary standard of care disadvantages those who may not be able to pay for health care. Physicians remain free, for the most part, to decline to treat those who cannot pay, and "an outright refusal to treat an indigent patient, in contrast to a decision to treat in a manner inconsistent with the unitary malpractice standard, rarely creates the threat of liability." [Siliciano, Wealth, Equity, and the Unitary Medical Malpractice Standard, 77 Va. L. Rev. 439, 457 (1991).] So, it has been argued that rather than assume the burden of paying for a patient's treatment, or the potential liability of providing some but not all possible care, the unitary standard makes it more likely that "providers will now sidestep the entire problem simply by refusing to accept some, or all, of such patients for treatment." [*Id.*]

On the other hand, it has been argued that permitting physicians to make medical decisions based on resource scarcity would compromise the fiduciary relationship between patient and physician, creating a conflict of interest because the patient's well-being would no longer be the physician's focus. The question is how the value judgments inherent in the development of the standard of care might evolve in response to a societal interest in controlling health care costs. It has been explained that a physician's initial value judgment, in treating a patient, is made in light of conclusions reached about the likely benefits that services would have had for the plaintiff patient. It involves an evaluation as to whether the services should have been provided given their likely benefits, the risk of iatrogenic harm, and the gravity of the problem experienced by the patient. Normally the value judgment does not involve an explicit consideration of the costs of caring for a patient, although economics are implicitly considered. Physicians do not do everything conceivably possible in caring for a patient—they draw what they consider to be reasonable boundary lines. . . .

In short, the traditional ethical norms of the medical profession and the legal demands of the customary standard of care impose significant restrictions on a physician's ability to consider the costs of treatment, despite significant and increasing pressure to contain those costs. Whether the legal standard of care should change to alleviate that conflict, and how it might change, has been the subject of considerable discussion. It has been suggested that the customary standard of care could evolve to permit the denial of marginally beneficial treatment—in other words, when high costs would not be justified by minor expected benefits. Others have suggested that the standard of care should evolve to consider two separate components: (1) a skill component, addressing the skill with which diagnoses are made and treatment is rendered, that would not vary by a patient's financial circumstances and (2) a resource component, addressing deliberate decisions about how much treatment to give a patient, that would vary so as to not demand more of physicians than is reasonable. It has been suggested that physicians should be permitted to rebut the presumption of a unitary standard of care when diminution of care arises by economic necessity instead of negligence. And many have suggested that custom should no longer be the benchmark for the standard of care; instead, practice standards or guidelines could be promulgated that would settle issues of resource allocation.

All of the concerns discussed above are serious, and they present difficult questions that courts will be required to confront in the future. But we do not confront them here, because under the unique facts of this case, they are not presented. Contrary to the district court's belief, this is not a case in which insurance company "bean counters" overrode the medical judgment of a patient's physicians or in which those physicians allowed their medical judgment to be subordinated to a patient's ability to pay for treatment. Nor is this a case in which the parties disputed the cost-effectiveness of the treatment at issue. Rather, UNMC's evidence was that its decision to wait to begin Flolan treatment was not economic—it was a medical decision, based on the health consequences to the patient if the treatment is interrupted.

. . . [M]ore fundamentally, the district court's concerns about health care policy, while understandable, are misplaced in a situation in which the patient's ability to continue to pay for treatment is still a medical consideration. In other words, even when the standard of care is limited to medical considerations relevant to the welfare of the patient, and not economic considerations relevant to the welfare of the health care provider, the standard of care articulated by UNMC's witnesses in this case was still consistent with a medical standard of care.

This case does not involve a conflict of interest between the physician and patient—there was no evidence, for instance, of a financial incentive for UNMC's physicians to control costs . . . because UNMC's physicians were not weighing the risk to Mary's health against the risk to her pocketbook, or UNMC's budget, or even a general social interest in controlling health care costs. UNMC's physicians were weighing the risk to Mary's health of delaying treatment against the risk to Mary's health of potentially interrupted treatment. Stated another way, this was not a case in which a physician refused to provide beneficial care—it was a case in which the physicians determined that the care would not be beneficial if it was later interrupted. In fact, it could be deadly.

[Gerrard, J., then concluded that it was a jury question whether the applicable standard of care "required Flolan to be administered immediately," so that it was wrong to order a new trial.]

Reversed.

NOTES

1. Revolution in health care provision. The traditional fee for service system of payments has been displaced by a complicated array of health care programs—Medicare, Medicaid, the Affordable Care Act of 2010—each with its own elaborate requirements for coverage and reimbursements. As *Murray* indicates, these complex financial constraints are only aggravated in the face of ever more expensive medical treatments of varying effectiveness. Is *Murray* right to leave these questions to the jury in each individual case? Should physicians and medical centers that have no direct financial interest in these cases be held exempt from coverage as a matter of law? For discussions on this question, see Morreim, Cost Containment and the Standard of Medical Care, 75 Cal. L. Rev. 1719 (1987); Henderson & Siliciano, Universal Health Care and the Continued Reliance on Custom in Determining Medical Malpractice, 79 Cornell L. Rev. 1382 (1994).

2. Empirical assessment of the medical malpractice system. How effective is the malpractice system in deterring physician and hospital negligence and in providing compensation to injured patients? What effect does malpractice liability have on health care costs, treatment options, and the way medicine is practiced?

Empirical evidence of a strong deterrent effect from medical malpractice liability is hard to find. One comprehensive review of all tort systems, Dewees & Trebilcock, The Efficacy of the Tort System and Its Alternatives: A Review of the Empirical Evidence, 30 Osgoode Hall L.J. 57 (1992), notes that Canadian doctors are only 20 percent as likely to be sued as U.S. doctors, and pay insurance premiums around 10 percent of those paid by U.S. doctors, yet "there appears to be no evidence that Canadian physicians are more careless than their U.S. counterparts." Dewees and Trebilcock conclude that the medical malpractice system fares badly, both in absolute terms and in comparison with automobile insurance, in providing compensation to injured parties and in meeting the concerns of corrective justice.

Weiler, Medical Malpractice on Trial 14 (1991), reports on two major studies—one in California during the 1970s, and one in New York from the late 1980s—that between them reviewed the patient records of some 50,000 hospitalizations (some 20,000 in California and 30,000 in New York). Both studies found that the instances of negligent treatment resulting in patient harm far exceeded the number of malpractice claims filed, and, by greater margins, the number of cases in which recovery occurred. The New York investigation (in which Weiler took part), for example, estimated that about one in 100 patients suffered serious injury or death attributable to negligent medical treatment, yet suit was filed for only one in every eight valid claims, with compensation paid in only half those claims. Moreover, "a substantial proportion of the claims actually filed were for cases in which we had concluded on the basis of hospital records that no medical injury at all had occurred, much less one caused by medical negligence." It was not possible to determine whether the compensation actually paid was in the meritorious cases. Stated otherwise, these studies suggest that the liability system picks out the wrong cases for suit.

More recent empirical work by Studdert et al., Claims, Errors, and Compensation Payments in Medical Malpractice Litigation, 354 New Eng. J. Med. 2024, 2024 (2006), suggests that concerns regarding frivolous claims are overstated. Based upon physician review of a random sample of 1,452 closed malpractice claims, including paid claims, from five different liability insurers in 2006, the researchers concluded that "[c]laims that lack evidence of error are not uncommon, but most are denied compensation."

Hyman et al., Does Tort Reform Affect Physician Supply? Evidence from Texas, 43 Int'l Rev. L. & Econ. 203 (2015), examines the impact of the substantial Texas medical malpractice reforms of 2003, and concludes that there is no evidence that these reforms had many effects. "Physician supply was not measurably stunted prior to reform, and it did not measurably improve after reform. This is true for all patient care physicians in Texas, high-malpractice-risk specialties, primary care physicians, and rural physicians." Need the same results apply for the willingness of physicians to take on difficult cases, or alter their fees for services? Most states have nonetheless responded legislatively to the perceived need to curb malpractice liability. For a comprehensive compendium of the most prevalent tort reforms between 1980 and 2014 in the United States, see Avraham, Database of State Law Tort Reforms (Northwestern Law & Econ. Research Paper No. 06-08; U. of Tex. Law, Law and Econ. Research Paper No. 184), *available at* http://ssrn.com/abstract=902711. In The Poor State of Health Care Quality in the U.S.: Is Malpractice Liability Part of the Problem or Part of the Solution?, 90 Cornell L. Rev. 893, 895-896 (2005), Hyman and Silver complain:

The most popular proposals—damages caps, credits for payments from collateral sources, heightened requirements for expert witnesses, and limits on contingency fees—have more to do with provider and insurer self-interest than with health care quality. Their purpose is to reduce insurance costs in the short run, not to improve delivery systems in ways that address low-quality care or decrease the frequency of harmful errors.

Other more systemic reforms proposed by scholars have not fared well. Mello & Brennan, Deterrence of Medical Errors: Theory and Evidence for Malpractice Reform, 80 Tex. L. Rev. 1595, 1616-1617 (2002), concludes that "experience rating"—correlating physicians' medical liability insurance rates to malpractice claims against them—has generally been rejected as "unworkable," given the poor correlation between malpractice claims and negligence, the year-to-year variation in claims, the relatively small rate increases applied, and the ability of physicians simply to switch insurance carriers.

Peter Schuck, Rethinking Informed Consent
103 Yale L.J. 899, 900-903 (1994)

The doctrine requiring physicians to obtain a patient's informed consent before undertaking treatment is relatively young, having first appeared in a recognizable, relatively robust form only in 1957. Yet the values that underlie the doctrine have an ancient pedigree. The consent norm had occupied a prominent and honored place in our legal thought for many centuries before the courts began to develop a jurisprudence of informed consent in health care. Also well established was the cognate notion that consent must be informed or knowledgeable in some meaningful sense if we are to accord it legal or moral significance. . . .

When Americans think of informed consent, however, they probably think of consent to risks of personal injury from medical treatment and from exposure to dangerous products. In these contexts, informed consent does not simply pursue the contract law goals of individual autonomy, efficiency, and anti-statism; it also advances two related ideas, fault and duty, that pervade and moralize tort law. These ideas, which took root and flourished during the heyday of traditional liberalism in the nineteenth century, hold that as long as one who suffers harm consents (in some legally meaningful sense) to bear the risk that leads to it, the injurer is not under a duty to protect the victim and is not at fault if an injury occurs. By relieving the injurer of a duty to the victim and negating the injurer's fault—in effect, replacing the negligence standard of care applicable to the injurer's actions with a new, less demanding standard—informed consent absolves her of tort liability. Informed consent claims arise at the private law intersection of torts and contracts, the laws which govern most workaday activities and choices. It is here that the social meaning of consent becomes most evident.

The doctrine of informed consent in health care shared in the more general expansion of American tort liability that proceeded well into the 1980's and that now appears to have stabilized. Everyone, it seems, favors the principle of informed consent; it is "only" the specific details and applications of the doctrine that arouse serious debate. In order to map and enlarge this debate, it is useful to distinguish three different versions of informed consent doctrine. The first is the letter and spirit of the doctrine as developed primarily by courts — the law "in books." The second is the doctrine as imagined, feared, and often caricatured by some physicians — the law "in the mind." The third version, a consequence both of the gap between the first two and of other situational constraints, is the doctrine as actually practiced by clinicians — the law "in action."

Canterbury v. Spence
464 F.2d 772 (D.C. Cir. 1972)

[The plaintiff-appellant first consulted Dr. Spence, the defendant-appellee, after experiencing severe back pain in December 1958. After a preliminary examination, Dr. Spence had the appellant undergo a myelogram — a procedure in which dye is injected into the spinal column which is then examined for disease or other disorder — that revealed that the appellant suffered from a "filling defect" in the region of his fourth thoracic vertebra. Dr. Spence told the appellant that he needed a laminectomy — an operation on the posterior arch of the vertebra — to correct what he suspected was a ruptured disc. He did not tell the appellant the details of the proposed operation, nor did the appellant inquire about them. Next, Dr. Spence contacted the appellant's mother and told her, when asked, that the operation he proposed was a serious one, but "not any more than any other operation." Dr. Spence performed the operation on February 11, 1959, only to discover that the appellant's spinal cord was swollen and in very poor condition. He did what he could to relieve the pressure on the cord and left the appellant in bed to recuperate.

For the first day or so, the appellant's recuperation proceeded normally. However, at least according to appellant's testimony, he was allowed, contrary to Dr. Spence's original instructions, to void unattended. While doing so, he slipped off the side of the bed, there being no one to assist and no side rail to break his fall. Several hours later the appellant had difficulty breathing and suffered near-complete paralysis from the waist down. Dr. Spence performed another emergency operation that night, and the appellant's condition improved thereafter. "Despite extensive medical care, [the appellant] has never been what he was before. Instead of the back pain, even years later, he hobbled about on crutches, a victim of paralysis of the bowels and urinary incontinence. In a very real sense this lawsuit is an understandable search for reasons."]

ROBINSON, J. Appellant filed suit in the District Court on March 7, 1963, four years after the laminectomy and approximately two years after he attained his majority. The complaint stated several causes of action against each defendant. Against Dr. Spence it alleged, among other things, negligence in the performance of the laminectomy and failure to inform him beforehand of the risk involved. Against the hospital the complaint charged negligent post-operative care in permitting appellant to remain unattended after the laminectomy, in failing to provide a nurse or orderly to assist him at the time of his fall, and in failing to maintain a side rail on his bed. . . .

. . . Appellant introduced no evidence to show medical and hospital practices, if any, customarily pursued in regard to the critical aspects of the case, and only Dr. Spence, called as an adverse witness, testified on the issue of causality. Dr. Spence described the surgical procedures he utilized in the two operations and expressed his opinion that appellant's disabilities stemmed from his pre-operative condition as symptomized by the swollen, nonpulsating spinal cord. He stated, however, that neither he nor any of the other physicians with whom he consulted was certain as to what that condition was, and he admitted that trauma can be a cause of paralysis. Dr. Spence . . . testified that . . . paralysis can be anticipated "somewhere in the nature of one percent" of the laminectomies performed, a risk he termed "a very slight possibility." He felt that communication of that risk to the patient is not good medical practice because it might deter patients from undergoing needed surgery and might produce adverse psychological reactions which could preclude the success of the operation.

At the close of appellant's case in chief, each defendant moved for a directed verdict and the trial judge granted both motions. The basis of the ruling, he explained, was that appellant had failed to produce any medical evidence indicating negligence on Dr. Spence's part in diagnosing appellant's malady or in performing the laminectomy; that there was no proof that Dr. Spence's treatment was responsible for appellant's disabilities; and that notwithstanding some evidence to show negligent post-operative care, an absence of medical testimony to show causality precluded submission of the case against the hospital to the jury. The judge did not allude specifically to the alleged breach of duty by Dr. Spence to divulge the possible consequences of the laminectomy.

We reverse. The testimony of appellant and his mother that Dr. Spence did not reveal the risk of paralysis from the laminectomy made out a prima facie case of violation of the physician's duty to disclose which Dr. Spence's explanation did not negate as a matter of law. . . .

There was also testimony from which the jury could have found that the laminectomy was negligently performed by Dr. Spence, and that appellant's fall was the consequence of negligence on the part of the hospital. The record, moreover, contains evidence of sufficient quantity and quality to tender jury issues as to whether and to what extent any such negligence was causally related to appellant's post-laminectomy condition. These considerations entitled appellant to a new trial. . . .

Suits charging failure by a physician adequately to disclose the risks and alternatives of proposed treatment are not innovations in American law. They date back a good half-century, and in the last decade they have multiplied rapidly. There is, nonetheless, disagreement among the courts and the commentators on many major questions, and there is no precedent of our own directly in point. For the tools enabling resolution of the issues on this appeal, we are forced to begin at first principles.

The root premise is the concept, fundamental in American jurisprudence, that "[e]very human being of adult years and sound mind has a right to determine what shall be done with his own body. . . ." Schloendorff v. Soc'y of N.Y. Hosp., 105 N.E. 92, 93 (N.Y. 1914). True consent to what happens to one's self is the informed exercise of a choice, and that entails an opportunity to evaluate knowledgeably the options available and the risks attendant upon each. The average patient has little or no understanding of the medical arts, and ordinarily has only his physician to whom he can look for enlightenment with which to reach an intelligent decision. From these almost axiomatic considerations springs the need, and in turn the requirement, of a reasonable divulgence by physician to patient to make such a decision possible.[15] . . .

A reasonable revelation in these respects is not only a necessity but, as we see it, is as much a matter of the physician's duty. It is a duty to warn of the dangers lurking in the proposed treatment, and that is surely a facet of due care. It is, too, a duty to impart information which the patient has every right to expect.[27] The patient's reliance upon the physician is a trust of the kind which traditionally has exacted obligations beyond those associated with arms-length transactions. His dependence upon the physician for information affecting his well-being, in terms of contemplated treatment, is well-nigh abject. . . .

Thus the physician has long borne a duty, on pain of liability for unauthorized treatment, to make adequate disclosure to the patient.[36] The evolution of the obligation to communicate for the patient's benefit as well as the physician's protection has hardly involved an extraordinary restructuring of the law.

Duty to disclose has gained recognition in a large number of American jurisdictions, but more largely on a different rationale. The majority of courts dealing

---

15. In duty-to-disclose cases, the focus of attention is more properly upon the nature and content of the physician's divulgence than the patient's understanding or consent. Adequate disclosure and informed consent are, of course, two sides of the same coin — the former a sine qua non of the latter. But the vital inquiry on duty to disclose relates to the physician's performance of an obligation, while one of the difficulties with analysis in terms of "informed consent" is its tendency to imply that what is decisive is the degree of the patient's comprehension. . . . [T]he physician discharges the duty when he makes a reasonable effort to convey sufficient information although the patient, without fault of the physician, may not fully grasp it.

27. Some doubt has been expressed as to ability of physicians to suitably communicate their evaluations of risks and the advantages of optional treatment, and as to the lay patient's ability to understand what the physician tells him. Karchmer, Informed Consent: . . . We do not share these apprehensions. The discussion need not be a disquisition, and surely the physician is not compelled to give his patient a short medical education; the disclosure rule summons the physician only to a reasonable explanation. That means generally informing the patient in nontechnical terms as to what is at stake: the therapy alternatives open to him, the goals expectably to be achieved, and the risks that may ensue from particular treatment and no treatment. . . . So informing the patient hardly taxes the physician, and it must be the exceptional patient who cannot comprehend such an explanation at least in a rough way.

36. We discard the thought that the patient should ask for information before the physician is required to disclose. Caveat emptor is not the norm for the consumer of medical services. Duty to disclose is more than a call to speak merely on the patient's request, or merely to answer the patient's questions; it is a duty to volunteer, if necessary, the information the patient needs for intelligent decision. The patient may be ignorant, confused, overawed by the physician or frightened by the hospital, or even ashamed to inquire. . . . Perhaps relatively few patients could in any event identify the relevant questions in the absence of prior explanation by the physician. Physicians and hospitals have patients of widely divergent socio-economic backgrounds, and a rule which presumes a degree of sophistication which many members of society lack is likely to breed gross inequities.

with the problem have made the duty depend on whether it was the custom of physicians practicing in the community to make the particular disclosure to the patient. If so, the physician may be held liable for an unreasonable and injurious failure to divulge, but there can be no recovery unless the omission forsakes a practice prevalent in the profession. We agree that the physician's noncompliance with a professional custom to reveal, like any other departure from prevailing medical practice, may give rise to liability to the patient. We do not agree that the patient's cause of action is dependent upon the existence and nonperformance of a relevant professional tradition.

There are, in our view, formidable obstacles to acceptance of the notion that the physician's obligation to disclose is either germinated or limited by medical practice. To begin with, the reality of any discernible custom reflecting a professional consensus on communication of option and risk information to patients is open to serious doubt. We sense the danger that what in fact is no custom at all may be taken as an affirmative custom to maintain silence, and that physician-witnesses to the so-called custom may state merely their personal opinions as to what they or others would do under given conditions. . . . Nor can we ignore the fact that to bind the disclosure obligation to medical usage is to arrogate the decision on revelation to the physician alone. Respect for the patient's right of self-determination on particular therapy demands a standard set by law for physicians rather than one which physicians may or may not impose upon themselves. . . .

. . . We hold that the standard measuring performance of that duty [to disclose] by physicians, as by others, is conduct which is reasonable under the circumstances.

Once the circumstances give rise to a duty on the physician's part to inform his patient, the next inquiry is the scope of the disclosure the physician is legally obliged to make. The courts have frequently confronted this problem but no uniform standard defining the adequacy of the divulgence emerges from the decisions. Some have said "full" disclosure, a norm we are unwilling to adopt literally. It seems obviously prohibitive and unrealistic to expect physicians to discuss with their patients every risk of proposed treatment—no matter how small or remote and generally unnecessary from the patient's viewpoint as well. Indeed, the cases speaking in terms of "full" disclosure appear to envision something less than total disclosure, leaving unanswered the question of just how much.

The larger number of courts, as might be expected, have applied tests framed with reference to prevailing fashion within the medical profession. Some have measured the disclosure by "good medical practice," others by what a reasonable practitioner would have bared under the circumstances, and still others by what medical custom in the community would demand. We have explored this rather considerable body of law but are unprepared to follow it. . . .

In our view, the patient's right of self-decision shapes the boundaries of the duty to reveal. That right can be effectively exercised only if the patient possesses enough information to enable an intelligent choice. The scope of the physician's communications to the patient, then, must be measured by the patient's need, and that need is the information material to the decision. Thus the test for determining whether a particular peril must be divulged is its materiality to the patient's decision: all risks potentially affecting the decision must be unmasked. And to safeguard the patient's interest in achieving his own determination on treatment, the law must itself set the standard for adequate disclosure.

Optimally for the patient, exposure of a risk would be mandatory whenever the patient would deem it significant to his decision, either singly or in combination with other risks. Such a requirement, however, would summon the physician to second-guess the patient, whose ideas on materiality could hardly be known to the physician. That would make an undue demand upon medical practitioners, whose conduct, like that of others, is to be measured in terms of reasonableness. Consonantly with orthodox negligence doctrine, the physician's liability for non-disclosure is to be determined on the basis of foresight, not hindsight; no less than any other aspect of negligence, the issue on nondisclosure must be approached from the viewpoint of the reasonableness of the physician's divulgence in terms of what he knows or should know to be the patient's informational needs. If, but only if, the fact-finder can say that the physician's communication was unreasonably inadequate is an imposition of liability legally or morally justified. . . .

From these considerations we derive the breadth of the disclosure of risks legally to be required. The scope of the standard is not subjective as to either the physician or the patient; it remains objective with due regard for the patient's informational needs and with suitable leeway for the physician's situation. In broad outline, we agree that "[a] risk is thus material when a reasonable person, in what the physician knows or should know to be the patient's position, would be likely to attach significance to the risk or cluster of risks in deciding whether or not to forego the proposed therapy."

The topics importantly demanding a communication of information are the inherent and potential hazards of the proposed treatment, the alternatives to that treatment, if any, and the results likely if the patient remains untreated. The factors contributing significance to the dangerousness of a medical technique are, of course, the incidence of injury and the degree of the harm threatened. A very small chance of death or serious disablement may well be significant; a potential disability which dramatically outweighs the potential benefit of the therapy or the detriments of the existing malady may summon discussion with the patient.[86]

There is no bright line separating the significant from the insignificant; the answer in any case must abide a rule of reason. Some dangers — infection, for example — are inherent in any operation; there is no obligation to communicate those of which persons of average sophistication are aware. Even more clearly, the physician bears no responsibility for discussion of hazards the patient has

---

86. See Bowers v. Talmage, 159 So. 2d 888 (Fla. App. 1963) (3% chance of death, paralysis or other injury, disclosure required); Scott v. Wilson, 396 S.W.2d 532 (Tex. Civ. App. 1965), aff'd, 412 S.W.2d 299 (Tex. 1967) (1% chance of loss of hearing, disclosure required). Compare, where the physician was held not liable: Stottlemire v. Cawood, 213 F. Supp. 897 (D.D.C. 1963) (1/800,000 chance of aplastic anemia); Yeates v. Harms, 393 P.2d 982 (Kan. 1964) (1.5% chance of loss of eye); Starnes v. Taylor, 272 N.C. 386, 158 S.E.2d 339, 344 (1968) (1/250 to 1/500 chance of perforation of esophagus).

already discovered, or those having no apparent materiality to patients' decision on therapy. The disclosure doctrine, like others marking lines between permissible and impermissible behavior in medical practice, is in essence a requirement of conduct prudent under the circumstances. Whenever nondisclosure of particular risk information is open to debate by reasonable-minded men, the issue is for the finder of the facts.

Two exceptions to the general rule of disclosure have been noted by the courts. Each is in the nature of a physician's privilege not to disclose, and the reasoning underlying them is appealing. . . . The first comes into play when the patient is unconscious or otherwise incapable of consenting, and harm from a failure to treat is imminent and outweighs any harm threatened by the proposed treatment. When a genuine emergency of that sort arises, it is settled that the impracticality of conferring with the patient dispenses with need for it. Even in situations of that character the physician should, as current law requires, attempt to secure a relative's consent if possible. But if time is too short to accommodate discussion, obviously the physician should proceed with the treatment.

The second exception obtains when risk-disclosure poses such a threat of detriment to the patient as to become unfeasible or contraindicated from a medical point of view. It is recognized that patients occasionally become so ill or emotionally distraught on disclosure as to foreclose a rational decision, or complicate or hinder the treatment, or perhaps even pose psychological damage to the patient. Where that is so, the cases have generally held that the physician is armed with a privilege to keep the information from the patient, and we think it clear that portents of that type may justify the physician in action he deems medically warranted. The critical inquiry is whether the physician responded to a sound medical judgment that communication of the risk information would present a threat to the patient's well-being.

The physician's privilege to withhold information for therapeutic reasons must be carefully circumscribed, however, for otherwise it might devour the disclosure rule itself. The privilege does not accept the paternalistic notion that the physician may remain silent simply because divulgence might prompt the patient to forego therapy the physician feels the patient really needs. That attitude presumes instability or perversity for even the normal patient, and runs counter to the foundation principle that the patient should and ordinarily can make the choice for himself.

No more than breach of any other legal duty does nonfulfillment of the physician's obligation to disclose alone establish liability to the patient. . . . [A]s in malpractice actions generally, there must be a causal relationship between the physician's failure to adequately divulge and damage to the patient.

A causal connection exists when, but only when, disclosure of significant risks incidental to treatment would have resulted in a decision against it. The patient obviously has no complaint if he would have submitted to the therapy notwithstanding awareness that the risk was one of its perils. On the other hand, the very purpose of the disclosure rule is to protect the patient against consequences which, if known, he would have avoided by foregoing the treatment. The more difficult question is whether the factual issue on causality calls for an objective or a subjective determination.

It has been assumed that the issue is to be resolved according to whether the fact-finder believes the patient's testimony that he would not have agreed to the treatment if he had known of the danger which later ripened into injury. We think a technique which ties the factual conclusion on causation simply to the assessment of the patient's credibility is unsatisfactory. To be sure, the objective of risk-disclosure is preservation of the patient's interest in intelligent self-choice on proposed treatment, a matter the patient is free to decide for any reason that appeals to him. When, prior to commencement of therapy, the patient is sufficiently informed on risks and he exercises his choice, it may truly be said that he did exactly what he wanted to do. But when causality is explored at a post-injury trial with a professedly uninformed patient, the question whether he actually would have turned the treatment down if he had known the risks is purely hypothetical: "Viewed from the point at which he had to decide, would the patient have decided differently had he known something he did not know?" And the answer which the patient supplies hardly represents more than a guess, perhaps tinged by the circumstance that the uncommunicated hazard has in fact materialized.

In our view, this method of dealing with the issue on causation comes in second-best. It places the physician in jeopardy of the patient's hindsight and bitterness. It places the factfinder in the position of deciding whether a speculative answer to a hypothetical question is to be credited. It calls for a subjective determination solely on testimony of a patient-witness shadowed by the occurrence of the undisclosed risk.

Better it is, we believe, to resolve the causality issue on an objective basis: in terms of what a prudent person in the patient's position would have decided if suitably informed of all perils bearing significance. If adequate disclosure could reasonably be expected to have caused that person to decline the treatment because of the revelation of the kind of risk or danger that resulted in harm, causation is shown, but otherwise not. The patient's testimony is relevant on that score of course but it would not threaten to dominate the findings. . . .

[The court ordered a new trial because: (1) the appellant testified that he was not told of the hazards of the operation; (2) his mother was told that the laminectomy was no more serious than any other operation; (3) Dr. Spence himself testified about the 1 percent risk of paralysis; and (4) there was no evidence that appellant's "emotional makeup was such that concealment of the risk of paralysis was medically sound.[138]"]

---

138. Dr. Spence's opinion—that disclosure is medically unwise—was expressed as to patients generally, and not with reference to traits possessed by appellant. His explanation was:

I think that I always explain to patients the operations are serious, and I feel that any operation is serious. I think that I would not tell patients that they might be paralyzed because of the small percentage, one per cent, that exists. There would be a tremendous percentage of people that would not have surgery and would not therefore be benefited by it, the tremendous percentage that get along very well, 99 per cent.

NOTES

1. The case on remand. What issues were left to be resolved in *Canterbury* on remand? If the risk of paralysis from falling out of bed is common knowledge, does it make a difference that the defendant did not disclose the risk of paralysis from the operation itself? How ought Canterbury's prior condition be taken into account in assessing damages? On retrial the jury found for the defendants on liability. Its decision was affirmed on appeal, without opinion. 509 F.2d 537 (D.C. Cir. 1975).

2. Materiality of risk. What level of risk is needed to trigger the duty to disclose? In Kozup v. Georgetown University, 663 F. Supp. 1048, 1053-1054 (D.D.C. 1987), the parents of the decedent, Matthew Kozup, brought an informed consent claim against the defendant hospital, which in 1983 transfused Matthew at birth with blood contaminated with the human immunodeficiency virus (HIV), from which he died three years later. Flannery, J., dismissed the suit against the hospital, holding that the risk of AIDS from HIV was not material in 1983. The court stressed that in January 1983, only a single case of possible transfusion-related AIDS had been diagnosed out of the 3.5 million annual blood donations. Moreover, its viral agent HTLV-III would only be identified 15 months later. It then addressed the causation question as follows:

> However, in addition to this flaw in plaintiffs' theory, a second equally fatal problem remains. Even if plaintiffs could show that the risk of AIDS would have been material to their decision regarding Matthew's transfusions, plaintiffs must also show that the hospital's failure to warn of that risk *caused* the injury involved. That is, plaintiffs must show that "disclosure of significant risks incidental to treatment would have resulted in a decision against it." *Canterbury.* No reasonable jury could conclude on the facts of this case that, had the Kozups been informed of a one in 3.5 million possibility of contracting AIDS, they would have declined to permit Georgetown's physicians to transfuse blood into their son. Matthew was premature and his birth was accompanied by many complications including hypovolemia. The transfusions were absolutely necessary to save his life.

On appeal, Kozup v. Georgetown University, 851 F.2d 437 (D.C. Cir. 1988), the court agreed that the informed consent count failed on materiality, but remanded the case for a new trial on an alternative battery count, noting that no parental consent had been obtained at all. It rejected, at least for summary judgment purposes, the hospital's theory that "there is no necessity to obtain parent consent for life-saving treatment." If the claim were valid, what are the damages?

In subsequent cases, expert evidence established that blood banks were negligent in failing to perceive material transfusion risks of AIDS in early 1983. See, e.g., United Blood Services v. Quintana, 827 P.2d 509 (Colo. 1992). Knowledge advanced so rapidly between January and May of 1983 that the focus of attention at the latter time was not on informed consent but on developing effective institutional safeguards against the transmission of HIV. Note that conformity with professional blood bank testing standards is not an absolute defense after *The*

T.J. Hooper. What safeguards, if any, should be introduced to deal with the risk of 20/20 hindsight?

3. *Particularity of disclosure.*   Courts have commonly resisted demands for disclosure of the full range of treatment alternatives in complex cases. In Valles v. Albert Einstein Medical Center, 805 A.2d 1232, 1239-1240 (Pa. 2002), the decedent, Lope Valles, was admitted into the defendant medical center for treatment of a suspected abdominal aortic aneurysm—a weakness in the wall of the aorta. When surgery was postponed due to subsequent loss of kidney function, the treating physicians recommended the use of a "Permacath" device, suitable for prolonged dialysis. The surgical resident advised Valles of certain risks associated with the insertion of Permacath, "including bleeding, infection, collapsing of a lung and death," but he did not discuss the relative advantages and disadvantages from different placements in veins in the neck, chest, or groin. When one treating physician, Dr. Morros, tried inserting the Permacath in a chest vein, Valles suffered adverse reactions, went into cardiac arrest, and died. The trial court kept the informed consent case from the jury, but the Superior Court reversed, and allowed the case to go to the jury, saying that "informed consent applies to the method or manner of surgery and the risks associated therewith." The Pennsylvania Supreme Court rebuffed this position:

> We recently reiterated . . . that "the doctrine of informed consent is a limited one." In light of this limited scope, we find that the manner or method in which the surgeon performs the proposed procedure is not encompassed within the purview of the informed consent doctrine. Although there were several methods of performing the particular surgery, there was only one surgery proposed: the insertion of a Permacath. Appellant does not dispute that Valles was adequately informed of the risks attending the surgery: bleeding, lung collapse, and death. That the subclavian vein [in the chest] may not have been the optimum site is not an issue of informed consent, but of negligence in the physician's decision to place the Permacath at that site.

The dissent insisted that "the patient should be advised of those alternative types of treatment, i.e., the viable locations for the surgery, as well as the risks associated with each location." Who is right?

With *Valles,* contrast Felton v. Lovett, 388 S.W.3d 656 (Tex. 2012), where the defendant, a chiropractor, performed "forceful manipulation" on the plaintiff after which he "suffered a stroke resulting from a vertebral artery dissection." At trial, the plaintiff's expert witness testified that

- vertebral artery dissection is a known risk of neck adjustments but occurs only if the patient's artery is unhealthy or if the adjustment is performed improperly;
- chiropractors have been aware of the risk for a long time;
- there are safer alternatives to manual adjustment that do not run the risk of stroke;
- about 10 to 20% of vertebral dissections are preceded by chiropractic manipulation of the spine. . . .

On the strength of this evidence, Hecht, J., concluded:

> The same kind of injury may occur in other patients undergoing the same kind
> of treatment. The risk that a patient will not respond well to treatment is clearly
> one that inheres in the treatment. And as the evidence indicated, and the jury
> found, the possibility of vertebral artery dissection and stroke is precisely the kind
> of information a reasonable patient would be expected to want to know before
> deciding whether to risk such severe consequences in order to alleviate neck pain.

On the general duty of informed consent for chiropractors, see Hannemann
v. Boyson, 698 N.W.2d 714, 718 (Wis. 2005).

4. Expert testimony in informed consent cases. *Canterbury* held that "[l]ay witness
testimony can competently establish a physician's failure to disclose particular
risk information, the patient's lack of knowledge of the risk, and the adverse
consequences following the treatment. Experts are unnecessary to a showing of
the materiality of a risk to a patient's decision on treatment, or to the reasonably,
expectable effect of risk disclosure on the decision."

In Bly v. Rhoads, 222 S.E.2d 783, 787-788 (Va. 1976), the plaintiff sued under
an informed consent theory for the adverse consequences of a hysterectomy. The
court followed *Canterbury* insofar as it allowed the plaintiff "to establish by lay evidence that his physician did not disclose particular risk information and that he, the
patient, had no knowledge of the risk." It also agreed that lay evidence was sometimes admissible "to show the adverse consequences following treatment," and it left
open the possibility that infrequently "the duty of disclosure is so obvious that expert
testimony should not be required." But it broke with *Canterbury* in requiring expert
evidence on the full range of complex issues raised by the disclosure question.

> We believe the better rule, which we now adopt, is to require a patient-plaintiff to
> show by qualified medical experts whether and to what extent information should
> be disclosed by the physician to his patient. This rule would not, contrary to what
> *Canterbury* suggests, impose an undue burden upon the patient-plaintiff. After all,
> in the usual case, the patient unquestionably will have obtained experts to estab-
> lish the negligent treatment phase of his malpractice action.

Bly represents the majority view on expert evidence, which is often codified. See,
e.g., Ark. Code Ann. §16-114-206(b) (2015), which was sustained against a constitutional challenge in Eady v. Lansford, 92 S.W.3d 57, 61 (Ark. 2002), in the absence of
any showing "that the legislation is *not* rationally related to achieving any legitimate
objective of the government. . . ." Indeed, the court intimated that protecting the
medical profession against vexatious litigation justified both requiring expert testimony and adopting the customary care standard rejected in *Canterbury.*

5. Full disclosure forms. In Garcia v. Robinson, 349 P.3d 415 (Haw. Ct. App.
2015), the plaintiff claimed that the defendant physician had told him that he
would be "'dancing in a couple of days after surgery.'" The defendant introduced
into evidence the form that the defendant had signed that tracked exactly the
disclosures required under Haw. Rev. Stat. §671(3)(b). That form read as follows:

FULL DISCLOSURE
I AGREE THAT MY PHYSICIAN HAS INFORMED ME OF THE:
    a) DIAGNOSIS OR PROBABLE DIAGNOSIS.
    b) NATURE OF THE TREATMENT OR PROCEDURES RECOMMENDED.
    c) RISKS OR COMPLICATIONS INVOLVED IN SUCH TREATMENT OR PROCEDURES.
    d) ALTERNATIVE FORMS OF TREATMENT, INCLUDING NON-TREATMENT, AVAILABLE.
    e) ANTICIPATED RESULTS OF TREATMENT.

In affirming a summary judgment for the defendant, the court concluded simply in line with *Bly*: "The circuit court did not err in holding that Garcia's informed consent claim required expert testimony to establish the materiality of the risk asserted."

6. Legislative response to informed consent. In the wake of *Canterbury*, many legislatures codified the law of informed consent, often at the request of insurance companies and medical organizations. The New York statute (New York Pub. Health Law §2805-d (McKinney 2015)) provides that "[l]ack of informed consent means the failure of the person providing the professional treatment or diagnosis to disclose to the patient such alternatives thereto and the reasonably foreseeable risks and benefits involved as a reasonable medical . . . practitioner under similar circumstances would have disclosed, in a manner permitting the patient to make a knowledgeable evaluation." Recovery for malpractice "based on a lack of informed consent is limited to those cases involving either (a) non-emergency treatment, procedure or surgery, or (b) a diagnostic procedure which involved invasion or disruption of the integrity of the body." Additionally, a viable defense exists when "the medical . . . practitioner, after considering all of the attendant facts and circumstances, used reasonable discretion as to the manner and extent to which such alternatives or risks were disclosed to the patient because he reasonably believed that the manner and extent of such disclosure could reasonably be expected to adversely and substantially affect the patient's condition." How does this statutory regime differ from *Canterbury*? Is the statute preferable to a general good-faith standard whereby doctors make whatever disclosures they regard as appropriate under the circumstances?

Are further legislative reforms sensible in light of modern developments in medical science and health care delivery? Twerski & Cohen, The Second Revolution in Informed Consent: Comparing Physicians to Each Other, 94 Nw. U. L. Rev. 1 (1999), would require managed care organizations to disclose "comparative statistics," which assess the relative risks associated with an individual's *providers* who perform a particular procedure, to plan participants. Comparing informed consent in the treatment and research contexts, Grimm, Informed Consent for All! No Exceptions, 37 N.M. L. Rev. 39 (2007), argues that medical research requirements should be significantly more stringent, and permit no exceptions, to ensure sufficient protection for personal autonomy. On the other side, howls of protest have been raised against the excessive delays in experimental research stemming from highly restrictive protocols that drive research away.

Hamburger, The New Censorship: Institutional Review Boards, 2004 Sup. Ct. Rev. 271. For a wide range of opinions on this issue, see Symposium, 101 Nw. U. L. Rev. 837 (2007).

7. *The British rejection of* Canterbury. The duty to disclose, now widely accepted in the United States, has run into strong hostility in England. In Sidaway v. Bethlem Royal Hospital, [1985] All Eng. Rep. 1018, 1030, 1031, the English Court of Appeal explicitly rejected *Canterbury* in a case in which the defendant surgeon did tell a patient undergoing an elective laminectomy of the 1 or 2 percent risk of minor nerve damage, but decided not to mention the under-one-percent risk of permanent damage to the spinal cord. The dismissal of the plaintiff's suit below was affirmed on appeal with Dunn, L.J., saying:

> I confess that I reach this conclusion with no regret. The evidence in this case showed that a contrary result would be damaging to the relationship of trust and confidence between doctor and patient, and might well have an adverse effect on the practice of medicine. It is doubtful whether it would be of any significant benefit to patients, most of whom prefer to put themselves unreservedly in the hands of their doctors. This is not in my view "paternalism," to repeat an evocative word used in argument. It is simply an acceptance of the doctor/patient relationship as it has developed in this country. The principal effect of accepting the proposition advanced by the plaintiff would be likely to be an increase in the number of claims for professional negligence against doctors. This would be likely to have an adverse effect on the general standard of medical care, since doctors would inevitably be concerned to safeguard themselves against such claims, rather than to concentrate on their primary duty of treating their patients.

British judges remain more skeptical of informed consent cases. In Pearce v. United Bristol Healthcare NHS Trust, 48 BMLR 118 (1998), Lord Woolf MR reiterated the concerns raised in *Bethlem* only to conclude that "a significant event" did not include an increased risk of one to two in 1,000 that a child might be stillborn if not delivered.

8. *Contracts and causation in informed consent cases.* A more radical approach to the informed consent issue would allow physicians and patients to determine the proper scope of disclosure by private agreement. Arguments supporting that conclusion are found in Epstein, Medical Malpractice: The Case for Contract, 1 Am. B. Found. Res. J. 87, 119-128 (1976). A more bittersweet evaluation is found in Schuck, *supra* at 205, 957-958, which notes the tension between the defense of autonomous choices and the use of the prudent patient standard for disclosure:

> Like the "reasonable person" standard and other objective standards in tort law, the existing uniform approach to informed consent has two virtues: it is cheaper to know and administer, and it seeks to protect patients against gross inequalities of bargaining power vis-à-vis providers. But a doctrine that treats all patients and physician-patient relationships as essentially homogenous when in fact they are not exacts a price. Specifically, the law requires a level of informed consent that is different from the level that many consumers or groups of consumers want and for which they would be willing to pay if the choice were presented to them. The

existing doctrine, then, suffers from an ironic, if endemic vice: it deprives patients of choice in the name of choice.

The tension between objective and subjective tests spills over to the question of causation. In Cobbs v. Grant, 502 P.2d 1 (Cal. 1972), the court adopted the objective causation standard of *Canterbury*, notwithstanding its tension with the autonomy principle, because it declined to place the "physician in jeopardy of the patient's bitterness and disillusionment" resulting from "20/20 hindsight." But in Arena v. Gingrich, 748 P.2d 547 (Or. 1988), Linde, J., held that Oregon's informed consent statute (Or. Rev. Stat. §677.097 (2005)), precluded the objective standard: "The statute having defined the standard of disclosure without requiring reference to what a prudent patient reasonably would want to know, we shall not reintroduce that hypothetical prudent patient by the back door of 'causation.'"

SECTION E. STATUTES AND REGULATIONS

This section explores the ways in which statutes can add precision to the general negligence standard of reasonable care. Typically a statute involved in a negligence case provides for the state to administer some penalty in the case of violation, usually a fine, but sometimes incarceration or, on occasion, injunctive relief. The term "statute" is broadly construed to include not only state legislative acts, but also local ordinances, federal laws, and state and federal administrative regulations. RTT:LPEH §14, comment *a*. Traditionally this inquiry was raised in connection with traffic accidents, where violation of motor vehicle laws remains central to the negligence determination. RTT:LPEH §14, comment *d*. Litigation now frequently extends to the full range of health and safety statutes characteristic of the modern democratic state.

Analytically the first question is how any statute comes to be a source of private rights. When the statute expressly creates a private remedy for one injured by its violation, a court merely has to follow the explicit statutory command. Frequently, however, statutes are silent on whether they create private rights of action, so that the first judicial task is to set some "default" rule for statutory construction: Where the statute is silent, when should the private right of action be inferred? Sometimes courts assume that a private action is authorized by some "overriding" legislative intention. Yet that inference is contestable since the statutory silence is compatible with the opposite position that direct criminal penalties are the sole remedy for statutory violations. Given the wide variety of statutes on the books, it is doubtful that either extreme position (automatic creation or automatic denial of a private right of action) represents the best judicial accommodation in the absence of more specific legislative guidance. What principles help determine when courts should infer private rights of action? If the court determines that a statute *does not* create a private right of action, is it nonetheless still relevant in setting the general standard of reasonable care in a common law negligence suit?

Anon.
87 Eng. Rep. 791 (K.B. 1703)

HOLT, C.J. [F]or wherever a statute enacts anything, or prohibits anything, for the advantage of any person, that person shall have remedy to recover the advantage given him, or to have satisfaction for the injury done him contrary to law by the same statute; for it would be a fine thing to make a law by which one has a right, but no remedy but in equity. . . .

Ezra Ripley Thayer, Public Wrong and Private Action
27 Harv. L. Rev. 317, 321-322 (1914), *reprinted in* Selected Essays on the Law of Torts 276, 280-281 (1924)

Before the ordinance the plaintiff, injured by the runaway horse, must have based his action on negligence. Whether the defendant was negligent in leaving the horse unhitched would have been for the jury to say, unless this was so clear one way or the other that the court must deal with it as a "question of law" (so-called); i.e., as a point on which fair minds could reach but one conclusion. In any situation less extreme the whole matter would have been within the jury's province. And the jury was bound in deciding it to use the test of the "ordinary prudent man." They could not acquit the defendant of negligence without saying that an ordinary prudent man would have left his horse unhitched under these circumstances; that with such a horse as this, and in such a place, the prudent man would have foreseen no danger to others—for the foresight of the prudent man in the defendant's position (in other words, the probability of danger from his standpoint) is the test of negligence. The jury was justified either in accepting or rejecting the theory that he was negligent, for the mere fact of submitting the issue of negligence to them means that a finding either way is warranted by the evidence. The reasonableness of the defendant's conduct was thus in the eye of the law an open question, depending on the circumstances and the inferences fairly to be drawn from them.

Suppose now the situation to be changed by the single circumstance of the ordinance, all other facts remaining the same. Can the issue of negligence any longer be left to the jury? Not unless they would be justified in finding for either party; and what must a finding for the defendant on this issue mean? That an ordinary prudent man, knowing the ordinance—for upon familiar principles he can claim no benefit from his ignorance of the law—would have chosen to break it, "reasonably" believing that damage would not result from his action. It must then, upon this view, be deemed consistent with ordinary prudence for an individual to set his own opinion against the judgment authoritatively pronounced by constituted public authority, for the ordinance has prohibited leaving *all* horses unhitched, without exception, and has done this in order to prevent just such consequences as have occurred. It has thus declared the danger to be so serious and constant that a less sweeping prohibition would be inadequate.

And when eminent courts, using familiar phraseology, state that the breach of the ordinance is not "negligence per se," but only "evidence of negligence," and leave the question of negligence as a fact to the jury, they are doing nothing less than informing that body that it may properly stamp with approval, as reasonable conduct, the action of one who has assumed to place his own foresight above that of the legislature in respect of the very danger which it was legislating to prevent.

NOTES

1. Thayer in action.   The power of statutory commands still retains the force that Thayer attributed to them nearly 100 years ago. The Third Restatement proclaims that "courts, exercising their common law duty to develop tort doctrine, not only should regard the actor's statutory violation as evidence admissible against the actor, but should treat that violation as actually determining the actor's negligence." RTT:LPEH §14, *comment c.* In Schmitz v. Canadian Pacific Ry. Co., 454 F.3d 678, 684 (7th Cir. 2006), the plaintiff inspector fell into a hole alongside the tracks when defendant had not cleared away the vegetation as required by federal regulation. The trial judge did not instruct the jury on the mandatory force of the regulation, and his decision was reversed on appeal.

> There can be little doubt that the omission of an instruction on [the regulation] prejudiced Schmitz's case. Canadian Pacific argues that the jury still heard the essence of Schmitz's claim regarding the regulation—that Schmitz alleged the railroad was negligent because it did not keep the vegetation trimmed. But there is a world of difference between telling the jury that Schmitz alleged the railroad should have taken a particular precaution and telling the jury that federal law *required* the railroad to take that very precaution. By not instructing the jury on the federal regulation, the district judge left it up to the jury to decide whether the railroad had a duty to keep the vegetation trimmed. The regulation answers that question in the affirmative—the railroad was required under federal law to keep the vegetation trimmed. The jury should have been deciding only whether the railroad violated the regulation and whether the violation was a cause of Schmitz's injury.

Blomquist, The Trouble with Negligence Per Se, 61 S.C. L. Rev. 221, 279 (2009), criticizes the dominant rule for requiring judges to engage in "relatively abstract considerations of legislative purpose . . . in a highly manipulable process that leads to divergent and unpredictable results," and for impinging upon the domain of the jury in negligence determinations.

2. Defective statutes as a source of duty.   Thayer relies on the common notion of legislative supremacy to justify the rule that noncompliance with a statute counts as negligence per se. The Third Restatement likewise privileges "the judgment of the legislature, as the authoritative representative of the community" over the jury's assessment of reasonable conduct. RTT:LPEH §14, comment *c.* One test of this thesis examines the role of statutory provisions not currently in force. Assume that an otherwise valid criminal safety statute is invalid because of a technical defect in the enacting procedure. On Thayer's view, could it set the standard of care in a negligence action? In Clinkscales v. Carver, 136 P.2d 777,

778-779 (Cal. 1943), Traynor, J., held that while the state could not criminally enforce its laws when it erected a stop sign pursuant to a defective statute, nonetheless for a highway user it "was negligence as a matter of law to disregard the stop sign."

> If a through artery has been posted with stop signs by the public authorities in the customary way and to all appearances by regular procedure, any reasonable man should know that the public naturally relies upon their observance. If a driver from a side street enters the ostensibly protected boulevard without stopping, in disregard of the posted safeguards, contrary to what drivers thereon could reasonably have expected him to do, he is guilty of negligence regardless of any irregularity attending the authorization of the signs.

Osborne v. McMasters
41 N.W. 543 (Minn. 1889)

MITCHELL, J. Upon the record in this case it must be taken as the facts that defendant's clerk in his drug-store, in the course of his employment as such, sold to plaintiff's intestate a deadly poison without labeling it "Poison," as required by statute; that she, in ignorance of its deadly qualities, partook of the poison, which caused her death. Except for the ability of counsel and the earnestness with which they have argued the case, we would not have supposed that there could be any serious doubt of defendant's liability on this state of facts. It is immaterial for present purposes whether section 329 of the Penal Code or section 14, c. 147, Laws 1885, or both, are still in force, and constitute the law governing this case. The requirements of both statutes are substantially the same, and the sole object of both is to protect the public against the dangerous qualities of poison. It is now well settled, certainly in this state, that where a statute or municipal ordinance imposes upon any person a specific duty for the protection or benefit of others, if he neglects to perform that duty he is liable to those for whose protection or benefit it was imposed for any injuries of the character which the statute or ordinance was designed to prevent, and which were proximately produced by such neglect. . . .

Defendant contends that this is only true where a right of action for the alleged negligent act existed at common law; that no liability existed at common law for selling poison without labeling it, and therefore none exists under this statute, no right of civil action being given by it. Without stopping to consider the correctness of the assumption that selling poison without labeling it might not be actionable negligence at common law, it is sufficient to say that, in our opinion, defendant's contention proceeds upon an entire misapprehension of the nature and gist of a cause of action of this kind. The common law gives a right of action to every one sustaining injuries caused proximately by the negligence of another. The present is a common-law action, the gist of which is defendant's negligence, resulting in the death of plaintiff's intestate. Negligence is the breach of legal duty. It is immaterial whether the duty is one imposed by the rule of common law requiring the exercise of ordinary care not to injure another, or is imposed by a statute designed for the protection of others. In either case the failure to perform the duty constitutes negligence, and renders the party liable for injuries resulting from it. The only difference is that in the one case the measure of legal duty is to be determined upon common-law principles, while in the other the statute fixes it, so that the violation of the statute constitutes conclusive evidence of negligence, or, in other words, negligence per se. The action in the latter case is not a statutory one, nor does the statute give the right of action in any other sense except that it makes an act negligent which otherwise might not be such, or at least only evidence of negligence. All that the statute does is to establish a fixed standard by which the fact of negligence may be determined. The gist of the action is still negligence, or the non-performance of a legal duty to the person injured.

Judgment affirmed.

NOTES

1. Statutory causes of action versus negligence per se.   *Osborne* identifies three possible functions of a statute in a tort action. First, as described in the introduction to Section E, the statute can *create* a private right of action by providing that an individual injured by a violation of the statute can sue the offender. Second, as in *Osborne*, the plaintiff can bring a common law negligence suit for her injuries. In that case, the defendant's violation of a relevant statute may constitute "negligence per se." The court adopts the statute as the standard of reasonable care, and the defendant's violation is, by definition, negligent. Third, even if the defendant's statutory violation does not constitute negligence per se (usually because the situation does not satisfy criteria that limit the scope of the doctrine), the plaintiff can still argue that the defendant's underlying conduct was negligent. *See* RTT:LPEH §14, comment *f*.

Restatement of the Law (Second) of Torts

§286. WHEN STANDARD OF CONDUCT DEFINED BY LEGISLATION OR REGULATION WILL BE ADOPTED

The court may adopt as the standard of conduct of a reasonable man the requirements of a legislative enactment or an administrative regulation whose purpose is found to be exclusively or in part
(a) to protect a class of persons which includes the one whose interest is invaded, and
(b) to protect the particular interest which is invaded, and
(c) to protect that interest against the kind of harm which has resulted, and
(d) to protect that interest against the particular hazard from which the harm results.

Restatement of the Law (Third) of Torts: Liability for Physical and Emotional Harm

§14. STATUTORY VIOLATIONS AS NEGLIGENCE PER SE

An actor is negligent if, without excuse, the actor violates a statute that is designed to protect against the type of accident the actor's conduct causes, and if the accident victim is within the class of persons the statute is designed to protect.

California Evidence Code (West 2009)

§669(A). DUE CARE; FAILURE TO EXERCISE

The failure of a person to exercise due care is presumed if:
   (1) He violated a statute, ordinance, or regulation of a public entity;
   (2) The violation proximately caused death or injury to person or property;
   (3) The death or injury resulted from an occurrence of the nature which the statute, ordinance, or regulation was designed to prevent; and
   (4) The person suffering the death or the injury to his person or property was one of the class of persons for whose protection the statute, ordinance, or regulation was adopted.

2. Who is protected?   Even where the statute supports a negligence action, the plaintiff must show that she falls within the class of protected individuals, which is easier to do when a single statute is found to serve multiple purposes. In Stimpson v. Wellington Service Corp., 246 N.E.2d 801, 805 (Mass. 1969), the defendant drove a 137-ton rig over city streets without having obtained the needed statutory permit. The weight of defendant's truck dislocated and broke the pipes in plaintiff's building, flooding the premises. The court found that the statute had a dual purpose. "Undoubtedly the primary purpose of the statute was to protect the ways themselves from injury from overloaded vehicles. But the Cambridge authorities, in considering an application for a permit under the statute, should have weighed as well other possible effects of the proposal, particularly because of the prohibition of the city ordinance against moving over city streets vehicles so loaded as to be likely to injure property. Failure to apply for a permit meant that the appropriate authority did not have the opportunity to appraise the risks and probabilities and to refuse the permit or impose conditions."

3. Actions "for any injuries of the character which the statute or ordinance was designed to prevent."   In Gorris v. Scott, L.R. 9 Ex. 125, 129 (1874), the plaintiff had shipped a number of sheep with the defendant shipowner who failed to pen them in accordance with the requirement of the Contagious Disease (Animals) Act of 1869. The animals were washed overboard in a storm and "were lost by reason of the neglect to comply" with administrative orders issued pursuant to the statute. Notwithstanding this causal connection between plaintiff's harm and defendant's breach of statutory duty, Kelly, C.B., denied plaintiff's recovery:

> [I]f we could see that it was the object, or among the objects of this Act, that the owners of sheep and cattle coming from a foreign port should be protected by the means described against the danger of their property being washed overboard, or lost by the perils of the sea, the present action would be within the principle.
>
> But, looking at the Act, it is perfectly clear that its provisions were all enacted with a totally different view; there was no purpose, direct or indirect, to protect against such damage; but, as is recited in the preamble, the Act is directed against the possibility of sheep or cattle being exposed to disease on their way to this country. . . . That being so, if by reason of the default in question the plaintiffs' sheep had been overcrowded, or had been caused unnecessary suffering, and so had arrived in this country in a state of disease, I do not say that they might not have maintained this action. But the damage complained of here is something totally apart from the object of the Act of Parliament, and it is in accordance with all the authorities to say that the action is not maintainable.

Could the plaintiff have maintained an action for breach of the contract of carriage? What about a common claim for negligence action in not having pens, irrespective of the statute?

In Abrahams v. Young & Rubicam, Inc., 79 F.3d 234, 237 (2d Cir. 1996), Winter, J., stressed the difference between the two types of negligence cases: "At common law, so long as the plaintiff category is foreseeable, there is no requirement that the risk of injury to the plaintiff, and the risk of the harm that actually occurred, were what made the defendant's actions wrongful in the first place. With statutory claims, the issue is, instead, one of statutory intent: was the plaintiff (even though foreseeably injured) in the category the statute meant to protect, and was the harm that occurred (again, even if foreseeable), the 'mischief' the statute sought to avoid."

The distinction between common law duties of care and statutory duties was questioned by Posner, J., in Shadday v. Omni Hotels Management Corp., 477 F.3d 511, 517-518 (7th Cir. 2007):

> The violation of a statutory standard of care is negligence; so is a violation of a common law duty of care. In either case, the puzzle of the line of cases that descends from *Gorris* is why the defendant, having been negligent, should get off scot-free just because the harm that would have been averted had he been careful was not foreseeable. No doubt the framers of the Contagious Diseases (Animals) Act made no judgment that the cost of pens was less than the expected cost of a mass drowning of unpenned animals, but that seems irrelevant. Given that the

ship-owner was under a legal duty to pen the sheep, why should he not be liable for a disaster that would have been averted if only he had complied with his duty?

4. Violation of licensing requirements. The question frequently arises whether lack of license—for example, to practice medicine, or to operate a motor vehicle on the highway—standing alone constitutes negligence. Noting that "the immediate reason for the person's lack of a license is [often] unrelated to the state's general safety purpose," the Third Restatement concludes that the lack of a required license is neither negligence per se, nor evidence of negligence, unless the evidence indicates that the defendant has also violated the "substantive safety standards" enforced by the licensing requirement. RTT:LPEH §14, comment *h*. In Michaels v. Avitech, 202 F.3d 746, 752 (2000), a case involving a plane flown by an unlicensed pilot that crashed and killed all four passengers on board, the Fifth Circuit noted that "the violation of licensing regulations is often an exception to the general rule that the violation of a safety regulation or statute is negligence per se. . . . One reason . . . is that there may be reasons a license has not been renewed that do not relate to the operator's lack of skill."

Licensing raises urgent issues with medical devices subject to regulation by the Food and Drug Administration. In Talley v. Danek Med., Inc., 179 F.3d 154, 159-161 (4th Cir. 1999), a "well-known surgeon and professor . . . specializing in spinal surgery" used a Dyna-Lok internal fixation device manufactured by defendant, which failed when several of its screws came loose. Plaintiff's claim rested in part on the ground that the FDA had not approved this device for general use, which she argued violated the Federal Food, Drug, and Cosmetic Act. According to the plaintiff, this violation established negligence per se. Niemeyer, J., rejected her claim:

> [W]here a particular statutory requirement does not itself articulate a standard of care but rather requires only regulatory approval, or a license, or a report for the administration of a more general underlying standard, violation of that administrative requirement itself is not a breach of a standard of care. This violation rather indicates only a failure to comply with an administrative requirement, not the breach of a tort duty. . . . [W]e must determine whether Danek's alleged violation of statute amounted to the breach of an administrative requirement or the breach of a standard of care and whether such a breach proximately caused Talley's injury.

He then concluded:

> The administrative requirement that a given device be approved by the FDA before being marketed—as opposed to a specific substantive requirement that a device be safe and effective—is only a tool to facilitate administration of the underlying regulatory scheme. Because it lacks any independent substantive content, it does not impose a standard of care, the breach of which could form the basis of a negligence per se claim. Its breach is analogous to the failure to have a driver's license.

5. Causation in licensing cases. In Brown v. Shyne, 151 N.E. 197 (N.Y. 1926), the defendant chiropractor, who had no license to practice medicine, held himself out as licensed to practice medicine when he operated on the plaintiff's spine, which led to her paralysis. The plaintiff asked for a jury instruction that said that the physician should be held liable for the accident no matter what level of care was provided because the injury would not have occurred if he had not attempted to treat her back. That position was rejected by Lehman, J.:

> True, if the defendant had not practiced medicine in this State, he could not have injured the plaintiff, but the protection which the statute was intended to provide was against risk of injury by the unskilled or careless practitioner, and unless the plaintiff's injury was caused by carelessness or lack of skill, the defendant's failure to obtain a license was not connected with the injury.

On this view, the physician who practices without a license may be subject to a fine for a misdemeanor, but his conduct is judged by the same standard of negligence used to evaluate the conduct of a licensed physician. The dissent of Crane, J., took the opposite view:

> The law, to insure against ignorance and carelessness, has laid down a rule to be followed, namely, examinations to test qualifications, and a license to practice. If a man, in violation of this statute, takes his chances in trying to cure disease, and his acts result directly in injury, he should not complain if the law, in a suit for damages, says that his violation of the statute is some evidence of his incapacity.

RTT:LPEH §14, comment *h*, appears to endorse the outcome in *Brown*: "In light, then, of the combination of the statutory-purpose doctrine and ordinary principles of scope of liability, the lack of a license is not negligence per se on the part of the actor, nor is it evidence tending to show the actor's negligence."

Compare this view with section 4504 of the New York Civil Practice Law and Rules (Consol. 2007):

> (d) Proof of negligence; unauthorized practice of medicine. In any action for damages for personal injuries or death against a person not authorized to practice medicine . . . for any act or acts constituting the practice of medicine, when such act or acts were a competent producing proximate or contributing cause of such injuries or death, the fact that such person practiced medicine without being so authorized shall be deemed prima facie evidence of negligence.

6. Private rights of action under federal statutes. In recent times, one vital question is whether plaintiffs may maintain tort actions for defendant's breach of a *federal* statute or regulation under either federal or state law, in light of the federalism concerns that arise whenever a state court infers a private right of action from a federal statute. See RTT:LPEH §14, comment *c*, Reporter's Note. At the federal level, the earlier tendency was to freely imply causes of action, as is done in state courts dealing with state statutes. See J.I. Case Co. v. Borak, 377 U.S. 426 (1964). Subsequently, however, the Supreme Court has taken a much more restrictive view of the availability of federal relief. In the watershed case of Cort v. Ash, 422 U.S. 66, 78 (1975), the Court held:

In determining whether a private remedy is implicit in a statute not expressly providing one, several factors are relevant. First, is the plaintiff "one of the class for whose *especial* benefit the statute was enacted," . . . that is, does the statute create a federal right in favor of the plaintiff? Second, is there any indication of legislative intent, explicit or implicit, either to create such a remedy or to deny one? . . . Third, is it consistent with the underlying purposes of the legislative scheme to imply such a remedy for the plaintiff? . . . And finally, is the cause of action one traditionally relegated to state law, in an area basically the concern of the States, so that it would be inappropriate to infer a cause of action based solely on federal law?

Subsequent Supreme Court decisions confirm the hostile attitude to implying private rights of action in federal statutes. See, e.g., City of Milwaukee v. Illinois, 451 U.S. 304 (1981), where the Court refused to allow a private cause of action for nuisance, which it held was inconsistent with the comprehensive scheme of control imposed by the federal water pollution acts.

Assuming the federal statute at issue does not expressly or impliedly preempt state tort law liability (see Chapter 8, Section F, *infra*), is the state free to adopt or reject the federal standard as a basis for a private suit? As the Supreme Court noted in Grable & Sons v. Darue Engineering & Manufacturing, 545 U.S. 308, 318 (2005), "violation of federal statutes and regulations is commonly given negligence per se effect in state tort proceedings" (quoting Draft No. 1 of the Restatement (Third) of Torts, Reporters' Notes to §14, comment *a*). Lowe v. General Motors Corp., 624 F.2d 1373, 1379 (5th Cir. 1980), illustrates the majority position, by holding that the plaintiff stated a valid state law cause of action when he alleged that the recall and notice practices of the defendant, General Motors, did not comply with the National Traffic and Motor Vehicle Safety Act, 15 U.S.C.A. §1402(a), because Cort v. Ash was inapplicable to a wrongful death action maintained under Alabama law. "This Court has often held that violation of a Federal law or regulation can be evidence of negligence, and even evidence of negligence per se." Contrast with the minority position espoused by Miller v. E.I. DuPont de Nemours and Co., 880 F. Supp. 474, 480 (S.D. Miss. 1994): "[S]ince Congress did not intend to create a private right of action . . . then any alleged violation of that statute by defendant cannot provide a basis for a negligence per se claim."

Martin v. Herzog
126 N.E. 814 (N.Y. 1920)

[The decedent was killed in a collision between the buggy he was driving and defendant's automobile. The accident occurred after dark, and decedent was driving the buggy without any lights, in violation of a statute. The defendant requested a ruling that the absence of a light on the plaintiff's vehicle was "prima facie evidence of contributory negligence." This request was refused, and the jury was instructed that it might consider the absence of lights as some evidence of negligence, but not conclusive evidence of negligence. The plaintiff next requested a charge that "the fact that the plaintiff's intestate was driving without a light is not negligence in itself," and to this the court acceded. The jury found the defendant liable and the decedent free from contributory negligence and the plaintiff had judgment. The appellate division reversed for error in the instructions. Affirmed.]

CARDOZO, J. We think the unexcused omission of the statutory signals is more than some evidence of negligence. It *is* negligence in itself. Lights are intended for the guidance and protection of other travelers on the highway (Highway Law, sec. 329a). By the very terms of the hypothesis, to omit, willfully or heedlessly, the safeguards prescribed by law for the benefit of another that he may be preserved in life or limb, is to fall short of the standard of diligence to which those who live in organized society are under a duty to conform. . . . In the case at hand, we have an instance of the admitted violation of a statute intended for the protection of travelers on the highway, of whom the defendant at the time was one. Yet the jurors were instructed in effect that they were at liberty in their discretion to treat the omission of lights either as innocent or as culpable. They were allowed to "consider the default as lightly or gravely" as they would (Thomas, J., in the court below). They might as well have been told that they could use a like discretion in holding a master at fault for the omission of a safety appliance prescribed by positive law for the protection of a workman. Jurors have no dispensing power by which they may relax the duty that one traveler on the highway owes under the statute to another. It is error to tell them that they have. The omission of these lights was a wrong, and being wholly unexcused was also a negligent wrong. No license should have been conceded to the triers of the facts to find it anything else.

We must be on our guard, however, against confusing the question of negligence with that of the causal connection between the negligence and the injury. A defendant who travels without lights is not to pay damages for his fault unless the absence of lights is the cause of the disaster. A plaintiff who travels without them is not to forfeit the right to damages unless the absence of lights is at least a contributing cause of the disaster. To say that conduct is negligence is not to say that it is always contributory negligence. "Proof of negligence in the air, so to speak, will not do." (Pollock Torts (10th Ed.) p. 472).

We think, however, that evidence of a collision occurring more than an hour after sundown between a car and an unseen buggy, proceeding without lights, is evidence from which a causal connection may be inferred between the collision and the lack of signals. If nothing else is shown to break the connection, we have a case, prima facie sufficient, of negligence contributing to the result.

. . . A statute designed for the protection of human life is not to be brushed aside as a form of words, its commands reduced to the level of cautions, and the duty to obey attenuated into an option to conform.

NOTES

1. Negligence per se and excuses. Tedla v. Ellman, 19 N.E.2d 987, 989 (N.Y. 1939), offers an instructive contrast with *Martin.* The plaintiff and her brother, a deaf mute, were walking along a divided highway shortly after dark, pushing baby carriages filled with junk that they had collected for sale as part of their regular business. Instead of walking on the far left-hand side of the double highway, as required by statute so as to face oncoming traffic, they walked on the far right-hand side so that the traffic going in their direction approached them from behind. The defendant struck them with his car, hurting the plaintiff and killing her brother. The defendant's negligence was clearly established at trial and judgment was entered for plaintiff. The only issue on appeal was "whether, as matter of law, disregard of the statutory rule that pedestrians shall keep to the left of the center line of a highway constitutes contributory negligence which bars any recovery by the plaintiff." To answer that question, Lehman, J., noted that prior to the enactment of the statute, the common law custom usually required pedestrians to walk against traffic in order to be alert to dangers from oncoming traffic. The general customary rule, however, also contained a customary exception that required pedestrians to walk with the traffic when the traffic coming from behind was much lighter than the oncoming traffic. The case thus presented a knotty issue of statutory construction: Should the court read a customary exception to a statute that embodied the customary rule? If the statute had defined "specified safeguards against recognized dangers," Lehman, J., would have applied the rule in Martin v. Herzog. But since this statute was designed to "codify, supplement or even change common-law rules," themselves designed to prevent accidents, Lehman, J., implied this exception to the statute for the plaintiff's benefit. In an argument that appears to turn on legislative intent, Lehman, J., rebuffed the defendant as follows:

> Disregard of the statutory rule of the road and observance of a rule based on immemorial custom, it is said, is negligence which as matter of law is a proximate cause of the accident, though observance of the statutory rule might, under the circumstances of the particular case, expose a pedestrian to serious danger from which he would be free if he followed the rule that had been established by custom. If that be true, then the Legislature has decreed that pedestrians must observe the general rule of conduct which it has prescribed for their safety even under circumstances where observance would subject them to unusual risk; that pedestrians are to be charged with negligence as matter of law for acting as prudence dictates. It is unreasonable to ascribe to the Legislature an intention that the statute should have so extraordinary a result, and the courts may not give to a statute an effect not intended by the Legislature.

The one-sentence dissent argued that the plaintiff's action should have been dismissed on the authority of Martin v. Herzog.

The Second Restatement §288A, comment *i*, illus. 6 endorses the court's position in *Tedla*, as does RTT:LPEH §15(e), covering cases in which "the actor's compliance with the statute would involve a greater risk of physical harm to the actor or to others than noncompliance." Both Restatements also provide that violations of a statute may be excused by necessity or emergency, or by reason of incapacity, as is the case with various forms of common law negligence. In addition, the Third Restatement states that statutory causes of action should be judged by negligence, and not strict liability standards, by providing that a statutory violation is excused when "the actor exercises reasonable care in attempting to comply with the statute." RTT:LPEH §15(b). "Accordingly, the common law recognizes that the person can rebut negligence per se by showing that the person made a reasonable effort to comply with the statute," as with the driver who makes reasonable efforts to inspect or maintain brakes that fail. *Id.*, comment *c*.

2. Statutory duty and proximate cause.   The general principles of proximate cause were tested in Ross v. Hartman, 139 F.2d 14, 15-16 (D.C. Cir. 1943), where the defendant's agent left an unlocked car in a public alley with keys in the ignition. He intended for the car to be taken into an overnight garage, but did not notify anyone at the garage of his intention. Within two hours, a thief stole the car and negligently ran over the plaintiff. The defendant's conduct was in breach of an ordinance that made it illegal to allow an unlocked car "to stand or remain unattended on any street or in any public place." Edgerton, J., held that the deliberate intervention by the thief did not take the case outside the statutory prohibition:

> The particular ordinance involved here is one of a series which require, among other things, that motor vehicles be equipped with horns and lamps. Ordinary bicycles are required to have bells and lamps, but they are not required to be locked. The evident purpose of requiring motor vehicles to be locked is not to prevent theft for the sake of owners or the police, but to promote the safety of the public in the streets. An unlocked motor vehicle creates little more risk of theft than an unlocked bicycle, or for that matter an unlocked house, but it creates much more risk that meddling by children, thieves, or others will result in injuries to the public. The ordinance is intended to prevent such consequences. Since it is a safety measure, its violation was negligence. This negligence created the hazard and thereby brought about the harm which the ordinance was intended to prevent. It was therefore a legal or "proximate" cause of the harm. Both negligence and causation are too clear in this case, we think, for submission to a jury.
>
> There are practical as well as theoretical reasons for not excusing him. The rule we are adopting tends to make the streets safer by discouraging the hazardous conduct which the ordinance forbids. It puts the burden of the risk, as far as may be, upon those who create it. Appellee's agent created a risk which was both obvious and prohibited. Since appellee was responsible for the risk, it is fairer to hold him responsible for the harm than to deny a remedy to the innocent victim.

The opposite result was reached on similar facts in Richards v. Stanley, 271 P.2d 23, 26-27 (Cal. 1954), but there the San Francisco Municipal Code contained a proviso that barred the use of the ordinance in a private tort action. Traynor, J., also held that plaintiff had no action for common law negligence, noting that simply because an owner left a key in the ignition "does not assure that it will be driven, as he does when he lends it to another." Unless, therefore, he had some special reason to think that the car would be left in a dangerous locale, he was not subject to any general duty of care:

> In view of the fact that the risk of negligent driving she created was less than the risk she might intentionally have created without negligence by entrusting her car to another, and in the light of the rule that she owed no duty to protect plaintiff from harm resulting from the activities of third persons, we conclude that her duty to exercise reasonable care in the management of her automobile did not encompass a duty to protect plaintiff from the negligent driving of a thief.

The two dissenting judges would have left the plaintiff's common law claim to the jury. What if thieves are far more likely than guests to drive dangerously? If Justice Traynor's position is rejected, what result if the thief non-negligently struck the plaintiff?

3. Dram shop statutes. Causation issues also loom large in so-called dram shop litigation. When the basic statute makes it illegal to sell alcoholic beverages to a customer, is the provider of the alcohol responsible if the customer thereafter injures either a third person or himself while driving under the influence? The early common law rule treated the driver as the sole cause of the accident. "The rule was based on the obvious fact that one cannot be intoxicated by reason of liquor furnished him if he does not drink it." Nolan v. Morelli, 226 A.2d 383, 386 (Conn. 1967). In Vesely v. Sager, 486 P.2d 151 (Cal. 1971), the court repudiated the traditional rule, and followed *Ross, supra* at 230, by holding that the deliberate wrong by a third person did not sever the causal connection between the defendant's breach of statutory duty under California Business and Professions Code §25602(a) not to sell alcoholic beverages "to any habitual or common drunkard or to any obviously intoxicated person is guilty of a misdemeanor" and the injuries suffered by the plaintiff.

Dram statute liability did not go down well with California voters, and *Vesely* was overruled by name in 1978.

California Businesss & Professions Code §25602 (West 2015)

§25602. SALES TO DRUNKARD OR INTOXICATED PERSON; OFFENSE; CIVIL LIABILITY

(a) Every person who sells, furnishes, gives, or causes to be sold, furnished, or given away, any alcoholic beverage to any habitual or common drunkard or to any obviously intoxicated person is guilty of a misdemeanor.

(b) No person who sells, furnishes, gives, or causes to be sold, furnished, or given away, any alcoholic beverage pursuant to subdivision (a) of this section shall be civilly liable to any injured person or the estate of such person for injuries inflicted on that person as a result of intoxication by the consumer of such alcoholic beverage. . . .

Should social hosts be held responsible if commercial hosts are?

Local statutory variations in dram shop laws make it almost impossible to state the common law in this area. See generally 3 Harper, James & Gray, Torts §17.5 n.21.

Uhr v. East Greenbush Cent. Sch. Dist.
720 N.E.2d 886 (N.Y. 1999)

ROSENBLATT, J.

Education Law §905(1) requires school authorities in the State of New York to examine students between 8 and 16 years of age for scoliosis at least once in each school year. The principal issue on this appeal is whether the statute authorizes a private right of action.

[In the 1992-1993 school year the plaintiff, a pupil in the East Greenbush Central School District, was screened for scoliosis, but the tests were negative. In the following school year, she was not so checked. However, in 1995, as a ninth grader, an examination for scoliosis detected the condition.] Her parents, who are also plaintiffs in this action, then had her examined by an orthopedic doctor who concluded that her scoliosis had progressed to the point that surgery was required instead of the braces that often can be utilized when the condition is diagnosed earlier. The infant [i.e., minor] plaintiff underwent surgery in July 1995. [The plaintiffs then sued both under Education Law §905 and for common law negligence. The lower courts rejected both claims.]

Education Law §905(1) states that "[m]edical inspectors or principals and teachers in charge of schools in this state shall . . . examine all . . . pupils between eight and sixteen years of age for scoliosis, at least once in each school year." Education Law §905(2) provides that "[n]otwithstanding any other provisions of any general, special or local law, the school authorities charged with the duty of making such tests or examinations of pupils for the presence of scoliosis pursuant to this section shall not suffer any liability to any person as a result of making such test or examination, which liability would not have existed by any provision of law, statutory or otherwise, in the absence of this section." Finally, Education Law §911 charges the Commissioner of Education with the duty of enforcing the provisions of sections 901 through 910 of the Education Law and authorizes the Commissioner to "adopt rules and regulations" for such purpose.

THE TEST FOR THE AVAILABILITY OF A PRIVATE RIGHT OF ACTION

As plaintiffs point out, the District's obligation to examine for scoliosis is plain enough. [Given that the statute did not explicitly authorize a private right of action, the court then asked] whether creation of such a right would be consistent with the legislative scheme. . . .

Plaintiffs argue that a private right of action is not only consistent with Education Law §905(1) but also necessary for its operation. They assert that the statute offers no other practical means of enforcement and that a private right of action is imperative, in order to give it life. We disagree and conclude that a private right of action would not be consistent with the statutory scheme. To begin with, the statute carries its own potent official enforcement mechanism. The Legislature has expressly charged the Commissioner of Education with the duty to implement Education Law §905(1) and has equipped the Commissioner with authority to adopt rules and regulations for such purpose. Moreover, the Legislature has vested the Commissioner with power to withhold public funding from noncompliant school districts. Thus, the Legislature clearly contemplated administrative enforcement of this statute. The question then becomes whether, in addition to administrative enforcement, an implied private right of action would be consistent with the legislative scheme.

It would not. The evolution of Education Law §905(2) is compelling evidence of the Legislature's intent to immunize the school districts from any liability that might arise out of the scoliosis screening program. By the language of Education Law §905(2) the Legislature deemed that the school district "shall not suffer any liability to any person as a result of *making* such test or examination" (emphasis added). Plaintiffs contend that by implication, the District is denied immunity for *failing* to perform the examination. In effect, plaintiffs would interpret the statute as conferring immunity for misfeasance but not nonfeasance. On the other hand, the District contends that it would be incongruous for the Legislature to accord immunity for one circumstance but not the other.

Plaintiffs' reading of the statute might have some appeal if we did not have persuasive evidence as to the Legislature's intent to immunize the school districts for both nonfeasance and misfeasance. . . . Revealingly, the Legislature evidently saw no need to amend Education Law §905 in any other way, although obviously aware of [two Appellate Division decisions that had refused to create a private right of action.] Its failure to otherwise amend the statute is strong evidence of the Legislature's conclusion that the Appellate Divisions had correctly interpreted the statute's immunity provision.

There is also the matter of cost to the school districts, as evidenced by the Legislature's expressed sensitivity in that regard. Orthopedists through the New York State Society of Orthopaedic Surgeons and other professionals from the Scoliosis Association, Inc. agreed to volunteer their time and expertise to train existing school personnel on the relatively simple examination procedure. In forecasting its cost, the Legislature anticipated that the program would have minimal financial impact on school districts. Allowing a private right of action against the government as opposed to a private entity has direct and obvious financial consequences to the public.

Given the Legislature's concern over the possible costs to the school districts—as evidenced by the statutory immunity provision and the other legislative statements reflecting those concerns—we conclude that the Legislature did not intend that the districts bear the potential liability for a program that benefits a far wider population. If we are to imply such a right, we must have clear evidence of the Legislature's willingness to expose the governmental entity to liability that it might not otherwise incur. The case before us reveals no such legislative intent.

In sum, we conclude that a private right of action to enforce Education Law §905(1) is inconsistent with the statute's legislative scheme and therefore cannot be fairly implied.

COMMON-LAW NEGLIGENCE

Plaintiffs contend that the lower courts erred in holding that they failed to state a claim for common-law negligence. Essentially, plaintiffs argue that the District assumed a duty to the infant plaintiff and her parents by creating a special relationship with them in connection with the Education Law §905(1) program and that it breached its duty by failing to perform the examination during the 1993-1994 school year. We agree with the courts below that plaintiffs have failed as a matter of law to state a claim for common-law negligence.

[Affirmed.]

NOTE

1. Statutory causes of action under complex administrative schemes. *Uhr* represents the modern judicial reluctance to infer private rights of action from the breach of statutory duties imposed under complex administrative schemes. An early glimpse of this trend is found in Lucy Webb Hayes National Training School v. Perotti, *supra* at 191, which distinguished Ross v. Hartman, *supra* at 230. The decedent killed himself by jumping through a glass window shortly after he was committed to the defendant institution. The 1909 regulations for private hospitals prohibited them from keeping "any delirious or maniacal patient" in a room "not properly barred or closed." The court did not dwell on the question of proximate cause raised previously in *Ross*. Rather, it refused to create the private right of action at all:

> The traffic ordinance in *Ross* was one directed straight to the motoring public, who were expected to know and heed its requirements. In this case, the regulation related to the licensing of private hospitals in the District of Columbia.
>
> The Department of Public Health, which apparently is responsible for the enforcement of the regulation involved, approved the design of Sibley Memorial Hospital, . . . and recommended that the Commissioners of the District of Columbia license its operation, which they did. . . .
>
> Regulations relating to a licensing process are often enacted with the reasonable expectation that the licensing authority will exercise some judgment in applying the general rule to the specific case. To invoke a doctrine of negligence per se in such circumstances robs the regulation of the flexibility that its draftsmen may well have envisioned for it. We conclude that in this case the instruction that violation of the regulation would be negligence per se was erroneous, and requires a new trial. The correct standard . . . is that the hospital's negligence should be "decided on all relevant evidence, including violation of any safety regulation found to be applicable, and consequently admissible in evidence, but including also facts tending to show due care" on the part of the hospital in the construction and operation of [its facilities].

A similar hostility was expressed in Elliot v. City of New York, 747 N.E.2d 760 (N.Y. 2001). The plaintiff fell out of a bleacher seat that was not protected by a guardrail, as required by the city building code. The trial judge had held that the breach of the municipal building code amounted to negligence per se. The Court of Appeals reversed on the ground that a breach of the rules of a "subordinate rule-making body" did not count as negligence per se because only the state had power to pass a statute:

> [C]haracterizing the vast multitude of ordinances that have been adopted by New York City as State statutes would result in considerable fragmentation and uncertainty in the application of the common law of our State. Furthermore, since the City retains the authority to amend or repeal its Administrative Code provisions, including [that applicable here], without the need of State legislative action, we decline to transform the status of this provision from that of a local enactment to a State statute. In the absence of a violation of a statutorily imposed duty in this case, a negligence per se finding was unwarranted and defendants are entitled to a reversal and a new trial.

On the other hand, negligence per se actions have been allowed for violations of Medicare and Medicaid regulations. In McLain v. Mariner Health Care, Inc., 631 S.E.2d 435, 438 (Ga. 2006), Judy McLain alleged that a nursing home's violation of multiple health and safety regulations resulted in the wrongful death of her father. Johnson, J., reversing the lower court, observed that even in the absence of a private cause of action under the federal statute, McLain could assert a claim of negligence per se arising from the violation of regulations:

> It is obvious that as a resident of the nursing home owned by Mariner, McLain's father belonged to the class of persons for whom these statutes and regulations were intended to protect, and that the injuries set forth in the complaint, and which we assume to have occurred for purposes of a motion to dismiss, were among those these same statutes and regulations were designed to prevent. Likewise, the complaint's allegations of violations of the same statutes and regulations would be competent evidence of Mariner's breach of duty under a traditional negligence action.

And so it is back to first principles governing common law negligence.

SECTION F. JUDGE AND JURY

The law of negligence (indeed the entire law of tort) does more than articulate standards for liability. It also develops a wide range of legal institutions to apply its basic commands to individual cases. Our legal system divides the responsibility for deciding questions of fact between judge and jury. That divided system necessarily prevents either judge or jury from taking complete control over the individual case, unless both parties to the dispute waive a jury trial. Yet, by the same token, the division of responsibility is not arbitrary, for the jury is not simply told: "You are to decide, on the basis of all you have heard and in terms of your sense of fairness, whether the defendant should pay for the damage sustained by the plaintiff in this case." That total delegation of judicial responsibility has been rejected for two reasons. First, judges fear that the jury might abuse its unlimited power by deciding cases contrary to established principles of law, especially when motivated by obvious passion and prejudice, or even by more subtle forms of class, social, or economic bias. Second, judges believe that unlimited jury discretion repudiates or at least undermines the central principle of distributive justice — that like cases should be treated alike, no matter what substantive principles apply.

One form of judicial control is found in the judge's instructions to the jury on the relevant principles of substantive law, given at the close of the case. Substantive

Exhibit 3.5   The "Vanishing Trial" Phenomenon

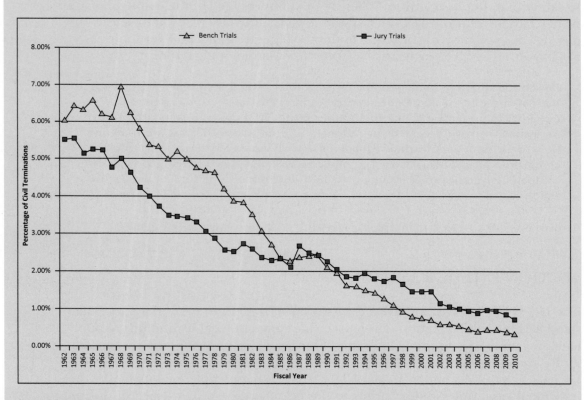

Percentage of Civil Terminations by Bench and Jury Trials
U.S. District Courts, 1962-2010

Source: Galanter & Frozena, The Continuing Decline of Civil Trials in American Courts, Forum for State Appellate Court Judges, Pound Civil Justice Institute 4 fig.2 (2011)

law is often made when the lawyers for either party challenge those instructions on appeal. Appellate courts set aside jury verdicts based on erroneous and prejudicial instructions precisely because they believe that juries should and do follow their instructions.

Sometimes mistakes seem quite minor. In Louisville & Nashville R.R. v. Gower, 3 S.W. 824, 827 (Tenn. 1887), the plaintiff, an employee of the defendant railroad, was hurt while attempting to couple two cars. Snodgrass, J., speaking for the court, reversed a judgment for the plaintiff and ordered a new trial:

> The charge was otherwise incorrect and misleading, particularly in defining the care necessary to have been exercised by Plaintiff Gower in order to entitle him to recovery. The Court, after telling the jury that "it was the duty of the plaintiff to exercise such a degree of care in making the coupling as a man of ordinary prudence" would have done, adds: "Just such care as one of you, similarly employed, would have exercised under such circumstances. If he exercised that degree of care, and was nevertheless injured, he is entitled to your verdict. If he failed to exercise that degree of care, he can not recover."
>
> The charge as to the exercise of such care as a man of ordinary prudence would have done was correct, but it was thought not full enough by the judge, who illustrated what he meant by reference to the care which each one of the jurymen would have exercised. His charge, so limited, was erroneous. It does not appear that all or any of the members of the jury were men of ordinary prudence, and yet the judge tells them that what he means by the "exercise of such care as a man of ordinary prudence would have exercised" is that it was the exercise of such care as one of them would have exercised if similarly situated. Under this instruction, if any member of the jury thought he would have done what Gower did in the coupling, he would of course have determined that Gower acted with the care required, and was entitled to recover. This illustration, used to define what he meant by "the care of a man of ordinary prudence" and thereby becoming its definition, was erroneous. The care he was required to exercise was that of a man of ordinary prudence in that dangerous situation, and not "just such care as one of the jury similarly situated" would have done, be that much or little as each member might be very prudent or very imprudent.

A second form of judicial control lies in the court's power to keep certain questions of fact from the jury. In Metropolitan Railway v. Jackson, 3 A.C. 193, 197 (1877), the issue on appeal was, "Was there at the trial any evidence of negligence by the defendant that ought to have been left to a jury?" Chancellor Cairns remarked as follows:

> There was not, at your Lordships' bar, any serious controversy as to the principles applicable to a case of this description. The Judge has a certain duty to discharge, and the jurors have another and a different duty. The Judge has to say whether any facts have been established by evidence from which negligence *may be* reasonably inferred; the jurors have to say whether, from those facts, when submitted to them, negligence *ought to be* inferred. It is, in my opinion, of the greatest importance in the administration of justice that these separate functions should be maintained, and should be maintained distinct. It would be a serious inroad on the province of

the jury, if, in a case where there are facts from which negligence may reasonably be inferred, the Judge were to withdraw the case from the jury upon the ground that, in his opinion, negligence ought not to be inferred; and it would, on the other hand, place in the hands of the jurors a power which might be exercised in the most arbitrary manner, if they were at liberty to hold that negligence might be inferred from any state of facts whatever.

As *Metropolitan Railway* suggests, the jury's traditional role is to find the "facts" to which it then applies the "law." In negligence cases, the jury's role fits uneasily into this sharp dichotomy between *law* and *fact*. Is it helpful to think of negligence as a "mixed issue of law and fact," as it is frequently called? Abraham elaborates in The Trouble with Negligence, 54 Vand. L. Rev. 1187, 1190-1191 (2001):

> [In negligence cases] the task of the finder of fact involves three steps, not just two. In logical order, the finder of fact must (1) find the empirical facts, including what the defendant did; (2) determine how much and what kind of care was reasonable given these facts; and (3) apply the law of negligence to these findings, by deciding whether the defendant behaved in accordance with the norm identified in step (2). It has long been recognized that step (2) involves a very different function than step (1), because the former is entirely empirical, whereas the latter is evaluative. In recognition of this difference, steps (2) and (3) together have been referred to as deciding a "mixed question of fact and law."

This section develops several themes: What is the role of the jury in law and in actual practice in setting the standard of care? What difference does it make who decides this issue? How does the court limit or control the jury's exercise of discretion? Is there any way to assure uniformity of jury decisions in similar cases? Are concerns about the objectivity and competence of juries well founded? Do juries ever nullify the legal rules articulated in appellate decisions? See generally James, Functions of Judge and Jury in Negligence Cases, 58 Yale L.J. 667 (1949).

Oliver Wendell Holmes, The Common Law
110-111, 120-124 (1881)

If, now, the ordinary liabilities in tort arise from failure to comply with fixed and uniform standards of external conduct, which every man is presumed and required to know, it is obvious that it ought to be possible, sooner or later, to formulate these standards at least to some extent, and that to do so must at last be the business of the court. It is equally clear that the featureless generality, that the defendant was bound to use such care as a prudent man would do under the circumstances, ought to be continually giving place to the specific one, that he was bound to use this or that precaution under these or those circumstances. The standard which the defendant was bound to come up to was a standard of specific acts or omissions, with reference to the specific circumstances in which he found himself. If in the whole department of unintentional wrongs the courts arrived at no further utterance than the question of negligence, and left every case, without rudder or compass, to the jury, they would simply confess their inability to state a very large part of the law which they required the defendant to know, and would assert, by implication, that nothing could be learned by experience. But neither courts nor legislatures have ever stopped at that point. . . .

The principles of substantive law which have been established by the courts are believed to have been somewhat obscured by having presented themselves oftenest in the form of rulings upon the sufficiency of evidence. When a judge rules that there is no evidence of negligence, he does something more than is embraced in an ordinary ruling that there is no evidence of a fact. He rules that the acts or omissions proved or in question do not constitute a ground of legal liability, and in this way the law is gradually enriching itself from daily life, as it should. Thus, in Crafter v. Metropolitan Railway Co.[, L.R. 1 C.P. 300 (1866)], the plaintiff slipped on the defendant's stairs and was severely hurt. The cause of his slipping was that the brass nosing of the stairs had been worn smooth by travel over it, and a builder testified that in his opinion the staircase was unsafe by reason of this circumstance and the absence of a hand-rail. There was nothing to contradict this except that great numbers of persons had passed over the stairs and that no accident had happened there, and the plaintiff had a verdict. The court set the verdict aside, and ordered a non-suit. The ruling was in form that there was no evidence of negligence to go to the jury; but this was obviously equivalent to saying, and did in fact mean, that the railroad company had done all that it was bound to do in maintaining such a staircase as was proved by the plaintiff. A hundred other equally concrete instances will be found in the text-books. . . .

Many have noticed the confusion of thought implied in speaking of such cases as presenting mixed questions of law and fact. No doubt, as has been said above, the averment that the defendant has been guilty of negligence is a complex one: first, that he has done or omitted certain things; second, that his alleged conduct does not come up to the legal standard. And so long as the controversy is simply on the first half, the whole complex averment is plain matter for the jury without special instructions, just as a question of ownership would be where the only dispute was as to the fact upon which the legal conclusion was founded. But when a controversy arises on the second half, the question whether the court or the jury ought to judge of the defendant's conduct is wholly unaffected by the accident, whether there is or is not also a dispute as to what that conduct was. If there is such a dispute, it is entirely possible to give a series of hypothetical instructions adapted to every state of facts which it is open to the jury to find. If there is no such dispute, the court may still take their opinion as to the standard. The problem is to explain the relative functions of court and jury with regard to the latter.

When a case arises in which the standard of conduct, pure and simple, is submitted to the jury, the explanation is plain. It is that the court, not entertaining any clear views of public policy applicable to the matter, derives the rule to be applied from daily experience, as it has been agreed that the great body of the law of tort has been derived. But the court further feels that it is not itself possessed of sufficient practical experience to lay down the rule intelligently. It conceives that twelve men taken from the practical part of the community can aid its judgment. Therefore it aids its conscience by taking the opinion of the jury.

But supposing a state of facts often repeated in practice, is it to be imagined that the court is to go on leaving the standard to the jury forever? Is it not manifest, on the contrary, that if the jury is, on the whole, as fair a tribunal as it is represented to be, the lesson which can be got from that source will be learned? Either the court will find that the fair teaching of experience is that the conduct complained of usually is or is not blameworthy, and therefore, unless explained, is or is not a ground of liability; or it will find the jury oscillating to and fro, and will see the necessity of making up its mind for itself. There is no reason why any other such question should not be settled, as well as that of liability for stairs with smooth strips of brass upon their edges. The exceptions would mainly be found where the standard was rapidly changing, as, for instance, in some questions of medical treatment.

If this be the proper conclusion in plain cases, further consequences ensue. Facts do not often exactly repeat themselves in practice; but cases with comparatively small variations from each other do. A judge who has long sat at nisi prius ought gradually to acquire a fund of experience which enables him to represent the common sense of the community in ordinary instances far better than an average jury. He should be able to lead and to instruct them in detail, even where he thinks it desirable, on the whole, to take their opinion. Furthermore, the sphere in which he is able to rule without taking their opinion at all should be continually growing.

Baltimore and Ohio R.R. v. Goodman
275 U.S. 66 (1927)

HOLMES, J. This is a suit brought by the widow and administratrix of Nathan Goodman against the petitioner for causing his death by running him down at a grade crossing. The defence is that Goodman's own negligence caused the death. At the trial, the defendant asked the Court to direct a verdict for it, but the request, and others looking to the same direction, were refused, and the plaintiff got a verdict and a judgment which was affirmed by the Circuit Court of Appeals. 10 F.(2d) 58.

Goodman was driving an automobile truck in an easterly direction and was killed by a train running southwesterly across the road at a rate of not less than sixty miles an hour. The line was straight, but it is said by the respondent that Goodman "had no practical view" beyond a section house two hundred and forty three feet north of the crossing until he was about twenty feet from the first rai or, as the respondent argues, twelve feet from danger, and that then the engir was still obscured by the section house. He had been driving at the rate of ten twelve miles an hour, but had cut down his rate to five or six miles at about fc feet from the crossing. It is thought that there was an emergency in which, sc as appears, Goodman did all that he could.

We do not go into further details as to Goodman's precise situation, be mentioning that it was daylight and that he was familiar with the crossing, appears to us plain that nothing is suggested by the evidence to relieve Goo from responsibility for his own death. When a man goes upon a railroad track he knows that he goes to a place where he will be killed if a train comes upon him before he is clear of the track. He knows that he must stop for the train, not the train stop for him. In such circumstances it seems to us that if a driver cannot be sure otherwise whether a train is dangerously near he must stop and get out of his vehicle, although obviously he will not often be required to do more than to stop and look. It seems to us that if he relies upon not hearing the train or any signal and takes no further precaution he does so at his own risk. If at the last moment Goodman found himself in an emergency it was his own fault that he did not reduce his speed earlier or come to a stop. It is true as said in Flannelly v. Delaware & Hudson Co., 225 U.S. 597 [1912], that the question of due care very generally is left to the jury. But we are dealing with a standard of conduct, and when the standard is clear it should be laid down once for all by the Courts. See Southern Pacific Co. v. Berkshire, 254 U.S. 415 [1921].

Judgment reversed.

Pokora v. Wabash Ry.
292 U.S. 98 (1934)

[The defendant operated four tracks at a level crossing. As plaintiff approached them, these included a switch track, a through track, and then two more switch tracks. Because of the boxcars on the first track, he could not see the main track. Plaintiff stopped, tried to look, and listened, but he heard no bell or whistle. He did not get out of his truck to obtain a better view, as the dictum in Baltimore & Ohio R.R. v. Goodman seemed to require under such circumstances. "Still listening, he crossed the switch, and reaching the main track was struck by a passenger train coming from the north at a speed of twenty-five to thirty miles an hour." The trial court directed a verdict for defendant on its finding that plaintiff had been contributorily negligent and this judgment was affirmed below. Reversed and remanded.]

CARDOZO, J. Standards of prudent conduct are declared at times by courts, but they are taken over from the facts of life. To get out of a vehicle and reconnoitre is an uncommon precaution, as everyday experience informs us. Besides being uncommon, it is very likely to be futile, and sometimes even dangerous. If the driver leaves his vehicle when he nears a cut or curve, he will learn nothing by getting out about the perils that lurk beyond. By the time he regains his seat and sets his car in motion, the hidden train may be upon him. . . . Often the added safeguard will be dubious though the track happens to be straight, as it seems that this one was, at all events as far as the station, about five blocks to the north. A train traveling at a speed of thirty miles an hour will cover a quarter of a mile in the space of thirty seconds. It may thus emerge out of obscurity as the driver turns his back to regain the waiting car, and may then descend upon him suddenly when his car is on the track. Instead of helping himself by getting out, he might do better to press forward with all his faculties alert. So a train at a neighboring station, apparently at rest and harmless, may be transformed in a few seconds into an instrument of destruction. At times the course of safety may be different. One can figure to oneself a roadbed so level and unbroken that getting out will be a gain. Even then the balance of advantage depends on many circumstances and can be easily disturbed. Where was Pokora to leave his truck after getting out to reconnoitre? If he was to leave it on the switch, there was the possibility that the box cars would be shunted down upon him before he could regain his seat. The defendant did not show whether there was a locomotive at the forward end, or whether the cars were so few that a locomotive could be seen. If he was to leave his vehicle near the curb, there was even stronger reason to believe that the space to be covered in going back and forth would make his observations worthless. One must remember that while the traveler turns his eye in one direction, a train or a loose engine may be approaching from the other.

Illustrations such as these bear witness to the need for caution in framing standards of behavior that amount to rules of law. The need is the more urgent when there is no background of experience out of which the standards have emerged. They are then, not the natural flowerings of behavior in its customary forms, but rules artificially developed, and imposed from without. Extraordinary situations may not wisely or fairly be subjected to tests or regulations that are fitting for the common-place or normal. In default of the guide of customary conduct, what is suitable for the traveler caught in a mesh where the ordinary safeguards fail him is for the judgment of a jury. The opinion in Goodman's case has been a source of confusion in the federal courts to the extent that it imposes a standard for application by the judge, and has had only wavering support in the courts of the states. We limit it accordingly.

NOTES

1. Stop, look, and listen. *Goodman* and *Pokora* illustrate the difficulty in fashioning a uniform rule for railroad crossing accidents. Notwithstanding *Pokora*'s respectful disapproval of *Goodman*, since 1927, *Goodman* has been cited hundreds of times, often with approval. Most critically, plaintiffs today face a rough time in cases involving collisions with trains moving through open country on single tracks. For instance, the court in Ridgeway v. CSX Transportation, Inc., 723 So. 2d 600 (Ala. 1998), emphatically upheld a contributory negligence defense as a matter of law in a single-track wrongful death case. It concluded that the statutory requirement to "stop, look, and listen" was "firmly rooted in our caselaw." Consistent with that view, the court in Jewell v. CSX Transportation, Inc., 135 F.3d 361, 364 (6th Cir. 1998), held that plaintiffs could not recover on the ground that an intersection was "extra-hazardous" when the plaintiffs' family car, traveling east across a railroad track on an elevated portion of the road, was struck by a train as it crossed the track (which ran at an "acute" angle to the road of 45 to 47 degrees). The court held that the narrow test for an extra-hazardous crossing under Kentucky law is whether there is a "real and substantial" obstruction to sight or hearing, which in turn "requires an actual physical inability to see or hear, and not merely such human factors as a disinclination to look for a train due to the angle of the intersection, distractions or diversions." Subsequently, in Norfolk Southern Railway Co. v. Johnson, 75 So. 3d 624, 641 (Ala. 2011), the court noted that the "stop, look, and listen" rule was embedded in Ala. Laws §32-5A-150, which it then applied against a plaintiff who was familiar with the crossing, was aware that boxcars could obscure his view, and knew it "was active with trains traveling both northbound and southbound along the track at the crossing."

In contrast, plaintiffs enjoy their greatest success in cases like *Pokora* when it is no longer clear that the railroad has the right of way. In Toschi v. Christian, 149 P.2d 848, 851 (Cal. 1944), plaintiff was hurt when the truck he was driving was struck at a crossing by defendant's train. The crossing was located in the heart of the business district, and the defendant customarily employed flagmen whose job was to signal drivers that the tracks were not clear, so as to warn them that it was unsafe for any drivers to cross them. At the time of this particular accident, defendant's flagman was literally experimenting with mirrors, and without the flagman's guidance, plaintiff drove his truck across the tracks. "As he drove onto the first track . . . light from the mirror, with which the flagman was still playing, was flashed in his eyes, blinding him. He stopped, and immediately his truck was struck. . . ."

Schauer, J., noted:

> The "stop, look and listen" rule, urged by defendants, will not be applied to factual bases where its application would be unreasonable. In the circumstances of this case, which comprise a six-track railroad yard crossing, switching operations progressing almost constantly, the employment of two flagmen by the railroad, whose duties involve traffic control on the highway and to some extent on the railroad, and a practical necessity for travelers on the highway to rely on the flagmen's signals because ordinarily it would be impossible for such travelers after they had observed railroad traffic approaching to know whether it would cross or stop short of the highway, the "stop, look and listen" rule is not wholly appropriate and cannot operate to establish contributory negligence as a matter of law.

Pokora is followed in the Third Restatement, which rejects the idea that uniform rules can decide concrete cases: "[W]hat looks at first to be a constant or recurring issue of conduct in which many parties engage may reveal on closer inspection many variables that can best be considered on a case-by-case basis. Tort law . . . requires that actual moral judgments be based on the circumstances of each individual situation. Tort law's affirmation of this requirement highlights the primary role necessarily fulfilled by the jury." RTT:LPEH §8, comment *c*.

2. Jury determinations in FELA cases. Today, juries are given broad discretion in suits in finding negligence for industrial accidents brought under the Federal Employers' Liability Act, 45 U.S.C. §51 et seq. (2012). This Act makes every interstate railroad liable in damages for injuries to its employees caused by the negligence of the railroad through any of its officers, agents, or employees, "or by reason of any defect or insufficiency" in any of its premises or equipment. FELA's 1939 amendments eliminated the defense of assumption of risk in all its forms and provided that contributory negligence should not bar an employee's action, but only that "the damages shall be diminished by the jury in proportion to the amount of negligence attributable to such employee."

In Wilkerson v. McCarthy, 336 U.S. 53, 62-64 (1949), the plaintiff was injured when he slipped on a board covered with oil and grease while taking a shortcut over a pit in the repair shop, even after the railroad had chained off the board-walk to prevent employees from using it. The Utah Supreme Court overturned the jury verdict for the plaintiff, but a badly fractured Supreme Court reinstated its verdict. Justice Black upheld that jury verdict, by insisting that courts should not assume that "juries will fall short of a fair performance of their constitutional function."

Chief Justice Vinson would have kept the case from the jury, saying in a brief dissent: "In my view of the record, there is no evidence, nor any inference which reasonably may be drawn from the evidence when viewed in the light most favorable to the petitioner, which could sustain a verdict for him." Justice Jackson then offered a fuller defense of the decision of the Utah Supreme Court to take the case from the jury:

> This record shows that both the wheel pit into which plaintiff fell and the board on which he was trying to cross over the pit were blocked off by safety chains strung between posts. Plaintiff admits he knew the chains were there to keep him from crossing over the pit and to require him to go a few feet farther to walk around it. After the chains were put up, any person undertaking to use the board as a cross walk had to complete involved contortions and gymnastics, particularly when, as was the case with petitioner, a car was on the track 23½. A casual examination of the model filed as an exhibit in this Court shows how difficult was such a passage. Nevertheless, the Court holds that if employees succeeded in disregarding the chains and forced passage frequently enough to be considered "customary," and the railroad took no further action, its failure so to do was negligence. The same rule would no doubt apply if the railroad's precautions had consisted of a barricade, or an armed guard.

Subsequent cases have confirmed that so long as the employer's negligence has played "any part, even the slightest" in bringing about the injury, then recovery under the FELA is appropriate. See Rogers v. Missouri Pacific R.R., 352 U.S. 500 (1957).

3. Should tort actions be left to the jury?   Why should any negligence case, or indeed any tort action, be tried by juries at all? Does the outcome in *Wilkerson* support Justice Frankfurter's view that the entire FELA system should be displaced by a workers' compensation law? Most civil law countries do not use juries to assess either liability or damages, and even the English courts rely on juries for those functions only in exceptional cases. Ward v. James, [1966] 1 Q.B. 273, 295. "Whenever a man is on trial for serious crime, or when in a civil case a man's honour or integrity is at stake, or when one or other party must be deliberately lying, then the trial by jury has no equal. But in personal injury cases trial by jury has given place of late to trial by judge alone, the reason being simply this, that in these cases trial by a judge alone is more acceptable to the great majority of people." Recently, however, "a striking number of countries have seriously debated or adopted new ways of incorporating ordinary citizens as decision makers in their legal systems." Hans, Jury Systems Around the World, 4 Ann. Rev. L. & Soc. Sci. 9.1, 9.1 (2008). Not all countries adopt the U.S. model; some use "mixed tribunals" of professional judges and laypersons, others are experimenting with tribunals composed of judges and private citizens who possess relevant substantive expertise.

Arguments for and against the use of juries are hotly debated. On the positive side, juries bring the common sense of the community to the difficult estimations of reasonable care required under a negligence system. Some jury advocates go further to suggest that juries add value to the litigation process by making significant contributions to accuracy in both fact-finding and legal decision making. Juries also provide a check against the domination of the legal system by government officials and professional people.

Jury detractors claim the jury system is expensive and time consuming. Juries may be subject to passion and prejudice, and, even when fair-minded, find themselves overwhelmed with the complex technical issues raised by medical malpractice or product liability claims. These critics also maintain that juries are pro-plaintiff decision makers, too easily swayed by emotion, and likely to award high amounts in damages.

4. Empirical studies. It has proved difficult to assemble hard empirical data on jury behavior, for it is generally considered unethical to monitor the deliberations of actual juries and too expensive to impanel enough mock juries to obtain a reliable data base. The Arizona Jury Project, a small pilot program, did enable a videotaped study of juror behavior in 50 civil cases. See Diamond & Vidmar, Jury Room Rumination on Forbidden Topics, 87 Va. L. Rev. 1857, 1869-1872 (2001). Here is an overview of some key empirical findings in some notable studies:

a. *Judge versus jury decision making.* The extensive Kalven and Zeisel Chicago jury study, based upon questionnaires sent to judges presiding over 4,000 state and federal civil jury trials nationwide in the 1950s, yielded data showing a 78 percent agreement between judge and jury on liability. Kalven defended civil juries on the ground that they usually reach the same results as judges sitting as triers of facts, leaving judges themselves generally pleased with their behavior. See Kalven, The Dignity of the Civil Jury, 50 Va. L. Rev. 1055 (1964). This judge-jury correspondence has been replicated in more recent studies. Clermont & Eisenberg, Trial by Jury or Judge: Transcending Empiricism, 77 Cornell L. Rev. 1124 (1992).

If juries typically reach the same conclusions as judges, do they add anything more to the system than higher costs? In The Georgia Jury and Negligence: The View from the Trenches, 28 Ga. L. Rev. 1 (1993), Sentelle relied on survey data of trial lawyers and found a significant (but far from unanimous) sentiment that today many judges are more pro-plaintiff than juries, at least on the issue of liability. On damages, however, judges were generally thought less likely to award "runaway verdicts" than a jury. See Clermont & Eisenberg,

Litigation Realities, 88 Cornell L. Rev. 119, 145 (2002), which found that, in product liability and medical malpractice cases, plaintiffs prevail "at a much higher rate before judges (48%) than they do before juries (28%)."

b. *"Deep pockets."* Some evidence suggests that, with injuries held constant, the size of the plaintiff's recovery depends largely on the identity of the defendant. Thus one study found that juries ratcheted up awards against defendants with "deep pockets."

> Compared with individual defendants, our model predicts that corporate defendants pay 34 percent larger awards, after controlling for plaintiffs' injuries and type of legal case. If the plaintiff is permanently and severely injured, the deep-pocket effect is much stronger—a corporate defendant pays almost 4.5 times as much as an individual, on average. Similarly, government defendants are estimated to pay 50 percent more than individuals (averaged over all plaintiff injuries; there were too few cases of permanently and severely injured plaintiffs suing government defendants to analyze these separately). Finally, medical malpractice awards against doctors are almost 2.5 times as great as awards against other individuals in average case types, and awards against hospitals are 85 percent larger. . . .
>
> There are several plausible explanations for the observed jury behavior. First, jurors may balance the benefit of greater compensation for the plaintiff against the harm to the defendant. While a relatively modest award against an individual defendant might cause him great financial hardship, the same award against a corporation would impose only miniscule losses on each of its stockholders. In addition, it may be impossible for jurors to separate the insult implicit in a tort from the harm to the plaintiff. Thus jurors may require doctors to provide greater compensation to victims of malpractice, not only because doctors are usually heavily insured and are wealthier than other defendants, but also because of the special trust a patient places in his or her doctor.

Hammitt, Carroll & Relles, Tort Standards and Jury Decisions, 14 J. Legal Stud. 751, 754-756 (1985). But see Hans, Business on Trial: The Civil Jury and Corporate Responsibility 23 (2000), which reports juror interviews and experimental studies that failed to detect a "deep pockets" effect.

c. *Hindsight bias.* Individual judgments by jurors (and judges) are often subject to so-called hindsight bias, wherein events that have actually occurred are thought to have been more likely than in fact they really were. The difficulties that bias poses for the administration of a negligence system are discussed in Rachlinski, A Positive Psychological Theory of Judging in Hindsight, 65 U. Chi. L. Rev. 571, 572 (1998).

> The hindsight bias clearly has implications for the legal system. Consider, for example, the dilemma of a defendant who, despite taking reasonable care, has caused an accident and has been sued. The defendant's level of care will be reviewed by a judge or jury who already knows that it proved inadequate to avoid the plaintiff's injury. Consequently, the defendant's level of care will seem less reasonable in hindsight than it did in foresight. Reasonableness must

be determined from the perspective of the defendant at the time that the precautions were taken, but the hindsight bias ensures that subsequent events will influence that determination. The law relies on a process that assigns liability in a biased manner. . . .

Rachlinski notes that hindsight bias in effect moves the negligence standard closer to a "quasi-strict" liability rule, because defendants may be held liable even when they take adequate precautions. Traditional methods for controlling bias, like jury instructions and creating a high burden of persuasion, do not remedy the problem. Although courts are unable to eliminate hindsight bias, Rachlinski argues that they have done a "remarkable job" of creating effective (if second-best) institutional responses. One response is to suppress evidence of information learned, and precautions taken, *after* the relevant time period. *Id.* at 624. Another response is to substitute ex ante standards, like relevant industry custom and regulations, for the standard of reasonable care. *Id.* at 608. What are the costs and benefits of these judicial solutions? Does the answer depend in part on the type of accident involved (e.g., medical malpractice versus highway accident)?

d. Anchoring. Perhaps the best-documented bias is "anchoring," or the process by which an initial numerical value or "anchor" disproportionately influences the decision maker's ultimate award. See Chapman & Bornstein, The More You Ask For, the More You Get: Anchoring in Personal Injury Verdicts, 10 Applied Cognitive Psychol. 519 (1996); Marti & Wissler, Be Careful What You Ask For: The Effects of Anchors on Personal Injury Damages Awards, 6 J. Exp. Psychol. 91 (2001).

Should we expect judges or juries to be more susceptible to this bias? Guthrie et al., Blinking on the Bench: How Judges Decide Cases, 93 Cornell L. Rev. 1, 20-26, 31 (2007), remind us that judges are people, too: Judges "generally make intuitive decisions" that expose their decision making to hindsight and anchoring biases, "impressionistic" evaluation of statistical evidence, and the unconscious influence of factors like race and gender.

Will concerns about systematic biases make actors take excessive care to avoid large adverse judgments?

5. Reform proposals. In order to reduce the cost of jury trials, courts have been urged to impanel smaller juries of six or eight instead of 12 jurors. However, the price of reducing the direct costs of jury operation is to decrease the level of community participation, diversity, and reliability of jury efforts. For evaluations of proposals to reduce jury size, see Diamond & Zeisel, "Convincing Empirical Evidence" on the Six-Member Jury, 41 U. Chi. L. Rev. 281 (1974); Vidmar, The Performance of the American Civil Jury: An Empirical Perspective, 40 Ariz. L. Rev. 849 (1998); Saks, The Smaller the Jury, the Greater the Unpredictability, 79 Judicature 263 (1996).

To control for juror bias, "blindfolding" the jury to certain information has been proposed. See generally Diamond & Casper, Blindfolding the Jury to Verdict Consequences: Damages, Experts and the Civil Jury, 26 Law & Soc'y Rev. 513, 557

(1992). Jurors are rarely told whether and how much liability insurance a defendant has, whether other parties to the dispute have settled and for how much, what settlement offers were made and rejected, and whether the court will modify the jury's award (as it is in certain types of cases). Alternatively, jurors may also be instructed to use information for certain purposes only. Diamond & Vidmar, *supra*, are skeptical that such tactics are effective; indeed, the authors suggest withholding such information may be the root cause of wide variability in jury verdicts.

More drastic proposals call for the removal of certain decisions from the purview of juries. Specialized "health courts" composed of neutral expert panels to adjudicate medical malpractice claims are backed by influential health policy organizations and are under consideration by Congress and several states. Peters, Health Courts?, 88 B.U. L. Rev. 227, 230 (2008), describes the procedure:

> Patients seeking to make a claim arising out of a hospital stay would start the process by filing their claim at the hospital or with its liability insurer. . . . A group of medical experts convened by the hospital would then evaluate the claim to decide whether the care given to the patient met the standard of care. . . . In the event of an appeal, an administrative law judge specializing in health court adjudications would review the claim de novo using all available materials, including a live hearing, if requested. After input from a court-appointed medical expert, the health court judge would render a verdict and produce a written opinion with precedential authority.

SECTION G. PROOF OF NEGLIGENCE

1. Methods of Proof

Success in prosecuting or defending negligence actions typically hinges on what the parties can prove at trial. With respect to offering evidence on the question of negligence, Clarence Morris has observed that "the plaintiff has usually exhausted the possibilities of proof once he has shown: (1) what defendant did, (2) how dangerous it was, (3) defendant's opportunity to discern danger, (4) availability of safer alternatives, and (5) defendant's opportunity to know about safer alternatives." Morris, Proof of Negligence, 47 Nw. U. L. Rev. 817, 834 (1953). In most negligence actions, plaintiffs get their cases to juries by proving that defendants failed to take specific precautions that would have averted the accident and resulting harm. Most modern litigation, especially in medical malpractice and products liability cases, also requires expert evidence to address issues such as the proper standard of care or causation. This section, however, is not primarily concerned with these general matters of proof, which are properly taken up in courses on evidence, trial practice, or clinical education.

One question of proof has, however, a long and close association with the law of tort. The doctrine of res ipsa loquitur—literally, Latin for "the thing speaks for itself"—is frequently invoked when the plaintiff seeks to establish the defendant's negligence by circumstantial evidence. Instead of proving that the defendant committed a specific act of negligence, a plaintiff invoking res ipsa loquitur argues that the jury should *infer* negligence from the very fact of the accident or injury. In some cases, the plaintiff seeks to reach and persuade a jury on the strength of the doctrine itself, relying on the jury's common knowledge. At other times, the plaintiff combines the doctrine with lay and expert testimony. This section traces the development and use of the doctrine, first with ordinary accident cases, and then in medical malpractice cases.

2.   Res Ipsa Loquitur

Byrne v. Boadle
159 Eng. Rep. 299 (Ex. 1863)

[Plaintiff's complaint stated that he was passing along the highway in front of defendant's premises when he was struck and badly hurt by a barrel of flour that was apparently being lowered from a window above, which was on the premises of the defendant, a dealer in flour. Several witnesses testified that they saw the barrel fall and hit plaintiff. The defendant claimed "that there was no evidence of negligence for the jury." The trial court, agreeing, nonsuited plaintiff after the jury had assessed the damages at £50. On appeal in the Court of Exchequer, the plaintiff argued that the evidence was sufficient to support a verdict in his favor. In response, the defendant's lawyer argued that it was consistent with the evidence that the purchaser of the flour or some complete stranger was supervising the lowering of the barrel of flour and that its fall was not attributable in any way to defendant or his servants. Pollock, C.B.: "The presumption is that the defendant's servants were engaged in removing the defendant's flour. If they were not it was competent to the defendant to prove it." Defendant's attorney replied, "Surmise ought not to be substituted for strict proof when it is thought to fix a defendant with serious liability. The plaintiff should establish his case by affirmative evidence. . . . The plaintiff was bound to give affirmative proof of negligence. But there was not a scintilla of evidence, unless the occurrence is of itself evidence of negligence." Pollock, C.B.: "There are certain cases of which it may be said res ipsa loquitur and this seems one of them. In some cases the Court had held that the mere fact of the accident having occurred is evidence of negligence, as, for instance, in the case of railway collisions."]

POLLOCK, C.B. We are all of opinion that the rule must be absolute [i.e., immediate and unconditional] to enter the verdict for the plaintiff. The learned counsel was quite right in saying that there are many accidents from which no presumption of negligence can arise, but I think it would be wrong to lay down as a rule that in no case can presumption of negligence arise from the fact of an accident. Suppose in this case the barrel had rolled out of the warehouse and fallen on the plaintiff, how could he possibly ascertain from what cause it occurred? It is the duty of persons who keep barrels in a warehouse to take care that they do not roll out, and I think that such a case would, beyond all doubt, afford prima facie evidence of negligence. A barrel could not roll out of a warehouse without some negligence, and to say that a plaintiff who is injured by it must call witnesses from the warehouse to prove negligence seems to me preposterous. So in the building or repairing a house, or putting pots on the chimneys, if a person passing along the road is injured by something falling upon him, I think the accident alone would be prima facie evidence of negligence. Or if an article calculated to cause damage is put in a wrong place and does mischief, I think that those whose duty it was to put it in the right place are prima facie responsible, and if there is any state of facts to rebut the presumption of negligence, they must prove them. The present case upon the evidence comes to this, a man is passing in front of the premises of a dealer in flour, and there falls down upon him a barrel of flour. I think it apparent that the barrel was in the custody of the defendant who occupied the premises, and who is responsible for the acts of his servants who had the control of it; and in my opinion the fact of its falling is prima facie evidence of negligence, and the plaintiff who was injured by it is not bound to show that it could not fall without negligence, but if there are any facts inconsistent with negligence it is for the defendant to prove them. [Judgment below reversed.]

NOTES

1. Historical origins. Baron Pollock's judicial aside in *Byrne* gave the doctrine its enduring Latin tag. Shortly thereafter, Chief Justice Erle supplied one standard account of res ipsa loquitur in Scott v. London & St. Katherine Docks Co., 159 Eng. Rep. 665 (Ex. 1865). "There must be reasonable evidence of negligence; but where the thing is shown to be under the management of the defendant or his servants, and the accident is such as in the ordinary course of things does not happen if those who have the management use proper care, it affords reasonable evidence, in the absence of explanation by the defendants, that the accident arose from want of care." In Wakelin v. London & S.W. Ry., [1886] 12 A.C. 41, 45-46 (H.L.E.), the plaintiff's deceased was struck and killed by one of defendant's trains. The view of the track was unobstructed at the time of the accident, and there was no specific evidence of any negligent act or omission by the defendant. The trial judge allowed the case to go to the jury, which returned a verdict for the plaintiff. The House of Lords overturned the decision, with Lord Halsbury noting:

> In this case I am unable to see any evidence of how this unfortunate calamity occurred. One may surmise, and it is but surmise and not evidence, that the unfortunate man was knocked down by a passing train while on the level crossing; but assuming in the plaintiff's favour that fact to be established, is there anything to shew that the train ran over the man rather than that the man ran against the train? I understand the admission in the answer to the sixth interrogatory to be simply an admission that the death of the plaintiff's husband was caused by contact with the train. If there are two moving bodies which come in contact, whether ships, or carriages, or even persons, it is not uncommon to hear the person complaining

of the injury describe it as having been caused by his ship, or his carriage, or himself having been run into, or run down, or run upon; but if a man ran across an approaching train so close that he was struck by it, is it more true to say that the engine ran down the man, or that the man ran against the engine? Neither man nor engine were intended to come in contact, but each advanced to such a point that contact was accomplished. . . .

Does res ipsa loquitur as formulated in *Scott* help the plaintiff in *Wakelin*?

2. From the terrace, hotel, etc. In *Byrne*, was the critical difficulty in establishing negligence in how the barrel was handled, or in showing that the person who dropped the barrel was someone for whom the defendant was responsible? Could the plaintiff have recovered if a thief had dropped the barrel out of the window?

In Larson v. St. Francis Hotel, 188 P.2d 513, 515 (Cal. App. 1948), the plaintiff, while walking on the sidewalk next to the hotel, was hit by a chair apparently thrown out of one of the hotel's windows as "the result of the effervescence and ebullition of San Franciscans in their exuberance of joy on V-J Day, August 14, 1945." Bray, J., refused to apply res ipsa loquitur:

> While, as pointed out by plaintiff, the rule of exclusive control "is not limited to the actual physical control but applies to the right of control of the instrumentality which causes the injury" it is not clear to us how this helps plaintiff's case. A hotel does not have exclusive control, either actual or potential, of its furniture. Guests have, at least, partial control. Moreover, it cannot be said that with the hotel using ordinary care "the accident was such that in the ordinary course of events . . . would not have happened." On the contrary, the mishap would quite as likely be due to the fault of a guest or other person as to that of defendants. The most logical inference from the circumstances shown is that the chair was thrown by some such person from a window. It thus appears that this occurrence is not such as ordinarily does not happen without the negligence of the party charged, but, rather, one in which the accident ordinarily might happen despite the fact that the defendants used reasonable care and were totally free from negligence. To keep guests and visitors from throwing furniture out windows would require a guard to be placed in every room in the hotel, and no one would contend that there is any rule of law requiring a hotel to do that.

Contrast Connolly v. Nicollet Hotel, 95 N.W.2d 657, 669 (Minn. 1959), in which defendant's hotel was "taken over" by a Junior Chamber of Commerce national convention, whose antics gave the management ample notice of drinking, revelry, and hooliganism on the premises. Plaintiff was injured when struck by some unidentified falling object. *Connolly* distinguished *Larson* as a case with a surprise celebration. In an opinion that never used the words "res ipsa loquitur," Murphy, J., reinstated the jury's $30,000 verdict for the plaintiff. Placing heavy reliance on "circumstantial evidence," he reversed the trial judge's judgment notwithstanding the verdict for defendant.

3. Doctrinal standards. How would you characterize the significant differences between the Prosser standard and the Second and Third Restatement formulations? Which standard should courts adopt? The vast majority of modern courts

suggested that the ship might have sunk because of a sudden redistribution of its weight after the catch had been taken aboard. The Court of Appeals approved the district court's refusal to submit res ipsa loquitur to the jury, noting that "the sea itself contains many hazards, and an inference of liability of the shipowner for the mysterious loss of his vessel should not be lightly drawn." One such hazard mentioned at trial was that of striking "deadheads," such as partially submerged logs. Could it be possible that the decedent's own negligence contributed to the harm?

Conversely, in some cases, a plaintiff presents enough circumstantial evidence to obtain a directed verdict under res ipsa loquitur. In Newing v. Cheatham, 540 P.2d 33 (Cal. 1975), the plaintiff's decedent was killed when a plane owned and piloted by the defendant's decedent crashed in mountainous terrain about 13 miles east of Tijuana, Mexico. The plaintiff's evidence indicated that the only possible cause of the crash was the negligence of the defendant in running out of fuel while in flight. The defendant had been drinking beer for about an hour on the morning of the crash. When the wreckage of the plane was examined, the smell of alcohol was found on the pilot's breath, as well as on the breath of a second passenger. None was found on plaintiff's decedent's breath. Eight or nine empty beer cans were also uncovered. Visibility was excellent; the weather was calm; there was no evidence of a midair collision; the plane's clock indicated that the crash took place at a time when it could be reasonably expected for the plane's fuel supply to be exhausted; and after the crash the plane's fuel tanks did not contain sufficient fuel to feed the motor.

The evidence also pointed to the pilot's exclusive control over the plane. He owned the plane; he was the only licensed pilot on board the aircraft; he was at the controls when the crash took place; and the applicable federal air regulations imposed upon him ultimate responsibility while airborne. Finally, no evidence suggested that the plaintiff's decedent's voluntary conduct could have contributed to the crash, since he did not know how to fly and at the time of the crash was seated in a rear seat, out of reach of the controls. The California Supreme Court upheld the trial court's decision to take the case from the jury and to direct a verdict for the plaintiff. Why did res ipsa loquitur apply in *Newing* but not in *Walston?* According to Grady, Res Ipsa Loquitur and Compliance Error, 142 U. Pa. L. Rev. 887, 910 (1994), "accidents in areas with the most safety equipment are the strongest res ipsa cases." Better technology reduces the number of accidents, but in the accidents that do occur, it makes it easier to rule out natural events or plaintiff's error.

> Since crab boat technology is so primitive, there are many hazards that will lead to its destruction without anyone having been negligent. Indeed, the cruder safety technology leads to a higher rate of unavoidable accident than there is in the air. Also, with more rudimentary technology, the required rate of precaution is lower than on a commercial aircraft. Hence, the possibilities for compliance error are lower at sea. A strong res ipsa case is one in which the expected rate of compliance error is high relative to the normal rate of unavoidable accident.

Colmenares Vivas v. Sun Alliance Insurance Co.
807 F.2d 1102 (1st Cir. 1986)

BOWNES, C.J. Appellants are plaintiffs in a diversity action to recover damages for injuries they suffered in an accident while riding an escalator. After the parties had presented their evidence, the defendants moved for and were granted a directed verdict. The court held that there was no evidence of negligence and that the doctrine of res ipsa loquitur, which would raise a presumption of negligence, did not apply. We reverse the directed verdict and remand the case to the district court because we hold that res ipsa loquitur does apply.

I. BACKGROUND

The relevant facts are not in dispute. On February 12, 1984, Jose Domingo Colmenares Vivas and his wife, Dilia Arreaza de Colmenares, arrived at the Luis Muñoz Marín International Airport in Puerto Rico. They took an escalator on their way to the Immigration and Customs checkpoint on the second level. Mrs. Colmenares was riding the escalator on the right-hand side, holding the moving handrail, one step ahead of her husband. When the couple was about halfway up the escalator, the handrail stopped moving, but the steps continued the ascent, causing Mrs. Colmenares to lose her balance. Her husband grabbed her from behind with both hands and prevented her from falling, but in doing so, he lost his balance and tumbled down the stairs. Mr. and Mrs. Colmenares filed a direct action against the Sun Alliance Insurance Company (Sun Alliance), who is the liability insurance carrier for the airport's owner and operator, the Puerto Rico Ports Authority (Ports Authority). Sun Alliance brought a third-party contractual action against Westinghouse Electric Corporation (Westinghouse) based on a maintenance contract that required Westinghouse to inspect, maintain, adjust, repair, and replace parts as needed for the escalator and handrails, and to keep the escalator in a safe operating condition. . . .

The trial was conducted on January 30 and 31, 1986. Appellants called four witnesses. The Ports Authority's contract and maintenance supervisor testified about his daily weekday inspections of the escalator, about the maintenance contract with Westinghouse, about inspection and maintenance procedures, and about the accident report and subsequent repair and maintenance of the escalator. The Ports Authority's assistant chief of operations testified about the accident report. Appellants' testimony concerned the accident and their injuries.

. . . After hearing the parties' arguments, the court ruled that there was no evidence that the Ports Authority had been negligent, and that the case could not go to the jury based on res ipsa loquitur because at least one of the requirements for its application—that the injury-causing instrumentality was within the exclusive control of the defendant—was not met. . . .

II. RES IPSA LOQUITUR

Under Puerto Rico law, three requirements must be met for res ipsa loquitur ("the thing speaks for itself") to apply: "(1) the accident must be of a kind which ordinarily does not occur in the absence of someone's negligence; (2) it must be caused by an agency or instrumentality within the exclusive control of the defendant; [and] (3) it must not be due to any voluntary action on the part of the plaintiff." Community Partnership v. Presbyterian Hosp., 88 P.R.R. 379, 386 (1963). If all three requirements are met, the jury may infer that the defendant was negligent even though there is no direct evidence to that effect.

A. THE FIRST REQUIREMENT: INFERENCE OF NEGLIGENCE

The first requirement that must be met for res ipsa loquitur to apply is that "the accident must be such that in the light of ordinary experience it gives rise to an inference that someone has been negligent." It is not clear to us whether the district court decided that this requirement was met, although the court did suggest that it was giving the benefit of the doubt on this question to the appellants. We hold that this requirement was met because an escalator handrail probably would not stop suddenly while the escalator continues moving unless someone had been negligent.[2]

This requirement would not be met if appellants had shown nothing more than that they had been injured on the escalator, because based on this fact alone it would not be likely that someone other than the appellants had been negligent. Here, it was not disputed that the handrail malfunctioned and stopped suddenly, an event that foreseeably could cause riders to lose their balance and get injured. Thus, the evidence gave rise to an inference that someone probably had been negligent in operating or maintaining the escalator, and the first requirement for the application of res ipsa loquitur was met.

B. THE SECOND REQUIREMENT: EXCLUSIVE CONTROL

The second requirement for res ipsa loquitur to apply is that the injury-causing instrumentality — in this case, the escalator — must have been within the exclusive control of the defendant. The district court found that this requisite was not met, despite the parties' stipulation that "[t]he escalator in question is property of and is under the control of the Puerto Rico Ports Authority." We agree that this stipulation was not by itself enough to satisfy the res ipsa loquitur requirement. It did not exclude the possibility that someone else also had control over the escalator; indeed, the stipulation said that Westinghouse maintained the escalator. We hold, however, that the Ports Authority effectively had exclusive control over the escalator because the authority in control of a public area had a nondelegable duty to maintain its facilities in a safe condition.

Few courts have required that control literally be "exclusive." . . . The exclusive control requirement, then, should not be so narrowly construed as to take from

---

2. In some jurisdictions, the courts have taken the position that escalator operators are common carriers owing the highest degree of care to their passengers. . . . To our knowledge, the Puerto Rico courts have not equated escalators to common carriers, and such a determination is not properly made by this court in the first instance. For the purposes of this appeal, however, it would not matter if the stricter standard did apply, because we hold that an inference of negligence has been raised even under the lower reasonable care standard.

the jury the ability to infer that a defendant was negligent when the defendant was responsible for the injury-causing instrumentality, even if someone else might also have been responsible. The purpose of the requirement is not to restrict the application of the res ipsa loquitur inference to cases in which there is only one actor who dealt with the instrumentality, but rather "to eliminate the possibility that the accident was caused by a *third party*." It is not necessary, therefore, for the defendant to have had actual physical control; it is enough that the defendant, and not a third party, was ultimately responsible for the instrumentality. Thus, res ipsa loquitur applies even if the defendant shares responsibility with another, or if the defendant is responsible for the instrumentality even though someone else had physical control over it. It follows that a defendant charged with a nondelegable duty of care to maintain an instrumentality in a safe condition effectively has exclusive control over it for the purposes of applying res ipsa loquitur. Unless the duty is delegable, the res ipsa loquitur inference is not defeated if the defendant had shifted physical control to an agent or contracted with another to carry out its responsibilities.

We hold that the Ports Authority could not delegate its duty to maintain safe escalators. There are no set criteria for determining whether a duty is nondelegable; the critical question is whether the responsibility is so important to the community that it should not be transferred to another. The Ports Authority was charged with such a responsibility. It was created for a public purpose, which included the operation and management of the airport. A concomitant of this authority is the duty to keep the facilities it operates in a reasonably safe condition. The public is entitled to rely on the Ports Authority — not its agents or contractors — to see that this is done. The Ports Authority apparently recognized this responsibility, for its maintenance and contract supervisor conducted daily weekday inspections of the escalators despite the maintenance contract with Westinghouse.

Duties have been seen as nondelegable in several analogous situations. For example, a public authority may not delegate to an independent contractor its responsibility to see that work in a public place is done carefully. Also, a government may not delegate its responsibility to maintain safe roads and similar public places. Finally, an owner has a nondelegable duty to keep business premises safe for invitees. These examples demonstrate a general tort law policy not to allow an entity to shift by contract its responsibility for keeping an area used by the public in a safe condition. It would be contrary to this policy to allow the owner and operator of an airport terminal to delegate its duty to keep its facility safe. We hold, therefore, that the district court erred in ruling that the exclusive control requirement was not met.

C. THE THIRD REQUIREMENT: THE PLAINTIFF'S ACTIONS

The third requirement that must be met for res ipsa loquitur to apply is that the accident must not have been due to the plaintiff's voluntary actions. The district court found, and we agree, that there was no evidence that Mr. and Mrs. Colmenares caused the accident. Indeed, there is no indication that they did anything other than attempt to ride the escalator in the ordinary manner. Therefore, we hold that all three requirements were met and that the jury should have been allowed to consider whether the Ports Authority was liable based on the permissible inference of negligence raised by the application of res ipsa loquitur. . . .

TORRUELLA, C.J. I must regretfully dissent. . . .

In my view, *solely* because the handrail stopped and Mrs. Colmenares fell, without further evidence as to why or how the handrail malfunctioned, does not give rise to an inference of *negligence* by the Ports Authority. . . .

The malfunctioning of an escalator presents an even stronger argument against the raising of an inference of negligence without additional proof as to the cause of the malfunction. Although a court can take notice that an escalator is a complicated piece of machinery, it has no basis of common knowledge for inferring that its malfunction is the result of the operator's negligence. . . .

NOTES

1. A difference of views?   What result in *Colmenares* if both the handrails and the steps had stopped simultaneously? With *Colmenares*, contrast Holzhauer v. Saks & Co., 697 A.2d 89, 93 (Md. 1997), where plaintiff was injured when he tumbled back down the steps after the escalator on which he was riding suddenly stopped. Chasanow, J., refused to allow the plaintiff to use res ipsa loquitur:

> For safety reasons, the escalator in question was equipped with two emergency stop buttons, located at the top and bottom of the escalator, respectively. When either button is pushed, if the escalator is functioning as intended, the escalator will stop. The buttons are safety devices designed to stop the escalator quickly should a hand, foot, or article of clothing become caught; thus, ready accessibility to the buttons is only sensible. We cannot say that the escalator would not stop in the absence of Appellees' negligence because the escalator would also stop whenever any person pushed one of the emergency stop buttons.
>
> The record is silent as to whether anyone did, in fact, push one of the stop buttons, but this is of little concern. The facts need not show that a stop button definitely was pushed to preclude reliance on *res ipsa;* they need only show that something other than Appellees' negligence was just as likely to cause the escalator to stop. The fact that the escalator had never malfunctioned before the day in question, and has not malfunctioned since, makes it equally likely, if not slightly more likely, that the escalator did not malfunction on the day in question but, rather, that it stopped because somebody intentionally or unintentionally pushed an emergency stop button.

In addition, the court held that the plaintiff could not satisfy the exclusive control requirement of res ipsa loquitur, observing: "Hundreds of Saks & Co.'s customers have unlimited access to the emergency buttons each day." Is this case distinguishable from *Colmenares*?

The disputes over escalators also arise with automatic doors. In the leading case of Rose v. New York Port Authority, 293 A.2d 371, 375 (N.J. 1972), the plaintiff claimed damages when struck by an automatic glass door while moving about

Kennedy Airport. "Here the occurrence bespeaks negligence. Members of the public passing through automatic doors, whether in an airport, office building or supermarket do so generally without sustaining injury. What happened to the plaintiff here is fortunately unusual and not commonplace. It strongly suggests a malfunction which in turn suggests negligence." But that inference was not drawn in Kmart v. Bassett, 769 So. 2d 282 (Ala. 2000), in which the plaintiff, an 83-year-old woman who used a cane, stepped on a rubber mat outside a Kmart to activate the automatic doors. As she progressed one third of the way, the door closed on her, resulting in a fall that led to a fractured hip. The Alabama Supreme Court reversed a jury verdict of $289,000 for plaintiff. It refused to find negligence in Kmart's decision not to have a regular maintenance contract and to wait for signs of trouble before calling for repairs, and it further rejected the argument that failures of this sort could not happen in the absence of negligence, noting that "a mere malfunction would be insufficient to invoke the doctrine of res ipsa loquitur under Alabama law." Should it make a difference if the door worked after the accident or not? Should the door be designed so as to avoid closing if someone is on the mat, no matter how slowly she moves?

Finally, in Jones v. Sheraton Atlantic City Convention Center Hotel, No. A-3827-12T4, 2014 WL 3375526 (N.J. Super. Ct. App. Div. July 11, 2014), the plaintiff sued to recover for personal injuries that she claimed were caused when she was struck by a malfunctioning elevator door while entering the elevator. The court first held that the defendant had a nondelegable duty to maintain the elevator, and concluded that the doctrine of res ipsa loquitur applied even though the parties disagreed about the length of "dwell time" between the time that the elevator doors opened and the plaintiff entered. Can the plaintiff satisfy the requirement that her conduct did not cause the harm?

2. Exclusive control.   In McGriff v. Gramercy Capital Corp., No. 2:13CV152, 2013 WL 1856233, at *4 (E.D. Va. Apr. 29, 2013), the elevator that the plaintiff had just entered suddenly plunged for several floors, causing serious injuries. The court refused to allow the case to go to the jury, noting, "While Virginia will permit a case against multiple defendants to go forward to determine *which* defendant had control, there is no precedent for permitting an action to proceed on the basis of joint exclusive control."

The extreme opposite view was taken in Miles v. St. Regis Paper Co., 467 P.2d 307, 310 (Wash. 1970), which involved the complex interaction between the tort and workers' compensation law. In general, the exclusive remedy provision of the workers' compensation statutes prevents an injured party from suing his employer in tort. To meet this challenge, the plaintiff often claims that res ipsa loquitur applies because some third-party defendant has "exclusive" control of the dangerous instrumentality. The decedent, an employee of the "D" Street Rafting Company, was crushed to death by a load of logs that suddenly rolled off the defendant railroad's flatcar while he was releasing one of its binders. Even though the decedent's employer directed the loading operations, a divided court found that the railroad company, which responded to the orders of employees of the rafting company, had "exclusive control" over the movement of the train, observing "the ultimate decision to move the train was made by employees of the railroad."

Does a finding of "exclusive control" in *Colmenares* require the same finding here?

3. Plaintiff's conduct and conduct of a third party. In many negligence actions the dangerous instrumentality in question has passed through the hands of a third party, only to cause injury while being used by the plaintiff. In these cases, "the plaintiff's mere possession of a chattel which injures him does not prevent a res ipsa case where it is made clear that he has done nothing abnormal and *has used the thing only for the purpose for which it was intended.*" Prosser, Res Ipsa Loquitur in California, 37 Cal. L. Rev. 183, 201-202 (1949).

Similarly, res ipsa loquitur was invoked in Benedict v. Eppley Hotel Co., 65 N.W.2d 224, 229 (Neb. 1954). The plaintiff-appellee was injured when a folding chair collapsed after she had been sitting on it for some 20 or 30 minutes while participating in a bingo game. After the accident it was discovered that the screws and bolts on one side of the chair were missing.

> [Plaintiff's] acts in reference to the chair were limited to transportation of it from where she first saw it in the hallway connecting the Embassy Room and the ball-room of the Rome Hotel to the table in the latter room where the game was in progress and sitting on it. She occupied the chair as an invitee of appellant. She had no right or duty to examine it for defects. She had a right to assume it was a safe instrumentality for the use she had been invited by appellant to make of it. Appellant had the ownership, possession, and control of the chair under the circumstances of this case and it was obligated to maintain it in a reasonably safe condition for the invited use made of it by the appellee. The fact that the chair when it was being properly used for the purpose for which it was made available gave way permits an inference that it was defective and unsafe and that appellant had not used due care in reference to it.

Formerly, res ipsa loquitur was only available when the plaintiff had not contributed in any way to the accident. RTT:LPEH §17, comment *h*, explains the modern rule that plaintiff's conduct only bears on the application of the doctrine when it may have disrupted the alleged causal sequence between the defendant's actions and the harm. Where this is not the case (for example, a plaintiff has been inattentive but cannot possibly have set the accident in motion), the plaintiff's negligence may reduce the amount of damages awarded, but it does not affect the operation of the doctrine in establishing the defendant's negligence. Thus the plaintiff in *Colmenares* can only rely on the doctrine by excluding his own conduct as a source of the escalator malfunction. But the possible contributory negligence of the plaintiff in Byrne v. Boadle does not prevent the use of res ipsa loquitur since the plaintiff had no control whatsoever over the barrel of flour.

What happens when the defendant has acquired the dangerous instrumentality from a third party? The Third Restatement takes a strong stand against the preservation of the exclusive control requirement, noting that it functions as a poor "proxy" for negligence. For example, an injured pedestrian should not normally be able to rely on res ipsa loquitur in a suit against a driver if his car's brakes fail a day after purchase. Although the driver has exclusive control over the car at the time of the accident, there is a high likelihood that the manufacturer is responsible for the brake failure. RTT:LPEH §17, comment *b.*

4. Assessing the probabilities of negligence.   Conceptually the most difficult part of the res ipsa loquitur test comes from attaching a precise meaning to the phrase "ordinarily does not occur in the absence of negligence." Most courts intuit whether this test is satisfied. Thus, in McDougald v. Perry, 716 So. 2d 783, 786 (Fla. 1998), the court used res ipsa loquitur when the defendant's 130-pound spare tire fell out from its angled cradle underneath the defendant's tractor-trailer as it was being driven over some railroad tracks. It bounced in the air, and struck the plaintiff's jeep. The incident "is the type of accident which, on the basis of common experience and as a matter of general knowledge, would not occur but for the failure to exercise reasonable care by the person who had control of the spare tire."

How strong must the inference of the defendant's negligence be before the plaintiff must introduce evidence to negate the likelihood of alternative causes? The Third Restatement offers a quantitative example:

> . . . [I]f a type of accident is caused by defendant negligence 70 percent of the time, the plaintiff's res ipsa case can proceed even without evidence from the plaintiff negating any of the remaining causes. But for another type of accident, defendant negligence may be implicated only 45 percent of the time; two other causes are 30 percent and 25 percent possibilities. In such cases the plaintiff must offer evidence negating at least one of these causes in order to render the res ipsa claim acceptable.

RTT:LPEH §17, comment *d.*

The Third Restatement shows further sensitivity to this difficulty by requiring the plaintiff to negotiate special hurdles created by issues of compound probabilities. Thus, if a given accident of a certain class only occurs two-thirds of the time with negligence, and that negligence is attributable to the defendant only two-thirds of the time, then res ipsa loquitur should not apply. Even if the accident does not ordinarily happen without the occurrence of negligence, it ordinarily happens without the negligence of this defendant, since the evidence establishes that the defendant is likely to be the responsible party only four-ninths (two-thirds multiplied by two-thirds) of the time. RTT:LPEH §17, comment *b.*

The phrase "ordinarily does not occur in the absence of negligence" is fraught with additional difficulties. Linguistically, the expression has generally been taken to signify either "(1) that the probability of the injury given the exercise of reasonable care is quite small, or (2) that the probability of the injury given reasonable care is smaller than the probability of the injury given negligence, or (3) that the probability of the injury given reasonable care is much smaller than the probability of the injury given negligence." Kaye, Probability Theory Meets Res Ipsa Loquitur, 77 Mich. L. Rev. 1456, 1465 (1979). However, as Kaye points out, none of these three commonsense statements captures the ultimate issue, namely, whether the probability that the defendant was negligent, given the occurrence of the injury, is greater than 50 percent. The first expression only notes that the probability of accident is quite small when there is reasonable care, but if the defendant exercises reasonable care an overwhelming proportion of the time, it could still prove more likely than not that reasonable care was in fact exercised in the particular case.

Thus suppose that it is established that a hand grenade has exploded prematurely because it contains a defective fuse. See, e.g., McGonigal v. Gearhart Industries, Inc., 788 F.2d 321 (5th Cir. 1986). Assume further liability turns solely on whether the defective fuse escaped detection because the manufacturer's employees negligently inspected it before shipment. To analyze this situation, consider two examples. First, suppose there is a one-in-one-thousand chance of a defective grenade slipping through a reasonable inspection and a one-in-two chance of a defective grenade slipping through a negligent inspection. If the defendant is careful 99.9 percent of the time, then for every one million units produced, 999,000 of them are properly inspected. Of these, we should expect to see 999 instances of failure, none of which are attributable to defendant's negligence. By the same token, we should expect to see an additional 500 failures (half of the 1,000 units that remain), all of which are attributable to negligence. To be sure, any negligently prepared unit is much more likely to be defective than a carefully manufactured one (as in Kaye's proposition (2)), for a 50 percent failure rate is 500 times a 0.1 percent failure rate. Yet—and the point is critical—by the same token it is more likely (by odds of 999 to 500) that any defective unit comes from the group of carefully inspected grenades than from the group of negligently inspected grenades, and thus would not satisfy the "ordinarily does not occur in the absence of negligence" requirement.

That conclusion, however, is very sensitive to the choice of numbers. Suppose now that the defendant's inspections were careful only 99 percent of the time, and careless 1 percent of the time. If the probability of a bad grenade slipping through the careful inspection remains 0.1 percent, then 990 defective grenades would be produced when care was exercised (one one-thousandth of 990,000). In addition, however, 5,000 defective units (half of 10,000) would be produced with negligence, making it better than five-to-one odds that the grenade came from the badly inspected batch.

These two examples illustrate the problem with inferring negligence from the occurrence of an accident based only on the knowledge that negligence frequently produces accidents like the one that has occurred. Kaye's article contains a formal demonstration, invoking the use of Bayes' theorem, of why in general that inference should be made only in the third situation set out above, namely, the probability of injury when defendant takes due care is much smaller than the probability of injury when the defendant is negligent. On the intricacies of statistical inference, see also Comment, Mathematics, Fuzzy Negligence and the Logic of Res Ipsa Loquitur, 75 Nw. U. L. Rev. 147 (1980).

In Guthrie, Rachlinski & Wistrich, Inside the Judicial Mind, 86 Cornell L. Rev. 777, 808-809 (2001), the authors surveyed federal magistrate judges on a variation of this problem that assumed that a barrel (à la *Byrne)* breaks loose only 1 percent of the time if properly handled, but 90 percent of the time if improperly handled, and employees handle the barrels properly 99.9 percent of the time. The judges were asked to state the odds that the fall of the barrel was attributable to negligence. About 41 percent of the judges said that the barrel's fall attributable to negligence fell between zero and 25 percent of the cases; 8.8 percent chose the interval between 25 and 50 percent; 10.1 percent chose the interval between 51 and 75 percent, and 40.3 percent chose 76 and 100 percent. The right answer is 8.3 percent. To calculate this, assume that there are 100,000 lifts. The 99,900 safe lifts result in breakage 999 times (99,900 multiplied by 0.01), while the 100 improper lifts result in breakage 90 times (100 multiplied by 0.9). The 90 breaks due to improper handling constitute roughly 8.3 percent of the 1,089 total breaks (90 divided by (90 plus 990)). Note that the size of the intervals makes it doubtful that the judges who picked the right answer correctly made the needed calculations. But query, if taught the basic insight about base rates first, could they have calculated the right answer?

Ybarra v. Spangard
154 P.2d 687 (Cal. 1944)

GIBSON, C.J. This is an action for damages for personal injuries alleged to have been inflicted on plaintiff by defendants during the course of a surgical operation. The trial court entered judgments of nonsuit as to all defendants and plaintiff appealed.

On October 28, 1939, plaintiff consulted defendant Dr. Tilley, who diagnosed his ailment as appendicitis, and made arrangements for an appendectomy to be performed by defendant Dr. Spangard at a hospital owned and managed by defendant Dr. Swift. Plaintiff entered the hospital, was given a hypodermic injection, slept, and later was awakened by Doctors Tilley and Spangard and wheeled into the operating room by a nurse whom he believed to be defendant Gisler, an employee of Dr. Swift. Defendant Dr. Reser, the anesthetist, also an employee of Dr. Swift, adjusted plaintiff for the operation, pulling his body to the head of the operating table and, according to plaintiff's testimony, laying him back against two hard objects at the top of his shoulders, about an inch below his neck. Dr. Reser then administered the anesthetic and plaintiff lost consciousness. When he awoke early the following morning he was in his hospital room attended by defendant Thompson, the special nurse, and another nurse who was not made a defendant.

Plaintiff testified that prior to the operation he had never had any pain in, or injury to, his right arm or shoulder, but that when he awakened he felt a sharp pain about half way between the neck and the point of the right shoulder. He complained to the nurse, and then to Dr. Tilley, who gave him diathermy treatments while he remained in the hospital. The pain did not cease, but spread down to the lower part of his arm, and after his release from the hospital the condition grew worse. He was unable to rotate or lift his arm, and developed paralysis and atrophy of the muscles around the shoulder. He received further treatments from Dr. Tilley until March, 1940, and then returned to work, wearing his arm in a splint on the advice of Dr. Spangard.

Plaintiff also consulted Dr. Wilfred Sterling Clark, who had X-ray pictures taken which showed an area of diminished sensation below the shoulder and atrophy and wasting away of the muscles around the shoulder. In the opinion of Dr. Clark, plaintiff's condition was due to trauma or injury by pressure or strain, applied between his right shoulder and neck.

Plaintiff was also examined by Dr. Fernando Garduno, who expressed the opinion that plaintiff's injury was a paralysis of traumatic origin, not arising from pathological causes, and not systemic, and that the injury resulted in atrophy, loss of use and restriction of motion of the right arm and shoulder.

Plaintiff's theory is that the foregoing evidence presents a proper case for the application of the doctrine of res ipsa loquitur, and that the inference of negligence arising therefrom makes the granting of a nonsuit improper. Defendants take the position that, assuming that plaintiff's condition was in fact the result of an injury, there is no showing that the act of any particular defendant, nor any particular instrumentality, was the cause thereof. They attack plaintiff's action as an attempt to fix liability "en masse" on various defendants, some of whom were not responsible for the acts of others; and they further point to the failure to show which defendants had control of the instrumentalities that may have been involved. Their main defense may be briefly stated in two propositions: (1) that where there are several defendants, and there is a division of responsibility in the use of an instrumentality causing the injury, and the injury might have resulted from the separate act of either one of two or more persons, the rule of res ipsa loquitur cannot be invoked against any one of them; and (2) that where there are several instrumentalities, and no showing is made as to which caused the injury or as to the particular defendant in control of it, the doctrine cannot apply. We are satisfied, however, that these objections are not well taken in the circumstances of this case.

The doctrine of res ipsa loquitur has three conditions: "(1) the accident must be of a kind which ordinarily does not occur in the absence of someone's negligence; (2) it must be caused by an agency or instrumentality within the exclusive control of the defendant; (3) it must not have been due to any voluntary action or contribution on the part of the plaintiff." (Prosser, Torts, p. 295.) It is applied in a wide variety of situations, including cases of medical or dental treatment and hospital care. . . .

There is, however, some uncertainty as to the extent to which res ipsa loquitur may be invoked in cases of injury from medical treatment. This is in part due to the tendency, in some decisions, to lay undue emphasis on the limitations of the doctrine, and to give too little attention to its basic underlying purpose. The result has been that a simple, understandable rule of circumstantial evidence, with a sound background of common sense and human experience, has occasionally been transformed into a rigid legal formula, which arbitrarily precludes its application in many cases where it is most important that it should be applied. If the doctrine is to continue to serve a useful purpose, we should not forget that "the particular force and justice of the rule, regarded as a presumption throwing upon the party charged the duty of producing evidence, consists in the circumstance that the chief evidence of the true cause, whether culpable or innocent, is practically accessible to him but inaccessible to the injured person." (9 Wigmore, Evidence [3d ed. 1940], §2509, p. 382.)

The present case is of a type which comes within the reason and spirit of the doctrine more fully perhaps than any other. The passenger sitting awake in a railroad car at the time of a collision, the pedestrian walking along the street and struck by a falling object or the debris of an explosion, are surely not more entitled to an explanation than the unconscious patient on the operating table. Viewed from this aspect, it is difficult to see how the doctrine can, with any justification, be so restricted in its statement as to become inapplicable to a patient who submits himself to the care and custody of doctors and nurses, is rendered unconscious, and receives some injury from instrumentalities used in his treatment. Without the aid of the doctrine a patient who received permanent injuries of a serious character, obviously the result of someone's negligence, would be entirely unable to recover unless the doctors and nurses in attendance voluntarily chose to disclose the identity of the negligent person and the facts of establishing liability. If this were the state of the law of negligence, the courts, to avoid gross injustice, would be forced to invoke the principles of absolute liability, irrespective of negligence, in actions by persons suffering injuries during the course of treatment under anesthesia. But we think this juncture has not yet been reached, and the doctrine of res ipsa loquitur is properly applicable to the case before us.

The condition that the injury must not have been due to the plaintiff's voluntary action is of course fully satisfied under the evidence produced herein; and the same is true of the condition that the accident must be one which ordinarily does not occur unless someone was negligent. We have here no problem of negligence in treatment, but of distinct injury to a healthy part of the body not the subject of treatment, nor within the area covered by the operation. The decisions in this state make it clear that such circumstances raise the inference of negligence, and call upon the defendant to explain the unusual result. . . .

The argument of defendants is simply that plaintiff has not shown an injury caused by an instrumentality under a defendant's control, because he has not shown which of the several instrumentalities that he came in contact with while in the hospital caused the injury; and he has not shown that any one defendant or his servants had exclusive control over any particular instrumentality. Defendants assert that some of them were not the employees of other defendants, that some did not stand in any permanent relationship from which liability in tort would follow, and that in view of the nature of the injury, the number of defendants and the different functions performed by each, they could not all be liable for the wrong, if any.

We have no doubt that in a modern hospital a patient is quite likely to come under the care of a number of persons in different types of contractual and other relationships with each other. For example, in the present case it appears that Doctors Smith, Spangard and Tilley were physicians or surgeons commonly

placed in the legal category of independent contractors and Dr. Reser, the anesthetist, and defendant Thompson, the special nurse, were employees of Dr. Swift
and not of the other doctors. But we do not believe that either the number or
relationship of the defendants alone determines whether the doctrine of res ipsa
loquitur applies. Every defendant in whose custody the plaintiff was placed for
any period was bound to exercise ordinary care to see that no unnecessary harm
came to him and each would be liable for failure in this regard. Any defendant
who negligently injured him, and any defendant charged with his care who so
neglected him as to allow injury to occur, would be liable. The defendant employers would be liable for the neglect of their employees and the doctor in charge of
the operation would be liable for the negligence of those who became his temporary servants for the purpose of assisting in the operation.

In this connection, it should be noted that while the assisting physicians and
nurses may be employed by the hospital, or engaged by the patient, they normally
become the temporary servants or agents of the surgeon in charge while the
operation is in progress, and liability may be imposed upon him for their negligent acts under the doctrine of respondeat superior. Thus a surgeon has been
held liable for the negligence of an assisting nurse who leaves a sponge or other
object inside a patient, and the fact that the duty of seeing that such mistakes do
not occur is delegated to others does not absolve the doctor from responsibility
for their negligence. . . .

It may appear at the trial that, consistent with the principles outlined above,
one or more defendants will be found liable and others absolved, but this should
not preclude the application of the rule of res ipsa loquitur. The control, at one
time or another, of one or more of the various agencies or instrumentalities
which might have harmed the plaintiff was in the hands of every defendant or of
his employees or temporary servants. This, we think, places upon them the burden of initial explanation. Plaintiff was rendered unconscious for the purpose of
undergoing surgical treatment by the defendants; it is manifestly unreasonable
for them to insist that he identify any one of them as the person who did the
alleged negligent act.

The other aspect of the case which defendants so strongly emphasize is that
plaintiff has not identified the instrumentality any more than he has the particular guilty defendant. Here, again, there is a misconception which, if carried to the
extreme for which defendants contend, would unreasonably limit the application
of the res ipsa loquitur rule. It should be enough that the plaintiff can show an
injury resulting from an external force applied while he lay unconscious in the
hospital; this is as clear a case of identification of the instrumentality as the plaintiff may ever be able to make.

[The court then discusses a series of precedents.]

In the face of these examples of liberalization of the tests for res ipsa loquitur,
there can be no justification for the rejection of the doctrine in the instant case.
As pointed out above, if we accept the contention of defendants herein, there
will rarely be any compensation for patients injured while unconscious. A hospital today conducts a highly integrated system of activities, with many persons

contributing their efforts. There may be, e.g., preparation for surgery by nurses and interns who are employees of the hospital; administering of an anesthetic by a doctor who may be an employee of the hospital, an employee of the operating surgeon, or an independent contractor; performance of an operation by a surgeon and assistants who may be his employees, employees of the hospital, or independent contractors; and post surgical care by the surgeon, a hospital physician, and nurses. The number of those in whose care the patient is placed is not a good reason for denying him all reasonable opportunity to recover for negligent harm. It is rather a good reason for re-examination of the statement of legal theories which supposedly compel such a shocking result.

We do not at this time undertake to state the extent to which the reasoning of this case may be applied to other situations in which the doctrine of res ipsa loquitur is invoked. We merely hold that where a plaintiff receives unusual injuries while unconscious and in the course of medical treatment, all those defendants who had any control over his body or the instrumentalities which might have caused the injuries may properly be called upon to meet the inference of negligence by giving an explanation of their conduct.

The judgment is reversed.

NOTES

1. Procedural role of res ipsa loquitur. The standard justification for res ipsa loquitur is that it offers injured plaintiffs a method of proving defendants' negligence even when there is no way to know (or no evidence to prove) exactly what happened. RTT:LPEH §17, comment *a*. In Morejon v. Rais Construction Co., 851 N.E.2d 1143, 1146, 1146-1147 (N.Y. 2006), Rosenblatt, J., described courts' confusion over the procedural effects of the doctrine: "Courts, including ours, used 'prima face case,' 'presumption of negligence,' and 'inference of negligence' interchangeably even though the phrases can carry different procedural consequences." *Morejon* affirmed the conventional view that the doctrine is "nothing more than a brand of circumstantial evidence." *Id.* at 1149. On this view, "only in the rarest of res ipsa loquitur cases may a plaintiff win summary judgment or a directed verdict. That would happen only when the plaintiff's circumstantial proof is so convincing and the defendant's response so weak that the inference of defendant's negligence is inescapable."

Ybarra is one of a number of exceptional cases in which courts shift the burden of production to the defendants. One early defense of the use of res ipsa loquitur in medical malpractice cases was as a tool to overcome the "conspiracy of silence" among physicians. "One may suspect that the courts are not reluctant to use res ipsa loquitur as a deliberate instrument of policy to even the balance against the professional conspiracy of silence; but with two exceptions the decisions give no hint of anything more than the obvious inference from the circumstantial evidence alone," Prosser, Selected Topics on the Law of Torts 346 (1954), citing *Ybarra*. The Third Restatement endorses the use of res ipsa loquitur to "smoke out" the culpable defendant in surgery cases, at least when all are simultaneously present in the operating room, noting that one defendant can escape liability by pointing a finger at another. RTT:LPEH §17, comment *f*. Today, however, the rise of modern discovery devices and the active market in expert testimony have quieted these conspiratorial concerns, such that the Third Restatement treats res ipsa loquitur as a doctrine of circumstantial evidence unrelated to any differential of knowledge between the parties. "The plaintiff may invoke res ipsa even though the defendant is as ignorant of the facts of the accident as the plaintiff is." RTT:LPEH §17, comment *i*.

While most states treat res ipsa loquitur as creating only a permissive inference that a jury is entitled to make, a few states treat it as a rebuttable presumption, which requires the defendant to come forward with exonerating evidence or suffer a judgment as a matter of law. See RTT:LPEH §17, comment *j*; see also Cox v. Paul, 828 N.E.2d 907, 912 (Ind. 2005), noting the difference. What defendant would remain silent even if res ipsa loquitur created only a permissive inference of negligence?

On retrial in *Ybarra*, the defendants testified that to their knowledge nothing had gone wrong in the operation. The California Court of Appeal held that the trial judge could still find for the plaintiff on the strength of the circumstantial evidence in the case. *Ybarra* v. Spangard, 208 P.2d 445 (Cal. App. 1949). For criticism of *Ybarra*, see Seavey, Res Ipsa Loquitur: Tabula in Naufragio, 63 Harv. L. Rev. 643 (1950).

2. Common knowledge, expert testimony, and res ipsa loquitur. Should *Ybarra* be treated as a pure res ipsa loquitur case given that Dr. Clark testified that he believed that the source of the injury was pressure applied between the shoulder and neck? In fact, modern anesthesiologists guard against just such pressure by cushioning that area, especially in long operations. What result if this risk was not fully understood when the operation took place? In modern practice, many medical malpractice plaintiffs mount a doubled-edged attack, using expert testimony to prove specific negligence, while invoking res ipsa loquitur in the alternative. Most courts will allow this two-front attack to proceed, see RTT:LPEH §17, comment *g*, but the strategy could easily backfire if the plaintiff prevails at trial only for an appellate court to reverse the judgment on the ground that the res ipsa loquitur instruction was improper.

The Third Restatement takes the position that the "better rule, now accepted by most courts, is that expert testimony is admissible in a medical-malpractice res ipsa loquitur case, and indeed is frequently necessary in order to justify submitting the res ipsa claim to the jury." RTT:LPEH §17, comment *c*. A key exception to the modern rule requiring expert testimony arises when the jury has "common knowledge" that the harm would not have occurred without defendant's negligence, as, for example, when a misapplied hot water bottle burns the plaintiff. However, the common knowledge exception rarely applies when complex medical judgments and procedures are at issue.

In Farber v. Olkon, 254 P.2d 520 (Cal. 1953), the plaintiff, who was mentally incompetent, suffered broken bones after being subjected to electroshock therapy. The court explicitly distinguished *Ybarra* as a case where "plaintiff while unconscious on an operating table received injuries to a healthy part of his body, not subject to treatment or within the area covered by his operation." It then refused to apply the common knowledge test given the undisputed testimony by the defendant's experts that "electroshock therapy is designed to have 'an effect upon the entire body'" in the hope that the convulsion will improve the patient's mental condition. Compare Bardessono v. Michels, 478 P.2d 480, 486 (Cal. 1971), in which the plaintiff received a series of injections of cortisone and local anesthetic for the treatment of tendonitis in his shoulder. All the injections caused the plaintiff excruciating pain, and shortly after their completion he developed partial paralysis. The court held that the jury was properly instructed when told that "it could infer negligence from the happening of the accident alone." The court allowed a jury to rely on common knowledge "if the routine medical procedure is relatively commonplace and simple, rather than special, unusual and complex." If the needle damaged one of the plaintiff's nerves, does that establish negligence or only causation? In *Bardessono*, the defendant testified that she had made the same sort of injection hundreds of times without adverse effects. How should the jury have weighed that evidence?

With *Bardessono*, contrast Greenberg v. Michael Reese Hospital, 396 N.E.2d 1088, 1094 (Ill. App. 1979), *aff'd in part and rev'd in part*, 415 N.E.2d 390, 397 (Ill. 1980). Plaintiff had been treated with radiation for enlarged tonsils and adenoids during the 1940s and 1950s, when such treatment was routine at Michael Reese Hospital. The treatment was discontinued when it was discovered that it could result in tumorous growths in or near the thyroid gland. The court rejected an analogy between these cases and radiation burn cases to which res ipsa loquitur applies:

> In the radiation burn cases, the reasoning takes two steps: first, that there is no medical reason to use radiation sufficient to cause extensive burns and, second, that the doctor in fact used excess radiation and therefore was negligent. Here, however, plaintiffs concede that irradiation of tonsils was a widely used therapeutic treatment, specifically chosen by the referring physician in the light of surgical dangers and poliomyelitic implications. The only possible inference which res ipsa loquitur could provide in the case at bar is that tumors, having resulted in some percentage of cases from either organic or external stimulus, are the result of negligent medical judgment. Res ipsa loquitur arises from a clearly negligent act (i.e., application of excessive doses of radiation) which leads to an almost certain outcome (radiation burns). Unlike these radiation burn cases, the original diagnostic decision to use tonsillar irradiation is at best debatably negligent. Whether or not a medical judgment to use an alternative form of therapy is legally negligent is properly contested at trial, and should not be subject to a presumption of negligence arising solely from the bad result.

The Illinois Supreme Court remanded on the res ipsa question, stating only that "we are unable to say that no set of facts can be proved which will entitle plaintiff to recover," without addressing the difference between excess radiation and tumor cases.

Finally, even in medical malpractice cases, it is possible to find situations where courts will use res ipsa loquitur to give plaintiffs a judgment as a matter of law. In

Quinby v. Plumsteadville Family Practice, Inc., 907 A.2d 1061, 1077 (Pa. 2006), the decedent, a quadriplegic for over 25 years, was placed on his right side for an operation to remove a small lesion from the left side of his head. When the operation was completed, the decedent, who had been left unattended, somehow fell off the bed, sustaining injuries that led to his death. The trial judge refused to instruct on res ipsa loquitur. On appeal, Baer, J., held that the plaintiff was entitled to a directed verdict on defendant's negligence:

> The only fact that was in dispute during trial was the positioning of Decedent on the table. This fact, however, is inconsequential to assessing Defendants' negligence. Even if Decedent was placed on his back in the center of the table as Defendants maintain, the fact remains that Decedent fell from the table to the floor, and Defendants have not offered any evidence explaining the cause of the fall. Pursuant to the above discussion, this is not the type of event that occurs without negligence; the evidence sufficiently eliminates other causes; and the negligence was within the scope of Defendants' duty to Decedent.

3. Statutory modification of res ipsa loquitur in medical malpractice cases.   Res ipsa loquitur has led medical groups to fear that the doctrine will become (as it often is in stranger cases) the opening wedge to a doctrine of strict liability that functions poorly in medical malpractice contexts. In order to limit its scope, and that of the use of common knowledge, medical groups have obtained passage of statutes, such as Nev. Rev. Stat. §41A.100 (2010). How would this statute apply to the cases discussed in this section?

Nevada Revised Statutes Annotated (West 2010)

§41A.100. REQUIRED EVIDENCE; EXCEPTIONS; REBUTTABLE PRESUMPTION OF NEGLIGENCE

1. Liability for personal injury or death is not imposed upon any provider of medical care based on alleged negligence in the performance of that care unless evidence consisting of expert medical testimony, material from recognized medical texts or treatises or the regulations of the licensed medical facility wherein the alleged negligence occurred is presented to demonstrate the alleged deviation from the accepted standard of care in the specific circumstances of the case and to prove causation of the alleged personal injury or death, except that such evidence is not required and a rebuttable presumption that the personal injury or death was caused by negligence arises where evidence is presented that the personal injury or death occurred in any one or more of the following circumstances:

> (a) A foreign substance other than medication or a prosthetic device was unintentionally left within the body of a patient following surgery;
>
> (b) An explosion or fire originating in a substance used in treatment occurred in the course of treatment;
>
> (c) An unintended burn caused by heat, radiation or chemicals was suffered in the course of medical care;
>
> (d) An injury was suffered during the course of treatment to a part of the body not directly involved in the treatment or proximate thereto; or
>
> (e) A surgical procedure was performed on the wrong patient or the wrong organ, limb or part of a patient's body.

4. Conditional res ipsa loquitur. In many malpractice cases, determining causation requires a two-step inquiry. First, was the patient's death or injury caused by the defendant's conduct or by a natural event? Second, if the former, was the defendant negligent? In dealing with these cases, res ipsa loquitur may be inapplicable for the first question, but relevant to the second, under the doctrine of conditional res ipsa loquitur, which Allendorf v. Kaiserman Enterprises, 630 A.2d 402, 405 (N.J. Super. Ct. App. Div. 1993), explained as follows:

> If the evidence presents a factual issue as to how an accident occurred, and the res ipsa loquitur doctrine would be applicable under only one version of the accident, the court should give a "conditional" res ipsa loquitur instruction, under which the jury is directed first to decide how the accident happened and to consider res ipsa loquitur only if it finds that the accident occurred in a manner which fits the doctrine.

More recently, the New Jersey Supreme Court reconsidered the propriety of conditional res ipsa instructions in medical malpractice cases where the underlying disputed issue of fact is the source of disagreement between the parties' experts. In Khan v. Singh, 975 A.2d 389, 402-403 (N.J. 2009), the plaintiff underwent a "thermal energy discectomy," in which a "thin radiofrequency needle" was inserted into a herniated disc in his spine; it was subsequently discovered that the nerve root in the treated disc was completely destroyed. Experts for both parties agreed that burning the nerve root during the discectomy would be negligent; they disagreed about whether the nerve was in fact burned. Worried about the possibility that conditional res ipsa charges would become "routine" in medical malpractice cases where parties' experts typically offer conflicting opinions, Hoens, J., rejected plaintiff's request for a conditional res ipsa instruction:

> By suggesting that the jury be told first to decide whether the nerve root was burned and then to apply a *res ipsa* analysis, plaintiff attempts to transform a conclusion

offered by an expert, that the jury can accept or reject in accordance with ordinary negligence concepts, into a fact for the jury to decide as a predicate for affording him the inference of negligence itself.

Could special verdicts guard against the confusion of a conditional res ipsa loquitur instruction? If so, how might one have been framed in *Khan*?

5. *Res ipsa loquitur and multiple defendants.*   *Ybarra* also has been extended to actions against multiple defendants sued under different substantive theories. In Anderson v. Somberg, 338 A.2d 1, 5, 9-10 (N.J. 1975), the plaintiff suffered serious injuries when the tip of a surgical forceps (a rongeur) broke off in his spinal canal and remained lodged there despite the efforts of defendant physician to remove it. The plaintiff brought actions against four separate defendants: against the physician, for negligence in the operation; against the hospital, for negligently furnishing a defective instrument; against the medical distributor who supplied the rongeur, on a warranty theory; and against the manufacturer of the rongeur, on a strict products liability theory. The jury returned a verdict in favor of each of the four defendants against the plaintiff; the decision was reversed by the appellate division, which held that the jury was obligated to impose liability on at least one of the named defendants. The New Jersey Supreme Court, by a four-to-three vote, applied res ipsa loquitur to this case of multiple defendants, noting that this "development represents a substantial deviation from earlier conceptions of res ipsa loquitur and has more accurately been called 'akin to res ipsa loquitur,' or 'conditional res ipsa loquitur.'" The dissent noted that other surgeons, perhaps numbering 20, could have created the defect but were not joined as defendants.

The New Jersey Court unanimously reaffirmed *Anderson* in Chin v. St. Barnabas Medical Center, 734 A.2d 778, 783 (N.J. 1999). The decedent, a 45-year-old woman, died of a massive air embolism that occurred during a routine "diagnostic hysteroscopy"—a procedure used to determine abnormalities in the uterus. The procedure in question required the cooperation of many physicians and nurses, and the evidence suggested that a hysteroscope had been misused by one of two nurses charged with hooking it up to various devices, so that gas instead of fluid was pumped into her uterus. Because the tubes had been disconnected before an investigation could be made, no one could determine which nurse had erred. Handler, J., held that under *Anderson*, given that Chin "was unconscious, helpless, and utterly blameless," "the air embolism could have been caused only by negligent use of the hysteroscope," and "[a]ll the potential defendants, that is, all those who participated in the chain of events leading up to Ms. Chin's injury, were sued in this case," the jury had to come back with a verdict against at least one defendant. The jury then exonerated the manufacturer, but on the basis of common knowledge, and without expert testimony, divided responsibility between two nurses, the treating physician, and the hospital.

With *Anderson* and *Chin*, contrast Darrah v. Bryan Memorial Hospital, 571 N.W.2d 783, 786 (Neb. 1998). The plaintiff suffered ulnar nerve damage at the site where an intravenous line was inserted postoperatively. The court upheld summary judgment for the defendant, and affirmed the trial court's refusal to grant a res ipsa loquitur instruction because "the district court found that the damage to Darrah's ulnar nerve could have occurred during or after surgery while he was hospitalized at BMH. . . . '[T]he requirement of exclusive control cannot be satisfied in view of the absence of the operating surgeons and the anesthesiologist as party defendants. These are parties who control the activities during surgery and they are neither agents [n]or employees of the defendant hospital.'"

CHAPTER 4

PLAINTIFF'S CONDUCT

SECTION A. INTRODUCTION

This chapter examines the ways that the plaintiff's own conduct affects her right to recover damages for her harms. This inquiry comes to the fore once the defendant claims that the plaintiff's harm was "her own fault." As is often the case with legal principles, however, this commonsense observation resists any easy transformation into workable legal rules, given its internal ambiguity. Thus, when the plaintiff is the only person involved in bringing about the accident, the defendant can simply deny his own responsibility, and say truthfully that the plaintiff was the sole cause of her own harm. In the absence of any prima facie case, questions of plaintiff's contributory negligence or assumption of risk do not and cannot arise.

The defendant's claim that the plaintiff should not recover because her injury was her own fault also arises when the defendant's actions were plainly involved in bringing about the plaintiff's harm, as when the defendant negligently runs over the plaintiff who has darted into the street from between two parked cars. Now the question is whether the plaintiff's conduct bars or reduces the amount of damages that she can recover.

This chapter explores the two major versions of the "plaintiff's conduct" defense: contributory negligence and assumption of risk. Contributory negligence is established when the plaintiff has not taken reasonable care for her own safety. If she has not, the further inquiry considers the causal connection between her want of care and her own injuries. At common law, the plaintiff's negligence, if established on the facts, generally barred her from *any* recovery despite the defendant's negligence, subject to a number of important exceptions regarding the defendant's "last clear chance" to avoid the harm, or to his willfulness in causing it.

The second key defense is assumption of risk. Unlike contributory negligence, assumption of risk asks whether the plaintiff has *deliberately and voluntarily encountered a known risk* created by the defendant's negligence. If so, the defense bars plaintiff's recovery for her consequent harm. Notwithstanding its intuitive plausibility, the assumption of risk defense has generated protracted analysis and often bitter controversy. Its place in tort law has been passionately defended in the name of laissez-faire economics that favors individual responsibility. With equal passion, it also has been denounced as an exploitive doctrine inconsistent with modern social norms of responsibility. Some scholars have even argued that, properly understood, assumption of risk has no place at all in a mature system of tort law, insisting that in most cases it is best understood as a variant of the contributory negligence defense. See, e.g., James, Assumption of Risk, 61 Yale L.J. 141 (1952).

With the contours of contributory negligence and assumption of risk thus established, we will investigate the pronounced movement, both by legislation and at common law, toward *comparative negligence*. That principle holds that the plaintiff's negligence should not typically bar her cause of action, but should only reduce the amount of damages recoverable. We will have to examine, therefore, how the various forms of the comparative negligence principle interact with both contributory negligence and assumption of risk, and how they mesh with a strict liability system.

SECTION B. CONTRIBUTORY NEGLIGENCE

1. Basic Doctrine

Butterfield v. Forrester
103 Eng. Rep. 926 (K.B. 1809)

This was an action on the case for obstructing a highway, by means of which obstruction the plaintiff, who was riding along the road, was thrown down with his horse, and injured, &c. At the trial before Bayley, J., at Derby, it appeared that the defendant, for the purpose of making some repairs to his house, which was close by the road side at one end of the town, had put up a pole across this part of the road, a free passage being left by another branch or street in the same direction. That the plaintiff left a public house not far distant from the place in question at 8 o'clock in the evening in August, when they were just beginning to light candles, but while there was light enough left to discern the obstruction at 100 yards distance: and the witness, who proved this, said that if the plaintiff had not been riding very hard he might have observed and avoided it: the plaintiff however, who was riding violently, did not observe it, but rode against it, and fell with his horse and was much hurt in consequence of the accident; and there was no evidence of his being intoxicated at the time. On this evidence Bayley, J., directed the jury, that if a person riding with reasonable and ordinary care could have seen and avoided the obstruction; and if they were satisfied that the plaintiff was riding along the street extremely hard, and without ordinary care, they should find a verdict for the defendant: which they accordingly did.

Vaughan Serjt. now objected to this direction, on moving for a new trial; and referred to Buller's Ni. Pri. 26, where the rule is laid down, that "if a man lay logs of wood across a highway though a person may with care ride safely by, yet if by means thereof my horse stumble and fling me, I may bring an action."

BAYLEY, J. The plaintiff was proved to be riding as fast as his horse could go, and this was through the streets of Derby. If he had used ordinary care he must have seen the obstruction so that the accident appeared to happen entirely from his own fault.

LORD ELLENBOROUGH, C.J. A party is not to cast himself upon an obstruction which has been made by the fault of another, and avail himself of it, if he do not himself use common and ordinary caution to be in the right. In cases of persons riding upon what is considered to be the wrong side of the road, that would not authorise another purposely to ride up against them. One person being in fault will not dispense with another's using ordinary care for himself. Two things must concur to support this action, an obstruction in the road by the fault of the defendant, and no want of ordinary care to avoid it on the part of the plaintiff.

Per Curiam. Rule refused.

Beems v. Chicago, Rock Island & Peoria R.R.
12 N.W. 222 (Iowa 1882)

BECK, J. . . . We will now consider the action of the court in overruling the [railroad's] motion for judgment non-obstante. The intestate met his death in making an attempt to uncouple the tender from a car. The special findings of the jury show that when he went between the cars to uncouple them they were moving at an improper and unusual rate of speed. Counsel for defendant insist that this finding establishes the fact of contributory negligence on the part of the intestate. The petition alleges that defendant's employees in charge of the engine were negligent, in failing to obey a direction given them by a signal made by the intestate to check the speed of the cars. The testimony tends to support this allegation. The jury were authorized to find from the testimony that deceased made two attempts to uncouple the cars while they were moving. After the first attempt he came out from between the cars, and signaled directions to check their speed; he immediately went again between the cars to make the second attempt to uncouple them. His signal was not obeyed. He was authorized to believe that the motion of the car would be checked, and he was not required to wait, before acting, to discover whether obedience would be given to his signal. The jury could have found that after the signal had been given, and after he had gone between the cars, if their speed had been checked, he would not have been exposed to danger. His act, therefore, in going between the cars after having made the signal to check their speed, was not necessarily contributory negligence. . . .

The court instructed the jury that if intestate's foot was caught between the rails and he "was thus held and run over, *without any negligence on the part of the other employees of defendant,* such as is charged in the petition, then the plaintiff cannot recover anything." The defendant asked an instruction, which was refused, to the effect that if the intestate's foot was caught between the rails the defendant is not liable, even though the jury should find the negligence charged in the petition. The instruction given is correct. If intestate was run over by reason of defendant's negligence, surely it cannot be claimed that defendant is not liable, because intestate's foot was caught between the rails. It would be a strange doctrine to hold that defendant could back its trains with unusual speed, without obeying signals to move more slowly, and thus negligently run over a brakesman, and would not be liable, for the reason that the unfortunate man was fastened to the spot by his foot being held between the rails. Whatever was the intestate's condition at the time of the accident, whether free to move, or fastened to the place, the defendant is liable if its cars were negligently driven over him.

Gary Schwartz, Tort Law and the Economy in Nineteenth-Century America: A Reinterpretation
90 Yale L.J. 1717, 1759-1762 (1981)

Professor Friedman describes the tort defense of contributory negligence as a "cunning trap" set by courts for nineteenth-century accident victims;[310] Professor Malone argues that nineteenth-century courts frequently were aggressive in withdrawing the contributory negligence issue from the jury in order carefully to monitor industry liability.[311] These assessments are contradicted, however, by the nineteenth-century experience in New Hampshire and California.

Each state's Supreme Court from an early date accepted the traditional rule of contributory negligence as a complete defense. Both Courts were openly ambivalent about the rule, however. . . .

The California Court placed the contributory-negligence burden of proof on the defendant, and regarded a technical misassignment of the burden of proof as reversible error, even when the defendant was the Central Pacific. . . . When allocating decisionmaking between judge and jury, the New Hampshire Court specified that the contributory negligence issue could be taken away from the jury only in "extraordinary" circumstances; the California Court frequently used language almost as strong.

---

310. Friedman, A History of American Law (1973), at 411–412. According to Professor Levy, nineteenth-century plaintiffs making "a misstep, however slight, from the ideal standard of conduct," were routinely and unfairly denied recoveries. L. Levy, The Law of the Commonwealth and Chief Justice Shaw (1957) at 319. For acceptance of the doctrine of "slight" contributory negligence, see W. Prosser, Law of Torts 421 (4th ed. 1971).

311. Malone, The Formative Era of Contributory Negligence, at 151, 152, 182. Professors Levy and Ursin—supposedly writing about California law specifically—claim that "the nineteenth-century [contributory negligence] doctrine could fairly have been called the rule of railroad and industrial immunity." Levy & Ursin, Tort Law in California: At the Crossroads, 67 Calif. L. Rev. 497, 509 (1979).

In administering tort appeals, the two states' Courts developed a variety of maxim-like ideas emphasizing the lenient and forgiving quality of the contributory negligence standard. Thus, a plaintiff was not required to exercise "great care" or to behave in a "very timid or cautious" way; contributory negligence was not proven by an "indiscretion" or a mere "error of judgment," let alone by a "misjudgment" in retrospect. If the plaintiff was "startled and alarmed," that was taken into account in evaluating the reasonableness of his conduct. Momentary distraction is a "most common occurrence" on city streets and "falls far short" of contributory negligence. If the plaintiff forgot what he knew about the particular danger, the Court could say that "people are liable to lapses of memory." Attenuating maxims like these were almost totally lacking in the Courts' opinions dealing with the possible negligence of tort defendants, who were frequently held to a standard of the "utmost care." Whatever, then, the symmetry in form of the doctrines of negligence and contributory negligence, they were administered under an emphatic, if implicit, double standard. . . .[333]

[Professor Schwartz then observes that a detailed analysis of the disposition of all contributory negligence cases in California and New Hampshire is consistent with the impression created by judicial language. Contributory negligence is rarely found as a matter of law; jury verdicts for the plaintiff on the issue are both frequent and usually upheld; jury verdicts for defendants are often set aside, typically because of a defect in jury instructions.]

NOTE

The scope and function of contributory negligence.   Professor Schwartz continues his attack on the proposition that American tort law gave special protection to industry and corporations in Schwartz, The Character of Early American Tort Law, 36 UCLA L. Rev. 641 (1989).

Apart from the history, scholars have had an extensive debate over whether any defense based upon plaintiff's misconduct is needed. To see what is at stake, it is useful to divide cases into stranger cases (including highway accidents) and consensual cases (including the employer/employee relation). *Butterfield* illustrates the first class of cases, while *Beems* illustrates the latter class. In the first situation, the ability of each party to act prudently does not depend on cooperation with the other. In the second situation, coordination is the order of the day. With the first case, therefore, it becomes more likely that the standards of care imposed on plaintiffs and defendants will be the same, as was the case when infant plaintiffs were charged with contributory negligence measured by objective standards in highway cases.

---

333. That is, when the conduct of the defendant and the plaintiff combined to expose the plaintiff to a major risk, the Courts subjected the defendant to a stern negligence obligation even while defining the plaintiff's contributory negligence obligation in a mild and permissive way.

What rules ought to govern these cases? One possibility is to eliminate the defense of contributory negligence altogether. See Landes & Posner, The Economic Structure of Tort Law 75-76 (1987). Under the Hand formula, they argue, the defendant can always escape liability by showing that he took cost-justified precautions against accidents. The "no-negligence" defense, therefore, provides the rational defendant with all the protection needed against unwarranted suits. Notwithstanding this argument, the defense is retained in practice because the defendant's negligence may be hotly contested in cases in which the plaintiff's negligence is evident. The use of the contributory negligence defense thus offers a buffer against the uncertainties in the basic negligence calculation.

In stranger cases, a strict liability rule could also be adopted. Owing to the greater scope of potential liability, some affirmative defense based on the plaintiff's conduct would then be needed. Contributory negligence might play a more critical role, lest the plaintiff take great risks at the defendant's expense. But marrying strict liability with a contributory negligence system is oddly asymmetrical when both parties start from a position of initial parity. See, e.g., Brown, Toward an Economic Theory of Liability, 2 J. Legal Stud. 323, 351 (1973). Suppose two cars crash head-on when neither driver is negligent. Under strict liability with contributory negligence, each driver must compensate the other for his loss: The relative extent of the two sets of injuries, itself largely a matter of luck, is simply reversed by legal action. Note, however, that a comprehensive system of strict liability escapes this inelegance. The negligence of both parties is irrelevant, but causation is not. If the prima facie case was that the defendant struck the plaintiff, then the causal defense is that the plaintiff blocked the defendant's right of way, as by entering an intersection when the light was red or by crossing the midline of the highway. The defendant need not show that the plaintiff's violation of the rule of the road was brought about by her negligence or wrongful intention. See the excerpt from Ross, Settled Out of Court, *supra* Chapter 3, at 178. It is of course odd to speak of "strict liability defenses" because a person cannot be liable to himself. Yet once it is recognized that causal principles operate on both sides, the rules of fairness require apportionment between the causal contributions of the two parties, based on the force at impact and the rights of way of the two vehicles. For an account of joint causation under a thoroughgoing system of strict liability, see Epstein, Defenses and Subsequent Pleas in a System of Strict Liability, 3 J. Legal Stud. 165, 174-185 (1974).

This analysis need not carry over to consensual relationships, in which the parties may have differential access to knowledge and a different ability to take care. In *Beems*, the court was clearly moved by the dependence that the hapless plaintiff below the cars had on the decisions made by his coworkers who were safely above. There was little need to create legal incentives for the plaintiff to do the right thing in light of his evident peril; more so for the defendant's employees who occupied a position of relative safety. But in other cases, the plaintiff's capacity to avoid a known hazard may well be far greater. In those cases, should the level of responsibility be raised to be commensurate with the degree of control?

Gyerman v. United States Lines Co.
498 P.2d 1043 (Cal. 1972)

[The plaintiff, a longshoreman employed by the Associated Banning Company, was injured while unloading fishmeal sacks that had just been brought into the warehouse of the defendant, United States Lines. Fishmeal is a very difficult cargo to handle, because it is packaged in sacks that have a tendency to rip and spill. To combat this danger, several common precautions are usually taken: Only 18 to 22 sacks of fishmeal are placed on any one pallet, and then only three or four layers high; the sacks are "bulkheaded," or tied together, to prevent them from falling; and, for maximum stability, they are aligned as are bricks in a wall, with no sack directly on top of another. The plaintiff had been assigned to "break down" the sacks into units that were only two pallets high. Before he began work, he noted that the sacks were not properly arranged. There were 30 sacks per pallet; the sacks were not bulkheaded; and they were not arrayed in brick-like fashion. He complained to Noel, the United States Lines chief marine clerk, that it was dangerous to proceed with the work in question, but was told that nothing could be done about it.

Fishmeal, stacked similarly as described in *Gyerman*
Source: Julio Etchart / Alamy

At no time, however, did the plaintiff speak to his own supervisor, even though the union contract with his employer provided, first, that "Longshoremen shall not be required to work when in good faith they believe that to do so is to immediately endanger health and safety," and established a grievance procedure "to determine whether a condition is safe or unsafe," and, second, that a joint labor-management committee should be immediately convened to resolve any outstanding safety issue. During the first three days of his work, an unusually large number of sacks fell off the forklift, but no harm resulted. On the afternoon of the fourth day, about 12 sacks simultaneously fell off a load that he was moving, and one of them, after bumping into the others, came toward him. Although the exact physical sequence of events was never established, the plaintiff did sustain injuries to his back and legs as a result of the incident. The trial judge, sitting without a jury, found that the defendant, United States Lines, was negligent in its failure to stack the fishmeal sacks in a safe way, conduct that was also a violation of the statutory duty to furnish every employee a "safe" place of employment. He found further that the defendant's negligence was a proximate cause of the plaintiff's harm. But he also found that the plaintiff's negligence in failing to stop work in the face of a known danger barred his cause of action. After disposing of two preliminary procedural points, the California Supreme Court considered the effect of plaintiff's contributory negligence upon his cause of action.]

SULLIVAN, J. . . .

3. CONTRIBUTORY NEGLIGENCE . . .

"Contributory negligence is conduct on the part of the plaintiff which falls below the standard to which he should conform for his own protection, and which is a legally contributing cause co-operating with the negligence of the defendant in bringing about the plaintiff's harm." (Rest. 2d Torts (1965) §463). The question of contributory negligence is ordinarily one of fact for the determination of the trier of fact.

"A plaintiff is required to exercise only that amount of care which would be exercised by a person of ordinary prudence in the same circumstances." Where a person must work under possibly unsafe or dangerous conditions, the amount of care he must exercise for his own safety may well be less than would otherwise be required by reason of the necessity of his giving attention to his work. The burden of proving that the plaintiff was negligent and that such negligence was a proximate cause of the accident is on the defendant.

In the instant case, absent evidence of the contract governing plaintiff's employment and of the custom and practice affecting stevedoring, we doubt that the record would provide evidentiary support for the finding that plaintiff violated a standard of due care for his own safety. Considered in the light of the realities of his working life, the laborer's duty may become considerably restricted in scope. In some instances he may find himself powerless to abandon the task at hand with impunity whenever he senses a possible danger; in others, he may be uncertain as to which person has supervision of the job or control of the place of employment, and therefore unsure as to whom he should direct his complaint; in still others, having been encouraged to continue working under conditions where danger lurks but has not materialized, he may be baffled in making an on-the-spot decision as to the imminence of harm. All of these factors enter into a determination whether his conduct falls below a standard of due care.

In the case before us the standard of due care required of laborers in general is explicated by evidence of duty imposed by contract and by custom upon the particular type of laborer involved. Custom alone, of course, does not create the standard of proper diligence. "Indeed in most cases reasonable prudence is in fact common prudence but strictly it is never its measure. . . ." (*The T.J. Hooper*). Nevertheless, although custom does not fix the standard of care, evidence of custom is ordinarily admissible for its bearing upon contributory negligence.

[The court then reviewed the facts of the case and concluded that the evidence supported the finding that the plaintiff failed to use ordinary care for his own protection.]

We must now inquire whether defendant sustained its burden of establishing that plaintiff's failure to report the unsafe condition was a "legally contributing cause . . . in bringing about the plaintiff's harm." (Rest. 2d Torts, §463.)

As previously noted, the trial court appears to have determined that plaintiff's failure was a proximate cause of his injuries because if plaintiff had reported the condition it would have been corrected. . . .

On this issue the positions of the parties may be summarized thusly: Plaintiff argues that the burden was on defendant to prove that if plaintiff had reported the condition to his own supervisor instead of to defendant's supervisor, the condition would have been corrected or made safer. Defendant asserts that it was not incumbent upon it to prove that the condition complained of was correctable and that in any event there is evidence supporting the trial court's finding.

The burden of proof rests on each party to a civil action as to each fact essential to his claim or defense. A party claiming a person failed to exercise due care has the burden of proof on that issue. The burden of proving all aspects of the affirmative defense of contributory negligence, including causation, rests on the defendant, unless the elements of the defense may be inferred from the plaintiff's evidence. The burden must be met by more than conjecture or speculation. Merely because plaintiff asserts that his own negligence, if any, could not have caused his injury, does not shift to him the burden of proof on the issue. Otherwise denial of any essential element of the defense case would shift the burden of proof on that issue to the plaintiff. . . .

We turn now to the facts of the case before us. It is obvious, of course, from what we have said that plaintiff did not create or maintain the dangerous and unsafe conditions of storage. The trial court found upon substantial evidence that defendant negligently maintained and operated its warehouse under those conditions. It was defendant who had control of the cargo and directed its disposition and high stacking throughout the warehouse. Defendant alone created this risk of harm which materialized in the toppling of the stacks.

Nor did the trial court find that plaintiff was negligent in his operation of the forklift or in his "breaking down" the particular stack of fishmeal whose sacks fell from the top of the load and injured him. In short there is no finding that any negligent conduct of plaintiff, operating with defendant's negligence, brought about the shifting and eventual dislodging of the sacks. According to the trial court's findings, plaintiff's negligence consisted solely in his failure to report the dangerous condition to his own supervisor. Our task then is to find in the record evidence showing, or from which it can be reasonably inferred, that this omission was a substantial factor in bringing about plaintiff's harm.

Defendant's theory of causation is that if plaintiff had reported the dangerous condition to his Associated Banning supervisor, that firm would have made the condition safer. An examination of the record, however, discloses no evidence establishing this theory. Indeed, although defendant vigorously asserts that the record supports a finding of proximate cause, it points to only one page of the extensive record for such evidence. At this part of the record, defendant's witness Hargett [manager of labor relations for Associated Banning, whose "duties were to represent not only Associated Banning but the industry as a whole in negotiations and disputes pertaining to contracts between the longshoremen and the various employers belonging to the Pacific Maritime Association"] responded on direct examination to a question about what a longshoreman should do upon encountering an unsafe condition. Hargett replied that he would have to get another lot to work on or "have supervision called, . . . and we would have sent men there to take care of the situation, if he was in such a condition he couldn't operate."

In our view this testimony does not show that the stacks would have been made safer. Although it indicates that the problem would have received immediate attention, it provides no clue as to what, if anything, could have been done to break down the stacks of fishmeal more safely than by the use of forklifts. Indeed, other than the vague statement as to sending "men there to take care of the situation" no evidence at all was offered as to specific measures that would be taken. Nor does evidence as to the existence of a grievance procedure, formalized in the ILWU-PMA contract constitute proof that in the particular situation culminating in plaintiff's injury, steps would have been taken to make the situation safer. Finally the trial court's suggestions made in its memorandum of decision that the offending bags could have been removed by using ladders or having other forklift drivers remove them one at a time are not based upon evidence in the record and therefore do not support the finding. Indeed such suggestions only point up the complete lack of defense evidence in the record on this critical issue. The record does not establish that plaintiff's failure to report the dangerous condition was a substantial factor in bringing about the fall of the sacks.

In view of the foregoing we conclude that defendant did not meet its burden of proving that plaintiff's contributory negligence was a proximate cause of his injuries.

[The court then remanded the case for a retrial on the questions of the plaintiff's contributory negligence and its causal connection to the plaintiff's own harm. It noted that, though the plaintiff's negligence had been sufficiently established by evidence below, the court was "not satisfied" that in the instant case the two issues were so "separate and distinct" that the issue of proximate cause could not be tried alone "without such confusion or uncertainty as would amount to a denial of a fair trial."]

The issue of defendant's negligence has been properly determined and we see no reason why it should be relitigated. Retrial should be had on the issue of plaintiff's contributory negligence (including the issue of whether such negligence, if any, was the proximate cause of the accident) and, if such issue is resolved favorably to plaintiff, on the issue of damages.

The judgment is reversed and the cause is remanded with directions for a new trial limited to the issues of plaintiff's contributory negligence and of damages. Each party shall bear his or its own costs on appeal.

WRIGHT, C.J., MCCOMB, PETERS, TOBRINER, and BURKE, JJ., concurred.

NOTES

1. Burden of proof on contributory negligence. *Gyerman* follows the universal modern rule that the defendant bears the burden of proof on the issues of contributory negligence and its causal relationship to the plaintiff's harm. See

RTT: Apportionment of Liability [RTT:AL] §4, comment *a*: Burden of proof. Nevertheless, a significant minority of states once required the plaintiff to establish her freedom from contributory negligence as a part of the basic cause of action. The rule probably arose when the intervening negligence of another actor, including the plaintiff, severed the causal connection between the defendant's negligence and the plaintiff's harm. See the discussion of the last clear chance rule, *infra* at 296. Because the plaintiff bore the burden of proof on proximate cause, it was but a small step to say that she bore the burden of proof on contributory negligence. That rule in turn created genuine difficulties in wrongful death actions when the decedent could not defend her own conduct. Initially, the courts shifted that burden back to the defendant in death cases, and over time the exception expanded into the current rule. Today, death cases are often governed by a rule that holds: "[I]n the absence of any evidence as to the conduct of a person who died of injuries received in an accident, there is the presumption that he, acting on the instinct of self-preservation, was in the exercise of ordinary care," and thus a decedent is in a stronger position than an injured plaintiff. Thompson v. Mehlhaff, 698 N.W.2d 512, 526 (S.D. 2005).

2. *Contributory negligence and breach of statutory duty.* In *Gyerman*, do the particulars of how best to deal with the stacking of the fishmeal stacks matter if the plaintiff could have refused to work on them as of right under the labor contract? Should the defense of contributory negligence be excluded because the improper stacking of the fishmeal sacks violated the defendant's statutory duty to provide a safe place to work? In Koenig v. Patrick Construction Corp., 83 N.E.2d 133, 135 (N.Y. 1948), the court refused to allow the defenses of either contributory negligence or assumption of risk when the plaintiff was a member of the class of persons for whose benefit a particular statute, the state Scaffold Law, §240(1), was enacted:

> Workmen such as the present plaintiff, who ply their livelihoods on ladders and scaffolds, are scarcely in a position to protect themselves from accident. They usually have no choice but to work with the equipment at hand, though danger looms large. The legislature recognized this and to guard against the known hazards of the occupation required the employer to safeguard the workers from injury caused by faulty or inadequate equipment. If the employer could avoid this duty by pointing to the concurrent negligence of the injured worker in using the equipment, the beneficial purpose of the statute might well be frustrated and nullified.

Why can't workers decline risky employment? Receive additional compensation for dangerous work? Are individual employees powerless when represented by a union that routinely bargains with the employer over safety issues?

Cases often come out quite differently in the absence of a specialized safety statute. In O'Neill v. Windshire-Copland Associates, L.P, 595 S.E.2d 281, 282 (Va. 2004), the defendant apartment building owner constructed its railings at 32 inches when the building code required 48 inches. The plaintiff became quadriplegic after he fell backward over the railing while drunk. Because Virginia law continues to treat contributory negligence as a total bar, the court denied the plaintiff any recovery. Lacy, J., followed Restatement (Second) Torts §483, which provides that "when a defendant's negligence consists of the violation of a statute, a plaintiff's contributory negligence bars his recovery for injuries caused by the negligence of the defendant 'unless the effect of the statute is to place the entire responsibility for such harm as has occurred upon the defendant.' " She then held that a building code statute did not so shift the loss.

The defense of contributory negligence may be established as a matter of law when it is the *plaintiff* who is in breach of statutory duty. Thus in Blake v. Securitas Securities Services, 962 F. Supp. 141, 146-147 (D.D.C. 2013), the plaintiff, a 17-year-old boy, while attending his high school prom, got high on marijuana and jumped or fell from a third-story balcony, sustaining serious injuries. Boasberg, J., noted that District of Columbia law made it a misdemeanor for any person "whether in or on public or private property . . . [, to] be intoxicated and endanger the safety of himself, herself, or any other person or property." He then sidestepped the question of whether this statutory breach was contributory negligence as a matter of law, by noting that Blake had also endangered himself when after smoking the marijuana he "then proceeded to break away from a school administrator, run down a hallway, and climb under protective cables and over a railing onto the exposed balcony from which he ultimately fell." The judge further rejected the defense that the plaintiff was entitled to the lower standard of care normally afforded children.

3. Contributory negligence in medical malpractice actions. In Cavens v. Zaberdac, 849 N.E.2d 526, 529-530 (Ind. 2006), the decedent suffered from chronic asthma, which the emergency room physician Dr. Cavens claimed was attributable in part to her "excessive use of medication and delay in seeking treatment." The defendants asked for this instruction: "A patient may not recover in a malpractice action where the patient is contributorily negligent by failing to follow the defendant physician's instructions if such contributory negligence is simultaneous with and unites with the fault of the defendant to proximately cause the injury." Dickson, J., first acknowledged that "the patient is contributorily negligent by failing to follow the defendant physician's instructions if such contributory negligence is simultaneous with and unites with the fault of the defendant to proximately cause the injury." Thereafter he continued:

> Permitting medical malpractice defendants to assert the defense of contributory negligence by reason of a patient's negligence prior to the defendant physician's treatment of the patient conflicts with a long-standing common law principle: "It is a staple of tort law that the tortfeasor takes her victim as she finds him."
>
> It is people who are sick or injured that most often seek medical attention. Many of these infirmities result, at least in part, from the patients' own carelessness (e.g. negligent driving or other activities, failure to regularly exercise, unhealthy diet, smoking, etc.). To permit healthcare providers to assert their patients' pre-treatment negligent conduct to support a contributory negligence defense would absolve such providers from tort responsibility in the event of medical negligence and thus operate to undermine substantially such providers' duty of reasonable care.

May a physician introduce evidence of excessive use of medication or delay in seeking care to undermine the claim that his negligence, if any, was causally responsible for the plaintiff's loss?

4. Contributory negligence and custodial care. What level of care should be required of people who, by virtue of being in custodial care, have demonstrated their inability to act reasonably on their own behalf? In Padula v. State, 398 N.E.2d 548, 551 (N.Y. 1979), the two plaintiffs, inmates at the Iroquois Narcotic Rehabilitation Center, and several of their friends were able, through the negligence of the center's guards, to gain access to the center's printing room. There they found some Ditto fluid, rich in methyl alcohol, which they drank after mixing it "with an orange preparation called Tang." One plaintiff died and the second became blind. The Court of Appeals held that their suit was not barred. The court first held that actions done under an irresistible impulse, even without specific proof of a mental disease, do not sever causal connection. It continued:

> [W]hatever the contributory or comparative negligence rule may ultimately be held to be as to a person under the influence of drugs in a noncustodial situation as to which we express no opinion, we think that in relation to persons in the custody of the State for treatment of a drug problem, contributory (or comparative) negligence should turn not on whether the drug problem or its effects be categorized as a mental disease nor on whether the injured person understood what he was doing, but on whether based upon the entire testimony presented (including objective behavioral evidence, claimant's subjective testimony and the opinions of experts) the trier of fact concludes that the injured person was able to control his actions.

The court was particularly impressed by the clear testimony that "not only Padula and Modaferi [the blind claimant] but six other residents drank the Ditto-Tang concoction notwithstanding that the warning [which spoke of death or blindness] had been read to them." Any action against the supplier of the methyl alcohol? Is there any analogy to the position of the plaintiff in *Beems?* In *Gyerman?*

5. Contributory negligence and private necessity. Should the defense of contributory negligence be available against a plaintiff who runs into the path of a negligently speeding car on the public highway to escape from a gang attack? In Raimondo v. Harding, 341 N.Y.S.2d 679 (App. Div. 1973), the court reversed the decision below, noting that a "person faced with an emergency and who acts, without opportunity for deliberation, to avoid an accident may not be charged with contributory negligence if he acts as a reasonably prudent person would act under the same emergency circumstances, even though it appears afterwards that he did not take the safest course or exercise the best judgment." The Third Restatement adopts this basic position, noting, for plaintiffs and defendants alike, that the law of negligence takes into account "an unexpected emergency requiring rapid response." RTT:LPEH §9. The standard caveat to this position is that no party can rely on an emergency created by his prior negligence. *Id.,* comment *d.* Is *Raimondo* consistent with Vincent v. Lake Erie, *supra* at 44?

6. Causation and contributory negligence. The causal complications with contributory negligence are well illustrated by two famous Connecticut cases. In Smithwick v. Hall & Upson Co., 21 A. 924 (Conn. 1890), the plaintiff was working on a narrow platform erected in front of the defendant's icehouse, about 15 feet above the ground. The defendant's foreman warned plaintiff to stay away from the east side of the platform, which had no railing, because he feared that the plaintiff could slip on the ice. Plaintiff disregarded that instruction, but was hurt when the east portion of the icehouse buckled. The defendant's negligence in maintaining the icehouse was conceded, but the plaintiff's contributory negligence was not treated as causally relevant because the resulting harm was "not within the risk," that is, the class of events that made it dangerous for the plaintiff to venture to the east side in the first place. See discussion of *Wagon Mound, infra* at 423. What was the risk of plaintiff working on the east side of the platform? Would the plaintiff still have been injured if he had followed orders?

Restatement of the Law (Third) of Torts: Apportionment of Liability

§4. PROOF OF PLAINTIFF'S NEGLIGENCE AND LEGAL CAUSATION

The defendant has the burden to prove plaintiff's negligence, and may use any of the methods a plaintiff may use to prove defendant's negligence. Except as otherwise provided in Topic 5 [Apportionment of Liability When Damages Can Be Divided by Causation], the defendant also has the burden to prove that the plaintiff's negligence, if any, was a legal cause of the plaintiff's damages.

In Mahoney v. Beatman, 147 A. 762, 768 (Conn. 1929), plaintiff was driving a Rolls-Royce around 60 miles per hour, while it was still daylight, on a gravel-shouldered, two-lane concrete turnpike, with a clear view in both directions. The defendant was approaching in a Nash from the other direction. He turned to speak to somebody in the backseat and permitted the Nash to cross over the middle of the highway into the plaintiff's lane. The plaintiff, to avoid a head-on collision, pulled the Rolls-Royce partly off onto the shoulder. Nonetheless, the Nash grazed the Rolls-Royce, causing an estimated $200 worth of damage. The Rolls-Royce proceeded for about 125 feet along the road, and then suddenly turned across the highway, climbed a small bank, and hit a tree and a stone wall, sustaining about $5,650 in additional damage.

The trial court, sitting without a jury, found that the defendant's Nash was on the wrong side of the road, that the speed of the Rolls-Royce was "unreasonable but it did not contribute to the collision which was due entirely to the negligence of the defendant," but that the speed of the Rolls-Royce did "materially hamper plaintiff's chauffeur in controlling the car after the collision and owing to it he completely lost control of it." The trial court then awarded "nominal damages" of $200 to the plaintiff. On appeal, the plaintiff was given judgment for $5,850 for damage to his car. The Supreme Court of Connecticut treated the defendant's negligence as the proximate cause of plaintiff's entire damage. Does this case illustrate the distinction between causation and coincidence? To be sure, the plaintiff's speeding did not contribute to the collision, which could have happened had he been driving at 45 miles per hour at that same location. Yet the plaintiff's speeding did cause the plaintiff to lose control after the collision, thus contributing to the balance of the damage to the Rolls-Royce. What result under comparative negligence? See Epstein, Defenses and Subsequent Pleas in a System of Strict Liability, 3 J. Legal Stud. 165, 181-184 (1974).

LeRoy Fibre Co. v. Chicago, Milwaukee & St. Paul Ry.
232 U.S. 340 (1914)

[As part of its business of making flax, the plaintiff stored about 700 tons of straw in 230 stacks on its own land. The stacks were lined up in two rows. The defendant's right of way ran about 70 feet from the first row and 85 feet from the second. One day, a high wind carried sparks from a passing train to one of the stacks of flax located in the row farther from the tracks. That fire eventually consumed all the flax. The jury found first that the defendant's servants had negligently operated its locomotive by allowing it to emit large quantities of sparks and live cinders, and second, that this act of negligence was a cause of the plaintiff's harm. Consistent with its instructions, the jury also found the plaintiff guilty of contributory negligence by placing the exposed stacks within 100 feet of the railroad's right of way. The Supreme Court was asked to decide whether there was any question of contributory negligence to leave to the jury.]

McKENNA, J. . . . It will be observed, the [plaintiff's] use of the land was of itself a proper use—it did not interfere with nor embarrass the rightful operation of the railroad. It is manifest, therefore, the questions certified . . . are but phases of the broader one, whether one is limited in the use of one's property by its proximity to a railroad or, to limit the proposition to the case under review, whether one is subject in its use to the careless as well as to the careful operation of the road. We might not doubt that an immediate answer in the negative should be given if it were not for the hesitation of the Circuit Court of Appeals evinced by its questions, and the decisions of some courts in the affirmative. That one's uses of his property may be subject to the servitude of the wrongful use by another of his property seems an anomaly. It upsets the presumptions of law and takes from him the assumption and the freedom which comes from the assumption, that the other will obey the law, not violate it. It casts upon him the duty of not only using his own property so as not to injure another, but so to use his own property that it may not be injured by the wrongs of another. How far can this subjection be carried? Or, confining the question to railroads, what limits shall be put upon their immunity from the result of their wrongful operation? In the case at bar, the property destroyed is described as inflammable, but there are degrees of that quality; and how wrongful must be the operation? In this case, large quantities of sparks and "live cinders" were emitted from the passing engine. Houses may be said to be inflammable, and may be, as they have been, set on fire by sparks and cinders from defective or carelessly handled locomotives. Are they to be subject as well as stacks of flax straw, to such lawless operation? And is the use of farms also, the cultivation of which the building of the railroad has preceded? Or is that a use which the railroad must have anticipated and to which it hence owes a duty, which it does not owe to other uses? And why? The question is especially pertinent and immediately shows that the rights of one man in the use of his property cannot be limited by the wrongs of another. The doctrine of contributory negligence is entirely out of place. Depart from the simple requirement of the law, that every one must use his property so as not to injure others, and you pass to refinements and confusing considerations. There is no embarrassment in the principle even to the operation of a railroad. Such operation is a legitimate use of property; other property in its vicinity may suffer inconveniences and be subject to risks by it, but a risk from wrongful operation is not one of them. . . .

HOLMES, J., partially concurring. . . . If a man stacked his flax so near to a railroad that it obviously was likely to be set fire to by a well-managed train, I should say that he could not throw the loss upon the road by the oscillating result of an inquiry by the jury whether the road had used due care. I should say that although of course he had a right to put his flax where he liked upon his own land, the liability of the railroad for a fire was absolutely conditioned upon the stacks being at a reasonably safe distance from the train. . . .

If I am right so far, a very important element in determining the right to recover is whether the plaintiff's flax was so near to the track as to be in danger from even a prudently managed engine. Here certainly, except in a clear case, we should call in the jury. I do not suppose that anyone would call it prudent to stack flax within five feet of the engines or imprudent to do it at a distance of half a mile, and it would not be absurd if the law ultimately should formulate an exact measure, as it has tended to in other instances; but at present I take it that if the question I suggest be material we should let the jury decide whether seventy feet was too near by the criterion that I have proposed. . . .

I do not think we need trouble ourselves with the thought that my view depends upon differences of degree. The whole law does so as soon as it is civilized. Negligence is all degree—that of the defendant here degree of the nicest sort; and between the variations according to distance that I suppose to exist and the simple universality of the rules in the Twelve Tables or the Leges Barbarorum, there lies the culture of two thousand years.

I am authorized to say that the Chief Justice concurs in the opinion that I express.

NOTES

Reciprocal causation.   *LeRoy Fibre* illustrates the close connection between property rights and causation. Unlike joint causation cases, this case does not involve a collision caused by two moving parties, or by any action of the plaintiff that blocked or hindered the operation of the railroad. In the Court's view, therefore, the issue of contributory negligence cannot arise because the plaintiff (even by stacking his flax close to the tracks) has done nothing to invade physically the railroad's right of way. The case is similar to Smith v. Kenrick, *supra* Chapter 2, at 103, which held that a mine owner was under no duty to erect a barrier to keep "foreign" water discharged by the defendant from flooding his mine. Thus it differs sharply from cases of joint causation that arise, say, in highway accidents between two vechicles.

On the other side, the majority position is vulnerable because it gives no incentives for victims to reduce their storage activities to appropriate levels. See Meese, The Externality of Victim Care, 68 U. Chi. L. Rev. 1201, 1218 (2001). That position is hinted at in Holmes' dissent, which stresses less the absence of physical invasion (here by plaintiff of defendant's property) and more the cheaper precautions that the plaintiff could have taken to prevent the fire. His position had in fact received a fair bit of support in some of the earlier nineteenth-century cases that imposed duties on farmers to minimize their losses from fires set by passing locomotives, even at distances that Holmes thought were outside the danger zone. Thus, in Kansas Pacific Ry. v. Brady, 17 Kan. 380, 386

"It's a mixed-use facility: retail space, low-rent housing, luxury apartments, and an area set aside for making steel."

(1877), the defendant railroad set fire to the plaintiff's hay, which was stacked between one and one-half and two miles away from the tracks. The court first found that there was evidence of the defendant's negligence in the operation of its train, and then turned to the question of contributory negligence:

> If the defendant was negligent at all as against the plaintiffs, it was really as much because said hay was stacked in a dangerous place, and because dry grass was allowed to intervene all the way from the stack to the railway track, as because said fire was permitted to escape. Now as the burning of said hay was the result of the acts and omissions of both the plaintiffs and the defendant, it would seem that the acts and omissions of both parties should have been submitted to the jury. Both parties may have been negligent, and the acts and omissions of both should have been subject to the scrutiny of the jury. But it is claimed that the plaintiffs could not under any circumstances be considered negligent. It is claimed that they had a right to stack their hay as they did stack it, in a dangerous place, with dry grass all around it, and without taking any precautions for its protection. And this is claimed upon the theory that every man has a right to use his own property as he pleases without reference to the great inconvenience he may thereby impose upon others. Is this theory, or rather the plaintiffs' application thereof, correct? . . . Why should any person be allowed to invite the destruction of his own property by his own negligence, so that he might by recovering for the loss thereof lessen the estate of another to that extent? Why should any person be allowed to so use his own property that in the natural course of things he would most likely injure the estate of another to the extent of the value of such property? Or, why should he have it

within his power to so use his own property as to make it so hazardous for others to use theirs that such others must necessarily abandon the use of theirs?

In Svea Insurance Co. v. Vicksburg, S. & P. Ry., 153 F. 774 (W.D. La. 1907), the court noted that fire cases required the jury to take into account the "reciprocal duties" of both parties. This theme of reciprocity has received its most famous elaboration in Coase, The Problem of Social Cost, 3 J.L. & Econ. 1, 2 (1960).

> The question is commonly thought of as one in which *A* inflicts harm on *B* and what has to be decided is: how should we restrain *A*? But this is wrong. We are dealing with a problem of a reciprocal nature. To avoid the harm to *B* would inflict harm on *A*. The real question that has to be decided is: should *A* be allowed to harm *B* or should *B* be allowed to harm *A*? The problem is to avoid the more serious harm. I instanced . . . the case of a confectioner the noise and vibrations from whose machinery disturbed a doctor in his work. To avoid harming the doctor would inflict harm on the confectioner. The problem posed by this case was essentially whether it was worth while, as a result of restricting the methods of production which could be used by the confectioner, to secure more doctoring at the cost of a reduced supply of confectionery products. Another example is afforded by the problem of straying cattle which destroy crops on neighbouring land. If it is inevitable that some cattle will stray, an increase in the supply of meat can only be obtained at the expense of a decrease in the supply of crops. The nature of the choice is clear: meat or crops. What answer should be given is, of course, not clear unless we know the value of what is obtained as well as the value of what is sacrificed to obtain it. To give another example, Professor George J. Stigler instances the contamination of a stream. If we assume that the harmful effect of the pollution is that it kills the fish, the question to be decided is: is the value of the fish lost greater or less than the value of the product which the contamination of the stream makes possible.

Is Coase correct to assume that the only question to decide is whether *A* should be allowed to harm *B*, or *B* to harm *A*? What about a rule that allows *A* to harm (i.e., to invade *B*'s premises) only if he compensates *B* for his loss? Put otherwise, should the railroad be required to purchase an easement to cause fire over the land of the neighboring farmers? For a general discussion of these fire cases, see Grady, Common Law Control of Strategic Behavior: Railroad Sparks and the Farmer, 17 J. Legal Stud. 15 (1988), which attacks the rigid property rights logic of McKenna, J., in *LeRoy Fibre*.

Derheim v. N. Fiorito Co.
492 P.2d 1030 (Wash. 1972)

[The plaintiff's car collided with the defendant's truck when the defendant made a left turn in violation of the rules of the road. The plaintiff was not wearing a seat belt at the time of the accident. The defendant sought to introduce expert evidence at trial to establish that the plaintiff's conduct was a form of contributory negligence, which at the very least should be taken into account to reduce damages under the doctrine of avoidable consequences. The trial judge, however, refused to allow the defendant to raise the seat belt defense in its amended answer. He also refused to allow the defendant's expert to testify that if the plaintiff had worn his seat belt at the time of the accident, he would not have suffered the injuries for which the suit was brought. After a verdict and judgment for the plaintiff, the case was certified for immediate hearing by the Washington Supreme Court.]

HUNTER, J. . . . We are thus called upon to determine the rule in this state with respect to the so-called "seat belt defense." No subject in the field of automobile accident litigation, with the possible exception of no-fault insurance, has received more attention in recent years than has the seat or lap belt defense. The question being one of first impression in this state, we have reviewed the published material extensively, concluding that while the research and statistical studies indicate a far greater likelihood of serious injuries in the event of nonuse, nevertheless the courts have been inconsistent in their handling of the defense. This inconsistency seems to result from the fact that the defense does not fit conveniently into the familiar time-honored doctrines traditionally used by the courts in deciding tort cases. Thus, the conduct in question (failure to buckle up) occurs before defendant's negligence, as opposed to contributory negligence which customarily is thought of in terms of conduct contributing to the accident itself. While more precisely, contributory negligence is conduct contributing, with the negligence of the defendant in bringing about the plaintiff's harm, it is a rare case indeed where the distinction need be made. Furthermore, while states with comparative negligence do not have the problem to the same extent, contributory negligence in many states (such as Washington) is a complete bar to any recovery by a plaintiff — an obvious unjust result to apply in seat belt cases. The same result would be reached if the defense were presented in terms of assumption of risk, that is, that one who ventures upon the highway without buckling up is voluntarily assuming the risk of more serious injuries resulting from a possible accident proximately caused by the negligence of another.

The doctrine of avoidable consequences has been suggested as a possible solution to this conceptual dilemma, but here again, the problem is one of appearing to stretch the doctrine to fit an unusual fact pattern. As a legal theory, avoidable consequences is closely akin to mitigation of damages, and customarily is applied when plaintiff's conduct after the occurrence fails to meet the standards of due care. Moreover, courts have traditionally said that a defendant whose negligence proximately causes an injury to plaintiff, "takes the plaintiff as he finds him."

The practical implications of allowing seat belt evidence has also given the courts pause. For example, most automobiles are now manufactured with shoulder straps in addition to seat belts, and medical evidence could be anticipated in certain cases that particular injuries would not have resulted if both shoulder belts and seat belts had been used. Additionally, many automobiles are now equipped with headrests which are designed to protect one from the so-called whiplash type of injury. But to be effective, its height must be adjusted by the occupant. Should the injured victim of a defendant's negligence be penalized in ascertainment of damages for failure to adjust his headrest? Furthermore, the courts are aware that other protective devices and measures are undergoing testing in governmental and private laboratories, or are on the drawing boards. The concern is, of course, that if the seat belt defense is allowed, would not the same analysis require the use of all safety devices with which one's automobile is equipped? A further problem bothers the courts, and that is the effect of injecting the seat belt issue into the trial of automobile personal injury cases. The courts are concerned about unduly lengthening trials and if each automobile accident trial is to provide an arena for a battle of safety experts, as well as medical experts, time and expense of litigation might well be increased.

These problems, legal and practical, are found in reviewing the most recent cases decided by other jurisdictions confronting the issue. . . .

[The court then reviewed a series of then recent cases in other jurisdictions, some accepting and some rejecting the "seat belt defense," and continued:]

We believe the cases in those jurisdictions rejecting the "seat belt defense" are the better reasoned cases. It seems extremely unfair to mitigate the damages of one who sustains those damages in an accident for which he was in no way responsible, particularly when, as in this jurisdiction, there is no statutory duty to wear seat belts.

For the reasons heretofore stated, we believe the trial court was correct in refusing admission of evidence on the "seat belt defense."

The judgment of the trial court is affirmed.

NOTES

1. The seat belt defense. Should the opposite result be reached in *Derheim* if seat belt use were mandated by statute, as it now is (with varying qualifications) in every state except New Hampshire? If it could be shown that overall accident rates and insurance premiums would drop if some seat belt defense were allowed? Contrast *Derheim* with the following observations of Gabrielli, J., in Spier v. Barker, 323 N.E.2d 164, 167-168 (N.Y. 1974):

> We today hold that nonuse of an available [i.e., already installed] seat belt, and expert testimony in regard thereto, is a factor which the jury may consider, in light of all the other facts received in evidence, in arriving at its determination as to whether the plaintiff has exercised due care, not only to avoid injury to himself, but to mitigate any injury he would likely sustain. However, as the trial court observed in its charge, the plaintiff's nonuse of an available seat belt should be strictly limited to the jury's determination of the plaintiff's damages and should not be considered by the triers of fact in resolving the issue of liability. Moreover, the burden of pleading and proving that nonuse thereof by

the plaintiff resulted in increasing the extent of his injuries and damages, rests upon the defendant. That is to say, the issue should not be submitted to the jury unless the defendant can demonstrate, by competent evidence, a causal connection between the plaintiff's nonuse of an available seat belt and the injuries and damages sustained. . . .

Since section 383 of the Vehicle and Traffic Law does not require occupants of a passenger car to make use of available seat belts, we hold that a plaintiff's failure to do so does not constitute negligence per se. . . . Likewise, we do not subscribe to the holdings of those cases in which the plaintiff's failure to fasten his seat belt may be determined by the jury to constitute contributory negligence as a matter of common law. In our view, the doctrine of contributory negligence is applicable only if the plaintiff's failure to exercise due care causes, in whole or in part, *the accident,* rather than when it merely exacerbates or enhances the severity of his injuries. That being the case, holding a nonuser contributorily negligent would be improper since it would impose liability upon the plaintiff for all his injuries though use of a seat belt might have prevented none or only a portion of them.

. . . We concede that the opportunity to mitigate damages prior to the occurrence of an accident does not ordinarily arise, and that the chronological distinction, on which the concept of mitigation damages rest, is justified in most cases. However, in our opinion, the seat belt affords the automobile occupant an unusual and ordinarily unavailable means by which he or she may minimize his or her damages *prior* to the accident. Highway safety has become a national concern; we are told to drive defensively and to "watch out for the other driver." When an automobile occupant may readily protect himself, at least partially, from the consequences of a collision, we think that the burden of buckling an available seat belt may, under the facts of the particular case, be found by the jury to be less than the likelihood of injury when multiplied by its accompanying severity.

Another objection frequently raised is that the jury will be unable to segregate the injuries caused by the initial impact from the injuries caused by the plaintiff's failure to fasten his seat belt. In addition to underestimating the abilities of those trained in the field of accident reconstruction, this argument fails to consider other instances in which the jury is permitted to apportion damages (i.e., as between an original tort-feasor and a physician who negligently treats the original injury).

2. Statutory response to the seat belt defense. The availability of the seat belt defense in tort litigation is today heavily regulated by statute, as almost 40 states have adopted different regimes, most of which sharply restrict the availability of defense. For a tally, see Schwartz, Comparative Negligence §4.06 (5th ed. 2010). For a good analysis, see Comment, The Seatbelt Defense: A Doctrine Based in Common Sense, 38 Tulsa L. Rev. 405, 416 n.121, 421 n.156 (2002), which reports that of the 39 statutes that deal with the question, 24 decline to allow the defense. Some of the remaining states cap the defense at some small fraction of the plaintiff's recovery, e.g., 2 percent. Others require defendant to plead and prove the defense. What is wrong with a rule that reduces the plaintiff's recovery by 25 percent in all cases in which her failure to wear the seatbelt contributes to her injury?

Is there any reason to treat a motorcyclist's failure to wear a required helmet differently from her failure to wear a seatbelt? In Dare v. Sobule, 674 P.2d 960, 963 (Colo. 1984), the court excluded the helmet defense to bar or diminish damages after the legislature repealed its law requiring helmets in 1977.

The rise and fall of helmet statutes has been influenced by federal intervention. In 1966, the federal government tied the distribution of funds for highway construction to states' willingness to pass motorcycle helmet laws. These were adopted in 47 states by 1975, and the number of motorcycle fatalities fell by half, from about 12 per 10,000 riders to about six per 10,000 riders. Schuster, Riding Without a Helmet: Liability, Social Efficiency, and the More Perfect Wisconsin Compromise to Motorcycle Helmet Liability, 89 Iowa L. Rev. 1391 (2004). The Department of Transportation reports, without explanation, that "[u]se of DOT-compliant motorcycle helmets decreased significantly to 54 percent in 2010 from 67 percent in 2009." National Highway Traffic Safety Administration, Department of Transportation, Motorcycle Helmet Use in 2010 — Overall Results (2010), *available at* http://www-nrd.nhtsa.dot.gov/Pubs/811419.pdf.

2. Last Clear Chance

Fuller v. Illinois Central R.R.
56 So. 783 (Miss. 1911)

[Decedent, a man of over 70, was riding his one-horse wagon on a north-south dirt road that crossed a straight stretch of railroad track that ran perpendicular to it. The decedent had his head down; he did not stop, look, or listen, and did not observe defendant's oncoming train. This train, a light one, came down the tracks 30 minutes late, at around 40 miles per hour, faster than usual or appropriate. The decedent was in plain view on the track some 660 feet from the crossing, and the uncontradicted evidence was that the defendant's engineer could have stopped the light train within 200 feet. The record was silent as to what the engineer of the train did or thought when the decedent came into plain view on the tracks, but he did not slow the train down. The only signal he gave was a routine whistle blast some 20 seconds before the train crashed into the wagon. The decedent was instantly killed. In response to contributory negligence, the plaintiff alleged that the defendant's servant had the last clear chance to avoid injury either by braking or promptly sounding a warning whistle. At trial judgment was given for the defendant.]

McLAIN, J. . . . The rule is settled beyond controversy or doubt, first, that all that is required of the railroad company as against a trespasser is the abstention from wanton or willful injury, or that conduct which is characterized as gross negligence; second, although the injured party may be guilty of contributory negligence, yet this is no defense if the injury were willfully, wantonly, or reck-lessly done or the party inflicting the injury was guilty of such conduct as to characterize it as gross; and, third, that the contributory negligence of the party injured will not defeat the action if it is shown that the defendant might by the exercise of reasonable care and prudence have avoided the consequence of the injured party's negligence. This last principle is known as the doctrine of the "last clear chance." The origin of this doctrine is found in the celebrated case of Davies v. Mann, 10 Mees & W. 545, [152 Eng. Rep. 588 (Ex. 1842)]. The plaintiff in that case fettered the front feet of his donkey, and turned him into the public highway to graze. The defendant's wagon, coming down a slight descent at a "smartish" pace, ran against the donkey, and knocked it down, the wheels of the wagon passing over it, and the donkey was killed. In that case Lord Abinger, C.B., says: "The defendant has not denied that the ass was lawfully in the highway, and therefore we must assume it to have been lawfully there. But, even were it otherwise, it would have made no difference, for, as the defendant might by proper care have avoided injuring the animal and did not, he is liable for the consequences of his negligence, though the animal might have been improperly there." While Park, B., says: "Although the ass might have been wrongfully there, still the defendant was bound to go along the road at such a pace as would be likely to prevent mischief. Were this not so, a man might justify the driving over goods left on the public highway or even a man lying asleep there, or probably running against the carriage going on the wrong side of the road." It is impossible to follow this case through its numerous citations in nearly every jurisdiction subject to Anglo-American jurisprudence. For the present it will be sufficient to say that the principle therein announced has met with practically almost universal favor. It has been severely criticized by some textwriters. The groans, ineffably and mournfully sad, of Davies' dying donkey, have resounded around the earth. The last lingering gaze from the soft, mild eyes of this docile animal, like the last parting sunbeams of the softest day in spring, has appealed to and touched the hearts of men. There has girdled the globe a band of sympathy for Davies' immortal "critter." Its ghost, like Ban-quo's ghost, will not down at the behest of the people who are charged with inflicting injuries, nor can its groanings be silenced by the rantings and exco-riations of carping critics. The law as enunciated in that case has come to stay. The principle has been clearly and accurately stated in 2 Quarterly Law Review, p. 207, as follows: "The party who last has a clear opportunity of avoiding the accident, notwithstanding the negligence of his opponent, is considered solely responsible for it." . . .

. . . The facts in the instant case show that for a distance of six hundred and sixty feet west of the crossing where Mr. Fuller was run over and injured the track was perfectly straight; that there were no obstructions; that there was nothing to prevent those in charge of the train from seeing the perilous position of the plaintiff, and it may be that, if the engineer and fireman were on the lookout, they saw, or by the exercise of reasonable care and diligence might have seen, the perilous position of the plaintiff. No alarm was given. Nothing was done to warn the deceased of the approaching train. He evidently was unconscious of its approach.

The only warning that was given him was too late to be of any benefit whatever, as the train was upon him at the time the two short blasts of the whistle were given. . . . Even if the engineer had not made an effort to stop or check his train, but had contented himself with giving the alarm at the point when he did see, or could have seen by the exercise of reasonable care on his part, the catastrophe in all probability could have been averted.

It must be observed that this is not the case of a pedestrian who approaches or who is on the track. In such cases the engineer has the right ordinarily to act upon the assumption that the party will get out of danger. Mr. Fuller was in a wagon, and the engineer could have seen that he was going to cross the track, and could only with difficulty extricate himself from his perilous position. . . .

Reversed and remanded.

Restatement of the Law (Second) of Torts

§479. LAST CLEAR CHANCE: HELPLESS PLAINTIFF

A plaintiff who has negligently subjected himself to a risk of harm from the defendant's subsequent negligence may recover for harm caused thereby if, immediately preceding the harm,

(a) the plaintiff is unable to avoid it by the exercise of reasonable vigilance and care, and

(b) the defendant is negligent in failing to utilize with reasonable care and competence his then existing opportunity to avoid the harm, when he

(i) knows of the plaintiff's situation and realizes or has reason to realize the peril involved in it or

(ii) would discover the situation and thus have reason to realize the peril, if he were to exercise the vigilance which it is then his duty to the plaintiff to exercise.

§480. LAST CLEAR CHANCE: INATTENTIVE PLAINTIFF

A plaintiff who, by the exercise of reasonable vigilance, could discover the danger created by the defendant's negligence in time to avoid the harm to him, can recover if, but only if, the defendant

(a) knows of the plaintiff's situation, and

(b) realizes or has reason to realize that the plaintiff is inattentive and therefore unlikely to discover his peril in time to avoid the harm, and

(c) thereafter is negligent in failing to utilize with reasonable care and competence his then existing opportunity to avoid the harm.

Compare to:

Restatement of the Law (Third) of Torts: Apportionment of Liability

§3. LAST CLEAR CHANCE: HELPLESS PLAINTIFF

. . . Special ameliorative doctrines for defining plaintiff's negligence are abolished.

Comment b. Timing of the plaintiff's and defendant's conduct: last clear chance, mitigation of damages, and avoidable consequences: . . . The timing of the plaintiff's and defendant's conduct may be relevant to the degree of responsibility the factfinder assigns to a plaintiff. . . . It may also be relevant to whether the plaintiff's injury was within the scope of liability of either the plaintiff's or defendant's conduct.

Do rules or standards work better in this context?

NOTES

1. Sequential conduct. The doctrine of last clear chance attaches great significance to sequential conduct, that is, situations in which the action of one party takes place after the other person has completed his conduct or has irrevocably committed himself to a given course of conduct, as in *Fuller*. The basic insight in this area is that once the defendant becomes aware of the plaintiff's peril, he then becomes obligated to react to that danger by taking prudent steps to avoid it. The conduct that was optimal without knowledge of the peril is no longer so once that knowledge is acquired or evident to the senses. The problem is in a sense reciprocal to the one in *Gyerman*, where the victim had the last clear chance to avoid the harm. In these sequential cases, should one regard the last party as the cheaper cost avoider, best able to bear the loss? The attractiveness of that position has made the doctrine something of a favorite of law and economics scholars, even though many lawyers regard last clear chance as a transitional doctrine on the road to a comparative negligence regime. See James, Last Clear Chance—Transitional Doctrine, 47 Yale L.J. 704 (1938).

The potential use of the doctrine is conveniently illustrated by Davies v. Mann, 152 Eng. Rep. 588 (Ex. 1842), so poignantly retold in *Fuller*. The plaintiff first left his donkey in plain view on the highway, only to have it run over by the defendant's wagon. Making contributory negligence an absolute bar reduces the likelihood that the plaintiff will leave his donkey in the road in the first place. Necessarily, however, the contributory negligence defense reduces the defendant's incentive to avoid killing the donkey, even when the defendant knows or has reason to know of the danger. Yet the defendant cannot take advantage of that position once either of those two conditions are satisfied. The last clear chance exception applies only in a small fraction of cases, so the plaintiff can hardly count on it to protect her interests in most cases when deciding where to leave her donkey. Thus the exception to the contributory negligence rule only arises when it is likely to be most effective.

For general discussions of this problem, see Shavell, Torts in Which Victim and Injurer Act Sequentially, 26 J.L. & Econ. 589 (1983); Wittman, Optimal Pricing of Sequential Inputs: Last Clear Chance, Mitigation of Damages, and Related Doctrines in the Law, 10 J. Legal Stud. 65 (1981).

2. Scope of the last clear chance doctrine. To make good her case on last clear chance, the plaintiff usually must show that the defendant was guilty of something more than ordinary negligence, which, as the Restatement implied, presupposes either knowledge that the plaintiff is in peril or "negligence so reckless as to betoken indifference to knowledge." Woloszynowski v. New York Central R.R., 172 N.E. 471, 472 (N.Y. 1930). The plaintiff met that burden in the grisly case of Kumkumian v. City of New York, 111 N.E.2d 865, 868 (N.Y. 1953), a wrongful death action in which the City's subway train ran over the decedent, who was lying on the track some 1,400 feet before the station's entrance. The train had halted three times after its tripping device came in contact with something on the tracks. After the first two stops, the brakeman inspected the tracks but found nothing. Only after the third time did the brakeman and engineer discover the decedent's mangled corpse, "actually steaming," on the track. Some evidence suggested that the fatal injuries were incurred only when the decedent was struck by the tripcocks of the third and fourth cars. Froessel, J., held that the trial judge properly left the case to the jury on a theory of last clear chance:

> Surely we cannot say, as a matter of law, under the last clear chance doctrine, that the motorman and conductor were not negligent in *twice* disregarding the emergency equipment, which is not placed in service to be ignored, and were merely chargeable with an error of judgment. At least it became a question of fact as to whether such conduct constitutes "negligence so reckless as to betoken indifference to knowledge" and whether they "ignored the warning" while there was still opportunity to avoid the accident. It matters not that they received the warning through a faultless mechanical instrumentality rather than a human agency, so long as they had "the requisite knowledge upon which a reasonably prudent man would act." The jury was entitled to find that lack of knowledge on the part of defendant's employees as to decedent's position of danger did not come about

through mere lack of vigilance in observing the tracks, but rather as the result of their own willful indifference to the emergency called to their attention by the automatic equipment, to which clear warning they paid no heed. When they did belatedly carry out their plain duty to investigate, they found decedent, and it may be inferred that they would have seen him had they carried out that duty after the second stop—still belatedly, yet in time to have saved his life. We are of the opinion that plaintiff made out at least a prima facie case under the doctrine of last clear chance.

Judge Fuld wrote a brief dissent denying the applicability of last clear chance. "Certainly, neither the motorman nor the conductor knew that any person was in peril in time to have prevented his death, and the evidence is insufficient to support the inference that they *should* have known."

SECTION C. IMPUTED CONTRIBUTORY NEGLIGENCE

The cases thus far considered have focused on whether an individual plaintiff could be held responsible in part for the harms that she has suffered. The issue of imputed contributory negligence asks whether the negligence of some other person should be charged or "imputed" to the plaintiff, at which point the traditional rules bar any right to recover. Traditional nineteenth-century doctrine drew that inference by holding, for example, that the owner of a wagon could be barred from recovery if her servant had carelessly guided the coach. The open question was whether that imputation applied to any other types of relationships between the plaintiff and some third person. In Thorogood v. Bryan, 137 Eng. Rep 452 (1849), the driver of the horse-drawn omnibus stopped in the middle of the road, instead of on the curb. As the decedent stepped off, he was killed when hit by another omnibus that was traveling too fast. The court first held that the driver's negligence should be imputed to the passenger because of the close "identification" between them. The court then further insisted that since the decedent had the choice of omnibuses in which to ride, he could not disclaim the responsibility in question.

Initially, *Thorogood* was adopted in most American states, but it was sternly rejected in Little v. Hackett, 116 U.S. 366, 375 (1886), by Field, J.:

> The truth is, the decision in Thorogood v. Bryan rests upon indefensible ground. The identification of the passenger with the negligent driver or the owner, without his personal co-operation or encouragement, is a gratuitous assumption. There is no such identity. The parties are not in the same position. The owner of a public conveyance is a carrier, and the driver or the person managing it is his servant. Neither of them is the servant of the passenger, and his asserted identity with them is contradicted by the daily experience of the world.

Two years later, *Thorogood* was also decisively repudiated in England in Mills v. Armstrong (the *Bernina*), [1888] 13 A.C. 1, when Lord Herschell denounced the doctrine on the ground that no one had ever used the identification test to hold the passenger vicariously liable to a stranger for the wrongs of the coach's driver: "[T]he identification appears to be effective only to the extent of enabling another person whose servants have been guilty of negligence to defend himself by the allegation of contributory negligence on the part of the person injured. The general rejection of *Thorogood* is subject to one critical exception. When the defendant can establish that the passenger and the driver have entered into some relationship that makes the passenger vicariously liable for the driver's torts, as was manifestly not the case in the *Bernina,* some courts impute the negligence of the driver to the passenger. Although such "joint enterprise" could conceivably arise from the simple driver-passenger relationship, most courts have tended to require more, sometimes dwelling on the "community of interest" that such an enterprise presupposes. See RST §491, comments *b* & *g*.

The hostile attitude toward the joint enterprise rule is well illustrated by Dashiell v. Keauhou-Kona Co., 487 F.2d 957, 959-961 (9th Cir. 1973). Mr. Dashiell was injured, jointly through the negligence of his wife, who was driving a golf cart in which he was a passenger, and the negligence of the defendant. By a two-to-one vote, the court reversed the judgment given to the defendant below, holding the joint enterprise defense inapplicable as a matter of law:

> We find that on the facts of this case, at no time did the relationship of joint enterprise or joint venture exist between Mr. and Mrs. Dashiell within the meaning of imputed negligence. This is not a typical case of a business venture of a character similar to a partnership where two or more parties undertake, for some pecuniary purpose, a contractual obligation resulting in the liability of each for the negligence of the other. . . .
>
> Additionally, applying the concept of imputed contributory negligence to the facts of this case would needlessly frustrate some basic policies of tort law. Mr. Dashiell was found by the jury to be blameless, and since negligence law is based on personal fault, it would be both illogical and inequitable to deny him recovery unless he were under a duty to control the actions of Mrs. Dashiell as she drove the golf cart. The record reflects no basis on which to find any duty of control. The original purpose of defining the joint enterprise relationship was vicarious liability, in order to increase the number of those liable to provide a financially responsible person to injured third parties. That purpose is absent when related to the Dashiells; in fact, application of the imputed contributory negligence rule would have the opposite effect of freeing from liability another party who is at fault even though the person denied recovery is blameless.

Dashiell reflects the modern dissatisfaction with the once fashionable "both ways test," which provided that if *A* could be held vicariously liable for the torts of *B*, then the contributory negligence of *B* should be imputed to *A*, barring *A*'s recovery. Despite the uneasiness, RTT: Apportionment of Liability adopts the "both ways test." See RTT:AL §5 and §5 comment *b*. Should Mr. Dashiell be vicariously liable if Mrs. Dashiell had injured the defendant? What result in *the Bernina* under the both ways test?

The doctrine of imputed contributory negligence was also applied in parent-child relationships in the early case of Hartfield v. Roper, 21 Wend. 615, 618-619 (N.Y. 1839). There the court barred the action of a two- or three-year-old infant because of his parents' negligence in allowing him to wander into a roadway, where he was struck and injured by a sleigh driven by defendants Roper and Newall, owing in part to "folly and gross neglect" of the child's parents in allowing him to wander into the road. While conceding that such parental foolishness could not excuse or justify either any deliberate injury or gross neglect of the defendants, the court nonetheless denied that plaintiff's recovery: "An infant is not *sui juris*. He belongs to another, to whom discretion in the care of his person is exclusively confided. That person is keeper and agent for this purpose; and in respect to third persons, his act must be deemed that of the infant; his neglect, the infant's neglect." Should the parents also be vicariously liable for the child's tort? *Hartfield* has been repudiated by either common law decision or statute in virtually all jurisdictions. New York, for example, overturned the rule by statute in 1935. N.Y. Dom. Rel. Law §73, now N.Y. Gen. Oblig. Law §3-111 (McKinney 2011). See generally Gregory, Vicarious Responsibility and Contributory Negligence, 41 Yale L.J. 831 (1932); 2 Harper, James & Gray, Torts ch. 23. Does the parental imputation rule make more sense in a regime of comparative negligence?

SECTION D. ASSUMPTION OF RISK

Lamson v. American Axe & Tool Co.
58 N.E. 585 (Mass. 1900)

Tort, under the employers' liability act, St. 1887, c. 270, for personal injuries occasioned to the plaintiff while in the defendant's employ. Trial in the Superior Court, before Lawton, J., who directed the jury to return a verdict for the defendant; and the plaintiff alleged exceptions, which appear in the opinion.

HOLMES, C.J. This is an action for personal injuries caused by the fall of a hatchet from a rack in front of which it was the plaintiff's business to work at painting hatchets, and upon which the hatchets were to be placed to dry when painted. The plaintiff had been in the defendant's employment for many years. About a year before the accident new racks had been substituted for those previously in use, and it may be assumed that they were less safe and were not proper, but were dangerous on account of the liability of the hatchets to fall from the pegs upon the plaintiff when the racks were jarred by the motion of machinery near by. The plaintiff complained to the superintendent that the hatchets were more likely to drop off than when the old racks were in use, and that now they might fall upon him, which they could not have done from the old racks. He was answered in substance that he would have to use the racks or leave. The accident which he feared happened, and he brought this suit.

304 Chapter 4. Plaintiff's Conduct

The plaintiff, on his own evidence, appreciated the danger more than any one else. He perfectly understood what was likely to happen. That likelihood did not depend upon the doing of some negligent act by people in another branch of employment, but solely on the permanent conditions of the racks and their surroundings and the plaintiff's continuing to work where he did. He complained, and was notified that he could go if he would not face the chance. He stayed and took the risk. . . . He did so none the less that the fear of losing his place was one of his motives.

Exceptions overruled.

NOTES

1. The fellow servant rule. *Lamson* represents only one manifestation of the assumption of risk defense in the area of its birth, the law of industrial accidents. The assumption of risk defense found its initial expression in the common employment (or fellow servant) rule, endorsed by Chief Justice Shaw (following the English decision of Priestley v. Fowler, 150 Eng. Rep. 1030 (Ex. 1837)) nearly 60 years before *Lamson* in Farwell v. Boston & Worcester R.R. Corp., 45 Mass. 49, 58-59 (1842). In *Farwell,* the defendant employed the plaintiff as an engineer. While engaged in his work, the plaintiff lost his right hand when another of the defendant's servants carelessly threw the wrong switch down the line. The employer had not been negligent in the selection and supervision of the "trusty" switchman. The court had to decide whether the railroad could be charged with its employee's negligence when sued by that employee's fellow servant. Shaw, J., conceded that a stranger could hold the railroad vicariously liable for the wrongs of its servant, but he denied that the principle could benefit the plaintiff, who in his view had assumed the risk: "[T]he implied contract of the master does not extend to indemnify the servant against the negligence of anyone but himself." Shaw, J., then contrasted the position of an employee with that of a passenger:

> The liability of passenger carriers is founded on similar considerations. They are held to the strictest responsibility for care, vigilance and skill, on the part of themselves and all persons employed by them, and they are paid accordingly. The rule is founded on the expediency of throwing the risk upon those who can best guard against it. Story on Bailments, §590 et seq.

Shaw, J., then concluded as follows:

> In applying these principles to the present case, it appears that the plaintiff was employed by the defendants as an engineer, at the rate of wages usually paid in that employment, being a higher rate than the plaintiff had before received as a machinist. It was a voluntary undertaking on his part, with a full knowledge of the risks incident to the employment; and the loss was sustained by means of an ordinary casualty, caused by the negligence of another servant of the company. Under these circumstances, the loss must be deemed to be the result of a pure accident, like those to which all men, in all employments, and at all times, are more

or less exposed; and like similar losses from accidental causes, it must rest where it first fell, unless the plaintiff has a remedy against the person actually in default; of which we give no opinion.

The fellow servant rule was, if anything, far more uncompromising than the assumption of risk rule in *Lamson*. In *Farwell*, for example, the risk was assumed by status alone, since the plaintiff was totally ignorant of the dangerous condition that could cause harm. In an unavailing effort to escape the fellow servant rule, the plaintiff's counsel in *Farwell* sought to confine it to the conditions applicable in Priestley v. Fowler, in which the two servants (jointly loading a butcher's wagon) were in face-to-face contact, and not under the immediate supervision of their common employer. Shaw, J., resisted any such compromise by extending the rule to employees who worked in "different departments" of the same business, however defined.

The common employment rule did not long retain its pristine simplicity in *Farwell*. Perhaps its most important refinement was the "vice principal" exception, whereby certain duties of the employer discharged by supervisory personnel were regarded as nondelegable: the duty to supply the proper equipment, to furnish a safe work place, and the like. For a comparison to the duties of common carriers, see Kelly v. Manhattan Ry., *supra* Chapter 3, at 181. The precise delineation of this exception generated many inconsistent judicial decisions, collected in Labatt, Master & Servant §§1433-1553 (2d ed. 1913). Indeed, Lord Cairns repudiated the whole vice principal exception in England in the celebrated (or infamous) case of Wilson v. Merry, 1 L.R.-S. & D. App. 326 (H.L.E. 1868), which reaffirmed *Priestley* in its original rigor.

Mere compromises in the basic principle did not, however, satisfy the critics of the fellow servant rule. In 1 Shearman & Redfield, Negligence vi, vii (5th ed. 1898), the authors denounced the rule in these words:

> A small number of able judges, devoted, from varying motives, to the supposed interests of the wealthy classes, and caring little for any others, boldly invented an exception to the general rule of masters' liability, by which servants were deprived of its protection. Very appropriately, this exception was first announced in South Carolina, then the citadel of human slavery. It was eagerly adopted in Massachusetts, then the centre of the factory system, where some decisions were then made in favor of great corporations, so preposterous that they have been disregarded in every other State, without even the compliment of refutation. It was promptly followed in England, which was then governed exclusively by landlords and capitalists. . . .
>
> As the courts, while asserting unlimited power to create new and bad law, denied their power to correct their own errors, the legislature intervened, and to a large extent the whole defence of "common employment" has been taken away in Great Britain. And now, not a single voice is raised in Great Britain in justification of the doctrine once enforced by the unanimous opinions of the English courts. The infallible Chief Justice Shaw and Chancellor Cairns have fallen so low, on *this* point at least, that "there are none so poor as to do them reverence. . . ."

Twentieth-century writers have uniformly rejected the doctrine. See Friedman, A History of American Law 413, 414 (1973); see also Schwartz, Tort Law and the Economy in Nineteenth-Century America: A Reinterpretation, 90 Yale L.J. 1717, 1768-1775 (1981). For a defense of the rule on the contractual grounds originally advanced by Shaw, see Posner, A Theory of Negligence, 1 J. Legal Stud. 29, 67-71 (1972); for an exhaustive account of its origins in Priestley v. Fowler, see Stein, Priestley v. Fowler (1837) and the Emerging Tort of Negligence, 44 B.C. L. Rev. 689 (2003), disputing *Priestley*'s role in the origin of common employment.

2. *Employer liability acts.*   *Lamson* was brought not at common law, but under the Massachusetts Employers' Liability Act. Based on an English statute of the same name (43 Vict. c. 42 (1880)), that Act, among other things, held employers to a general rule of negligence liability and abolished the fellow servant rule. See generally Epstein, The Historical Origins and Economic Structure of Workers' Compensation Law, 16 Ga. L. Rev. 775, 778 (1982). Rejection of the fellow servant rule, however, did not by itself prevent the common law version of assumption of risk from being read into the ELA, as happened in *Lamson*, or in the parallel English decisions; see, e.g., Thomas v. Quartermaine, 18 Q.B.D. 685 (1887); Smith v. Baker, [1891] A.C. 325.

The surviving version of assumption of risk, however, depended critically on the employee's continued willingness to work in the face of known risks, often after complaints had been voiced and rejected. In St. Louis Cordage Co. v. Miller, 126 F. 495 (8th Cir. 1903), Sanborn, J., defended assumption of risk as a manifestation of freedom of contract. Lord Bramwell took a similar stance in Smith v. Baker & Sons, [1891] A.C. 325, 344, in which the plaintiff, while engaged in his employment, was injured when a stone that was being lifted over his head fell and hit him. The House of Lords accepted the plaintiff's contention that he did not assume the risk because he had no specific knowledge that he was about to be struck, but Bramwell, that staunch and unreconstructed defender of laissez-faire, dissented, putting his case in the language of the bargain.

> It is a rule of good sense that if a man voluntarily undertakes a risk for a reward which is adequate to induce him, he shall not, if he suffers from the risk, have a compensation for which he did not stipulate. He can, if he chooses, say, "I will undertake the risk for so much, and if hurt, you must give me so much more, or an equivalent for the hurt." But drop the maxim. Treat it as a question of bargain. The plaintiff here thought the pay worth the risk, and did not bargain for a compensation if hurt: in effect, he undertook the work, with its risks, for his wages and no more. He says so. Suppose he had said, "If I am to run this risk, you must give me 6s. a day and not 5s.," and the master agreed, would he in reason have a claim if he got hurt? Clearly not. What difference is there if the master says, "No I will only give you 5s."? None. I am ashamed to argue it.

How does Bramwell know that this workplace bargain precluded compensation for injury? How could he, or the majority of the House of Lords, find out whether it did? In one sense, the larger issue in *Smith* was not whether this plaintiff had assumed this risk, but whether as a matter of law he, or any other employee, was allowed under the law to assume it by contract. The legal willingness to ban or limit the assumption of risk defense in industrial accident cases advanced by degrees, and culminated in its abolition by a 1939 amendment to the Federal Employers' Liability Act (45 U.S.C. §54). The defense is also eliminated under the standard workers' compensation statutes adopted in most states shortly after World War I. But the defense continues to operate in actions brought against third parties not covered by these statutes. See, e.g., Dullard v. Berkeley Associates Co., 606 F.2d 890 (2d Cir. 1979) (general contractors); Pomer v. Schoolman, 875 F.2d 1262 (7th Cir. 1989) (farmer). For the early developments, see Bohlen, Voluntary Assumption of Risk, 20 Harv. L. Rev. 14, 17-18 (1906).

Source: Guy & Rodd / Distributed by Universal Uclick for UFS via CartoonStock.com

3. *Risk premium.* Both Shaw in *Farwell* and Bramwell in *Smith* alluded to the possibility that higher wages compensate for risky employment. Much modern research holds that workers in dangerous employments receive a "risk premium" to cover their added risk before any loss occurs. Measuring the risk premium today is a chancy business at best. Some of the most careful empirical work on this question has been done by Viscusi, Risk by Choice 43-44 (1983), who reports as follows:

> In my study of workers' subjective risk perceptions, I found that workers who believed that they were exposed to dangerous or unhealthy conditions received over $900 annually (1980 prices) [or about $2,600 in 2015] in hazard pay. It is especially noteworthy that an almost identical figure was obtained when I used an objective industry injury risk measure. . . . The similarity of the findings using subjective and objective measures of risk lends strong empirical support to the validity of the risk premium analysis.
>
> Unfortunately, these results do not enable us to conclude that markets work perfectly. Is the premium less or more than would prevail if workers and employers were fully cognizant of the risks? The size of the premium only implies that compensating differentials are one element of market behavior. A more meaningful index is the wage premium per unit of risk. If it is very likely that a worker will be killed or injured, a $900 risk premium can be seen as a signal that the compensating differential process is deficient. The average blue-collar worker, however, faces an annual occupational death risk of only about 1/10,000 and a less than 1/25 risk of an injury severe enough to cause him to miss a day or more of work.

Consequently, the observed premium per unit of risk is quite substantial, with the implicit value of life being [roughly] $2 million . . . for many workers. [Or about $5.75 million in 2015 dollars.]

The safety incentives created by market mechanisms are much stronger than those created by OSHA standards; a conservative estimate of the total job risk premiums for the entire private sector is $69 billion, or almost 3,000 times the total annual penalties now levied by OSHA. Whereas OSHA penalties are only 34 cents per worker, market risk premiums per worker are $925 [(roughly $2,694 in 2015 dollars)] annually.

What happens to the risk premium when the OSHA protections are increased along with workers' compensation benefits? In Lott & Manning, Have Changing Liability Rules Compensated Workers Twice for Occupational Hazards? Earnings Premiums and Cancer Risks, 29 J. Legal Stud. 99 (2000), the authors note that the risk premium for workers declined between 43 and 108 percent as the level of workers' compensation increased. Kniesner et al., Policy Relevant Heterogeneity in the Value of Statistical Life: New Evidence from Panel Data Quantile Regressions, 40 J. Risk & Uncertainty 15 (2010), finds a "reasonable average" cost per life of $7 million to $8 million, but also finds that the value of statistical life varies across the labor force. More recent evidence from Viscusi points to a $9 million figure. See Hersch & Viscusi, Assessing the Insurance Role of Tort Liability After Calabresi, 77 Law & Contemp. Probs. 135, 156 (2014).

Murphy v. Steeplechase Amusement Co.
166 N.E. 173 (N.Y. 1929)

CARDOZO, C.J. The defendant, Steeplechase Amusement Company, maintains an amusement park at Coney Island, New York. One of the supposed attractions is known as "The Flopper." It is a moving belt, running upward on an inclined plane, on which passengers sit or stand. Many of them are unable to keep their feet because of the movement of the belt, and are thrown backward or aside. The belt runs in a groove, with padded walls on either side to a height of four feet, and with padded flooring beyond the walls at the same angle as the belt. An electric motor, driven by current furnished by the Brooklyn Edison Company, supplies the needed power.

Plaintiff, a vigorous young man, visited the park with friends. One of them, a young woman, now his wife, stepped upon the moving belt. Plaintiff followed and stepped behind her. As he did so, he felt what he describes as a sudden jerk, and was thrown to the floor. His wife in front and also friends behind him were thrown at the same time. Something more was here, as every one understood, than the slowly-moving escalator that is common in shops and public places. A fall was foreseen as one of the risks of the adventure. There would have been no point to the whole thing, no adventure about it, if the risk had not been there. The very name above the gate, the Flopper, was warning to the timid. If the name was not enough, there was warning more distinct in the experience of others. We are told by the plaintiff's wife that the members of her party stood looking at the sport before joining in it themselves. Some aboard the belt were able, as she viewed them, to sit down with decorum or even to stand and keep their footing; others jumped or fell. The tumbling bodies and the screams and laughter supplied the merriment and fun. "I took a chance," she said when asked whether she thought that a fall might be expected.

Plaintiff took the chance with her, but, less lucky than his companions, suffered a fracture of a knee cap. He states in his complaint that the belt was dangerous to life and limb in that it stopped and started violently and suddenly and was not properly equipped

The Flopper
Source: Courtesy of Kenneth W. Simmons, from the Record on Appeal

to prevent injuries to persons who were using it without knowledge of its dangers, and in a bill of particulars he adds that it was operated at a fast and dangerous rate of speed and was not supplied with a proper railing, guard or other device to prevent a fall therefrom. No other negligence is charged.

We see no adequate basis for a finding that the belt was out of order. It was already in motion when the plaintiff put his foot on it. He cannot help himself to a verdict in such circumstances by the addition of the facile comment that it threw him with a jerk. One who steps upon a moving belt and finds his heels above his head is in no position to discriminate with nicety between the successive stages of the shock, between the jerk which is a cause and the jerk, accompanying the fall, as an instantaneous effect. There is evidence for the defendant that power was transmitted smoothly, and could not be transmitted otherwise. If the movement was spasmodic, it was an unexplained and, it seems, an inexplicable departure from the normal workings of the mechanism. An aberration so extraordinary, if it is to lay the basis for a verdict, should rest on something firmer than a mere descriptive epithet, a summary of the sensations of a tense and crowded moment. But the jerk, if it were established, would add little to the case. Whether the movement of the belt was uniform or irregular, the risk at greatest was a fall. This was the very hazard that was invited and foreseen.

Volenti non fit injuria. One who takes part in such a sport accepts the dangers that inhere in it so far as they are obvious and necessary, just as a fencer accepts the risk of a thrust by his antagonist or a spectator at a ball game the chance of contact with the ball. The antics of the clown are not the paces of the cloistered cleric. The rough and boisterous joke, the horseplay of the crowd, evokes its own guffaws, but they are not the pleasures of tranquillity. The plaintiff was not seeking a retreat for meditation. Visitors were tumbling about the belt to the merriment of onlookers when he made his choice to join them. He took the chance of a like fate, with whatever damage to his body might ensue from such a fall. The timorous may stay at home.

A different case would be here if the dangers inherent in the sport were obscure or unobserved, or so serious as to justify the belief that precautions of some kind must have been taken to avert them. Nothing happened to the plaintiff except what common experience tells us may happen at any time as the consequence of a sudden fall. Many a skater or a horseman can rehearse a tale of equal woe. A different case there would also be if the accidents had been so many as to show that the game in its inherent nature was too dangerous to be continued without change. The president of the amusement company says that there had never been such an accident before. A nurse employed at an emergency hospital maintained in connection with the park contradicts him to some extent. She says that on other occasions she had attended patrons of the park who had been injured at the Flopper, how many she could not say. None, however, had been badly injured or had suffered broken bones. Such testimony is not enough to show that the game was a trap for the unwary, too perilous to be endured. According to the defendant's estimate, two hundred and fifty thousand visitors were at the Flopper in a year. Some quota of accidents was to be looked for in so great a mass. One might as well say that a skating rink should be abandoned because skaters sometimes fall.

There is testimony by the plaintiff that he fell upon wood, and not upon a canvas padding. He is strongly contradicted by the photographs and by the witnesses for the defendant, and is without corroboration in the testimony of his companions who were witnesses on his behalf. If his observation was correct, there was a defect in the equipment, and one not obvious or known. The padding should have been kept in repair to break the force of any fall. The case did not go to the jury, however, upon any such theory of the defendant's liability, nor is the defect fairly suggested by the plaintiff's bill of particulars, which limits his complaint. The case went to the jury upon the theory that negligence was dependent upon a sharp and sudden jerk.

The judgment of the Appellate Division and that of the Trial Term [for the plaintiff] should be reversed, and a new trial granted, with costs to abide the event.

POUND, CRANE, LEHMAN, KELLOGG and HUBBS, JJ., concur; O'BRIEN, J., dissents.

NOTES

1. Historical criticisms of Murphy.   For a strong "dissenting" opinion, see Simon, Murphy v. Steeplechase Amusement Co.: While the Timorous Stay at Home, the Adventurous Ride the Flopper, *in* Tort Stories 179 (Rabin & Sugarman eds., 2003). The article argues that the Flopper was more dangerous than Cardozo suggested. It was only 16 inches wide and had to be entered while moving at a speed of seven miles per hour, in contrast to the one to 1.5 miles per hour of the standard escalator, and the evidence of the sudden jerk was more persuasive than Cardozo acknowledged. But at the same time, it may have been safer than other rides (e.g., the Whirlpool or Human Roulette Wheel) in standard use at Coney Island, then the amusement capital of the world. Why, on this record, grant a new trial?

2. *Primary and secondary assumption of risk.* In Meistrich v. Casino Arena Attractions, Inc., 155 A.2d 90 (N.J. 1959), the plaintiff fell while skating on the defendant's rink. The plaintiff's evidence showed that "defendant departed from the usual procedure in preparing the ice, with the result that it became too hard and hence too slippery for the patron of average ability using skates sharpened for the usual surface." Weintraub, C.J., speaking for a unanimous court, held that a jury could infer that the defendant's negligence was a proximate cause of the accident. It also held that a "jury could permissibly find [the plaintiff] carelessly contributed to his injury when, with that knowledge, he remained on the ice and skated cross-hand with another." He nonetheless ordered a new trial because of what he regarded as a faulty instruction below on assumption of risk, namely the trial court's instruction: "that assumption of risk may be found if plaintiff knew or reasonably should have known of the risk, notwithstanding that a reasonably prudent man would have continued in the face of the risk."

Weintraub, C.J., critically reviewed the history of assumption of risk in industrial accidents, and in the course of his opinion articulated the distinction between primary and secondary assumption of risk as follows:

> [Apart from intentional or contractually addressed harms], assumption of risk has two distinct meanings. In one sense (sometimes called its "primary" sense), it is an alternative expression for the proposition that defendant was not negligent, i.e., either owed no duty or did not breach the duty owed. In its other sense (sometimes called "secondary"), assumption of risk is an affirmative defense to an established breach of duty. In its primary sense, it is accurate to say plaintiff assumed the risk whether or not he was "at fault," for the truth thereby expressed in alternate terminology is that defendant was not negligent. But in its secondary sense, i.e., as an affirmative defense to an established breach of defendant's duty, it is incorrect to say plaintiff assumed the risk whether or not he was at fault. . . .
>
> In applying assumption of risk in its secondary sense in areas other than that of master and servant, our cases have consistently recognized the ultimate question to be whether a reasonably prudent man would have moved in the face of a known risk, dealing with the issue as one of law or leaving it to the jury upon the same standard which controls the handling of the issue of contributory negligence. . . .

One consequence of this definition is that the cases from Chapter 1, *supra* at 25, Note 2, that hold that the plaintiff must show defendant's intentional or reckless behavior to recover from the defendant are all cases of assumption of risk in its primary sense, as there is no ordinary duty of care. *Meistrich* differs from these cases because the action is brought not against a competitor or participant, but the owner or occupier of established premises who generally owes a duty of care. In its secondary sense, assumption of risk is only an aspect of contributory negligence. Unlike the situation in *Lamson* or *Murphy*, the plaintiff in *Meistrich* knew that the defendant was in breach of its obligation to provide a safe skating surface before he fell. Why then is he not under an obligation to leave the ice? If he does, can he get his money back? Is *Murphy* a case of primary or secondary assumption of risk?

3. Assumption of risk and the duty to warn.   One important issue in these amusement park cases is the extent to which assumption of risk can survive the recent expansion of the duty to warn. In Russo v. The Range, Inc., 395 N.E.2d 10, 13-14 (Ill. App. 1979), the plaintiff was injured while riding down the "giant slide" owned and operated by the defendant. Before entering the amusement park, he purchased a ticket that on the reverse side read: "[T]he person using this ticket so assumes all risk of personal injury." At the top of the slide, defendant placed a warning and instructions for its proper use. The plaintiff also admitted that he had taken several similar rides at the amusement park before the accident, but claimed that he had "no knowledge that the slide would cause his body to fly in the air as he rode it—the event which he says caused his injury." The court allowed the plaintiff's case to reach the jury. "From these same facts the Range relies on it is possible to infer that Russo's ride down the slide was an abnormal occurrence caused by some danger unknown to him and a risk he did not assume. It is the presence of this possibility which precludes summary judgment."

Modern providers of rides routinely take aggressive steps to deal with the risks, often using bold signs to that effect. Thus, in Anderson v. Hedstrom Corp., 76 F. Supp. 2d 422 (S.D.N.Y. 1999), the plaintiff sued for injuries suffered in a trampoline accident. The product came with this warning:

> **WARNING!** MISUSE AND ABUSE OF THIS TRAMPOLINE IS DANGEROUS AND CAN CAUSE SERIOUS INJURIES. DO NOT DO SOMERSAULTS. DO NOT LAND ON NECK OR HEAD. PERMIT ONLY **ONE** PERSON AT A TIME ON THIS TRAMPOLINE. MORE THAN ONE PERSON AT A TIME ON THIS TRAMPOLINE INCREASES THE CHANCE OF INJURY.

Smith, J., denied the defendant's motion for summary judgment saying:

> Whether those warnings should have specified, for example, the specific danger of paralysis from neck injury, rather than only the danger of "serious injuries," is a question upon which reasonable people could disagree. . . . Similarly, in light of defendants' own contention that plaintiff's injuries were caused by his failure to bounce in the center of the trampoline, a jury could reasonably decide that the absence, on the trampoline labels, of any warning to bounce only in the center, constituted a failure to adequately warn, even though a statement in the Owner's Manual did advise, "Avoid bouncing too high. Stay low until you can control your bounce and repeatedly land in the center of the trampoline."

Can anyone draft a warning good enough to support a summary judgment? Should the jury also be instructed to note that many of the risks subject to a warning are also obvious?

4. Spectator sports and assumption of risk.   A large body of cases relies on the assumption of risk defense to deny recovery to spectators injured at sporting events. The defense proceeds at two levels. First, at the wholesale level, courts hold that all spectators share the common knowledge of injury from attending these events. Second, at the retail level, particularized evidence tends to confirm that any individual plaintiff has this knowledge, such as the risk of being hit by a hockey puck, Moulas v. PBC Productions, Inc., 570 N.W.2d 739 (Wis. App. 1997), *aff'd by an equally divided court,* 576 N.W.2d 929 (Wis. 1998), a baseball, or a golf ball.

The chinks in the armor of this defense arise in special settings where spectators are said to be induced into letting down their guard. Thus, in Maisonave v. The Newark Bears, Gourmet Services, 852 A.2d 233, 236 (N.J. Super. Ct. App. Div. 2004), the plaintiff spectator was struck in the face by a foul ball as he stood before a vending cart operated by the defendant Gourmet Dining Service, which had a concession contract from the team. The carts were needed because the concession areas were still under construction. By agreement between the defendants, they were positioned close to the field so that customers could continue to watch the game. The plaintiff, himself an experienced baseball player and long-time fan, was hit while reaching into his wallet to pay for his purchase. Building on precedents that require operators of sports facilities to screen high-risk places, Coleman, J., held that the plaintiff was entitled to a jury trial on the question of whether the defendants had breached their duty:

> While watching the game, either seated or standing in an unprotected viewing area, spectators reasonably may be expected to pay attention and to look out for their own safety; but the activities and ambiance of a concession area predictably draw the attention of even the most experienced and the most wary fan from the action on the field of play. It is not only foreseeable, but inevitable, that in the process of placing orders or reaching for money or accepting the purchases or striking up conversations with others on line, spectators will be distracted from the action on the field and the risk of injury from flying objects will be increased significantly. The defendants are engaged in a commercial venture which by its nature induces spectators to let down their guard. They have a concomitant duty to exercise reasonable care to protect them during such times of heightened vulnerability. The imposition of a duty under these circumstances, particularly where it involves a temporary arrangement, is not only fair but reasonable.

What result if a fan sitting in the stands is injured while reaching for his wallet to buy a hot dog from a roving vendor?

5. Professional sports and assumption of risk. In Maddox v. City of New York, 487 N.E.2d 553, 556-557 (N.Y. 1985), the plaintiff was an outfielder for the New York Yankees whose professional career was effectively ended after he sustained severe damage to his knee when he slipped in the "wet and muddy" outfield while chasing after a fly ball. He sued the Yankees as his employer, the Mets as lessees of Shea Stadium, and New York City as the stadium's owner. The plaintiff knew about the general condition of the field, and the court held that "[h]is continued participation in the game in light of that awareness constituted assumption of risk as a matter of law, entitling defendants to a summary judgment." The court reasoned as follows:

> There is no question that the doctrine requires not only knowledge of the injury-causing defect but also appreciation of the resultant risk, but awareness of the risk is not to be determined in a vacuum. It is, rather, to be assessed against the

background of the skill and experience of the particular plaintiff, and in that assessment a higher degree of awareness will be imputed to a professional than to one with less than professional experience in the particular sport. In that context plaintiff's effort to separate the wetness of the field, which he testified was above the grassline, from the mud beneath it in which his foot became lodged must be rejected for not only was he aware that there was "some mud" in the centerfield area, but also it is a matter of common experience that water of sufficient depth to cover grass may result in the earth beneath being turned to mud. We do not deal here . . . with a hole in the playing field hidden by grass, but with water, indicative of the presence of mud, the danger of which plaintiff was sufficiently aware to complain to the grounds keepers. It is not necessary to the application of assumption of risk that the injured plaintiff have foreseen the exact manner in which his or her injury occurred, so long as he or she is aware of the potential for injury of the mechanism from which the injury results.

6. Assumption of risk and abandonment of rights. Many cases address assumption of risk in its secondary sense when the defendant has negligently or unlawfully created a dangerous condition that the plaintiff must endure in the exercise of her ordinary rights. In Marshall v. Ranne, 511 S.W.2d 255, 260 (Tex. 1974), the court refused to find that the plaintiff had assumed the risk of being bitten by the defendant's vicious boar that bit the plaintiff while the plaintiff was walking from his house to his car:

> We hold that there was no proof that plaintiff had a free and voluntary choice, because he did not have a free choice of alternatives. He had, instead, only a choice of evils, both of which were wrongfully imposed upon him by the defendant. He could remain a prisoner inside his own house or he could take the risk of reaching his car before defendant's hog attacked him. Plaintiff could have remained inside his house, but in doing so, he would have surrendered his legal right to proceed over his own property to his car so he could return to his home in Dallas. The latter alternative was forced upon him against his will and was a choice he was not legally required to accept.

See RST §496E.

The problem of implicit coercion in secondary assumption of risk cases also surfaced in ADM Partnership v. Martin, 702 A.2d 730 (Md. 1997). The plaintiff, Martin, was injured when she fell on a walkway covered with snow and ice while making a delivery to the defendant's premises. The court held that the plaintiff had, as a matter of law, known, appreciated, and voluntarily confronted the risk in question even though she had claimed that she used the walkway "as a result of being coerced by the economic necessity of securing a service contract for her employer and for her continued employment." The court rejected that proposition as a matter of law when the plaintiff could produce no objective evidence that she had ever been threatened with a loss of her job. The court then quoted its earlier decision in Gibson v. Beaver, 226 A.2d 273, 276 (Md. 1967):

> The plaintiff takes a risk voluntarily . . . where the defendant has a right to face him with the dilemma of "take it or leave"—in other words, where [the] defendant is

under no duty to make the conditions of their association any safer than they appear to be. In such a case it does not matter that the plaintiff is coerced to assume the risk by some force not emanating from defendant, such as poverty, dearth of living quarters, or a sense of moral responsibility.

Suppose she braved the snow because she was under an employer ultimatum, what then?

7. Assumption of risk: The fireman's rule. Assumption of risk remains relevant with the so-called fireman's rule, which covers police officers and other public officials who enter private premises in order to maintain public order by responding to a fire or burglar alarm. "[O]ne who has knowingly and voluntarily confronted a hazard cannot recover for injuries sustained thereby." Walters v. Sloan, 571 P.2d 609, 612 (Cal. 1979). The public policy reasons behind the principle were well set out by Weintraub, C.J., shortly after his opinion in *Meistrich,* in Krauth v. Geller, 157 A.2d 129, 130-131 (N.J. 1960):

> [I]t is the fireman's business to deal with that very hazard [the fire] and hence, perhaps by analogy to the contractor engaged as an expert to remedy dangerous situations, he cannot complain of negligence in the creation of the very occasion for his engagement. In terms of duty, it may be said there is none owed the fireman to exercise care so as not to require the special services for which he is trained and paid. Probably most fires are attributable to negligence, and in the final analysis the policy decision is that it would be too burdensome to charge all who carelessly cause or fail to prevent fires with the injuries suffered by the expert retained with public funds to deal with those inevitable, although negligently created, occurrences. Hence, for that risk, the fireman should receive appropriate compensation from the public he serves both in pay which reflects the hazard and in workmen's compensation benefits for the consequences of the inherent risks of the calling.

For a critique of the fireman's rule, see Heidt, When Plaintiffs Are Premium Planners for Their Injuries: A Fresh Look at the Fireman's Rule, 82 Ind. L.J. 745 (2007).

Dalury v. S-K-I Ltd.
670 A.2d 795 (Vt. 1995)

JOHNSON, J: We reverse the trial court's grant of summary judgment for defendants S-K-I, Ltd. and Killington, Ltd. in a case involving an injury to a skier at a resort operated by defendants. We hold that the exculpatory agreements which defendants require skiers to sign, releasing defendants from all liability resulting from negligence, are void as contrary to public policy.

While skiing at Killington Ski Area, plaintiff Robert Dalury sustained serious injuries when he collided with a metal pole that formed part of the control maze for a ski lift line. Before the season started, Dalury had purchased a midweek season pass and signed a form releasing the ski area from liability. The relevant portion reads:

RELEASE FROM LIABILITY AND CONDITIONS OF USE

1. I accept and understand that Alpine Skiing is a hazardous sport with many dangers and risks and that injuries are a common and ordinary occurrence of the sport. As a condition of being permitted to use the ski area premises, I freely accept and voluntarily assume the risks of injury or property damage and release Killington Ltd., its employees and agents from any and all liability for personal injury or property damage resulting from negligence, conditions of the premises, operations of the ski area, actions or omissions of employees or agents of the ski area or from my participation in skiing at the area, accepting myself the full responsibility for any and all such damage or injury of any kind which may result.

Plaintiff also signed a photo identification card that contained this same language.

Dalury and his wife filed a complaint against defendants, alleging negligent design, construction, and replacement of the maze pole. Defendants moved for summary judgment, arguing that the release of liability barred the negligence action. The trial court, without specifically addressing plaintiffs' contention that the release was contrary to public policy, found that the language of the release clearly absolved defendants of liability for their own negligence. . . .

[W]e hold the agreement is unenforceable. . . .

I

This is a case of first impression in Vermont. While we have recognized the existence of a public policy exception to the validity of exculpatory agreements, in most of our cases, enforceability has turned on whether the language of the agreement was sufficiently clear to reflect the parties' intent. . . .

Even well-drafted exculpatory agreements, however, may be void because they violate public policy. . . .

The leading judicial formula for determining whether an exculpatory agreement violates public policy was set forth by Justice Tobriner of the California Supreme Court. Tunkl v. Regents of Univ. of Cal., 383 P.2d 441, 445-46, (Cal. 1963). An agreement is invalid if it exhibits some or all of the following characteristics:

[1.] It concerns a business of a type generally thought suitable for public regulation. [2.] The party seeking exculpation is engaged in performing a service of great importance to the public, which is often a matter of practical necessity for some members of the public. [3.] The party holds itself out as willing to perform this service for any member of the public who seeks it, or at least for any member coming within certain established standards. [4.] As a result of the essential nature of the service, in the economic setting of the transaction, the party invoking exculpation possesses a decisive advantage of bargaining strength against any member of the public who seeks [the party's] services. [5.] In exercising a superior bargaining power the party confronts the public with a standardized adhesion contract of exculpation, and makes no provision whereby a purchaser may pay additional reasonable fees and obtain protection against negligence. [6.] Finally, as a result of the transaction, the person or property of the purchaser is placed under the control of the seller, subject to the risk of carelessness by the seller or [the seller's] agents.

Applying these factors, the court concluded that a release from liability for future negligence imposed as a condition for admission to a charitable research hospital was invalid. Numerous courts have adopted and applied the *Tunkl* factors. . . .

Other courts have incorporated the *Tunkl* factors into their decisions. . . . In Jones [v. Dressel, 623 P.2d 370, 376 (Colo. 1981)], the court concluded, based on the *Tunkl* factors, that no duty to the public was involved in air service for a parachute jump, because that sort of service does not affect the public interest. Using a similar formula, the Wyoming Supreme Court concluded that a ski resort's sponsorship of an Ironman Decathlon competition did not invoke the public interest. Milligan v. Big Valley Corp., 754 P.2d 1063, 1066-67 (Wyo. 1988).

On the other hand, the Virginia Supreme Court recently concluded, in the context of a "Teflon Man Triathlon" competition, that a preinjury release from liability for negligence is void as against public policy because it is simply wrong to put one party to a contract at the mercy of the other's negligence. Hiett v. Lake Barcroft Community Ass'n, 418 S.E.2d 894, 897 (Va. 1992). . . .

II

Defendants urge us to uphold the exculpatory agreement on the ground that ski resorts do not provide an essential public service. They argue that they owe no duty to plaintiff to permit him to use their private lands for skiing, and that the terms and conditions of entry ought to be left entirely within their control. Because skiing, like other recreational sports, is not a necessity of life, defendants contend that the sale of a lift ticket is a purely private matter, implicating no public interest. We disagree.

Whether or not defendants provide an essential public service does not resolve the public policy question in the recreational sports context. The defendants' area is a facility open to the public. They advertise and invite skiers and nonskiers of every level of skiing ability to their premises for the price of a ticket. At oral argument, defendants conceded that thousands of people buy lift tickets every day throughout the season. Thousands of people ride lifts, buy services, and ski the trails. Each ticket sale may be, for some purposes, a purely private transaction. But when a substantial number of such sales take place as a result of the seller's general invitation to the public to utilize the facilities and services in question, a legitimate public interest arises.

The major public policy implications are those underlying the law of premises liability. In Vermont, a business owner has a duty "of active care to make sure that its premises are in safe and suitable condition for its customers." . . . We have already held that a ski area owes its customers the same duty as any other business—to keep its premises reasonably safe.

The policy rationale is to place responsibility for maintenance of the land on those who own or control it, with the ultimate goal of keeping accidents to the minimum level possible. Defendants, not recreational skiers, have the expertise and opportunity to foresee and control hazards, and to guard against the negligence of their agents and employees. They alone can properly maintain and inspect their premises, and train their employees in risk management. They alone can insure against risks and effectively spread the cost of insurance among their thousands of customers. Skiers, on the other hand, are not in a position to discover and correct risks of harm, and they cannot insure against the ski area's negligence.

If defendants were permitted to obtain broad waivers of their liability, an important incentive for ski areas to manage risk would be removed, with the public bearing the cost of the resulting injuries. It is illogical, in these circumstances, to undermine the public policy underlying business invitee law and allow skiers to bear risks they have no ability or right to control. . . .

Defendants argue that the public policy of the state, as expressed in the "Acceptance of inherent risks" statute, 12 V.S.A. 1037,[2] indicates a willingness on the part of the Legislature to limit ski area liability. Therefore, they contend that public policy favors the use of express releases such as the one signed by plaintiff. On the contrary, defendants' allocation of responsibility for skiers' injuries is at odds with the statute. The statute places responsibility for the "inherent risks" of any sport on the participant, insofar as such risks are obvious and necessary. A ski area's own negligence, however, is neither an inherent risk nor an obvious and necessary one in the sport of skiing. Thus, a skier's assumption of the inherent risks of skiing does not abrogate the ski area's duty "to warn of or correct dangers which in the exercise of reasonable prudence in the circumstances could have been foreseen and corrected."

Reversed and remanded.

NOTES

1. Exculpation clauses at ski resorts. A different attitude toward exculpation clauses was taken in Chepkevich v. Hidden Valley Resort, L.P., 2 A.3d 1174, 1190 (Pa. 2010). The plaintiff, Lori Chepkevich, was an experienced skier who held a season pass at Hidden Valley Resort. On the day of the injury, she agreed with her other family members that she would take her six-year-old nephew back to the family's condominium when he complained of being cold. The ski lift they used had only one speed, and the plaintiff was afraid that her nephew could not board it safely. She therefore got the lift operator to agree to stop the lift twice, once to let the plaintiff and her nephew get in position to board the lift, and the second time to board it. The first part of the plan was successfully executed, but the

---

2. "Notwithstanding the provisions of section 1036 of this title, a person who takes part in any sport accepts as a matter of law the dangers that inhere therein insofar as they are obvious and necessary." 12 V.S.A. §1037.

second was not. As the plaintiff and her nephew boarded the moving lift, both lost their balance and fell off. The plaintiff sustained a dislocated shoulder and a fractured hip. The plaintiff testified that she took her own seven-year-old son to a variable-speed lift when helping him down the mountain.

The release document recited that skiing was "a dangerous sport with inherent risks" from the natural terrain, the manmade structures on the course, and the actions of other skiers, all of which "present the risk of serious or fatal injury." It concluded by stating: "By accepting this Season Pass I agree to accept all these risks and agree not to sue Hidden Valley Resort or their employees if injured while using their facilities regardless of any negligence on their part."

The trial court held that the release was binding because it explicitly covered cases of the defendant's negligence, but its decision was reversed in the Superior Court on the ground that injuries getting on and off lifts were not "inherent" in skiing. In the Pennsylvania Supreme Court, Castille, J., reinstated the judgment of the trial court:

> [T]he panel herein plainly erred in suggesting that the Release could be deemed to be an unenforceable contract of adhesion. Indeed, voluntary participation in inherently dangerous sporting activities does not easily lend itself to a claim that an exculpatory agreement governing that activity is an invalid adhesion contract. . . .
>
> As we have stated, downhill skiing—like auto racing—is a voluntary and hazardous activity, and that fact is acknowledged in the Act as discussed above. Moreover, an exculpatory agreement conditioning use of a commercial facility for such activities has not been construed as a typical contract of adhesion. The signer is under no compulsion, economic or otherwise, to participate, much less to sign the exculpatory agreement, because it does not relate to essential services, but merely governs a voluntary recreational activity.
>
> In addition, the Release cannot be said to contravene any policy of the law. Indeed, the clear policy of this Commonwealth, as embodied by the Act, is to encourage the sport and to place the risks of skiing squarely on the skier. 42 Pa. C.S. §7102(c)(2) [*infra* at 337]. Furthermore, Pennsylvania courts have upheld similar releases respecting skiing and other inherently dangerous sporting activities [such as tubing and motorcycling]. . . . And, finally, the Release Lori signed is a contract between the ski resort and Lori relating to their private affairs, specifically Lori's voluntary use of the resort's facilities.

Chepkevich was followed in Bell v. Dean, 5 A.3d 266, 272 (Pa. Super Ct. 2010). There the plaintiff skier was making slow S-turns while going slowly down an expert slope, when he was struck by a speeding snowboarder. The plaintiff argued "the risk of another skier or snowboarder's negligence is not a risk inherent to the sport of downhill skiing." Lazarus, J., held that nothing in the statutory language [42 Pa. Cons. Stat. Ann. §7102(c) (*infra* at 337)] precluded its application to negligence actions between patrons (whether they be skiers or snowboarders) of the ski resort or ski area. Moreover, the statute preserved the assumption of risk defense between skiers.

> Rarely, is it the case that a skier finds him or herself traversing the slopes alone, unaccompanied by others. Each participant on the slope is of varying age,

coordination, and skill. Some are beginners, some are more experienced, but few are experts or professionals. Moreover, participants travel down the mountain at different speeds. Some travel down the slope in a straight line with greater speed than those who slalom down the mountain in a wide S-type pattern. That this varied group of skiers and snowboarders alike, for recreation, proceed voluntarily down the side of a mountain together, simultaneously, creates the obvious danger for mishaps leading to collisions among them. The causes of such mishaps would certainly include incidents, similar to Bell's allegations, of ordinary carelessness or inadvertence. Indeed, general allegations of this sort could serve as the basis upon which many skiing or snowboarding collisions occur.

2. Assumption of risk by contract: other contexts.   It is perhaps instructive that the court in *Chepkevich* ignored the basic framework for exculpation clauses set out in *Tunkl*, on which the Vermont court in *Dalury* so heavily relied. Elsewhere, courts have invoked *Tunkl* in passing on the validity of contractual waivers outside the medical context. Wagenblast v. Odessa School District No. 105-157-166J, 758 P.2d 968 (Wash. 1988), invoked *Tunkl's* six criteria to strike down an agreement whereby parents released the school district from all liability in negligence related to their children's participation in interscholastic athletics, preferring to examine liability on a case-by-case basis. In contrast, in Zivich v. Mentor Soccer Club, Inc., 696 N.E.2d 201, 205 (Ohio 1998), the court upheld a similar exemption clause when the plaintiff was hurt while swinging from an unanchored soccer goal shortly after winning an intrasquad contest. The court wanted to spare the huge number of volunteer members in such organizations as the Little League and the American Youth Soccer Organization "the risks and overwhelming costs of litigation." Should different rules apply to schools and nonprofit leagues? See generally Developments in the Law—Nonprofit Corporations, 105 Harv. L. Rev. 1578 (1992).

Note too that even if exculpation clauses pass muster on substantive grounds, they can be challenged on the ground that the exculpation clause was not brought clearly to the attention of the plaintiff. See Obstetrics & Gynecologists Ltd. v. Pepper, 693 P.2d 1259, 1260 (Nev. 1985), which refused to enforce, as an improper contract of adhesion, an arbitration clause that it inserted in all its contracts because the plaintiff testified that she assigned the agreement without first having its terms explained to her, and thus "had no opportunity to modify any of its terms; her choices were to sign the agreement as it stood or to forego treatment at the clinic." With *Pepper*, contrast Madden v. Kaiser Foundation Hospitals, 552 P.2d 1178, 1185 (Cal. 1976), which upheld an arbitration clause contained in a contract between a state employee and the defendant foundation—noting that the employer intermediate was able to protect the interest of its employees. But in Engalla v. Permanente Medical Group, Inc., 938 P.2d 903, 909, 911, 912-913 (Cal. 1997), Mosk, J., held that the individual patient could sue to set aside a medical malpractice arbitration plan on grounds of fraud and bias in the selection of the arbitrator.

3. Contracting out of medical malpractice liability generally.   Arbitration clauses represent only the tip of the iceberg in the larger dispute over whether the parties can contract out of the tort rules that now govern medical malpractice litigation. Professor Robinson puts the case for market freedom of contract on all issues of liability forcefully:

> In terms of utilitarian efficiency, contractual arrangements allow parties to achieve the most efficient combination of efforts to manage risk in accordance with their respective comparative advantages and their respective risk preferences. The moral argument proceeds along similar lines but emphasizes the fact that contractual allocation promotes individual freedom of choice, constrained only by the need to accommodate the divergent interests of the contracting parties. To justify private ordering one need not suppose that it always yields "good" or "fair" results. It is enough that, in general, private parties are likely to achieve results that are at least as good and fair for themselves as would be achieved by paternalistic intervention.

Robinson, Rethinking the Allocation of Medical Malpractice Risks Between Patients and Providers, 49 Law & Contemp. Probs. 172, 189 (1986). Robinson's article (as well as others by Danzon, Epstein, and Havighurst) provoked the following response from an English scholar in Atiyah, Medical Malpractice and the Contract/Tort Boundary, 49 Law & Contemp. Probs. 287, 296 (1986):

> The real market enthusiasts appear to envisage a situation in which a competitive market offers a range of benefit and risk packages suitable to the individual desires, risk-averseness, and wallets of various patients. If all the bargaining is in practice to be done collectively (by employers and unions whose interests of course are not always identical with those of employees), however, the reality is that the rules which will govern the physician/patient relationship will not be tailored to the individual patient's needs at all. They will be fixed by third parties, just as much as the tort rules are. There may, it is true, be more choice available in the market, but this argument takes us back to our starting point about information, risk evaluation, and bargaining power. If the patient does not understand the differences in the packages offered to him, choice by itself means little, and the presumption of efficiency in outcome is rebutted.

See generally Symposium, Medical Malpractice: Can the Private Sector Find Relief?, 49 Law & Contemp. Probs. 1-348 (Spring 1986). See also Danzon, Medical Malpractice: Theory, Evidence, and Public Policy 208-217 (1985), for a qualified endorsement of the contract solution, and Weiler, Medical Malpractice on Trial 113 (1991), for a "highly dubious [view] of the brave new world of no-liability," which Weiler thinks will emerge from any contractual regime. See also Arlen, Contracting over Liability: Medical Malpractice and the Cost of Choice, 158 U. Pa. L. Rev. 957 (2010), who argues against the contract solution as being unable to keep up with the myriad physician actions that could in principle be subject to negligence liability.

SECTION E. COMPARATIVE NEGLIGENCE

1. At Common Law

Lombard Laws, King Liutprand
Law 136.VII. (A.D. 733)

It has likewise been made known to us that a certain man has a well in his courtyard and, according to custom, it has a prop and lift for raising the water. Another man who came along stood under that lift and, when yet another man came to draw water from the well and incautiously released the lift, the weight came down on the man who stood under it, and he was killed. The question then arose over who should pay composition for this death, and it has been referred to us. It seems right to us and to our judges that the man who was killed, since he was not an animal but had the power of reason like other men, should have noticed where he stood or what weight was above his head. Therefore, two-thirds of the amount of his composition shall be assessed to him [the dead man], and one-third of the amount at which he was valued according to law shall be paid as composition by the man who incautiously drew the water. He shall pay the composition to the children or to the near relatives who are the heirs of the dead man, and the case shall be ended without any feud or grievance since it was done unintentionally. Moreover, no blame should be placed on the man who owns the well because if we placed the blame on him, no one hereafter would permit other

Liutprand (at left), 712-744 A.D.
Source: Wikimedia Commons

men to raise water from their wells, and since all men cannot have a well, those who are poor would die and those who are traveling through would also suffer need.

Charles Beach, Contributory Negligence
12-13 (2d ed. 1892)

The reasons of the rule which denies relief to a plaintiff guilty of contributory negligence have been previously stated. The common law refuses to apportion damages which arise from negligence. This it does upon considerations of public convenience and public policy, and upon this principle, it is said, depends also the rule which makes the contributory negligence of a plaintiff a complete defense. For the same reason, when there is an action in tort, where injury results from the negligence of two or more persons, the sufferer has a full remedy against any one of them, and no contribution can be enforced between the tort feasors. The policy of the law in this respect is founded upon the inability of human tribunals to mete out exact justice. A perfect code would render each man responsible for the unmixed consequences of his own default; but the common law, in view of the impossibility of assigning all effects to their respective causes, refuses to interfere in those cases where negligence is the issue, at the instance of one whose hands are not free from the stain of contributory fault, and where accordingly the impossibility of apportioning the damage between the parties does not exist, the rule is held not to apply.

William Prosser, Comparative Negligence
41 Cal. L. Rev. 1, 3-4 (1953)

There has been much speculation as to why the rule thus declared found such ready acceptance in later decisions, both in England and in the United States. The explanations given by the courts themselves never have carried much conviction. Most of the decisions have talked about "proximate cause," saying that the plaintiff's negligence is an intervening, insulating cause between the defendant's negligence and the injury. But this cannot be supported unless a meaning is assigned to proximate cause which is found nowhere else. If two automobiles collide and injure a bystander, the negligence of one driver is not held to be a superseding cause which relieves the other of liability; and there is no visible reason for any different conclusion when the action is by one driver against the other. It has been said that the defense has a penal basis, and is intended to punish the plaintiff for his own misconduct; or that the court will not aid one who is himself at fault, and he must come into court with clean hands. But this is no explanation of the many cases, particularly those of the last clear chance, in which a plaintiff clearly at fault is permitted to recover. It has been said that the rule is intended to discourage accidents, by denying recovery to those who fail to use proper care for their own safety; but the assumption that the speeding motorist is, or should be, meditating on the possible failure of a lawsuit for his possible injuries lacks all reality, and it is quite as reasonable to say that the rule promotes accidents by encouraging the negligent defendant. Probably the true explanation lies merely in the highly individualistic attitude of the common law of the early nineteenth century. The period of development of contributory negligence was that of the industrial revolution, and there is reason to think that the courts found in this defense, along with the concepts of duty and proximate cause, a convenient instrument of control over the jury, by which the liabilities of rapidly growing industry were curbed and kept within bounds.

Li v. Yellow Cab Co. of California
532 P.2d 1226 (Cal. 1975)

[The accident in question resulted from the negligence of both parties. The plaintiff had attempted to cross three lanes of oncoming traffic to enter a service station; the defendant's driver was traveling at an excessive speed when he ran a yellow light just before striking the plaintiff's car. The trial court held that the plaintiff was barred from recovery by her own contributory negligence.]

SULLIVAN, J. In this case we address the grave and recurrent question whether we should judicially declare no longer applicable in California courts the doctrine of contributory negligence, which bars all recovery when the plaintiff's negligent conduct has contributed as a legal cause in any degree to the harm suffered by him, and hold that it must give way to a system of comparative negligence, which assesses liability in direct proportion to fault. As we explain in detail infra, we conclude that we should. In the course of reaching our ultimate decision we conclude that: (1) The doctrine of comparative negligence is preferable to the "all-or-nothing" doctrine of contributory negligence from the point of view of logic, practical experience, and fundamental justice; (2) judicial action in this area is not precluded by the presence of section 1714 of the Civil Code, which has been said to "codify" the "all-or-nothing" rule and to render it immune from attack in the courts except on constitutional grounds; (3) given the possibility of judicial action, certain practical difficulties attendant upon the adoption of comparative negligence should not dissuade us from charting a new course—leaving the resolution of some of these problems to future judicial or legislative action; (4) the doctrine of comparative negligence should be applied in this state in its so-called "pure" form under which the assessment of liability in proportion to fault proceeds in spite of the fact that the plaintiff is equally at fault as or more at fault than the defendant and finally; (5) this new rule should be given a limited retrospective application.

I

[The court then notes that the once dominant common law rule treated contributory negligence as an absolute defense subject to a limited last clear chance exception.]

It is unnecessary for us to catalogue the enormous amount of critical comment that has been directed over the years against the "all-or-nothing" approach of the doctrine of contributory negligence. The essence of that criticism has been constant and clear: the doctrine is inequitable in its operation because it fails to distribute responsibility in proportion to fault. Against this have been raised several arguments in justification, but none have proved even remotely adequate to the task [quoting Prosser's 1953 article]. The basic objection to the doctrine—grounded in the primal concept that in a system in which liability is based on fault, the extent of fault should govern the extent of liability—remains irresistible to reason and all intelligent notions of fairness.

Furthermore, practical experience with the application by juries of the doctrine of contributory negligence has added its weight to analyses of its inherent shortcomings: "Every trial lawyer is well aware that juries often do in fact allow recovery in cases of contributory negligence, and that the compromise in the jury room does result in some diminution of the damages because of the plaintiff's fault. But the process is at best a haphazard and most unsatisfactory one." (Prosser, Comparative Negligence.) . . . It is manifest that this state of affairs, viewed from the standpoint of the health and vitality of the legal process, can only detract from public confidence in the ability of law and legal institutions to assign liability on a just and consistent basis. . . .

It is in view of these theoretical and practical considerations that to this date 25 states, have abrogated the "all-or-nothing" rule of contributory negligence and have enacted in its place general apportionment statutes calculated in one manner or another to assess liability in proportion to fault. In 1973 these states were joined by Florida, which effected the same result by judicial decision. (Hoffman v. Jones (Fla. 1973) 280 So. 2d 431.) We are likewise persuaded that logic, practical experience, and fundamental justice counsel against the retention of the doctrine rendering contributory negligence a complete bar to recovery—and that it should be replaced in this state by a system under which liability for damage will be borne by those whose negligence caused it in direct proportion to their respective fault. . . .[6a]

II

It is urged that any change in the law of contributory negligence must be made by the Legislature, not by this court. Although the doctrine of contributory negligence is of judicial origin—its genesis being traditionally attributed to the opinion of Lord Ellenborough in Butterfield v. Forrester (K.B. 1809) 103 Eng. Rep. 926—the enactment of section 1714 of the Civil Code in 1872 codified the

---

6a. In employing the generic term "fault" throughout this opinion we follow a usage common to the literature on the subject of comparative negligence. In all cases, however, we intend the term to import nothing more than "negligence" in the accepted legal sense. [Footnote 6a did not appear in the original advance sheets. There, the court stated a comparative negligence test that would allocate liability "in direct proportion to the extent of the parties' causal responsibility." 119 Cal. Rptr. 858 (1975), advance sheets only.—Eds.]

doctrine as it stood at that date and, the argument continues, rendered it invulnerable to attack in the courts except on constitutional grounds.

[The court then exhaustively examined section 1714 of the California Civil Code, which provides: "Everyone is responsible, not only for the result of his willful acts, but also for an injury occasioned to another by his want of ordinary care or skill in the management of his property or person, except so far as the latter has, willfully or by want of ordinary care, brought the injury upon himself. The extent of liability in such cases is defined by the Title on Compensatory Relief." The court concluded that "it was not the intention of the Legislature in enacting section 1714 of the Civil Code, as well as other sections of that code declarative of the common law, to insulate the matters therein expressed from further judicial development; rather it was the intention of the Legislature to announce and formulate existing common law principles and definitions for purposes of orderly and concise presentation and with a distinct view toward continuing judicial evolution."]

III

We are thus brought to the second group of arguments which have been advanced by defendants and the amici curiae supporting their position. Generally speaking, such arguments expose considerations of a practical nature which, it is urged, counsel against the adoption of a rule of comparative negligence in this state even if such adoption is possible by judicial means.

The most serious of these considerations are those attendant upon the administration of a rule of comparative negligence in cases involving multiple parties. One such problem may arise when all responsible parties are not brought before the court: it may be difficult for the jury to evaluate relative negligence in such circumstances, and to compound this difficulty such an evaluation would not be res judicata in a subsequent suit against the absent wrongdoer. Problems of contribution and indemnity among joint tortfeasors lurk in the background.

A second and related major area of concern involves the administration of the actual process of fact-finding in a comparative negligence system. The assigning of a specific percentage factor to the amount of negligence attributable to a particular party, while in theory a matter of little difficulty, can become a matter of perplexity in the face of hard facts.

The temptation for the jury to resort to a quotient verdict in such circumstances can be great. These inherent difficulties are not, however, insurmountable. Guidelines might be provided the jury which will assist it in keeping focussed upon the true inquiry and the utilization of special verdicts or jury interrogatories can be of invaluable assistance in assuring that the jury has approached its sensitive and often complex task with proper standards and appropriate reverence.

The third area of concern, the status of the doctrines of last clear chance and assumption of risk, involves less the practical problems of administering a particular form of comparative negligence than it does a definition of the theoretical outline of the specific form to be adopted. Although several states which apply comparative negligence concepts retain the last clear chance doctrine, the better reasoned position seems to be that when true comparative negligence is adopted, the need for last clear chance as a palliative of the hardships of the "all-or-nothing" rule disappears and its retention results only in a windfall to the plaintiff in direct contravention of the principle of liability in proportion to fault. As for assumption of risk, we have recognized in this state that this defense overlaps that of contributory negligence to some extent and in fact is made up of at least two distinct defenses. "To simplify greatly, it has been observed . . . that in one kind of situation, to wit, where a plaintiff unreasonably undertakes to encounter a specific known risk imposed by a defendant's negligence, plaintiff's conduct, although he may encounter that risk in a prudent manner, is in reality a form of contributory negligence. . . . Other kinds of situations within the doctrine of assumption of risk are those, for example, where plaintiff is held to agree to relieve defendant of an obligation of reasonable conduct toward him. Such a situation would not involve contributory negligence but rather a reduction of defendant's duty of care." We think it clear that the adoption of a system of comparative negligence should entail the merger of the defense of assumption of risk into the general scheme of assessment of liability in proportion to fault in those particular cases in which the form of assumption of risk involved is no more than a variant of contributory negligence.

Finally there is the problem of the treatment of willful misconduct under a system of comparative negligence. In jurisdictions following the "all-or-nothing" rule, contributory negligence is no defense to an action based upon a claim of willful misconduct (see Rest. 2d Torts, §503), and this is the present rule in California.[19] As Dean Prosser has observed, "[this] is in reality a rule of comparative fault which is being applied, and the court is refusing to set up the lesser fault against the greater." (Prosser, Torts, *supra* 426, at §65.) The thought is that the difference between willful and wanton misconduct and ordinary negligence is one of kind rather than degree in that the former involves conduct of an entirely different order,[20] and under this conception it might well be urged that comparative negligence concepts should have no application when one of the parties has been guilty of willful and wanton misconduct. It has been persuasively argued, however, that the loss of deterrent effect that would occur upon application of comparative fault concepts to willful and wanton misconduct as well as ordinary negligence would be slight, and that a comprehensive system of comparative

---

19. BAJI No. 3.52 (1971 re-revision) currently provides: "Contributory negligence of a plaintiff is not a bar to his recovery for an injury caused by the wilful or wanton misconduct of a defendant. (¶) Wilful or wanton misconduct is intentional wrongful conduct, done either with knowledge, express or implied, that serious injury to another will probably result, or with a wanton and reckless disregard of the possible results. An intent to injure is not a necessary element of wilful or wanton misconduct. (¶) To prove such misconduct it is not necessary to establish that defendant himself recognized his conduct as dangerous. It is sufficient if it be established that a reasonable man under the same or similar circumstances would be aware of the dangerous character of such conduct."

20. "Disallowing the contributory negligence defense in this context is different from last clear chance; the defense is denied not because defendant had the last opportunity to avoid the accident but rather because defendant's conduct was so culpable it was different in 'kind' from the plaintiff's. The basis is culpability rather than causation." (Schwartz, *supra*, §5.1, p. 100; fn. omitted.)

negligence should allow for the apportionment of damages in all cases involving misconduct which falls short of being intentional. The law of punitive damages remains a separate consideration. . . .

The existence of the foregoing areas of difficulty and uncertainty has not diminished our conviction that the time for a revision of the means for dealing with contributory fault in this state is long past due and that it lies within the province of this court to initiate the needed change by our decision in this case. Two of the indicated areas (i.e., multiple parties and willful misconduct) are not involved in the case before us, and we consider it neither necessary nor wise to address ourselves to specific problems of this nature which might be expected to arise. . . .

Our decision in this case is to be viewed as a first step in what we deem to be a proper and just direction, not as a compendium containing the answers to all questions that may be expected to arise. Pending future judicial or legislative developments, we are content for the present to assume the position taken by the Florida court in this matter: "We feel the trial judges of this State are capable of applying [a] comparative negligence rule without our setting guidelines in anticipation of expected problems. The problems are more appropriately resolved at the trial level in a practical manner instead of a theoretical solution at the appellate level. The trial judges are granted broad discretion in adopting such procedures as may accomplish the objectives and purposes expressed in this opinion." (280 So. 2d at pp. 439-440.)

It remains to identify the precise form of comparative negligence which we now adopt for application in this state. Although there are many variants, only the two basic forms need be considered here. The first of these, the so-called "pure" form of comparative negligence, apportions liability in direct proportion to fault in all cases. This was the form adopted by the Supreme Court of Florida in Hoffman v. Jones, supra, and it applies by statute in Mississippi, Rhode Island, and Washington. Moreover it is the form favored by most scholars and commentators. The second basic form of comparative negligence, of which there are several variants, applies apportionment based on fault up to the point at which the plaintiff's negligence is equal to or greater than that of the defendant—when that point is reached, plaintiff is barred from recovery. Nineteen states have adopted this form or one of its variants by statute. The principal argument advanced in its favor is moral in nature: that it is not morally right to permit one more at fault in an accident to recover from one less at fault. Other arguments assert the probability of increased insurance, administrative, and judicial costs if a "pure" rather than a "50 percent" system is adopted, but this has been seriously questioned.

We have concluded that the "pure" form of comparative negligence is that which should be adopted in this state. In our view the "50 percent" system simply shifts the lottery aspect of the contributory negligence rule to a different ground. As Dean Prosser has noted, under such a system "[i]t is obvious that a slight difference in the proportionate fault may permit a recovery and there has been much justified criticism of a rule under which a plaintiff who is charged with 49 percent of the total negligence recovers 51 percent of his damages, while one who is charged with 50 percent recovers nothing at all."[22] (Prosser, Comparative Negligence.) In effect "such a rule distorts the very principle it recognizes, i.e., that persons are responsible for their acts to the extent their fault contributes to an injurious result. The partial rule simply lowers, but does not eliminate, the bar of contributory negligence."

We also consider significant the experience of the State of Wisconsin, which until recently was considered the leading exponent of the "50 percent" system. There that system led to numerous appeals on the narrow but crucial issue whether plaintiff's negligence was equal to defendant's. Numerous reversals have resulted on this point, leading to the development of arcane classifications of negligence according to quality and category. (See cases cited in Vincent v. Pabst Brewing Co., 177 N.W.2d 513, at 513 [(Wis. 1970)] (dissenting opn.).) . . .

[The court then held its rule should apply in all cases in which the trial had not yet begun. It noted that there was some unfairness in denying the benefits of the comparative negligence rule to other plaintiffs who had sought to raise the issue on appeal while granting them to Nga Li, but justified its result for creating a good incentive in future cases for parties to "raise issues involving renovation of unsound or outmoded legal doctrines." The judgment was reversed. Mosk, J., concurring and dissenting, took exception to that portion of the opinion that held the rule of comparative negligence should apply to all cases in which the trial had not yet begun. Clark, J. (with McComb, J., concurring), dissented on the ground that section 1714 of the Civil Code codified the common law rule on contributory negligence, which could only be displaced by other legislation.]

NOTES

1. Historical origins of the comparative negligence system.   Although comparative negligence has met with widespread favor only since the late 1960s, Georgia enacted a comparative negligence statute as early as 1855; Mississippi adopted pure comparative negligence in 1910; and Wisconsin introduced comparative negligence by legislation in 1931. From its humble roots, comparative negligence has become a veritable giant. As recently as 1968, only five states had adopted some form of comparative negligence by statute. Then the dam broke. Between 1969 and 1973, 19 additional states adopted some form of comparative negligence by legislation so that by the time Hoffman v. Jones and *Li* were decided, the common law rule had been abandoned in about half the states. Today, virtually all states have some form of comparative negligence, usually by legislation and occasionally by judicial decision. Indeed, the only jurisdictions not to have some form of the doctrine are Alabama, District of Columbia, Maryland, North Carolina, and

---

22.   This problem is compounded when the injurious result is produced by the combined negligence of several parties. For example in a three-car collision a plaintiff whose negligence amounts to one-third or more recovers nothing; in a four-car collision the plaintiff is barred if his negligence is only one-quarter of the total. [The original 1931 Wisconsin comparative negligence statute contained the words "not as great as" instead of the current words "not greater than." — Eds.]

Virginia. For detailed tallies, see Schwartz, Comparative Negligence, Appendix A (5th ed. 2010); Woods & Deere, Comparative Fault, Appendix (3d ed. 1996 & Supp. 2007).

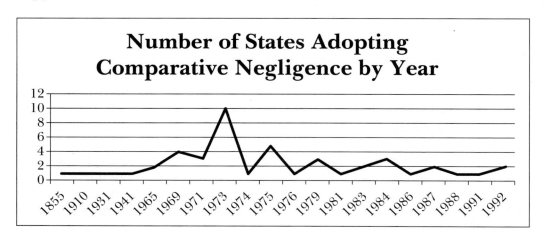

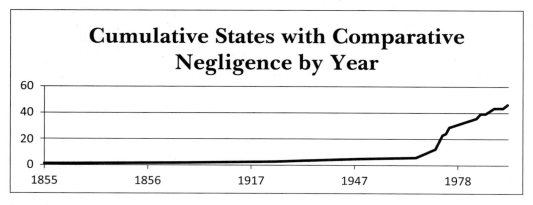

Source: Schwartz & Rowe, Comparative Negligence, Appendix A (5th ed. 2012); data table available from Sam Schoenburg

Table based on following data of when states adopted comparative negligence:

Year	Adopt	Cumulative
1855	1	1
1910	1	2
1931	1	3
1941	1	4
1965	2	6
1969	4	10
1971	3	13
1973	10	23
1974	1	24
1975	5	29

Year	Adopt	Cumulative
1976	1	30
1979	3	33
1981	1	34
1983	2	36
1984	3	39
1986	1	40
1987	2	42
1988	1	43
1991	1	44
1992	2	46

For a comment on *Li*, see Fleming, Foreword: Comparative Negligence at Last—by Judicial Choice, 64 Cal. L. Rev. 239 (1976).

2. Doctrinal complications—revisited. The rise of comparative negligence has forced courts to revisit many of the legal issues that arose when contributory negligence and assumption of risks were absolute defenses. What follows is a sampler of reactions to those problems.

a. Last clear chance. An overwhelming majority of cases have followed *Li*'s lead in jettisoning the separate last clear chance doctrine. In Spahn v. Town of Port Royal, 499 S.E.2d 205, 208 (S.C. 1998), the South Carolina Supreme Court, an early holdout, joined the parade, finding that the critical "authorities are persuasive that the rationalization for last clear chance as a matter of proximate cause is simply unnecessary where the jury may compare the parties' negligence." See generally Calabresi & Cooper, New Directions in Tort Law, 30 Val. U. L. Rev. 859, 872 (1996) ("The doctrine of last clear chance, which ameliorated the harshness of the all-or-nothing contributory negligence rule, typically disappears under comparative negligence."). In apportioning damages, should the jury be instructed to attach greater weight to defendant's conduct when he has had the last clear chance?

b. Assumption of risk. The traditional distinction, endorsed in *Li*, between primary and secondary assumption of risk has held fast. In Knight v. Jewett, 834 P.2d 696 (Cal. 1992), the plaintiff broke her little finger in a casual coed game of touch football after she had cautioned the defendant "not to play so rough," and threatened to quit the game. On the next play, the defendant leaped to intercept a pass; he touched the ball, came down on the plaintiff's back, and fell on the plaintiff's hand, breaking her little finger. The trial judge granted the defendant's motion for summary judgment on the ground that "reasonable implied assumption of risk" continues to operate after *Li*. In upholding that ruling, George, J., treated this case as one of primary assumption of risk because the defendant owed the plaintiff only a duty to avoid reckless misbehavior, but was at most guilty of ordinary negligence, effectively cutting out the plaintiff's cause of action.

Kennard, J., dissented on the ground that the categorical rule should not apply. In her view, it is important to determine assumption of risk on an individual basis. "To establish the defense a defendant must prove that the plaintiff voluntarily accepted a risk with knowledge and appreciation of that risk." One possible way to reconcile the two opinions is to hold that the recklessness rule constitutes the basic default position, which can be displaced if a defendant agreed to observe some higher standard of care in the individual case. Did that displacement of the basic norm take place in *Knight*?

A similar development took place in New York, in Morgan v. State, 685 N.E.2d 202, 208 (N.Y. 1997). The plaintiffs in this consolidated action challenged the application of *Murphy* under the comparative negligence regime. Bellacosa, J., rejected that invitation, noting that assumption of risk in its primary "no duty" sense survived the advent of comparative negligence, subject to the usual caveat that "an undue interposition of the assumption of risk doctrine is that participants will not be deemed to have assumed the risks of reckless or intentional conduct or concealed or unreasonably increased risks."

c. Intentional torts.   In Morgan v. Johnson, 976 P.2d 619 (Wash. 1999), the plaintiff and the defendant, never married, had a child some years before, and resumed a stormy and complex relationship after their daughter, who had lived with her mother, became curious about her biological father. One evening, both the plaintiff and the defendant left a bar together while drunk. It appeared that the defendant had threatened the plaintiff with a knife, dragged her to the car, and beat her with the interior rearview mirror. The court rejected the defendant's argument that the plaintiff's intoxication should be a defense to an intentional tort, noting that the term "fault" under Wash. Rev. Code §4.22.015 (West 2015) covered all acts or omissions that were negligent or reckless, or that were the subject of a strict liability or product liability claim. "The statute does not mention intentional torts. Our prior cases interpreting the statute confirm this omission was intentional. . . . The definition is intended to encompass all degrees of fault in tort actions short of intentionally caused harm."

In Blazovic v. Andrich, 590 A.2d 222, 231 (N.J. 1991), a case arising out of a barroom brawl, the court deviated from the majority view, stating:

> [W]e reject the concept that intentional conduct is "different in kind" from both negligence and wanton and willful conduct, and consequently cannot be compared with them. Instead, we view intentional wrongdoing as "different in degree" from either negligence or wanton and willful conduct. To act intentionally involves knowingly or purposefully engaging in conduct "substantially certain" to result in injury to another. In contrast, wanton and willful conduct poses a highly unreasonable risk of harm likely to result in injury. Neither that difference nor the divergence between intentional conduct and negligence precludes comparison by a jury. The different levels of culpability inherent in each type of conduct will merely be reflected in the jury's apportionment of fault. By viewing the various types of tortious conduct in that way, we adhere most closely to the guiding principle of comparative fault — to distribute the loss in proportion to the respective faults of the parties causing that loss.

The court then reduced plaintiff's recovery against the owner of a bar to reflect the intentional wrongs of its patrons who had previously settled with the plaintiff.

d. Violation of safety act.   In Hardy v. Monsanto Enviro-Chem Systems, Inc., 323 N.W.2d 270, 273, 274 (Mich. 1982), the court relied on the advent of Michigan's comparative negligence scheme to reject its earlier view, in Funk v. General Motors Corp., 220 N.W.2d 641 (Mich. 1974), that refused to treat the plaintiff's violation of a safety act as a form of contributory negligence. *Hardy* held:

Since the defense of comparative negligence serves not to undermine but to enhance safety in the workplace, we are of the view that comparative negligence is available in those cases where *Funk* . . . formerly prohibited the application of the contributory negligence defense. . . .

[A]t some point a worker must be charged with *some* responsibility for his own safety-related behavior. If a worker continues to work under extremely unsafe conditions when a reasonable worker under all the facts and circumstances would "take a walk," the trier of fact might appropriately reduce the plaintiff's recovery under comparative negligence. Comparative negligence enhances the goal of safety in the workplace under these conditions since it gives the worker some financial incentive to act in a reasonable and prudent fashion.

e. Seat belt defense.   In Amend v. Bell, 570 P.2d 138 (Wash. 1977), the Washington Supreme Court held that Derheim v. Fiorito, *supra* at 292, rejecting the seat belt defense, remained good law even under the state's pure comparative negligence rule. In the absence of a statutory requirement, the court did not want to enmesh itself in "a veritable battle of experts" over the nature and effects of the seat belt defense. That result was codified by statute, Wash. Rev. Code §46.61.688(6) (2015), enacted in 1986.

f. Imputed negligence.   In LaBier v. Pelletier, 665 A.2d 1013 (Me. 1995), a car struck a four-year-old child while his mother talked to a neighbor. The trial court instructed the jury to return a verdict for the plaintiffs only if the combined causative negligence of the child and his mother was less than that of the defendant. The Maine Supreme Court, finding these instructions erroneous, set aside the jury's verdict in favor of the defendant and remanded for a new trial. The court adopted the Restatement (Second) of Torts §488, which provides that "[a] child who suffers physical harm is not barred from recovery by the negligence of his parent, either in the parent's custody of the child or otherwise."

Other states have rejected imputed parental (and spousal) negligence by statute. Wash. Rev. Code §4.22.020 (West 2015) provides:

> The contributory fault of one spouse . . . shall not be imputed to the other spouse . . . or the minor child of the spouse . . . to diminish recovery in an action by the other spouse . . . or the minor child of the spouse . . . , or his or her legal representative, to recover damages caused by fault resulting in death or in injury to the person or property, whether separate or community, of the spouse. . . . In an action brought for wrongful death or loss of consortium, the contributory fault of the decedent or injured person shall be imputed to the claimant in that action.

3. Comparative negligence in admiralty.   Traditionally courts of admiralty apportioned damages under a rule of "divided damages," whereby an equal division of property damage was required whenever two ships were guilty of negligence, no matter what their relative degrees of fault. See The Schooner Catharine v.

Dickinson, 58 U.S. 170 (1854). In United States v. Reliable Transfer Co., 421 U.S. 397, 405, 411 (1975), the plaintiff's tanker, the *Mary A. Whalen* (which, as the last of its kind, is docked at Red Hook, Brooklyn), crashed into the rocks after the captain attempted dangerous turning maneuvers that failed in part because the Coast Guard had failed to maintain its breakwater lights. "The District Court found that the vessel's grounding was caused 25% by the failure of the Coast Guard to maintain the breakwater light and 75% by the fault of the Whalen," but owing to the admiralty rules, divided damages equally. A unanimous Supreme Court jettisoned the rule of divided damages in favor of the pure form of comparative negligence less than two months before Li v. Yellow Cab. Justice Stewart wrote:

> An equal division of damages is a reasonably satisfactory result only where each vessel's fault is approximately equal and each vessel thus assumes a share of the collision damages in proportion to its share of the blame, or where proportionate degrees of fault cannot be measured and determined on a rational basis. The rule produces palpably unfair results in every other case. For example, where one ship's fault in causing a collision is relatively slight and her damages small, and where the second ship is grossly negligent and suffers extensive damage, the first ship must still make a substantial payment to the second. "This result hardly commends itself to the sense of justice any more appealingly than does the common law doctrine of contributory negligence. . . ." G. Gilmore & C. Black, The Law of Admiralty 528 (2d ed. 1975). . . .

Reliable Transfer brought the admiralty rules in United States courts into conformity with those applied by all other leading maritime nations. See the Maritime Conventions Act, 1 & 2 Geo. V., c. 57 (1911), and the comparative negligence rules applicable in personal injury actions under the Jones Act, 46 U.S.C. §30104 (2012).

4. *"Impure" comparative negligence by judicial action.*   In Bradley v. Appalachian Power Co., 256 S.E.2d 879, 885 (W. Va. 1979), the West Virginia Supreme Court adopted comparative negligence by judicial action, but declined to follow *Li* in its choice of the pure form.

> We do not accept the major premise of pure comparative negligence that a party should recover his damages regardless of his fault, so long as his fault is not 100 percent. Without embarking on an extended philosophical discussion of the nature and purpose of our legal system, we do state that in the field of tort law we are not willing to abandon the concept that where a party substantially contributes to his own damages, he should not be permitted to recover for any part of them. We do recognize that the present rule that prohibits recovery to the plaintiff if he is at fault in the slightest degree is manifestly unfair, and in effect rewards the substantially negligent defendant by permitting him to escape any responsibility for his negligence.
>
>   Our present judicial rule of contributory negligence is therefore modified to provide that a party is not barred from recovering damages in a tort action so long

as his negligence or fault does not equal or exceed the combined negligence or fault of the other parties involved in the accident.

Note that this rule creates a huge discontinuity as the plaintiff who is 49 percent negligent recovers 51 percent of the injury but the one who is 51 percent negligent recovers nothing. Matters are even more strained because on matters this imprecise juries can pick as their focal point a 50/50 split, which could go either way under this rule. Note that under pure comparative negligence, the 49 percent versus 51 percent yields only a 2 percent difference, and the focal 50 percent division just calls for dividing the losses equally. Nonetheless, the impure rule has gained traction. As of 2015, 32 states have adopted some version of the 50-percent rule, compared to only 13 states having adopted the pure comparative approach, which is approved in RTT:AL §7. Does the *Bradley* rule encourage the plaintiff to join as many parties to the suit as possible? What should be done if, for example, a landlord and tenant are joined in a suit arising out of a single incident on common property?

5. *Economic analysis of comparative negligence.* The efficiency analysis of comparative negligence has been, on balance, somewhat more tentative than the fairness arguments made in its favor. Once again, the issue is how to coordinate the behavior of two parties, each of whom will vary the level of care provided as a function of the level of care provided by the other side. At one level, therefore, the familiar paradox of the Hand formula reasserts itself in this context. When both parties and the court all possess full information, neither party, if fully rational, will behave negligently. Suppose that the expected loss is $100, and the optimal levels of joint precautions are $30 by the plaintiff and $40 by the defendant. If comparative negligence were to leave the plaintiff with 20 percent of the expected loss, it might appear that she would not take the precaution, because her cost of avoidance ($30) is greater than her residual loss ($20). Nonetheless, this analysis is incomplete, because it ignores the response of the defendant who will prefer to spend $40 on precaution to avoid $80 worth of loss. Yet once that step is taken, the plaintiff may now prefer to take precautions as well, for the $30 spent could avoid a $100 loss that might otherwise occur.

This stylized account is highly sensitive to its initial assumptions. If the defendant thought he would have to spend $50 to avoid a 40 percent chance of a $100 loss, he would not take precautions and thus would be held negligent. But if the plaintiff knew or had reason to believe that the defendant would make this blunder, then her informed decision would not be to take care because the $30 precaution is now more expensive than the $20 in unrecoverable losses. On the other hand, if the precautions taken by the two parties are independent, the defendant's unilateral action could reduce the risk of loss to the point where it no longer makes sense from an economic point of view to make these adjustments.

See Posner, Economic Analysis of Law 198-202 (9th ed. 2014). See also Shavell, An Economic Analysis of Accident Law 15-16 (1987); Haddock & Curran, An

Economic Theory of Comparative Negligence, 14 J. Legal Stud. 49 (1985); Cooter & Ulen, An Economic Case for Comparative Negligence, 61 N.Y.U. L. Rev. 1067 (1986).

The analysis, however, is still more rarified because neither party knows whether both parties will be at fault if an accident occurs when they are deciding on acting. Both also face the possibility of injuring only themselves, or being involved in accidents in which only one party is negligent. Nor do the parties have any reliable information on the relation between the dollar cost of precautions and expected damages when making their initial decisions. Worse still, virtually no one knows what legal regime applies in any state. (The differential incentive effects of the various rules are virtually impossible to plot out, in light of practical concerns, such as (a) the risk that the defendant will be insolvent, (b) the possibility of jury error, (c) the payment of contingent fees and other expenses of suit, (d) the lower standard for contributory negligence, (e) the role of fines and other sanctions in influencing behavior, and (f) the internal difficulties of the Hand formula.) See generally Schwartz, Contributory and Comparative Negligence: A Reappraisal, 87 Yale L.J. 697 (1978).

How would the analysis be altered under the old admiralty rule of even division? Under the 50 percent negligence threshold, as in Wisconsin and West Virginia?

2.   By Legislation

As the decision of the California Supreme Court in Li v. Yellow Cab points out, since 1970 there has been a massive legislative move toward comparative negligence. A representative sample of the possible forms of comparative negligence legislation is given below. For a full collection of the statutes, see Schwartz, Comparative Negligence, Appendix B (5th ed. 2010). Woods & Deere, Comparative Fault, Appendix (3d ed. 1996 & Supp. 2007). A sampler follows.

Federal Employers' Liability Act
35 Stat. 66 (1908), 45 U.S.C. §53 (2012)

§53. That in all actions hereafter brought against any such common carrier or railroad under or by virtue of any of the provisions of this Act to recover damages for personal injuries to an employee, or where such injuries have resulted in his death, the fact that the employee may have been guilty of contributory negligence shall not bar a recovery, but the damages shall be diminished by the jury in proportion to the amount of negligence attributable to such employee: Provided, that no such employee who may be injured or killed shall be held to have been guilty of contributory negligence in any case where the violation by such common carrier of any statute enacted for the safety of employees contributed to the injury or death of such employee.

New York

N.Y. Civil Practice Law and Rules §§1411-1412 (McKinney 2015)

§1411. In any action to recover damages for personal injury, injury to property, or wrongful death, the culpable conduct attributable to the claimant or to the decedent, including contributory negligence or assumption of risk, shall not bar recovery, but the amount of damages otherwise recoverable shall be diminished in the proportion which the culpable conduct attributable to the claimant or decedent bears to the culpable conduct which caused the damages.

§1412. Culpable conduct claimed in diminution of damages, in accordance with section fourteen hundred eleven, shall be an affirmative defense to be pleaded and proved by the party asserting the defense.

Pennsylvania

42 Pa. Cons. Stat. Ann. §7102 (Purdon 2015)

(a) General rule. In all actions brought to recover damages for negligence resulting in death or injury to person or property, the fact that the plaintiff may have been guilty of contributory negligence shall not bar a recovery by the plaintiff or his legal representative where such negligence was not greater than the causal negligence of the defendant or defendants against whom recovery is sought, but any damages sustained by the plaintiff shall be diminished in proportion to the amount of negligence attributed to the plaintiff.

(b) Recovery against joint defendant; contribution. Where recovery is allowed against more than one defendant, each defendant shall be liable for that proportion of the total dollar amount awarded as damages in the ratio of the amount of his causal negligence to the amount of causal negligence attributed to all defendants against whom recovery is allowed. The plaintiff may recover the full amount of the allowed recovery from any defendant against whom the plaintiff is not barred from recovery. Any defendant who is so compelled to pay more than his percentage share may seek contribution.

(c) Downhill skiing.

(1) The General Assembly finds that the sport of downhill skiing is practiced by a large number of citizens of this Commonwealth and also attracts to this Commonwealth large numbers of nonresidents significantly contributing to the economy of this Commonwealth. It is recognized that as in some other sports, there are inherent risks in the sport of downhill skiing.

(2) The doctrine of voluntary assumption of risk as it applies to downhill skiing injuries and damages is not modified by subsections (a) and (b).

Wisconsin

Wis. Stat. Ann. §895.045 (West 2015)

§895.045. Contributory negligence shall not bar recovery in an action by any person or his legal representative to recover damages for negligence resulting in death or in injury to person or property, if that negligence was not greater than the negligence of the person against whom recovery is sought, but any damages allowed shall be diminished in the proportion to the amount of negligence attributable to the person recovering. The negligence of the plaintiff shall be measured separately against the negligence of each person found to be causally negligent. The liability of each person found to be causally negligent whose percentage of causal negligence is less than 51% is limited to the percentage of the total causal negligence attributed to that person. A person found to be causally negligent whose percentage of causal negligence is 51% or more shall be jointly and severally liable for the damages allowed.*

> ### Restatement (Third) of Torts: Apportionment of Liability
>
> #### §7. EFFECT OF PLAINTIFF'S NEGLIGENCE WHEN PLAINTIFF SUFFERS AN INDIVISIBLE INJURY
>
> Plaintiff's negligence (or the negligence of another person for whose negligence the plaintiff is responsible) that is a legal cause of an indivisible injury to the plaintiff reduces the plaintiff's recovery in proportion to the share of responsibility the factfinder assigns to the plaintiff (or other person for whose negligence the plaintiff is responsible).

NOTES

1. PROBLEM: Computational exercises. In examining the respective merits of the principal comparative negligence systems, see how they apply to the following hypothetical five situations, assuming that the negligence of each of the parties contributed causally to the total damage sustained. Does a comparison of the particular numerical results suggest any reason to prefer one system to another?

I. *A*, who is 10 percent negligent, suffers $10,000 damages; *B*, who is 90 percent negligent, suffers no damage.

II. *A*, who is 60 percent negligent, suffers $10,000 damages; *B*, who is 40 percent negligent, suffers no damage.

III. *A*, who is 30 percent negligent, suffers $2,000 damages; *B*, who is 70 percent negligent, suffers $8,000 damages.

IV. *A*, who is approximately 50 percent negligent, suffers $2,000 damages; *B*, who is approximately 50 percent negligent, suffers $8,000 damages.

V. *A* and *B* are equally negligent; *A* suffers $10,000 damages, while *B* suffers no damage.

---

* The original 1931 Wisconsin comparative negligence statute contained the words "not as great as" instead of the current words "not greater than." —Eds.

2. Comparative negligence and the control of juries.   Special verdicts play an important role in administering a comparative negligence system given that the plaintiff's final damages award depends upon both the extent of her total damages and her degree of negligence. A verdict that states only a dollar figure for the plaintiff's award becomes difficult to interpret after trial. An award of $60,000 to a plaintiff who suffered $150,000 damages could be attacked as inadequate if a finding of contributory negligence totally bars the plaintiff's recovery, since the jury has no valid reason for awarding only partial compensation. Under pure comparative negligence, however, that verdict is consistent with a finding that the plaintiff was 60 percent negligent. General verdicts conceal a jury's thought processes from both the trial judge and the appellate court. Special verdicts promise greater judicial oversight.

Should courts require special verdicts on both the degree of negligence of each party and on the total amount of the plaintiff's? Or should special verdicts be ordered only at the request of either party or otherwise be left to the discretion of the court? Note that an Idaho statute allows any party to request the court to "direct the jury to find separate special verdicts determining the amount of damages and the percentage of negligence or comparative responsibility attributable to each party," after which the court makes the appropriate reduction in damages for the successful plaintiff. Idaho Code §6-802 (West 2015). The Idaho statute only allows recovery when the plaintiff's negligence "was not as great as the negligence, gross negligence or comparative responsibility of the person against whom recovery is sought." Idaho Code §6-801 (West 2015). Is there a greater need for the special verdict here or under pure comparative negligence?

3. Insurance complications.   One collateral complication under comparative negligence concerns the amount of damages that can be recovered when, as so often happens in routine collision cases, each party is a tortfeasor as well as an accident victim. When contributory negligence was an absolute bar, it was difficult, if not impossible, for both parties to obtain judgment, because if both were at fault, typically neither could recover. Accident cases, therefore, resulted in a single judgment against one defendant that was then discharged by the insurance carrier up to its policy limits. Today, comparative negligence makes it possible for each party to recover from the other. Thus assume that *A* has $100,000 in damages and was 25 percent responsible for her loss, while *B* has $200,000 in damages and was 75 percent responsible for his loss. If *A* alone were injured, she should recover $75,000 in damages from *B*. Likewise, if *B* alone were injured, he should be able to recover $50,000 in damages from *A*. In Jess v. Herrmann, 604 P.2d 208, 212 (Cal. 1979), the California Supreme Court had to decide whether, as the statute seemed to require, the two damage awards should be set off against each other, so that the insurer of *B* pays *A* $25,000, or whether, in the alternative, *A*'s insurer should pay *B* $50,000 and *B*'s insurer should pay *A* $75,000.

Tobriner, J., held that the statutory setoff was available only when the parties in question were not covered by insurance. In his view, the insurance function would not be well served if the application of the mandatory setoff rule were allowed to produce "the anomalous situation in which a liability insurer's responsibility under its policy depends as much on the extent of injury suffered by its own insured as on the amount of damages sustained by the person its insured has negligently injured." Manual, J., in dissent argued that the court misconstrued the applicable statutory language, and that it did not explain the way in which the rule was to operate in situations in which either or both parties had limited insurance coverage.

CHAPTER 5

CAUSATION

SECTION A. INTRODUCTION

This chapter examines the topic of causation, which, in one form or another, is an indispensable element in every tort case. Once the plaintiff has established that the defendant has engaged in some wrongful conduct, she must link that conduct to her harm. In practice, that requirement of causal linkage generally raises two distinct issues: cause in fact and proximate cause. For the distinction, see RTT:LPEH §26, comment *a*.

> *Restatement of the Law (Third) of Torts: Liability for Physical and Emotional Harm*
>
> ### §26. FACTUAL CAUSE
>
> Tortious conduct must be a factual cause of harm for liability to be imposed. Conduct is a factual cause of harm when the harm would not have occurred absent the conduct. . . .
>
> **Comment b. "But-for" standard for factual cause:** . . . With recognition that there are multiple factual causes of an event, see Comment c, a factual cause can also be described as a necessary condition for the outcome. . . .
>
> **Comment c. Tortious conduct need only be one of the factual causes of harm:** An actor's tortious conduct need only be *a* [as opposed to *the*] factual cause of the other's harm. . . .

The "cause in fact" rubric addresses the sequence of events that plaintiff claims links the two parties together. In the ordinary highway collision case, for example, the defendant will triumph on the cause in fact question if he can show that the plaintiff's injury occurred before the collision. The defendant did not cause (in fact) any of that preexisting harm; nor is the defendant responsible for any harm attributable to some independent event, such as another automobile or a natural event. A similar analysis carries over to far more complex causal chains, including those involving the drugs and chemicals whose ingestion or exposure may have brought about the plaintiff's disease or disability. In the modern setting, moreover, issues of cause in fact are no longer confined to the plaintiff's search for some discrete cause of a known and certain harm. Especially thorny issues arise when the plaintiff claims that the defendant's conduct only increased the risk of injury—the so-called lost chance of survival—for harms like cancer that are themselves compensable.

The factual causation inquiry is further complicated when multiple defendants may have contributed to a plaintiff's injury, so that it becomes necessary to apportion damages among them. One important variation on this theme arises when a plaintiff can establish that one of a group of defendants caused her harm, without knowing which one. Thus the law must develop rules to allocate causal responsibility when it is unclear which of a given group of manufacturers produced a fungible product that caused harm to one or more plaintiffs, none of whom can identify which defendant (if any of those joined in the action) manufactured or supplied the particular product that injured her.

The extensive discussion of factual causation sets up the second inquiry: what counts as a "proximate" cause of the harm. The Second Restatement substituted the bland term "legal cause" for proximate cause, but that verbal innovation has never been widely accepted, so the term "proximate cause" has been retained, RTT:LPEH §26, comment *a*, although with evident reluctance. Chapter 6 of the Third Restatement, entitled "Scope of Liability (Proximate Cause)," contains this notable caveat: "The Institute fervently hopes that the Restatement Fourth of Torts will not find the parenthetical necessary." Ironically, whatever one's views on the ingrained legal terminology, any literal reading of "proximate" as "nearest" misstates the function of the doctrine, which is to see whether more distant acts or events, in either time or space, create a prima facie case for liability. Here the issues are not factual but conceptual: Once the facts are laid out, for what harms is the defendant responsible when his own actions are combined, often in long and tortuous chains, with those of other persons and/or natural events?

The traditional account of proximate cause asks whether the defendant's conduct should be regarded as a "substantial factor" in bringing about the plaintiff's harm. But that terminology too is disfavored in the Third Restatement. See RTT:LPEH §26, comment *j*, which dismisses the phrase as "confusing" and sticks with the but-for or necessary condition accounts of causation. The phrase continues to be deployed nonetheless. See, e.g., Turcios v. DeBruler Co., 32 N.E.3d 1117 (Ill. 2015), in which the court approved the substantial factor test in connection with both negligence and intentional torts. No matter what the rubric, the much-ingrained substantial factor test asks whether any of the intervening or concurrent human actions or natural events sever the causal connection between the defendant's conduct and the plaintiff's injury. The analysis begins typically in negligence cases, but must also be adapted to the cases of strict liability. The same issues of causation also arise with the various no-fault systems considered in Chapter 10, *infra*.

Analytically the problem of proximate cause can be addressed in two distinct ways. The forward-looking approach asks whether the chain of events that in fact occurred was sufficiently "foreseeable," "natural" or "probable" for the defendant to be held liable for the ultimate harm. That judgment is made from the standpoint of the defendant *at the time* the tortious act was committed, and denies recovery for those harms that do not fall "within the risk." The approach has an obvious connection with the negligence standard of liability, which generally refuses to hold a defendant liable for improbable or unforeseeable acts. The second approach starts with the injury and works back toward the wrongful action of the defendant, seeking to determine whether any act of a third party or the plaintiff, or any natural event, severs the causal connection between the harm and the defendant's wrongful conduct. Here the question is only whether, when all the evidence is in, it is permissible to say that the defendant "did it," that is, brought about the plaintiff's harm. This approach dominated both Roman law and the early common law, and was used in strict liability and negligence cases. The interaction between the "foresight" and "directness" perspectives, as they are respectively called, is the subject of Section C of this chapter. These materials trace the historical evolution and permutation of the basic doctrine from its nineteenth-century origins to its contemporary applications. The first part of this section deals with physical injuries; the second with negligent infliction of emotional distress.

As a rough generalization, the cause in fact issues appear to have gained in importance relative to the proximate cause issues in the past generation. Why might this be so?

SECTION B. CAUSE IN FACT

1. The "But For" Test

New York Central R.R. v. Grimstad
264 F. 334 (2d Cir. 1920)

Action of Elfrieda Grimstad, administratrix of the estate of Angell Grimstad, deceased, against the New York Central Railroad Company. Judgment for plaintiff, and defendant brings error. Reversed.

WARD, C.J. This is an action under the Federal Employers' Liability Act (Comp. St. Sec. 8657-8665) to recover damages for the death of Angell Grimstad, captain of the covered barge *Grayton,* owned by the defendant railroad company. The charge of negligence is failure to equip the barge with proper life-preservers and other necessary and proper appliances, for want of which the decedent, having fallen into the water, was drowned.

The barge was lying on the port side of the steamer *Santa Clara,* on the north side of Pier 2, Erie Basin, Brooklyn, loaded with sugar in transit from Havana to St. John, N.B. The tug *Mary M,* entering the slip between Piers 1 and 2, bumped against the barge. The decedent's wife, feeling the shock, came out from the cabin, looked on one side of the barge, and saw nothing, and then went across the deck to the other side of the barge, and discovered her husband in the water about 10 feet from the barge holding up his hands out of the water. He did not know how to swim. She immediately ran back into the cabin for a small line, and when she returned with it he had disappeared.

It is admitted that the decedent at the time was engaged in interstate commerce. The court left it to the jury to say whether the defendant was negligent in not equipping the barge with life-preservers and whether, if there had been a life-preserver on board, Grimstad would have been saved from drowning.

The jury found as a fact that the defendant was negligent in not equipping the barge with life-preservers. Life-preservers and life belts are intended to be put on the body of a person before getting into the water, and would have been of no use at all to the decedent. On the other hand, life buoys are intended to be thrown to a person when in the water, and we will treat the charge in the complaint as covering life buoys.

Obviously the proximate cause of the decedent's death was his falling into the water, and in the absence of any testimony whatever on the point, we will assume that this happened without negligence on his part or on the part of the defendant. On the second question, whether a life buoy would have saved the decedent from drowning, we think the jury were left to pure conjecture and speculation. A jury might well conclude that a light near an open hatch or rail on the side of a vessel's deck would have prevented a person's falling into the hatch or into the water, in the dark. But there is nothing whatever to show that the decedent was not drowned because he did not know how to swim, nor anything to show that, if there had been a life buoy on board, the decedent's wife would have got it in time, that is, sooner than she got the small line, or, if she had, that she would have thrown it so that her husband could have seized it, or, if she did, that he would have seized it, or that, if he did, it would have prevented him from drowning.

The court erred in denying the defendant's motion to dismiss the complaint at the end of the case.

Judgment reversed.

NOTES

1. The life you save. In Ford v. Trident Fisheries Co., 122 N.E. 389, 390 (Mass. 1919), the decedent fell overboard from his shipping vessel and drowned. The plaintiff alleged that the defendant was negligent because its rescue boat was "lashed to the deck instead of being suspended from davits" from which it could be easily lowered. The court held that even if the defendants were negligent, "there is nothing to show they in any way contributed to Ford's death. He disappeared when he fell from the trawler, and it does not appear that if the boat had been suspended from davits and a different method of propelling it had been used he could have been rescued."

What is the precedential value of *Grimstad?* In Kirincich v. Standard Dredging Co., 112 F.2d 163, 164 (3d Cir. 1940), "the deceased fell off a dredge close to shore and was carried away by the falling tide while shipmates tried to save him with inadequate lifesaving equipment, such inadequacy of equipment being the negligence alleged." The trial judge had dismissed plaintiff's cause of action, but the Third Circuit reversed and remanded for trial. Clark, C.J., observed in part:

> In the light, then, of this logic and these examples, would Kirincich have drowned even if a larger and more buoyant object than the inch heaving line had been thrown within two feet of him? If he could swim, even badly, there would be no doubt. Assuming he could not, we think he might (the appropriate grammatical mood) have saved himself through the help of something which he could more easily grasp. We can take judicial notice of the instinct of self-preservation that at first compensates for lack of skill. A drowning man comes to the surface and clutches at what he finds there — hence the significance of size and buoyancy in life saving apparatus. In other words, we prefer the doctrine of Judge Learned Hand in the case of Zinnel v. United States Shipping Board Emergency Fleet Corp., 10 F.2d 47, 49 [(2d Cir. 1925)]: "There of course remains the question whether they might have also said that the fault caused the loss. About that we agree no certain conclusion was possible. Nobody could, in the nature of things, be sure that the intestate would have seized the rope, or, if he had not, that it would have stopped his body. But we are not dealing with a criminal case, nor are we justified, where certainty is impossible, in insisting upon it. . . . [W]e think it a question about which reasonable men might at least differ whether the intestate would not have been saved, had it been there," to that of his colleague, Judge Hough, dissenting in that case, and concurring in the earlier case of New York Central R. Co. v. Grimstad, 2 Cir., 264 F. 334, 335.

The modern cases explicitly give the jury broad powers of decision in cases of rescue at sea. In Reyes v. Vantage Steamship Co., 609 F.2d 140, 144 (5th Cir. 1980), the decedent, while drunk, jumped off his boat and tried to swim to a mooring buoy some several hundred feet away. Immediately after striking the water members of the crew saw that he was in mortal danger. The decedent struggled against a strong current only to drown, his energy spent, some 20 feet from the buoy. Since the ship was under a duty of maritime rescue, liability depended on showing the causal connection between the failed rescue and the decedent's drowning. Coast Guard regulations required a ship to have a rocket-powered line-throwing appliance capable of throwing at least 1,500 feet of line. The district court first denied relief. On appeal the court initially entered a judgment for the plaintiff, but on rehearing reversed and remanded for a jury finding on causation. "The District Court on remand must be prepared to determine whether there was time for a crew member to go to the hypothetical storage location, obtain the hypothetical line-throwing appliance, move it to the appropriate firing location, and fire the appliance—all before Reyes went limp in the water." The court also noted that the jury had to take into account "some possibility that a line or lines fired over or near Reyes might have harmed him or perhaps impeded his labored swimming," the likelihood that the line would have reached Reyes and, the chances he "would have obeyed an order" to take it. The court then refused to place "the difficult burden of proving causation on the widow of the deceased seaman." On remand, the district court entered a judgment for the plaintiff, finding that defendant's negligence was 15 percent of the cause of death. The Third Restatement endorses the hypothetical, or counterfactual approach, noting the serious factual difficulties in marginal cases where the defendant's deviation from the accepted standard of care is slight. RTT:LPEH §26, comment *e*.

2. *Slip-and-fall cases.*   Difficult questions of cause in fact are also raised in so-called slip-and-fall cases. In Reynolds v. Texas & Pacific Ry., 37 La. Ann. 694, 698 (1885), plaintiff, a 250-pound woman, after hurrying out of a lighted waiting room, fell down the unlighted steps leading to the train platform. The defendant argued that "she might well have made the mis-step and fallen even had it been broad daylight," but the court affirmed judgment for plaintiff, noting:

> We concede that this is possible, and recognize the distinction between post hoc and propter hoc. But where the negligence of the defendant greatly multiplies the chances of accident to the plaintiff, and is of a character naturally leading to its occurrence, the mere possibility that it might have happened without the negligence is not sufficient to break the chain of cause and effect between the negligence and the injury. Courts, in such matters, consider the natural and ordinary course of events, and do not indulge in fanciful suppositions. The whole tendency of the evidence connects the accident with the negligence.

3. *Products liability cases: Seatbelts.*   In Engberg v. Ford Motor Co., 205 N.W.2d 104, 106 (S.D. 1973), the plaintiff's husband was killed when he drove his station wagon, purchased two weeks earlier from the defendant, off the highway into a ditch. No other cars were involved in the accident, and the parties were unable to establish the precise sequence of events leading up to the decedent's death. The plaintiff supported her claim that the defendant's seatbelt was of insufficient strength to withstand the impact of a crash by introducing evidence that the belt was found "buckled but broken" after the fatal crash, and that no blood was found inside the car. Her expert witnesses further testified that

> the seat belt severed in this case because the boot and belt were rubbing on the frame of the seat causing them to give way under the pressure of less than expectable force. He also stated that in his opinion, the design of the assembly and the installation of the belt was improper to prevent the rubbing that caused the severance. He further testified, over the defendant's objection, that the absence of internal damage to the vehicle indicated that the fatal injury occurred outside of the car and that had the seat belt remained intact and the decedent remained inside the car, the amount of injury would have been minor.

[The defendant's expert witness in turn] testified that the boot and seat belt could not in any way come into contact with the frame of the seat. [He] also testified that based upon the type and location of the cut, it was his opinion that the seat belt had been severed by the metal capsule that ties together the wires of the seat and that the capsule had been moved from where it was originally installed by the manufacturer.

Additional evidence suggested that the decedent did not properly adjust his seat belt before the crash, leaving ample room for him to slip out under the belt when the crash took place.

The court held that the case was properly left for the jury because defendant could not show that plaintiff's version of the case was "contradicted by its undisputed physical facts," and it further rejected the defendant's contention that it was pure "speculation" to conclude that the decedent would have survived if the seat belt had remained intact. What additional facts need to be established in order for the defendant to be entitled to a directed verdict? For the plaintiff to be entitled to a directed verdict?

4. Products liability cases: Baseball.   In Sanchez v. Hillerich & Bradsby Co., 128 Cal. Rptr. 2d 529, 538-541 (Ct. App. 2002), the plaintiff, a pitcher for California State University, Northridge, was struck by a line-drive hit by Correa, a University of Southern California batter, using an aluminum Air Attack 2 bat, manufactured by the defendant. The bat contained "a pressurized air bladder which, according to its designer, substantially increases the speed at which the ball leaves the surface of the bat." The trial judge dismissed the case on the ground that "because the speed of the ball leaving the bat was never established, no causation attributed to the increased risk of use of the [bat] could be established." The Court of Appeal held that once the increased speed was established, the plaintiff's case should reach the jury: "[A]bsent other factors (none are suggested) it follows that the ball must have reached the appellant sooner than if Correa had used a bat other than the Air Attack 2. Dr. Kent [plaintiff's expert] opined that the ball which hit Correa was traveling at a speed of up to 107.8 miles per hour, giving appellant a reaction time of .32 and .37 seconds, below the acceptable minimum time recognized by the NCAA." Must it also be shown that the plaintiff pitcher could have reacted in time to avoid the injury had the batter been using another bat?

Sanchez was distinguished in Yeaman v. Hillerich & Bradsby Co., 570 Fed. Appx. 728, 737-741 (10th Cir. 2014), where the plaintiff, another star pitcher, was badly hurt when struck by a hit ball. Dr. Kent, the same plaintiff's expert as in *Sanchez*, estimated the ball was traveling at between 100 and 105 miles per hour when it struck the plaintiff. The plaintiff claimed that defendant's 33-inch, 30-ounce Louisville Slugger Exogrid bat, Model No. CB71X, was defective because its design featured a stiff handle and flexible barrel for "maximum trampoline effect" or "rebound." O'Brien, J., upheld the grant of a judgment for the defendant notwithstanding the jury verdict for the plaintiff: "[W]ithout any objective evidence as to the ball exit speed expected by the ordinary baseball bat consumer or the ball exit speed produced by the Exogrid, there was no basis for a rational jury to reasonably find the Exogrid to be dangerous beyond that expected by the ordinary bat consumer." The plaintiff's case failed on causation because Kent did not take into account the "numerous variables" that could have influenced the outcome, including "the speed and type of pitch and the ability and swing speed of the batter." The court distinguished *Sanchez* because there "the plaintiffs' evidence included the testimony of the bat's designer who said "the bat allowed a batter to hit balls at speeds in excess of that which would allow a pitcher sufficient time to react." Cannot the same argument be made in *Yeaman*? Should any bat approved for use in league games, in this instance, by National Federation of High Schools Athletic Association, ever be regarded as defective?

Zuchowicz v. United States
140 F.3d 381 (2d Cir. 1998)

CALABRESI, J. The defendant, the United States of America, appeals from a judgment of the United States District Court for the District of Connecticut (Warren W. Eginton, Judge). This suit under the Federal Tort Claims Act, 28 U.S.C. §§1346(b), 2671-2680, was originally filed by Patricia Zuchowicz, who claimed to have developed primary pulmonary hypertension, a fatal lung condition, as a result of the defendant's negligence in prescribing an overdose of the drug Danocrine. Following Mrs. Zuchowicz's death in 1991, her husband, Steven, continued the case on behalf of his wife's estate, claiming that the defendant was responsible for her death. After a bench trial, the district court awarded the plaintiff $1,034,236.02 in damages. . . .

I. BACKGROUND

A.   DRUG, ILLNESS, AND DEATH

1.   The Overdose

The facts, as determined by the district court, are as follows. On February 18, 1989, Mrs. Zuchowicz filled a prescription for the drug Danocrine at the Naval Hospital pharmacy in Groton, Connecticut. The prescription erroneously instructed her to take 1600 milligrams of Danocrine per day, or twice the maximum recommended dosage. The defendant has stipulated that its doctors and/or pharmacists were negligent and violated the prevailing standard of medical care by prescribing this wrong dosage.

Mrs. Zuchowicz took the 1600 milligrams of Danocrine each day for the next month. Thereafter, from March 24 until May 30, she took 800 milligrams per day. While taking Danocrine she experienced abnormal weight gain, bloating, edema, hot flashes, night sweats, a racing heart, chest pains, dizziness, headaches, acne, and fatigue. On May 30, she was examined by an obstetrician/gynecologist in private practice who told her to stop taking the Danocrine. During the summer, she continued to experience severe fatigue and chest tightness and pain, and began having shortness of breath. In October 1989, she was diagnosed with primary pulmonary hypertension ("PPH"), a rare and fatal disease in which increased pressure in an individual's pulmonary artery causes severe strain on the right side of the heart. At the time she was diagnosed with the disease, the median life expectancy for PPH sufferers was 2.5 years. Treatments included calcium channel blockers and heart and lung transplantation.

Mrs. Zuchowicz was on the waiting list for a lung transplant when she became pregnant. Pregnant women are not eligible for transplants, and pregnancy exacerbates PPH. Mrs. Zuchowicz gave birth to a son on November 21, 1991. She died one month later, on December 31, 1991. . . .

B. THE EXPERT TESTIMONY . . .

[Plaintiff's expert] Dr. Matthay testified that he was confident to a reasonable medical certainty that the Danocrine caused Mrs. Zuchowicz's PPH. When pressed, he added that he believed the *overdose* of Danocrine to have been responsible for the disease. His conclusion was based on the temporal relationship between the overdose and the start of the disease and the differential etiology method of excluding other possible causes. While Dr. Matthay did not rule out *all* other possible causes of pulmonary hypertension, he did exclude all the causes of secondary pulmonary hypertension. On the basis of Mrs. Zuchowicz's history, he also ruled out all previously known drug-related causes of primary pulmonary hypertension.

Dr. Matthay further testified that the progression and timing of Mrs. Zuchowicz's disease in relation to her overdose supported a finding of drug-induced PPH. Dr. Matthay emphasized that, prior to the overdose, Mrs. Zuchowicz was a healthy, active young woman with no history of cardiovascular problems, and that, shortly after the overdose, she began experiencing symptoms of PPH such as weight gain, swelling of hands and feet, fatigue, and shortness of breath. He described the similarities between the course of Mrs. Zuchowicz's illness and that of accepted cases of drug-induced PPH, and he went on to discuss cases involving classes of drugs that are known to cause other pulmonary diseases (mainly anticancer drugs). He noted that the onset of these diseases, which are recognized to be caused by the particular drugs, was very similar in timing and course to the development of Mrs. Zuchowicz's illness. . . .

II

B. WERE THE DISTRICT COURT'S FACTUAL FINDINGS WITH RESPECT TO CAUSATION CLEARLY ERRONEOUS? . . .

4. Was Danocrine a But For Cause of Mrs. Zuchowicz's Illness and Death? . . .

We hold that, on the basis of Dr. Matthay's testimony alone, the finder of fact could have concluded—under Connecticut law—that Mrs. Zuchowicz's PPH was, more likely than not, caused by Danocrine. While it was not possible to eliminate all other possible causes of pulmonary hypertension, the evidence presented showed that the experts had not only excluded all causes of secondary pulmonary hypertension, but had also ruled out all the previously known drug-related causes of PPH. In addition, Dr. Matthay testified, based on his expertise in pulmonary diseases, that the progression and timing of Mrs. Zuchowicz's illness in relationship to the timing of her overdose supported a finding of *drug-induced* PPH to a reasonable medical certainty. In this respect, we note that in the case before us, unlike many toxic torts situations, there was not a long latency period between the onset of symptoms and the patient's exposure to the drug that was alleged to have caused the illness. Rather, as Dr. Matthay testified, the plaintiff began exhibiting symptoms typical of drug-induced PPH shortly after she started taking the Danocrine. Under the circumstances, we cannot say that the fact finder was clearly erroneous in determining that, more probably than not, the Danocrine caused Mrs. Zuchowicz's illness.

5.   Was the Overdose a But For Cause of Mrs. Zuchowicz's Illness and Death?

To say that Danocrine caused Mrs. Zuchowicz's injuries is only half the story, however. In order for the causation requirement to be met, a trier of fact must be able to determine, by a preponderance of the evidence, that the defendant's *negligence* was responsible for the injury. In this case, defendant's negligence consisted in prescribing an overdose of Danocrine to Mrs. Zuchowicz. For liability to exist, therefore, it is necessary that the fact finder be able to conclude, more probably than not, that the *overdose* was the cause of Mrs. Zuchowicz's illness and ultimate death. The mere fact that the exposure to Danocrine was likely responsible for the disease does not suffice.

The problem of linking defendant's negligence to the harm that occurred is one that many courts have addressed in the past. A car is speeding and an accident occurs. That the car was involved and was a cause of the crash is readily shown. The accident, moreover, is of the sort that rules prohibiting speeding are designed to prevent. But is this enough to support a finding of fact, in the individual case, that *speeding* was, in fact, more probably than not, the cause of the accident? The same question can be asked when a car that was driving in violation of a minimum speed requirement on a super-highway is rear-ended. Again, it is clear that the car and its driver were causes of the accident. And the accident is of the sort that minimum speeding rules are designed to prevent. But can a fact finder conclude, without more, that the driver's negligence in *driving too slowly* led to the crash? To put it more precisely—the defendant's negligence was strongly causally linked to the accident, and the defendant was undoubtedly a *but for* cause of the harm, but does this suffice to allow a fact finder to say that the defendant's *negligence* was a *but for* cause?

At one time, courts were reluctant to say in such circumstances that the wrong could be deemed to be the cause. They emphasized the logical fallacy of *post hoc, ergo propter hoc,* and demanded some direct evidence connecting the defendant's wrongdoing to the harm. . . .

All that has changed, however. And, as is so frequently the case in tort law, Chief Judge Cardozo in New York and Chief Justice Traynor in California led the way. In various opinions, they stated that: if (a) a negligent act was deemed wrongful *because* that act increased the chances that a particular type of accident would occur, and (b) a mishap of that very sort did happen, this was enough to support a finding by the trier of fact that the negligent behavior caused the harm. Where such a strong causal link exists, it is up to the negligent party to bring in evidence denying *but for* cause and suggesting that in the actual case the wrongful conduct had not been a substantial factor.

Thus, in a case involving a nighttime collision between vehicles, one of which did not have the required lights, Judge Cardozo stated that lights were mandated precisely to reduce the risk of such accidents occurring and that this fact sufficed to show causation unless the negligent party demonstrated, for example, that in the particular instance the presence of very bright street lights or of a full moon rendered the lack of lights on the vehicle an unlikely cause. See Martin v. Herzog. . . .

The case before us is a good example of the above-mentioned principles in their classic form. The reason the FDA does not approve the prescription of new drugs at above the dosages as to which extensive tests have been performed is because all drugs involve risks of untoward side effects in those who take them. Moreover, it is often true that the higher the dosage the greater is the likelihood of such negative effects. At the approved dosages, the benefits of the particular drug have presumably been deemed worth the risks it entails. At greater than approved dosages, not only do the risks of tragic side effects (known and unknown) increase, but there is no basis on the testing that has been performed for supposing that the drug's benefits outweigh these increased risks. . . . It follows that when a negative side effect is demonstrated to be the result of a drug, and the drug was wrongly prescribed in an unapproved and excessive dosage (*i.e.* a strong causal link has been shown), the plaintiff who is injured has generally shown enough to permit the finder of fact to conclude that the excessive dosage was a substantial factor in producing the harm.

In fact, plaintiff's showing in the case before us, while relying on the above stated principles, is stronger. For plaintiff introduced some direct evidence of causation as well. On the basis of his long experience with drug-induced pulmonary diseases, one of plaintiff's experts, Dr. Matthay, testified that the timing of Mrs. Zuchowicz's illness led him to conclude that the overdose (and not merely Danocrine) was responsible for her catastrophic reaction.

Under the circumstances, we hold that defendant's attack on the district court's finding of causation is meritless. . . .

Affirmed.

NOTES

1. Incremental risk and causal connections. As Calabresi, J., stressed, in an overdose case, the plaintiff must prove that the excess dosage caused her injury. In

Zuchowicz, is it relevant that the current labels list the maximum permissible daily dosage for Danocrine at 400 milligrams for some conditions and 200 milligrams for others, with a strict warning against double dosing in the event that one dose was missed? More concretely, how did Calabresi, J., decide that the excess dosage of Danocrine made the difference? Suppose that the incremental dosage supplied only a 5 percent benefit, but increased the risk of death from 10 to 11 percent, and that no one thinks that this extra benefit is worth the extra risk. Does the 1 percent statistical increase suffice to show causation? If not, what level of increase should be required to reach a jury? For a recognition of the different causal inquiry for "incremental risk" in overdose cases, see RTT:LPEH §26, comment *f*, and illustrations 1 & 2.

2. *Switching the burden of proof on causation.* In Haft v. Lone Palm Hotel, 478 P.2d 465, 474-475 (Cal. 1970), the plaintiffs brought wrongful death actions when a father and son drowned in the pool at the defendant's Palm Springs motel. The applicable statute provided that "lifeguard service shall be provided or signs shall be erected clearly indicating that such service is not provided." The defendant neither provided the lifeguard service nor posted the signs, and no evidence explained how the deaths actually took place. The court, through Tobriner, J., first observed that "to hold that a pool owner, who has failed to satisfy either of the section's alternative requirements, may limit his liability to that resulting from his 'lesser' failure to erect a sign, would of course effectively read out of the section the primary requirement of providing lifeguard service." (Is this a reasonable interpretation of the statute?) He then addressed the burden of proof on causation as follows:

> The troublesome problems concerning the causation issue in the instant case of course arise out of the total lack of direct evidence as to the precise manner in which the drownings occurred. Although the paucity of evidence on causation is normally one of the burdens that must be shouldered by a plaintiff in proving his case, the evidentiary void in the instant action results primarily from defendants' failure to provide a lifeguard to observe occurrences within the pool area. The main purpose of the lifeguard requirement is undoubtedly to aid those in danger, but an attentive guard does serve the subsidiary function of witnessing those accidents that do occur. The absence of such a lifeguard in the instant case thus not only stripped decedents of a significant degree of protection to which they were entitled, but also deprived the present plaintiffs of a means of definitively establishing the facts leading to the drownings.
>
> Clearly, the failure to provide a lifeguard greatly enhanced the chances of the occurrence of the instant drownings. In proving (1) that defendants were negligent in this respect, and (2) that the available facts, at the very least, strongly suggest that a competent lifeguard, exercising reasonable care, would have prevented the deaths, plaintiffs have gone as far as they possibly can under the circumstances in proving the requisite causal link between defendants' negligence and the accidents. To require plaintiffs to establish "proximate causation" to a greater certainty than they have in the instant case, would permit defendants to gain the advantage of the lack of proof inherent in the lifeguardless situation which they have created. Under these circumstances the burden of proof on the issue of causation should be shifted to defendants to absolve themselves if they can.

Haft's burden-shifting is one of several solutions proposed by Levmore, Probabilistic Recoveries, Restitution, and Recurring Wrongs, 19 J. Legal Stud. 691, 707-710 (1990), to the "recurring miss" problem—whereby application of the preponderance of the evidence standard leads to systematic underdeterrence in repeat situations where an actor's negligence is less than 50 percent likely to have caused a particular plaintiff's injury.

Haft's burden-shifting rationale was not applied in the grisly case of Jimenez v. Morbark, Inc., 2013 WL 5585402 (Cal. Ct. App. 2013), where the decedent, an experienced tree trimmer, was pulverized when his body was drawn into the feed wheel of the defendant's brush chipper. No witness saw exactly how the decedent was drawn into the feed chute, but one witness saw him being drawn in. The plaintiff claimed that the incident could have happened when the decedent's glove was drawn into the machine while loading brush. On this view, a "knee bar" device might have allowed him to stop the machine before he was pulled in. The defendant's theory was that the decedent, contrary to all instructions, had climbed onto the feed tray in order to clear a jam, only to get drawn in. The plaintiff's effort to rely on the burden-shifting device in *Haft* to resolve the conflict was sternly rebuked by Grimes, J.:

> This case is not like *Haft.* Unlike *Haft,* there was no violation of a statute intended to prevent the very injury that occurred. Unlike *Haft,* the available facts did not "strongly suggest" that a knee bar would have prevented Mr. Jimenez's death. Unlike *Haft,* the lack of proof of causation is not "inherent" in the absence of a knee bar (as it was in the lifeguardless situation). Unlike *Haft,* the "absence of definite evidence on causation" is not "a direct and foreseeable result of the defendants' negligent failure to provide" a knee bar. Indeed, in *Haft* the court observed that "this record comes very close to, and may well succeed in, establishing that the absence of a lifeguard was an actual cause of the deaths as a matter of law even without a shift in the burden of proof. . . ." This is not such a case.

2. Joint and Several Liability and Multiple Causes

a. Joint and Several Liability

Before discussing multiple and indeterminate causes of a plaintiff's injury, it is useful to understand the methods used to apportion liability and their relationship to cause in fact determinations. Under joint liability each of several obligors—any person who bears an obligation—can be responsible for the entire loss if the others are unable to pay. Under several liability each person has an obligation to pay only a proportionate share, thereby casting onto the plaintiff the risk of the insolvency of the other defendants. The traditional method of apportionment for multiple causes is joint and several liability. The first term captures the notion that if all defendants are present, each pays only his proportionate share. The second requires any one of multiple defendants that contributed to the plaintiff's injury to pay for the full amount of the plaintiff's damages, no matter how small his contribution. See Restatement (Third) of Torts: Apportionment of Liability [RTT:AL] §17.

The first common law case to endorse joint liability was Merryweather v. Nixan, 101 Eng. Rep. 1337 (K.B. 1799). The plaintiff sued two defendants for conversion of machinery belonging to the plaintiff's mill. The headnote announced: "If *A* recover in tort against two defendants, and levy the whole damages on one, that one cannot recover a moiety against the other for his contribution; aliter, in assumpsit [otherwise in contract]." *Merryweather* offers no explanation for why one defendant has a claim against the other in contract cases, but lacks any such contribution claim in tort cases. The usual explanation for the difference is that the law of partnership and voluntary guarantees routinely provided for the pro rata division of responsibility among defendants, an objective easily achieved for monetizable obligations. Tort claims, however, did not offer that easy mode of division, so that the hostility toward apportionment in contributory negligence cases carried over to disputes between codefendants based on the common law principle that no wrongdoer could bring suit against another party whose wrong was no greater than its own. The tort plaintiff could decide which of two solvent defendants had to bear the entire loss: If *A* recovered $100 from *B*, *B* in turn could not recover $50 from his codefendant, even if the two were equally to blame. As a matter of initial expectations, both defendants might be equally at risk. But in practice, the plaintiff could extract her full pound of flesh from either defendant to the exclusion of the other. In addition, if one defendant made only partial payment, the plaintiff could then sue the second defendant for the remainder. Although *Merryweather* only applied to intentional conversions, in time the no-contribution rule was extended to ordinary negligence actions as well.

The defendant saddled with full liability could at times seek indemnity, as opposed to contribution, from his codefendant for the full loss. Such indemnities have long been and are still allowed by contract, see RTT:AL §22. Should indemnification also be allowed in the absence of a contractual agreement? If so, under what circumstances?

Union Stock Yards Co. of Omaha v. Chicago, Burlington, & Quincy R.R.
196 U.S. 217 (1905)

[The plaintiff terminal company was responsible for moving the switching cars for the defendant railroad in its yard. One of the cars under its control had a defective nut, which either the terminal company or the railroad could have discovered by reasonable inspection. Both parties were found negligent in failing to carry out that inspection, consequently injuring the plaintiff's employee. Plaintiff then paid its employee damages, which it sought to recover from the defendant.]

MR. JUSTICE DAY. . . .

Coming to the very question to be determined here, the general principle of law is well settled that one of several wrongdoers cannot recover against another wrongdoer, although he may have been compelled to pay all the damages for the wrong done. In many instances, however, cases have been taken out of this general rule, and it has been held inoperative in order that the ultimate loss may be visited upon the principal wrongdoer, who is made to respond for all the damages, where one less culpable, although legally liable to third persons, may escape the payment of damages assessed against him by putting the ultimate loss upon the one principally responsible for the injury done. These cases have, perhaps, their principal illustration in that class wherein municipalities have been held responsible for injuries to persons lawfully using the streets in a city, because of defects in the streets or sidewalks caused by the negligence or active fault of a property owner. In such cases, where the municipality has been called upon to respond because of its legal duty to keep public highways open and free from nuisances, a recovery over has been permitted for indemnity against the property owner, the principal wrongdoer, whose negligence was the real cause of the injury. . . .

In a case cited and much relied upon at the bar, Gray v. Boston Gas Light Co., 114 Mass. 149 (1873), a telegraph wire was fastened to the plaintiff's chimney without his consent, and, the weight of the wire having pulled the chimney over into the street, to the injury of a passing traveler, an action was brought against the property owner for damages, and notice was duly given to the gas company, which refused to defend. Having settled the damages at a figure which the court thought reasonable, the property owner brought suit against the gas company, and it was held liable. In the opinion the court said:

> When two parties, acting together, commit an illegal or wrongful act the party who is held responsible for the act cannot have indemnity or contribution from the other, because both are equally culpable or *particeps criminis*, and the damage results from their joint offense. This rule does not apply when one does the act or creates the nuisance, and the other does not join therein, but is thereby exposed to liability and suffers damage. He may recover from the party whose wrongful act has thus exposed him. In such cases the parties are not in *pari delicto* as to each other, though, as to third persons, either may be held liable. . . .

Other cases might be cited, which are applications of the exception engrafted upon the general rule of non-contribution among wrongdoers, holding that the law will inquire into the facts of a case of the character shown with a view to fastening the ultimate liability upon the one whose wrong has been primarily responsible for the injury sustained. . . .

The case then stands in this wise: The railroad company and the terminal company have been guilty of a like neglect of duty in failing to properly inspect the car before putting it in use by those who might be injured thereby. We do not perceive that, because the duty of inspection was first required from the railroad company, the case is thereby brought within the class which holds the one primarily responsible, as the real cause of the injury, liable to another less culpable, who may have been held to respond for damages for the injury inflicted. It is not like the case of the one who creates a nuisance in the public streets; or who furnishes a defective dock; or the case of the gas company, where it created the condition of unsafety by its own wrongful act; or the case of the defective boiler, which blew out because it would not stand the pressure warranted by the manufacturer. In all these cases the wrongful act of the one held finally liable created the unsafe or dangerous condition from which the injury resulted. The principal and moving cause, resulting in the injury sustained, was the act of the first wrongdoer, and the other has been held liable to third persons for failing to discover or correct the defect caused by the positive act of the other.

In the present case the negligence of the parties has been of the same character. Both the railroad company and the terminal company failed by proper inspection to discover the defective brake. The terminal company, because of its fault, has been held liable to one sustaining an injury thereby. We do not think the case comes within that exceptional class which permits one wrongdoer who has been mulcted in damages to recover indemnity or contribution from another.

[Judgment for defendant affirmed.]

NOTE

Contribution versus indemnity. In *Union Stock Yards,* should an action for contribution or indemnity have been allowed if the cost of inspection was low to the railroad and high to the stockyard? How does *Union Stock Yards* come out if the passive party (the party exposed to liability for setting the stage for the wrongful act of another) may obtain contribution or indemnity from the active one (the party that performed the wrongful act from which liability arises)? Under a rule that allows the party secondarily responsible to obtain contribution or indemnity from the party primarily responsible? What is the distinction between these rules and under what circumstances would the rules produce a different result?

California Civil Procedure Code [enacted 1957]

§§875-877.5 (West 2015)

SECTION 875. JUDGMENT AGAINST TWO OR MORE DEFENDANTS; CONTRIBUTION; SUBROGATION BY INSURER; RIGHT OF INDEMNITY; SATISFACTION OF JUDGMENT IN FULL.

(a) Where a money judgment has been rendered jointly against two or more defendants in a tort action there shall be a right of contribution among them as hereinafter provided.

(b) Such right of contribution shall be administered in accordance with the principles of equity.

(c) Such right of contribution may be enforced only after one tortfeasor has, by payment, discharged the joint judgment or has paid more than his pro rata share thereof. It shall be limited to the excess so paid over the pro rata share of the person so paying and in no event shall any tortfeasor be compelled to make contribution beyond his own pro rata share of the entire judgment.

(d) There shall be no right of contribution in favor of any tortfeasor who has intentionally injured the injured person.

(e) A liability insurer who by payment has discharged the liability of a tort-feasor judgment debtor shall be subrogated to his right of contribution.

(f) This title shall not impair any right of indemnity under existing law, and where one tortfeasor judgment debtor is entitled to indemnity from another there shall be no right of contribution between them.

(g) This title shall not impair the right of a plaintiff to satisfy a judgment in full as against any tortfeasor judgment debtor.

SECTION 876. DETERMINATION OF PRO RATA SHARE.

(a) The pro rata share of each tortfeasor judgment debtor shall be determined by dividing the entire judgment equally among all of them.

(b) Where one or more persons are held liable solely for the tort of one of them or of another, as in the case of the liability of a master for the tort of his servant, they shall contribute a single pro rata share, as to which there may be indemnity between them.

SECTION 877. RELEASE OF ONE OR MORE JOINT TORTFEASORS OR CO-OBLIGORS; EFFECT UPON LIABILITY OF OTHERS.

[The section provides inter alia that a release shall not discharge any third party "unless its terms so provide."]

SECTION 877.5. SLIDING SCALE RECOVERY AGREEMENT; DISCLOSURE TO COURT AND JURY; SERVICE OF NOTICE OF INTENT TO ENTER.

[This section requires prompt disclosure to the court of any agreement whereby the liability of a party will be reduced if it testifies as a witness for the plaintiff. The court shall disclose to the jury the "existence and content" of that agreement, unless disclosure will cause unfair prejudice or mislead the jury. Unless the judge rules otherwise for good cause, the agreement is only effective if other parties receive notice of an intent to enter an agreement at least 72 hours prior to entering that agreement.]

NOTE

Statutory repudiation of the joint and several liability rule.   In contrast to the stark all-or-nothing allocations of the common law, the California statute adopted a regime of pro rata liability that allowed each defendant to recover from his code-fendants any amount above his own share. Thus, if one defendant paid the full $100, he could recoup $50 in a separate action from the second defendant, so long as judgment had been entered against both. Statutory contribution was not available for intentional harms, nor did it displace any available indemnity actions. Other rules governed cases of vicarious liability. The California statute was initially passed in 1957 before the adoption of pure comparative negligence in Li v. Yellow Cab Co., 532 P.2d 1226 (Cal. 1975), discussed *supra* at 324. Does it make sense to have a regime of pure comparative negligence between plaintiffs and defendants and a regime of pro rata apportionment among defendants? How might the differing rules affect each litigant's settlement incentives?

American Motorcycle Association v. Superior Court
578 P.2d 899 (Cal. 1978)

[In this case, the California Supreme Court addressed the proper apportionment of liability in suits against multiple defendants. At the outset, the court stated its conclusions as follows:

1. The doctrine subjecting multiple defendants to "joint and several liability" to a single plaintiff was neither abolished nor limited by the decision in *Li*.
2. A doctrine of partial equitable indemnity should be adopted at common law to permit apportionment of loss among codefendants on pure comparative principles.
3. The California contribution statutes do not "preclude" the development of a common law doctrine of comparative indemnity.
4. Under this system of equitable contribution, any defendant may maintain an action against any other party, whether or not joined in the original suit, but that the trial judge may postpone trial of the indemnity action in order "to avoid unduly complicating the plaintiff's suit."]

TOBRINER, J., . . . In light of these determinations, we conclude that a writ of mandate should issue, directing the trial court to permit petitioner-defendant to file a cross-complaint for partial indemnity against previously unjoined alleged concurrent tortfeasors.

1.   THE FACTS

[The plaintiff, Glen Gregos, was injured in a novice motorcycle race that he claimed was negligently organized and run by two defendants, the American Motorcycle Association (AMA) and the Viking Motorcycle Club (Viking). When he sued the AMA, it sought leave of the court to file a cross-complaint against Gregos' parents, alleging their negligence and improper supervision of their minor son. It also asked declaratory relief that its portion of the judgment be reduced by the amount of the "allocable negligence" of the parents.]

2.   THE ADOPTION OF COMPARATIVE NEGLIGENCE IN LI DOES NOT WARRANT THE ABOLITION OF JOINT AND SEVERAL LIABILITY OF CONCURRENT TORTFEASORS . . .

In the instant case AMA argues that the *Li* decision, by repudiating the all-or-nothing contributory negligence rule and replacing it by a rule which simply diminishes an injured party's recovery on the basis of his comparative fault, in effect undermined the fundamental rationale of the entire joint and several liability doctrine as applied to concurrent tortfeasors. . . .

AMA argues that after *Li* (1) there *is* a basis for dividing damages, namely on a comparative negligence basis, and (2) a plaintiff is no longer necessarily "innocent," for *Li* permits a negligent plaintiff to recover damages. AMA maintains that in light of these two factors it is logically inconsistent to retain joint and several liability of concurrent tortfeasors after *Li*. As we explain, for a number of reasons we cannot accept AMA's argument.

First, the simple feasibility of apportioning fault on a comparative negligence basis does not render an indivisible injury "divisible" for purposes of the joint and several liability rule. [A] concurrent tortfeasor is liable for the whole of an indivisible injury whenever his negligence is a proximate cause of that injury. In many instances, the negligence of each of several concurrent tortfeasors may be sufficient, in itself, to cause the entire injury; in other instances, it is simply impossible to determine whether or not a particular concurrent tortfeasor's negligence, acting alone, would have caused the same injury. Under such circumstances, a defendant has no equitable claim vis-à-vis an injured plaintiff to be relieved of liability for damage which he has proximately caused simply because some other tortfeasor's negligence may also have caused the same harm. In other words, the mere fact that it may be possible to assign some percentage figure to the relative culpability of one negligent defendant as compared to another does not in any way suggest that each defendant's negligence is not a proximate cause of the entire indivisible injury.

Second, abandonment of the joint and several liability rule is not warranted by AMA's claim that, after *Li*, a plaintiff is no longer "innocent." Initially, of course, it is by no means invariably true that after *Li* injured plaintiffs will be guilty of negligence. In many instances a plaintiff will be completely free of all responsibility for the accident, and yet, under the proposed abolition of joint and several liability, such a completely faultless plaintiff, rather than a wrongdoing defendant, would be forced to bear a portion of the loss if any one of the concurrent tortfeasors should prove financially unable to satisfy his proportioned share of the damages.

Moreover, even when a plaintiff is partially at fault for his own injury, a plaintiff's culpability is not equivalent to that of a defendant. In this setting, a plaintiff's negligence relates only to a failure to use due care for his own protection, while a defendant's negligence relates to a lack of due care for the safety of others. Although we recognized in *Li* that a plaintiff's self-directed negligence would justify reducing his recovery in proportion to his degree of fault for the accident,[2] the fact remains that insofar as the plaintiff's conduct creates only a risk of self-injury, such conduct, unlike that of a negligent defendant, is not tortious.

---

2. A question has arisen as to whether our *Li* opinion, in mandating that a plaintiff's recovery be diminished in proportion to the plaintiff's negligence, intended that the plaintiff's conduct be compared with each individual tortfeasor's negligence, with the cumulative negligence of all named defendants or with all other negligent conduct that contributed to the injury. The California BAJI Committee, which specifically addressed this issue after *Li*, concluded that "the contributory negligence of the plaintiff must be proportioned to the combined negligence of plaintiff and of all the tortfeasors, whether or not joined as parties . . . whose negligence proximately caused or contributed to plaintiff's injury."

We agree with this conclusion, which finds support in decisions from other comparative negligence jurisdictions. In determining to what degree the injury was due to the fault of the plaintiff, it is logically essential that the plaintiff's negligence be weighed against the combined total of all other causative negligence; moreover, inasmuch as a plaintiff's actual damages do not vary by virtue of the particular defendants who happen to be before the court, we do not think that the damages which a plaintiff may recover against defendants who are joint and severally liable should fluctuate in such a manner.

Finally, from a realistic standpoint, we think that AMA's suggested abandonment of the joint and several liability rule would work a serious and unwarranted deleterious effect on the practical ability of negligently injured persons to receive adequate compensation for their injuries. One of the principal by-products of the joint and several liability rule is that it frequently permits an injured person to obtain full recovery for his injuries even when one or more of the responsible parties do not have the financial resources to cover their liability. In such a case the rule recognizes that fairness dictates that the "wronged party should not be deprived of his right to redress," but that "[t]he wrongdoers should be left to work out between themselves any apportionment." See Summers v. Tice 199 P.2d 1, 5 (1948) [discussed *infra* at 372]. The *Li* decision does not detract in the slightest from this pragmatic policy determination.

[The court then noted that the overwhelming weight of judicial and academic opinion supports its conclusion.]

3. UPON REEXAMINATION OF THE COMMON LAW EQUITABLE INDEMNITY DOCTRINE IN LIGHT OF THE PRINCIPLES UNDERLYING *LI*, WE CONCLUDE THAT THE DOCTRINE SHOULD BE MODIFIED TO PERMIT PARTIAL INDEMNITY AMONG CONCURRENT TORTFEASORS ON A COMPARATIVE FAULT BASIS . . .

In California, as in most other American jurisdictions, the allocation of damages among multiple tortfeasors has historically been analyzed in terms of two, ostensibly mutually exclusive, doctrines: contribution and indemnification. In traditional terms, the apportionment of loss between multiple tortfeasors has been thought to present a question of contribution; indemnity, by contrast, has traditionally been viewed as concerned solely with whether a loss should be entirely shifted from one tortfeasor to another, rather than whether the loss should be shared between the two. As we shall explain, however, the dichotomy between the two concepts is more formalistic than substantive, and the common goal of both doctrines, the equitable distribution of loss among multiple tortfeasors, suggests a need for a reexamination of the relationship of these twin concepts.

Early California decisions, relying on the ancient law that "the law will not aid a wrongdoer," embraced the then ascendant common law rule denying a tortfeasor any right to contribution whatsoever. [The court then reviewed the 1957 legislation set out above.]

[T]he equitable indemnity doctrine originated in the common sense proposition that when two individuals are responsible for a loss, but one of the two is more culpable than the other, it is only fair that the more culpable party should bear a greater share of the loss. Of course, at the time the doctrine developed, common law precepts precluded any attempt to ascertain comparative fault; as a consequence, equitable indemnity, like the contributory negligence doctrine, developed as an all-or-nothing proposition.

Because of the all-or-nothing nature of the equitable indemnity rule, courts were, from the beginning, understandably reluctant to shift the entire loss to a party who was simply slightly more culpable than another. As a consequence, throughout the long history of the equitable indemnity doctrine courts have struggled to find some linguistic formulation that would provide an appropriate test for determining when the relative culpability of the parties is sufficiently disparate to warrant placing the entire loss on one party and completely absolving the other.

A review of the numerous California cases in this area reveals that the struggle has largely been a futile one. . . .

Indeed, some courts, as well as some prominent commentators, after reviewing the welter of inconsistent standards utilized in the equitable indemnity realm, have candidly eschewed any pretense of an objectively definable equitable indemnity test. . . .

If the fundamental problem with the equitable indemnity doctrine as it has developed in this state were simply a matter of an unduly vague or imprecise linguistic standard, the remedy would be simply to attempt to devise a more definite verbal formulation. In our view, however, the principal difficulty with the current equitable indemnity doctrine rests not simply on a question of terminology, but lies instead in the all-or-nothing nature of the doctrine itself. . . .

In order to attain such a system in which liability for an indivisible injury caused by concurrent tortfeasors will be borne by each individual tortfeasor "in direct proportion to [his] respective fault," we conclude that the current equitable indemnity rule should be modified to permit a concurrent tortfeasor to obtain partial indemnity from other concurrent tortfeasors on a comparative fault basis. In reaching this conclusion, we point out that in recent years a great number of courts, particularly in jurisdictions which follow the comparative negligence rule, have for similar reasons adopted, as a matter of common law, comparable rules providing for comparative contribution or comparative indemnity. . . .

CLARK, J., dissenting. . . . The majority reject the *Li* principle in two ways. First, they reject it by adopting joint and several liability holding that each defendant—including the marginally negligent one—will be responsible for the loss attributable to his codefendant's negligence. To illustrate, if we assume that the plaintiff is found 30 percent at fault, the first defendant 60 percent, and a second defendant 10 percent, the plaintiff under the majority's decision is entitled to a judgment for 70 percent of the loss against each defendant, and the defendant found only 10 percent at fault may have to pay 70 percent of the loss if his codefendant is unable to respond in damages.

The second way in which the majority reject *Li*'s irresistible principle is by its settlement rules. Under the majority opinion, a good faith settlement releases the settling tortfeasor from further liability, and the "plaintiff's recovery from nonsettling tortfeasors should be diminished only by the amount that the plaintiff has actually recovered in a good faith settlement, rather than by an amount measured by the settling tortfeasor's proportionate responsibility for the injury." The settlement rules announced today may turn *Li*'s principle upside down—the extent of dollar liability may end up in inverse relation to fault.

[Clark, J., then noted that the inversion takes place under the credit rule when a central defendant settles for a small sum. Thus, if *P* is 30 percent responsible,

D_1 is 10 percent responsible, and D_2 60 percent responsible, if D_2 settles for 20 percent, D_1 could be held responsible for 50 percent of the loss, notwithstanding his 10 percent share of responsibility. Under the carve-out rule, P could pursue D_1 only for 10 percent of the loss no matter how much she obtained from D_2. Clark, J., also argued that if D_2 was insolvent, P could recover only 25 percent of the loss—10 percent from P compared to 30 percent from D_1].

I do not suggest return to the old contributory negligence system. The true criticism of that system remains valid: one party should not be required to bear a loss which by definition two have caused. However, in departing from the old system of contributory negligence numerous approaches are open, but the Legislature rather than this court is the proper institution in a democratic society to choose the course. . . .

NOTES

1. Insolvent defendants in joint tortfeasor cases.   Further complications arise with the insolvency of one or more multiple defendants. *American Motorcycle* seems to hold that the remaining defendants bear *all* of the risk of an insolvent codefendant, but Evangelatos v. Superior Court (Van Waters & Rogers, Inc., RPI), 753 P.2d 585, 590 (Cal. 1988), applied a different rule: "[M]ore recent decisions also make clear that if one or more tortfeasors prove to be insolvent and are not able to bear their fair share of the loss, the shortfall created by such insolvency should be apportioned equitably among the remaining culpable parties—both defendants and plaintiffs."

To revert to Justice Clark's 30/60/10 hypothetical, if the 60 percent defendant is insolvent, *American Motorcycle* placed 70 percent of the loss on the 10 percent defendant. *Evangelatos* splits that 60 percent loss between plaintiff and defendant in accordance with their responsibility, so that the plaintiff can recover only 25 percent of her loss from the solvent defendant, representing his own 10 percent responsibility plus one-quarter (10 divided by 40) of the remaining 60 percent of the loss, or 15 percent. The Third Restatement adopts a similar rule: "[I]f a defendant establishes that a judgment for contribution cannot be collected fully from another defendant, the court reallocates the uncollectible portion of the damages to all other parties, including the plaintiff, in proportion to the percentages of comparative responsibility assigned to the other parties." RTT:AL §21(a). The exceptions to this rule cover intentional tortfeasors (*id.* §12), persons acting in concert (*id.* §15), vicarious liability (*id.* §13), and persons who fail to protect plaintiff from the specific risk of an intentional tort (*id.* §14).

2. Several liability for multiple defendants?   The Restatement's approach of partial reapportionment was not applied in Brown v. Keill, 580 P.2d 867, 873-874 (Kan. 1978), a car accident case involving two parties. In that case, the court held that the Kansas comparative negligence statute (Kan. Stat. Ann. §60-258a (2007)), allowing recovery if plaintiff's negligence "was less than" defendant's causal negligence, abrogated the traditional rule of joint and several liability, and created several liability only. Subsection (d) provides:

Where the comparative negligence of the parties in any action is an issue and recovery is allowed against more than one party, each such party shall be liable for that portion of the total dollar amount awarded as damages to any claimant in the proportion that the amount of such party's causal negligence bears to the amount of the causal negligence attributed to all parties against whom such recovery is allowed.

The court first held that the plain language of the statute compelled the result. It then argued that a limitation of losses for defendants was not inconsistent with sound social policy:

The perceived purpose in adopting K.S.A. 60-258a is fairly clear. The legislature intended to equate recovery and duty to pay to degree of fault. Of necessity, this involved a change of both the doctrine of contributory negligence and of joint and several liability. There is nothing inherently fair about a defendant who is 10% at fault paying 100% of the loss, and there is no social policy that should compel defendants to pay more than their fair share of the loss. Plaintiffs now take the parties as they find them. . . . Previously, when the plaintiff had to be totally without negligence to recover and the defendants had to be merely negligent to incur an obligation to pay, an argument could be made which justified putting the burden of seeking contribution on the defendants. Such an argument is no longer compelling because of the purpose and intent behind the adoption of the comparative negligence statute.

Under Clark's, J., hypothetical, in the event of the insolvency of the 60 percent defendant, the 10 percent defendant continues to bear 10 percent of the loss, with the rest being borne by the plaintiff. Does joint and several liability make as much sense with 100 defendants in a cumulative trauma case as with two in an accident case?

3. Statutory modifications of joint and several liability.   The common law rule of joint and several liability has proved to be a priority for legislative reform. A chief concern has been the marginal defendant whose tiny fraction of responsibility has required it to bear the full damages attributable to more culpable, but wholly or largely insolvent, defendants. One possible response to this problem is to abolish the rule outright, as was done by statute in Colorado, Utah, and Wyoming. See Colo. Rev. Stat. §13-21-111.5 (West 2015); Utah Code Ann. §78B-5-818 (West 2014); Wyo. Stat. §1-1-109 (West 2014). A second response is to relieve the plight of marginal defendants with ad hoc fixes. Thus, Iowa abolished joint liability for defendants found to be less than 50 percent at fault, but retained joint liability for economic damages for defendants 50 percent or more at fault. Iowa Code §668.4 (West 2015). New Jersey set a 60 percent threshold for joint and several liability for both economic and noneconomic damages. New Jersey Stat. §2A:15-5.3 (West 2015). Finally, New Hampshire allows a judgment for the full amount of damages to be entered against a codefendant found 50 or more percent at fault, but allows only for several liability against a codefendant found less than 50 percent at fault. N.H. Rev. Stat. Ann. §507:7-e (West 2015).

At this point, the choice lay between the last two rules, neither of which allows for contribution against settling defendants. Under the credit, or pro tanto, rule, the award against the nonsettling defendant is reduced by the actual amount paid by the settling defendant. Thus, if defendant *A* pays $30,000 in settlement, the plaintiff, who then receives an award of $100,000 against the second defendant, gets to recover $70,000. As Justice Stevens noted, "the settlement figure is likely to be significantly less than the settling defendant's equitable share of the loss, because settlement reflects the uncertainty of trial and provides the plaintiff with a 'war chest' with which to finance the litigation against the remaining defendants." The advantage of the rule is that it sets out a precise number for the second defendant to pay. Its disadvantage is that it encourages the first defendant to settle early so that the second defendant will hold the bag, which leads to the inversions between relative culpability and settlement referred to by Justice Clark in his *AMA* dissent.

The third rule, the proportionate share rule, eliminates that incentive. Under this rule, the plaintiff is treated as having two divisible claims, each with its set value. Thus, if each defendant has a 50 percent share of the loss, the initial settlement of $30,000 makes one-half of the claim disappear so that the second defendant now is only responsible for $50,000, no matter how much or little the first defendant settled for. At this point, there is no longer any benefit for either defendant to settle early. Nor is the plaintiff likely to take a discount on its claim, knowing that it cannot recover the larger fraction from the second defendant.

The Achilles heel of this proposal is that someone has to determine the relative shares of the two parties to make this system work, and it is not clear when that determination should be made. The administration of the proportionate share rule, however, is easier under the older admiralty rule rejected in *Reliable Transfer*, which holds each defendant liable for a pro rata share of the loss. Notwithstanding this difficulty, Justice Stevens opted for the proportionate share rule:

> It seems to us that a plaintiff's good fortune in striking a favorable bargain with one defendant gives other defendants no claim to pay less than their proportionate share of the total loss. In fact, one of the virtues of the proportionate share rule is that, unlike the *pro tanto* rule, it does not make a litigating defendant's liability dependent on the amount of a settlement negotiated by others without regard to its interests.

6. Bargaining under the pro tanto rule. How do the strategic bargaining opportunities play out under the pro tanto or credit rule? Kornhauser & Revesz, Settlements Under Joint and Several Liability, 68 N.Y.U. L. Rev. 427, 433 (1993), show that settlement strategies under the pro tanto method depend on the correlation in the success rates on the two claims. One extreme possibility is that the risks of liability for the two defendants are *independent*—that is, the success against one defendant "does not depend upon whether the plaintiff prevails against, loses to, or settles with the other defendant." The other extreme occurs when the two risks are perfectly *correlated*—that is, success or failure against one defendant implies the same result against the other. The difference between these two situations matters for the likelihood of settlement. In general, it is easier to arrange settlements whereby all parties are left better off when the risks are correlated than when they are independent. For the mathematical demonstration, see Kornhauser & Revesz, *supra*, at 447.

How do the settlement dynamics play out when the plaintiff declines to sue one defendant? In Murphy v. Florida Keys Electric Cooperative Association, Inc., 329 F.3d 1311, 1313, 1315 (11th Cir. 2003), three people were in a small boat piloted by a member of the Ashman family, which collided with an "electrical pole abutment support structure" owned by defendant Florida Keys Co-op Association. The injured passenger and the family of the decedent, the other passenger, sued and settled their claim with Florida Keys on a proportionate share basis under *McDermott*. Florida Keys then promptly sued the Ashmans, whom the plaintiffs had declined to sue, for indemnity and contribution in a third-party complaint. Carnes, J., first noted that the law on the status of the third-party claim "[has] lurched back and forth like a drunken sailor." He held "that a settling defendant cannot bring a suit for contribution against a nonsettling defendant who was not released from liability to the plaintiff by the settlement agreement." He explained the situation as follows:

> There are two ways to look at what Florida Keys is seeking to do, and both are telling. One way is that Florida Keys is seeking to escape the bargain it struck with the Murphys about the extent of its liability, trying to litigate with the Ashmans the issue of how much it should have paid the Murphys and then recover from the Ashmans any excess it did pay. That will not do, because the Ashmans are not responsible for the bargain Florida Keys struck with the Murphys. The other way to look at Florida Keys' position is that it is seeking to recover from the Ashmans the amount of the settlement it paid to the Murphys that is attributable to the Ashmans' liability. That will not do either, because none of the settlement is attributable to the Ashmans' liability, which was not released in whole or part. We hold Florida Keys to its bargain: it paid for a discharge of its liability to the Murphys, and that is all it got.

b. Multiple Sufficient Causes

Kingston v. Chicago & N.W. Ry.
211 N.W. 913 (Wis. 1927)

Owen, J., . . . We therefore have this situation: The northeast fire was set by sparks emitted from defendant's locomotive. This fire, according to the finding of the jury, constituted a proximate cause of the destruction of plaintiff's property. This finding we find to be well supported by the evidence. We have the northwest fire, of unknown origin. This fire, according to the finding of the jury, also constituted a proximate cause of the destruction of the plaintiff's property. This finding we also find to be well supported by the evidence. We have a union of these two fires 940 feet north of plaintiff's property, from which point the united fire bore down upon and destroyed the property. We therefore have two separate, independent, and distinct agencies, each of which constituted the proximate cause of plaintiff's damage, and either of which, in the absence of the other, would have accomplished such result.

It is settled in the law of negligence that any one of two or more joint tortfeasors, or one of two or more wrongdoers whose concurring acts of negligence result in injury, are each individually responsible for the entire damage resulting from their joint or concurrent acts of negligence. This rule also obtains "where two causes, each attributable to the negligence of a responsible person, concur in producing an injury to another, either of which causes would produce it regardless of the other, . . . because, whether the concurrence be intentional, actual, or constructive, each wrongdoer, in effect, adopts the conduct of his co-actor, and for the further reason that it is impossible to apportion the damage or to say that either perpetrated any distinct injury that can be separated from the whole. The whole loss must necessarily be considered and treated as an entirety." Cook v. M., St. P. & S.S.M.R. Co., 74 N.W. 561, 566 (1898). That case presented a situation very similar to this. One fire, originating by sparks emitted from a locomotive, united with another fire of unknown origin and consumed plaintiff's property. There was nothing to indicate that the fire of unknown origin was not set by some human agency. The evidence in the case merely failed to identify the agency. In that case it was held that the railroad company which set one fire was not responsible for the damage committed by the united fires because the origin of the other fire was not identified [and could well have been of natural, not human origins]. . . .

From our present consideration of the subject we are not disposed to criticise the doctrine which exempts from liability a wrongdoer who sets a fire which unites with a fire originating from natural causes, such as lightning, not attributable to any human agency, resulting in damage. It is also conceivable that a fire so set might unite with a fire of so much greater proportions, such as a raging forest fire, as to be enveloped or swallowed up by the greater holocaust, and its identity destroyed, so that the greater fire could be said to be an intervening or superseding cause. But we have no such situation here. These fires were of comparatively equal rank. If there was any difference in their magnitude or threatening aspect, the record indicates that the northeast fire was the larger fire and was really regarded as the menacing agency. At any rate there is no intimation or suggestion that the northeast fire was enveloped and swallowed up by the northwest fire. We will err on the side of the defendant if we regard the two fires as of equal rank.

According to well settled principles of negligence, it is undoubted that if the proof disclosed the origin of the northwest fire, even though its origin be attributed to a third person, the railroad company, as the originator of the northeast fire, would be liable for the entire damage. There is no reason to believe that the northwest fire originated from any other than human agency. It was a small fire. It had traveled over a limited area. It had been in existence but for a day. For a time it was thought to have been extinguished. It was not in the nature of a raging forest fire. The record discloses nothing of natural phenomena which could have given rise to the fire. It is morally certain that it was set by some human agency.

Now the question is whether the railroad company, which is found to have been responsible for the origin of the northeast fire, escapes liability because the origin of the northwest fire is not identified, although there is no reason to believe that it had any other than human origin. An affirmative answer to that question would certainly make a wrongdoer a favorite of the law at the expense of an innocent sufferer. The injustice of such a doctrine sufficiently impeaches the logic upon which it is founded. Where one who has suffered damage by fire proves the origin of a fire and the course of that fire up to the point of the destruction of his property, one has certainly established liability on the part of the originator of the fire. Granting that the union of that fire with another of natural origin, or with another of much greater proportions, is available as a defense, the burden is on the defendant to show that by reason of such union with a fire of such character the fire set by him was not the proximate cause of the damage. No principle of justice requires that the plaintiff be placed under the burden of specifically identifying the origin of both fires in order to recover the damages for which either or both fires are responsible. . . .

While under some circumstances a wrongdoer is not responsible for damage which would have occurred in the absence of his wrongful act, even though such wrongful act was a proximate cause of the accident, that doctrine does not obtain "where two causes, each attributable to the negligence of a responsible person, concur in producing an injury to another, either of which causes would produce it regardless of the other." This is because "it is impossible to apportion the damage or to say that either perpetrated any distinct injury that can be separated from the whole," and to permit each of two wrongdoers to plead the wrong of the other as a defense to his own wrongdoing would permit both wrongdoers to escape and penalize the innocent party who has been damaged by their wrongful acts.

The fact that the northeast fire was set by the railroad company, which fire was a proximate cause of plaintiff's damage, is sufficient to affirm the judgment. This conclusion renders it unnecessary to consider other grounds of liability stressed in respondent's brief.

By the Court. —Judgment affirmed.

NOTES

1. Fires: Human and natural.   *Kingston* addresses two situations: one in which both fires are set by humans, and a second in which only one such fire is set. Is it wise to adopt a rule of joint and several liability when both fires are of human origin and a rule of no liability when only one fire is so set? Why not a rule of several liability that holds the named defendant responsible for half of the damage regardless of how the other fire was set? Which rule gives the railroad the proper incentives to take the optimal level of care?

What weight should be attached when the two fires cause harm to plaintiff at slightly different times? Consider these three situations. Case 1: Fire *A*, of natural origin, burns plaintiff's premises. Minutes later, fire *B*, set by defendant, reaches plaintiff's property. Fire *B* would have destroyed plaintiff's property if fire *A* had not destroyed it first. Case 2: Same sequence of events, only fire *A* is of human origin and *B* is of natural origin. Should the twice-cursed plaintiff be better off in the second case than she is in the first? Case 3: Same as above, only both fires are of human origin.

2. Restatement views on the joint causation cases.   The Third Restatement strongly endorses the view that all joint tortfeasors are fully responsible for the undivided consequences of their own actions.

> ### *Restatement of the Law (Third) of Torts: Liability for Physical and Emotional Harm*
>
> #### §27. MULTIPLE SUFFICIENT CAUSES
>
> If multiple acts occur, each of which under §26 alone would have been a factual cause of the physical harm at the same time in the absence of the other act(s), each act is regarded as a factual cause of the harm.
>
> The Restatement separately discusses a number of different types of cause and conduct:
>
> - **Synergistic cause:** Where two or more causes' combined effect is greater than the sum of their parts. For example, when neither of two fires alone would be sufficient to destroy the plaintiff's property, each defendant's negligence is a factual cause of the harm. *Id.*, comment *a*.
>
> - **Overdetermined cause:** All actors held liable where a subset of them committing that act would have sufficed to cause the harm at issue. For example, if three men combine to push a car over a cliff, all are liable even if the force applied by any two would have been sufficient. *Id.*, comment *f*.

3. Apportionment of damages.   In many cases of multiple causation, no portion of the harm is uniquely attributable to any particular defendant. But what if some causal segregation is possible? On that question RST §433A has proved hugely influential.

The Third Restatement also endorses apportionment when there is a "reasonable basis for the factfinder to determine . . . the amount of damages separately caused" by each party. See RTT:AL §26(b).

Restatement of the Law (Second) of Torts

§433A. APPORTIONMENT OF HARM TO CAUSES

(1) Damages for harm are to be apportioned among two or more causes where
  (a) there are distinct harms, or
  (b) there is a reasonable basis for determining the contribution of each cause to a single harm.
(2) Damages for any other harm cannot be apportioned among two or more causes.

Comment d. Divisible harm: . . . [W]here the cattle of two or more owners trespass upon the plaintiff's land and destroy his crop, the aggregate harm is a lost crop, but it may nevertheless be apportioned among the owners of the cattle, on the basis of the number owned by each, and the reasonable assumption that the respective harm done is proportionate to that number. . . .

Restatement of the Law (Third) of Torts: Apportionment of Liability

§26. APPORTIONMENT OF LIABILITY WHEN DAMAGES CAN BE DIVIDED BY CAUSATION

(b) Damages can be divided by causation when the evidence provides a reasonable basis for the factfinder to determine:
  (1) that any legally culpable conduct of a party or other relevant person to whom the factfinder assigns a percentage of responsibility was a legal cause of less than the entire damages for which the plaintiff seeks recovery and
  (2) the amount of damages separately caused by that conduct. Otherwise, the damages are indivisible and thus the injury is indivisible. . . .

The cases that address these apportionment problems are legion. In Smith v. J.C. Penney Co., Inc., 525 P.2d 1299, 1305-1306 (Or. 1974), the plaintiff was wearing a coat purchased from J.C. Penney made of flammable material supplied, as the jury found, by defendant Bunker-Ramo. The coat was set ablaze by a fire started through the negligence of another defendant's service station employees. Bunker-Ramo contended that because "there is no way to segregate the damages as between the various defendants," plaintiff should not recover from any of them. The court, however, thought otherwise:

There was evidence in this case that as a practical matter plaintiff's injuries were indivisible; that is, the jury could not make any reasonable determination that certain injuries were caused by the gasoline fire and other injuries were caused by the coat.

An employee of the Enco Service Station had gasoline sprayed on his trousers and was engulfed in the same fire as plaintiff, yet suffered only minor burns to his legs. The jury could infer from this that plaintiff would not have incurred severe burns to her lower extremities if she had not been wearing the coat. There was evidence that burning material dripped from the coat, although there was no direct evidence that such dripping material landed on plaintiff's legs or feet. There was evidence that the burning coat radiated such heat that the jury could find it burned plaintiff's lower extremities. There also was testimony that the fierce burning of the coat and the emission of gases in the process would have impeded a wearer from rapidly escaping a fire.

Most important is that there is evidence that the greatest injury to plaintiff arises out of the totality of her condition. There is testimony that she is physically and psychologically permanently disabled and unable to lead a normal life. This cannot be attributed to a burn on her foot, her head, or her body but only to her entire condition.

Should the gasoline station be held liable for the full extent of the damage, given that its employee suffered only minor burns from the same fire?

More recently the apportionment issues under RST §433A have surfaced on the question whether it is proper to apportion damages for injuries caused by both smoking and asbestos exposure. In Carter v. Wallace & Gale Asbestos Settlement Trust, 96 A.3d 147, 151 (Md. 2013), the plaintiffs sued only asbestos and not tobacco companies. Green, J., refused to allow apportionment, holding on the strength of expert evidence that it was not possible to "differentiate between the two causes because the two exposures 'are not just additive, they are synergistic which means they multiply exposures.'" The decision rested in part on Maryland's continued treatment of contributory negligence as a total bar against recovery, which in turn rests on the difficulty of apportionment in scenarios such as these. On this ground, should the plaintiff be totally barred from all recovery by contributory negligence or assumption of risk? Is it true that apportionment is impossible in synergistic cases? Suppose that the probability of harm given A's acts alone is 40 percent, and that the probability of harm given B's acts alone is 20 percent. When both acts occur, should the losses be allocated by two-to-one ratio? See Rizzo & Arnold, Causal Apportionment in the Law of Torts: An Economic Theory, 80 Colum. L. Rev. 1399 (1980).

3. Indeterminate Causes

a. Alternative Liability

Summers v. Tice
199 P.2d 1 (Cal. 1948)

CARTER, J. Each of the two defendants appeals from a judgment against them in an action for personal injuries. Pursuant to stipulation the appeals have been consolidated.

Plaintiff's action was against both defendants for an injury to his right eye and face as the result of being struck by bird shot discharged from a shotgun. The case was tried by the court without a jury and the court found that on November 20, 1945, plaintiff and the two defendants were hunting quail on the open range. Each of the defendants was armed with a 12 gauge shotgun loaded with shells containing 7-½ size shot. Prior to going hunting plaintiff discussed the hunting procedure with defendants, indicating that they were to exercise care when shooting and to "keep in line." In the course of hunting plaintiff proceeded up a hill, thus placing the hunters at the points of a triangle. The view of defendants with reference to plaintiff was unobstructed and they knew his location. Defendant Tice flushed a quail which rose in flight to a 10-foot elevation and flew between plaintiff and defendants. Both defendants shot at the quail, shooting in plaintiff's direction. At that time defendants were 75 yards from plaintiff. One shot struck plaintiff in his eye and another in his upper lip. Finally it was found by the court that as the direct result of the shooting by defendants the shots struck plaintiff as above mentioned and that defendants were negligent in so shooting and plaintiff was not contributorily negligent.

[The court upheld the findings below on defendants' negligence and plaintiff's lack of contributory negligence and assumption of risk.]

The problem presented in this case is whether the judgment against both defendants may stand. It is argued by defendants that they are not joint tort feasors, and thus jointly and severally liable, as they were not acting in concert, and that there is not sufficient evidence to show which defendant was guilty of the negligence which caused the injuries—the shooting by Tice or that by Simonson. Tice argues that there is evidence to show that the shot which struck plaintiff came from Simonson's gun because of admissions allegedly made by him to third persons and no evidence that they came from his gun. Further in connection with the latter contention, the court failed to find on plaintiff's allegation in his complaint that he did not know which one was at fault—did not find which defendant was guilty of the negligence which caused the injuries to plaintiff.

Considering the last argument first, we believe it is clear that the court sufficiently found on the issue that defendants were jointly liable and that thus the negligence of both was the cause of the injury or to that legal effect. It found that both defendants were negligent and "That as a direct and proximate result of the shots fired by *defendants, and each of them,* a birdshot pellet was caused to and did lodge in plaintiff's right eye and that another birdshot pellet was caused to and did lodge in plaintiff's upper lip." In so doing the court evidently did not give credence to the admissions of Simonson to third persons that he fired the shots, which it was justified in doing. It thus determined that the negligence of both defendants was the legal cause of injury—or that both were responsible. Implicit in such finding is the assumption that the court was unable to ascertain whether the shots were from the gun of one defendant or the other or one shot from each of them. The one shot that entered plaintiff's eye was the major factor in assessing damages and that shot could not have come from the gun of both defendants. It was from one or the other only.

It has been held that where a group of persons are on a hunting party, or otherwise engaged in the use of firearms, and two of them are negligent in firing in the direction of a third person who is injured thereby, both of those so firing are liable for the injury suffered by the third person, although the negligence of only one of them could have caused the injury. (Moore v. Foster, 182 Miss. 15 [(1938)]; Oliver v. Miles, 144 Miss. 852 [(1926)].) These cases speak of the action of defendants as being in concert as the ground of decision, yet it would seem they are straining that concept and the more reasonable basis appears in Oliver v. Miles, supra. There two persons were hunting together. Both shot at some partridges and in so doing shot across the highway injuring plaintiff who was travelling on it. The court stated they were acting in concert and thus both were liable. The court then stated: "We think that . . . each is liable for the resulting injury to the boy, although no one can say definitely who actually shot him. *To hold otherwise would be to exonerate both from liability, although each was negligent, and the injury resulted from such negligence.*" [Emphasis added.]

When we consider the relative position of the parties and the results that would flow if plaintiff was required to pin the injury on one of the defendants only, a requirement that the burden of proof on that subject be shifted to defendants becomes manifest. They are both wrongdoers—both negligent toward plaintiff. They brought about a situation where the negligence of one of them injured the plaintiff, hence it should rest with them each to absolve himself if he can. The injured party has been placed by defendants in the unfair position of pointing to which defendant caused the harm. If one can escape, the other may also and plaintiff is remediless. Ordinarily defendants are in a far better position to offer evidence to determine which one caused the injury. . . .

Cases are cited for the proposition that where two or more tort feasors acting independently of each other cause an injury to plaintiff, they are not joint tort feasors and plaintiff must establish the portion of the damage caused by each, even though it is impossible to prove the portion of the injury caused by each. In view of the foregoing discussion it is apparent that defendants in cases like the present one may be treated as liable on the same basis as joint tort feasors, and hence the last-cited cases are distinguishable inasmuch as they involve independent tort feasors.

In addition to that, however, it should be pointed out that the same reasons of policy and justice shift the burden to each of defendants to absolve himself if he can—relieving the wronged person of the duty of apportioning the injury to a particular defendant, apply here where we are concerned with whether plaintiff is required to supply evidence for the apportionment of damages. If defendants are independent tort feasors and thus each liable for the damage caused by him alone, and, at least, where the matter of apportionment is incapable of proof, the innocent wronged party should not be deprived of his right to redress. The wrongdoers should be left to work out between themselves any apportionment. Some of the cited cases refer to the difficulty of apportioning the burden of damages between the independent tort feasors, and say that where factually a correct division cannot be made, the trier of fact may make it the best it can, which would be more or less a guess, stressing the factor that the wrongdoers are not in a position to complain of uncertainty. . . .

The judgment is affirmed.

NOTE

Alternative liability.   Prior to *Summers,* some courts were more reluctant to indulge in the fancy footwork needed to apportion harm. In Adams v. Hall, 2 Vt. 9, 11 (1829), the plaintiff's sheep were killed by two dogs, each owned by two separate defendants. Once the evidence showed that the two dogs did not have a common owner, the court refused to allow the plaintiff to recover against either. "Hall was under no obligation to keep the other defendant's dog from killing sheep; nor *vice versa.* Then, shall each become liable for the injury done by the other's dog, merely because the dogs, without the knowledge or consent of the owners did the mischief in company? We think not." Hutchinson, J., then analogized the case to one where two servants of different owners combined to destroy property without the knowledge and consent of their masters, and concluded that there too neither master would be liable.

Summers differs from *Kingston,* in which *both A and B* are causally responsible, because in *Summers either A or B, but not both* is causally responsible for the plaintiff's harm. Is a regime of joint and several liability equally appropriate for both situations? A regime whereby each defendant is liable only for 50 percent of the harm? On the court's reasoning in *Summers,* what result if ten persons were in the hunting party? One hundred? How would the decision look if both defendants were covered by liability insurance issued by the same carrier?

Summers v. Tice has been endorsed by RST §433B(3), and RTT:LPEH §28(b), comment *f,* so long as both defendants acted "tortiously." *Id.,* comment *i.*

Restatement of the Law (Third) of Torts: Liability for Physical and Emotional Harm

§28. BURDEN OF PROOF

(b) When the plaintiff sues all of multiple actors and proves that each engaged in tortious conduct that exposed the plaintiff to a risk of harm and that the tortious conduct of one or more of them caused the plaintiff's harm but the plaintiff cannot reasonably be expected to prove which actor or actors caused the harm, the burden of proof, including both production and persuasion, on factual causation is shifted to the defendants.

Illustration 6: Reed, a pedestrian, was injured by a sofa that was negligently or intentionally thrown from an upper-story hotel room during the celebration of an NCAA basketball championship. Reed sues all of the occupants of the 47 rooms from which the sofa might have been thrown. Reed must prove which of the defendants was responsible for throwing the sofa; the burden shifting provided in this Subsection is unavailable to Reed in his suit because he has not shown that the occupants of each of the 47 rooms acted tortiously. The result would be the same if two sofas fell simultaneously, one thrown negligently or intentionally from one room and the other not due to negligence of the occupant of the other room, and Reed, not knowing from where the sofa that fell on him came, sued the occupants of both rooms. Each of the possible causes of harm must be tortious for this Subsection to be invoked.

b. Market Share Liability

Sindell v. Abbott Laboratories
607 P.2d 924 (Cal. 1980)

MOSK, J. This case involves a complex problem both timely and significant: may a plaintiff, injured as the result of a drug administered to her mother during pregnancy, who knows the type of drug involved but cannot identify the manufacturer of the precise product, hold liable for her injuries a maker of a drug produced from an identical formula?

Plaintiff Judith Sindell brought an action against eleven drug companies . . . on behalf of herself and other women similarly situated.* The complaint alleges as follows:

Between 1941 and 1971, defendants were engaged in the business of manufacturing, promoting, and marketing diethylstilbesterol (DES), a drug which is a synthetic compound of the female hormone estrogen. [After the drug entered the public domain in 1938, perhaps as many as 300 national, regional, and local producers manufactured the identical drug.] The drug was administered to plaintiff's mother and the mothers of the class she represents [other women and girls from California who were exposed to DES in utero], for the purpose of preventing miscarriage. In 1947, the Food and Drug Administration authorized the marketing of DES as a miscarriage preventative, but only on an experimental basis, with a requirement that the drug contain a warning label to that effect. . . .

In 1971, the Food and Drug Administration ordered defendants to cease marketing and promoting DES for the purpose of preventing miscarriages, and to warn physicians and the public that the drug should not be used by pregnant women because of the danger to their unborn children.

During the period defendants marketed DES, they knew or should have known that it was a carcinogenic substance, that there was a grave danger after varying periods of latency it would cause cancerous [adenocarcinoma] and precancerous

---

* [The California Supreme Court noted that class certification was not discussed in the trial court: "The plaintiff class alleged consists of 'girls and women who are residents of California and who have been exposed to DES before birth and who may or may not know that fact or the dangers' to which they were exposed."—EDS.]

growths [adenosis] in the daughters of the mothers who took it, and that it was ineffective to prevent miscarriage. Nevertheless, defendants continued to advertise and market the drug as a miscarriage preventative. They failed to test DES for efficacy and safety; the tests performed by others, upon which they relied, indicated that it was not safe or effective. In violation of the authorization of the Food and Drug Administration, defendants marketed DES on an unlimited basis rather than as an experimental drug, and they failed to warn of its potential danger.

Because of defendants' advertised assurances that DES was safe and effective to prevent miscarriage, plaintiff was exposed to the drug prior to her birth. She became aware of the danger from such exposure within one year of the time she filed her complaint. As a result of the DES ingested by her mother, plaintiff developed a malignant bladder tumor which was removed by surgery. She suffers from adenosis and must constantly be monitored by biopsy or colposcopy to insure early warning of further malignancy.

The first cause of action alleges that defendants were jointly and individually negligent in that they manufactured, marketed and promoted DES as a safe and efficacious drug to prevent miscarriage, without adequate testing or warning, and without monitoring or reporting its effects.

A separate cause of action alleges that defendants are jointly liable regardless of which particular brand of DES was ingested by plaintiff's mother because defendants collaborated in marketing, promoting and testing the drug, relied upon each other's tests, and adhered to an industry-wide safety standard. DES was produced from a common and mutually agreed upon formula as a fungible drug interchangeable with other brands of the same product; defendants knew or should have known that it was customary for doctors to prescribe the drug by its generic rather than its brand name and that pharmacists filled prescriptions from whatever brand of the drug happened to be in stock. . . .

Each cause of action alleges that defendants are jointly liable because they acted in concert, on the basis of express and implied agreements, and in reliance upon and ratification and exploitation of each other's testing and marketing methods.

Plaintiff seeks compensatory damages of $1 million and punitive damages of $10 million for herself. For the members of her class, she prays for equitable relief in the form of an order that defendants warn physicians and others of the danger of DES and the necessity of performing certain tests to determine the presence of disease caused by the drug, and that they establish free clinics in California to perform such tests. . . .

We begin with the proposition that, as a general rule, the imposition of liability depends upon a showing by the plaintiff that his or her injuries were caused by the act of the defendant or by an instrumentality under the defendant's control. The rule applies whether the injury resulted from an accidental event or from the use of a defective product.

There are, however, exceptions to this rule. Plaintiff's complaint suggests several bases upon which defendants may be held liable for her injuries even though she cannot demonstrate the name of the manufacturer which produced the DES actually taken by her mother. The first of these theories, classically illustrated by

Summers v. Tice[, 199 P.2d 1 (Cal. 1948),] places the burden of proof of causation upon tortious defendants in certain circumstances. The second basis of liability emerging from the complaint is that defendants acted in concert to cause injury to plaintiff. There is a third and novel approach to the problem, sometimes called the theory of "enterprise liability," but which we prefer to designate by the more accurate term of "industry-wide" liability, which might obviate the necessity for identifying the manufacturer of the injury-causing drug. We shall conclude that these doctrines, as previously interpreted, may not be applied to hold defendants liable under the allegations of this complaint. However, we shall propose and adopt a fourth basis for permitting the action to be tried, grounded upon an extension of the *Summers* doctrine.

I

Plaintiff places primary reliance upon cases which hold that if a party cannot identify which of two or more defendants caused an injury, the burden of proof may shift to the defendants to show that they were not responsible for the harm. This principle is sometimes referred to as the "alternative liability" theory.

[The court then discusses *Summers v. Tice* and *Ybarra v. Spangard,* 154 P.2d 687 (1944), *supra* at 263, as seminal cases in the development of "alternative liability."]

Defendants assert that these principles are inapplicable here. First, they insist that a predicate to shifting the burden of proof under *Summers-Ybarra* is that the defendants must have greater access to information regarding the cause of the injuries than the plaintiff, whereas in the present case the reverse appears. . . .

Here, as in *Summers,* the circumstances of the injury appear to render identification of the manufacturer of the drug ingested by plaintiff's mother impossible by either plaintiff or defendants, and it cannot reasonably be said that one is in a better position than the other to make the identification. Because many years elapsed between the time the drug was taken and the manifestation of plaintiff's injuries she, and many other daughters of mothers who took DES, are unable to make such identification. Certainly there can be no implication that plaintiff is at fault in failing to do so—the event occurred while plaintiff was *in utero,* a generation ago.

On the other hand, it cannot be said with assurance that defendants have the means to make the identification. In this connection, they point out that drug manufacturers ordinarily have no direct contact with the patients who take a drug prescribed by their doctors. Defendants sell to wholesalers, who in turn supply the product to physicians and pharmacies. Manufacturers do not maintain records of the persons who take the drugs they produce, and the selection of the medication is made by the physician rather than the manufacturer. Nor do we conclude that the absence of evidence on this subject is due to the fault of defendants. While it is alleged that they produced a defective product with delayed effects and without adequate warnings, the difficulty or impossibility of identification results primarily from the passage of time rather than from their allegedly negligent acts of failing to provide adequate warnings. Thus *Haft v. Lone Palm Hotel*[, 478 P.2d 465 (Cal. 1970), *supra* at 352], upon which plaintiff relies, is distinguishable.

It is important to observe, however, that while defendants do not have means superior to plaintiff to identify the maker of the precise drug taken by her mother, they may in some instances be able to prove that they did not manufacture the injury-causing substance. In the present case, for example, one of the original defendants was dismissed from the action upon proof that it did not manufacture DES until after plaintiff was born.

Thus we conclude the fact defendants do not have greater access to information which might establish the identity of the manufacturer of the DES which injured plaintiff does not per se prevent application of the *Summers* rule.

Nevertheless, plaintiff may not prevail in her claim that the *Summers* rationale should be employed to fix the whole liability for her injuries upon defendants, at least as those principles have previously been applied. There is an important difference between the situation involved in *Summers* and the present case. There, all the parties who were or could have been responsible for the harm to the plaintiff were joined as defendants. Here, by contrast, there are approximately 200 drug companies which made DES, any of which might have manufactured the injury-producing drug.

Defendants maintain that, while in *Summers* there was a 50 percent chance that one of the two defendants was responsible for the plaintiff's injuries, here since any one of 200 companies which manufactured DES might have made the product which harmed plaintiff, there is no rational basis upon which to infer that any defendant in this action caused plaintiff's injuries, nor even a reasonable possibility that they were responsible.

These arguments are persuasive if we measure the chance that any one of the defendants supplied the injury-causing drug by the number of possible tortfeasors. In such a context, the possibility that any of the five defendants supplied the DES to plaintiff's mother is so remote that it would be unfair to require each defendant to exonerate itself. There may be a substantial likelihood that none of the five defendants joined in the action made the DES which caused the injury, and that the offending producer not named would escape liability altogether. While we propose, *infra*, an adaptation of the rule in *Summers* which will substantially overcome these difficulties, defendants appear to be correct that the rule, as previously applied, cannot relieve plaintiff of the burden of proving the identity of the manufacturer which made the drug causing her injuries.

II

The second principle upon which plaintiff relies is the so-called "concert of action" theory. . . .

. . . The gravamen of the charge of concert is that defendants failed to adequately test the drug or to give sufficient warning of its dangers and that they relied upon the tests performed by one another and took advantage of each others' promotional and marketing techniques. These allegations do not amount to a charge that there was a tacit understanding or a common plan among defendants to fail to conduct adequate tests or give sufficient warnings, and that they substantially aided and encouraged one another in these omissions. . . .

III

[The court rejects an "enterprise theory" of liability in the DES cases.]

IV

If we were confined to the theories of *Summers* and [a case about enterprise theory], we would be constrained to hold that the judgment must be sustained [for the defendant]. Should we require that plaintiff identify the manufacturer which supplied the DES used by her mother or that all DES manufacturers be joined in the action, she would effectively be precluded from any recovery. As defendants candidly admit, there is little likelihood that all the manufacturers who made DES at the time in question are still in business or that they are subject to the jurisdiction of the California courts. There are, however, forceful arguments in favor of holding that plaintiff has a cause of action.

In our contemporary complex industrialized society, advances in science and technology create fungible goods which may harm consumers and which cannot be traced to any specific producer. The response of the courts can be either to adhere rigidly to prior doctrine, denying recovery to those injured by such products, or to fashion remedies to meet these changing needs. Just as Justice Traynor in his landmark concurring opinion in *Escola v. Coca Cola Bottling Co.*[, 150 P.2d 436 (1944), *infra* at 656], recognized that in an era of mass production and complex marketing methods the traditional standard of negligence was insufficient to govern the obligations of manufacturer to consumer, so in these recurring circumstances. The Restatement comments that modification of the *Summers* rule may be necessary in a situation like that before us.

The most persuasive reason for finding plaintiff states a cause of action is that advanced in *Summers*: as between an innocent plaintiff and negligent defendants, the latter should bear the cost of the injury. Here, as in *Summers*, plaintiff is not at fault in failing to provide evidence of causation, and although the absence of such evidence is not attributable to the defendants either, their conduct in marketing a drug the effects of which are delayed for many years played a significant role in creating the unavailability of proof.

From a broader policy standpoint, defendants are better able to bear the cost of injury resulting from the manufacture of a defective product. As was said by Justice Traynor in *Escola*, "[t]he cost of an injury and the loss of time or health may be an overwhelming misfortune to the person injured, and a needless one, for the risk of injury can be insured by the manufacturer and distributed among the public as a cost of doing business." 150 P.2d at 441. The manufacturer is in the best position to discover and guard against defects in its products and to warn of harmful effects; thus, holding it liable for defects and failure to warn of harmful effects will provide an incentive to product safety. These considerations are particularly significant where medication is involved, for the consumer is virtually helpless to protect himself from serious, sometimes permanent, sometimes fatal, injuries caused by deleterious drugs.

Where, as here, all defendants produced a drug from an identical formula and the manufacturer of the DES which caused plaintiff's injuries cannot be identified through no fault of plaintiff, a modification of the rule of *Summers* is warranted. As we have seen, an undiluted *Summers* rationale is inappropriate to shift the burden of proof of causation to defendants because if we measure the chance that any particular manufacturer supplied the injury-causing product by the number of producers of DES, there is a possibility that none of the five defendants in this case produced the offending substance and that the responsible manufacturer, not named in the action, will escape liability.

But we approach the issue of causation from a different perspective: we hold it to be reasonable in the present context to measure the likelihood that any of the defendants supplied the product which allegedly injured plaintiff by the percentage which the DES sold by each of them for the purpose of preventing miscarriage bears to the entire production of the drug sold by all for that purpose. Plaintiff asserts in her briefs that Eli Lilly and Company and 5 or 6 other companies produced 90 percent of the DES marketed. If at trial this is established to be the fact, then there is a corresponding likelihood that this comparative handful of producers manufactured the DES which caused plaintiff's injuries, and only a 10 percent likelihood that the offending producer would escape liability.[28]

If plaintiff joins in the action the manufacturers of a substantial share of the DES which her mother might have taken, the injustice of shifting the burden of proof to defendants to demonstrate that they could not have made the substance which injured plaintiff is significantly diminished. While 75 to 80 percent of the market is suggested as the requirement by [Comment, DES and a Proposed Theory of Enterprise Liability, 46 Fordham L. Rev. 963, 996 (1978) [hereinafter Fordham Comment]], we hold only that a substantial percentage is required.

The presence in the action of a substantial share of the appropriate market also provides a ready means to apportion damages among the defendants. Each defendant will be held liable for the proportion of the judgment represented by its share of that market unless it demonstrates that it could not have made the product which caused plaintiff's injuries. In the present case, as we have seen, one DES manufacturer was dismissed from the action upon filing a declaration that it had not manufactured DES until after plaintiff was born. Once plaintiff has met her burden of joining the required defendants, they in turn may cross-complaint against other DES manufacturers, not joined in the action, which they can allege might have supplied the injury-causing product.

---

28. The Fordham Comment explains the connection between percentage of market share and liability as follows: "[I]f X Manufacturer sold one-fifth of all the DES prescribed for pregnancy and identification could be made in all cases, X would be the sole defendant in approximately one-fifth of all cases and liable for all the damages in those cases. Under alternative liability, X would be joined in all cases in which identification could not be made, but liable for only one-fifth of the total damages in these cases. X would pay the same amount either way. Although the correlation is not, in practice, perfect [footnote omitted], it is close enough so that defendants' objections on the ground of fairness lose their value." [Comment, DES and a Proposed Theory of Enterprise Liability, 46 Fordham L. Rev. 963, 994 (1978).]

Under this approach, each manufacturer's liability would approximate its responsibility for the injuries caused by its own products. Some minor discrepancy in the correlation between market share and liability is inevitable; therefore, a defendant may be held liable for a somewhat different percentage of the damage than its share of the appropriate market would justify. It is probably impossible, with the passage of time, to determine market share with mathematical exactitude. But just as jury cannot be expected to determine the precise relationship between fault and liability in applying the doctrine of comparative fault (Li v. Yellow Cab Co.) or partial indemnity (American Motorcycle Ass'n v. Superior Court), the difficulty of apportioning damages among the defendant producers in exact relation to their market share does not seriously militate against the rule we adopt. As we said in *Summers* with regard to the liability of independent tortfeasors, where a correct division of liability cannot be made "the trier of fact may make it the best it can." 199 P.2d at 5.

We are not unmindful of the practical problems involved in defining the market and determining market share, but these are largely matters of proof which properly cannot be determined at the pleading stage of these proceedings. Defendants urge that it would be both unfair and contrary to public policy to hold them liable for plaintiff's injuries in the absence of proof that one of them supplied the drug responsible for the damage. Most of their arguments, however, are based upon the assumption that one manufacturer would be held responsible for the products of another or for those of all other manufacturers if plaintiff ultimately prevails. But under the rule we adopt, each manufacturer's liability for an injury would be approximately equivalent to the damages caused by the DES it manufactured.

The judgments are reversed.

RICHARDSON, J., dissenting. . . . With particular reference to the matter before us, and in the context of products liability, the requirement of a causation element has been recognized as equally fundamental . . . . Indeed, an inability to prove this causal link between defendant's conduct and plaintiff's injury has proven fatal in prior cases brought against manufacturers of DES by persons who were situated in positions identical to those of plaintiffs herein . . . . According to the majority, in the present case plaintiffs have openly conceded that they are unable to identify the particular entity which manufactured the drug consumed by their mothers. In fact, plaintiffs have joined only *five* of the approximately *two hundred* drug companies which manufactured DES. Thus, the case constitutes far more than a mere factual variant upon the theme composed in *Summers v. Tice,* wherein plaintiff joined as codefendants the *only* two persons who could have injured him . . . . In the present case, in stark contrast, it remains wholly speculative and conjectural whether *any* of the five named defendants actually caused plaintiffs' injuries.

The fact that plaintiffs cannot tie defendants to the injury-producing drug does not trouble the majority for it declares that the *Summers* requirement of proof of actual causation by a named defendant is satisfied by a joinder of those defendants who have *together* manufactured "*a substantial percentage*" of the DES which has been marketed. Notably lacking from the majority's expression of its new rule, unfortunately, is any definition or guidance as to what should constitute a "substantial" share of the relevant market. The issue is entirely open-ended and the answer, presumably, is anyone's guess . . . .

In adopting the foregoing rationale the majority rejects over 100 years of tort law which required that before tort liability was imposed a "matching" of defendant's conduct and plaintiff's injury was absolutely essential. Furthermore, in bestowing on plaintiffs this new largess the majority sprinkles the rain of liability upon all the joined defendants alike — those who may be tortfeasors and those who may have had nothing at all to do with plaintiffs' injury — and an added bonus is conferred. Plaintiffs are free to pick and choose their targets . . . .

NOTES

1. Calculating market shares.   Calculating market shares has proven difficult because DES was sold for many different uses in many different tablet sizes, making a firm's gross DES sales a poor indicator of its share of the DES market directed to pregnant women. In addition, the plaintiffs were born in different years in which the market composition varied. Half were also born outside California. *Sindell* settled in September 1983, before discovery was taken on any of these factual issues. The partial information on market shares led the court in McCormack v. Abbott Laboratories, 617 F. Supp. 1521, 1527 (D. Mass. 1985), to proceed as follows: First, let each defendant establish its (small) share and then divide the remainder equally among the remaining defendants. "Assume hypothetically, five prima facie defendants, of whom one shows an actual share of 12%. The four remaining defendants will each be potentially liable for 22%." This system of allocation prevents any plaintiff from charging any defendant the share attributable to absent third parties. "Assume hypothetically, five prima facie defendants who show that their actual shares are, respectively, 5%, 10%, 15%, 20% and 25%. Plaintiff could recover a maximum of 75% of her damages."

Sindell originally held that each defendant could be held liable for the shares of absent or insolvent defendants no matter how small its share of the market. The California Supreme Court stepped back from that holding in two stages. In Murphy v. E.R. Squibb & Sons, Inc., 710 P.2d 247, 255 (Cal. 1985), it held that the "substantial share" requirement of *Sindell* was not met when the plaintiff sued only one manufacturer, Squibb, with a 10 percent market share. Subsequently, in Brown v. Superior Court (Abbott Laboratories, RPI), 751 P.2d 470 (Cal. 1988), Mosk, J., held that defendant was responsible only for its proportionate share of the loss, so that the entire loss could not be thrown on a defendant with an "insignificant" market share.

2. Exculpation evidence?   In Hymowitz v. Eli Lilly & Co., 539 N.E.2d 1069, 1078 (N.Y. 1989), the New York Court of Appeals first noted that *Sindell* based the proportionate liability of each defendant pharmaceutical company on its sales in the "national market" for DES used in pregnancy. *Hymowitz* then concluded that since liability was "based on the over-all risk produced" no exculpation evidence could be allowed in individual cases. Thus a defendant could be found liable even if it could demonstrate with certainty that it did not produce the tablets in question. The court reasoned that, while defendant's exculpation evidence, if permitted, would allow it to escape liability in a given case, that evidence would not reduce its overall burden, because its *increased* share of liability for the remaining cases in the pool exactly offset its saving in the individual case. Since gains and losses net out, it is cheaper administratively in the long run if *no one* can exonerate himself in the individual case. Is the *Hymowitz* approach dependent upon all DES victims' seeking compensation for their injuries? On all jurisdictions adopting the same approach to market share calculation?

3. *Market share liability in lead cases.*   In Skipworth v. Lead Industries Ass'n, 690 A.2d 169, 172, 173 (Pa. 1997), the parents of a child who was treated for lead poisoning five times in three years sued several manufacturers of lead pigment (contained in paint) and a trade association, Lead Industries Association, Inc. (LIA). Plaintiff invoked multiple theories of liability, including market share liability. The trial court granted summary judgment in favor of defendants and the Superior Court affirmed. The Pennsylvania Supreme Court declined to adopt market share liability and distinguished lead pigment from DES:

> Pennsylvania . . . follows the general rule that a plaintiff, in order to recover, must establish that a particular defendant's negligence was the proximate cause of her injuries. Adoption of the market share liability theory would result in a significant departure from this rule . . . . Application of market share liability to lead paint cases such as this one would lead to a distortion of liability which would be so gross as to make determinations of culpability arbitrary and unfair.

The court focused on two key differences between the lead pigment and DES cases. "First, the relevant time period in question is far more extensive than the relevant time period in a DES case [nine months of pregnancy]." The plaintiff in *Skipworth* did not know which application of paint in her residence had caused the lead poisoning, and could not narrow the relevant time span from the time the house was built (1870) to the last time paint was applied (1977). Second, "lead paint, as opposed to DES, is not a fungible product."

> [The lack of fungibility] is . . . fatal to [plaintiff's] claim. . . . Market share liability is grounded on the premise that it ensures that "each manufacturer's liability would approximate its responsibility for the injuries caused by its own products." *Sindell*, 607 P.2d at 937. Yet, in this case, apportioning liability based upon a manufacturer defendant's share of the market . . . would not serve to approximate that defendant's responsibility for injuries caused by its lead paint. For example, a manufacturer whose lead product had a lower bioavailability than average would have caused less damage that its market share would indicate. Thus, application of market share to such a manufacturer would impose on it a disproportionately high share of the damages awarded.

The suits against manufacturers of lead pigment, rebuffed in *Skipworth*, received a much warmer reception in Thomas v. Mallett, 701 N.W.2d 523, 562, 563

(Wis. 2005), where Butler, J., allowed an infant plaintiff injured by lead poisoning to sue, in addition to the family landlord, the lead pigment manufacturers under a risk-contribution theory—a variation on *Sindell*'s market-share liability. Butler, J., first held that lead carbonate, the active agent in the defendants' pigment, was a fungible product, as lead pigments differed only in "degree, not function," because "white lead carbonates were produced utilizing 'virtually identical chemical formulas' such that all white lead carbonates were 'identically defective.'" He then addressed the defendants' other objections to the risk-contribution theory:

> [The] Pigment Manufacturers contend that the risk-contribution theory should not be extended because Thomas's lead poisoning could have been caused from many different sources. We agree that the record indicates that lead poisoning can stem from the ambient air, many foods, drinking water, soil, and dust.
>
> Further, the Pigment Manufacturers argue that the risk-contribution theory should not be extended because lead poisoning does not produce a "signature injury." As alternate explanations for Thomas's cognitive deficits, the Pigment Manufacturers have brought forth evidence that genetics, birth complications causing damage to the central nervous system, severe environmental deprivation, inadequate parenting, parental emotional disorders, and child abuse could all, in varying ways, cause such impairments.
>
> These arguments have no bearing on whether the risk-contribution theory should be extended to white lead carbonate claims. Harm is harm, whether it be "signature" or otherwise. Even under the risk-contribution theory, the plaintiff still retains a burden of establishing causation. . . .
>
> [In addition,] the record is replete with evidence that shows the Pigment Manufacturers actually magnified the risk through their aggressive promotion of white lead carbonate, even despite the awareness of the toxicity of lead.

The bottom line was that the considerations that proved decisive in *Skipworth* became jury questions in *Thomas*. Wilcox, J., dissented:

> It is often said that bad facts make bad law. Today's decision epitomizes that ancient legal axiom. The end result of the majority opinion is that the defendants, lead pigment manufacturers, can be held liable for a product they may or may not have produced, which may or may not have caused the plaintiff's injuries, based on conduct that may have occurred over 100 years ago when some of the defendants were not even part of the relevant market.

For the academic inspiration in *Thomas*, see Rostron, Beyond Market Share Liability: A Theory of Proportional Share Liability for Nonfungible Products, 52 UCLA L. Rev. 151 (2004). In 2013, in response to the ruling in *Thomas*, the Wisconsin legislature enacted a law that imposed a number of limiting factors—e.g., the manufacturer must have produced the product within 25 years of "the date that the claimant's cause of action accrued," and the product in question must have been distributed without any labeling that identified the manufacturer or distributor—which effectively withdrew the risk-contribution theory of liability from the majority of toxic tort cases. See Wis. Stat. Ann. §895.046 (West 2015).

Thomas' risk-contribution theory was challenged on constitutional grounds in Gibson v. American Cyanamid, 760 F.3d 600, 604-605 (7th Cir. 2014). The District Court held "that risk-contribution theory violates the substantive component of the Due Process Clause," and granted the defendants a summary judgment. That decision was overturned by Chang, J., "in light of the broad deference that the Constitution grants to the development of state common law."

4. Market share: Beyond DES. A few states have been willing to extend market share liability beyond DES cases. The Hawaii Supreme Court held that market share liability applied against defendant manufacturers of blood products, from which the plaintiff, a hemophiliac, allegedly contracted the AIDS virus. Smith v. Cutter Biological, Inc., 823 P.2d 717 (Haw. 1991). A federal district court applying Florida law also imposed market share liability in a blood products case. Ray v. Cutter Laboratories, 754 F. Supp. 193 (M.D. Fla. 1991).

In other cases, the courts have taken their cue from *Skipworth*, by refusing to extend *Sindell* beyond fungible products like DES. In Pooshs v. Philip Morris USA, Inc., 904 F. Supp. 2d 1009, 1032 (N.D. Cal. 2012), the court refused to apply market share liability to cigarettes, holding that they were not fungible. In DiCola v. White Bros. Perf. Prods., Inc., 158 Cal. App. 4th 666, 677 (2008), the point was generalized when the court refused to apply market share liability to a product that was not a "generic item produced by several manufacturers." In Shackil v. Lederle Laboratories, 561 A.2d 511, 523 (N.J. 1989), the New Jersey Supreme Court held the market share doctrine did not apply to the diphtheria-pertussis-tetanus (DPT) vaccine, whose pertussis component caused the infant plaintiff to have a seizure disorder resulting in serious and permanent brain damage. Not all DPT vaccines were prepared in the same way, so they did not necessarily hold out the same level of risk. Similarly, courts have rejected the theory in asbestos cases, in light of the nonfungible natures of the exposures. Finally, in Hamilton v. Beretta U.S.A. Corp., 750 N.E. 2d 1055, 1067 (N.Y. 2001), the New York Court of Appeals refused to extend *Hymowitz* to cases of manufacturer's potential gun liability, noting that "guns are not identical, fungible products. . . . [G]iven the negligent marketing theory on which plaintiffs tried this case—plaintiffs have never asserted that the manufacturers' marketing techniques were uniform. . . . Defendants engaged in widely-varied conduct creating varied risks."

Even though market share liability has been truncated, market share evidence was allowed to establish causation in In re Methyl Tertiary Butyl Ether (MTBE) Products Liability Litigation, 725 F.3d 65, 115-116 (2d Cir. 2013). New York City sued Exxon Corporation, among other oil companies, for contamination of its water by the ongoing release of MTBE "into the ground, contaminating ground water supplies." The releases took place from the early 1980s until 2005, when the chemical was banned under federal law. Carney, J., held that the district court was correct to instruct the jury that it could "consider as circumstantial evidence [Exxon's] percentage share of the retail and/or supply market for gasoline containing MTBE in Queens or [in] any other region that you determine is relevant." According to Carney, J., "[t]he District Court did not impose market-share liability upon Exxon; it simply permitted the jury to draw upon market-share data as one piece of circumstantial evidence that Exxon caused the City's injury." How much of the total losses in question can be recovered by such circumstantial evidence, if the market share theory is not invoked?

c. Loss of Chance of Survival

Herskovits v. Group Health Cooperative
664 P.2d 474 (Wash. 1983)

DORE, J. This appeal raises the issue of whether an estate can maintain an action for professional negligence as a result of failure to timely diagnose lung cancer, where the estate can show probable reduction in statistical chance for survival but cannot show and/or prove that with timely diagnosis and treatment, decedent probably would have lived to normal life expectancy.

Both counsel advised that for the purpose of this appeal we are to *assume* that the respondent Group Health Cooperative of Puget Sound and its personnel negligently failed to diagnose Herskovits' cancer on his first visit to the hospital and *proximately* caused a 14 percent reduction in his chances of survival. It is undisputed that Herskovits had less than a 50 percent chance of survival at all times herein.

The main issue we will address in this opinion is whether a patient, with less than a 50 percent chance of survival, has a cause of action against the hospital and its employees if they are negligent in diagnosing a lung cancer which reduces his chances of survival by 14 percent. . . . [The trial judge granted defendant's motion for summary judgment.]

I

. . . Dr. Ostrow [plaintiff's expert] testified that if the tumor was a "stage 1" tumor in December 1974, Herskovits' chance of a 5-year survival would have been 39 percent. In June 1975, his chances of survival were 25 percent assuming the tumor had progressed to "stage 2." Thus, the delay in diagnosis may have reduced the chance of a 5-year survival by 14 percent. . . .

Plaintiff contends that medical testimony of a reduction of chance of survival from 39 percent to 25 percent is sufficient evidence to allow the proximate cause issue to go to the jury. Defendant Group Health argues conversely that Washington law does not permit such testimony on the issue of medical causation and requires that medical testimony must be at least sufficiently definite to establish that the act complained of "probably" or "more likely than not" caused the subsequent disability. It is Group Health's contention that plaintiff must prove that Herskovits "probably" would have survived had the defendant not been allegedly negligent; that is, the plaintiff must prove there was at least a 51 percent chance of survival. . . .

II

This court has held that a person who negligently renders aid and consequently increases the risk of harm to those he is trying to assist is liable for any physical damages he causes. Brown v. MacPherson's, Inc., 545 P.2d 13 (Wash. 1975). In *Brown,* the court cited Restatement (Second) of Torts §323 (1965), which reads:

> One who undertakes . . . to render services to another which he should recognize as necessary for the protection of the other's person or things, is subject to liability to the other for physical harm resulting from his failure to exercise reasonable care to perform his undertaking, if
> (a) his failure to exercise such care increases the risk of such harm, . . .

This court heretofore has not faced the issue of whether, under section 323(a), proof that the defendant's conduct increased the risk of death by decreasing the chances of survival is sufficient to take the issue of proximate cause to the jury. Some courts in other jurisdictions have allowed the proximate cause issue to go to the jury on this type of proof. These courts emphasized the fact that defendants' conduct deprived the decedents of a "significant" chance to survive or recover, rather than requiring proof that with absolute certainty the defendants' conduct caused the physical injury. The underlying reason is that it is not for the wrongdoer, who put the possibility of recovery beyond realization, to say afterward that the result was inevitable.

Other jurisdictions have rejected this approach, generally holding that unless the plaintiff is able to show that it was *more likely than not* that the harm was caused by the defendant's negligence, proof of a decreased chance of survival is not enough to take the proximate cause question to the jury. Cooper v. Sisters of Charity, Inc., 272 N.E.2d 97 (Ohio 1971). These courts have concluded that the defendant should not be liable where the decedent more than likely would have died anyway.

The ultimate question raised here is whether the relationship between the increased risk of harm and Herskovits' death is sufficient to hold Group Health responsible. Is a 36 percent (from 39 percent to 25 percent) reduction in the decedent's chance for survival sufficient evidence of causation to allow the jury to consider the possibility that the physician's failure to timely diagnose the illness was the proximate cause of his death? We answer in the affirmative. To decide otherwise would be a blanket release from liability for doctors and hospitals any time there was less than a 50 percent chance of survival, regardless of how flagrant the negligence.

CONCLUSION

. . . We reject Group Health's argument that plaintiffs *must show* that Herskovits "probably" would have had a 51 percent chance of survival if the hospital had not been negligent. We hold that medical testimony of a reduction of chance of survival from 39 percent to 25 percent is sufficient evidence to allow the proximate cause issue to go to the jury.

Causing reduction of the opportunity to recover (loss of chance) by one's negligence, however, does not necessitate a total recovery against the negligent party for all damages caused by the victim's death. Damages should be awarded to the injured party or his family based only on damages caused directly by premature death, such as lost earnings and additional medical expenses, etc.

We reverse the trial court and reinstate the cause of action.

PEARSON, J., concurring. I agree with the majority that the trial court erred in granting defendant's motion for summary judgment. I cannot, however, agree with the majority's reasoning in reaching this decision.

[Pearson, J., then conducted an exhaustive review of the cases and explicitly adopted the position in King, Causation, Valuation, and Chance in Personal Injury Torts Involving Preexisting Conditions and Future Consequences, 90 Yale L.J. 1353 (1981).]

King's basic thesis is explained in the following passage, which is particularly pertinent to the case before us.

> Causation has for the most part been treated as an all-or-nothing proposition. Either a loss was caused by the defendant or it was not. . . . A plaintiff ordinarily should be required to prove by the applicable standard of proof that the defendant caused the loss in question. *What* caused a loss, however, should be a separate question from what the *nature and extent* of the loss are. This distinction seems to have eluded the courts, with the result that lost chances in many respects are compensated either as certainties or not at all.
>
> To illustrate, consider the case in which a doctor negligently fails to diagnose a patient's cancerous condition until it has become inoperable. Assume further that even with a timely diagnosis the patient would have had only a 30% chance of recovering from the disease and surviving over the long term. There are two ways of handling such a case. Under the traditional approach, this loss of a not-better-than-even chance of recovering from the cancer would not be compensable because it did not appear more likely [than] not that the patient would have survived with proper care. Recoverable damages, if any, would depend on the extent to which it appeared that cancer killed the patient sooner than it would have with timely diagnosis and treatment, and on the extent to which the delay in diagnosis aggravated the patient's condition, such as by causing additional pain. A more rational approach, however, would allow recovery for the loss of the chance of cure even though the chance was not better than even. The probability of long-term survival would be reflected in the amount of damages awarded for the loss of the chance. While the plaintiff here could not prove by a preponderance of the evidence that he was denied a cure by the defendant's negligence, he could show by a preponderance that he was deprived of a 30% chance of a cure. [90 Yale L.J. at 1363-1364.]

Under the all-or-nothing approach typified by Cooper v. Sisters of Charity, Inc., a plaintiff who establishes that but for the defendant's negligence the decedent had a 51-percent chance of survival may maintain an action for that death. The defendant will be liable for all damages arising from the death, even though there was a 49-percent chance it would have occurred despite his negligence. On the other hand, a plaintiff who establishes that but for the defendant's negligence the decedent had a 49-percent chance of survival recovers nothing.

[The dissent of Brachtenberg, J., is omitted.]

DOLLIVER, J., dissenting. . . . I favor the opposing view and believe the reasoning in Cooper v. Sisters of Charity, Inc., also cited by the majority, is more persuasive. In discussing the rule to be adopted the Ohio Supreme Court stated:

> . . . Traditional proximate cause standards require that the trier of the facts, at a minimum, must be provided with evidence that a result was more likely than not to have been caused by an act, in the absence of any intervening cause.
>
> Lesser standards of proof are understandably attractive in malpractice cases where physical well being, and life itself, are the subject of litigation. The strong intuitive sense of humanity tends to emotionally direct us toward a conclusion that in an action for wrongful death an injured person should be compensated for the loss of any chance for survival, regardless of its remoteness. However, we have trepidations that such a rule would be so loose that it would produce more injustice than justice. Even though there exists authority for a rule allowing recovery based upon proof of causation by evidence not meeting the standard of probability, we are not persuaded by their logic. . . .

We consider the better rule to be that in order to comport with the standard of proof of proximate cause, plaintiff in a malpractice case must prove that defendant's negligence, *in probability,* proximately caused the death. (Citations omitted.) *Cooper,* at 251-252.

NOTES

1. Judicial response to the lost chance doctrine.   The "lost chance" doctrine continues to divide the courts. A recent tally indicated that 22 states have adopted lost chance, 16 have rejected it, six have deferred on deciding the issue, and six have not yet addressed the issue. Koch, Comment, Whose Loss Is It Anyway? Effects of the "Lost-Chance" Doctrine on Civil Litigation and Medical Malpractice, 88 N.C. L. Rev. 595, 606-611 (2010). If the doctrine is accepted, how should it be applied? More concretely, what is the relevance of the 36 percent "reduction in survival" figure to Dore's, J., analysis? How does the case come out if we posit that the missed diagnosis increased the risk of death from 61 percent to 75 percent? What result if the lost chance reduced the five-year survival rate from 5 percent to zero? Or increased the chance of death from 95 percent to 100 percent?

The lost chance doctrine is addressed in RTT:LPEH §26, comment *n,* in line with recent cases that have invoked it to cover situations of missed diagnosis, on the one hand, or inappropriate or delayed treatment, on the other. In Holton v. Memorial Hospital, 679 N.E.2d 1202, 1213 (Ill. 1997), the court embraced the lost chance doctrine, in part out of its concerns with incentives: "Disallowing tort recovery in medical malpractice actions on the theory that a patient was already too ill to survive or recover may operate as a disincentive on the part of health care providers to administer quality medical care to critically ill or injured patients." In most cases, the measure of damages is computed simply by looking at the percentage reduction in the value of life or limb involved in the individual case, allowing for a 14 percent recovery (39 percent minus 25 percent) in *Herskovits.*

> ### Restatement of the Law (Third) of Torts: Liability for Physical and Emotional Harm
>
> #### §26. FACTUAL CAUSE
>
> ***Comment n. Lost opportunity or lost chance as harm:*** Concomitant with [the] re-conceptualization of the harm for a plaintiff unable to show a probability in excess of 50 percent is an adjustment of the damages to which the plaintiff is entitled. Rather than full damages for the adverse outcome, the plaintiff is only compensated for the lost opportunity. . . . These decisions are a response to inadequate (and unavailable) information about what would have been the course of a specific patient's medical condition if negligence, typically in failing to diagnose, refer, or otherwise provide proper treatment, had not occurred. Lost chance thus serves to ameliorate what would otherwise be insurmountable problems of proof. . . .

Lost chance cases often raise complex factual disputes relating both to whether the defendant was negligent and what kind of lost chance was created. In Dickhoff v. Green, 836 N.W.2d 321 (Minn. 2013), Anderson, J., allowed the lost chance doctrine. At issue in the case was whether defendant should have diagnosed the newborn plaintiff's cancer when it was a small lump, possibly a cyst, on her initial, or other early, well-baby care visit. An early detection would have allowed for about a 60 percent chance of recovery. The late detection, over a year later, when the tumor was advanced, made it highly likely that the plaintiff would die. The parties differed on how often the plaintiff's mother made reference to the lump, and the plaintiff conceded that painful therapy was needed even with an early diagnosis. But the court concluded that it "should be beyond dispute that a patient regards a chance to survive or achieve a more favorable medical outcome as something of value." Should the lost chance doctrine be applied to lost sales in a competitive market? The probability of winning a contest?

2. The incentive effects of the lost chance doctrine. The states that still reject the lost chance rule do so out of a concern over how it fits into the larger system of damage compensation. See Fennell v. Southern Maryland Hospital Center, Inc., 580 A.2d 206, 214 (Md. 1990), in which the court wrote:

> If loss of chance damages are to be recognized, amendments to the wrongful death statute should also be considered. As a class, medical malpractice plaintiffs benefit from the fact that they are entitled to recover 100% of their damages from a defendant whose negligence caused only 51% of their loss because it is more probable than not that the defendant's negligence caused the loss. Reciprocally, a defendant whose negligence caused less than 50% of a plaintiff's loss pays nothing because it is [more] probable that the negligence did not cause the loss. If a plaintiff whose decedent had a 49% chance of survival, which was lost through negligent treatment, is permitted to recover 49% of the value of the decedent's

life, then a plaintiff whose decedent had a 51% chance of survival, which was lost through negligent treatment, perhaps ought to have recovery limited to 51% of the value of the life lost. The latter result would require a change in our current wrongful death statute.

For a statutory endorsement of the no lost chance position, see Mich. Comp. Laws Ann. §600.2912a(2) (West 2015): "In an action alleging medical malpractice . . . the plaintiff cannot recover for loss of an opportunity to survive or an opportunity to achieve a better result unless the opportunity was greater than 50%."

What about other tort actions? *Fennell's* concern can be recast as an inquiry into the optimal level of deterrence under the tort law. Under the lost chance doctrine, errors in individual cases will not "cancel out" in the long run, so that defendants may be systematically overtaxed for harms that they did *not* cause. Consider a group of 100 cases. Defendant has a 25 percent chance of causing the death in 50 of them and a 75 percent chance of causing the death in the other 50. On balance, the defendant has caused half the deaths $[(0.25 \times 50) + (0.75 \times 50) = 50]$. Yet under the *Herskovits* rule, the defendant will be charged for 62.5 deaths $[(0.25 \times 50) + (1 \times 50) = 62.5]$, which leads to overdeterrence. The *Fennell* rule tends to yield better results because, even though the defendants are undercharged when the chance of loss is less than 50 percent, they are overcharged when it is more. The two errors balance each other out, at least if the losses are symmetrically distributed about a mean of 50 percent probability, in which case the all-or-nothing rule reduces the level of error below what it would be with a proportionate share rule. See Kaye, The Limits of the Preponderance of the Evidence Standard: Justifiably Naked Statistical Evidence and Multiple Causation, 1982 Am. B. Found. Res. J. 487.

This conclusion does not hold, however, in the "recurring miss" situation (see *supra* at 353) when the defendant undertakes a large number of similar actions, each of which is less than 50 percent likely to cause harm. The refusal to allow any plaintiff to recover now results in systematic underdeterrence, because a defendant who is, say, 40 percent responsible for loss in each of 100 cases pays nothing at all. See Shavell, Economic Analysis of Accident Law 117 (1987), who criticizes the 50 percent threshold on the ground that it "will result in injurers' never being liable for the losses they cause; it may thus provide grossly inadequate incentives to reduce risk." What should be done if the percentage reduction in life chances is uncertain?

3. Compensation for future tortious risk only. The probabilistic tests of causation also can be pressed into service to calculate current awards for tortious risk that has not ripened into actual injury. Suppose a release of radioactive materials increases by 10 percent the expected number of cancers in a community over the next 30 years, from 100 to 110. The 50 percent cutoff denies recovery in all cases, and thus leads to the underdeterrence noted by Levmore (see *supra* at 353) and Shavell. Yet holding the defendant liable in all 110 cancer cases would force the defendant to pay for 100 cancers that he did not cause, thereby inducing him to take excessive precautions.

One way to get the incentives aligned is to require the defendant to compensate the "tortious risk" today, without the occurrence of actual injury. Professor Robinson so argues in Probabilistic Causation and Compensation for Tortious Risk, 14 J. Legal Stud. 779 (1985). Should, for example, a 10 percent increase in risk trigger 110 actions today, each for about 9 percent of present discounted value, necessarily barring all future claims when they arise? Most courts have avoided this huge administrative hassle when no one can quantify the increase in risk or identify which individuals fall into the exposed class. One variation on this theme was allowed in Jackson v. Johns-Manville Sales Corp., 781 F.2d 394, 413, 414 (5th Cir. 1986), where a plaintiff, who had already contracted asbestosis, was awarded a recovery for "probable future consequences" in light of the 50 percent chance of contracting cancer thereafter.

4. Enhanced risk of injury and medical monitoring.   The enhanced risk of future injury has led to many class actions to recover the costs of medical monitoring of potential future diseases. The first case that recognized this item of damages was Friends for All Children, Inc. v. Lockheed Aircraft Corp., 746 F.2d 816, 818 (D.C. Cir. 1984), in which Starr, J., held that Lockheed had to supply diagnostic tests to about 40 adopted Vietnamese children living in France prior to final judgment because they "faced irreparable injury unless they promptly obtained diagnostic examinations." Allowing costs for medical monitoring was stoutly rejected as a matter of federal common law in Metro-North Commuter Railroad Co. v. Buckley, 521 U.S. 424 (1997). Several states have followed suit. In Henry v. Dow Chemical Co., 701 N.W.2d 684, 690-691 (Mich. 2005), the plaintiffs sought to recover medical monitoring expenses for their exposure to the dioxin component of Agent Orange that Dow manufactured. Noting that a physical injury has long been a part of the negligence claim, Corrigan, J., continued:

> The requirement of a present physical injury to person or property serves a number of important ends for the legal system. First, such a requirement defines more clearly who actually possesses a cause of action. In allowing recovery only to those who have actually suffered a present physical injury, the fact-finder need not engage in speculations about the extent to which a plaintiff possesses a cognizable legal claim. Second, such a requirement reduces the risks of fraud, by setting a clear minimum threshold — a present physical injury — before a plaintiff can proceed on a claim.
>
> Finally, [in] the absence of such a requirement, it will be inevitable that judges, as in the instant case, will be required to answer questions that are more appropriate for a legislative than a judicial body: How far from the Tittibawassee River must a plaintiff live in order to have a cognizable claim? What evidence of exposure to dioxin will be required to support such a claim? What level of medical research is sufficient to support a claim that exposure to dioxin, in contrast to exposure to another chemical, will give rise to a cause of action?

More recent cases have been more receptive to medical monitoring claims. In Exxon Mobil Corp. v. Albright, 71 A.3d 30, 81-82 (Md. 2013), the plaintiffs sought, among other relief, the costs of medical monitoring for medical illnesses for conditions derived from a massive leak of over 26,000 gallons of gasoline. In line with the recent decisions in many other jurisdictions, Harrell, J., held that recovery for medical monitoring did not create a standalone cause of action, but could be an appropriate remedy for tortious behavior: "[A] plaintiff must show that reasonable medical costs are necessary due to a reasonably certain and significant[ly] increased risk of developing a latent disease as a result of exposure to a toxic substance." In determining whether to award medical monitoring damages, the court continued, a trial judge must consider whether the plaintiff proved four factors:

> (1) that the plaintiff was significantly exposed to a proven hazardous substance through the defendant's tortious conduct; (2) that, as a proximate result of significant exposure, the plaintiff suffers a significantly increased risk of contracting a latent disease; (3) that increased risk makes periodic diagnostic medical examinations reasonably necessary; and (4) that monitoring and testing procedures exist which make the early detection and treatment of the disease possible and beneficial.

These decisions followed earlier cases such as Donovan v. Philip Morris USA, Inc., 914 N.E.2d 891, 901 (Mass. 2009), urging that late nineteenth-century tort law "must adapt to the growing recognition that exposure to toxic substances and radiation may cause substantial injury which should be compensable even if the full effects are not immediately apparent." See generally Geistfeld, The Analytics of Duty: Medical Monitoring and Related Forms of Economic Loss, 88 Va. L. Rev. 1921 (2002).

4.   Proof of Factual Causation

General Electric Co. v. Joiner
522 U.S. 136 (1997)

CHIEF JUSTICE REHNQUIST delivered the opinion of the court.

We granted certiorari in this case to determine what standard an appellate court should apply in reviewing a trial court's decision to admit or exclude expert testimony under Daubert v. Merrell Dow Pharmaceuticals, Inc., 509 U.S. 579 (1993). We hold that abuse of discretion is the appropriate standard. We apply this standard and conclude that the District Court in this case did not abuse its discretion when it excluded certain proffered expert testimony.

I

Respondent Robert Joiner began work as an electrician in the Water & Light Department of Thomasville, Georgia (City) in 1973. This job required him to work with and around the City's electrical transformers, which used a mineral-based dielectric fluid as a coolant. Joiner often had to stick his hands and arms into the fluid to make repairs. The fluid would sometimes splash onto him, occasionally getting into his eyes and mouth. In 1983 the City discovered that the fluid in some of the transformers was contaminated with polychlorinated biphenyls (PCB's). PCB's are widely considered to be hazardous to human health. Congress, with limited exceptions, banned the production and sale of PCB's in 1978.

Joiner was diagnosed with small cell lung cancer in 1991. He sued petitioners in Georgia state court the following year. Petitioner Monsanto manufactured PCB's from 1935 to 1977; petitioners General Electric and Westinghouse Electric manufactured transformers and dielectric fluid. In his complaint Joiner linked his development of cancer to his exposure to PCB's and their derivatives, polychlorinated dibenzofurans (furans) and polychlorinated dibenzodioxins (dioxins). Joiner had been a smoker for approximately eight years, his parents had both been smokers, and there was a history of lung cancer in his family. He was thus perhaps already at a heightened risk of developing lung cancer eventually. The suit alleged that his exposure to PCB's "promoted" his cancer; had it not been for his exposure to these substances, his cancer would not have developed for many years, if at all.

Petitioners removed the case to federal court. Once there, they moved for summary judgment. They contended that (1) there was no evidence that Joiner suffered significant exposure to PCB's, furans, or dioxins, and (2) there was no admissible scientific evidence that PCB's promoted Joiner's cancer. . . .

The District Court ruled that there was a genuine issue of material fact as to whether Joiner had been exposed to PCB's. But it nevertheless granted summary judgment for petitioners because (1) there was no genuine issue as to whether Joiner had been exposed to furans and dioxins, and (2) the testimony of Joiner's experts had failed to show that there was a link between exposure to PCB's and small-cell lung cancer. The court believed that the testimony of respondent's experts to the contrary did not rise above "subjective belief or unsupported speculation." 864 F. Supp. 1310, 1326 (N.D. Ga. 1994). Their testimony was therefore inadmissible.

The Court of Appeals for the Eleventh Circuit reversed. 78 F.3d 524 (1996). It held that "[b]ecause the Federal Rules of Evidence governing expert testimony display a preference for admissibility, we apply a particularly stringent standard of review to the trial judge's exclusion of expert testimony." Id. at 529. Applying that standard, the Court of Appeals held that the District Court had erred in excluding the testimony of Joiner's expert witnesses. . . .

We granted petitioners' petition for a writ of certiorari, and we now reverse. . . .

II

. . . We have held that abuse of discretion is the proper standard of review of a district court's evidentiary rulings. . . . The Court of Appeals suggested that *Daubert* somehow altered this general rule in the context of a district court's decision to exclude scientific evidence. But *Daubert* did not address the standard of appellate review for evidentiary rulings at all. It did hold that the "austere" *Frye* standard of "general acceptance" had not been carried over into the Federal Rules of Evidence. But the opinion also said:

> That the *Frye* test was displaced by the Rules of Evidence does not mean, however, that the Rules themselves place no limits on the admissibility of purportedly scientific evidence. Nor is the trial judge disabled from screening such evidence. To the contrary, under the Rules the trial judge must ensure that any and all scientific testimony or evidence admitted is not only relevant, but reliable.

Thus, while the Federal Rules of Evidence allow district courts to admit a somewhat broader range of scientific testimony than would have been admissible under *Frye,* they leave in place the "gatekeeper" role of the trial judge in screening such evidence. A court of appeals applying "abuse-of-discretion" review to such rulings may not categorically distinguish between rulings allowing expert testimony and rulings disallowing it. We likewise reject respondent's argument that because the granting of summary judgment in this case was "outcome determinative," it should have been subjected to a more searching standard of review. On a motion for summary judgment, disputed issues of fact are resolved against the moving party—here, petitioners. But the question of admissibility of expert testimony is not such an issue of fact, and is reviewable under the abuse-of-discretion standard. . . .

III

We believe that a proper application of the correct standard of review here indicates that the District Court did not abuse its discretion. Joiner's theory of liability was that his exposure to PCB's and their derivatives "promoted" his development of small-cell lung cancer. In support of that theory he proffered the deposition testimony of expert witnesses. . . .

The District Court agreed with petitioners that the animal studies on which respondent's experts relied did not support his contention that exposure to PCB's had contributed to his cancer. The studies involved infant mice that had developed cancer after being exposed to PCB's. The infant mice in the studies had had massive doses of PCB's injected directly into their peritoneums or stomachs. Joiner was an adult human being whose alleged exposure to PCB's was far less than the exposure in the animal studies. The PCB's were injected into the mice in a highly concentrated form. The fluid with which Joiner had come into contact generally had a much smaller PCB concentration of between 0-500 parts per million. The cancer that these mice developed was alveologenic adenomas; Joiner had developed small-cell carcinomas. No study demonstrated that adult mice developed cancer after being exposed to PCB's. One of the experts admitted that no study had demonstrated that PCB's lead to cancer in any other species.

Respondent failed to reply to this criticism. Rather than explaining how and why the experts could have extrapolated their opinions from these seemingly far-removed animal studies, respondent chose "to proceed as if the only issue

[was] whether animal studies can ever be a proper foundation for an expert's opinion." *Joiner*, 864 F. Supp. at 1324. Of course, whether animal studies can ever be a proper foundation for an expert's opinion was not the issue. The issue was whether *these* experts' opinions were sufficiently supported by the animal studies on which they purported to rely. The studies were so dissimilar to the facts presented in this litigation that it was not an abuse of discretion for the District Court to have rejected the experts' reliance on them.

The District Court also concluded that the four epidemiological studies on which respondent relied were not a sufficient basis for the experts' opinions. The first such study involved workers at an Italian capacitor plant who had been exposed to PCB's. The authors noted that lung cancer deaths among ex-employees at the plant were higher than might have been expected, but concluded that "there were apparently no grounds for associating lung cancer deaths (although increased above expectations) and exposure in the plant." Id. at 172. Given that [the authors] were unwilling to say that PCB exposure had caused cancer among the workers they examined, their study did not support the experts' conclusion that Joiner's exposure to PCB's caused his cancer. [The Court then conducted similar reviews of three other studies.]

[Respondent] claims that because the District Court's disagreement was with the conclusion that the experts drew from the studies, the District Court committed legal error and was properly reversed by the Court of Appeals. But conclusions and methodology are not entirely distinct from one another. Trained experts commonly extrapolate from existing data. But nothing in either *Daubert* or the Federal Rules of Evidence requires a district court to admit opinion evidence that is connected to existing data only by the *ipse dixit* of the expert. A court may conclude that there is simply too great an analytical gap between the data and the opinion proffered. That is what the District Court did here, and we hold that it did not abuse its discretion in so doing.

[The Court then remanded for a determination of "whether Joiner was exposed to furans and dioxins, and whether if there was such exposure, the opinions of Joiner's experts would then be admissible. . . ."]

JUSTICE BREYER, concurring.

. . . [M]odern life, including good health as well as economic well-being, depends upon the use of artificial or manufactured substances, such as chemicals. And it may, therefore, prove particularly important to see that judges fulfill their *Daubert* gatekeeping function, so that they help assure that the powerful engine of tort liability, which can generate strong financial incentives to reduce, or to eliminate, production, points toward the right substances and does not destroy the wrong ones. [Justice Breyer then endorses a suggestion from the amici brief of the *New England Journal of Medicine* that judges "be strongly encouraged to make use of their inherent authority . . . to appoint experts."]

JUSTICE STEVENS, concurring in part and dissenting in part.

. . . Unlike the District Court, the Court of Appeals expressly decided that a "weight of the evidence" methodology was scientifically acceptable. To this extent, the Court of Appeals' opinion is persuasive. It is not intrinsically "unscientific" for experienced professionals to arrive at a conclusion by weighing all available scientific evidence—this is not the sort of "junk science" with which *Daubert* was concerned. After all, as Joiner points out, the Environmental Protection Agency (EPA) uses the same methodology to assess risks, albeit using a somewhat different threshold than that required in a trial. Petitioners' own experts used the same scientific approach as well. And using this methodology, it would seem that an expert could reasonably have concluded that the study of workers at an Italian capacitor plant, coupled with data from Monsanto's study and other studies, raises an inference that PCB's promote lung cancer. . . .

In any event, it bears emphasis that the Court has not held that it would have been an abuse of discretion to admit the expert testimony. . . .

NOTES

1. Beyond Daubert.   Within short order, *Joiner* was extended in Kumho Tire Co. v. Carmichael, 526 U.S. 137, 148 (1999), so that a district court's gatekeeper function under *Daubert* extended to technical as well as scientific evidence, in this case the engineering testimony about the possible causes of a tire blowout. Justice Breyer noted that

> it would prove difficult, if not impossible, for judges to administer evidentiary rules under which a gatekeeping obligation depended upon a distinction between "scientific" knowledge and "technical" or "other specialized" knowledge. There is no clear line that divides the one from the others. Disciplines such as engineering rest upon scientific knowledge. Pure scientific theory itself may depend for its development upon observation and properly engineered machinery.

Thereafter, in Weisgram v. Marley Co., 528 U.S. 440, 455-456 (2000), the plaintiff prevailed at trial by proving a product defect solely on the strength of expert evidence that the district court had ruled admissible. The Court of Appeals disqualified that expert testimony as speculative under *Daubert*, and then entered a judgment as a matter of law for the defendant. The Supreme Court rejected plaintiff's contention that he was entitled to an "automatic remand" in order to refurbish his case with additional evidence, noting that it "is implausible to suggest, post-*Daubert*, that parties will initially present less than their best expert evidence in the expectation of a second chance should their first try fail."

2. The Bendectin saga.   In *Daubert*, the defendant obtained summary judgment on the causation issue after the plaintiff's team of eight recognized experts were prepared to testify that Bendectin, a drug once commonly used to control nausea during pregnancy, could cause birth defects, largely by reinterpreting the data contained in peer review studies that had denied the causal association between Bendectin and birth defects. *Daubert* rejected the traditional test of Frye v. United States, 293 F. 1013, 1014 (D.C. Cir. 1923), which had allowed as admissible only expert testimony that had been "generally accepted" as reliable by the scientific community, in favor of allowing the introduction of relevant scientific testimony that has "a valid scientific connection to the pertinent inquiry." It then remanded the case for further consideration, noting that both lower courts erroneously "focused almost exclusively on 'general acceptance,' as gauged by publication and the decision of other courts," not taking into account sufficiently other measures of reliability and relevance, including the tightness of "fit" between the evidence presented and the charge to be proved.

In a bruising opinion on remand, Kozinski, J., broke with earlier decisions that had freely allowed plaintiff's expert to testify on the relationship between Bendectin and birth defects, see, e.g., Oxendine v. Merrell Dow Pharmaceuticals, Inc., 506 A.2d 1100, 1110 (D.C. 1986), and upheld summary judgment under the revised standard, noting that none of plaintiff's experts "are proposing to testify about matters growing naturally and directly out of research they have conducted independent of the litigation," and far from publishing their results in peer-reviewed journals, "the only place their theories and studies have been published is in the pages of federal and state reporters." See Daubert v. Merrell Dow Pharmaceuticals, Inc., 43 F.3d 1311, 1317, 1318 (9th Cir. 1995). In one sense his decision came too late, because Richardson-Merrell had already pulled Bendectin from the market due to its fear of continued lawsuits. "[W]hile Bendectin usage declined from 1 million new therapy starts in 1979 to zero in 1984, there has been no change in the incidence of birth defects." Lynch v. Merrell-National Laboratories, Inc., 830 F.2d 1190, 1194 (1st Cir. 1987).

3. The thimerosal litigation. Kozinski's, J., decision in *Daubert* proved highly influential in Doe v. Ortho-Clinical Diagnostics, 440 F. Supp. 2d 465, 474 (M.D.N.C. 2006), in which the plaintiff, an autistic child, sued Ortho-Clinical for negligence, breach of warranty, and negligent and intentional misrepresentation. Each claim rested on the assertion that thimerosal, a component in RhoGAM, the defendant's biologic — that is, a complex, large, living molecule often found in blood or vaccines — administered to the plaintiff's mother during pregnancy, caused the plaintiff's autism. That claim depended on showing, first, general causation (namely, that defendant's product was of the type that could have caused the injuries in question) and, second, specific causation (namely, making out that causal connection in the instant case). The court's exhaustive review of the qualifications and proffered testimony of the plaintiff's expert physicians reads like summary judgment for the defendant on both causal issues. For example, Beaty, J., observed that Dr. Geier did not have the formal qualifications as a pediatric neurologist to testify on the relevant causal issues. As did Kozinski, J., in *Daubert*, Beaty, J., also conducted his own extensive review "of a motley assortment of diverse literature" that Dr. Geier presented. He noted that "Dr. Geier could not point to a single study, including his own writing, that conclusively determined that the amount of thimerosal in RhoGAM when given not to the fetus but to the mother, as in this case, could cause autism. . . . Moreover, Dr. Geier's conclusion that the peer-reviewed literature he has relied upon supports his theory that autism can be caused by thimerosal is flatly contradicted by all of the epidemiological studies available at this time."

The link between thimerosal and autism also arises in litigation under the National Childhood Vaccine Injury Act of 1986, passed in response to a sharp increase in the price of vaccines that threatened to drive many vaccine makers out of the critical children's marketplace. The NCVIA establishes a complex system of no-fault compensation, paying up to $250,000 for children suffering particular side effects from certain vaccines within specified time limits. 42 U.S.C. §300aa (2012). In some instances, the statute adopts explicit tests for determining whether compensation is owed. For example, the recipient of a measles vaccine who suffers an anaphylactic shock within 24 hours of inoculation can receive payment. Also, under the statute people who meet the conditions for no-fault recovery may nonetheless reject the payment and sue for tort damages. The largest statutory award has been $8.4 million, and the average award has been around $833,000, where autism claims have uniformly been rejected by the Institute of Medicine for the want of any proof of causal connection. Nonetheless, an FDA report, Thimerosal in Vaccines, http://www.fda.gov/cber/vaccine/thimerosal.htm, first noted that preliminary results from the CDC indicated "no change in autism rates relative to the amount of thimerosal a child received during the first six months of life" and then lauded recent efforts to remove thimerosal from its traditional role as a preservative for vaccines.

The issue of causation in vaccine cases arises also in other contexts. Thus, in Pafford v. Secretary of Health and Human Services, 451 F.3d 1252 (Fed. Cir. 2006), Rader, C.J., rejected the claim that a suite of vaccines—DTaP (diphtheria, tetanus (commonly known as lockjaw), and pertussis (commonly known as whooping cough)), MMR (measles, mumps, and rubella), and OPV (oral poliovirus)—resulted in the occurrence of systematic juvenile rheumatoid arthritis from a condition known as Still's disease. That condition was not on the "table" of listed events, and it was not a "signature disease" associated with any of the vaccines that the plaintiff took. Her claim was rejected because she could not make out her case on a three-part causation test identical to that used in tort cases:

(1)   a medical theory causally connecting the vaccination and the injury;
(2)   a logical sequence of cause and effect showing that the vaccination was the reason for the injury; and
(3)   . . . a proximate temporal relationship between the vaccine and injury.

Rader, C.J., agreed that coverage was possible if the vaccine was one of several joint causes of injury. But no close temporal evidence of that sort was presented, and, more specifically, the plaintiff could not rule out that other contemporaneous events unrelated to the vaccinations might have caused the injury.

("[A]bsent an appropriate time frame, the Court cannot find the mere temporal proximity of the vaccination and injury dispositive."). These contemporaneous events included: (1) a positive test for mycoplasma (a type of bacteria); (2) x-rays showing a thickening of the sinus membrane consistent with a sinus infection; (3) an earlier bout of tonsillitis; and (4) an earlier cold accompanied by diarrhea. Thus, according to the Special Master, Pafford did not prove by preponderant evidence that one or more of her vaccinations were a "but-for" cause of her contracting Still's disease.

4. State court response. Post-*Daubert*, state courts have had to decide whether to keep the somewhat higher *Frye* standard or to move toward the *Daubert* rule. In Goeb v. Tharaldson, 615 N.W.2d 800, 812-816 (Minn. 2000), the plaintiffs alleged that they were injured by harmful exposure to Dow Chemical's insecticide Dursban. The Minnesota court opted to adhere to the more restrictive *Frye* standard it had adopted in State v. Mack, 292 N.W.2d 764 (Minn. 1980). Blatz, C.J., first recognized that

> critics of the *Frye* general acceptance standard claim that it may at times exclude cutting-edge but otherwise demonstrably reliable, probative evidence, and thus represents a more conservative approach to the admissibility of scientific evidence. For example, the *Frye* standard might exclude a new, but reliable, methodology or test because of the inherent time lag between the development of a new scientific technique and its general acceptance in the field. . . .
>
> By comparison, because *Daubert* stresses a more liberal and flexible approach to the admission of scientific testimony, it has been viewed as relaxing the barriers to the admissibility of expert evidence. *See, e.g., Joiner.* . . .
>
> The *Frye* general acceptance standard has been criticized for other reasons, most notably that it improperly defers to scientists the legal question of admissibility of scientific evidence. . . . However, in repossessing the power to determine admissibility for the courts, *Daubert* takes from scientists and confers upon judges uneducated in science the authority to determine what is scientific. This approach which necessitates that trial judges be "amateur scientists," has also been frequently criticized. . . . By comparison, the *Frye* general acceptance standard ensures that the persons most qualified to assess scientific validity of a technique have the determinative voice.

Blatz, C.J., then opted for the *Frye* standard even though Rule 702 of the Minnesota Code was identical to the federal standard.

Just how great is the practical difference between *Daubert* and *Frye*? For the claim that *Daubert* has markedly increased the number of challenges to statistical data, see Kaye, The Dynamics of *Daubert*, 87 Va. L. Rev. 1933, 1936-1937 (2001), who cautions that the "'intellectual rigor' standard . . . must be applied with some caution lest it become a subterfuge for excluding expert testimony that is less than ideal but still within the range of reasonable scientific debate." A recent tabulation suggests that at present about 20 states opt for *Daubert + Kumho Tire*, eight for *Daubert* alone, eight for *Frye*, with the remaining 14 using a variety of other tests. Expert Witnesses in Civil Trials, Effective Preparation and Presentation §2:46 (2014-2015 ed.) (2014). How these different tests play out in practice is more difficult to determine. One study, Cheng & Yoon, Does *Frye* or *Daubert* Matter?: A Study of Scientific Admissibility Standards, 91 Va. L. Rev. 471, 475 (2005), concluded "that the choice between a *Frye* and *Daubert* standard does not make any practical difference."

5. The Agent Orange litigation. Proving causation in fact was also the central issue in suits brought mainly by servicemen and their offspring who claimed that Agent Orange (or more specifically, dioxin, a deadly byproduct of its production) caused a large class of serious but undifferentiated illnesses and birth defects. The individual suits were consolidated into a class before Weinstein, J., with individual plaintiffs having the right to opt out of the class. The main class settled for $180,000,000, with the moneys placed in a trust fund for distribution to the victims. In a subsequent action, Weinstein, J., anticipated *Joiner* and dismissed the suits of the opt-out plaintiffs because the evidence (including animal and epidemiological studies) did not support proof of causal connection. See In re "Agent Orange" Product Liability Litigation, 611 F. Supp. 1223, 1241 (E.D.N.Y. 1985). Why should the settlement have provided for any award given the summary judgment that followed? On Agent Orange generally, see Schuck, Agent Orange on Trial: Mass Toxic Disasters in the Courts (1986).

The Agent Orange cases illustrate the three levels of causation relevant in toxic torts cases. These are summarized by Professor Abraham in Individual Action and Collective Responsibility: The Dilemma of Mass Tort Reform, 73 Va. L. Rev. 845, 860, 867-868 (1987):

> To meet traditional burdens of proof in a regime that emphasizes individual responsibility, the plaintiff must show what I shall call *substance, source,* and *exposure* causation. That is, he must prove that the substance for which the defendant is responsible can cause his injury or disease, that the defendant and not someone else was the source of the substance, and that he was in fact exposed to the substance in a way that has caused his disease. In many cases, proof of some of these elements is simple; in some cases, proof of one automatically proves another. For example, when a particular disease is caused almost exclusively by a particular substance, the occurrence of the disease is the substance's "signature." Proof that the plaintiff has the disease, therefore, is also proof of both exposure and substance causation. In many cases, however, meeting the traditional burden of proof as to each of these elements is no minor accomplishment.

Abraham then expressed his doubt that the traditional tort models could work in cases like Agent Orange where no signature disease is found. How does Abraham's framework apply to asbestosis?

6. The Third Restatement on proof of factual causation. The Third Restatement offers an extended exegesis on proof of causation in toxic substance and disease cases that deliberately skirts the *Daubert* issue. RTT:LPEH §28, comment c.

> *Restatement of the Law (Third) of Torts: Liability for Physical and Emotional Harm*
>
> **§28. FACTUAL CAUSE**
>
> ***Comment c. Toxic substances and disease:*** . . . A few celebrated cases and case congregations, such as the Agent Orange and Bendectin litigations, led some courts to distrust juries' ability to resolve cases based on conflicting expert-opinion evidence. . . . The high-water mark for this overreliance on scientific thresholds occurred in the Bendectin litigation when one court announced a

blanket rule that a plaintiff could not make out a sufficient case without statistically significant epidemiologic evidence.

These courts may be relying on a view that "science" presents an "objective" method of establishing that, in all cases, reasonable minds cannot differ on the issue of factual causation. Such a view is incorrect. First, scientific standards for the sufficiency of evidence to establish a proposition may be inappropriate for the law. . . . Second, scientists report that an evaluation of data and scientific evidence to determine whether an inference of causation is appropriate requires judgment and interpretation. Scientists are subject to their own value judgments and preexisting biases that may affect their view of a body of evidence. . . .

SECTION C. PROXIMATE CAUSE (HEREIN OF DUTY)

1. Physical Injury

Francis Bacon, The Elements of the Common Lawes of England
(1630)

Reg. I. In jure non remota causa sed proxima spectatur. [In law, not the remote, but the proximate cause is to be looked at.] It were infinite for the law to judge the causes, and their impulsions one of another; therefore it contenteth it selfe with the immediate cause, and judgeth of acts by that, without looking to any further degree.

Thomas Atkins Street, Foundations of Legal Liability
Vol. I, p. 110 (1906)

The terms "proximate" and "remote" are thus respectively applied to recoverable and non-recoverable damages. . . . It is unfortunate that no definite principle can be laid down by which to determine this question. It is always to be determined on the facts of each case upon mixed considerations of logic, common sense, justice, policy and precedent. . . . The best use that can be made of the authorities on proximate cause is merely to furnish illustrations of situations which judicious men upon careful consideration have adjudged to be on one side of the line or the other.

Ryan v. New York Central R.R.
35 N.Y. 210 (1866)

On the 15th July 1854, in the city of Syracuse, the defendants, by the careless management, or through the insufficient condition, of one of their engines, set fire to their woodshed, and a large quantity of wood therein. The plaintiff's house, situated at a distance of one hundred and thirty feet from the shed, soon took fire from the heat and sparks, and was entirely consumed, notwithstanding diligent efforts were made to save it. A number of other houses were also burned by the spreading of the fire.

These facts having been proved on the part of the plaintiff, the defendants' counsel moved for a nonsuit, which was granted, and an exception taken. And the judgment having been affirmed at general term, the plaintiff appealed to this court.

HUNT, J. [after stating the facts]. The question may be thus stated: A house in a populous city takes fire, through the negligence of the owner or his servant; the flames extend to and destroy an adjacent building: Is the owner of the first building liable to the second owner for the damage sustained by such burning?

It is a general principle, that every person is liable for the consequences of his own acts; he is thus liable in damages for the proximate results of his own acts, but not for remote damages. It is not easy, at all times, to determine what are proximate and what are remote damages. . . .

[After discussing cases of direct ignition of plaintiff's property by defendants' negligence, the court continued:] Thus far the law is settled, and the principle is apparent. If, however, the fire communicates from the house of A. to that of B., and that is destroyed, is the negligent party liable for his loss? And if it spreads thence to the house of C., and thence to the house of D., and thence consecutively through the other houses, until it reaches and consumes the house of Z., is the party liable to pay the damages sustained by these twenty-four sufferers? The counsel for the plaintiff does not distinctly claim this, and I think it would not be seriously insisted, that the sufferers could recover in such case. Where, then, is the principle upon which A. recovers and Z. fails?

It has been suggested, that an important element exists in the difference between an intentional firing and a negligent firing merely; that when a party designedly fires his own house or his own fallow-land, not intending, however, to do any injury to his neighbor, but a damage actually results, that he may be liable for more extended damages than where the fire originated in accident or negligence. It is true, that the most of the cases where the liability was held to exist, were cases of an intentional firing. The case, however, of Vaughan v. Menlove (3 Bing. N.C. 468) was that of a spontaneous combustion of a hay-rick; the rick was burned, the owner's buildings were destroyed, and thence the fire spread to the plaintiff's cottage, which was also consumed; the defendant was held liable.

Without deciding upon the importance of this distinction, I prefer to place my opinion upon the ground, that, in the one case, to wit, the destruction of the building upon which the sparks were thrown by the negligent act of the party sought to be charged, the result was to have been anticipated, the moment the fire was communicated to the building; that its destruction was the ordinary and natural result of its being fired. In the second, third or twenty-fourth case, as supposed, the destruction of the building was not a natural and expected result of the first firing. That a building upon which sparks and cinders fall should be destroyed or seriously injured, must be expected, but that the fire should spread and other buildings be consumed, is not a necessary or a usual result. That it is possible, and that it is not unfrequent, cannot be denied. The result, however, depends, not upon any necessity of a further communication of the fire, but upon a concurrence of accidental circumstances, such as the degree of the heat, the state of the atmosphere, the condition and materials of the adjoining structures and the direction of the wind. These are accidental and varying circumstances; the party has no control over them, and is not responsible for their effects.

My opinion, therefore, is, that this action cannot be sustained, for the reason that the damages incurred are not the immediate but the remote result of the negligence of the defendants. The immediate result was the destruction of their own wood and sheds beyond that, it was remote. . . .

To sustain such a claim as the present, and to follow the same to its legitimate consequences, would subject to a liability against which no prudence could guard, and to meet which no private fortune would be adequate. Nearly all fires are caused by negligence, in its extended sense. In a country where wood, coal, gas and oils are universally used, where men are crowded into cities and villages, where servants are employed, and where children find their home in all houses, it is impossible, that the most vigilant prudence should guard against the occurrence of accidental or negligent fires. A man may insure his own house, or his own furniture, but he cannot insure his neighbor's building or furniture, for the reason that he has no interest in them. To hold that the owner must not only meet his own loss by fire, but that he must guaranty the security of his neighbors on both sides, and to an unlimited extent, would be to create a liability which would be the destruction of all civilized society. No community could long exist, under the operation of such a principle. In a commercial country, each man, to some extent, runs the hazard of his neighbor's conduct, and each, by insurance against such hazards, is enabled to obtain a reasonable security against loss. To neglect such precaution, and to call upon his neighbor, on whose premises a fire originated, to indemnify him instead, would be to award a punishment quite beyond the offence committed. It is to be considered, also, that if the negligent party is liable to the owner of a remote building thus consumed, he would also be liable to the insurance companies who should pay losses to such remote owners. The principle of subrogation would entitle the companies to the benefit of every claim held by the party to whom a loss should be paid.

. . . The remoteness of the damage, in my judgment, forms the true rule on which the question should be decided, and which prohibits a recovery by the plaintiff in this case. Judgment should be affirmed.

NOTES

1. Fire! The earlier common law cases took a much harder line toward the spread of fire. In Beaulieu v. Finglam, Y.B. 2 Hen. 4, f. 18, pl. 6 (1401), Markham, J., held that liability extended to the actions not only of the owner, but also of all his guests. He was insulated from liability only for fires set by strangers. The following dialogue then ensued: Hornby [the defendant's lawyer]: "The defendant will be undone and impoverished all his days if this action is to be maintained against him; for then twenty other such suits will be brought against him." Thirning, C.J.: "What is that to us? It is better that he should be undone than that the law be changed for him." Why this shift in view in *Ryan*, when the defendant is a railroad, not an individual landowner?

For a contemporary English contrast to *Ryan*, see Smith v. London & South Western Ry., 6 C.P. 14 (1870). A spark from defendant's engine started a fire in some heaps of the railway's cut grass. Fanned by a high wind, the flames spread through a stubble field not owned by the railroad until it consumed plaintiff's cottage. Kelly, C.B., allowed recovery, noting that "there was negligence in the defendants in not removing these trimmings, and that they thus become responsible for all the consequences of their conduct, and that the mere fact of the distance of this cottage from the point where the fire broke out does not affect their liability." The Supreme Court, in Milwaukee & St. Paul Ry. v. Kellogg, 94 U.S. 469, 474 (1876), also rejected *Ryan*'s view, stating, "[W]hen a building has been set on fire through the negligence of a party, and a second building has been fired from the first, it is a conclusion of law that the owner of the second has no recourse to the negligent wrong-doer, they have not been accepted as authority for such a doctrine, even in the States where the decisions were made."

See generally Schwartz, Tort Law and the Economy in Nineteenth-Century America: A Reinterpretation, 90 Yale L.J. 1717, 1746-1747 (1981). See also note to *Leroy Fibre, supra* at 290.

2. "Ordinary and natural result of defendant's negligence." *Ryan* placed a narrow construction on the phrase "ordinary and natural result" of the defendant's negligence. That phrase must be construed not only with intervening natural events, but also with intervening human conduct. In *City of Lincoln*, 15 P.D. 15, 18 (1889), the plaintiff's vessel, the *Albatross*, was totally disabled in a collision with the *City of Lincoln* wholly through the fault of the latter vessel. The *Albatross* lost its compass, log, log glass, and charts, and the captain was unsuccessful in his efforts to bring the ship to port. The court first noted that the "only inquiry in all these cases is whether the damage complained of is the natural and reasonable result of the defendant's act," and found the test satisfied if the damage was "such a consequence as in the ordinary course of things would flow from the act." Lindley, L.J., continued:

> We have then to consider what is the meaning of "the ordinary course of things." Sir Walter Phillimore has asked us to exclude from it all human conduct. I can do nothing of the kind. I take it that reasonable human conduct is part of the ordinary course of things. So far as I can see my way to any definite proposition I should say that the ordinary course of things does not exclude all human conduct, but includes at least the reasonable conduct of those who have sustained the damage, and who are seeking to save further loss. . . . Let us see, then, what occurred in the present case, and what was the real cause of the loss of this vessel. It was the fact that the captain was, by the collision, deprived of the means of ascertaining his position and of properly navigating his ship. He was deprived of his compass, his log-line, and his charts. His ship was not utterly unmanageable but she was in a

very bad state, and the necessary consequence of all this was that this captain lost his vessel without any negligence on his part. Under these circumstances the case falls within the rule I have laid down as to the term "ordinary course of things." Therefore, I am of opinion that the owners of the *City of Lincoln* must pay for the loss of the *Albatross*.

3. Plaintiff's response to emergencies. The problem of intervening actions also arises with sudden emergencies that require the plaintiff's immediate action. In Tuttle v. Atlantic City R.R., 49 A. 450, 451 (N.J. 1901), Vroom, J., held:

> The true rule governing cases of this character may be stated as follows: That if a defendant, by negligence, puts the plaintiff under a reasonable apprehension of personal physical injury, and plaintiff, in a reasonable effort to escape, sustains physical injury, a right of action arises to recover for the physical injury and the mental disorder naturally incident to its occurrence.

In other words, if the plaintiff acts in good faith to minimize the risk of loss from a dangerous situation of the defendant's making, then those actions do not sever causal connection: The defendant cannot complain when the plaintiff has done everything that the defendant would have done for himself to minimize the loss if he had been in the same situation.

In some instances, although now generally disfavored, courts have invoked a foresight limitation to bar recovery in these emergency cases, even when the plaintiff has undertaken a good-faith action. Thus, in Mauney v. Gulf Refining Co., 9 So. 2d 780, 782 (Miss. 1942), the plaintiff, hurrying to fetch her two-year-old child after being warned by neighbors that defendant's delivery truck was on fire and likely to explode, tripped over a chair in her husband's cafe and suffered a miscarriage. The court denied recovery on the ground that if the plaintiff "didn't see a chair in her own place of business, it would impose an inadmissible burden upon the defendants to say that they should have foreseen from across the street and through the walls of a building on another corner what appellant didn't see right at her feet. . . ." What degree of precision is required in working a foreseeability test? See, e.g., Williams, The Risk Principle, 77 Law Q. Rev. 179, 183 (1961): "The test of foreseeability does not require all the details of what happens to be foreseeable; it is enough if it is foreseeable in general outline." Is there any difficulty in holding the defendant liable under a directness standard?

Berry v. Sugar Notch Borough
43 A. 240 (Pa. 1899)

. . . Trespass for personal injuries. Before Woodward, P.J. . . .

Verdict and judgment for plaintiff for $3,162.50. Defendant appealed. . . .

FELL, J. The plaintiff was a motorman in the employ of the Wilkes-Barre and Wyoming Valley Traction Company on its line running from Wilkes-Barre to the borough of Sugar Notch. The ordinance by virtue of which the company was permitted to lay its track and operate its cars in the borough of Sugar Notch contained a provision that the speed of the cars while on the streets of the borough should not exceed eight miles an hour. On the line of the road, and within the borough limits, there was a large chestnut tree, as to the condition of which there was some dispute at the trial. The question of the negligence of the borough in permitting it to remain must, however, be considered as set at rest by the verdict. On the day of the accident the plaintiff was running his car on the borough street in a violent wind-storm, and as he passed under the tree it was blown down, crushing the roof of the car and causing the plaintiff's injury. There is some conflict of testimony as to the speed at which the car was running, but it seems to be fairly well established that it was considerably in excess of the rate permitted by the borough ordinance.

We do not think that the fact that the plaintiff was running his car at a higher rate of speed than eight miles an hour affects his right to recover. It may be that in doing so he violated the ordinance by virtue of which the company was permitted to operate its cars in the streets of the borough, but he certainly was not for that reason without rights upon the streets. Nor can it be said that the speed was the cause of the accident, or contributed to it. It might have been otherwise if the tree had fallen before the car reached it; for in that case a high rate of speed might have rendered it impossible for the plaintiff to avoid a collision which he either foresaw or should have foreseen. Even in that case the ground for denying him the right to recover would be that he had been guilty of contributory negligence, and not that he had violated a borough ordinance. The testimony however shows that the tree fell upon the car as it passed beneath. With this phase of the case in view, it was urged on behalf of the appellant that the speed was the immediate cause of the plaintiff's injury, inasmuch as it was the particular speed at which he was running which brought the car to the place of the accident at the moment when the tree blew down. This argument, while we cannot deny its ingenuity, strikes us, to say the least, as being somewhat sophistical. That his speed brought him to the place of the accident at the moment of the accident was the merest chance, and a thing which no foresight could have predicted. The same thing might as readily have happened to a car running slowly, or it might have been that a high speed alone would have carried him beyond the tree to a place of safety. It was also argued by the appellant's counsel that, even if the speed was not the sole efficient cause of the accident, it at least contributed to its severity, and materially increased the damage. It may be that it did. But what basis could a jury have for finding such to be the case and, should they so find, what guide could be given them for differentiating between the injury done this man and the injury which would have been done a man in a similar accident on a car running at a speed of eight miles an hour or less?

The judgment is affirmed.

NOTES

1. Coincidence and causation. In *Berry*, the plaintiff's breach of a safety ordinance was not causally connected with his injuries because the breach did not increase the risk or hazard of his being struck. Is it relevant that the increased speed reduced the time that the plaintiff was exposed to potential injury? Increased the possibility of damage in the event of a collision with a fallen log? With *Berry*, compare Mahoney v. Beatman, *supra* at 288. Note that the Third Restatement endorses the outcome in *Berry*. RTT:LPEH §30, comment *a*, illus. 1.

The problem of such coincidence between negligence and injury arose in a somewhat different form in Central of Georgia Ry. Co. v. Price, 32 S.E. 77, 77-78 (Ga. 1898). Through its negligence the railroad did not drop the plaintiff off at her station. She spent the night at a hotel to which she had been escorted by the railroad's conductor. At the hotel, she was given a furnished room outfitted with a kerosene lamp, which exploded and set fire to the mosquito netting covering the bed. In her efforts to put out the fire, the plaintiff severely burnt her hands. The court first rejected her argument that the railroad should be liable because the hotel proprietor was its agent. It then held that the plaintiff's harm was too remote from the railroad's negligence:

> The negligence of the company consisted in passing the station where the passenger desired to alight, without giving her an opportunity to get off. Taking her version of the manner in which she was injured, the injury was occasioned by the negligence of the proprietor of the hotel or his servants in giving her a defective lamp. The negligence of the company in passing her station was therefore not the natural and proximate cause of her injury. There was the interposition of a separate, independent agency, the negligence of the proprietor of the hotel, over whom, as we have shown, the railway company neither had nor exercised any control. The injuries to the plaintiff were not the natural and proximate consequences of carrying her beyond her station, but were unusual, and could not have been foreseen or provided against by the highest practicable care. The plaintiff was not entitled to recover for such injuries, and the court erred in overruling the motion for new trial.

In contrast, the defendant railroad was found liable for subjecting the plaintiff passenger to an increased risk in Hines v. Garrett, 108 S.E. 690, 692, 695 (Va. 1921). A railroad conductor negligently carried the 19-year-old plaintiff almost a mile past her stop at night, forcing her to walk back this distance through an area "habitually frequented and infested by hoboes, tramps, and questionable characters." During her walk back she was raped once by a soldier and once by a hobo, both unidentified. Allowing her to recover against the railroad, the court said, in part: "We do not wish to be understood as questioning the general proposition that no responsibility for a wrong attaches whenever an independent act of a third person intervenes between the negligence complained of and the injury. But . . . this proposition does not apply where the very negligence alleged consists of exposing the injured party to the act causing the injury. It is perfectly well settled and will not be seriously denied that whenever a carrier has reason to anticipate the danger of an assault upon one of its passengers, it rests under the duty of protecting such passenger against the same."

2. Dependent causes.   Still another variation on the causal theme arises when each of two successive acts is sufficient to harm the plaintiff, but the plaintiff is exposed to the second cause only because of the prior negligence of a separate actor involved in the first. In these situations, the second act is said to be "dependent" on the first, so that the second defendant is normally responsible only for the incremental damages, if any, brought about by his action. In Dillon v. Twin State Gas & Electric Co., 163 A. 111, 115 (N.H. 1932), the plaintiff's decedent, a boy of 14, lost his balance while trespassing on the superstructure of a bridge and grabbed the defendant's high-voltage wires as he fell. The current killed him and the shock apparently threw his body back onto the girder. The defendant power company was not found responsible for the boy's fall given his trespass, but it was found responsible for the boy's exposure to the uncovered charged wires. The defendant's motion for a directed verdict on the issue of liability was denied, and that decision was affirmed on appeal. Allen, J., wrote:

> In leaning over from the girder and losing his balance he was entitled to no protection from the defendant to keep from falling. Its only liability was in exposing him to the danger of the charged wires. If but for the current in the wires he would have fallen down on the floor of the bridge or into the river, he would without doubt have been either killed or seriously injured. Although he died from electrocution, yet, if by reason of his preceding loss of balance he was bound to fall except for the intervention of the current, he either did not have long to live or was to be maimed. In such an outcome of his loss of balance, the defendant deprived him not of a life of normal expectancy, but of one too short to be given pecuniary allowance, in one alternative, and not of normal but of limited, earning capacity, in the other. . . .

3. An apparent condition of safety.   Problems of causal intervention also arise when dangerous objects are passed from hand to hand. In Pittsburg Reduction Co. v. Horton, 113 S.W. 647, 648-649 (Ark. 1908), the defendant discarded a dynamite cap on its unenclosed plant premises near a public school. The cap was picked up by Charlie Copple, age ten, who placed it in a tin box with other caps and played with it on several occasions in his house. His mother, who later testified that she did not know what they were, would pick the caps up when Charlie was done playing. About a week after he found the cap, Charlie traded it to Jack Horton, age 13, for some writing paper. Horton thought that "the cap was the shell of a .22 cartridge that had been shot." He was picking the dirt out of the cap with a match when the cap exploded, so injuring his hand that it had to be amputated. Charlie's father, a miner, denied knowing that the cap was in the house until after the accident. Horton brought suit against the defendant company and its foreman, but his claim was denied.

> In the present case the facts are practically undisputed. Charlie Copple's father was an employee of a company engaged in a similar business to that of appellant company. Naturally, his avocation and the proximity of his residence to the mines made both himself and his wife familiar with the nature of explosives. True, Mrs.

Copple says that she did not know what the shells contained, but she did know that they were shells for some kind of explosives, that her son brought them home, and that he played with them. She admits that when he would leave them on the floor she would pick them up and lay them away for him. This continued for a week, and then, with her knowledge, he carried them to school. Her course of conduct broke the causal connection between the original negligent act of appellant and the subsequent injury of the plaintiff. It established a new agency, and the possession of Charlie Copple of the caps or shells was thereafter referable to the permission of his parents, and not to the original taking. Charlie Copple's parents having permitted him to retain possession of the caps, his further acts in regard to them must be attributable to their permission, and were wholly independent of the original negligence of appellants.

Horton and similar cases were analyzed in great detail in Beale, The Proximate Consequences of an Act, 33 Harv. L. Rev. 633, 650, 651, 656 (1920), which offered the following two generalizations:

> If the defendant's active force has come to rest, but in a dangerous position, creating a new or increasing an existing risk of loss, and the foreseen danger comes to pass, operating harmfully on the condition created by defendant and causing the risked loss, we say that the injury thereby created is a proximate consequence of the defendant's act. . . .
>
> On the other hand, where defendant's active force has come to rest in a position of apparent safety, the court will follow it no longer; if some new force later combines with this condition to create harm, the result is remote from the defendant's act.

With reference to cases like *Horton*, Beale concluded that "if the explosive gets into the hands of an adult the defendant's force has ceased to be an active danger; if the explosive thereafter gets into the hands of a child, defendant is not the proximate cause of anything this child may do with it." Should the result be the same even if the adult did not know that the cap was dangerous? The outcome in *Horton* has also been defended in Grady, Proximate Cause and the Law of Negligence, 69 Iowa L. Rev. 363, 420 (1984): "In situations when the last wrongdoer would feel especially disposed to remain at a low level of precaution because of an expectation that the original wrongdoer would be held liable for a lion's share of the expected harm that would result from their joint omissions, the direct-consequences doctrine cuts off the liability of the original wrongdoer and makes the last wrongdoer solely responsible for the damage. This was the result in the *Horton* case."

For a criticism of both Beale and Grady, see Epstein, Toward a General Theory of Tort Law: Strict Liability in Context, 3 J. Tort L. (Iss. 1, Art. 6) 6, 29 (2010). Epstein argues that the difficulty with the Bealean formulation is that its use of the phrase "active force" ties the theory of proximate causation too closely to claims for trespass, when the phrase "dangerous condition" better captures the situation. In response to Grady, Epstein urges:

[T]he flaw in Grady's argument is to assume that once the proximate cause arguments allow the suit against remote actor, all incentives on the intermediate party vanish. This is not the case, however, if the action for contribution or indemnity is allowed for the remote party against the party nearer in control.

Brower v. New York Central & H.R.R.
103 A. 166 (N.J. 1918)

SWAYZE, J. This is a case of a grade-crossing collision. We are clear that the questions of negligence and contributory negligence were for the jury. If there were nothing else, the testimony of the plaintiff as to signals of the flagman would carry the case to the jury. The only question that has caused us difficulty is that of the extent of the defendant's liability. The complaint avers that the horse was killed, the wagon and harness, and the cider and barrels with which the wagon was loaded, were destroyed. What happened was that as a result of the collision, aside from the death of the horse and the destruction of the wagon, the contents of the wagon, consisting of empty barrels and a keg of cider, were scattered and probably stolen by people at the scene of the accident. The driver, who was alone in charge for the plaintiff, was so stunned that one of the railroad detectives found him immediately after the collision in a fit. There were two railroad detectives on the freight train to protect the property it was carrying against thieves, but they did nothing to protect the plaintiff's property. The controversy on the question of damages is as to the right of the plaintiff to recover the value of the barrels, cider and blanket. . . . It is now argued that the defendant's negligence was not in any event the proximate cause of the loss of this property since the act of the thieves intervened. The rule of law which exempts the one guilty of the original negligence from damage due to an intervening cause is well settled. The difficulty lies in the application. Like the question of proximate cause, this is ordinarily a jury question. . . .

We think these authorities justified the trial judge in his rulings as to the recovery of the value of the barrels, cider and blanket. The negligence which caused the collision resulted immediately in such a condition of the driver of the wagon that he was no longer able to protect his employer's property; the natural and probable result of his enforced abandonment of it in the street of a large city was its disappearance and the wrongdoer cannot escape making reparation for the loss caused by depriving the plaintiff of the protection which the presence of the driver in his right senses would have afforded. "The act of a third person," said the Supreme Judicial Court of Massachusetts, "intervening and contributing a condition necessary to the injurious effect of the original negligence, will not excuse the first wrongdoer, if such act ought to have been foreseen." Lane v. Atlantic Works, 111 Mass. 136 [(1872)]. A railroad company which found it necessary or desirable to have its freight train guarded by two detectives against thieves is surely chargeable with knowledge that portable property left without a guard was likely to be made off with. Again, strictly speaking, the act of the thieves did not intervene between defendant's negligence and the plaintiff's loss; the two causes were to all practical intent simultaneous and concurrent; it is rather a case of a joint tort than an intervening cause. . . . An illustration will perhaps clarify the case. Suppose a fruit vendor at his stand along the street is rendered unconscious by the negligence of the defendant, who disappears, and boys in the street appropriate the unfortunate vendor's stock in trade; could the defendant escape liability for their value? We can hardly imagine a court answering in the affirmative. Yet the case is but little more extreme than the jury might have found the present case. . . .

GARRISON, J., dissenting. The collision afforded an opportunity for theft of which a thief took advantage, but I cannot agree that the collision was therefore the proximate cause of loss of the stolen articles. Proximate cause imports unbroken continuity between cause and effect, which, both in law and in logic, is broken by the active intervention of an independent criminal actor. This established rule of law is defeated if proximate cause be confounded with mere opportunity for crime. A maladjusted switch may be the proximate cause of the death of a passenger who was killed by the derailment of the train, or by the fire or collision that ensued, but it is not the proximate cause of the death of a passenger who was murdered by a bandit who boarded the train because of the opportunity afforded by its derailment. This clear distinction is not met by saying that criminal intervention should be foreseen, for this implies that crime is to be presumed and the law is directly otherwise.

NOTES

1. The last wrongdoer and beyond. Cases like *Brower* call into question the proper test of proximate causation. The earliest tests of proximate causation held the defendant liable only when he was the "last wrongdoer" whose conduct contributed to the loss: Criminal conduct by some third party obviously severed causal connection on this view. More generally, the last actor need not be the last wrongdoer, for his actions could be blameless or even praiseworthy. The efforts of the captain to save his ship in *City of Lincoln, supra* at 406, did not sever causal connection. Likewise, the actions of infants and incompetents do not break the chain of causation, at least in those cases where the law does not regard their actions as tortious. Nevertheless, the test is highly restrictive since it blocks causal recovery not only when the deliberate wrong of a third party intervenes but also when the negligence of a third party intervenes.

Although this "last wrongdoer" test had some early champions (see Beven, Negligence in Law 45 (3d ed. 1908)), it was necessarily circumvented whenever the negligence of one defendant did not sever causal connection to a prior actor. Thus, in Atherton v. Devine, 602 P.2d 634, 636-637 (Okla. 1979), the plaintiff was injured in a road accident attributable to the defendant's negligence. The ambulance that took the plaintiff to the hospital was involved in another collision, aggravating the original injuries. The Oklahoma Supreme Court, reversing the decision below, held that the first collision was a "substantial factor" in causing the subsequent injury, so the harm was not too remote:

It has long been the rule in Oklahoma that an original wrongdoer, negligently causing injury to another is liable for the negligence of a physician who treats the injured person where the negligent treatment results in the aggravation of injuries, so long as the injured person exercises good faith in the choice of his physician. . . .

As a matter of principle, there would seem to be no material distinction between medical treatment required because of the tortious act, and transportation required to reach an institution where medical treatment is available. The use of an ambulance, like the use of a surgeon's scalpel, is necessitated by the tortfeasor's wrong, and either may be used negligently.

Even after the negligence barrier was overcome, many causal theorists continued to believe that deliberate and malicious acts should in general negate causal connection. Thus, Hart and Honoré offer this general test of causation: "The general principle of the traditional doctrine is that *the free, deliberate and informed act or omission of a human being, intended to exploit the situation created by the defendant, negatives any causal connection.*" Causation in the Law 136 (2d ed. 1985) (italics in original). The commonsense defense of this position rests on the observation that the original actor did not constrain the conduct of the malicious intervenor, but only facilitated his mischief. Yet it was just the creation of additional opportunities for harm that allowed the plaintiff to recover against the railroad in Hines v. Garrett (*supra* at 409) or indeed in *Brower* itself, so this test also is generally regarded as too restrictive on recovery.

2. The Second Restatement approach. The Second Restatement establishes a "substantial factor" test for legal, or proximate, causation in RST §431.

Restatement of the Law (Second) of Torts

§431. WHAT CONSTITUTES LEGAL CAUSE

The actor's negligent conduct is a legal cause of harm to another if
  (a) his conduct is a substantial factor in bringing about the harm, and
  (b) there is no rule of law relieving the actor from liability because of the manner in which his negligence has resulted in the harm.

Comment a. Distinction between substantial cause and cause in the philosophic sense: In order to be a legal cause of another's harm, it is not enough that the harm would have not occurred had the actor not been negligent. Except as stated in §432(2) [dealing with joint causation], this is necessary, but it is not of itself sufficient. The negligence must also be a substantial factor in bringing about the plaintiff's harm. The word "substantial" is used to denote the fact that the defendant's conduct has such an effect in producing the harm as to lead reasonable men to regard it as a cause, using that word in the popular sense, in which there always lurks the idea of responsibility, rather than in the so-called "philosophic sense," which includes every one of the great number of events without which any happening would not have occurred. Each of these events is a cause in the so-called "philosophic sense," yet the effect of many of them is so insignificant that no ordinary mind would think of them as causes.

The role of deliberate third-party intervention is taken up in two critical provisions, RST §448 and RST §449.

Restatement of the Law (Second) of Torts

§448. INTENTIONALLY TORTIOUS OR CRIMINAL ACTS DONE UNDER OPPORTUNITY AFFORDED BY ACTOR'S NEGLIGENCE

The act of a third person in committing an intentional tort or crime is a superseding cause of harm to another resulting therefrom, although the actor's negligent conduct created a situation which afforded an opportunity to the third person to commit such a tort or crime, unless the actor at the time of his negligent conduct realized or should have realized the likelihood that such a situation might be created, and that a third person might avail himself of the opportunity to commit such a tort or crime.

Illustration 1: The A Railroad Company negligently runs down a truck driven by a servant of B and containing barrels of cider. The collision occurs at night and at a place where there have been frequent thefts from the company's freight cars. It results in the scattering of the barrels of cider along the road and the stunning of the driver. The cider is stolen by unknown thieves. The negligence of the A Railroad Company is a legal cause of the loss of the cider by the theft of the unknown persons.

Restatement of the Law (Second) of Torts

§449. TORTIOUS OR CRIMINAL ACTS THE PROBABILITY OF WHICH MAKES ACTOR'S CONDUCT NEGLIGENT

If the likelihood that a third person may act in a particular manner is the hazard or one of the hazards which makes the actor negligent, such an act whether innocent, negligent, intentionally tortious, or criminal does not prevent the actor from being liable for harm caused thereby.

Illustration 1: A is traveling on the train of the B Railway Company. Her ticket entitles her to ride only to Station X, but she intentionally stays on the train after it has passed that station. When she arrives at Station Y the conductor

> puts her off the train. This occurs late at night after the station has been closed and the attendants have departed. The station is situated in a lonely district, and the only way in which she can reach the neighboring town is by passing a place where to the knowledge of the conductor there is a construction camp. The construction crew is known to contain many persons of vicious character. While attempting to pass by this camp, A is attacked and ravished by some of the construction crew. The B Railway Company is subject to liability to A.

The Restatement holds that the defendant should be liable precisely because the third party *did* exploit the dangerous condition he created. *Brower* tacitly acknowledges distinct limits to causal responsibility, wholly without reference to foreseeability, even if the malicious acts of a third party do not sever causal connection. The consequences of the defendant's action cease once the railroad gathers up the barrels and places them under a competent guard.

The case law uniformly follows the Second Restatement. In Bigbee v. Pacific Telephone and Telegraph Co., 665 P.2d 947, 952 (Cal. 1983), the plaintiff was trapped in a telephone booth located in a parking lot 15 feet from a major thoroughfare. The plaintiff saw an oncoming car careening out of control. He was struck by Leona Roberts, a drunk driver, when he was unable to wrestle the door open in time to escape. After holding that the phone company could be found negligent both in its placement and its maintenance of the booth, Bird, C.J., brushed aside the defendant's proximate cause argument, noting that it "is of no consequence that the harm to the plaintiff came about through the negligent or reckless acts of Roberts," citing RST §449.

In Britton v. Wooten, 817 S.W.2d 443, 449 (Ky. 1991), a grocery store, in which the defendant had negligently stacked excessive amounts of flammable trash, was destroyed by possible third-party arson. The plaintiff had leased the building to the defendant. Relying on the Second Restatement, the court concluded, "[W]e reject any all-inclusive general rule that, as respondent contends, 'criminal acts of third parties . . . relieve the original negligent party from liability.'" Likewise in Bell v. Board of Education, 687 N.E.2d 1325, 1326 (N.Y. 1998), the defendant school board left the plaintiff behind at a sixth-grade drug awareness fair near her school. On her way back she was accosted by three boys and taken to the house of one, where she was raped and sodomized. The court affirmed a jury verdict for the plaintiff, holding that "we cannot say that the intervening act of rape was unforeseeable as a matter of law." Does *Bell* present the same increased risk or hazard as *Hines, supra* at 409?

3. The Third Restatement approach.   The conceptual terminology of the Second Restatement gets a rude reception in the Third Restatement. Typically the results in particular cases show no difference between the two Restatements, leaving it unclear whether the Third Restatement's preferred language will displace the ingrained usage of the Second.

Restatement of the Law (Third) of Torts: Liability for Physical and Emotional Harm

§34. INTERVENING ACTS AND SUPERSEDING CAUSES

An actor's liability is limited to those harms that result from the risks that made the actor's conduct tortious.

Comment a. History and Introduction: . . . Despite the continuing influence of the Second Restatement of Torts, much of the formalism of its treatment of superseding causes has been supplanted in the latter part of the 20th century with a recognition that there are always multiple causes of an outcome and that the existence of intervening causes does not ordinarily elide a prior actor's liability. . . .

Illustration 3: The Brown Transport Company negligently seals a container truck loaded with a highly flammable liquid. The liquid leaks onto the street, after its driver parks it there while eating lunch. The leaking fluid creates a risk of fire or explosion. A fire does occur when a passerby negligently strikes a match to light her cigar. The flame from the match ignites the vapors produced by the liquid, and the ensuing fire injures Gordon. The harm suffered by Gordon in the fire is within the scope of Brown's liability for its negligence.

Illustration 5: Same facts as Illustration 3, except that the smoker, seeing the liquid and appreciating its flammability, deliberately throws a match onto the liquid. Whether Gordon's harm is within the scope of Brown's liability for its negligence is an issue for the factfinder.

Wagner v. International Ry.
133 N.E. 437 (N.Y. 1921)

CARDOZO, J. [after a brief statement of preliminary facts about the electric railway's trestle:] Plaintiff and his cousin Herbert boarded a car at a station near the bottom of one of the trestles. Other passengers, entering at the same time, filled the platform, and blocked admission to the aisle. The platform was provided with doors, but the conductor did not close them. Moving at from six to eight miles an hour, the car, without slackening, turned the curve. There was a violent lurch, and Herbert Wagner was thrown out, near the point where the trestle changes to a bridge. The cry was raised, "Man overboard." The car went on across the bridge, and stopped near the foot of the incline. Night and darkness had come on. Plaintiff walked along the trestle, a distance of four hundred and forty-five feet, until he arrived at the bridge, where he thought to find his cousin's body. He says that he was asked to go there by the conductor. He says, too, that the conductor followed with a lantern. Both these statements the conductor denies. Several other persons, instead of ascending the trestle, went beneath it, and discovered under the bridge the body they were seeking. As they stood there, the plaintiff's body struck the ground beside them. Reaching the bridge, he had found upon a beam his cousin's hat, but nothing else. About him, there was darkness. He missed his footing, and fell.

The trial judge held that negligence toward Herbert Wagner would not charge the defendant with liability for injuries suffered by the plaintiff unless two other facts were found: First, that the plaintiff had been invited by the conductor to go upon the bridge; and second, that the conductor had followed with a light. Thus limited, the jury found in favor of the defendant. Whether the limitation may be upheld, is the question to be answered.

Danger invites rescue. The cry of distress is the summons to relief. The law does not ignore these reactions of the mind in tracing conduct to its consequences. It recognizes them as normal. It places their effects within the range of the natural and probable. The wrong that imperils life is a wrong to the imperiled victim; it is a wrong also to his rescuer. The state that leaves an opening in a bridge is liable to the child that falls into the stream, but liable also to the parent who plunges to its aid. . . . The railroad company whose train approaches without signal is a wrongdoer toward the traveler surprised between the rails, but a wrongdoer also to the bystander who drags him from the path (Eckert v. L.I.R.R. Co., 43 N.Y. 502). . . . The rule is the same in other jurisdictions. . . . The risk of rescue, if only it be not wanton, is born of the occasion. The emergency begets the man. The wrongdoer may not have foreseen the coming of a deliverer. He is accountable as if he had. . . .

The defendant says that we must stop, in following the chain of causes, when action ceases to be "instinctive." By this, is meant, it seems, that rescue is at the peril of the rescuer, unless spontaneous and immediate. If there has been time to deliberate, if impulse has given way to judgment, one cause, it is said, has spent its force, and another has intervened. In this case, the plaintiff walked more than four hundred feet in going to Herbert's aid. He had time to reflect and weigh; impulse had been followed by choice; and choice, in the defendant's view, intercepts and breaks the sequence. We find no warrant for thus shortening the chain of jural causes. We may assume, though we are not required to decide, that peril and rescue must be in substance one transaction; that the sight of the one must have aroused the impulse to the other; in short, that there must be unbroken continuity between the commission of the wrong and the effort to avert its consequences. If all this be assumed, the defendant is not aided. Continuity in such circumstances is not broken by the exercise of volition. . . . So sweeping an exception, if recognized, would leave little of the rule. "The human mind," as we have said (People v. Majone, 91 N.Y. 211, 212), "acts with celerity which it is sometimes impossible to measure." The law does not discriminate between the rescuer oblivious of peril and the one who counts the cost. It is enough that the act, whether impulsive or deliberate, is the child of the occasion.

The defendant finds another obstacle, however, in the futility of the plaintiff's sacrifice. [The court then discussed whether or not plaintiff was contributorily negligent and concluded that under the emergency conditions he was not.]

Whether Herbert Wagner's fall was due to the defendant's negligence, and whether plaintiff in going to the rescue, as he did, was foolhardy or reasonable in the light of the emergency confronting him, were questions for the jury.

NOTE

Danger invites rescue? Should the plaintiff's recovery be barred if the conductor had already mounted adequate rescue efforts without the plaintiff's assistance? If he had told the plaintiff to stay in the train? If Herbert were thought to be dead? Whatever its soundness, the "rescue doctrine" is well established today. See Espinoza v. Schulenberg, 129 P.3d 937, 939 (Ariz. 2006) (en banc). See RTT:LPEH §32, noting that any unreasonable rescue efforts by plaintiff should be covered by comparative negligence and not the doctrine of superseding cause. *Id.*, comment *a*. The functions of the rescue doctrine were described in McCoy v. American Suzuki Motor Corp., 961 P.2d 952, 956 (Wash. 1998), as follows:

First, it informs a tortfeasor it is foreseeable a rescuer will come to the aid of a person imperiled by the tortfeasor's actions, and, therefore, the tortfeasor owes the rescuer a duty similar to the duty he owes the person he imperils. Second, the rescue doctrine negates the presumption that the rescuer assumed the risk of injury when he knowingly undertook the dangerous rescue, so long as he does not act rashly or recklessly.

To achieve rescuer status one must demonstrate: (1) the defendant was negligent to the person rescued and such negligence caused the peril or appearance of peril to the person rescued; (2) the peril or appearance of peril was imminent; (3) a reasonably prudent person would have concluded such peril or appearance of peril existed; and (4) the rescuer acted with reasonable care in effectuating the rescue.

Is the "danger invites rescue" doctrine justified on economic grounds? According to Hylton, Duty in Tort Law: An Economic Approach, 75 Fordham L. Rev. 1501, 1515 (2006): "By relieving rescuers of the duty to take care for their own safety, courts effectively subsidize rescue attempts. This is justifiable on the theory that the societal benefits of high-stakes altruism are substantial." Is the subsidy needed if the conductor has matters well in hand?

In re Polemis & Furness, Withy & Co.
[1921] 3 K.B. 560

BANKES, L.J. By a time charterparty dated February 21, 1917, the respondents chartered their vessel to the appellants. Clause 21 of the charterparty was in these terms.

["The act of God, the King's enemies, loss or damage from fire on board in hulk or craft, or on shore, arrest and/or restraint of princes, rulers, and people, collision, an act, neglect, or default whatsoever of pilot, master, or crew in the management or navigation of the ship, and all and every of the dangers and accidents of the seas, canals, and rivers, and of navigation of whatever nature or kind always mutually excepted." This charterparty was the agreement whereby the shipowner leased the ship to the "charterers"—the appellants in this case. The "mutually excepted" language meant on its face that each side had to bear its own losses from the stated contingencies. The court first held that the language of clause 21 did not release the charterers from the consequences of their negligence.]

The vessel was employed by the charterers to carry a cargo to Casablanca in Morocco. The cargo included a quantity of benzine or petrol in cases. While discharging at Casablanca a heavy plank fell into the hold in which the petrol was stowed, and caused an explosion, which set fire to the vessel and completely destroyed her. The owners claimed the value of the vessel from the charterers, alleging that the loss of the vessel was due to the negligence of the charterers' servants. The charterers contended that they were protected by the exception of fire contained in clause 21 of the charterparty, and they also contended that the damages claimed were too remote. The claim was referred to arbitration, and the arbitrators stated a special case for the opinion of the Court. Their findings of fact are as follows.

(a) That the ship was lost by fire.

(b) That the fire arose from a spark igniting petrol vapour in the hold.

(c) That the spark was caused by the falling board coming into contact with some substance in the hold.

(d) That the fall of the board was caused by the negligence of the Arabs (other than the winchman) engaged in the work of discharging.

(e) That the said Arabs were employed by the charterers or their agents the Cie. Transatlantique on behalf of the charterers, and that the said Arabs were the servants of the charterers.

(f) That the causing of the spark could not reasonably have been anticipated from the falling of the board, though some damage to the ship might reasonably have been anticipated.

(g) There was no evidence before us that the Arabs chosen were known or likely to be negligent.

Then they state the damages, £196,165 1*s*. 11*d*. These findings are no doubt intended to raise the question whether the view taken, or said to have been taken, by Pollock, C.B., in Rigby v. Hewitt[, 155 Eng. Rep. 103 (Ex. 1850), and Greenland v. Chaplin (5 [Ex.] 243, 155 [Eng. Rep.] 104, [1850]), or the view taken by Channell, B., and Blackburn, J., in Smith v. London & South Western Ry. Co. (3 L. R. 6 C.P. 21 [(1870)]), is the correct one. . . .

Assuming the Chief Baron to have been correctly reported in the Exchequer Reports, the difference between the two views is this: According to the one view, the consequences which may reasonably be expected to result from a particular act are material only in reference to the question whether the act is or is not a negligent act; according to the other view, those consequences are the test whether the damages resulting from the act, assuming it to be negligent, are or are not too remote to be recoverable. [Bankes, L.J., then quoted from H.M.S. London, [1914] P. 72, in part, as follows:] ". . . In Smith v. London and South Western Ry. Co., Channell, B., said: 'Where there is no direct evidence of negligence, the question what a reasonable man might foresee is of importance in considering the question whether there is evidence for the jury of negligence or not . . . but when it has been once determined that there is evidence of negligence, the person guilty of it is equally liable for its consequences, whether he could have foreseen them or not.' And Blackburn, J., in the same case said: 'What the defendants might reasonably anticipate is only material with reference to the question, whether the defendants were negligent or not, and cannot alter their liability if they were guilty of negligence.' " . . .

In the present case the arbitrators have found as a fact that the falling of the plank was due to the negligence of the defendants' servants. The fire appears to me to have been directly caused by the falling of the plank. Under these circumstances I consider that it is immaterial that the causing of the spark by the falling of the plank could not have been reasonably anticipated. The appellants' junior counsel sought to draw a distinction between the anticipation of the extent of damage resulting from a negligent act, and the anticipation of the type of damage resulting from such an act. He admitted that it could not lie in the mouth of a person whose negligent act had caused damage to say that he could not reasonably have foreseen the extent of the damage, but he contended that the negligent person was entitled to rely upon the fact that he could not reasonably have anticipated the type of damage which resulted from his negligent act. I do not think that the distinction can be admitted. Given the breach of duty which constitutes the negligence, and given the damage as a direct result of that negligence, the anticipations of the person whose negligent act has produced the damage appear to me to be irrelevant. I consider that the damages claimed are not too remote.

WARRINGTON, L.J. [referring to a discussion by Beven on Negligence, observed:] . . . The result may be summarised as follows: The presence or absence of reasonable anticipation of damage determines the legal quality of the act as negligent or innocent. If it be thus determined to be negligent, then the question whether particular damages are recoverable depends only on the answer to the question whether they are the direct consequence of the act. Sufficient authority for the proposition is afforded by Smith v. London and South Western Ry. Co., in the Exchequer Chamber, and particularly by the judgments of Channell, B., and Blackburn, J. . . . In the present case it is clear that the act causing the plank to fall was in law a negligent act, because some damage to the ship might reasonably be anticipated. If this is so then the appellants are liable for the actual loss, that being on the findings of the arbitrators the direct result of the falling board. . . .

SCRUTTON, L.J. . . . The second defence is that the damage is too remote from the negligence, as it could not be reasonably foreseen as a consequence. On this head we were referred to a number of well known cases in which vague language, which I cannot think to be really helpful, has been used in an attempt to define the point at which damage becomes too remote from, or not sufficiently directly caused by, the breach of duty, which is the original cause of action, to be recoverable. For instance, I cannot think it useful to say the damage must be the natural and probable result. This suggests that there are results which are natural but not probable, and other results which are probable but not natural. I am not sure what either adjective means in this connection; if they mean the same thing, two need not be used; if they mean different things, the difference between them should be defined. And as to many cases of fact in which the distinction has been drawn, it is difficult to see why one case should be decided one way and one another. . . . To determine whether an act is negligent, it is relevant to determine whether any reasonable person would foresee that the act would cause damage; if he would not, the act is not negligent. But if the act would or might probably cause damage, the fact that the damage it in fact causes is not the exact kind of damage one would expect is immaterial, so long as the damage is in fact directly traceable to the negligent act, and not due to the operation of independent causes having no connection with the negligent act, except that they could not avoid its results. Once the act is negligent, the fact that its exact operation was not foreseen is immaterial. . . . In the present case it was negligent in discharging cargo to knock down the planks of the temporary staging, for they might easily cause some damage either to workmen, or cargo, or the ship. The fact that they did directly produce an unexpected result, a spark in an atmosphere of petrol vapour which caused a fire, does not relieve the person who was negligent from the damage which his negligent act so directly caused.

NOTES

1. The ex ante contract.   In light of the contractual exclusion of clause 21, *Polemis* presented a case of an incomplete contract between the owner and charterer because it did not specify the allocation of loss in the event of negligence by either party. What result if the contract had provided explicitly that all unforeseeable risks of the charterer's negligence were to be borne by the shipowner? Is that likely to have been the ex ante arrangement between the parties?

2. The directness test.   What are the arguments for imposing liability only if the unforeseeable harm results directly, rather than indirectly? Is it enough that this avoids factual problems of causal intervention and thereby simplifies the cause in fact inquiry? Whatever its merits, the *Polemis* approach has long had its American supporters. In Christianson v. Chicago, St. P., M. and O. Ry., 69 N.W. 640, 641 (Minn. 1896), the plaintiff was riding on the rear of a railroad's handcar, moving west. His handcar was being overtaken by a second car, driven by his foreman, going at a faster rate in the same direction. The plaintiff lost his balance and fell off the car, only to be struck and severely injured by the second handcar. Mitchell, J., upheld jury determinations that exonerated the plaintiff from charges of contributory negligence and found the defendant negligent. He continued:

> The main contention, however, of defendant's counsel, is that, conceding that those on the rear car were negligent, yet plaintiff's injuries were not the proximate result of such negligence; or, perhaps to state his position more accurately, that

it is not enough to entitle plaintiff to recover that his injuries were the natural consequence of this negligence, but that it must also appear that, under all the circumstances, it might have been reasonably anticipated that such injury would result. With this legal premise assumed, counsel argues that those on the rear car could not have reasonably anticipated that plaintiff would fall from the car. . . .

The doctrine contended for by counsel would establish practically the same rule of damages resulting from tort as is applied to damages resulting from breach of contract, under the familiar doctrine of Hadley v. Baxendale, 9 Exch. 341. This mode of stating the law is misleading, if not positively inaccurate. It confounds and mixes the definition of "negligence" with that of "proximate cause."

What a man may reasonably anticipate is important, and may be decisive, in determining whether an act is negligent, but is not at all decisive in determining whether that act is the proximate cause of an injury which ensues. . . . Consequences which follow in unbroken sequence, without an intervening efficient cause, from the original negligent act, are natural and proximate and for such consequences the original wrongdoer is responsible, even though he could not have foreseen the particular results which did follow. Smith v. Railway Co., L. R. 6 C. P. 14.

Tested by this rule, we think that it is clear that the negligence of those on the rear car was the proximate cause of plaintiff's injuries; at least, that the evidence justified the jury in so finding. Counsel admitted on the argument that if, by derailment or other accident, the front car had been suddenly stopped, and a collision and consequent injuries to plaintiff had resulted, the negligence of those on the rear car would have been the proximate cause. But we can see no difference in principle between the case supposed and the present case. The causal connection between the negligent act and the resulting injury would be the same in both cases. The only possible difference is that it might be anticipated that the sudden stoppage of the car was more likely to happen than the falling of one of its occupants upon the track.

What result under a modern foreseeability test? In a famous bon mot, Professor Seavey said, "Prima facie at least, the reasons for creating liability should limit it." Seavey, Mr. Justice Cardozo and the Law of Torts, 39 Colum. L. Rev. 20, 34; 52 Harv. L. Rev. 372, 386; 48 Yale L.J. 390, 404 (1939). How does Seavey's argument apply under a regime of strict liability?

Overseas Tankship (U.K.) Ltd. v. Morts Dock & Engineering Co., Ltd. (*Wagon Mound (No. 1)*)
[1961] A.C. 388 (P.C. Aust.)

[The appellants, defendants in the original cause of action, had carelessly discharged oil from their ship while it was berthed in Sydney Harbor. After their ship set sail, the oil was carried by the wind and tide to the plaintiff's wharf, which was used for repair work on other ships in the harbor. Plaintiff's supervisor was concerned about the spread of the oil, and he ordered his workmen to do no welding or burning in the area until further orders. He made some inquiries with the manager of the CalTex Oil Company, where the *Wagon Mound* was berthed, which, coupled with his own knowledge, satisfied him that the oil was not flammable.

Wagon Mound
Source: bulkers/photobucket

He accordingly instructed his men to resume their welding operations, and directed them as well to take care that no flammable material should fall off the wharf into the oil.

About two and one-half days later, the plaintiff's wharf was destroyed when the oil caught fire. "The outbreak of fire was due, as the trial judge found, to the fact that there was floating in the oil underneath the wharf a piece of debris on which lay some smouldering cotton waste or rag which had been set on fire by molten metal falling from the wharf: that the cotton waste or rag burst into flames: that the flames from the cotton waste set the floating oil afire either directly or by first setting fire to a wooden pile coated with oil, and that after the floating oil became ignited; the flames spread rapidly over the surface of the oil and quickly developed into a conflagration which severely damaged the wharf." "The trial judge also made the all-important finding, which must be set out in his own words: 'The *raison d'être* of furnace oil is, of course, that it shall burn, but I find the defendant did not know and could not reasonably be expected to have known that it was capable of being set afire when spread on water.'" The trial judge also found that the oil had caused, apart from the conflagration, some slight damage when it mucked up the plaintiff's wharf.]

VISCOUNT SIMONDS. . . . There can be no doubt that the decision of the Court of Appeal in *Polemis* plainly asserts that, if the defendant is guilty of negligence, he is responsible for all the consequences whether reasonably foreseeable or not. The generality of the proposition is perhaps qualified by the fact that each of the Lords Justices refers to the outbreak of fire as the direct result of the negligent act. There is thus introduced the conception that the negligent actor is not responsible for consequences which are not "direct," whatever that may mean. It has to be asked, then, why this conclusion should have been reached. The answer appears to be that it was reached upon a consideration of certain authorities, comparatively few in number, that were cited to the court. Of these, three are generally regarded as having influenced the decision. [The court then reviewed Smith v. London & South Western Railway Co. ((1870) L.R. 6 C.P. 14), *supra* at 406.] It would perhaps not be improper to say that the law of negligence as an independent tort was then of recent growth and that its implications had not been fully examined.

[The Privy Council then considered the H.M.S. London [1914] P. 72 and Weld Blundell v. Stephens [1970] A.C. 956, and concluded with a famous passage from the latter case by Lord Sumner:] "What a defendant ought to have anticipated as a reasonable man is material when the question is whether or not he was guilty of negligence, that is, of want of due care according to the circumstances. This, however, goes to culpability, not to compensation." [After discussion of some other English precedents, the opinion continues:]

The impression that may well be left on the reader of the scores of cases in which liability for negligence has been discussed is that the courts were feeling their way to a coherent body of doctrine and were at times in grave danger of being led astray by scholastic theories of causation and their ugly and barely intelligible jargon. . . .

Enough has been said to show that the authority of *Polemis* has been severely shaken though lip service has from time to time been paid to it. In their Lordships' opinion it should no longer be regarded as good law. It is not probable that many cases will for that reason have a different result, though it is hoped that the law will be thereby simplified, and that in some cases, at least, palpable injustice will be avoided. For it does not seem consonant with current ideas of justice or morality that for an act of negligence, however slight or venial, which results in some trivial foreseeable damage the actor should be liable for all consequences however unforeseeable and however grave, so long as they can be said to be "direct." It is a principle of civil liability, subject only to qualifications which have no present relevance, that a man must be considered to be responsible for the probable consequences of his act. To demand more of him is too harsh a rule, to demand less is to ignore that civilized order requires the observance of a minimum standard of behaviour.

This concept applied to the slowly developing law of negligence has led to a great variety of expressions which can, as it appears to their Lordships, be harmonized with little difficulty with the single exception of the so-called rule in *Polemis*. For, if it is asked why a man should be responsible for the natural or necessary or probable consequences of his act (or any other similar description of them) the answer is that it is not because they are natural or necessary or probable, but because, since they have this quality, it is judged by the standard of the reasonable man that he ought to have foreseen them. Thus it is that over and over again it has happened that in different judgments in the same case, and sometimes in a single judgment, liability for a consequence has been imposed on the ground that it was reasonably foreseeable or, alternatively, on the ground that it was natural or necessary or probable. The two grounds have been treated as coterminous, and so they largely are. But, where they are not, the question arises to which the wrong answer was given in *Polemis*. For, if some limitation must be imposed upon the consequences for which the negligent actor is to be held responsible—and all are agreed that some limitation there must be—why should that test (reasonable foreseeability) be rejected which, since he is judged by what the reasonable man ought to foresee, corresponds with the common conscience of mankind, and a test (the "direct" consequence) be substituted which leads to nowhere but the never-ending and insoluble problems of causation. "The lawyer," said Sir Frederick Pollock, "cannot afford to adventure himself with philosophers in the logical and metaphysical controversies that beset the idea of cause." Yet this is just what he has most unfortunately done and must continue to do if the rule in *Polemis* is to prevail. A conspicuous example occurs when the actor seeks to escape liability on the ground that the "chain of causation" is broken by a nova causa or novus actus interveniens. . . .

In the same connection may be mentioned the conclusion to which the Full Court finally came in the present case. Applying the rule in *Polemis* and holding therefore that the unforeseeability of the damage by fire afforded no defence, they went on to consider the remaining question. Was it a "direct" consequence? Upon this Manning, J., said: "Notwithstanding that, if regard is had separately to each individual occurrence in the chain of events that led to this fire, each occurrence was improbable and, in one sense, improbability was heaped upon improbability, I cannot escape from the conclusion that if the ordinary man in the street had been asked, as a matter of common sense, without any detailed analysis of the circumstances, to state the cause of the fire at Morts Dock, he would unhesitatingly have assigned such cause to spillage of oil by the appellant's employees." Perhaps he would, and probably he would have added: "I never should have thought it possible." But with great respect to the Full Court this is surely irrelevant, or, if it is relevant, only serves to show that the *Polemis* rule works in a very strange way. After the event even a fool is wise. But it is not the hindsight of a fool; it is the foresight of the reasonable man which alone can determine responsibility. The *Polemis* rule by substituting "direct" for "reasonably foreseeable" consequence leads to a conclusion equally illogical and unjust.

[Appeal allowed.]

NOTES

1. Foresight versus directness.   The abstract debate over the proper standard for remoteness of damage often obscures what is at stake in the two positions. An instructive way to approach this dispute over proximate cause is to ask whether *Wagon Mound (No. 1)* can be reconciled with *In re Polemis* even under the "direct consequences" test. To do so, it is necessary to examine the precise sequence of events between defendant's wrongful conduct and plaintiff's harm. In *Polemis*, no human act intervened between the dropping of the plank and the burning of the ship; the only causal complication was the antecedent presence of fumes in the ship's hold. In *Wagon Mound (No. 1)*, however, the causal chain contained at least two human acts between the oil spill from defendant's ship and the destruction of plaintiff's wharf: first, the consultations by plaintiff's dock supervisor with CalTex's manager, and second, the ignition of the fire by the oxyacetylene torches used by plaintiff's servants. If the conduct of plaintiff's servants amounts to either assumption of risk or contributory negligence, it is possible both to keep the directness test of *Polemis* and to defend the result in *Wagon Mound (No. 1)*. Note also that if either defense is feasible, the plaintiff must proceed gingerly on foreseeability, for if the defendant's servants could have foreseen the harm, so too could the plaintiff's.

The importance of the plaintiff's conduct is illustrated by the Privy Council's subsequent decision in Overseas Tankship (U.K.) Ltd. v. The Miller Steamship Co., [1967] 1 A.C. 617, 642-643, better known as *Wagon Mound (No. 2)*. The facts in that case were the same as in *Wagon Mound (No. 1)*, except that the plaintiff in *Wagon Mound (No. 2)* was the owner of a ship destroyed by the fire in *Wagon Mound (No. 1)*. The plaintiff shipowner was not, of course, bound by the prior decision; nor was he hampered by possible charges of contributory negligence or assumption of risk. As against the plaintiff, the conduct of the servants of Morts Dock (plaintiff in *Wagon Mound (No. 1)*) only went to the question of causal connection, where in the modern view it could not, as intervening negligence, be decisive. See *supra* at 413. Plaintiff, therefore, introduced evidence to show that some risk of harm by fire was reasonably foreseeable by defendant's engineer. Lord Reid, speaking for the Privy Council, distinguished *Wagon Mound (No. 1)* and affirmed a judgment for the plaintiff. He noted that the plaintiff lost in Bolton v. Stone, *supra* at 123, because the risk of harm was small and the activity that caused the harm was lawful, whereas:

> In the present case there was no justification whatever for discharging the oil into Sydney Harbour. Not only was it an offence to do so, but it involved considerable loss financially. If the ship's engineer had thought about the matter, there could have been no question of balancing the advantages and disadvantages. From every point of view it was both his duty and his interest to stop the discharge immediately. . . .
>
> The findings show that he [the ship's engineer] ought to have known that it is possible to ignite this kind of oil on water, and that the ship's engineer probably ought to have known that this had in fact happened before. The most that can be said to justify inaction is that he would have known that this could only happen in very exceptional circumstances. But that does not mean that a reasonable man would dismiss such a risk from his mind and do nothing when it was so easy to prevent it.

Does Lord Reid's argument amount to a repudiation of Bolton v. Stone? An adoption of the Hand formula for negligence? A belated acceptance of the judgment of Nares, J., in Scott v. Shepherd, Chapter 2, *supra* at 84? On the progression from *Polemis* to *Wagon Mound*, see Levmore, *The Wagon Mound Cases*: Foreseeability, Causation, and Mrs. Palsgraf, *in* Torts Stories 129, 142 (Rabin & Sugarman ed., 2003), suggesting that on grounds of causation the outcome of the two cases could easily be reversed.

2. The passing of causation.   The proponents of the foresight test insist that it allows courts to dispense with the technical and nearly insoluble conundrums of causation. Even if the argument is sound (is it?), the foresight test raises unique problems of its own, chiefly in describing the events that led to the plaintiff's harm. Professor Morris discusses this point in Torts 174-177 (1953):

> Once misconduct causes damage, a specific accident has happened in a particular way and has resulted in a discrete harm. When, after the event, the question is asked, "Was the particular accident and the resulting damages foreseeable?", the cases fall into the three classes:
>
>   (1) In some cases damages resulting from misconduct are so typical that judge and jurors cannot possibly be convinced that they were unforeseeable. . . .

(2) In some cases freakishness of the facts refuses to be downed and any description that minimizes it is viewed as misdescription. For example, in a recent Louisiana case [Lynch v. Fisher, 41 So. 2d 692 (La. App. 1949)] a trucker negligently left his truck on the highway at night without setting out flares. A car crashed into the truck and caught fire. A passerby came to the rescue of the car occupants — a man and wife. After the rescuer got them out of the car he returned to the car to get a floor mat to pillow the injured wife's head. A pistol lay on the mat rescuer wanted to use. He picked it up and handed it to the husband. The accident had unbeknownst to the rescuer, temporarily deranged the husband, and he shot rescuer in the leg. Such a consequence of negligently failing to guard a truck with flares is so unarguably unforeseeable that no judge or juror would be likely to hold otherwise. (Incidentally the Louisiana court held the trucker liable to the rescuer on the ground that foreseeability is not a requisite of liability.)

(3) Between these extremes are cases in which consequences are neither typical nor wildly freakish. In these cases unusual details are arguably — but only arguably significant. If they are held significant, then the consequences are unforeseeable; if they are held unimportant then the consequences are foreseeable.

Into which class does *Polemis* fall? *Wagon Mound?* Need the defendant only foresee "in a general way" the consequences of his act, and not the "precise details of its occurrence"?

3. A foreseeable kind of damage.   In the aftermath of *Wagon Mound (No. 1)*, the English courts struggled to determine whether the harm suffered by the plaintiff was foreseeable. In Doughty v. Turner Manufacturing Co., Ltd., [1964] 1 Q.B. 518, one of the defendant's employees knocked an asbestos cement cover into a vat of extremely hot solution of sodium cyanide — eight times as hot as boiling water. His conduct was negligent since the falling cover might have splashed some of the molten substance on someone standing nearby. In fact, nobody was hurt by the splash, but after a short time the asbestos cement cover caused an explosion in the vat that hurled the molten substance into the air, some of it hurting the plaintiff, who stood nearby. No one had any reason to suspect that the cover, when immersed, would explode. The trial judge allowed recovery given defendant's negligence, but the Court of Appeal reversed because the damage was the consequence of a risk or hazard about which defendant had not been negligent. Does *Doughty* present any problems of causal intervention?

Contrast *Doughty* with Hughes v. Lord Advocate, [1963] A.C. 837. Defendant's servants were working on an underground cable to which they had access through an open manhole nine feet deep. The manhole was covered by a shelter-tent. When defendant's servants left the work area, they left a ladder near the manhole, pulled a tarpaulin over the entrance to the tent, and lighted four paraffin warning lamps outside the tent. The plaintiff, aged eight, and his uncle, aged ten, came by and started to play with the equipment with a view toward descending into the manhole. Plaintiff tripped over one of the paraffin lamps, which he had brought into the tent, which then fell into the hole. An explosion ensued when, as best as could be determined, "paraffin escaped from the tank, formed vapour and was ignited by the flame." The explosion burned the plaintiff and knocked him into the hole, as a result of which the severity of his burns was greatly increased. The respondents argued that the explosion was unforeseeable even if some harm from burning by the lamp was foreseeable. The House of Lords rejected the argument, holding that the damage was not of a different type from that which was foreseeable given that paraffin lamps were a "known source of danger." Is the distinction between burning and explosion "too fine to warrant acceptance"? If so, why accept the distinction between splashing and exploding? Does *Hughes* present the troublesome questions of causal intervention referred to in *Wagon Mound (No. 1)*? Note that the defendant in *Hughes*, on appeal, did not claim that plaintiff's trespass barred his recovery.

4. The thin skull rule, or "you take your victim as you find him." One rule of tort law left unshaken by *Wagon Mound (No. 1)* is that the defendant takes his victim as he finds him. In Smith v. Brain Leech & Co. Ltd., [1962] 2 Q.B. 405, plaintiff's decedent was burned on his lip by splashing molten metal because defendant negligently failed to provide an adequate guard. Because of prior exposures of another kind in the past, the decedent had (according to the court) developed a tendency toward cancer. In any event, the burned lip developed a cancer from which he died. The court acknowledged that death by cancer was unforeseeable, but, notwithstanding *Wagon Mound (No. 1)*, it allowed recovery, expressing certainty that the Privy Council had no intention of changing the "take plaintiff as he is" principle or denying recovery to a plaintiff with a thin skull.

On the thin skull rule and its relationship to the problems of causal intervention, see Seavey, Mr. Justice Cardozo and the Law of Torts, 39 Colum. L. Rev. 20, 32-33; 52 Harv. L. Rev. 372, 384-385; 48 Yale L.J. 390, 402-403 (1939):

> [W]here the defendant has negligently struck a person whose skull is so fragile that it is broken by the comparatively slight blow, all courts are agreed that the defendant is liable for the wholly unexpected breaking. This is true not only with reference to physical harm but also other forms of harm. If a person were negligently to incapacitate another who has a yearly earning capacity of a hundred thousand dollars, there is liability for the resulting loss though so great a loss could not have been anticipated. It may be that this is a possible explanation for the reaction of the King's Bench in its famous but doubtful decision of the *Polemis* case, in which the defendant whose workman negligently dropped a plank into the hold of a ship filled with gasoline vapor was made liable for the destruction of the ship resulting from the ensuing explosion. In this, as in other cases, the courts are agreed that the negligent person takes his victims as they are.

The causal complications of the thin skull rule are graphically illustrated by Steinhauser v. Hertz Corp., 421 F.2d 1169, 1172 (2d Cir. 1970). Plaintiff, a 14-year-old child, was a passenger in her parents' car when it was wrongfully struck by the driver of defendant's car. The plaintiff suffered no physical injuries, but shortly thereafter she began to behave strangely; she became "highly agitated," "glassy-eyed," and "nervous." As her condition worsened, she was institutionally treated for schizophrenia. Even after her release she required further medical treatment, with reinstitutionalization a likely prospect. Two years prior to the accident, the plaintiff had suffered a mild concussion. Plaintiff's attorney argued that the accident was a "precipitating cause of a quiescent disease." The trial judge instructed the jury that recovery was permissible only if the plaintiff were normal before the accident, but not if "this plaintiff had this disease all along." Proximate cause was, in the words of the trial judge, "a big word" for what ordinary people call cause. The jury's verdict for defendant was reversed on appeal, with Friendly, J., writing as follows:

> The testimony was that before the accident Cynthia was *neither* a "perfectly normal child" *nor* a schizophrenic, but a child with some degree of pathology which was activated into schizophrenia by an emotional trauma although it otherwise might not have blossomed. Whatever the medical soundness of this theory may or may not be, and there does not seem in fact to have been any dispute about it, plaintiffs were entitled to have it fairly weighed by the jury. They could not properly be pinioned on the dilemma of having either to admit that Cynthia was already suffering from active schizophrenia or to assert that she was wholly without psychotic tendencies.

5. American response to Polemis *and* Wagon Mound (No. 1).   Friendly, J., also commented on the English debate over proximate cause in Petition of Kinsman Transit Co., 338 F.2d 708, 723-725 (2d Cir. 1964). A January thaw on the Buffalo River released large cakes of ice that, because of high water, banged into and loosened a negligently tied and improperly tended ship so that it started downstream, careening into another ship and knocking it loose. Both ships then drifted on and crashed into a drawbridge maintained by the city of Buffalo at a point before the river flows into Lake Erie. The two ships and the drawbridge made an effective dam against which floating ice accumulated, causing flooding for miles. This action was brought against the owner of the first ship and the city. The above events all occurred at night, when no traffic was expected on the river.

The crew tending the drawbridge was, or so the court held, under a statutory duty to raise the drawbridge not only for ships passing by in the course of navigation but also for drifting vessels. If the crew had displayed the requisite alertness by raising the bridge in time, all of the harm at issue could have been avoided. By a two-to-one vote, the court held both defendants jointly liable for plaintiff's damages. Judge Friendly made these observations about the rejection of *Polemis* in *Wagon Mound (No. 1)*:

> [We] find it difficult to understand why one who had failed to use the care required to protect others in the light of expectable forces should be exonerated when the very risks that rendered his conduct negligent produced other and more serious consequences to such persons than were fairly foreseeable when he fell short of what the law demanded. Foreseeability of danger is necessary to render conduct negligent where as here the damage was caused by just those forces whose existence required the exercise of greater care than was taken—the current, the ice, and the physical mass of the Shiras, the incurring of consequences other and greater than foreseen does not make the conduct less culpable or provide a reasoned basis for

insulation. The oft-encountered argument that failure to limit liability to foreseeable consequences may subject the defendant to a loss wholly out of proportion to his fault seems scarcely consistent with the universally accepted rule that the defendant takes the plaintiff as he finds him and will be responsible for the full extent of the injury even though a latent susceptibility of the plaintiff renders this far more serious than could reasonably have been anticipated. . . .

The weight of authority in this country rejects the limitation of damages to consequences foreseeable at the time of the negligent conduct when the consequences are "direct," and the damage, although other and greater than expectable, is of the same general sort that was risked. . . . Other American courts, purporting to apply a test of foreseeability to damages, extend that concept to such unforeseen lengths as to raise serious doubt whether the concept is meaningful; indeed, we wonder whether the British courts are not finding it necessary to limit the language of *The Wagon Mound* as we have indicated.

We see no reason why an actor engaging in conduct which entails a large risk of small damage and a small risk of other and greater damage, of the same general sort, from the same forces, and to the same class of persons, should be relieved of responsibility for the latter simply because the chance of its occurrence, if viewed alone, may not have been large enough to require the exercise of care. By hypothesis, the risk of the lesser harm was sufficient to render his disregard of it actionable; the existence of a less likely additional risk that the very forces against whose action he was required to guard would produce other and greater damage than could have been reasonably anticipated should inculpate him further rather than limit his liability.

Why is plaintiff's harm direct damage in *Kinsman?*

Palsgraf v. Long Island R.R.

162 N.E. 99 (N.Y. 1928)

Appeal from a judgment of the Appellate Division of the Supreme Court in the second judicial department, entered December 16, 1927, affirming a judgment in favor of plaintiff entered upon a verdict.

[The following excerpts are from the majority opinion of Seeger, J., in the Appellate Division, 222 App. Div. 166 (1927):]

The defendant contends that the accident was not caused by the negligence of the defendant.

The sole question of defendant's negligence submitted to the jury was whether the defendant's employees were "careless and negligent in the way they handled this particular passenger after he came upon the platform and while he was boarding the train." This question of negligence was submitted to the jury by a fair and impartial charge and the verdict was supported by the evidence. The jury might well find that the act of the passenger in undertaking to board a moving train was negligent, and that the acts of the defendant's employees in assisting him while engaged in that negligent act were also negligent. Instead of aiding or assisting the passenger engaged in such an act, they might better have discouraged and warned him not to board the moving train. It is quite probable that without their assistance the passenger might have succeeded in boarding the train and no accident would have happened, or without the assistance of these employees the passenger might have desisted in his efforts to board the train. In any event, the acts of defendant's employees, which the jury found to be negligent, caused the bundle to be thrown under the train and to explode. It is no answer or defense to these negligent acts to say that the defendant's employees were not chargeable with notice that the passenger's bundle contained an explosive. . . .

It must be remembered that the plaintiff was a passenger of the defendant and entitled to have the defendant exercise the highest degree of care required of common carriers.

[The dissenting opinion of Lazansky, P.J., in the appellate division reads as follows:]

The facts may have warranted the jury in finding the defendant's agents were negligent in assisting a passenger in boarding a moving train in view of the fact that a door of the train should have been closed before the train started, which would have prevented the passenger making the attempt. There was also warrant for a finding by the jury that as a result of the negligence of the defendant a package was thrown between the platform and train, exploded, causing injury to plaintiff, who was on the station platform. In my opinion, the negligence of defendant was not a proximate cause of the injuries to plaintiff. Between the negligence of defendant and the injuries, there intervened the negligence of the passenger carrying the package containing an explosive. This was an independent, and not a concurring act of negligence. The explosion was not reasonably probable as a result of defendant's act of negligence. The negligence of defendant was not a likely or natural cause of the explosion, since the latter was such an unusual occurrence. Defendant's negligence was a cause of plaintiff's injury, but too remote.

[The appellate division split three to two for plaintiff. The Court of Appeals reversed by a four-to-three vote.]

CARDOZO, C.J. Plaintiff was standing on a platform of defendant's railroad after buying a ticket to go to Rockaway Beach. A train stopped at the station, bound for another place. Two men ran forward to catch it. One of the men reached the platform of the car without mishap, though the train was already moving. The other man, carrying a package, jumped aboard the car, but seemed unsteady as if about to fall. A guard on the car, who had held the door open, reached forward to help him in, and another guard on the platform pushed him from behind. In this act, the package was dislodged, and fell upon the rails. It was a package of small size, about fifteen inches long, and was covered by a newspaper. In fact it contained fireworks, but there was nothing in its appearance to give notice of its contents. The fireworks when they fell exploded. The shock of the explosion threw down some scales at the other end of the platform, many feet away. The scales struck the plaintiff, causing injuries for which she sues.

Exhibit 3.2 Benjamin Cardozo

Benjamin Cardozo (1870-1938) was one of the foremost jurists of the early twentieth century, serving on the New York Court of Appeals (1914-1932) and the United States Supreme Court (1932-1938). During his tenure on the Court of Appeals, Cardozo wrote some of the most notable modern tort law decisions, including *Palsgraf*, Murphy v. Steeplechase Amusement Co., and MacPherson v. Buick Motor Co. Cardozo has been praised by Court of Appeals Chief Judge Judith Kaye for "look[ing] beyond the immediate facts to the future course of the law." Cardozo also believed that "there is an accuracy that defeats itself by the overemphasis of details," instead relying on sparse statements of facts to support an opinion's inevitable conclusion (as in *Palsgraf*).

Described as a "legal landmark" by Cardozo biographer Andrew L. Kaufman, *Palsgraf*'s "extraordinary events that linked Helen Palsgraf and Benjamin Cardozo" were not confined to the case itself. Over 60 years after the case was decided, in 1991, Lisa Newell, "the first cousin four times removed of Benajmin Cardozo, married J. Scott Garvey. Mr. Garvey is the great-grandson of Helen Palsgraf." Andrew L. Kaufman, Cardozo 303 (Harvard University Press, 1998).

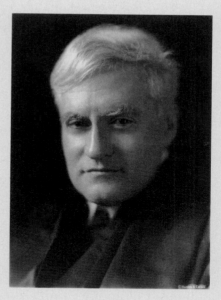

Bio source: Judith S. Kaye, Benjamin Nathan Cardozo (1870-1938) Court of Appeals 1914-1932 Chief Judge 1927-1932, 6 Jud. Notice 3 (2009)
Image source: Wikimedia Commons

The conduct of the defendant's guard, if a wrong in its relation to the holder of the package, was not a wrong in its relation to the plaintiff, standing far away. Relatively to her it was not negligence at all. Nothing in the situation gave notice that the falling package had in it the potency of peril to persons thus removed. Negligence is not actionable unless it involves the invasion of a legally protected interest, the violation of a right. "Proof of negligence in the air, so to speak, will not do" (Pollock, Torts, p. 455 [11th ed.]). The plaintiff as she stood upon the platform of the station might claim to be protected against intentional invasion of her bodily security. Such invasion is not charged. She might claim to be protected against unintentional invasion by conduct involving in the thought of reasonable men an unreasonable hazard that such invasion would ensue. These, from the point of view of the law, were the bounds of her immunity, with perhaps some rare exceptions, survivals for the most part of ancient forms of liability, where conduct is held to be at the peril of the actor. If no hazard was apparent to the eye of ordinary vigilance, an act innocent and harmless, at least to outward seeming, with reference to her, did not take to itself the quality of a tort because it happened to be a wrong, though apparently not one involving the risk of bodily insecurity, with reference to someone else. . . . The plaintiff sues in her own right for a wrong personal to her, and not as the vicarious beneficiary of a breach of duty to another.

A different conclusion will involve us, and swiftly too, in a maze of contradictions. A guard stumbles over a package which has been left upon a platform. It seems to be a bundle of newspapers. It turns out to be a can of dynamite. To the eye of ordinary vigilance, the bundle is abandoned waste, which may be kicked or trod on with impunity. Is a passenger at the other end of the platform protected by the law against the unsuspected hazard concealed beneath the waste? If not, is the result to be any different, so far as the distant passenger is concerned, when the guard stumbles over a valise which a truckman or a porter has left upon the walk? The passenger far away, if the victim of a wrong at all, has a cause of action, not derivative, but original and primary. His claim to be protected against invasion of his bodily security is neither greater nor less because the act resulting in the invasion is a wrong to another far removed. In this case, the rights that are said to have been violated, the interests said to have been invaded, are not even of the same order. The man was not injured in his person nor even put in danger. The purpose of the act, as well as its effect, was to make his person safe. If there was a wrong to him at all, which may very well be doubted, it was a wrong to a property interest only, the safety of his package. Out of this wrong to property, which threatened injury to nothing else, there has passed, we are told, to the plaintiff by derivation or succession a right of action for the invasion of an interest of another order, the right to bodily security. The diversity of interests emphasizes the futility of the effort to build the plaintiff's right upon the basis of a wrong to some one else. The gain is one of emphasis, for a like result would follow if the interests were the same. Even then, the orbit of the danger as disclosed to the eye of reasonable vigilance would be the orbit of the duty. One who jostles one's neighbor in a crowd does not invade the rights of others standing at the outer fringe when the unintended contact casts a bomb upon the ground. The wrongdoer as to them is the man who carries the bomb, not the one who explodes it without suspicion of the danger. Life will have to be made over, and human nature transformed, before prevision so extravagant can be accepted as the norm of conduct, the customary standard to which behavior must conform.

The argument for the plaintiff is built upon the shifting meanings of such words as "wrong" and "wrongful," and shares their instability. What the plaintiff must show is "a wrong" to herself, i.e. a violation of her own right, and not merely a wrong to someone else, nor conduct "wrongful" because unsocial, but not "a wrong" to any one. We are told that one who drives at reckless speed through a crowded city street is guilty of a negligent act and, therefore, of a wrongful one irrespective of the consequences. Negligent the act is, and wrongful in the sense that it is unsocial, but wrongful and unsocial in relation to other travelers, only because the eye of vigilance perceives the risk of damage. If the same act were to be committed on a speedway or a race course, it would lose its wrongful quality. The risk reasonably to be perceived defines the duty to be obeyed, and risk imports relation; it is risk to another or to others within the range of apprehension (Seavey, Negligence, Subjective or Objective, 41 H.L. Rv. 6). This does not mean, of course, that one who launches a destructive force is always relieved of liability if the force, though known to be destructive, pursues an unexpected path. "It was not necessary that the defendant should have had notice of the particular method in which an accident would occur, if the possibility of an accident was clear to the ordinarily prudent eye" (Munsey v. Webb, 231 U.S. 150, 156 [(1913)]). Some acts, such as shooting, are so imminently dangerous to any one who may come within reach of the missile, however unexpectedly, as to impose a duty of prevision not far from that of an insurer. Even today, and much oftener in earlier stages of the law, one acts sometimes at one's peril (Jeremiah Smith, Tort and Absolute Liability, 30 H.L. Rv. 328; Street, Foundations of Legal Liability, vol. 1, pp. 77, 78). Under this head, it may be, fall certain cases of what is known as transferred intent, an act willfully dangerous to *A* resulting by misadventure in injury to *B* (Talmage v. Smith, 101 Mich. 370, 374). These cases aside, wrong is defined in terms of the natural or probable, at least when unintentional (Parrot v. Wells-Fargo Co. [The Nitro-Glycerine Case], [82 U.S.] 15 Wall. [524 (1872)]). The range of reasonable apprehension is at times a question for the court, and at times, if varying inferences are possible, a question for the jury. Here, by concession, there was nothing in the situation to suggest to the most cautious mind that the parcel wrapped in newspaper would spread wreckage through the station. If the guard had thrown it down knowingly and willfully, he would not have threatened the plaintiff's safety, so far as appearances could warn him. His conduct would not have involved, even then, an unreasonable probability of invasion of her bodily security. Liability can be no greater where the act is inadvertent.

Negligence, like risk, is thus a term of relation. Negligence in the abstract, apart from things related, is surely not a tort, if indeed it is understandable at all. . . . The victim does not sue derivatively, or by right of subrogation, to vindicate an interest invaded in the person of another. Thus to view his cause of action [for negligence] is to ignore the fundamental difference between tort and crime. He sues for breach of a duty owing to himself.

The law of causation, remote or proximate, is thus foreign to the case before us. The question of liability is always anterior to the question of the measure of the consequences that go with liability. If there is no tort to be redressed, there is no occasion to consider what damage might be recovered if there were a finding of a tort. We may assume, without deciding, that negligence, not at large or in the abstract, but in relation to the plaintiff, would entail liability for any and all consequences, however novel or extraordinary. There is room for argument that a distinction is to be drawn according to the diversity of interests invaded by the act, as where conduct negligent in that it threatens an insignificant invasion of an interest in property results in an unforeseeable invasion of an interest of another order, as e.g., one of bodily security. Perhaps other distinctions may be necessary. We do not go into the question now. The consequences to be followed must first be rooted in a wrong.

[Reversed].

ANDREWS, J., dissenting. Assisting a passenger to board a train, the defendant's servant negligently knocked a package from his arms. It fell between the platform and the cars. Of its contents the servant knew and could know nothing. A violent explosion followed. The concussion broke some scales standing a considerable distance away. In falling they injured the plaintiff, an intending passenger.

Upon these facts may she recover the damages she has suffered in an action brought against the master? The result we shall reach depends upon our theory as to the nature of negligence. Is it a relative concept—the breach of some duty owing to a particular person or to particular persons? Or where there is an act which unreasonably threatens the safety of others, is the doer liable for all its proximate consequences, even where they result in injury to one who would generally be thought to be outside the radius of danger? This is not a mere dispute as to words. We might not believe that to the average mind the dropping of the bundle would seem to involve the probability of harm to the plaintiff standing many feet away whatever might be the case as to the owner or to one so near as to be likely to be struck by its fall. If, however, we adopt the second hypothesis we have to inquire only as to the relation between cause and effect. We deal in terms of proximate cause, not of negligence.

Negligence may be defined roughly as an act or omission which unreasonably does or may affect the rights of others, or which unreasonably fails to protect oneself from the dangers resulting from such acts. Here I confine myself to the first branch of the definition. Nor do I comment on the word "unreasonable." For present purposes it sufficiently describes that average of conduct that society requires of its members. . . .

But we are told that "there is no negligence unless there is in the particular case a legal duty to take care, and this duty must be one which is owed to the plaintiff himself and not merely to others." (Salmond, Torts, 24 [6th ed.].) This, I think too narrow a conception. Where there is the unreasonable act, and some right that may be affected there is negligence whether damage does or does not result. That is immaterial. Should we drive down Broadway at a reckless speed, we are negligent whether we strike an approaching car or miss it by an inch. The act itself is wrongful. It is a wrong not only to those who happen to be within the radius of danger but to all who might have been there—a wrong to the public at large. Such is the language of the street. Such is the language of the courts when speaking of contributory negligence. Such is again and again their language in speaking of the duty of some defendant and discussing proximate cause in cases where such a discussion is wholly irrelevant on any other theory. . . . Due care is a duty imposed on each one of us to protect society from unnecessary danger, not to protect *A, B* or *C* alone.

It may well be that there is no such thing as negligence in the abstract. "Proof of negligence in the air, so to speak, will not do." In an empty world negligence would not exist. It does involve a relationship between man and his fellows, but not merely a relationship between man and those whom he might reasonably expect his act would injure; rather, a relationship between him and those whom he does in fact injure. If his act has a tendency to harm some one, it harms him a mile away as surely as it does those on the scene. We now permit children to recover for the negligent killing of the father. It was never prevented on the theory that no duty was owing to them. A husband may be compensated for the loss of his wife's services. To say that the wrongdoer was negligent as to the husband as well as to the wife is merely an attempt to fit facts to theory. An insurance company paying a fire loss recovers its payment of the negligent incendiary. We speak of subrogation—of suing in the right of the insured. Behind the cloud of words is the fact they hide, that the act, wrongful as to the insured, has also injured the company. Even if it be true that the fault of father, wife or insured will prevent recovery, it is because we consider the original negligence not the proximate cause of the injury. (Pollock, Torts, 463 [12th ed.].)

In the well-known *Polemis Case*, Scrutton, L.J., said that the dropping of a plank was negligent for it might injure "workman or cargo or ship." Because of either possibility the owner of the vessel was to be made good for his loss. The act being wrongful the doer was liable for its proximate results. Criticized and explained as this statement may have been, I think it states the law as it should be and as it is.

The proposition is this. Every one owes to the world at large the duty of refraining from those acts that may unreasonably threaten the safety of others. Such an act occurs. Not only is he wronged to whom harm might reasonably be expected to result, but he also who is in fact injured, even if he be outside what would generally be thought the danger zone. There needs be duty due the one complaining but this is not a duty to a particular individual because as to him harm might be expected. Harm to some one being the natural result of the act, not only that one alone, but all those in fact injured may complain. . . . Unreasonable risk being taken, its consequences are not confined to those who might probably be hurt.

If this be so, we do not have a plaintiff suing by "derivation or succession." Her action is original and primary. Her claim is for a breach of duty to herself—not that she is subrogated to any right of action of the owner of the parcel or of a passenger standing at the scene of the explosion.

The right to recover damages rests on additional considerations. The plaintiff's rights must be injured, and this injury must be caused by the negligence. We build a dam, but are negligent as to its foundations. Breaking, it injures property down stream. We are not liable if all this happened because of some reason other than the insecure foundation. But when injuries do result from our unlawful act we are liable for the consequences. It does not matter that they are unusual, unexpected, unforeseen and unforeseeable. But there is one limitation. The damages must be so connected with the negligence that the latter may be said to be the proximate cause of the former.

These two words have never been given an inclusive definition. What is a cause in a legal sense, still more what is a proximate cause, depend in each case upon many considerations, as does the existence of negligence itself. Any philosophical doctrine of causation does not help us. A boy throws a stone into a pond. The ripples spread. The water level rises. The history of that pond is altered to all eternity. It will be altered by other causes also. Yet it will be forever the resultant of all causes combined. Each one will have an influence. How great only omniscience can say. You may speak of a chain, or if you please, a net. An analogy is of little aid. Each cause brings about future events. Without each the future would not be the same. Each is proximate in the sense it is essential. But that is not what we mean by the word. Nor on the other hand do we mean sole cause. There is no such thing.

Should analogy be thought helpful, however, I prefer that of a stream. The spring, starting on its journey, is joined by tributary after tributary. The river, reaching the ocean, comes from a hundred sources. No man may say whence any drop of water is derived. Yet for a time distinction may be possible. Into the clear creek, brown swamp water flows from the left. Later, from the right comes water stained by its clay bed. The three may remain for a space, sharply divided. But at last, inevitably no trace of separation remains. They are so commingled that all distinction is lost.

As we have said, we cannot trace the effect of an act to the end, if end there is. Again, however, we may trace it part of the way. A murder at Serajevo may be the necessary antecedent to an assassination in London twenty years hence. An overturned lantern may burn all Chicago. We may follow the fire from the shed to the last building. We rightly say the fire started by the lantern caused its destruction.

A cause, but not the proximate cause. What we do mean by the word "proximate" is, that because of convenience, of public policy, of a rough sense of justice, the law arbitrarily declines to trace a series of events beyond a certain point. This is not logic. It is practical politics. Take our rule as to fires. Sparks from my burning haystack set on fire my house and my neighbor's. I may recover from a negligent railroad. He may not. Yet the wrongful act as directly harmed the one as the other. We may regret that the line was drawn just where it was, but drawn somewhere it had to be. We said the act of the railroad was not the proximate cause of our neighbor's fire. Cause it surely was. The words we used were simply indicative of our notions of public policy. Other courts think differently. But somewhere they reach the point where they cannot say the stream comes from any one source. . . .

It is all a question of expediency. There are no fixed rules to govern our judgment. There are simply matters of which we may take account. We have in a somewhat different connection spoken of "the stream of events." We have asked whether that stream was deflected—whether it was forced into new and unexpected channels. This is rather rhetoric than law. There is in truth little to guide us other than common sense.

There are some hints that may help us. The proximate cause, involved as it may be with many other causes, must be, at the least, something without which the event would not happen. The court must ask itself whether there was a natural and continuous sequence between cause and effect. Was the one a substantial factor in producing the other? Was there a direct connection between them, without too many intervening causes? Is the effect of cause on result not too attenuated? Is the cause likely, in the usual judgment of mankind, to produce the result? Or by the exercise of prudent foresight could the result be foreseen? Is the result too remote from the cause, and here we consider remoteness in time and space. . . . Clearly we must so consider, for the greater the distance either in time or space, the more surely do other causes intervene to affect the result. When a lantern is overturned the firing of a shed is a fairly direct consequence. Many things contribute to the spread of the conflagration—the force of the wind, the direction and width of streets, the character of intervening structures, other factors. We draw an uncertain and wavering line, but draw it we must as best we can.

Once again, it is all a question of fair judgment, always keeping in mind the fact that we endeavor to make a rule in each case that will be practical and in keeping with the general understanding of mankind. . . .

This last suggestion is the factor which must determine the case before us. The act upon which defendant's liability rests is knocking an apparently harmless package onto the platform. The act was negligent. For its proximate consequences the defendant is liable. If its contents were broken, to the owner; if it fell upon and crushed a passenger's foot, then to him. If it exploded and injured one in the immediate vicinity, to him also. . . . Mrs. Palsgraf was standing some distance away. How far cannot be told from the record—apparently twenty-five or thirty feet. Perhaps less. Except for the explosion, she would not have been injured. We are told by the appellant in his brief "it cannot be denied that the explosion was the direct cause of the plaintiff's injuries." So it was a substantial factor in producing the result—there was here a natural and continuous sequence—direct connection. The only intervening cause was that instead of blowing her to the ground the concussion smashed the weighing machine which in turn fell upon her. There was no remoteness in time, little in space. And surely, given such an explosion as here it needed no great foresight to predict that the natural result would be to injure one on the platform at no greater distance from its scene than was the plaintiff. Just how no one might be able to predict. Whether by flying fragments, by broken glass, by wreckage of machines or structures no one could say. But injury in some form was most probable.

Under these circumstances I cannot say as a matter of law that the plaintiff's injuries were not the proximate result of the negligence. That is all we have before us. The court refused to so charge. No request was made to submit the matter to the jury as a question of fact, even would that have been proper upon the record before us.

The judgment appealed from should be affirmed, with costs.

NOTES

1. Questions raised by Palsgraf. *Palsgraf* has inspired extensive detective work to uncover its facts. Judge Noonan, Persons and Masks of the Law ch. 4 (1976), suggests that the "scales must have been toppled *not by the explosion* of the fireworks, but by the crowd running in panic on the platform." In Cardozo: A Study in Reputation 38-39 (1990), Judge Posner relies on a front-page *New York Times* report of the accident, "Bomb Blast Injures 13 in Station Crowd," (Aug. 25, 1924, at A1), to conclude that the explosion was not only loud enough to cause a stampede, but also violent enough to cause extensive damage to the train station, and to send several of the 13 people it injured to the hospital with minor injuries. Why didn't the defendant owe the plaintiff the highest duty of care since it was a common carrier and she was a passenger? See Prosser, *Palsgraf* Revisited, 52 Mich. L. Rev. 1, 4-5 (1953). Would the conductor have been negligent if he had knocked the package out of the passenger's arm while trying to prevent him from boarding the train while it was in motion? Should Palsgraf have recovered if she stood next to the passenger carrying the package, given that the railroad conductor had no notice of its contents? Should a total stranger, not a patron of the railroad, injured by the blast be able to recover from the railroad if its conductor had innocently set off the bomb? Could the railroad, if held liable, sue the passenger for indemnification if he were solvent?

Exhibit 5.2   What Really Happened on That Train Platform?

- "There was . . . much smoke and a fireball, and the force of the blast ripped up part of the wooden station platform. . . . The explosion shattered the glass in the scale and knocked the scale itself over onto Mrs. Palsgraf, bruising her. It also caused a stampede of the crowd on the platform. There is conjecture that the crowd, rather than the direct force of the explosion, knocked over the scale. . . . Mrs. Palsgraf was one of thirteen people on the platform who were injured by the explosion (or, conceivably, by the stampede that it sparked), none seriously, although several, not including her, were taken to hospitals in ambulances called to the scene."

  Posner, Cardozo: A Study in Reputation 34-35 (1990).

- The "scales must have been toppled *not by the explosion* of the fireworks, but by the crowd running in panic on the platform," and although the plaintiff "had been hit by the scales on the arm, hip and thigh," the chief source of her complaint was "a stammer and a stutter" that appeared about one week after the accident and may have been intensified by the litigation itself.

  Noonan, Persons and Masks of the Law ch. 4 (1976).

- "Several large explosions (likely six, but maybe twenty-four . . .) followed [the package at issue being jarred loose]. Panic and pandemonium apparently ensued, resulting in numerous injuries of varying severity. . . . About ten feet away

from the explosion, a large penny scale topped on Mrs. Palsgraf, who suffered contusions in the short term, and what we would today call post-traumatic stress disorder (stuttering, nervous fits) in the long term."

  Krauss, *Palsgraf*: The Rest of the Story, 9 Green Bag 2d 309, 310 (2006) (reviewing Manz, The *Palsgraf* Case: Courts, Law and Society in 1920s New York (2005)).

- "No witness saw this [i.e., the facts recounted in Cardozo's opinion]. There was testimony that afterward the scale was found to be 'blown right to pieces and knocked down, the glass was busted and blown — just simply laid down on the platform. . . . Mrs. Palsgraf's . . . daughter said that she heard the scale 'blow apart.' Notwithstanding all this, it is very probable, in line with the original theory of plaintiff's complaint, that the scale was in fact knocked over by the stampede of frightened passengers. There was an appreciable interval after the 'ball of fire' before the 'scale blew.' With the explosion occurring in the pit between the platform and the train, or under the wheels, it is difficult to see how the scale would not be completely protected from it. Although the platform was crowded, there is no indication in the Record that any other damage whatever was done by the explosion itself."

  Source: Prosser, Palsgraf *Revisited*, 52 Mich. L. Rev. 1, 3 n.9 (1953) (internal citations to *Palsgraf* record omitted).

With *Palsgraf*, compare The Nitro-Glycerine Case, Parrot v. Wells, Fargo & Co., 82 U.S. 524 (1872), in which an unmarked package containing nitroglycerine was delivered to the defendant's place of business, which was located in its landlord's building. When the defendant's servants tried to open the package, it exploded, killing them and damaging the building. The Supreme Court noted that different outcomes were required for the servants' wrongful death actions and the landlord's property damage claim. For property damage, the landlord could recover without proof of negligence, basing its case on a covenant in its lease with the defendant. For the death actions, however, the lease was inapplicable, and the cause of action failed for want of proof of negligence, given that the parcel gave no notice of its dangerous contents. For the suggestion that *Palsgraf* should be understood on those "notice" grounds only, see the opinion of Judge Friendly in Petition of Kinsman Transit Co., 338 F.2d 708 (2d Cir. 1964), from which excerpts are reprinted *supra* at 430.

2. *Harm within the risk.* Note that Second Restatement §281 appears to follow Cardozo on the duty requirement:

> *Comment c. Risk to class of which plaintiff is member.* . . . If the actor's conduct creates such a recognizable risk of harm only to a particular class of persons, the fact that it in fact causes harm to a person of a different class, to whom the actor could not reasonably have anticipated injury, does not make the actor liable to the persons so injured.

How does one decide to which class a particular person belongs? In examining this question, Professor Seavey poses a case in which the defendant leaves a ten-pound can of nitroglycerin on a table off of which it is knocked by a child. It hurts the child's foot but, miraculously, does not explode. If the defendant had left a can of water of similar size on the table, he could not be held negligent: Since the risk that materialized was unrelated to the explosive power of the nitroglycerin, the plaintiff could not recover. See Seavey, Mr. Justice Cardozo and the Law of Torts, 39 Colum. L. Rev. 20, 35; 52 Harv. L. Rev. 372, 385; 48 Yale L.J. 390, 405 (1939); compare RST §281, illus. 2.

A second scenario is put forth in Keeton, Legal Cause in the Law of Torts, 77 Harv. L. Rev. 595 (1963-1964). The defendant "negligently" places unlabeled rat poison on a shelf full of food. The shelf happens to be near a stove that gives off heat, and the heat causes the poison to explode, injuring the plaintiff. Keeton argues that this plaintiff should be denied recovery on grounds that the negligent *aspect* of the defendant's conduct is not the cause of the plaintiff's harm. For a consideration of several other scenarios and an argument that the foreseeable harm test provides the best limits on liability, see Williams, The Risk Principle, 77 Law Q. Rev. 179, 185-190 (1961).

The Third Restatement of Torts states its general test for the scope of liability (avoiding the term "proximate cause") in RTT:LPEH §29. Does this test support the position of Cardozo or Andrews in *Palsgraf?* Whatever that answer, the Third Restatement accepts the efforts of both Seavey and Keeton to isolate particular harms that fall outside the risk. Thus it holds as a matter of law that a defendant hunter who carelessly entrusts his loaded gun to a child is not liable if she drops it on her toe, breaking it. RTT:LPEH §29, comment *d,* illus. 3. Note the common thread in all these cases: It turns out after the fact that the aspect of the defendant's behavior that increased the risk of harm to the plaintiff never materialized. The nitroglycerin did not explode; the poison was not consumed; the gun did not go off. Are all of these cases distinguishable from *Palsgraf*, which involves the materialization of a risk from a dangerous but unknown condition? What about a solution that holds the railroad liable for triggering the explosives, with an action over against the person who carried it? For a sustained attack on the harm within the risk test for resulting in too many cases of undercompensation, see Hurd & Moore, Negligence in the Air, 3 Theoretical Inquiries in Law 333 (2002), calling for its abandonment "root and branch."

Restatement of the Law (Third) of Torts: Liability for Physical and Emotional Harm

§29. LIMITATIONS ON LIABILITY FOR TORTIOUS CONDUCT

An actor's liability is limited to those harms that result from the risks that made the actor's conduct tortious.

Comment d. Harm different from the harms risked by the tortious conduct: . . . [T]he jury should be told that, in deciding whether the plaintiff's harm is within the scope of liability, it should go back to the reasons for finding the defendant engaged in negligent or other tortious conduct. If the harms risked by that tortious conduct include the general sort of harm suffered by the plaintiff, the defendant is subject to liability for the plaintiff's harm. . . .

Illustration 3: Richard, a hunter, finishes his day in the field and stops at a friend's house while walking home. His friend's nine-year-old daughter, Kim, greets Richard, who hands his loaded shotgun to her as he enters the house. Kim drops the shotgun, which lands on her toe, breaking it. Although Richard is negligent for giving Kim his shotgun, the risk that makes Richard negligent is that Kim might shoot someone with the gun, not that she would drop it and hurt herself (the gun was neither especially heavy nor unwieldy). Kim's broken toe is outside the scope of Richard's liability, even though Richard's tortious conduct was a factual cause of Kim's harm.

---

3. Jury instructions on proximate causation.   The role of the Second Restatement's substantial factor test, discussed *supra* at 414, was examined in Mitchell v. Gonzales, 819 P.2d 872, 877-878 (Cal. 1991). The decedent, 12-year-old Damechie Mitchell, drowned while vacationing with the defendants and their 14-year-old son Luis. Damechie did not know how to swim, but with the Gonzales' permission, he went out on a raft with Luis and his sister Yoshi and drowned; the boys had engaged in horseplay on the raft while Luis's father slept on the beach. The decedent's parents charged Luis with negligence for his conduct on the raft and Luis' parents with negligent supervision. The jury found that the defendants were negligent, but that their negligence was not the proximate cause of the death.

At trial, the judge gave the defendants' requested instruction (BAJI 3.75), a "but for" test of cause in fact, which provided: "A proximate cause of injury is a cause which, in natural and continuous sequence, produces the injury and without which the injury would not have occurred." The test gets its name from the "without which" clause, and also adopts the precise language of the *Andrews* dissent. The rival "substantial factor" instruction (BAJI 3.76), requested by the plaintiff, read: "A legal cause of injury is a cause which is a substantial factor in bringing about the injury."

By a divided vote, the court treated the "but for" instruction as always prejudicial to the plaintiffs. The court also noted its dislike for the term "proximate cause," and adopted Prosser's view that the term was just an unfortunate "legacy of Sir Francis Bacon." It also pointed to experimental studies that indicated subjects interpreted the term as "'approximate cause,' 'estimated cause,' or some fabrication." The court then adopted the "substantial factor" test because it was largely free of these confusions, was generally intelligible to juries, and helped to clarify issues in joint causation. Accordingly, any but-for instruction was prejudicial error because it "overemphasized the condition temporally closest to the death" (Damechie's inability to swim) and downplayed how the negligent supervision of Mr. and Mrs. Gonzales contributed to the loss. Kennard, J., dissented on the ground that the court should not displace a standard instruction without developing a better alternative, noting that the substantial factor test fails to supply "meaningful guidance" on the proximate cause issue. What is wrong with asking whether the parents could have, to a reasonable certainty, prevented Damechie's death if they had properly watched the children at play? Forbidden them to go out on the raft? Asked the decedent if he knew how to swim?

The Second Restatement's terminology also received a mixed reception for its use of the term "superseding cause" to talk about events occurring after the defendant's negligence that break causal connection. See RST §442. In Barry v. Quality Steel Products, 820 A.2d 258, 266 (Conn. 2003), the court rejected any superseding cause instructions based on the Second Restatement because they only "serve to complicate what is fundamentally a proximate cause analysis." Accordingly, it reversed a directed verdict for the defendant manufacturer and seller of defective brackets, which had failed in part because the plaintiff's employer had improperly installed the roof brackets and failed to provide the needed scaffolding to protect the plaintiff from a fall. In the court's view, apportionment under a comparative negligence regime was the proper way to deal with multiple sources of negligence. "The test of proximate cause is whether the defendant's conduct is a substantial factor in bringing about the plaintiff's injuries." What result if sound brackets would have certainly failed given the employer's improper installation?

The substantial factor test rejected in *Barry* was revived in Snell v. Norwalk Yellow Cab, Inc., 2015 WL 4570799 (Conn. Super. Ct. June 24, 2015), a case in which the plaintiff suffered catastrophic injuries when struck by the defendant's car. The car was driven recklessly by two drunk teenage boys who stole the car after the defendant's driver left the keys in the ignition. It was unclear whether the engine was still running. Povodator, J., concluded: "We made clear [in *Barry*] that [o]ur conclusion does not necessarily affect those cases where the defendant claims that an unforeseeable intentional tort, force of nature, or criminal event supersedes its tortious conduct." With that conclusion, the court uneasily upheld a jury verdict that exonerated the defendant from liability. Why this exception to *Barry*? Is the result consistent with Beale's test, *supra* at 411, which requires that the situation return to a condition of safety?

The Third Restatement rejects all permutations of the substantial factor, intervening cause, and supervening cause language. See RTT:LPEH §26, comment *j*, and §34, comment *b*, dismissing both the phrases "intervening acts" and "superseding causes" as "conclusory labels." Can any single verbal account for causation work for all stranger (including explosion), rescue, malpractice, and supervision cases? If not, how should the causal element of each type of case be addressed? Which set of instructions would be appropriate in *Berry*? *Palsgraf*?

4. Proximate causation in FELA cases. In CSX Transportation, Inc. v. McBride, 131 S. Ct. 2630, 2643 (2011), the Supreme Court held that proximate cause did not apply in cases brought by injured railroad workers under the Federal Employers' Liability Act (FELA). Quoting the statute, Ginsburg, J., explained: "[R]ailroads are made answerable in damages for an employee's 'injury or death resulting in whole or in part from [carrier] negligence.'" And while "reasonable foreseeability of harm . . . is indeed an essential ingredient of [FELA] negligence, . . . [i]f negligence is proved . . . and is shown to have played any part, even the slightest, in producing the injury, then the carrier is answerable in damages even if the extent of the [injury] or the manner in which it occurred was not [p]robable or foreseeable." Roberts, C.J., criticized the majority for casting aside "the well established principle of [the common] law" and for treating FELA like a no-fault compensation scheme like most workers' compensation schemes. *Id.* at 2644. Is the rule in *CSX* a return to *In re Polemis*? For a critique of the FELA tests of causation, see Nolan, Are Railroads Liable When Lightning Strikes?, 79 U. Chi. L. Rev. 1513, 1515 (2012), arguing that "the *McBride* Court's statements about the role of foreseeability have led some courts to adopt a form of 'freestanding negligence,' leading to potentially limitless liability." For such an expansive interpretation, see Anderson v. BNSF Ry., 354 P.3d 1248, 1256 (Mont. 2015), noting: "The FELA thus calls for an interpretive approach that is significantly different from that which ordinarily prevails in suits involving common-law negligence claims, and the resulting interpretations often seem anomalous in comparison to the norms of tort law."

Marshall v. Nugent
222 F.2d 604 (1st Cir. 1955)

[A truck owned by the defendant oil company cut the corner as it headed north around a sharp curve on an icy New Hampshire highway, forcing off the road a southbound car driven by the plaintiff's son-in-law, Harriman. Prince, the driver of the truck, offered to help pull Harriman's car back onto the highway and suggested that the plaintiff go around the curve to the south to warn oncoming cars of the unexpected danger. As the plaintiff was getting into position on the west side of the highway, the defendant, Nugent, who was driving northbound, suddenly saw his way blocked by the oil truck on one side of the road and Prince and Harriman on the other. In an effort to avoid a collision with them, he pulled the car over to the left where it went into a skid, hit a plank guard fence on the west side of the highway, and glanced off it into the plaintiff, severely hurting him.

The jury returned a verdict for Nugent and another for Marshall against the oil company. The second contention of the oil company on appeal was that the wrongful conduct of its driver was not the proximate cause of the plaintiff's injury.]

MAGRUDER, C.J. . . . Coming then to contention (2) above mentioned, this has to do with the doctrine of proximate causation, a doctrine which appellant's arguments tend to make out to be more complex and esoteric than it really is. To say that the situation created by the defendant's culpable acts constituted "merely a condition," not a cause of plaintiff's harm, is to indulge in mere verbiage, which does not solve the question at issue, but is simply a way of stating the conclusions, arrived at from other considerations, that the casual relation between the defendant's act and the plaintiff's injury is not strong enough to warrant holding the defendant legally responsible for the injury.

The adjective "proximate," as commonly used in this connection, is perhaps misleading, since to establish liability it is not necessarily true that the defendant's culpable act must be shown to have been the next or immediate cause of the plaintiff's injury. In many familiar instances, the defendant's act may be more remote in the chain of events and the plaintiff's injury may more immediately have been caused by an intervening force of nature, or an intervening act of a third person whether culpable or not, or even an act by the plaintiff bringing himself in contact with the dangerous situation resulting from the defendant's negligence. Therefore, perhaps, the phrase "legal cause," as used in Am. L. Inst., Rest. of Torts §431, is preferable to "proximate cause"; but the courts continue generally to use "proximate cause," and it is pretty well understood what is meant.

Back of the requirement that the defendant's culpable act must have been a proximate cause of the plaintiff's harm is no doubt the widespread conviction that it would be disproportionately burdensome to hold a culpable actor potentially liable for all the injurious consequences that may flow from his act, i.e., that would not have been inflicted "but for" the occurrence of the act. This is especially so where the injurious consequence was the result of negligence merely. And so, speaking in general terms, the effort of the courts has been, in the development of this doctrine of proximate causation, to confine the liability of a negligent actor to those harmful consequences which result from the operation of the risk, or of a risk, the foreseeability of which rendered the defendant's conduct negligent.

Of course, putting the inquiry in these terms does not furnish a formula which automatically decides each of an infinite variety of cases. Flexibility is still preserved by the further need of defining the risk, or risks, either narrowly, or more broadly, as seems appropriate and just in the special type of case.

Regarding motor vehicle accidents in particular, one should contemplate a variety of risks which are created by negligent driving. There may be injuries resulting from a direct collision between the carelessly driven car and another vehicle. But such direct collision may be avoided, yet the plaintiff may fall and injure himself in frantically racing out of the way of the errant car. Or the plaintiff may be knocked down and injured by a human stampede as the car rushes toward a crowded safety zone. Or the plaintiff may faint from intense excitement stimulated by the near collision, and in falling sustain a fractured skull. Or the plaintiff may suffer a miscarriage or other physical illness as a result of intense nervous shock incident to a hair-raising escape. This bundle of risks could be enlarged indefinitely with a little imagination. In a traffic mix-up due to negligence, before the disturbed waters have become placid and normal again, the unfolding of events between the culpable act and the plaintiff's eventual injury may be bizarre indeed; yet the defendant may be liable for the result. In such a situation, it would be impossible for a person in the defendant's position to predict in advance just how his negligent act would work out to another's injury. Yet this in itself is no bar to recovery.

[Magruder, C.J., then notes that close cases on proximate cause are normally left to the jury.]

Exercising [our] judgment on the facts in the case at bar, we have to conclude that the district court committed no error in refusing to direct a verdict for the defendant Socony on the issue of proximate cause. . . .

Plaintiff Marshall was a passenger in the oncoming Chevrolet car, and thus was one of the persons whose bodily safety was primarily endangered by the negligence of Prince, as might have been found by the jury, in "cutting the corner" with the Socony truck in the circumstances above related. In that view, Prince's negligence constituted an irretrievable breach of duty to the plaintiff. Though this particular act of negligence was over and done with when the truck pulled up alongside of the stalled Chevrolet without having actually collided with it, still the consequences of such past negligence were in the bosom of time, as yet unrevealed. If the Chevrolet had been pulled back onto the highway, and Harriman and Marshall, having got in it again, had resumed their journey and had had a collision with another car five miles down the road, in which Marshall suffered bodily injuries, it could truly be said that such subsequent injury to Marshall was a consequence in fact of the earlier delay caused by the defendant's negligence, in the sense that but for such delay the Chevrolet car would not have been at the fatal intersection at the moment the other car ran into it. But on such assumed state of facts, the courts would no doubt conclude, "as a matter of law," that Prince's earlier negligence in cutting the corner was not the "proximate cause" of this later injury received by the plaintiff. That would be because the extra risks to which such negligence by Prince had subjected the passengers in the Chevrolet car were obviously entirely over; the situation had been stabilized and become normal, and, so far as one could foresee, whatever subsequent risks the Chevrolet might have to encounter in its resumed journey were simply the inseparable risks, no more and no less, that were incident to the Chevrolet's being out on the highway at all. But in the case at bar, the circumstances under which Marshall received the personal injuries complained of presented no such clear-cut situation.

As we have indicated, the extra risks created by Prince's negligence were not all over at the moment the primary risk of collision between the truck and the Chevrolet was successfully surmounted. Many cases have held a defendant, whose negligence caused a traffic tie-up, legally liable for subsequent property damage or personal injuries more immediately caused by an oncoming motorist. This would particularly be so where, as in the present case, the negligent traffic tie-up and delay occurred in a dangerous blind spot, and where the occupants of the stalled Chevrolet, having got out onto the highway to assist in the operation of getting the Chevrolet going again, were necessarily subject to risks of injury from cars in the stream of northbound traffic coming over the crest of the hill. It is true, the Chevrolet car was not owned by the plaintiff Marshall, and no doubt, without violating any legal duty to Harriman, Marshall could have crawled up onto the snowbank at the side of the road out of harm's way and awaited there, passive and inert, until his journey was resumed. But the plaintiff, who as a passenger in this Chevrolet car had already been subjected to a collision risk by the negligent operation of the Socony truck, could reasonably be expected to get out onto the highway and lend a hand to his host in getting the Chevrolet started again, especially as Marshall himself had an interest in facilitating the resumption of the journey in order to keep his business appointment in North Stratford. Marshall was therefore certainly not an "officious intermeddler," and whether or not he was barred by contributory negligence in what he did was a question for the jury, as we have already held. The injury Marshall received by being struck by the Nugent car was not remote, either in time or place, from the negligent conduct of defendant Socony's servant, and it occurred while the traffic mix-up occasioned by defendant's negligence was still persisting, not after the traffic flow had become normal again. In the circumstances presented we conclude that the district court committed no error in leaving the issue of proximate cause to the jury for determination.

NOTE

A resumption of normal conditions.   Why shouldn't the plaintiff get a directed verdict on the admitted facts of *Marshall?* Note that Magruder's decision stresses that causation has run its course with the dissipation of the extra risks created by defendant's negligence. In Union Pump Co. v. Allbritton, 898 S.W.2d 773 (Tex. 1995), a pump manufactured by the defendant caught fire in a Texaco Chemical plant in which the plaintiff worked as a trainee employee. The plaintiff assisted her supervisor in putting out the fire and, after it was extinguished, she followed him over an aboveground pipe rack, some two and one-half feet high, to make repairs on a broken valve. Once the valve was fixed, she followed him back over to the pipe rack, where she fell and injured herself. Her supervisor said that his "bad habits" led him to walk over the pipe instead of taking the safer alternative route around it. The plaintiff argued that the defective pump was a cause of her injuries. "But for the pump fire, she asserts, she would never have walked over the pipe rack, which was wet with water or firefighting foam." Owen, J., rejected her argument:

> Even if the pump fire were in some sense a "philosophic" or "but for" cause of Allbritton's injuries, the forces generated by the fire had come to rest when she fell off the pipe rack. The fire had been extinguished, and Allbritton was walking away from the scene. Viewing the evidence in the light most favorable to Allbritton, the pump fire did no more than create the condition that made Allbritton's injuries possible. We conclude that the circumstances surrounding her injuries are too remotely connected with Union Pump's conduct or pump to constitute a legal cause of her injuries.

Spector, J., argued in dissent:

> The record reflects that at the time Sue Albritton's injury occurred, the forces generated by the fire in question had *not* come to rest. Rather, the emergency situation was continuing. The whole area of the fire was covered in water and foam; in at least some places, the water was almost knee-deep. Allbritton was still wearing hip boots and other gear, as required to fight the fire. Viewing all the evidence in the light most favorable to Allbritton, . . . the pump defect was both a "but-for" cause and a substantial factor in bringing about Allbritton's injury, and was therefore a cause in fact.

What is the factual dispute in *Union Pump?* Do the conceptual arguments go beyond those advanced by Beale (discussed *supra* at 411, following *Berry*)? Should they?

Virden v. Betts and Beer Construction Company
656 N.W.2d 805 (Iowa 2003)

NEUMAN, J., Plaintiff, Ron Virden, worked in the maintenance department of Indianola High School. On the first day of school in 1997, Virden's supervisor asked him to reinstall an angle iron that had fallen from the ceiling of the school's new wrestling room. As Virden was bolting the angle iron into place, he fell from the top of the ten-foot ladder on which he was standing. He sustained severe injuries to his left leg, requiring several surgeries.

Virden sued the contractors, defendants Betts & Beer Construction and Stroh Corporation, who earlier in the year had installed the wrestling room ceiling. Over Virden's objection, the district court granted these defendants summary judgment. It held their negligence, if any, was not the proximate cause of Virden's injuries. Virden appealed and the court of appeals reversed. We granted further review and, now, vacate the court of appeals decision and affirm the judgment of the district court.

I. SCOPE OF REVIEW/ISSUE ON APPEAL

[The court noted that summary judgment on the question of proximate cause is granted only in exceptional cases, of which this is one.]

II. ANALYSIS

. . . The summary judgment record makes plain that neither Virden nor his employer contacted the defendants about the fallen angle iron before attempting to effect repairs. Virden also concedes that he sought no help in positioning or securing the ladder, even though several pieces of weight-lifting equipment hampered clear access to the repair site. With this record in mind, we turn to the disputed elements of Virden's claim: duty and causation.

A. DUTY

[As a building or construction contractor] the defendants had a duty to Virden, and others using the room, to construct a ceiling that did not fall apart and injure someone.

Virden did not suffer, however, from being hit by the angle iron or tripping over it once it fell from the ceiling. In his words, he was injured when the ladder he stood on to replace the fallen hardware "suddenly kicked out from under [him] and [he] fell." That brings us to the crux of the case.

B. CAUSATION

Defendants' breach of their duty of care only constitutes actionable negligence if it is "also the proximate cause of the injury." There are two components to the proximate-cause inquiry: "(1) the defendant's conduct must have in fact caused the damages; and (2) the policy of the law must require the defendant to be legally responsible for them."

With respect to the first component, a plaintiff must at a minimum prove that the damages would not have occurred *but for* the defendant's negligence. Here, viewing the facts in the light most favorable to Virden, we assume that but for the faulty weld in the angle iron he would not have been perched precariously upon a ladder attempting to fix it. So, minimally, the but-for test of causation would survive defendants' motion for summary judgment.

The but-for test is not the end of the inquiry, however. . . . Virden must also tender proof that defendants' negligent welding of the angle iron was a *substantial factor* in bringing about his injury. . . .

Here, the district court assessed defendants' role in Virden's mishap as remote rather than foreseeable. Its conclusion stemmed from the undisputed fact that the instrumentality causing Virden's injury was a tipping or collapsing ladder, not a defective angle iron. We agree.

. . . [W]e observe that the duty to construct a solid ceiling is not to protect repairmen from perching on tall ladders but to prevent collapsing parts of the ceiling from falling on persons below.

To summarize, the unfortunate outcome of Virden's self-help remedy cannot be said to fall naturally within the scope of the probable risk created by the defendants' failure to properly install the ceiling. Because Virden's fall was not a reasonably foreseeable or probable consequence of *defendants'* negligence, the district court correctly granted judgment in their favor. We therefore vacate the court of appeals' contrary decision and affirm the judgment of the district court.

Hebert v. Enos
806 N.E.2d 452 (Mass. App. 2004)

KAFKER, J., The plaintiff William Hebert (Hebert) brought an action to recover for personal injuries he suffered as a result of receiving a severe electric shock while lawfully on the defendant Carl Enos's property to water the defendant's flowers. Hebert claimed that the defendant's faulty repairs of a second-floor toilet caused the toilet to overflow. The flooding water then reacted with the home's electrical system, creating an electrical current that shocked and injured Hebert when he touched the outside water faucet. Hebert asserted a claim for negligence in his complaint, and his wife sought damages for loss of consortium. The defendant moved for summary judgment on the ground that Hebert's injuries were not a reasonably foreseeable consequence of any negligence on the defendant's part. The judge allowed the defendant's motion for summary judgment, finding that "the injury to [Hebert] was highly extraordinary and 'so remote in everyday life' as to preclude a finding that the alleged negligence was a legal cause of [Hebert's] injuries." We affirm.

. . . In their opposition to the defendant's motion for summary judgment, the plaintiffs provided an expert's report prepared by a professional engineer. It was the expert's opinion that "in the several days the water was flowing through the house, the water caused good [or already deteriorated] insulation on wires to break down allowing leakage current to flow into a grounded surface and thence through the water piping system."

When Hebert "came into contact with the water piping system (i.e. the turn-on handle)," he became "part of the electric circuit." Because Hebert was wet from perspiration and from having watered his own flowers, the amount of electricity that would have flowed through him was much greater than it would have been had he been dry. The expert opined to a "reasonable degree of engineering certainty" that the electrical current flowing through Hebert's body and causing his injury was "a direct result of the water overflow and accompanying flooded condition of the house." . . .

Discussion. When the facts and reasonable inferences therefrom are viewed in the light most favorable to the plaintiffs, we conclude that the plaintiffs submitted sufficient evidence to establish that faulty repairs of the toilet by the defendant resulted in flooding and severe electric shock to Hebert when he touched the faucet. Summary judgment is still appropriate, however, if a plaintiff has no reasonable expectation of proving that "the injury to the plaintiff was a foreseeable result of the defendant's negligent conduct."

In the instant case, when we consider the likelihood, character, and location of the harm, we conclude as matter of law that the injuries sustained by Hebert were a "highly extraordinary" consequence of a defective second-floor toilet. . . . We therefore conclude that Hebert's severe and unfortunate injuries were the consequence of the type of unforeseeable accident for which we do not hold the defendant responsible in tort. The harm Hebert suffered, even when the facts and reasonable inferences that could be drawn therefrom are viewed in the light most favorable to him, was so highly extraordinary that the defendant cannot be required to guard against it.

We briefly touch upon various subsidiary arguments raised by the plaintiffs. The plaintiffs argue that water and electricity have distinct places in the law, and that the motion judge should have recognized the foreseeability of the risk of injury due to the mixture of electricity and water "as a matter of common sense." We conclude that the motion judge held the defendant to the "proper standard of care [which] is . . . the usual one of traditional negligence theory: 'to exercise care that was reasonable in the circumstances.'"

Finally, the plaintiffs appear to suggest that so long as the defendant's negligence can be connected in an unbroken causal chain to the resultant harm, and no third party's negligence can be blamed for the injury, the harm is by definition proximate. This is not the law of proximate cause in Massachusetts, nor is it supported by the commentary upon which the plaintiffs rely. Here, the defendant could not have reasonably foreseen the harm that befell Hebert.

Judgment affirmed.

NOTE

A choice of theories? *Virden* and *Hebert* both result in summary judgment for the defendant. Yet in a sense they are polar opposites of each other. In *Virden*, the dangerous condition was obvious to the plaintiff who had a wide range of choices on whether, and if so how, to proceed in repairing the angle iron. In *Hebert*, the dangerous condition was wholly concealed from the plaintiff who acted in complete ignorance of the peril that befell him. How then do both of these cases result in the same outcome? How should these cases come out if one looks at the question of whether a voluntary and independent act of the defendant severed causal connection? If foresight of harm by the defendant is the appropriate test? Should it make a difference in *Hebert* that Hebert was doing a favor for Enos?

2. Emotional Distress

Thus far, the question of proximate causation has been addressed largely with physical injuries. In this section we ask whether other consequences, such as mental shock or emotional distress, can flow from wrongful conduct. As with physical injury claims, the first line of defense simply denies the connection between the distress and the defendant's conduct, blaming some other event for the plaintiff's emotional harm. The second line of defense, however, holds that even if defendant's conduct is the cause in fact of plaintiff's injury, that conduct is not the proximate cause. Over the past century, liability in emotional distress cases has expanded, but the area still retains its distinctive limitations on recovery.

Mitchell v. Rochester Ry.
45 N.E. 354 (N.Y. 1896)

MARTIN, J. The facts in this case are few, and may be briefly stated. On the 1st day of April, 1891, the plaintiff was standing upon a cross walk on Main Street, in the city of Rochester, awaiting an opportunity to board one of the defendant's cars which had stopped upon the street at that place. While standing there, and just as she was about to step upon the car, a horse car of the defendant came down the street. As the team attached to the car drew near, it turned to the right, and came close to the plaintiff, so that she stood between the horses' heads when they were stopped. She testified that from fright and excitement caused by the approach and proximity of the team she became unconscious, and also that the result was a miscarriage, and consequent illness. Medical testimony was given to the effect that the mental shock which she then received was sufficient to produce that result. Assuming that the evidence tended to show that the defendant's servant was negligent in the management of the car and horses, and that the plaintiff was free from contributory negligence, the single question presented is whether the plaintiff is entitled to recover for the defendant's negligence which occasioned her fright and alarm, and resulted in the injuries already mentioned. While the authorities are not harmonious upon this question, we think the most reliable and better-considered cases, as well as public policy, fully justify us in holding that the plaintiff cannot recover for injuries occasioned by fright, as there is no immediate personal injury. If it be admitted that no recovery can be had for fright occasioned by the negligence of another, it is somewhat difficult to understand how a defendant would be liable for its consequences. Assuming that fright cannot form the basis of an action, it is obvious that no recovery can be had for injuries resulting therefrom. That the result may be nervous disease, blindness, insanity, or even a miscarriage, in no way changes the principle. These results merely show the degree of right or the extent of the damages. The right of action must still depend upon the question whether a recovery may be had for fright. If it can, then an action may be maintained, however slight the injury. If not, then there can be no recovery, no matter how grave or serious the consequences. Therefore, the logical result of the respondent's concession would seem to be, not only that no recovery can be had for mere fright, but also that none can be had for injuries which are the direct consequences of it. If the right of recovery in this class of cases should be once established, it would naturally result in a flood of litigation in cases where the injury complained of may be easily feigned without detection, and where the damages must rest upon mere conjecture or speculation. The difficulty which often exists in cases of alleged physical injury, in determining whether they exist, and if so, whether they were caused by the negligent act of the defendant, would not only be greatly increased, but a wide field would be opened for fictitious or speculative claims. To establish such a doctrine would be contrary to principles of public policy.

Moreover, it cannot be properly said that the plaintiff's miscarriage was the proximate result of the defendant's negligence. Proximate damages are such as are the ordinary and natural results of the negligence charged, and those that are usual and may, therefore, be expected. It is quite obvious that the plaintiff's injuries do not fall within the rule as to proximate damages. The injuries to the plaintiff were plainly the result of an accidental or unusual combination of circumstances, which could not have been reasonably anticipated, and over which

(3)

the defendant had no control, and, hence, her damages were too remote to justify a recovery in this action. These considerations lead to the conclusion that no recovery can be had for injuries sustained by fright occasioned by the negligence of another, where there is no immediate personal injury.

[Reversed and dismissed.]

NOTES

1. Coping with the physical injury rule. Why should plaintiff's fright count as a superseding cause of the plaintiff's miscarriage? The early opposition to allowing recovery for negligently inflicted emotional distress rested on two distinct grounds. The first was that the damages were too "remote," and the second was the fear that allowing emotional distress claims would open the floodgates to fabricated claims. Which argument is stronger for disallowing recovery in the mere fright cases?

Historically, however, whenever the plaintiff showed physical impact, courts used that impact, however slight, as the foundation for the plaintiff's claim for emotional distress. In effect, courts treated the emotional distress as parasitic — *opportunistic?* damages upon the most nominal of invasions. In Comstock v. Wilson, 177 N.E. 431 (N.Y. 1931), recovery was allowed for a slight jolt in a very minor automobile collision. In Porter v. Delaware, L. & W. R.R., 63 A. 860 (N.J. 1906), the plaintiff recovered when "something" slight hit her neck and she got dust in her eyes. In Kenney v. Wong Len, 128 A. 343 (N.H. 1925), the requisite impact was found when a mouse hair in a spoonful of stew touched the roof of the plaintiff's mouth. In Christy Bros. Circus v. Turnage, 144 S.E. 680 (Ga. App. 1928), the hapless plaintiff recovered when one of defendant's horses "evacuated his bowels" in plaintiff's lap, "in full view of many people . . . all of whom laughed at the occurrence." Finally, in Deutsch v. Shein, 597 S.W.2d 141 (Ky. 1980), bombarding the plaintiff with x-rays met the requirements of the impact rule, which only required that the contact be "slight, trifling, or trivial."

2. Beyond physical impact. While some courts extended the impact rule, other courts reexamined its foundations. In Dulieu v. White & Sons, [1901] 2 K.B. 669, 677, 681, the court rejected both the proximate cause and floodgates arguments. The plaintiff gave premature birth to her child after nearly being run over by the defendant's team of horses while working behind the counter in her husband's public house. Kennedy, J., rejected *Mitchell*, making these observations about remoteness of damage:

> Why is the accompaniment of physical injury essential? For my own part, I should not like to assume it to be scientifically true that a nervous shock which causes serious bodily illness is not actually accompanied by physical injury, although it may be impossible, or at least difficult, to detect the injury at the time in the living subject. I should not be surprised if the surgeon or the physiologist told us that nervous shock is or may be in itself an injurious affection of the physical organism. Let it be assumed, however, that the physical injury follows the shock, but that the jury are satisfied upon proper and sufficient medical evidence that it follows the shock

as its direct and natural effect, is there any legal reason for saying that the damage is less proximate in the legal sense than damage which arises contemporaneously?

Thereafter Kennedy, J., rejected any concern about spurious claims, saying:

> I should be sorry to adopt a rule which would bar all such claims on grounds of policy alone, and in order to prevent the possible success of unrighteous or groundless actions. Such a course involves the denial of redress in meritorious cases, and it necessarily implies a certain degree of distrust, which I do not share, in the capacity of legal tribunals to get at the truth in this class of claim. My experience gives me no reason to suppose that a jury would really have more difficulty in weighing the medical evidence as to the effects of nervous shock through fright, than in weighing the like evidence as to the effects of nervous shock through a railway collision or a carriage accident, where, as often happens, no palpable injury, or very slight palpable injury, has been occasioned at the time.

Accordingly, Kennedy, J., nonetheless did impose this limitation: The plaintiff was not "entitled to maintain this action if the nervous shock was produced, not by the fear of bodily injury to herself, but by horror or vexation arising from the sight of mischief being threatened or done either to some other person, or to her own or her husband's property, by the intrusion of the defendant's van and horses." Is this defensible on proximate cause grounds?

Likewise, in Osborne v. Keeney, 399 S.W.3d 1, 17-18 (Ky. 2012), the Kentucky Supreme Court overruled its past support of the impact rule, declaring that its job was not to "maintain[] the watch as the law ossifies." The court pointed to advances in medical science and mental health treatment, as well as the fact that there had been no flood of litigation in other jurisdictions that had removed the impact requirement, to support its claim that the new standard is "more at home in our current societal and legal landscape."

3. Empirical complications.   Is the concern with fraud or error in nervous shock cases understated in *Dulieu?* In 1944, a doctor-lawyer surveyed all cases brought for physical injuries resulting from negligently inflicted fright and concluded:

> On the basis of all available factors, we thought at least 7/10 or 21/30 of the 301 cases examined should have been decided in defendant's favor. . . . [In practice, however], defendants prevailed in only 51 cases or 5/30 of the total series. Taking all cases decided between 1850 and 1944, the net balance of justice would have been greater had all courts denied damages for injury imputed to psychic stimuli alone.

Smith, Relation of Emotions to Injury and Disease: Legal Liability for Psychic Stimuli, 30 Va. L. Rev. 193, 284 (1944). Smith's conclusions are premised on his belief that liability should only result when a plaintiff suffered a normal response; otherwise, he believed that a plaintiff's "preexisting vulnerability" ought to bar recovery. For another view, see Chamallas & Kerber, Women, Mothers, and the Law of Fright: A History, 88 Mich. L. Rev. 814, 847-848 (1990), arguing that "Smith's medicalized notions of normality disadvantaged women. He believed that it was proper to classify pregnancy as 'a temporary idiosyncrasy' and that '[a]n actor should not be required to assume that every female in his path is about to become a mother.'"

Dillon v. Legg
441 P.2d 912 (Cal. 1968) (en banc)

[The defendant driver struck and killed Erin Lee Dillon, a child, as she was crossing a public street. Her death precipitated three separate claims. First, decedent's mother and minor sister, Cheryl, sued for wrongful death. Second, her mother sued for nervous shock and serious mental and physical pain suffered in consequence of defendant's negligence. Third, the minor sister, Cheryl, also sued for emotional and physical suffering. The evidence established that the mother was in "close proximity" to Erin Lee at the time of the collision, but that defendant's car never threatened her safety since she was outside the "zone of danger." The trial court dismissed the mother's action for emotional distress under *Amaya v. Home Ice, Fuel & Supply Co.*, 379 P.2d 513 (Cal. 1963), because her fright and distress did not arise out of fear for her own safety. However, Cheryl's parallel action was not dismissed because she might have been in the zone of danger or feared for her own safety. The mother appealed.

Noting that her claim rested on considerations of "natural justice," the court held it should not be "frustrated" because of judicial fears of fraudulent claims that "would involve the courts in the hopeless task of defining the extent of the tortfeasor's liability." It then critiqued *Amaya*.]

TOBRINER, J.* . . . [W]e can hardly justify relief to the sister for trauma which she suffered upon apprehension of the child's death and yet deny it to the mother merely because of a happenstance that the sister was some few yards closer to the accident. The instant case exposes the hopeless artificiality of the zone-of-danger rule. In the second place, to rest upon the zone-of-danger rule when we have rejected the impact rule becomes even less defensible. We have, indeed, held that impact is not necessary for recovery. The zone-of-danger concept must, then, inevitably collapse because the only reason for the requirement of presence in that zone lies in the fact that one within it will fear the danger of *impact*. At the threshold, then, we point to the incongruity of the rules upon which any rejection of plaintiff's recovery must rest.

We further note, at the outset, that defendant has interposed the defense that the contributory negligence of the mother, the sister, and the child contributed to the accident. If any such defense is sustained and defendant found not liable for the death of the child because of the contributory negligence of the mother, sister or child, we do not believe that the mother or sister should recover for the

---

* [Tobriner, J., while on the California Court of Appeal, wrote the opinion in *Amaya*, later reversed by the California Supreme Court, allowing the plaintiff to recover for nervous shock even though he was beyond the zone of danger. 23 Cal. Rptr. 131 (1962).—EDS.]

emotional trauma which they allegedly suffered. In the absence of the primary liability of the tort-feasor for the death of the child, we see no ground for an independent and secondary liability for claims for injuries by third parties. The basis for such claims must be the adjudicated liability and fault of defendant; that liability and fault must be the foundation for the tort-feasor's duty of due care to third parties who, as a consequence of such negligence, sustain emotional trauma.

We turn then to an analysis of the concept of duty, . . .

The history of the concept of duty in itself discloses that it is not an old and deep-rooted doctrine but a legal device of the latter half of the nineteenth century designed to curtail the feared propensities of juries toward liberal awards.

1.   *This court in the past has rejected the argument that we must deny recovery upon a legitimate claim because other fraudulent ones may be urged.* . . .

Indubitably juries and trial courts, constantly called upon to distinguish the frivolous from the substantial and the fraudulent from the meritorious, reach some erroneous results. But such fallibility, inherent in the judicial process, offers no reason for substituting for the case-by-case resolution of causes an artificial and indefensible barrier. Courts not only compromise their basic responsibility to decide the merits of each individually but destroy the public's confidence in them by using the broad broom of "administrative convenience" to sweep away a class of claims a number of which are admittedly meritorious. The mere assertion that fraud is possible, "a possibility [that] exists to some degree in all cases," does not prove a present necessity to abandon the neutral principles of foreseeability, proximate cause and consequential injury that generally govern tort law.

Indeed, we doubt that the problem of the fraudulent claim is substantially more pronounced in the case of a mother claiming physical injury resulting from seeing her child killed than in other areas of tort law in which the right to recover damages is well established in California. For example, a plaintiff claiming that fear for his own safety resulted in physical injury makes out a well recognized case for recovery.

Moreover, damages are allowed for "mental suffering," a type of injury, on the whole, less amenable to objective proof than the physical injury involved here; the mental injury can be in aggravation of, or "parasitic to," an established tort. In fact, fear for another, even in the absence of resulting physical injury, can be part of these parasitic damages. And emotional distress, if inflicted intentionally, constitutes an independent tort. The danger of plaintiffs' fraudulent collection of damages for nonexistent injury is at least as great in these examples as in the instant case.

In sum, the application of tort law can never be a matter of mathematical precision. In terms of characterizing conduct as tortious and matching a money award to the injury suffered as well as in fixing the extent of injury, the process cannot be perfect. Undoubtedly, ever since the ancient case of the tavern-keeper's wife who successfully avoided the hatchet cast by an irate customer (I. de S. et ux v. W. de S., Y.B. 22 Edw. iii, f. 99, pl. 60 (1348)), defendants have argued that plaintiffs' claims of injury from emotional trauma might well be fraudulent. Yet we cannot let the difficulties of adjudication frustrate the principle that there be a remedy for every substantial wrong.

2. *The alleged inability to fix definitions for recovery on the different facts of future cases does not justify the denial of recovery on the specific facts of the instant case; in any event, proper guidelines can indicate the extent of liability for such future cases. . . .*

Since the chief element in determining whether defendant owes a duty or an obligation to plaintiff is the foreseeability of the risk, that factor will be of prime concern in every case. Because it is inherently intertwined with foreseeability such duty or obligation must necessarily be adjudicated only upon a case-by-case basis. We cannot now predetermine defendant's obligation in every situation by a fixed category; no immutable rule can establish the extent of that obligation for every circumstance of the future. We can, however, define guidelines which will aid in the resolution of such an issue as the instant one.

We note, first, that we deal here with a case in which plaintiff suffered a shock which resulted in physical injury and we confine our ruling to that case. In determining, in such a case, whether defendant should reasonably foresee the injury to plaintiff, or, in other terminology, whether defendant owes plaintiff a duty of due care, the courts will take into account such factors as the following: (1) Whether plaintiff was located near the scene of the accident as contrasted with one who was a distance away from it. (2) Whether the shock resulted from a direct emotional impact upon plaintiff from the sensory and contemporaneous observance of the accident, as contrasted with learning of the accident from others after its occurrence. (3) Whether plaintiff and the victim were closely related, as contrasted with an absence of any relationship or the presence of only a distant relationship.

The evaluation of these factors will indicate the degree of the defendant's foreseeability: obviously defendant is more likely to foresee that a mother who observes an accident affecting her child will suffer harm than to foretell that a stranger witness will do so. Similarly, the degree of foreseeability of the third person's injury is far greater in the case of his contemporaneous observance of the accident than that in which he subsequently learns of it. The defendant is more likely to foresee that shock to the nearby, witnessing mother will cause physical harm than to anticipate that someone distant from the accident will suffer more than a temporary emotional reaction. All these elements, of course, shade into each other; the fixing of obligation, intimately tied into the facts, depends upon each case.

In light of these factors the court will determine whether the accident and harm was *reasonably* foreseeable. Such reasonable foreseeability does not turn on whether the particular defendant as an individual would have in actuality foreseen the exact accident and loss; it contemplates that courts, on a case-to-case basis, analyzing all the circumstances, will decide what the ordinary man under such circumstances should reasonably have foreseen. The courts thus mark out the areas of liability, excluding the remote and unexpected.

In the instant case, the presence of all the above factors indicates that plaintiff has alleged a sufficient prima facie case. Surely the negligent driver who causes the death of a young child may reasonably expect that the mother will not be far distant and will upon witnessing the accident suffer emotional trauma. . . .

The fear of an inability to fix boundaries has not impelled the courts of England to deny recovery for emotional trauma caused by witnessing the death or injury of another due to defendant's negligence. We set forth the holdings of some English cases merely to demonstrate that courts can formulate and apply such limitations of liability.

[The court then reviewed the English cases that are favorable to recovery in nervous shock cases.]

Thus we see no good reason why the general rules of tort law, including the concepts of negligence, proximate cause, and foreseeability, long applied to all other types of injury, should not govern the case now before us. . . .

In short, the history of the cases does not show the development of a logical rule but rather a series of changes and abandonments. Upon the argument in each situation that the courts draw a Maginot Line to withstand an onslaught of false claims, the cases have assumed a variety of postures. At first they insisted that there be no recovery for emotional trauma at all. Retreating from this position, they gave relief for such trauma only if physical impact occurred. They then abandoned the requirement for physical impact but insisted that the victim fear for her own safety, holding that a mother could recover for fear for her children's safety if she simultaneously entertained a personal fear for herself. They stated that the mother need only be in the "zone of danger." The final anomaly would be the instant case in which the sister, who observed the accident, would be granted recovery because she was in the "zone of danger," but the *mother*, not far distant, would be barred from recovery.

The successive abandonment of these positions exposes the weakness of artificial abstractions which bar recovery contrary to the general rules. . . .

Yet for some artificial reason this delimitation of liability is alleged to be unworkable in the most egregious case of them all: the mother's emotional trauma at the witnessed death of her child. If we stop at this point, however, we must necessarily question and reject not merely recovery here, but the viability of the judicial process for ascertaining liability for tortious conduct itself. To the extent that it is inconsistent with our ruling here, we therefore overrule Amaya v. Home Ice, Fuel & Supply Co.

To deny recovery would be to chain this state to an outmoded rule of the 19th century which can claim no current credence. No good reason compels our captivity to an indefensible orthodoxy.

The judgment is reversed.

TRAYNOR, C.J. I dissent for the reasons set forth in Amaya v. Home Ice, Fuel & Supply Co. In my opinion that case was correctly decided and should not be overruled.

BURKE, J., [dissenting, questioned the guidelines set forth in the majority opinion]. . . . What if the plaintiff was honestly *mistaken* in believing the third person to be in danger or to be seriously injured? What if the third person had assumed the risk involved? How "close" must the relationship be between the plaintiff and the third person? I.e., what if the third person was the plaintiff's beloved niece or nephew, grandparent, fiancé, or lifelong friend, more dear to the plaintiff than her immediate family? Next, how "near" must the plaintiff have been to the scene of the accident, and how "soon" must shock have been felt? Indeed, what is the magic in the plaintiff's being actually present? Is the shock any less real if the mother does not know of the accident until her injured child is brought into her home? On the other hand, is it any less real if the mother is physically present at the scene but is nevertheless unaware of the danger or injury to her child until after the accident has occurred? No answers to these questions are to be found in today's majority opinion. Our trial courts, however, will not so easily escape the burden of distinguishing between litigants on the basis of such artificial and unpredictable distinctions.

NOTES

1. Foreseeability in emotional distress cases.   In Tobin v. Grossman, 249 N.E.2d 419, 422-423 (N.Y. 1969), the plaintiff suffered "physical injuries caused by shock and fear" when her two-year-old son was seriously injured in an automobile accident. The plaintiff did not see the accident, but heard the screech of brakes and arrived on the scene, only a few feet away, moments later. In denying recovery for negligent infliction of emotional distress, or NIED, Breitel, J., took direct issue with *Dillon*'s heavy reliance on foreseeability, and predicted that actions, if allowed, could not in principle or practice be confined to close family members who witnessed the accident.

> On foreseeability, it is hardly cogent to assert that the negligent actor if he could foresee injury to the child that he should not also foresee at the same time harm to the mother who, especially in the case of children of tender years, is likely to be present or about. But foreseeability, once recognized, is not so easily limited. Relatives, other than the mother, such as fathers or grandparents, or even other caretakers, equally sensitive and as easily harmed, may be just as foreseeably affected. Hence, foreseeability would, in short order, extend logically to caretakers other than the mother, and ultimately to affected bystanders. . . .
>
>   The final and most difficult factor is any reasonable circumscription, within tolerable limits required by public policy, of a rule creating liability. Every parent who loses a child or whose child of any age suffers an injury is likely to sustain grievous psychological trauma, with the added risk of consequential physical harm. Any rule based solely on eyewitnessing the accident could stand only until the first case comes along in which the parent is in the immediate vicinity but did not see the accident. Moreover, the instant advice that one's child has been killed or injured, by telephone, word of mouth, or by whatever means, even if delayed, will have in most cases the same impact. The sight of gore and exposed bones is not necessary to provide special impact on a parent.

Judge Breitel's focus on the foreseeability prong of the *Dillon* test underestimated the resolve of the California courts on its explicit requirements of a close relationship and direct observation. In Elden v. Sheldon, 758 P.2d 582 (Cal. 1988), the California Supreme Court denied claims for the negligent infliction of emotional distress (and loss of consortium) of an unmarried cohabitant involved in an automobile accident, who not only witnessed his cohabitant's death but was injured himself. The court in *Elden* construed *Dillon's* third prong—that the plaintiff be "closely related" to the victim—to cover only spouses and siblings. Further, it held that *Dillon's* general foreseeability language did not include a "close friend" and concluded that unmarried cohabitants stood in no better position than close friends, given the "state's interest in promoting marriage."

public policy

In Thing v. La Chusa, 771 P.2d 814, 815 (Cal. 1989), the court refused to buckle on the direct observation requirement when it denied recovery for emotional distress to a mother who had not witnessed the automobile accident that injured her child. Eagleson, J., rejected *Dillon's* assertion that "foreseeability" was the touchstone of duty, treating the concept as "amorphous." Instead he opted for a "bright line" rule:

> In the absence of physical injury or impact to the plaintiff himself, damages for emotional distress should be recoverable only if the plaintiff: (1) is closely related to the injury victim; (2) is present at the scene of the injury-producing event at the time it occurs, and is then aware that it is causing injury to the victim and, (3) as a result suffers emotional distress beyond that which would be anticipated in a disinterested witness.

In defense of creating this "clear rule" for liability, Eagleson, J., reasoned:

> In so doing we balance the impact of arbitrary lines which deny recovery to some victims whose injury is very real against that of imposing liability out of proportion to culpability for negligent acts. We also weigh in the balance the importance to the administration of justice of clear guidelines under which litigants and trial courts may resolve disputes.

2. Another Maginot line? Dillon's *reception outside California.* *Dillon* and its progeny have been subject to intensive examination in other states. One state, Kentucky, recently overturned its acceptance of the impact rule in cases of severe or serious emotional distress, noting "that at least forty jurisdictions have either rejected the impact rule or abandoned it." See Osborne v. Keeney, 399 S.W.3d 1, 17-18 (Ky. 2012). One of the holdouts for the older rule is Engler v. Illinois Farmers Insurance Co., 706 N.W.2d 764, 771 (Minn. 2005), which adheres to the zone of danger test in RST §§313 and 436, chiefly because "it provides a bright line to limit recovery." In *Engler* the plaintiff experienced fright because the driver of the other car had threatened both her and her son. Blatz, C.J., allowed her to recover for the fright that she experienced, but not for the post-traumatic distress that she suffered because of the severe injuries to her son. Blatz, C.J., stated that NIED claims were allowable only

> if the plaintiff can prove that she: (1) was in the zone of danger of physical impact; (2) had an objectively reasonable fear for her own safety; (3) had severe emotional

distress with attendant physical manifestations; and (4) stands in a close relationship to the third-party victim. In addition, to succeed with such a claim, the plaintiff also must establish that the defendant's negligent conduct—the conduct that created an unreasonable risk of physical injury to the plaintiff—caused serious bodily injury to the third-party victim.

In his concurrence, Anderson, J., claimed that the majority position was too loose insofar as it allowed anyone with a "close relationship" to the injured person to recover, and would have permitted recovery only to a "spouse, parent, child, grandparent, grandchild, or sibling of the plaintiff."

Other courts following *Dillon* have read it restrictively. Hawaii first adopted the *Dillon* rule in Rodrigues v. State, 472 P.2d 509 (Haw. 1970). However, in Kelley v. Kokua Sales and Supply, Ltd., 532 P.2d 673 (Haw. 1975), a divided court denied recovery when the decedent, a California resident, died of a heart attack shortly after being informed by telephone that his daughter and grandchild had been killed in a road accident. The court, unquestionably motivated by the fear of unlimited liability, invoked the language of "duty of care" and "foresight of consequences" to justify its denial of recovery. In Dziokonski v. Babineau, 380 N.E.2d 1295, 1302 (Mass. 1978), the court held that "allegations concerning a parent who sustains substantial physical harm as a result of severe mental distress over some peril or harm to his minor child caused by the defendant's negligence state a claim for which relief might be granted, where the parent either witnesses the accident or soon comes on the scene while the child is still there."

3. Proper plaintiffs in emotional distress cases. Similarly, the class of eligible plaintiffs has been narrowly construed. In Trombetta v. Conkling, 626 N.E.2d 653, 654 (N.Y. 1993), the court denied an emotional distress claim brought by a niece who witnessed the death of her aunt who had raised her from age 11, concluding baldly: "Recovery of damages by bystanders for the negligent infliction of emotional distress should be limited only to the immediate family." Thompson v. Dhaiti, 103 A.D.3d 711 (N.Y. App. Div. 2013), construed "immediate family" not to include a stepdaughter. In Dunphy v. Gregor, 642 A.2d 372 (N.J. 1994), the New Jersey Supreme Court also split the difference. As in *Dillon*, it required a plaintiff to have observed the death or injury of another person, but it repudiated *Elden*, by extending the concept to an unmarried cohabitant. "The State's interest in marriage would not be harmed if unmarried cohabitants are permitted to prove on a case-by-case basis that they enjoy a steadfast relationship that is equivalent to a legal marriage and thus equally deserves legal protection." *Dunphy* was followed in McDougall v. Lamm, 48 A.3d 312 (N.J. 2012), which disallowed a pet owner an emotional distress claim arising from the death of his pet.

More recently, in Coleson v. City of New York, 24 N.E.3d 1074, 1079 (N.Y. 2014), the infant plaintiff brought an emotional distress claim against the New York City police department for injuries suffered when his estranged father stabbed his mother with a knife. The plaintiff claimed that he "was in the zone of danger because, although he was in a closet at the time his mother was stabbed, he saw Coleson [his father] with the knife and while in the closet heard his mother's screams." Abdus-Salaam, J., concluded that "the child was not in the zone of danger because he was in a broom closet while his mother was stabbed, and thus neither saw the incident nor was immediately aware of the incident at the time it occurred." The Third Restatement takes much the same hard line in RTT:LPEH §47.

Restatement of the Law (Third) of Torts: Liability for Physical and Emotional Harm

§47. NEGLIGENT CONDUCT DIRECTLY INFLICTING EMOTIONAL HARM ON ANOTHER

An actor whose negligent conduct causes serious emotional harm to another is subject to liability to the other if the conduct:

(a) places the other in danger of immediate bodily harm and the emotional harm results from the danger; or

(b) occurs in the course of specified categories of activities, undertakings, or relationships in which negligent conduct is especially likely to cause serious emotional harm.

Comment j. Physical consequences not required: Significant emotional harm may cause physical illness or other bodily harm. Some courts insist that plaintiff present with physical symptoms to ensure that the emotional harm claimed is genuine and serious. The rule stated in this Section, while requiring serious emotional harm, is not limited to cases in which there are physical manifestations. The requirements that the harm be serious, that the circumstances of the case be such that a reasonable person would suffer serious harm, and that there be credible evidence that the plaintiff has suffered such harm better serve the purpose of screening claims than a requirement of physical consequences.

---

4. The "at risk" plaintiff: Of drugs and toxic torts. One important variation on NIED cases involves individuals who are exposed to dangerous drugs or toxic substances and suffer distress, for fear of future harm to themselves. The Third Restatement notes the powerful judicial sentiment against awarding damages, for example, in cancer phobia, in part for the fear of multiple lawsuits—one for the fear and a second for the injury. RTT:LPEH §47, comment *k*. For example, an "at-risk" claim for emotional distress was rejected in Payton v. Abbott Labs, 437 N.E.2d 171, 181 (Mass. 1982), when brought by daughters exposed to DES in utero who stood between 1 in 1,000 and 1 in 10,000 chance of getting adenocarcinoma, a very serious form of cancer. The court insisted that the proper measure of damage was that which would be experienced by "a reasonable person, normally constituted," and then only for physical harm that "must be manifested by objective symptomatology and substantiated by expert medical testimony." Similarly, in Metro-North Commuter R.R. Co. v. Buckley, 521 U.S. 424 (1997), the Court disallowed a claim alleging fear of cancer after exposure to asbestos. *Buckley* was distinguished in Norfolk & Western Ry. Co. v. Ayers, 538 U.S. 135, 141 (2003), another FELA claim, by allowing mental anguish damages from fear of future cancer for a plaintiff who is actually suffering from asbestosis.

A parallel NIED claim arose in Potter v. Firestone Tire & Rubber Co., 863 P.2d 795, 800, 810, 826 (Cal. 1993), in which the defendant's local employees, in conscious violation of federal and state statutes, and internal company policy, dumped certain toxic wastes into an unauthorized dumpsite to cut costs. Firestone's toxins (unique to its manufacturing processes) made their way into the plaintiffs' wells. Informed of this risk, the plaintiff owners sought relief for emotional distress stemming from "significant increase in the risk of cancer" even though none of them suffered from cancerous or precancerous conditions. The defendants sought to limit recovery to persons who manifested some sign of physical injury from the ingested toxic substances.

Baxter, J., rejected both extremes and required, as in *Payton*, that the plaintiff "pleads and proves that the fear stems from a knowledge, corroborated by reliable medical and scientific opinion, that it is more likely than not that the feared cancer will develop in the future due to the toxic exposure." Generally, the court thought that in NIED cases only this limitation would confine liability to manageable limits, control insurance costs, and leave funds available for future serious cases of cancer. But owing to the defendant's malicious conduct the court allowed recovery even though plaintiffs' toxic intake from smoking was 2,500 times that found in the defendant's waste. Why credit the plaintiff's fears of the former to the exclusion of the latter?

5. Emotional distress in medical malpractice cases. In Squeo v. Norwalk Hosp. Ass'n, 113 A.3d 932, 935 (Conn. 2015), the plaintiffs sued a nurse and hospital for negligently discharging their suicidal son after completing an emergency psychiatric examination. The parents claimed that they suffered emotional distress from discovering that their son hung himself in their front yard. Palmer, J., affirmed summary judgment for the defendants concluding:

> [A] bystander to medical malpractice may bring a claim for the resulting emotional distress only when the injuries result from gross negligence such that it would be readily apparent to a lay observer. This additional element reflects our determination that bystander claims should be available in the medical malpractice context only under extremely limited circumstances. [We also] conclude that a bystander must suffer injuries that are severe and debilitating, such that they warrant a psychiatric diagnosis or otherwise substantially impair the bystander's ability to cope with life's daily routines and demands.

A still-developing area of law is that of reproductive harm. In Broadnax v. Gonzalez, 809 N.E.2d 645, 648-649 (N.Y. 2004), the plaintiff was advised by her obstetrician, Dr. Gonzalez, to travel 45 minutes to a hospital in New York City rather than seek immediate treatment at a suburban hospital. Upon arrival at Columbia Presbyterian Hospital in Manhattan, the plaintiff had to wait an additional 45 minutes for Dr. Gonzalez to show up, during which time the nurse-midwife who had accompanied the plaintiff from Westchester neglected to contact the on-call doctor. When Dr. Gonzalez arrived, he performed a sonogram that detected fetal heart rate decelerations, but he delayed in performing an emergency cesarean section. Three and a half hours after the plaintiff's initial arrival at the Westchester Birth Center, Dr. Gonzalez finally undertook a cesarean section, delivering a full-term stillborn girl. Reversing the grant of the defendants' summary judgment motion, the Court of Appeals noted the nonsensical nature of the longstanding reluctance to recognize NIED in cases of miscarriage or stillbirth resulting from medical malpractice, absent independent physical injury to the plaintiff:

> [The old rule] exposed medical caregivers to malpractice liability for in utero injuries when the fetus survived, but immunized them against any liability when their malpractice caused a miscarriage or stillbirth. . . . We therefore hold that, even in the absence of an independent injury, medical malpractice resulting in miscarriage or stillbirth should be construed as a violation of a duty of care to the expectant mother, entitling her to damages for emotional distress.

6. Direct victims. The Third Restatement extends liability to "specified categories of activities, undertakings, or relationships in which negligent conduct is especially likely to cause serious emotional harm." RTT:LPEH §47(b). In these cases, there is no requirement of the direct observation of a harm to some third person. "Specifically, courts have imposed liability on hospitals and funeral homes for negligently mishandling a corpse and on telegraph companies for negligently mistranscribing or misdirecting a telegram that informs the recipient, erroneously, about the death of a loved one." *Id.*, comment *b*.

Liability under this provision has also been extended to cover other cases in which the recipient of information is a "direct victim" of the harm. In Molien v. Kaiser Foundation Hospitals, 616 P.2d 813, 817 (Cal. 1980) (en banc), the defendant's employee, Dr. Kilbridge, negligently provided the plaintiff's wife with an erroneous report that she had contracted an infectious type of syphilis. She in turn had to undergo unnecessary medical treatment and became "upset and suspicious that her husband had engaged in extramarital sexual activities." Their marriage broke up from the ensuing tension and hostility, and the husband's suit for emotional distress was allowed, notwithstanding the limitations in *Dillon*, on the ground that the plaintiff was a "direct victim" of the defendant's erroneous report. Mosk, J., wrote:

> In the case at bar the risk of harm to plaintiff was reasonably foreseeable to defendants. It is easily predictable that an erroneous diagnosis of syphilis and its probable source would produce marital discord and resultant emotional distress to a married patient's spouse; Dr. Kilbridge's advice to Mrs. Molien to have her husband examined for the disease confirms that plaintiff was a foreseeable victim of the negligent diagnosis. Because the disease is normally transmitted only by sexual relations, it is rational to anticipate that both husband and wife would experience anxiety, suspicion, and hostility when confronted with what they had every reason to believe was reliable medical evidence of a particularly noxious infidelity.

Post-*Molien*, foresight is no longer the touchstone of duty. Instead, the California court asks whether the defendant has assumed some direct duty to the plaintiff. In Huggins v. Longs Drug Stores California, Inc., 862 P.2d 148, 152-153 (Cal. 1993), the court found that no direct relationship existed between the defendant pharmacy, which dispensed five times the prescribed dosage, and the parents whose child was harmed by the overdose. In Marlene F. v. Affiliated Psychiatric Medical Clinic, Inc., 770 P.2d 278 (Cal. 1989), a defendant psychotherapist that had treated both the plaintiff mother and her son for intrafamily difficulties owed duties to both, such that the mother's NIED claim against the psychotherapist for sexually molesting her son could proceed. More recently, in Eriksson v. Nunnink, 183 Cal. Rptr. 3d 234, 251-252 (Ct. App. 2015), the plaintiffs' child died while participating in an equestrian contest. The plaintiffs' NIED suit against the child's coach was dismissed on the ground that the release signed on behalf of the child also bound the parents. King, J., concluded:

> Because the defendant can owe no greater duty to the heirs than to the decedent the release can be asserted against the wrongful death plaintiffs to prove the absence of a duty of ordinary care. The same rationale should apply in bystander NIED cases. Accordingly, just as Nunnink may interpose the defense of express assumption of the risk to the Erikssons' wrongful death suit, she may interpose the same defense to their bystander action for NIED.

CHAPTER 6

AFFIRMATIVE DUTIES

SECTION A. INTRODUCTION

The previous five chapters have been largely, but not exclusively, devoted to understanding the rules for personal injury and property damage that result from the defendant's positive acts, such as hitting another person, or creating dangerous conditions that result in the harm of another. In this chapter, the focus shifts from liability for misfeasance, or misdeeds, to liability for nonfeasance, or failure to act. The difference between these two types of cases is often expressed in terms of duty.

In misfeasance cases, the basic duty of all individuals is to abstain from hurting other persons, both strangers and persons with whom the defendant has some special relationship. In the stranger setting, any invasion of the plaintiff's person or space by the defendant sets up a prima facie obligation to compensate under strict liability. And in the negligence system, the usual reference to a duty of care is to take care to avoid harm to another person by one's own affirmative acts. Within consensual arrangements, few defendants agree either expressly or impliedly to assume strict liability obligations.

In contrast, for cases of nonfeasance, the idea of negligence is subtly modified. The notion of care no longer refers to taking precautions to avoid harmful contact. Instead it requires rendering material aid or support to other persons. That duty of affirmative care is neatly divided in two halves. The first is directed to strangers and the second to individuals with whom the defendant stands in what is commonly termed a special relationship. These two strands of duty are reflected in the Third Restatement, which discusses the question of duty in connection with positive acts in §7, and the affirmative duties to aid in §§37-44.

In line with the distinction between affirmative care to strangers and to individuals in a special relationship, the first part of this chapter examines a hardy problem of enduring philosophical interest: When are individuals liable for failing to rescue strangers in imminent peril of life or limb? The so-called Good Samaritan cases are prominent in this area, in which the defendant was in no sense responsible for creating the dangerous condition or situation that brought forth the need to rescue in the first place. Thereafter, the discussion is extended to less controversial cases in which the defendant, either tortiously or nontortiously, has created the dangerous situation requiring rescue.

The second set of issues concerns the duties that landowners and occupiers owe to persons who enter their premises. These entries may be unlawful, as with trespassers, or lawful, as with persons who have received permission from the landowner. Despite fluctuations in judicial attitude, the law generally holds that the trespasser takes, at the very least, the risk of purely accidental injuries even if he is entitled to recover for deliberately and perhaps recklessly inflicted injuries. In contrast, the landowner clearly owes some duty of care to persons lawfully on the premises. The critical issues are how much care is owed and to which persons. The traditional common law cases distinguished between social guests (called "licensees") and business visitors (called "invitees"), and imposed a lower duty to the former—merely to warn of known latent defects—than it did to the latter—to take reasonable care to both discover danger and to keep the premises safe. Many states today reject this status distinction and impose a uniform duty of reasonable care for the benefit of licensees and invitees alike. In addition, courts have more frequently addressed how far the duties of occupiers extend beyond making the premises safe, such as by providing emergency assistance to persons in various states of distress.

The third set of issues involves gratuitous undertakings by the defendant to benefit or assist the plaintiff. These cases are, in a sense, contractual, as they rest upon the defendant's promise, express or implied, to the plaintiff. But the defendant's undertakings have not been bargained for by the plaintiff, and, for that reason, these cases have historically been treated as part of tort law.

The fourth set of issues arises whenever the defendant owes a duty to prevent harm to the plaintiff's person or property because the defendant stands in some sort of "special relationship" either with the plaintiff or with the person who threatens harm to the plaintiff. The first subclass of special relationship cases is an outgrowth of the premise liability cases and concerns, for example, the duties a landlord owes to his tenant, a hotel to its guests, a club to its members, or a university to its students. In these cases, the defendant may be called upon to guard against various contingencies, ranging from the simple loss or destruction of property entrusted to its care, to the defective conditions of premises under its control, or, in today's most contentious area, to the criminal act of a third party. The second subclass of special relationship cases arises when prisons and hospitals have charge of persons who, once released, commit acts of violence against third parties. Until recently, contemporary tort law had expanded the range of affirmative duties that large (and not-so-large) social institutions—schools, hotels, hospitals, landlords, common carriers—owe their customers and clients, but today the law shows evidence of stabilization and perhaps modest contraction.

SECTION B. THE DUTY TO RESCUE

Luke 10:30–37 (King James Translation)

A certain man went down from Jerusalem to Jericho, and fell among thieves which stripped him of his raiment, and wounded him, and departed, leaving him half dead. And by chance there came down a certain priest that way: and when he saw him, he passed by on the other side. And likewise a Levite, when he was at the place, came and looked at him, and passed by on the other side. But a certain Samaritan, as he journeyed, came where he was: and when he saw him, he had compassion on him, and went to him, and bound up his wounds, pouring in oil and wine, and set him on his own beast, and brought him to an inn, and took care of him. And on the morrow when he departed, he took out two pence, and gave them to the host and said unto him, Take care of him; and whatsoever thou spendest more, when I come again, I will repay thee. Which of these three, thinkest thou, was neighbour unto him that fell among the thieves. And he said, He that shewed mercy on him. Then said Jesus unto him, Go, do thou likewise.

Vincent van Gogh, "The Good Samaritan" (left) and Rembrandt Harmensz van Rijn, "The Good Samaritan at the Inn" (right)
Source: Public domain

Buch v. Amory Manufacturing Co.

44 A. 809 (N.H. 1897)

[The plaintiff, aged eight years, trespassed in defendant's mill, where weaving machinery was in operation. An overseer observed him there and told him to leave. Plaintiff did not go because he did not understand English. Nonetheless the overseer did not put him out, although the running machinery presented an obvious hazard to a child of plaintiff's age. Plaintiff had his hand crushed in a machine that his brother, age 13, an employee, was trying to teach him to run. The trial court denied a motion for a directed verdict for defendant. Defendant appealed. The verdict for plaintiff set aside and judgment was entered for defendant.]

CARPENTER, C.J. Assuming, then, that the plaintiff was incapable either of appreciating the danger or of exercising the care necessary to avoid it, is he, upon the facts stated, entitled to recover? He was a trespasser in a place dangerous to children of his age. In the conduct of their business and management of their machinery the defendants were without fault. The only negligence charged upon, or attributed to, them is that, inasmuch as they could not make the plaintiff understand a command to leave the premises, and ought to have known that they could not, they did not forcibly eject him. Actionable negligence is the neglect of a legal duty. The defendants are not liable unless they owed to the plaintiff a legal duty which they neglected to perform. With purely moral obligations the law does not deal. For example, the priest and Levite who passed by on the other side were not, it is supposed, liable at law for the continued suffering of the man who fell among thieves, which they might and morally ought to have prevented or relieved. Suppose *A*, standing close by a railroad, sees a two-year-old babe on the track and a car approaching. He can easily rescue the child with entire safety to himself, and the instincts of humanity require him to do so. If he does not, he may, perhaps, justly be styled a ruthless savage and a moral monster; but he is not liable in damages for the child's injury, or indictable under the statute for its death. . . .

What duties do the owners owe to a trespasser upon their premises? They may eject him, using such force and such only as is necessary for the purpose. They are bound to abstain from any other or further intentional or negligent acts of personal violence — bound to inflict upon him by means of their own active intervention no injury which by due care they can avoid. They are not bound to warn him against hidden or secret dangers arising from the condition of the premises, or to protect him against any injury that may arise from his own acts or those of other persons. In short, if they do nothing, let him entirely alone, in no manner interfere with him, he can have no cause of action against them for any injury that he may receive. On the contrary, he is liable to them for any damage that he by his unlawful meddling may cause them or their property. What greater or other legal obligation was cast on these defendants by the circumstance that the plaintiff was (as is assumed) an irresponsible infant?

If landowners are not bound to warn an adult trespasser of hidden dangers, — dangers which he by ordinary care cannot discover and, therefore, cannot avoid, — on what ground can it be claimed that they must warn an infant of open and visible dangers which he is unable to appreciate? No legal distinction is perceived between the duties of the owners in one case and the other. The situation of the adult in front of secret dangers which by no degree of care he can discover, and that of the infant incapable of comprehending danger, is in a legal aspect exactly the same. There is no apparent reason for holding that any greater or other duty rests upon the owners in one case than in the other.

There is a wide difference—a broad gulf—both in reason and in law, between causing and preventing an injury; between doing by negligence or otherwise a wrong to one's neighbor, and preventing him from injuring himself; between protecting him against injury by another and guarding him from injury that may accrue to him from the condition of the premises which he has unlawfully invaded. The duty to do no wrong is a legal duty. The duty to protect against wrong is, generally speaking and excepting certain intimate relations in the nature of a trust, a moral obligation only, not recognized or enforced by law. Is a spectator liable if he sees an intelligent man or an unintelligent infant running into danger and does not warn or forcibly restrain him? What difference does it make whether the danger is on another's land, or upon his own, in case the man or infant is not there by his express or implied invitation? If *A* sees an eight-year-old boy beginning to climb into his garden over a wall stuck with spikes and does not warn him or drive him off, is he liable in damages if the boy meets with injury from the spikes? I see my neighbor's two-year-old babe in dangerous proximity to the machinery of his windmill in his yard, and easily might, but do not, rescue him. I am not liable in damages to the child for his injuries, nor, if the child is killed, punishable for manslaughter by the common law or under the statute (P.S., c. 278, S. 8), because the child and I are strangers, and I am under no legal duty to protect him. Now suppose I see the same child trespassing in my own yard and meddling in like manner with the dangerous machinery of my own windmill. What additional obligation is cast upon me by reason of the child's trespass? The mere fact that the child is unable to take care of himself does not impose on me the legal duty of protecting him in the one case more than in the other. Upon what principle of law can an infant by coming unlawfully upon my premises impose upon me the legal duty of a guardian? None has been suggested, and we know of none.

An infant, no matter of how tender years, is liable in law for his trespasses. . . . If, then, the defendants' machinery was injured by the plaintiff's act in putting his hand in the gearing, he is liable to them for the damages in an action of trespass and to nominal damages for the wrongful entry. It would be no answer to such an action that the defendants might by force have prevented the trespass. It is impossible to hold that while the plaintiff is liable to the defendants in trespass, they are liable to him in case for neglecting to prevent the act which caused the injury both to him and them. Cases of enticement, allurement, or invitation of infants to their injury, or setting traps for them, and cases relating to the sufficiency of public ways, or to the exposure upon them of machinery attractive and dangerous to children, have no application here.

Danger from machinery in motion in the ordinary course of business cannot be distinguished from that arising from a well, pit, open scuttle, or other stationary object. The movement of the works is a part of the regular and normal condition of the premises. . . . The law no more compels the owners to shut down their gates and stop their business for the protection of a trespasser than it requires them to maintain a railing about an open scuttle or to fence in their machinery for the same purpose.

Hurley v. Eddingfield
59 N.E. 1058 (Ind. 1901)

BAKER, J. Appellant sued appellee for $10,000 damages for wrongfully causing the death of his intestate. The court sustained appellee's demurrer to the complaint; and this ruling is assigned as error.

The material facts alleged may be summarized thus: At and for years before decedent's death appellee was a practicing physician at Mace in Montgomery county, duly licensed under the laws of the State. He held himself out to the public as a general practitioner of medicine. He had been decedent's family physician. Decedent became dangerously ill and sent for appellee. The messenger informed appellee of decedent's violent sickness, tendered him his fees for his services, and stated to him that no other physician was procurable in time and that decedent relied on him for attention. No other physician was procurable in time to be of any use, and decedent did rely on appellee for medical assistance. Without any reason whatever, appellee refused to render aid to decedent. No other patients were requiring appellee's immediate service, and he could have gone to the relief of decedent if he had been willing to do so. Death ensued, without decedent's fault, and wholly from appellee's wrongful act.

The alleged wrongful act was appellee's refusal to enter into a contract of employment. Counsel do not contend that, before the enactment of the law regulating the practice of medicine, physicians were bound to render professional service to every one who applied. The act regulating the practice of medicine provides for a board of examiners, standards of qualification, examinations, licenses to those found qualified, and penalties for practicing without license. The act is a preventive, not a compulsive, measure. In obtaining the State's license (permission) to practice medicine, the State does not require, and the licensee does not engage, that he will practice at all or on other terms than he may choose to accept. Counsel's analogies, drawn from the obligations to the public on the part of innkeepers, common carriers, and the like, are beside the mark.

Judgment affirmed.

NOTE

My brother's tormentor.   Yania v. Bigan, 155 A.2d 343, 345, 346 (Pa. 1959), manifests a similar hostility toward the creation of affirmative duties. The decedent and defendant were operators of nearby strip mines. One day Yania was visiting Bigan's land to discuss business. Located on the land was a worked-out strip mine in which about 8 to 10 feet of water stood in a cut some 16 or 18 feet deep. Yania jumped into the cut and drowned, and the complaint in the wrongful death action that ensued charged Bigan "with three-fold negligence: (1) by urging, enticing, taunting and inveigling Yania to jump into the water; (2) by failing to warn Yania of a dangerous condition on the land; i.e., the cut wherein lay 8 to 10 feet of water; (3) by failing to go to Yania's rescue after he jumped into the water."

Jones, J., dismissed all three parts of the claim. The first count failed because the

complaint does not allege that Yania slipped or that he was pushed or that Bigan made any *physical* impact on his person. On the contrary, the only inference deducible from the facts alleged in the complaint is that Bigan, by the employment of cajolery and inveiglement, caused such a *mental* impact on Yania that the latter was deprived of his volition and freedom of choice and placed under a compulsion to jump into the water. Had Yania been a child of tender years or a person mentally deficient then it is conceivable that taunting and enticement could constitute actionable negligence if it resulted in harm. However to contend that such conduct directed to an adult in full possession of all his mental faculties constitutes actionable negligence is not only without precedent but completely without merit.

On the second count, Jones, J., held that Yania, as a strip-mine operator, was well aware of the obvious dangers of jumping into the water. The judge addressed the third claim as follows: "Lastly, it is urged that Bigan failed to take the necessary steps to rescue Yania from the water. The mere fact that Bigan saw Yania in a position of peril in the water imposed upon him no legal, although a moral, obligation or duty to go to his rescue unless Bigan was legally responsible in whole or in part, for placing Yania in the perilous position." It was his fault for undertaking a dangerous and reckless course of action. How should the law respond to these various situations?

Francis H. Bohlen, The Moral Duty to Aid Others as a Basis of Tort Liability
56 U. Pa. L. Rev. 217, 218-220 (1908)

There is no distinction more deeply rooted in the common law and more fundamental than that between misfeasance and non-feasance, between active misconduct working positive injury to others and passive inaction, a failure to take positive steps to benefit others, or to protect them from harm not created by any wrongful act of the defendant. This distinction is founded on that attitude of extreme individualism so typical of anglo-saxon thought.

James Barr Ames, Law and Morals
22 Harv. L. Rev. 97, 110-113 (1908)

The law is utilitarian. It exists for the realization of the reasonable needs of the community. If the interest of an individual runs counter to this chief object of the law, it must be sacrificed. That is why, in [some cases], the innocent suffer and the wicked go unpunished. . . .

It remains to consider whether the law should ever go so far as to give compensation or to inflict punishment for damage which would not have happened but for the wilful inaction of another. I exclude cases in which, by reason of some relation between the parties like that of father and child, nurse and invalid, master and servant and others, there is a recognized legal duty to act. In the case supposed the only relation between the parties is that both are human beings. As I am walking over a bridge a man falls into the water. He cannot swim and calls for help. I am strong and a good swimmer, or, if you please, there is a rope on the bridge, and I might easily throw him an end and pull him ashore. I neither jump in nor throw him the rope, but see him drown. Or, again, I see a child on the railroad track too young to appreciate the danger of the approaching train. I might easily save the child, but do nothing, and the child, though it lives, loses both legs. Am I guilty of a crime, and must I make compensation to the widow and children of the man drowned and to the wounded child? Macaulay, in commenting upon his Indian Criminal Code, puts the case of a surgeon refusing to go from Calcutta to Meerut to perform an operation, although it should be absolutely certain that this surgeon was the only person in India who could perform it, and that, if it were not performed, the person who required it would die.

We may suppose again that the situation of imminent danger of death was created by the act, but the innocent act, of the person who refuses to prevent the death. The man, for example, whose eye was penetrated by the glancing shot of the careful pheasant hunter, stunned by the shot, fell face downward into a shallow pool by which he was standing. The hunter might easily save him, but lets him drown.

In the first three illustrations, however revolting the conduct of the man who declined to interfere, he was in no way responsible for the perilous situation, he did not increase the peril, he took away nothing from the person in jeopardy, he simply failed to confer a benefit upon a stranger. As the law stands today there would be no legal liability, either civilly or criminally, in any of these cases. The law does not compel active benevolence between man and man. It is left to one's conscience whether he shall be the good Samaritan or not.

But ought the law to remain in this condition? Of course any statutory duty to be benevolent would have to be exceptional. The practical difficulty in such legislation would be in drawing the line. But that difficulty has continually to be faced in the law. We should all be better satisfied if the man who refuses to throw a rope to a drowning man or to save a helpless child on the railroad track could be punished and be made to compensate the widow of the man drowned and the wounded child. We should not think it advisable to penalize the surgeon who refused to make the journey. These illustrations suggest a possible working rule. One who fails to interfere to save another from impending death or great bodily harm, when he might do so with little or no inconvenience to himself, and the death or great bodily harm follows as a consequence of his inaction, shall be punished criminally and shall make compensation to the party injured or to his widow and children in case of death. The case of the drowning of the man shot by the hunter differs from the others in that the hunter, although he acted innocently, did bring about the dangerous situation. Here, too, the lawyer who should try to charge the hunter would lead a forlorn hope. But it seems to me that he could make out a strong case against the hunter on common law grounds. By the early law, as we have seen, he would have been liable simply because he shot the other. In modern times the courts have admitted as an affirmative defense the fact that he was not negligent. May not the same courts refuse to allow a defense, if the defendant did not use reasonable means to prevent a calamity after creating the threatening situation? Be that as it may, it is hard to see why such a rule should not be declared by statute, if not by the courts.

Richard A. Epstein, A Theory of Strict Liability
2 J. Legal Stud. 151, 198-200 (1973)

Under Ames' good Samaritan rule, a defendant in cases of affirmative acts would be required to take only those steps that can be done "with little or no inconvenience." But if the distinction between causing harm and not preventing harm is to be disregarded, why should the difference in standards between the two cases survive the reform of the law? The only explanation is that the two situations are regarded at bottom as raising totally different issues, even for those who insist upon the immateriality of this distinction. Even those who argue, as Ames does, that the law is utilitarian must in the end find some special place for the claims of egoism which are an inseparable byproduct of the belief that individual autonomy — individual liberty — is a good in itself not explainable in terms of its purported social worth. It is one thing to *allow* people to act as they please in the belief that the "invisible hand" will provide the happy congruence of the individual and the social good. Such a theory, however, at bottom must regard individual autonomy as but a means to some social end. It takes a great deal more to assert that men are *entitled* to act as they choose (within the limits of strict liability) even though it is certain that there will be cases where individual welfare will be in conflict with the social good. Only then is it clear that even freedom has its costs: costs revealed in the acceptance of the good Samaritan doctrine.

But are the alternatives more attractive? Once one decides that as a matter of statutory or common law duty, an individual is required under some circumstances to act at his own cost for the exclusive benefit of another, then it is very hard to set out in a principled manner the limits of social interference with individual liberty. Suppose one claims, as Ames does, that his proposed rule applies only in the "obvious" cases where everyone (or almost everyone) would admit that the duty was appropriate: to the case of the man upon the bridge who refuses to throw a rope to a stranger drowning in the waters below. Even if the rule starts out with such modest ambitions, it is difficult to confine it to those limits. Take a simple case first. *X* as a representative of a private charity asks you for $10 in order to save the life of some starving child in a country ravaged by war. There are other donors available but the number of needy children exceeds that number. The money means "nothing" to you. Are you under a legal obligation to give the $10? Or to lend it interest-free? Does $10 amount to a substantial cost or inconvenience within the meaning of Ames' rule? It is true that the relationship between the gift to charity and the survival of an unidentified child is not so apparent as is the relationship between the man upon the bridge and the swimmer caught in the swirling seas. But lest the physical imagery govern, it is clear that someone will die as a consequence of your inaction in both cases. Is there a duty to give, or is the contribution a matter of charity?

Consider yet another example where services, not cash, are in issue. Ames insists that his rule would not require the only surgeon in India capable of saving the life of a person with a given affliction to travel across the subcontinent to perform an operation, presumably because the inconvenience and cost would be substantial. But how would he treat the case if some third person were willing to pay him for all of his efforts? If the payment is sufficient to induce the surgeon to act, then there is no need for the good Samaritan doctrine at all. But if it is not, then it is again necessary to compare the costs of the physician with the benefits to his prospective patient. It is hard to know whether Ames would require the forced exchange under these circumstances. But it is at least arguable that under his theory forced exchanges should be required, since the payment might reduce the surgeon's net inconvenience to the point where it was trivial.

Once forced exchanges, regardless of the levels of payment, are accepted, it will no longer be possible to delineate the sphere of activities in which contracts (or charity) will be required in order to procure desired benefits and the sphere of activity in which those benefits can be procured as of right. Where tests of "reasonableness"—stated with such confidence, and applied with such difficulty—dominate the law of tort, it becomes impossible to tell where liberty ends and obligation begins; where contract ends, and tort begins. In each case, it will be possible for some judge or jury to decide that there was something else which the defendant should have done, and he will decide that on the strength of some cost-benefit formula that is difficult indeed to apply. These remarks are conclusive, I think, against the adoption of Ames' rule by judicial innovation, and they bear heavily on the desirability of the abandonment of the good Samaritan rule by legislation as well. It is not surprising that the law has, in the midst of all the clamor for reform, remained unmoved in the end, given the inability to form alternatives to the current position.

Richard A. Posner, Epstein's Tort Theory: A Critique
8 J. Legal Stud. 457, 460 (1979)

Suppose that if all the members of society could somehow be assembled they would agree unanimously that, as a reasonable measure of mutual protection, anyone who can warn or rescue someone in distress at negligible cost to himself (in time, danger, or whatever) should be required to do so. These mutual promises of assistance would create a contract that Epstein would presumably enforce since he considers the right to make binding contracts a fundamental one. However, there are technical obstacles—in this case insurmountable ones—to the formation of an actual contract among so many people. Transaction costs are prohibitive. If, moved by these circumstances, a court were to impose tort liability on a bystander who failed to assist a person in distress, such liability would be a means of carrying out the original desires of the parties just as if it were an express contract that was being enforced.

The point of this example is that tort duties can sometimes (perhaps, as we shall see, generally) be viewed as devices for vindicating the principles that underlie freedom of contract. It may be argued, however, that the contract analogy is inapplicable because the bystander would not be compensated for coming to the rescue of the person in distress. But this argument overlooks the fact that the consideration for the rescue is not payment when the rescue is effected but a commitment to reciprocate should the roles of the parties some day be reversed. Liability would create a mutual protective arrangement under which everyone was obliged to attempt a rescue when circumstances dictated and, in exchange, was entitled to the assistance of anyone who might be able to help him should he ever find himself in a position of peril.

Leslie Bender, An Overview of Feminist Torts Scholarship
78 Cornell L. Rev. 575, 580-581 (1993)

"No Duty to Rescue"

Tort law's view of human nature as highly individualistic, autonomous, and self-interested has generated a "no duty to rescue" doctrine. This doctrine states that an actor has no duty to aid or rescue an imperiled person even when the rescue could be performed with no risk to the rescuer, unless the actor directly caused the peril or is in a narrowly defined category of special relationships with the person in danger. Famous cases illustrating this doctrine are taught to most first year law students—stories of "moral monsters" who make no effort to stop young children from being mangled by machinery in factories and business competitors who stand by and watch a man drown in a trench on their property. In challenging that no duty rule, I rely on alternative conceptions of human nature, developed in some feminist theories, in order to transform this doctrine. Applying a feminist ethic of care and responsibility, I [have] argue[d] that "the recognition that we are all interdependent and connected and that we are by nature social beings who must interact with one another should lead us to judge conduct as tortious when it does not evidence responsible care or concern for another's safety, welfare, or health." Utilizing this analysis, the "no duty" doctrine might be transformed into a duty to exercise the "conscious care and concern of a responsible neighbor or social acquaintance," which would impose a duty to aid or rescue within one's capacity under the circumstances. Tort law would no longer condone the inhumane response of doing absolutely nothing to aid or rescue when one could save another person from dying. Finally, . . . feminist theory encourages us to challenge traditional modes of legal analysis and to rethink the questions we ask, including: who are the parties involved, whose interests are protected by tort law, what are appropriate forms of compensation, how should we allocate responsibility for harms and risks, and what assumptions and values underlie various tort doctrines?

NOTES

1. An affirmative duty to rescue.   Judge Posner returned to the Good Samaritan problem in Stockberger v. United States, 332 F.3d 479, 481 (7th Cir. 2003):

> Various rationales have been offered for the seemingly hardhearted common law rule: people should not count on nonprofessionals for rescue; the circle of potentially liable nonrescuers would be difficult to draw (suppose a person is drowning and no one on the crowded beach makes an effort to save him—should all be liable?); altruism makes the problem a small one and liability might actually reduce the number of altruistic rescues by depriving people of credit for altruism (how would they prove they hadn't acted under threat of legal liability?); people would be deterred by threat of liability from putting themselves in a position where they might be called upon to attempt a rescue, especially since a failed rescue might under settled common law principles give rise to liability, on the theory that a clumsy rescue attempt may have interfered with a competent rescue by someone else.

Applying Indiana law, Posner, J., refused to impose liability on coworkers of a hypoglycemic employee at a federal prison for allowing him to undertake his fatal drive home. The coworkers were familiar with the decedent's condition and had supplied him with Ensure, a nutritious liquid food substitute, which made him strong enough to start the drive home. Posner, J., treated this essentially as a stranger case, because otherwise "the exceptions to the rule that there is no 'good Samaritan' liability would have to be enlarged, to encompass the case in which an employee becomes ill at the workplace for reasons unrelated to his work and the employer fails to use due care to treat the illness."

On the complications of creating a generalized duty of rescue, see Epstein, Causation and Corrective Justice, A Reply to Two Critics, 8 J. Legal Stud. 477, 490-492 (1979). For the affirmative case for the duty of easy rescue, see Weinrib, The Case for a Duty to Rescue, 90 Yale L.J. 247 (1980); Hasen, The Efficient Duty to Rescue, 15 Int'l Rev. L. & Econ. 141 (1995).

2. Restitution and rescue.   As a common law matter, is it better to approach the rescue problem with restitution instead of tort doctrines? Restitution imposes on the party rescued an obligation to compensate the rescuer for his costs. Whereas the tort solution requires a large judgment against the able defendant who does not rescue, the restitution solution gives a much smaller payment to the enterprising person who does rescue. The restitution scheme reduces the level of legal intervention, and it eliminates the vexing problems of multiple causation that arise whenever many persons are in a position to undertake a rescue (or to call the police) and none in fact does. Yet how are the levels of compensation to be fixed? Should these be restricted to out-of-pocket costs, without allowance for time spent or personal risk incurred? Is it sound policy to pay rescuers out of public funds? See the thoughtful article by Dawson, Rewards for the Rescue of Human Life, *in* The Good Samaritan and the Law (Ratcliffe ed., 1966), which takes a cautious attitude toward creating restitution remedies. Note that restitution remedies have been allowed for professional rescuers who might be discouraged by the threat of tort suits from making the heavy investments necessary to carry out rescues at sea. See Landes & Posner, Salvors, Finders, Good Samaritans, and Other Rescuers: An Economic Study of Law and Altruism, 7 J. Legal Stud. 83, 119-127 (1978). For a broad exploration of other reward and penalty incentive structures to promote rescue, see Levmore, Waiting for Rescue, 72 Va. L. Rev. 879, 882-929 (1986).

3. *Legislation and the Good Samaritan.* Legislative responses to the Good Samaritan problem have typically been designed either to induce rescue by insulating the rescuer against liability for ordinary negligence or by imposing affirmative duties to rescue, subject to the payment of fines. In both cases the rescuer remains liable for willful misconduct. See, e.g., Kan. Stat. Ann. §§65-2891(a) & (d) (West 2015); N.J. Stat. Ann. §2A:62A-1 (West 2015). Similar immunities for similar reasons have been extended to laypersons who supply emergency care, such as driving injured people to the hospital. Swenson v. Waseca Mutual Insurance Co., 653 N.W.2d 794, 798 (Minn. App. 2002).

Kansas Statutes Annotated

§65-2891. EMERGENCY CARE BY HEALTH CARE PROVIDERS; LIABILITY; STANDARDS OF CARE APPLICABLE

(a) Any health care provider who in good faith renders emergency care or assistance at the scene of an emergency or accident including treatment of a minor without first obtaining the consent of the parent or guardian of such minor shall not be liable for any civil damages for acts or omissions other than damages occasioned by gross negligence or by willful and wanton acts or omissions by such persons in rendering emergency care. . . .

(d) Any provision herein contained notwithstanding, the ordinary standards of care and rules of negligence shall apply in those cases wherein emergency care and assistance is rendered in any physician's or dentist's office, clinic, emergency room or hospital with or without compensation.

New Jersey Statutes Annotated

§2A:62A-1. EMERGENCY CARE

Any individual, including a person licensed to practice any method of treatment of human ailments, disease, pain, injury, deformity, mental or physical condition, or licensed to render services ancillary thereto, or any person who is a volunteer member of a duly incorporated first aid and emergency or volunteer ambulance or rescue squad association, who in good faith renders emergency care at the scene of an accident or emergency to the victim or victims thereof, or while transporting the victim or victims thereof to a hospital or other facility where treatment or care is to be rendered, shall not be liable for any civil damages as a result of any acts or omissions by such person in rendering the emergency care.

A very different approach to the Good Samaritan problem was adopted in Vermont.

Vermont Statutes Annotated

§519. EMERGENCY MEDICAL CARE

(a) A person who knows that another is exposed to grave physical harm shall, to the extent that the same can be rendered without danger or peril to himself or without interference with important duties owed to others, give reasonable assistance to the exposed person unless that assistance or care is being provided by others.

(b) A person who provides reasonable assistance in compliance with subsection (a) of this section shall not be liable in civil damages unless his acts constitute gross negligence or unless he will receive or expects to receive remuneration. Nothing contained in this subsection shall alter existing law with respect to tort liability of a practitioner of the healing arts for acts committed in the ordinary course of his practice.

(c) A person who willfully violates subsection (a) of this section shall be fined not more than $100.00.

Does the Vermont statute adopt a straight negligence approach in rescue cases? Does it authorize the creation of a private cause of action? As of 2015, only three reported actions have been brought for failure to rescue under section (a), none of which succeeded. See, e.g., Kane v. Lamothe, 936 A.2d 1303 (Vt. 2007). See also Franklin, Vermont Requires Rescue: A Comment, 25 Stan. L. Rev. 51 (1972).

4. *Empirical study of duty to rescue.*   The movement for statutory duties to rescue has provoked this response in Hyman, Rescue Without Law: An Empirical Perspective on the Duty to Rescue, 84 Tex. L. Rev. 653, 712 (2006):

During the past decade, there have been an average of 1.6 documented cases of non-rescue each year in the entire United States. Every year, Americans perform at least 946 non-risky rescues and 243 risky rescues. Every year, at least sixty-five times as many Americans die while attempting to rescue someone else as die from a documented case of non-risky non-rescue. If a few isolated (and largely unverified and undocumented) cases of non-rescues have been deemed sufficient to justify legislative reform, one would think a total of approximately 1,200 documented cases of rescue every year should point rather decisively in the opposite direction. When it comes to the duty to rescue, leaving well enough alone is likely to be sufficient unto the day.

Uneasiness with the current law of rescue elicited a proposal to remove rescue cases from the tort liability system altogether by allowing injured rescuers to "recover compensatory damages under either a renter's or homeowner's insurance policy." See White, No Good Deed Goes Unpunished: The Case for Reform of the Rescue Doctrine, 97 Nw. U. L. Rev. 507 (2002). Why can't insurance companies just voluntarily supply the coverage?

Montgomery v. National Convoy & Trucking Co.
195 S.E. 247 (S.C. 1937)

[Defendants' trucks had stalled on an icy highway without their fault, blocking the road completely. About 15 minutes later plaintiff's car came over a hill and started down toward the trucks before either the plaintiff or plaintiff's driver could see them. The trucks were about 50 feet away, not being previously visible because they were obscured by the hill. In view of the icy condition of the road, the plaintiff's chauffeur could not stop the car in time. "The agents of the [defendants] operating the trucks knew, or had every reason to know, that once a car had passed the crest of the hill and started down the decline, . . . it would be impossible to stop such automobile or motor vehicle due to the icy condition of the highway, regardless of the rate of speed at which such automobile may be traveling." Defendants' drivers had ample time to place a warning signal at the top of the hill, where it could have been observed by the plaintiff's chauffeur who, well aware of the dangerous condition of the road, could have stopped before the collision that injured plaintiff. The defendants' motion for a directed verdict was refused, and the jury awarded plaintiff the full amount demanded, $3,000. The defendants appealed.]

BAKER, J. One may be negligent by acts of omission as well as of commission, and liability therefor will attach if the act of omission of a duty owed another, under the circumstances, is the direct, proximate and efficient cause of the injury. It is only where the evidence is susceptible of but one reasonable inference that the Court may declare what that inference is and take the case from the consideration of the jury. . . .

One of the acts of negligence alleged in the complaint is the failure of the appellants to warn approaching vehicles of the conditions existing, and this necessarily means that the warning should be given at a point where it would be effective. That appellants recognized that they owed a duty to others using the highway cannot be questioned, since they at some time put out flares and left the lights on their trucks. But if appellants owed a duty to others using the highway, and this cannot be disputed, the performance of such duty was not met by merely having lights at the point where the trucks blocked the highway, but it was incumbent on the appellants to take such precautions as would reasonably be calculated to prevent injury.

For the moment let us repeat some of the facts. There is a curve in the highway at the crest of a long hill. A short distance to the south of the curve and crest of the hill two trucks are stalled and block the entire road. It is a much-traveled highway. Respondent's chauffeur testified that due to the curve in the road and the hill, the lights of an automobile approaching from the north would not focus on the trucks until the automobile was within a little over fifty feet from the trucks. Once a car passed the crest of the hill and commenced to descend on the south side, it could not be stopped due to the ice on the highway — the slippery condition thereof, which was known or should have been known to appellants. No flagman nor warning of any description was placed at the crest of the hill to warn approaching cars. That a warning at the crest of the hill would have been effective and prevented the injury is fully demonstrated from other evidence had upon the trial. The danger of the situation was so self-evident that a jury could have concluded that the omission to warn approaching travelers from the north at a point where the warning would be effective, amounted not only to negligence, but to willfulness. However, the jury in this case have vindicated their intelligence and freedom from passion when they found only inadvertence.

NOTES

1. Misfeasance and nonfeasance. The distinction between misfeasance and nonfeasance articulated with such confidence by Bohlen, *supra,* is more difficult to draw when the defendant fails to neutralize a dangerous condition that he has created, as in *Montgomery* when defendants' stalled trucks, without fault, blocked the icy highway. How would Bohlen treat the case? What result if the defendants' drivers did not have time to place the flares at the top of the hill?

A similar situation arose in Newton v. Ellis, 119 Eng. Rep. 424 (K.B. 1855). The defendant, while under contract with the local board of health, dug a hole in a public highway that he left unlighted at night. Shortly thereafter the plaintiff, while driving, fell into the hole. The three judges who heard the case denied that plaintiff's action was for nonfeasance. Coleridge, J., remarked: "This is not a case of not doing: the defendant does something, omitting to secure protection for the public. He is not sued for not putting up a light, but for the complex act." Erle, J., agreed, saying: "Here the cause of action is the making the hole, compounded with the not putting up a light. When these two are blended, the result is no more than if two positive acts were committed, such as digging the hole and throwing out the dirt: the two would make up one act." Suppose that *A,* while driving, hits *B* because *A* has failed to apply the brakes. Can *A* argue that this is a simple case of nonfeasance for which he is not responsible? Why not?

Yet another variation of the Good Samaritan theme arose in Louisville & Nashville R.R. v. Scruggs, 49 So. 399 (Ala. 1909). The defendant's freight train was stopped, blocking a fire engine as it drove up to extinguish a fire in plaintiff's house just across the tracks. The defendant's employees refused to move the train except on the dispatcher's orders and, by the time the firemen arrived, plaintiff's house was destroyed. Because the defendant's use of its land was "merely passive," the Alabama Supreme Court denied recovery, adding that "[t]he law imposes no duty on one man to aid another in the preservation of the latter's property, but only the duty not to injure another's property in the use of his own." The court conceded that the defendant could be held liable for the loss of plaintiff's home if its engineer deliberately or negligently ran over a hose that already was laid across the tracks. One judge dissented, thinking the attitude of defendant's employees showed "an indifference to the situation and emergency that was little short of shocking." What if the local rules of the road give fire engines the right of way over all other traffic?

Scruggs provoked the following response in Hale, Prima Facie Torts, Combination, and Non-Feasance, 46 Colum. L. Rev. 196, 214 (1946):

> Perhaps judicial reluctance to recognize affirmative duties is based on one or both of two inarticulate assumptions. One of these is that a rugged, independent individual needs no help from others, save such as they may be disposed to render him out of kindness, or such as he can induce them to render by the ordinary process of bargaining, without having the government step in to make them help. All he is supposed to ask of the government is that it interfere to prevent others from doing him positive harm. The other assumption is that when a government *requires* a person to act, it is necessarily interfering more seriously with his liberty than when it places limits on his freedom to act—to make a man serve another is to make him a slave, while to forbid him to commit affirmative wrongs is to leave him still essentially a freeman. Neither of these assumptions is universally true. Neither was true in [*Scruggs*]. No matter how rugged the owner of the burning building, his property depended for its preservation on the affirmative acts of the railroad employees—acts which they were evidently not disposed to render out of kindness, and which he was in no position to induce them to perform by bargaining. Nor would a legal duty to move the train have subjected either the employees or the railroad company itself to anything having the slightest resemblance to slavery.

The Third Restatement has codified the rule in *Montgomery* in RTT: LPEH §39.

Restatement of the Law (Third) of Torts: Liability for Physical and Emotional Harm

§39. DUTY BASED ON PRIOR CONDUCT CREATING A RISK OF PHYSICAL HARM

When an actor's prior conduct, even though not tortious, creates a continuing risk of physical harm of a type characteristic of the conduct, the actor has a duty to exercise reasonable care to prevent or minimize the harm.

Could this duty attach if the defendant had no knowledge, or reason to know, of the risk of physical injury to others? Is there any reason, if knowledge is had, to limit the continuing duty of care to cases of "physical harm of a type characteristic of the conduct"? Note that the parallel provision in the Second Restatement only applied to a plaintiff who was rendered "helpless and in danger of further harm." RST §322. Any reason for the helpless limitation? Many state statutes impose particular obligations on motorists to render "reasonable assistance" to other persons involved in an accident, and to exchange information, names, and registration to facilitate subsequent resolution of any future litigation. See, e.g., Cal. Veh. Code §20003 (West 2015).

Just that principle was invoked as a common law matter in Podias v. Mairs, 926 A.2d 859, 866 (N.J. Super. Ct. App. Div. 2007). There the defendant Mairs fell asleep at the wheel and severely injured the decedent, who was left lying unattended on the public highway, making no movement or sound. Mairs and his two passengers, Newell and Swanson, all 18 years old, did nothing to provide assistance or call for help before they left the scene several minutes later, after which the decedent was struck and killed in an independent incident by the defendant Uribe. The trial court invoked the no-duty rule on behalf of Newell and Swanson. On appeal, Parrillo, J.A.D., overturned that summary judgment:

> [W]e are satisfied that the summary judgment record admits of sufficient facts from which a reasonable jury could find defendants breached a duty which proximately caused the victim's death. In the first place, the risk of harm, even death, to the injured victim lying helpless in the middle of a roadway, from the failure of defendants to summon help or take other precautionary measures was readily and clearly foreseeable. Not only were defendants aware of the risk of harm created by their own inaction, but were in a unique position to know of the risk of harm posed by Mairs' own omission in that regard, as well as Mairs' earlier precipatory conduct in driving after having consumed alcohol. Even absent any encouragement on their part, defendants had special reason to know that Mairs would not himself summon help, but instead illegally depart the scene of a hit-and-run accident.

2. Aid to the helpless: Once begun, then undone. In Zelenko v. Gimbel Bros., 287 N.Y.S. 134, 135 (Sup. Ct. 1935), Lauer, J., wrote:

> . . . Plaintiff's intestate was taken ill in defendant's store. We will assume that the defendant owed her no duty at all; that defendant could have let her be and die. But if a defendant undertakes a task, even if under no duty to undertake it, the defendant must not omit to do what an ordinary man would do in performing the task.
> Here the defendant undertook to render medical aid to the plaintiff's intestate. Plaintiff says that defendant kept his intestate for six hours in an infirmary without any medical care. If defendant had left plaintiff's intestate alone, beyond doubt some bystander, who would be influenced more by charity than by legalistic duty, would have summoned an ambulance. Defendant segregated this plaintiff's intestate where such aid could not be given and then left her alone.
> The plaintiff is wrong in thinking that the duty of a common carrier of passengers is the same as the duty of this defendant. The common carrier assumes its

duty by its contract of carriage. This defendant assumed its duty by meddling in matters with which legalistically it had no concern. The plaintiff is right in arguing that when the duty arose, the same type of neglect is actionable in both cases.

Does RTT:LPEH §44 prefer lofty indifference to honest but inept efforts to aid? Compare the following two cases: In the first, *A*, coming upon the scene of an accident, picks up *B*, who is helpless, and starts to drive him to a hospital. En route she drives negligently and has a collision, aggravating *B*'s injuries. In the second, *A* comes upon the scene of an accident and picks up *B*, who is helpless, and starts to drive him to a hospital. A moment later, *A* changes her mind and returns *B* to the scene of the accident. What result in each case if prompt medical care would have greatly reduced the harm to *B* and that this was obvious to *A*?

Restatement of the Law (Third) of Torts: Liability for Physical and Emotional Harm

§44. DUTY TO ANOTHER BASED ON TAKING CHARGE OF THE OTHER

(a) An actor who, despite no duty to do so, takes charge of another who reasonably appears to be:
(1) imperiled; and
(2) helpless or unable to protect himself or herself
has a duty to exercise reasonable care while the other is within the actor's charge.

(b) An actor who discontinues aid or protection is subject to a duty of reasonable care to refrain from putting the other in a worse position than existed before the actor took charge of the other and, if the other reasonably appears to be in imminent peril of serious physical harm at the time of termination, to exercise reasonable care with regard to the peril before terminating the rescue.

---

3. Cracks in the Good Samaritan doctrine.   In Soldano v. O'Daniels, 190 Cal. Rptr. 310 (Ct. App. 1983), the decedent was in imminent danger of being shot at Happy Jack's Saloon. Another patron ran across the street to the defendant's restaurant. He asked the defendant's bartender either to use the defendant's phone to call the police or, alternatively, to make the emergency call. The bartender refused both requests, and the decedent was killed. The court rebuffed the defendant's argument that there was no duty to aid or assist the plaintiff. It first agreed with Prosser that the common law rule denying the duty to rescue violates "common decency" and is "revolting to any moral sense." It then held that the defendant, while not required to rescue, was required "to permit the patron from Happy Jack's to place a call to the police or to place the call himself." Second Restatement section 327 renders any person who "knows or has reason to know that a third person is giving or is ready to give another aid necessary to prevent physical harm to [an endangered person]" tortiously liable if he "negligently prevents or disables the third person from giving such aid." Should it matter that the bartender in *Soldano* only prevented the third party from using its own phone, and did not block the use of any third person's phone? Eric J. v. Betty M., 90 Cal. Rptr. 2d 549, 560 (Ct. App. 1999), criticized *Soldano* for not distinguishing between "[i]nterference and refusal to allow one's property to be commandeered, even for a good purpose." Should *Soldano* be governed by the doctrine of private necessity in Vincent v. Lake Erie Transportation Co., *supra* at 44? Is it a suitable precedent for *Podias*, which cited it favorably?

Whatever its conceptual foundations, *Soldano* has sometimes received a rocky reception in other jurisdictions. In Iseberg v. Gross, 879 N.E.2d 278, 285, 291 (Ill. 2007), the plaintiff was shot by one Slavin when he answered his front door. Slavin had been a former partner of both the plaintiff and the two defendants Gross and Frank. The plaintiff alleged that the two defendants had a duty to warn him when Slavin had made threats against Iseberg's life in their presence. They pointed to *Soldano* "in support of their position that the current trend in the law is toward the abandonment of the no-duty rule and 'special relationship' exceptions," which was in turn based on the interplay of four factors: "foreseeability, likelihood of injury, magnitude of the burden, and consequences of placing the burden on the defendants." Burke, J., rebuffed that claim, noting that "the no-affirmative-duty rule, as a common law tort principle, has been retained in every jurisdiction," and given that the "abandonment of the no-duty rule would create a number of practical difficulties—defining the parameters of an affirmative obligation and enforcement, to name just two." How should a jury decide the instant case under plaintiff's proposed rule?

SECTION C. DUTIES OF OWNERS AND OCCUPIERS

Robert Addie & Sons (Collieries), Ltd. v. Dumbreck
[1929] A.C. 358 (Scot.)

[The defendant colliers (coal miners) operated a haulage system in their fields near a public road in order to remove coal ashes from the pithead, where mining operations were going on. The haulage system employed a continuous wire cable; at one end of the system, near the mouth of the mine, there was an eight-horsepower engine used intermittently to operate the system. At the other end, which was not visible to anyone working the electrical motor, was a large, heavy horizontal wheel around which the cable passed at a rate of two to two and one-half miles per hour when the system was in use. The wheel in question was protected only by four boards placed upon its top, leaving a space of eight or nine inches between the boards and the bed of ashes beneath the wheel. The court below found that the wheel was dangerous and attractive to children.

The haulage system was located in a field surrounded by a hedge that contained a number of gaps, making it inadequate for keeping little children away from the wheel. In fact, many people used the field as a shortcut and many children played there. Though the defendant's servants from time to time warned children to stay out of the field and admonished adults not to cross, they knew their warnings had little or no effect. The defendant's servants did maintain a watch over the field, but to protect the defendant's property, not the persons who trespassed on it. There were two gates to the field, at one of which was posted a notice that read "Trespassers will be prosecuted."

The plaintiff's son was a four-year-old boy whom the plaintiff had warned not to go into the field and not to play with the wheel. The exact circumstances of his death were not determined, but it appeared that he had either been "sitting on the cover of the wheel or in a position in front of and in close proximity to the pulley and rope, being caught and drawn into the mechanism when it was set in motion by the defendant's servants."

The court below had awarded the plaintiff judgment on the ground that the accident was due to the fault of the defendant in not taking suitable precautions to avoid accidents to persons using the fields before activating the haulage system.

The defendant appealed.]

HAILSHAM, L.C. . . . The first and in my opinion the only question which arises for determination is the capacity in which the deceased child was in the field and at the wheel on the occasion of the accident. There are three categories in which persons visiting premises belonging to another person may fall; they may go

1. By the invitation, express or implied, of the occupier;
2. With the leave and license of the occupier; and
3. As trespassers.

It was suggested in argument that there was a fourth category of persons who were not on the premises with the leave or license of the occupier, but who were not pure trespassers. I cannot find any foundation for this suggestion either in English or Scotch law, and I do not think that the category exists.

The duty which rests upon the occupier of premises towards the persons who come on such premises differs according to the category into which the visitor falls. The highest duty exists towards those persons who fall into the first category, and who are present by the invitation of the occupier. Towards such persons the occupier has the duty of taking reasonable care that the premises are safe.

In the case of persons who are not there by invitation, but who are there by leave and licence, express or implied, the duty is much less stringent — the occupier has no duty to ensure that the premises are safe, but he is bound not to create a trap or allow a concealed danger to exist upon the said premises, which is not apparent to the visitor, but which is known — or ought to be known — to the occupier.

Towards the trespasser the occupier has no duty to take reasonable care for his protection or even to protect him from concealed danger. The trespasser comes on to the premises at his own risk. An occupier is in such a case liable only where the injury is due to some wilful act involving something more than the absence

below, sustaining injuries. The court expressed an obvious distaste for a rule that treats alike all trespassers, from guileless infants to persistent poachers. While it did not upset the finding below that the plaintiff was a trespasser in the apartment, it held that the jury could properly find the defendants guilty of "wilful and wanton misconduct" in ignoring their statutory obligation to replace the defective screen after receiving urgent requests from Mrs. Dodd to do so. Although the statute only provided that the screens "be so maintained as to prevent effectively the entrance of flies and mosquitoes into the building," the court found that the defendant's statutory obligation "certainly comprehends, in the Washington summer when windows must be raised, screens which keep flies out and young children in."

2. Attractive nuisance doctrine: Origins.   The rigors of the common law rules regarding trespassers have also been eased by the widespread adoption of the attractive nuisance doctrine. Traditionally, this doctrine allows infant trespassers to recover when lured onto defendant's premises by some tempting condition created and maintained by the defendant, such as railway turntables, explosives, electrical conduits, smoldering fires, and rickety structures. Exposure to liability under the doctrine is, however, limited, for the case law tends to exclude "rivers, creeks, ponds, wagons, axes, plows, woodpiles, haystacks," and the like. Franich v. Great Northern Ry., 260 F.2d 599 (9th Cir. 1958).

During the nineteenth century some courts rejected the attractive nuisance doctrine on grounds that, once recognized, its scope could not be confined or limited. For example, Mitchell, J., in Twist v. Winona & St. Peter R.R., 39 N.W. 402, 404 (Minn. 1888), wrote:

> To the irrepressible spirit of curiosity and intermeddling of the average boy there is no limit to the objects which can be made attractive playthings. In the exercise of his youthful ingenuity, he can make a plaything out of almost anything, and then so use it as to expose himself to danger. If all this is to be charged to natural childish instincts, and the owners of property are to be required to anticipate and guard against it, the result would be that it would be unsafe for a man to own property, and the duty of the protection of children would be charged upon every member of the community except the parents or the children themselves.

Yet most courts, including the New Hampshire court in *Buch,* followed the Supreme Court in Sioux City & Pacific R.R. v. Stout, 84 U.S. 657, 661 (1873), when it allowed the plaintiff, a six-year-old child, to recover when his foot was caught between the fixed rail of the roadbed and the turning rail of a turntable while playing with friends. The Court wrote that "if from the evidence given it might justly be inferred by the jury that the defendant, in the construction, location, management, or condition of its machine had omitted that care and attention to prevent the occurrence of accidents which prudent and careful men ordinarily bestow, the jury was at liberty to find for the plaintiff." See also Smith, Liability of Landowners to Children Entering Without Permission, 11 Harv. L. Rev. 349 (1898).

3. Restatement reformulation of the attractive nuisance doctrine. The Second Restatement continues to exert enormous influence on the law of attractive nuisance. It seeks to reconcile "[t]he public interest in the possessor's free use of his land for his own purposes" (comment *n*) with the general law of negligence.

The Restatement position is narrower than the position staked out in *Stout.* First, as stated, the rule only applies to "artificial conditions on the land." While the Restatement itself takes no position on whether section 339 should apply to natural conditions, such as an ocean cove or steep cliff, most cases hold it does not. Nor does it apply to persons on the premises with the permission of the land-owner, who are treated as licensees, protected from latent defects. See Maalouf v. Swiss Confederation, 208 F. Supp. 2d 31, 41 (D.D.C. 2002).

Restatement of the Law (Second) of Torts

§339. ARTIFICIAL CONDITIONS HIGHLY DANGEROUS TO TRESPASSING CHILDREN

A possessor of land is subject to liability for physical harm to children trespassing thereon caused by an artificial condition upon the land if

(a) the place where the condition exists is one upon which the possessor knows or has reason to know that children are likely to trespass, and

(b) the condition is one of which the possessor knows or has reason to know and which he realizes or should realize will involve an unreasonable risk of death or serious bodily harm to such children, and

(c) the children because of their youth do not discover the condition or realize the risk involved in intermeddling with it or in coming within the area made dangerous by it, and

(d) the utility to the possessor of maintaining the condition and the burden of eliminating the danger are slight as compared with the risk to children involved, and

(e) the possessor fails to exercise reasonable care to eliminate the danger or otherwise to protect the children.

Second, the section only applies when the owner "knows or has reason to know that children are likely to trespass," which makes the possessor under no duty to investigate the land to determine whether trespassing children are present.

Third, the assumption of risk language in clause (c) bars many claims. See, e.g., Holland v. Baltimore & Ohio R.R., 431 A.2d 597 (D.C. 1981), which protected defendants against liability to a nine-year-old boy injured while jumping trains, given the obvious nature of the risk, even to a child of his age.

Nonetheless, the Restatement provisions allow cases involving very young children to reach the jury. In Carmona v. Hagerman Irrigation Co., 957 P.2d 44, 49 (N.M. 1998), the court reversed a summary judgment granted to the defendant irrigation company when a two-year-old boy drowned in a canal. Even though the court acknowledged that "it is virtually impossible to make an irrigation ditch inaccessible to trespassing children," it found genuine issues of fact under section 339 that precluded holding that "all irrigation ditches are categorically exempted from the doctrine of attractive nuisance." In Kessler v. Mortenson, 16 P.3d 1225 (Utah 2000), the court let the jury find an attractive nuisance with a six-year-old boy at a residential construction site, noting that "homebuilders and landowners will be encouraged to minimize or eliminate dangers that trespassing children may be exposed to on the site." Finally, in Bennett v. Stanley, 748 N.E.2d 41 (Ohio 2001), the court embraced section 339, holding that a swimming pool left unused for three years, filled with six feet of rainwater and covered with algae, could constitute an attractive nuisance to a five-year-old child.

More recently a theoretical debate broke out in S.W. v. Towers Boat Club, Inc., 315 P.3d 1257 (Colo. 2013), over the question whether the attractive nuisance doctrine under RST §339 could be invoked by a licensee, in this instance a child who suffered traumatic brain injuries and a broken arm and leg at a private party when he was blown into the air by an inflatable bungee only to come crashing down. Colorado statute §13-12-115(3.5) provides: "[T]he circumstances under which a licensee may recover include all of the circumstances under which a trespasser could recover and . . . the circumstances under which an invitee may recover include all of the circumstances under which a trespasser or a licensee could recover." Rice, J., held that this provision extended the protection that the attractive nuisance doctrine afforded child trespassers to child licensees and invitees. Eid, J., protested in dissent that the defendants were still entitled to a summary judgment because, even if the child were treated as a licensee, the defendant did not know or have reason to know about the dangerous condition that caused the harm. Should the duties of licensees extend beyond warning or correcting latent defects in the premises of which they know or have reason to know?

4. Licensees versus invitees.   Even though classical common law devoted considerable ingenuity to refining the difference between a licensee and an invitee, a host of marginal cases remained. The late Professor Harper observed:

> When a customer goes into a store to buy something and actually makes the purchase, the problem is easy. But how about the person who is merely "shopping" or who accompanies a friend who makes a purchase or children who accompany their parents or one who drops into a hotel or store to go to the toilet or use the telephone, or to mail a letter? And what of a worker looking for a job which he may or may not get? Then there is the problem of public officials of one kind or another who enter another's premises, not with his permission, but because they have legal authority to do so in the discharge of their duties.

Harper, Laube v. Stevenson: A Discussion: Licensor-Licensee, 25 Conn. B.J. 123, 131 (1951).

One response to these difficulties focuses not on the purpose of the visit but on the nature of the premises. Those who run business premises, or premises to which the public generally is invited, are subject to the rules for invitees; those who maintain private or residential premises are not. See Prosser, Business Visitors and Invitees, 26 Minn. L. Rev. 573 (1942), defending this position, which has been adopted in RST §332.

Restatement of the Law (Second) of Torts

§332. INVITEE DEFINED

(1) An invitee is either a public invitee or a business visitor.

(2) A public invitee is a person who is invited to enter or remain on land as a member of the public for a purpose for which the land is held open to the public.

(3) A business visitor is a person who is invited to enter or remain on land for a purpose directly or indirectly connected with business dealings with the possessor of the land.

Even under this view, private understandings might be found to alter the background standard of care. In Lemon v. Busey, 461 P.2d 145 (Kan. 1969), a five-year-old child was brought to the defendant church by her grandmother, a part-time church employee. The arrangement was "for the convenience of her grandmother and parents" and the church at no time supervised the child. While her grandmother was busy at work, the child wandered off and fell to her death from a roof that she had probably reached through an unlocked elevator door or fire escape. The court held that she was a licensee and denied recovery.

With *Lemon* contrast Post v. Lunney, 261 So. 2d 146 (Fla. 1972). The plaintiff bought a ticket for five dollars from a club for its tour of several estates in the area, including defendant Marjorie Merriweather Post's home. While touring the Post estate, she "tripped on a piece of transparent vinyl which had been placed over a valuable oriental rug, and she fractured her hip." The trial judge categorized the plaintiff as a licensee because the visit was not, as the older conception of invitee required, to their mutual economic advantage because the defendant received nothing for letting the plaintiff into her house. The Florida Supreme Court rejected that contention and treated the plaintiff as a public invitee, since Ms. Post had opened up her home for a paid public tour. Should it make any difference whether the vinyl was placed over the oriental rug solely in preparation for the tour? Does Ms. Post have an action over against the tour organizer?

In Olier v. Bailey, 164 So. 3d 982, 987-988 (Miss. 2015), defendant Bailey maintained a garden in which she allowed geese to run free, even though she knew that they had a tendency to bite people. The garden was posted with a "Beware—Attack Geese" sign. The defendant also maintained a row of five-gallon water buckets for the geese that also formed a protective barrier behind which anyone could stand. When plaintiff Olier first ventured into the garden, a goose came close to her, and she retreated behind the buckets, after which she was told by the defendant that she could venture forth again if she defended herself with a stick. When plaintiff went out a second time, she panicked when a goose attacked her in the "crotch area," dropped her stick, and injured herself when she tripped over one of the buckets while attempting to flee. Kitchen, J., held that plaintiff was a licensee as a matter of law because "Olier came at Bailey's invitation to view Bailey's plants. She did not assist Bailey with housework, help her move, take her somewhere, or do anything to benefit Bailey. Instead, she came entirely for her own benefit to look at Bailey's plants and perhaps take a sample home with her." Should her status matter given the interplay between the two women? Was defendant guilty of ordinary negligence? Plaintiff of contributory negligence?

5. Duties to licensees and invitees in slip-and-fall cases. Slip-and-fall cases offer a vivid contrast between the duties to licensees and invitees. The sources of danger in slip-and-fall cases are typically short-lived phenomena, such as spilled fluids. A licensor typically has no knowledge of these evanescent conditions and no duty to inspect for them, but lives instead in a self-help regime. The invitee's host, however, has an explicit duty to seek out and correct these conditions within a reasonable time after their occurrence. "Whether a dangerous condition has existed long enough for a reasonably prudent person to have discovered it is a question of fact for the jury, and the cases do not impose exact time limitations." Ortega v. Kmart Corp., 36 P.3d 11, 16 (Cal. 2001). That approach was also taken in Zuppardi v. Wal-Mart Stores, 770 F.3d 644 (7th Cir. 2014). The plaintiff slipped in a clear puddle of water on a concrete floor as she walked down a busy "action aisle" used by Wal-Mart employees for restocking shelves. There were no footprints or other signs of danger near the puddle. Wal-Mart's standard policy tasked all employees to carry "a towel in pocket" to clean up any spill they encountered. There were no personal witnesses to or video footage of the accident. On appeal, Kendall, J., affirmed the summary judgment. There was no evidence that the defendant caused the spill given that there "were no trails, tracks, or footprints leading to or from the puddle to any store display or freezer." Nor did Wal-Mart have constructive notice of the puddle given that plaintiff "present[ed] next to no evidence of how much time elapsed between the spill and the fall."

Rowland v. Christian
443 P.2d 561 (Cal. 1968)

[On November 30, 1963, the defendant, Nancy Christian, invited James Rowland to her apartment. While he was using the bathroom fixtures, the porcelain handle on one of the water faucets broke, severing the nerves and tendons of his right hand. The defendant knew of the crack in the faucet and two weeks before the incident had asked her landlord to repair it, but she did not warn the plaintiff of the danger. The defendant's affidavits did not show that the defect was "obvious or even nonconcealed" or that the plaintiff knew or had reason to know of the defect. The defendant moved for a summary judgment, alleging first that the plaintiff was a social guest and, second, that the twin defenses of assumption of risk and contributory negligence barred the action. The trial court granted the motion. Reversed.]

Δ arg.

PETERS, J. . . . Section 1714 of the Civil Code provides: "Every one is responsible, not only for the result of his willful acts, but also for an injury occasioned to another by his want of ordinary care or skill in the management of his property or person, except so far as the latter has, willfully or by want of ordinary care, brought the injury upon himself. . . ." This code section, which has been unchanged in our law since 1872, states a civil law and not a common law principle.

Nevertheless, some common law judges and commentators have urged that the principle embodied in this code section serves as the foundation of our negligence law. Thus in a concurring opinion, Brett, M.R., in Heaven v. Pender (1883) 11 Q.B.D. 503, 509, states: "whenever one person is by circumstances placed in such a position with regard to another that every one of ordinary sense who did think would at once recognise that if he did not use ordinary care and skill in his own conduct with regard to those circumstances he would cause danger of injury to the person or property of the other, a duty arises to use ordinary care and skill to avoid such danger."

general duty

Although it is true that some exceptions have been made to the general principle that a person is liable for injuries caused by his failure to exercise reasonable care in the circumstances, it is clear that in the absence of statutory provision declaring an exception to the fundamental principle enunciated by section 1714 of the Civil Code, no such exception should be made unless clearly supported by public policy.

A departure from this fundamental principle involves the balancing of a number of considerations; the major ones are the foreseeability of harm to the plaintiff, the degree of certainty that the plaintiff suffered injury, the closeness of the connection between the defendant's conduct and the injury suffered, the moral blame attached to the defendant's conduct, the policy of preventing future harm, the extent of the burden to the defendant and consequences to the community of imposing a duty to exercise care with resulting liability for breach, and the availability, cost, and prevalence of insurance for the risk involved.

Factors

One of the areas where this court and other courts have departed from the fundamental concept that a man is liable for injuries caused by his carelessness is with regard to the liability of a possessor of land for injuries to persons who have entered upon that land. It has been suggested that the special rules regarding liability of the possessor of land are due to historical considerations stemming from the high place which land has traditionally held in English and American thought, the dominance and prestige of the landowning class in England during the formative period of the rules governing the possessor's liability, and the heritage of feudalism.

The departure from the fundamental rule of liability for negligence has been accomplished by classifying the plaintiff either as a trespasser, licensee, or invitee and then adopting special rules as to the duty owed by the possessor to each of the classifications. Generally speaking a trespasser is a person who enters or remains upon land of another without a privilege to do so; a licensee is a person like a social guest who is not an invitee and who is privileged to enter or remain upon land by virtue of the possessor's consent, and an invitee is a business visitor who is invited or permitted to enter or remain on the land for a purpose directly or indirectly connected with business dealings between them.

General Rule

Although the invitor owes the invitee a duty to exercise ordinary care to avoid injuring him, . . . the general rule is that a trespasser and licensee or social guest are obliged to take the premises as they find them insofar as any alleged defective condition thereon may exist, and that the possessor of the land owes them only the duty of refraining from wanton or willful injury. The ordinary justification for the general rule severely restricting the occupier's liability to social guests is based on the theory that the guest should not expect special precautions to be made on his account and that if the host does not inspect and maintain his property the guest should not expect this to be done on his account.

Justification

Exception 1 "active operation"

An increasing regard for human safety has led to a retreat from this position, and an exception to the general rule limiting liability has been made as to active operations where an obligation to exercise reasonable care for the protection of the licensee has been imposed on the occupier of land. . . . In an apparent attempt to avoid the general rule limiting liability, courts have broadly defined active operations, sometimes giving the term a strained construction in cases involving dangers known to the occupier.

Thus in Hansen v. Richey, 46 Cal. Rptr. 909 [1965], an action for wrongful death of a drowned youth, the court held that liability could be predicated not upon the maintenance of a dangerous swimming pool but upon negligence "in the active conduct of a party for a large number of youthful guests in the light of knowledge of the dangerous pool." . . .

Exception 2 "Concealed trap"

Another exception to the general rule limiting liability has been recognized for cases where the occupier is aware of the dangerous condition, the condition amounts to a concealed trap, and the guest is unaware of the trap. In none of these cases, however, did the court impose liability on the basis of a concealed trap; in some liability was found on another theory, and in others the court concluded that there was no trap. A trap has been defined as a "concealed" danger, a danger with a deceptive appearance of safety. It has also been defined as something akin to a spring gun or steel trap. . . . [I]t is pointed out that the lack of definiteness in the application of the term "trap" to any other situation makes its use argumentative and unsatisfactory.

The cases dealing with the active negligence and the trap exceptions are indicative of the subtleties and confusion which have resulted from application of the common law principles governing the liability of the possessor of land. Similar confusion and complexity exist as to the definitions of trespasser, licensee, and invitee.

In refusing to adopt the rules relating to the liability of a possessor of land for the law of admiralty, the United States Supreme Court stated: "The distinctions which the common law draws between licensee and invitee were inherited from a culture deeply rooted to the land, a culture which traced many of its standards to a heritage of feudalism. In an effort to do justice in an industrialized urban society, with its complex economic and individual relationships, modern common-law courts have found it necessary to formulate increasingly subtle verbal refinements, to create subclassifications among traditional common-law categories, and to delineate fine gradations in the standards of care which the landowner owes to each. Yet even within a single jurisdiction, the classifications and subclassifications bred by the common law have produced confusion and conflict. As new distinctions have been spawned, older ones have become obscured. Through this semantic morass the common law has moved, unevenly and with hesitation, towards 'imposing on owners and occupiers a single duty of reasonable care in all circumstances.'" (Footnotes omitted.) (Kermarec v. Compagnie Generale, 358 U.S. 625, 630-631 (1959)....

There is another fundamental objection to the approach to the question of the possessor's liability on the basis of the common law distinctions based upon the status of the injured party as a trespasser, licensee, or invitee. Complexity can be borne and confusion remedied where the underlying principles governing liability are based upon proper considerations. Whatever may have been the historical justifications for the common law distinctions, it is clear that those distinctions are not justified in the light of our modern society and that the complexity and confusion which has arisen is not due to difficulty in applying the original common law rules—they are all too easy to apply in their original formulation—but is due to the attempts to apply just rules in our modern society within the ancient terminology.

Without attempting to labor all of the rules relating to the possessor's liability, it is apparent that the classifications of trespasser, licensee, and invitee, the immunities from liability predicated upon those classifications, and the exceptions to those immunities, often do not reflect the major factors which should determine whether immunity should be conferred upon the possessor of land. Some of those factors, including the closeness of the connection between the injury and the defendant's conduct, the moral blame attached to the defendant's conduct, the policy of preventing future harm, and the prevalence and availability of insurance, bear little, if any, relationship to the classifications of trespasser, licensee, and invitee and the existing rules conferring immunity.

Although in general there may be a relationship between the remaining factors and the classifications of trespasser, licensee, and invitee, there are many cases in which no such relationship may exist. Thus, although the foreseeability of harm to an invitee would ordinarily seem greater than the foreseeability of harm to a trespasser, in a particular case the opposite may be true. The same may be said of the issue of certainty of injury. The burden to the defendant and consequences to the community of imposing a duty to exercise care with resulting liability for breach may often be greater with respect to trespassers than with respect to invitees, but it by no means follows that this is true in every case. In many situations, the burden will be the same, i.e., the conduct necessary upon the defendant's part to meet the burden of exercising due care as to invitees will also meet his burden with respect to licensees and trespassers. The last of the major factors, the cost of insurance, will, of course, vary depending upon the rules of liability adopted, but there is no persuasive evidence that applying ordinary principles of negligence law to the land occupier's liability will materially reduce the prevalence of insurance due to increased cost or even substantially increase the cost.

Considerations such as these have led some courts in particular situations to reject the rigid common law classifications and to approach the issue of the duty of the occupier on the basis of ordinary principles of negligence. (E.g., Gould v. DeBeve, 330 F.2d 826, 829-830 (1964).) And the common law distinctions after thorough study have been repudiated by the jurisdiction of their birth. (Occupiers' Liability Act, 1957, 5 and 6 Eliz. 2, ch. 31.)

A man's life or limb does not become less worthy of protection by the law nor a loss less worthy of compensation under the law because he has come upon the land of another without permission or with permission but without a business purpose. Reasonable people do not ordinarily vary their conduct depending upon such matters, and to focus upon the status of the injured party as a trespasser, licensee, or invitee in order to determine the question whether the landowner has a duty of care, is contrary to our modern social mores and humanitarian values. The common law rules obscure rather than illuminate the proper considerations which should govern determination of the question of duty. . . .

We decline to follow and perpetuate such rigid classifications. The proper test to be applied to the liability of the possessor of land in accordance with section 1714 of the Civil Code is whether in the management of his property he has acted as a reasonable man in view of the probability of injury to others, and, although the plaintiff's status as a trespasser, licensee, or invitee may in the light of the facts giving rise to such status have some bearing on the question of liability, the status is not determinative.

Once the ancient concepts as to the liability of the occupier of land are stripped away, the status of the plaintiff relegated to its proper place in determining such liability, and ordinary principles of negligence applied, the result in the instant case presents no substantial difficulties. As we have seen, when we view the matters presented on the motion for summary judgment as we must, we must assume defendant Miss Christian was aware that the faucet handle was defective and dangerous, that the defect was not obvious, and that plaintiff was about to come in contact with the defective condition, and under the undisputed facts she neither remedied the condition nor warned plaintiff of it. Where the occupier of land is aware of a concealed condition involving in the absence of precautions an unreasonable risk of harm to those coming in contact with it and is aware that a person on the premises is about to come in contact with it, the trier of fact can reasonably conclude that a failure to warn or to repair the condition constitutes negligence. Whether or not a guest has a right to expect that his host will remedy dangerous conditions on his account, he should reasonably be entitled to rely upon a warning of the dangerous condition so that he, like the host, will be in a position to take special precautions when he comes in contact with it. . . .

The judgment is reversed.

TRAYNOR, C.J., and TOBRINER, MOSK, and SULLIVAN, JJ., concur.

BURKE, J., dissenting. I dissent. In determining the liability of the occupier or owner of land for injuries, the distinctions between trespassers, licensees and invitees have been developed and applied by the courts over a period of many years. They supply a reasonable and workable approach to the problems involved, and one which provides the degree of stability and predictability so highly prized in the law. The unfortunate alternative, it appears to me, is the route taken by the majority in their opinion in this case that such issues are to be decided on a case by case basis under the application of the basic law of negligence, bereft of the guiding principles and precedent which the law has heretofore attached by a virtue of the relationship of the parties to one another.

Liability for negligence turns upon whether a duty of care is owed, and if so, the extent thereof. Who can doubt that the corner grocery, the large department store, or the financial institution owes a greater duty of care to one whom it has invited to enter its premises as a prospective customer of its wares or services than it owes to a trespasser seeking to enter after the close of business hours and for a nonbusiness or even an antagonistic purpose? I do not think it unreasonable or unfair that a social guest (classified by the law as a licensee, as was plaintiff here) should be obliged to take the premises in the same condition as his host finds them or permits them to be. Surely a homeowner should not be obliged to hover over his guests with warnings of possible dangers to be found in the condition of the home (e.g., waxed floors, slipping rugs, toys in unexpected places, etc., etc.). Yet today's decision appears to open the door to potentially unlimited liability despite the purpose and circumstances motivating the plaintiff in entering the premises of another, and despite the caveat of the majority that the status of the parties may "have some bearing on the question of liability . . . ," whatever the future may show that language to mean.

In my view, it is not a proper function of this court to overturn the learning, wisdom and experience of the past in this field. Sweeping modifications of tort liability law fall more suitably within the domain of the Legislature, before which all affected interests can be heard and which can enact statutes providing uniform standards and guidelines for the future.

I would affirm the judgment for defendant.

NOTES

1. Response to Rowland v. Christian. Is it necessary to abolish the distinction between licensees and invitees in order to deny the defendant's motion for summary judgment? Should the court have granted summary judgment to the plaintiff on the question of liability? Should Burke's, J., decision properly have been a concurrence? Note that prior to *Rowland*, California had not accepted the standard view stated in RST §342 that the possessor of real property was under a duty to warn a licensee of concealed dangerous conditions. See, e.g., Fisher v. General Petroleum Corp., 267 P.2d 841 (Cal. App. 1954); Hansen v. Richey, 46 Cal. Rptr. 909 (Ct. App. 1965). On remand in *Rowland*, will the plaintiff be able to prevail if the defendant can show that the defect was patent? Will the defendant escape liability if the defect was concealed? Does it make a difference if Rowland's apartment was a pigsty when she moved in so that the crack in the faucet was concealed under grime? For a discussion of the origins and influence of the case, see Rabin, *Rowland v. Christian*: Hallmark of an Expansionary Era, *in* Torts Stories 73 (Rabin & Sugarman eds., 2003). For an argument that, in recent years, "[t]he categorical approach to questions of duties owed to entrants onto real property is quietly being resurrected" by California courts, see Esper & Keating, Abusing "Duty," 79 S. Cal. L. Rev. 265, 322 (2006).

Rowland has received a mixed response elsewhere. In Mallet v. Pickens, 522 S.E.2d 436 (W. Va. 1999), West Virginia abandoned the invitee/licensee distinction, while preserving the traditional common law rules for trespassers. It summarized the current state of authority as follows:

> Broad generalizations about the state of premises liability law in other jurisdictions are always subject to caveats and limitations. Several states have special rules for invited social guests; others limit landowner liability via recreational use statutes, or employ a distinction between "active" and "passive" negligence. Having said that, our research reveals that at least 25 jurisdictions have abolished or largely abandoned the licensee/invitee distinction. Among these 25 jurisdictions that have broken with past tradition, at least 17 have eliminated or fundamentally altered the distinction. Another eight of the 25 have eliminated even the trespasser distinction. And, of those retaining the old scheme, judges in at least five of those states have authored vigorous dissents or concurrences arguing for change.

The courts that have defended the older distinctions have tended to do so without an elaborate statement of reasons. Thus, in Gladon v. Greater Cleveland Regional Transit Authority, 662 N.E.2d 287 (Ohio 1996), the court noted that it was "not inclined to reject" the classic distinctions. It held that a railroad passenger who exceeded the scope of his invitation by entering areas near the track lost his status as an invitee, and was properly treated as either a licensee or trespasser. Hylton, Tort Duties of Landowners: A Positive Theory, 44 Wake Forest L. Rev. 1049 (2009), takes a stab at providing an economic justification for the common law categories. Drawing upon traditional assumption-of-risk theory, he argues that "[l]icensees, typically social guests, are likely to know more about the landowner than would the typical invitee," and are thus able to foresee and protect against possible dangers.

Critics of the established order have been more vocal. Thus, in Koenig v. Koenig, 766 N.W.2d 635, 643-645 (Iowa 2009), the court wrote:

> The primary advantage of abolishing the invitee-licensee distinction is to avoid confusion. . . . [The cases are] replete with examples of the difficulties appellate courts have experienced in attempting to fit modern human interaction into rigid categories developed three centuries ago. Such confusion is likely to only increase in the future. . . . As a result, retention of the common-law system has not fulfilled its goal of predictability, but rather has "produced confusion and conflict." . . .

The fungible and unpredictable nature of the classifications makes it impossible for landowners to conform their behavior to current community standards. . . . Contrary to courts that have upheld the trichotomy, there is nothing to fear about jury involvement. . . . [B]oth logic and almost forty years of practice suggest that there is no reason to question a jury's ability to perform in the area of premises liability as opposed to any other area of tort law. . . . Finally, abandonment of this common-law distinction recognizes a higher valuation of public safety over property rights.

2. Duties to trespassers after Rowland v. Christian.   As noted above, *Rowland* has met with greater resistance on its extension of the ordinary duty of care to trespassers. Thus the Minnesota Supreme Court, in Peterson v. Balach, 199 N.W.2d 639, 642 (Minn. 1972), observed:

[T]he considerations governing a landowner's or occupant's liability to trespassers may be fundamentally different from his duty to those whom he has expressly or by implication invited onto his property. Burglars are trespassers; vandals are trespassers. We have criminal statutes governing trespassers. Minn. St. 609.605. Sweeping away all distinction between trespassers and social guests and business invitees is a drastic step to take because there may be, and often is, good reason to distinguish between a trespasser and a social guest. There is little or no reason to distinguish between a social guest and a business invitee.

The Massachusetts Supreme Judicial Court, however, cast its lot with *Rowland* in Pridgen v. Boston Housing Authority, 308 N.E.2d 467, 476-477 (Mass. 1974). The plaintiff, an 11-year-old boy, lifted an escape hatch in the ceiling of an elevator and climbed into the elevator shaft. He slipped off the elevator roof and became trapped. His mother, having learned of her son's predicament, asked one of the defendant's servants to turn off "the lights" to keep her son from being injured, but he failed to shut down the power in time to prevent the boy's legs from being crushed by the moving elevator. The court, much troubled by the influence of the Good Samaritan doctrine on the common law, observed:

In the context of the relationship between an owner or occupier (owner) of the property and a trapped, imperiled and helpless trespasser thereon, we reject any rule which would exempt the owner from liability if he knowingly refrains from taking reasonable action which he is in a position to take and which would prevent injury or further injury to the trespasser. It should not be, it cannot be, and surely it is not now the law of this Commonwealth that the owner in such a situation is rewarded with immunity from liability as long as he ignores the plight of the trapped trespasser and takes no affirmative action to help him. Thus, in the case before us it is unthinkable to have a rule which would hold the authority liable if one of its employees, acting in the course of his employment, pushed the "go" button on the elevator although he knew Joseph Pridgen was trapped in the elevator shaft, but would not hold it liable if, being reasonably able to do so, the employee knowingly failed or refused to turn off the switch to the electrical power for the same elevator.

How would *Pridgen* be decided under Addie v. Dumbreck, or under Excelsior Wire Rope Ltd. v. Callan?

Other states have flip-flopped on the question. Thus, in Mariorenzi v. Joseph DiPonte, Inc., 333 A.2d 127, 133 n.4 (R.I. 1975), the court stressed the malleable nature of the categories to abolish the special rules toward trespassers:

> A canvasser who comes on your premises without your consent is a trespasser. Once he has your consent, he is a licensee. Not until you do business with him is he an invitee. Even when you have done business with him, it seems rather strange that your duty towards him should be different when he comes up to your door from what it is when he goes away. Does he change his colour in the middle of the conversation? What is the position when you discuss business with him and it comes to nothing? No confident answer can be given to these questions. Such is the morass into which the law has floundered in trying to distinguish between licensees and invitees.

Twenty years later, in Tantimonico v. Allendale Mutual Insurance Co., 637 A.2d 1056, 1061 (R.I. 1994), the boundary questions did not seem as pressing, and the court backed off its earlier position with respect to trespassers. It denied recovery to two trespassing motorcyclists who apparently collided head-on while riding in opposite directions on defendant's circular trail. "It is almost impossible to entertain the notion that anyone other than plaintiffs themselves is responsible for their injuries. To hold the property owner liable for injuries brought about by a plaintiff's negligent behavior would be patently ludicrous." *Tantimonico* adopts the position toward flagrant trespassers taken in RTT:LPEH §52, comment *a*.

3. Statutory abolition of the invitee/licensee distinction. In some cases, the abolition of the categories is done by statute. The first move in this direction took place in England with the Occupiers' Liability Act, 1957 (5 & 6 Eliz. II, c. 31), which abolished the distinction between invitees and licensees but left untouched the rules governing the occupier's liability to trespassers. Likewise Illinois (740 Ill. Comp. Stat. Ann. 130/2 (West 2015)) abolishes the distinction between invitees and licensees and toughens up the standard of liability, by noting that "[t]he duty of reasonable care under the circumstances which an owner or occupier of land owes to such entrants does not include any of the following: a duty to warn of or otherwise take reasonable steps to protect such entrants from conditions on the premises that are known to the entrant, are open and obvious, or can reasonably be expected to be discovered by the entrant; a duty to warn of latent defects or dangers or defects or dangers unknown to the owner or occupier of the premises; or a duty to protect such entrants from their own misuse of the premises or anything affixed to or located on the premises."

In Ward v. K-Mart Corp., 554 N.E.2d 223, 230-231, 233 (Ill. 1990), the plaintiff sustained injuries to his face and partial loss of vision when he walked into a concrete post located about 19 inches from the rear wall of the K-Mart store. On entering the store, plaintiff had noticed the post, but he had forgotten about it momentarily while leaving the store carrying a large bathroom mirror that obscured his view. The trial judge overruled a jury verdict for the plaintiff for

$68,000, but the Illinois Supreme Court reinstated the verdict. Ryan, J., refused to hold that the defendant had automatically discharged its duty of care for dangerous conditions that are open and obvious, saying:

> [I]n the case at bar it was reasonably foreseeable that a customer would collide with the post while exiting defendant's store carrying merchandise which could obscure view of the post. . . . It should be remembered that the post was located immediately outside the entrance to the Home Center section of defendant's store. Defendant had every reason to expect that customers would carry large, bulky items through that door, particularly where, as here, the large overhead door was closed. The burden on the defendant of protecting against this danger would be slight. A simple warning or a relocation of the post may have sufficed. It is also relevant that there were no windows or transparent panels on the customer entrance doors to permit viewing of the posts from the interior of the store.

Could this defect be treated as latent to the plaintiff even if patent to the world?

4. Recreational land statutes. Many states have also passed statutes that relax the liability of owners for recreational or rural lands. N.J. Stat. Ann. §§2A:42A-3 et seq. (West 2011), provides:

> a. An owner, lessee or occupant of premises, whether or not posted . . . and whether or not improved or maintained in a natural condition, or used as part of a commercial enterprise, owes no duty to keep the premises safe for entry or use by others for sport and recreational activities, or to give warning of any hazardous condition of the land or in connection with the use of any structure or by reason of any activity on such premises to persons entering for such purposes;
>
> b. An owner, lessee or occupant of premises who gives permission to another to enter upon such premises for a sport or recreational activity or purpose does not thereby (1) extend any assurance that the premises are safe for such purpose, or (2) constitute the person to whom permission is granted an invitee to whom a duty of care is owed, or (3) assume responsibility for or incur liability for any injury to person or property caused by any act of persons to whom the permission is granted.

"Sport and recreational activities" as statutory terms are to "be liberally construed to serve as an inducement to the owners, lessees and occupants of property, that might otherwise be reluctant to do so for fear of liability, to permit persons to come onto their property for sport and recreational activities." *Id.* §2A:42A-5.1. This statute did not, however, protect a landowner against suit by a Good Samaritan who drowned while trying to rescue two 15-year-old boys who had fallen through thin ice on the defendant's reservoir on the first day of the skating season because the rescuer was not engaged in recreational activities. Harrison v. Middlesex Water Co., 403 A.2d 910, 914 (N.J. 1979).

See generally Carroll et al., Recreational User Statutes and Landowner Immunity: A Comparison Study of State Legislation, 17 J. Legal Aspects Sport 163 (2007).

5. Duties to strangers after Rowland v. Christian. Rowland has also impacted the liability of owners and occupiers to persons who have not entered their land.

As in attractive nuisance cases, a critical distinction is between natural and artificial conditions upon the land. Artificial conditions raise no special problems because they satisfy the normal "act" requirement of both negligence and strict liability theories. Natural conditions are more problematic because now the "act" requirement is not (at least obviously) satisfied. Nor can any stranger rely upon affirmative duties born of the informal consensual arrangements with invitees and licensees. In consequence, the duty issue becomes a stumbling block in the path of the stranger's recovery.

Most American cases refuse to impose liability for natural conditions, except harm caused by falling trees. See, e.g., Taylor v. Olsen, 578 P.2d 779 (Or. 1978). See also Noel, Nuisances from Land in Its Natural Condition, 56 Harv. L. Rev. 772, 796-797 (1943), in which the author observed: "Where a planted tree has become dangerous to persons on the highway or on adjoining land, and causes harm, the fault lies not in the planting of the tree but in permitting it to remain after it has become unsafe."

The judicial acceptance of a no-liability regime for natural conditions has decreased in recent years, at least in urban settings. In Sprecher v. Adamson Co., 636 P.2d 1121, 1125, 1126 (Cal. 1981), the court was prepared to impose an affirmative duty on one Malibu landowner to prevent a mudslide after heavy rains that would damage the home of his downhill neighbor. Bird, C.J., showed her obvious hostility to the misfeasance-nonfeasance distinction at common law and placed heavy reliance upon *Rowland,* noting the "inherent injustice . . . in allowing a landowner may escape all liability for serious damage to his neighbors [or those using a public highway], merely by allowing nature to take its course. . . . Whatever the rule may once have been, it is now clear that a duty to exercise due care can arise out of possession alone." Richardson, J., concurred, finding it "exceedingly difficult to imagine what respondents *reasonably* could have done to prevent or reduce the damage caused by the natural condition here present." *Id.* at 1136. *Sprecher* was relied on in Contra Costa County v. Pinole Point Properties, LLC, 186 Cal. Rptr. 3d 109, 122 (Ct. App. 1 Dist. 2015), to impose liability on a landowner for failing to take affirmative action to prevent debris buildup in a drainage channel. "Although this latter situation is less common, liability can be based on an *omission* or *inaction* when the failure to act is an *unreasonable* use of the property." Is *Contra Costa* an example of the "compound act" in Newton v. Ellis, *supra* at 482?

Sprecher was relied on outside California in Whitt v. Silverman, 788 So. 2d 210 (Fla. 2001), when one pedestrian was killed and another injured when struck by a driver leaving the defendant's gas station. The driver's view of the highway was obscured by heavy foliage located exclusively on the defendant's property. The court refused to follow the so-called agrarian rule, whereby a landowner owes no duty of care to a stranger for harm caused by the natural condition of his land. The owners of ordinary businesses have specific knowledge of the "continuous flow of traffic entering and exiting the premises for the commercial benefit of the landowners," where their control over their own premises undercuts any claim "that it would have been unduly burdensome for the landowners to have maintained this foliage consistent with the safe egress and ingress of vehicles attracted to the business and persons affect thereby."

SECTION D.   GRATUITOUS UNDERTAKINGS

Coggs v. Bernard
92 Eng. Rep. 107 (K.B. 1703)

[The action was brought in assumpsit, Latin for "he has undertaken," which allowed for the recovery of damages for breach of a simple contract. The defendant had moved casks of brandy owned by the plaintiff from one cellar to another. Through the defendant's negligence, some of the casks were split open and great quantities of brandy were lost. The defendant sought to overturn the judgment in plaintiff's favor because plaintiff had not alleged that the defendant was a common porter or that he had received any reward or consideration. Notwithstanding, the plaintiff had judgment.]

GOULD, J. I think this is a good declaration [complaint]. The objection that has been made is, because there is not any consideration laid. But I think it is good either way, and that any man, that undertakes to carry goods, is liable to an action, be he a common carrier, or whatever he is, if through his neglect they are lost, or come to any damage: and if a praemium be laid to be given, then it is without question so. The reason of the action is, the particular trust reposed in the defendant, to which he has concurred by his assumption, and in the executing which he has miscarried by his neglect. But if a man undertakes to build a house, without any thing to be had for his pains, an action will not lie for non-performance, because it is nudum pactum. . . .

HOLT, C.J. . . .

[After his review of the six different types of bailments in Roman law, discussed *supra* at 143, he continues]: If it had appeared that the mischief happened by any person that met the cart in the way, the bailee had not been chargeable. As if a drunken man had come by in the streets, and had pierced the cask of brandy; in this case the defendant had not been answerable for it, because he was to have nothing for his pains. Then the bailee having undertaken to manage the goods and having managed them ill, and so by his neglect a damage had happened to the bailor, which is the case in question, what will you call this?

In Bracton, lib. 3,100, it is called *mandatum*. It is an obligation which arises *ex mandato*. It is what we call in English an acting commission. And if a man acts by his commission for another and in executing his commission behaves himself negligently, he is answerable. . . . [I]t is supported by good reason and authority. The reasons are, first, because in such a case, a neglect is a deceit to the bailor. For when he intrusts the bailee upon his undertaking to be careful, he has put a fraud upon the plaintiff by being negligent, his pretence of care being the persuasion that induced the plaintiff to trust him. And a breach of a trust undertaken voluntarily will be a ground for an action. . . .

But secondly it is objected, that there is no consideration to ground this promise upon, and therefore the undertaking is but *nudum pactum*. But to this I answer, that the owner's trusting him with the goods is a sufficient consideration to oblige him to a careful management. Indeed if the agreement had been executory, to carry these brandies from the one place to the other such a day, the defendant had not been bound to carry them. But this is a different case, for *assumpsit* does not only signify a future agreement, but in such a case as this, it signifies an actual entry upon the thing, and taking the trust upon himself. And if a man will do that, and miscarries in the performance of his trust, an action will lie against him for that, though no body could have compelled him to do the thing.

NOTES

1. Contract without consideration.   *Coggs*, also discussed *supra* at 144, Note 3, on the issue of degrees of negligence, bears as well on the question whether gratuitous promises can be a source of affirmative duties. Holt, C.J., attacks this point in two ways. He first claims that the case has overtones of deceit and pretense, both of which seem to be unlikely on the facts on the case. He next claims that consideration can be "found" in this essentially gratuitous transaction, given that the general formula requires a benefit to the promisor or a detriment to the promise. Note too that civil law treats these cases as contract cases without invoking the idea of consideration. Thus the plaintiff may recover on contractual grounds for the improper performance of the duty even though the promisor can withdraw from his engagement if he changes his mind before performance was due. The doctrine of consideration functions in the civil law mainly as the test for enforceability of fully executory agreements, not as the test of whether the parties formed any contract at all.

The interaction between tort and contract is illustrated again by the famous early case of Thorne v. Deas, 4 Johns. 84 (N.Y. Sup. Ct. 1809). The plaintiff was captain of a ship and, as he was about to leave on a voyage, he suggested to his co-owner, the defendant, that they insure the ship before leaving. Defendant told plaintiff to go ahead and sail—that he would insure the ship on plaintiff's departure. Relying on defendant's promise, plaintiff left port. Defendant failed to insure the ship, which was subsequently wrecked. On his return home, plaintiff sued defendant for his loss. The court denied recovery. Kent, C.J., following the rule announced by Gould, J., *supra*, noted that this was "an action on the case, for a *non-feasance*" and that it could not lie because of "the want of a consideration for the promise," even though the plaintiff's case was good under Roman contract law under the contract of mandate—essentially a gratuitous agency.

Because the contract option was foreclosed by the English consideration rules, the plaintiff tried to frame his action in tort. Kent refused to first deny recovery for breach of a promise unsupported by consideration, only to turn around and allow recovery by calling defendant's conduct a tort. However, plaintiff could recover, according to Kent, by showing that defendant had engaged in misfeasance—i.e., he had actually started to perform and had done so negligently. Would the actions (incorrectly filling out papers) of the defendant have been tortious without reference to the former promise? If not, why does the ineffective promise make these ministerial mishaps actionable? What if defendant fails to finish the job he started, as by failing to supply the insurer with a certificate of title?

2. *Promissory estoppel.*   Section 90 of the Restatement (Second) of Contracts provides:

§90. PROMISE REASONABLY INDUCING ACTION OR FORBEARANCE

(1) A promise which the promisor should reasonably expect to induce action or forbearance on the part of the promisee or a third person and which does induce such action or forbearance is binding if injustice can be avoided only by enforcement of the promise. The remedy granted for breach may be limited as justice requires.

Does this section help the plaintiff in *Coggs* or *Thorne*? On section 90 and this area in general, see Seavey, Reliance upon Gratuitous Promises or Other Conduct, 64 Harv. L. Rev. 913, 926-927 (1951), who observed: "The colloquial explanation for the rule of the section is that it creates 'promissory estoppel.' Estoppel is basically a tort doctrine and the rationale of the section is that justice requires the defendant to pay for the harm caused by foreseeable reliance upon the performance of his promise. The wrong is not primarily in depriving the plaintiff of the promised reward but in causing the plaintiff to change position to his detriment. . . . In a case like Thorne v. Deas, however, the continuing representation becomes fraudulent when the promisor decides not to perform and does not inform the plaintiff, knowing that he still relies upon performance." What if the defendant simply forgot his promise?

How does reliance on voluntary undertakings work for promises made to the public at large?

Erie Railroad Co. v. Stewart
40 F.2d 855 (6th Cir. 1930)

HICKENLOOPER, C.J. Stewart, plaintiff below, was a passenger in an automobile truck, sitting on the front seat to the right of the driver, a fellow employee of the East Ohio Gas Company. He recovered a judgment in the District Court for injuries received when the truck was struck by one of the defendant's trains at the 123d Street crossing in the city of Cleveland. Defendant maintained a watchman at this crossing, which was

An Erie Railroad "Berkshire" locomotive
Source: Wikimedia Commons

admittedly heavily traveled, but the watchman was either within the shanty or just outside of it as the train approached, and he gave no warning until too late to avoid the accident. . . .

The second contention of appellant presents the question whether the court erred in charging the jury that the absence of the watchman, where one had been maintained by the defendant company at a highway crossing over a long period of time to the knowledge of the plaintiff, would constitute negligence as a matter of law. In the present case it is conceded that the employment of the watchman by the defendant was voluntary upon its part, there being no statute or ordinance requiring the same, and that plaintiff had knowledge of this practice and relied upon the absence of the watchman as an assurance of safety and implied invitation to cross. We are not now concerned with the extent of the duty owing to one who had no notice of the prior practice, nor, in this aspect of the case, with the question of contributory negligence and the extent to which the plaintiff was relieved from the obligation of vigilance by the absence of the watchman. The question is simply whether there was any positive duty owing to the plaintiff in respect to the maintenance of such watchman, and whether a breach of such duty is so conclusively shown as to justify a peremptory charge of negligence. The question whether such negligence was the proximate cause of the injury was properly submitted to the jury.

Where the employment of a watchman or other precaution is required by statute, existence of an absolute duty to the plaintiff is conclusively shown, and failure to observe the statutory requirement is negligence per se. . . . Conversely, where there is no duty prescribed by statute or ordinance, it is usually a question for the jury whether the circumstances made the employment of a watchman necessary in the exercise of due care. Where the voluntary employment of a watchman was unknown to the traveler upon the highway, the mere absence of such watchman could probably not be considered as negligence toward him as a matter of law, for in such case there is neither an established duty positively owing to such traveler as a member of the general public, nor had he been led into reliance upon the custom. The question would remain simply whether the circumstances demanded such employment. But where the practice is known to the traveler upon the highway, and such traveler has been educated into reliance upon it, some positive duty must rest upon the railway with reference thereto. The elements of invitation and assurance of safety exist in this connection no less than in connection with contributory negligence. The company has established for itself a standard of due care while operating its trains across the highway, and, having led the traveler into reliance upon such standard, it should not be permitted thereafter to say that no duty required, arose from or attached to these precautions.

This duty has been recognized as not only actual and positive, but as absolute, in the sense that the practice may not be discontinued without exercising reasonable care to give warning of such discontinuance, although the company may thereafter do all that would otherwise be reasonably necessary. Conceding for the purposes of this opinion that, in cases where a watchman is voluntarily employed by the railway in an abundance of precaution, the duty is not absolute, in the same sense as where it is imposed by statute, still, if there be some duty, it cannot be less than that the company must use reasonable care to see that reliance by members of the educated public upon its representation of safety is not converted into a trap. Responsibility for injury will arise if the service be negligently performed or abandoned without other notice of that fact. . . .

So, in the present case, the evidence conclusively establishes the voluntary employment of a watchman, knowledge of this fact and reliance upon it by the plaintiff, a duty, therefore, that the company, through the watchman, will exercise reasonable care in warning such travelers as plaintiff, the presence of the watchman thereabouts, and no explanation of the failure to warn. Therefore, even though the duty be considered as qualified, rather than absolute, a prima facie case was established by plaintiff, requiring the defendant to go forward with evidence to rebut the presumption of negligence thus raised, or else suffer a verdict against it on this point. . . . No such evidence was introduced by defendant. No other inference than that of negligence could therefore be drawn from the evidence. If, perhaps, the rule was stated more broadly than this in the charge, the error, if any, was harmless as applied to the present case. . . .

[Affirmed.]

TUTTLE, J. I concur in the result reached by the opinion of the majority of the court. I cannot, however, concur in the views, expressed in that opinion, which would make the actionable negligence of the defendant dependent upon the knowledge of the plaintiff, previous to his injury, of the custom of the defendant in maintaining a watchman at the crossing where such injury occurred. It is settled law that a railroad company operating trains at high speed across a public highway owes to travelers properly using such highway the duty to exercise reasonable care to give such warning of approaching trains as may be reasonably required by the particular circumstances. It is equally well settled that the standard of duty thus owed to the public, at least where not otherwise prescribed by statutory law, consists of that care and prudence which an ordinarily prudent person would exercise under the same circumstances. I am satisfied that where, as here, a railroad company has established a custom, known to the general public, of maintaining a watchman at a public crossing with instructions to warn the traveling public of the approach of trains, such railroad company, in the exercise of that reasonable care which it owes to the public, should expect, and is bound to expect, that any member of the traveling public approaching such crossing along the public highway is likely to have knowledge of and to rely upon the giving of such warning. Such knowledge, with the consequent reliance, may be acquired by a traveler at any time, perhaps only a moment before going upon the crossing, and this also the railroad company is bound to anticipate. Having, in effect, given notice to the public traveling this highway that it would warn them of trains at this crossing, I think that it was bound to assume (at least in the absence of knowledge to the contrary) that every member of such public would receive, and rely on, such notice. Under such circumstances such a railroad company, in my opinion, owes to every traveler so approaching this crossing a duty to give such a warning, if reasonably possible, and a reasonably prudent railroad company would not fail, without sufficient cause, to perform that duty. It follows that the unexplained failure, as in the present case, of the defendant to give this customary warning to the plaintiff, a traveler on the highway approaching this crossing, indicates, as a matter of law, actionable negligence for which it is liable. While undoubtedly lack of reliance by plaintiff upon the custom of the defendant has an important bearing and effect upon the question whether the plaintiff was guilty of contributory negligence, it seems to me clear that the knowledge or lack of knowledge of the plaintiff, unknown to the defendant, concerning such customs cannot affect the nature or extent of the duty owed to the plaintiff by the defendant or the performance of such duty. As therefore the conclusions expressed in the opinion of a majority of the court are, to the extent which I have thus indicated, not in accord with my own views in this connection, I have felt it my duty to briefly state such views in this separate concurring opinion.

NOTES

1. The scope of voluntary undertakings. What exactly is the point of disagreement between Judges Hickenlooper and Tuttle? If reliance is required in cases where promises or representations are made to a single person, should any member of the public who is injured be required to show that she was aware of the prior practice in order to make good her claim for "negative" reliance?

The limits of *Erie Railroad* are evident in Martin v. Twin Falls School District #411, 59 P.3d 317 (Idaho 2002). There the plaintiff children were struck by a pick-up truck driven by one Ryan Canoy as they were walking through a designated school crossing, properly equipped with signs and flashing lights, located about two blocks from their school. The plaintiffs claimed that the school district had a duty to supply crossing guards at this intersection because it had provided crossing guards at other intersections. Eismann, J., rejected that contention, noting: "By providing crossing guards at certain intersections or pedestrian crossings, the school district did not thereby assume the duty to provide guards at any other intersections or crossings." This decision is approved in the Third Restatement, which notes: "The scope of an undertaking can be determined only from the facts and circumstances of the case. When reasonable minds can differ about whether the risk or negligence was within the scope of the undertaking, it is a question of fact for the factfinder." RTT:LPEH §42, comment *g*.

The reluctance to recognize special relationships beyond situations in which the defendant has direct charge of the plaintiff is evident in Beers v. Corporation of President of Church of Jesus Christ of Latter-Day Saints [COP], 316 P.3d 92, 100-101 (Idaho 2013). Heidi Beers, a 13-year-old girl, who had attended a church retreat without her parents, was severely injured when she jumped off a bridge. At that time she was with several adults who had marked out a place safe for jumping. Heidi jumped in at an uninspected location. In affirming a grant of summary judgment for defendants below, Horton, J., first denied that there was a special relationship between the plaintiff and COP that generated a duty of protection under RST §315(b):

Here, the COP's only affirmative actions were extending an open invitation to all Ward members to attend a campout and planning two meals and a devotional. These actions do not reflect the assumption of a duty by the Ward to supervise Heidi jumping from a bridge a mile away from the location of the Ward campout upon which she could reasonably rely.

Horton, J., further held that the individual church members who were at the bridge supervising their own children did not assume a duty to supervise Heidi.

2. Special precautions for rabies inspections. In Marsalis v. LaSalle, 94 So. 2d 120 (La. App. 1957), the plaintiff had been bitten or scratched by the defendant's cat in defendant's store. After the bite, the plaintiff asked the defendant to keep the cat "under observation" and "locked up" for two weeks until it could be determined whether or not it had rabies. The defendants, however, took no special precautions to keep the cat in. About four days later the cat escaped. It was found about one month later, free of any rabies symptom. In the interim, the plaintiff, on the advice of her neighbor, a neurologist, received rabies shots, to which she developed a severe allergic reaction. The shots would have been completely unnecessary if the cat had been properly held in. The court recognized (soundly?) that the plaintiff could not recover for the simple cat bite or scratch, but adopted the rule "that one who voluntarily undertakes to care for, or to afford relief or assistance to, an ill, injured, or helpless person is under a legal obligation to use reasonable care and prudence in what he does." It then explained:

> Perhaps the defendant, LaSalle, initially owed no duty whatever to Mrs. Marsalis, but when he once agreed to restrain and keep the cat under observation, he was bound to use reasonable care and prudence in doing so and to assume and exercise reasonable care and common humanity. It may be that Mrs. Marsalis had open to her some other course by which she could have had the cat incarcerated and examined in order to determine if it was rabid, but she unquestionably and in good faith relied upon defendant to carry out the agreement which he voluntarily made, thus foregoing such other possible available protection. It was of extreme importance to know if the cat had rabies so she could regulate her course of conduct with reference to the injury. . . .

In light of the decision in *Montgomery* and RTT:LPEH §39, *supra* at 481, is the voluntary undertaking necessary to impose the duty of care on the LaSalles? What result in *Marsalis* if the defendant's cat had in fact been rabid?

The Third Restatement's principle of duty based on undertaking is frequently invoked today in suits against the government for breach of its various regulatory duties. In the leading case of Indian Towing v. United States, 350 U.S. 61, 64-65 (1955), the U.S. Coast Guard operated a lighthouse whose light was negligently allowed to go out, whereupon the plaintiff's barge ran aground. The plaintiff brought suit under the Federal Tort Claims Act, which imposes upon the government the duties of a private party acting under like circumstances. Frankfurter, J., allowed the cause of action, noting that "it is hornbook tort law that one who undertakes to warn the public of danger and thereby induces reliance must perform his 'good Samaritan' task in a careful manner."

> ### Restatement (Third) of Torts: Liability for Physical and Emotional Harm
>
> #### §42. DUTY BASED ON UNDERTAKING
>
> An actor who undertakes to render services to another that the actor knows or should know reduce the risk of physical harm to the other has a duty of reasonable care to the other in conducting the undertaking if:
>
> (a) the failure to exercise such care increases the risk of harm beyond that which existed without the undertaking, or
>
> (b) the person to whom the services are rendered or another relies on the actor's exercising reasonable care in the undertaking.

Moch Co. v. Rensselaer Water Co.
159 N.E. 896 (N.Y. 1928)

CARDOZO, C.J. The defendant, a water works company under the laws of this State, made a contract with the city of Rensselaer for the supply of water during a term of years. Water was to be furnished to the city for sewer flushing and street sprinkling; for service to schools and public buildings; and for service at fire hydrants, the latter service at the rate of $42.50 a year for each hydrant. Water was to be furnished to private takers within the city at their homes and factories and other industries at reasonable rates, not exceeding a stated schedule. While this contract was in force, a building caught fire. The flames, spreading to the plaintiff's warehouse near by, destroyed it and its contents. The defendant according to the complaint was promptly notified of the fire, "but omitted and neglected after such notice, to supply or furnish sufficient or adequate quantity of water, with adequate pressure to stay, suppress or extinguish the fire before it reached the warehouse of the plaintiff, although the pressure and supply which the defendant was equipped to supply and furnish, and had agreed by said contract to supply and furnish, was adequate and sufficient to prevent the spread of the fire to and the destruction of the plaintiff's warehouse and its contents." By reason of the failure of the defendant to "fulfill the provisions of the contract between it and the city of Rensselaer," the plaintiff is said to have suffered damage, for which judgment is demanded. A motion, in the nature of a demurrer, to dismiss the complaint, was denied at Special Term. The Appellate Division reversed by a divided court.

Liability in the plaintiff's argument is placed on one or other of three grounds. The complaint, we are told, is to be viewed as stating: (1) A cause of action for breach of contract within Lawrence v. Fox (20 N.Y. 268 [1859]); (2) a cause of action for a common-law tort, within MacPherson v. Buick Motor Company (217 N.Y. 382 [1916]); or (3) a cause of action for the breach of a statutory duty. These several grounds of liability will be considered in succession.

(1) We think the action is not maintainable as one for breach of contract.

No legal duty rests upon a city to supply its inhabitants with protection against fire. That being so, a member of the public may not maintain an action under Lawrence v. Fox against one contracting with the city to furnish water at the hydrants, unless an intention appears that the promisor is to be answerable to individual members of the public as well as to the city for any loss ensuing from the failure to fulfill the promise. No such intention is discernible here. On the contrary, the contract here is significantly divided into two branches: One a promise to the city for the benefit of the city in its corporate capacity, in which branch is included the service at the hydrants; and the other a promise to the city for the benefit of private takers, in which branch is included the service at their homes and factories. In a broad sense it is true that every city contract, not improvident or wasteful, is for the benefit of the public. More than this, however, must be shown to give a right of action to a member of the public not formally a party. The benefit, as it is sometimes said, must be one that is not merely incident and secondary. It must be primary and immediate in such a sense and to such a degree as to bespeak the assumption of a duty to make reparation directly to the individual members of the public if the benefit is lost. The field of obligation would be expanded beyond reasonable limits if less than this were demanded as a condition of liability. A promisor undertakes to supply fuel for heating a public building. He is not liable for breach of contract to a visitor who finds the building without fuel, and thus contracts a cold. . . .

[Cardozo then notes that the overwhelming authority treats the benefit to the public under these contracts as incidental and secondary.] An intention to assume an obligation of indefinite extension to every member of the public is seen to be the more improbable when we recall the crushing burden that the obligation would impose. . . . If the plaintiff is to prevail, one who negligently omits to supply sufficient pressure to extinguish a fire started by another assumes an obligation to pay the ensuing damage, though the whole city is laid low. A promisor will not be deemed to have had in mind the assumption of a risk so overwhelming for any trivial reward. . . .

(2) We think the action is not maintainable as one for a common-law tort.

"It is ancient learning that one who assumes to act, even though gratuitously, may thereby become subject to the duty of acting carefully, if he acts at all" (Glanzer v. Shepard, 233 N.Y. 236, 239 [1922]). The plaintiff would bring its case within the orbit of that principle. The hand once set to a task may not always be withdrawn with impunity though liability would fail if it had never been applied at all. A time-honored formula often phrases the distinction as one between misfeasance and nonfeasance. Incomplete the formula is, and so at times misleading. Given a relation involving in its existence a duty of care irrespective of a contract, a tort may result as well from acts of omission as of commission in the fulfillment of the duty thus recognized by law. What we need to know is not so much the conduct to be avoided when the relation and its attendant duty are established as existing. What we need to know is the conduct that engenders the relation. It is here that the formula, however incomplete, has its value and significance. If conduct has gone forward to such a stage that inaction would commonly result, not negatively merely in withholding a benefit, but positively or actively in working an injury, there exists a relation out of which arises a duty to go forward. So the surgeon who operates without pay is liable though his negligence is in the omission to sterilize his instruments; the engineer, though his fault is in the failure to shut off steam; the maker of automobiles, at the suit of some one other than the buyer, though his negligence is merely in inadequate inspection (*Mac-Pherson*). The query always is whether the putative wrongdoer has advanced to such a point as to have launched a force or instrument of harm, or has stopped where inaction is at most a refusal to become an instrument for good.

The plaintiff would have us hold that the defendant, when once it entered upon the performance of its contract with the city, was brought into such a relation with every one who might potentially be benefited through the supply of water at the hydrants as to give to negligent performance, without reasonable notice of a refusal to continue, the quality of a tort. . . . We are satisfied that liability would be unduly and indeed indefinitely extended by this enlargement of the zone of duty. The dealer in coal who is to supply fuel for a shop must then answer to the customers if fuel is lacking. The manufacturer of goods, who enters upon the performance of his contract, must answer, in that view, not only to the buyer, but to those who to his knowledge are looking to the buyer for their own sources of supply. Everyone making a promise having the quality of a contract will be under a duty to the promisee by virtue of the promise, but under another duty, apart from contract, to an indefinite number of potential beneficiaries when performance has begun. The assumption of one relation will mean the involuntary assumption of a series of new relations, inescapably hooked together. Again we may say in the words of the Supreme Court of the United States: "The law does not spread its protection so far" (Robins Dry Dock & Repair Co. v. Flint, 275 U.S. 303 [1927]; cf. Byrd v. English, 117 Ga. 191 [1903]). We do not need to determine now what remedy, if any, there might be if the defendant had withheld the water or reduced the pressure with a malicious intent to do injury to the plaintiff or another. We put aside also the problem that would arise if there had been reckless and wanton indifference to consequences measured and foreseen. Difficulties would be present even then, but they need not now perplex us. What we are dealing with at this time is a mere negligent omission, unaccompanied by malice or other aggravating elements. The failure in such circumstances to furnish an adequate supply of water is at most the denial of a benefit. It is not the commission of a wrong.

(3) We think the action is not maintainable as one for the breach of a statutory duty.

The defendant, a public service corporation, is subject to the provisions of the Transportation Corporations Act. The duty imposed upon it by that act is in substance to furnish water, upon demand by the inhabitants, at reasonable rates, through suitable connections at office, factory or dwelling, and to furnish water at like rates through hydrants or in public buildings upon demand by the city, all according to its capacity. We find nothing in these requirements to enlarge the zone of liability where an inhabitant of the city suffers indirect or incidental damage through deficient pressure at the hydrants. The breach of duty in any case is to the one to whom service is denied at the time and at the place where services to such one is due. The denial, though wrongful, is unavailing without more to give a cause of action to another. We may find a helpful analogy in the law of common carriers. A railroad company is under a duty to supply reasonable facilities for carriage at reasonable rates. It is liable, generally speaking, for breach of a duty imposed by law if it refuses to accept merchandise tendered by a shipper. The fact that its duty is of this character does not make it liable to some one else who may be counting upon the prompt delivery of the merchandise to save him from loss in going forward with his work. If the defendant may not be held for a tort at common law, we find no adequate reason for a holding that it may be held under the statute.

The judgment should be affirmed with costs.

NOTES

1. *The privity limitation and the waterworks cases.* *Moch* represents an uneasy mixture of a gratuitous and a commercial transaction. On the one hand, the contract required the city to reimburse the water company for the services it provided. On the other hand, the plaintiff, a stranger to the contract, did not pay for any services even as a taxpayer of the local community that funded the contract. Cardozo addresses both sides of the dilemma. He first refuses to treat the plaintiff as a third-party beneficiary. He refuses to impose upon the defendant a duty to act carefully toward the plaintiff in what is, as to it, a gratuitous undertaking.

The decision has met with a divided press. It was criticized in Seavey, Reliance upon Gratuitous Promises or Other Conduct, 64 Harv. L. Rev. 913, 920-921 (1951), on the ground that "it is difficult to differentiate this type of case from that where a person has negligently broken a water main and is held responsible for harm caused by the consequent lack of pressure. The earlier cases, however, were decided at a time when nonfeasance and lack of privity were sufficient to prevent liability and the subsequent cases have followed these precedents. Even Cardozo, in what is perhaps his most unsatisfactory opinion in the field of torts, rested his decision, in part, upon the nonfeasance of the waterworks company." In contrast, Gregory, Gratuitous Undertakings and the Duty of Care, 1 DePaul L. Rev. 30, 59-60 (1951), defended *Moch* on the grounds that it placed the burden of the loss on the fire insurance companies who would otherwise assert their subrogation rights—which allow them to stand in the shoes of their insureds after paying the underlying claims—against the water company. "Cardozo thought the sum of $42.50 insufficient to warrant the conclusion that a negligent water company should be made to relieve a fire insurance company from bearing the ultimate risk of loss by fire. . . ." Would Gregory's logic preclude liability even if the water company's own employee accidentally broke the water main while making repairs?

Should the plaintiff in *Moch* be able to recover on the strength of RTT:LPEH §42(a) or (b), *supra*, given that the breakdown in services was in the water supply to the plaintiff's neighbor? RTT:LPEH §42, comment *f* observes: "This [reliance] requirement is often met because the plaintiff or another relied on the actor's performing the undertaking in a nonnegligent manner and declined to pursue an alternative means for protection."

Note that the comments to the Third Restatement explicitly question *Moch's* nonfeasance rationale:

> The difficulty with [*Moch*] is that the provision of utilities fundamentally changes the landscape, creating an expectation of and reliance on continued service. When the utility ceases to supply service, the omission is much like ceasing to provide warning signals at a railroad crossing. Put another way, reliance on the utility's continuing to provide its services is a cause of the harm. Moreover, the policies supporting the no-duty-to-rescue rule do not apply to a commercial enterprise that is engaged in the business of supplying services to customers.
>
> The better explanation for limitations on the duty of public utilities is concern about the huge magnitude of liability to which a utility might be exposed from a single failure to provide service that affects hundreds, thousands, or, in the case of an electrical blackout, millions of people. In addition, when the harm is property damage, often the plaintiff will have first-party insurance that covers the loss.

2. Judicial developments since Moch.   Judicial developments since *Moch* largely anticipated the uneasiness now expressed in the Third Restatement. Most notably, in Doyle v. South Pittsburgh Water Co., 199 A.2d 875, 878 (Pa. 1964), Musmanno, J., held that waterworks cases fell "squarely within the rule that where a party to a contract assumes a duty to the other party to the contract, and it is foreseeable that a breach of that duty will cause injury to some third person not a party to the contract, the contracting party owes a duty to all those falling within the foreseeable orbit of risk of harm."

New York courts, however, have followed *Moch.* Strauss v. Belle Realty Co., 482 N.E.2d 34, 38 (N.Y. 1985), arose out of the great New York City power failure of 1977, for which the defendant, Consolidated Edison, had been found grossly negligent. The power failure cut off the pumps used to circulate water upstairs in defendant Belle Realty's building. The plaintiff, a 77-year-old tenant in Belle's building, was injured when he fell in the dark on some defective basement stairs in search of water. Both the plaintiff and Belle were customers of Con Ed, but only Belle had a contract

New York City blackout of 1977
Source: Dan Farrell / New York Daily News Archive via Getty Images

with the utility. The court refused to extend the utility's liability in negligence to the plaintiff tenant:

> [W]e deal here with a system-wide power failure occasioned by what has already been determined to be the utility's gross negligence. If liability could be found here, then in logic and fairness the same result must follow in many similar situations. For example, a tenant's guests and invitees, as well as persons making deliveries or repairing equipment in the building, are equally persons who must use the common areas, and for whom they are maintained. Customers of a store and occupants of an office building stand in much the same position with respect to Con Edison as tenants of an apartment building. In all cases the numbers are to a certain extent limited and defined, and while identities may change, so do those of apartment dwellers. While limiting recovery to customers in this instance can hardly be said to confer immunity from negligence on Con Edison, permitting recovery to those in plaintiff's circumstances would, in our view, violate the court's responsibility to define an orbit of duty that places controllable limits on liability. . . .

3. Affirmative duties and the role of insurance. The availability of insurer's subrogation rights led to a partial retreat from Cardozo's no-duty rule in Weinberg v. Dinger, 524 A.2d 366, 378 (N.J. 1987). The court first noted its concern with the high insurance costs that water companies might have to bear, and wrote as follows:

> We believe that the imposition on a water company of liability for subrogation claims of carriers who pay fire losses caused by the company's negligent failure to maintain adequate water pressure would inevitably result in higher water rates paid by the class of consumers that paid for the fire insurance. The result of imposing subrogation-claim liability on water companies in such cases would be to shift the risk from the fire-insurance company to the water company, and, ultimately, to the consumer in the form of increased water rates. Thus, the consumer would pay twice—first for property insurance premiums, and then in the form of higher water rates to fund the cost of the water company's liability insurance. We find this result contrary to public policy.
>
> Accordingly, we abrogate the water company's immunity for losses caused by the negligent failure to maintain adequate water pressure for fire fighting only to the extent of claims that are uninsured or underinsured. To the extent that such claims are insured and thereby assigned to the insurance carrier as required by statute, *N.J.S.A.* 17:36-5:20, we hold that the carrier's subrogation claims are unenforceable against the water company.

Note that the water company contract at issue in *Weinberg* provided as follows:

> 8. The Company will use due diligence at all times to provide continuous service of the character or quality proposed to be supplied but in case the service shall be interrupted or irregular or defective or fail, the Company shall be liable and obligated only to use reasonably diligent efforts in light of the circumstances then existing to restore or correct its characteristics. . . .

10. The standard terms and conditions contained in this tariff are a part of every contract for service entered into by the Company and govern all classes of service where applicable.

What result if homeowner fire insurance contracts are redrafted to deny coverage shall exist for fires that the water company could avoid by exercising due care?

The tariff limitation referred to above played a prominent role in Los Angeles Cellular Telephone Company v. Superior Court (Spielholz RPI), 76 Cal. Rptr. 2d 894 (Ct. App. 1998). Spielholz could not get a connection on defendant's cellular system to call 911 as she was pursued by two men, one of whom subsequently shot her. The defendant company interposed its tariff that had been approved by the state's Public Utility Commission. That tariff explicitly and unambiguously limited the defendant's liability to $5,000 per incident. The court, without resort to common law principles of nonfeasance, unhesitatingly applied the damage limitation noting: "A condition imposed by a tariff binds a utility's customers without regard to whether a contract is signed by the customer and without regard to the customer's actual knowledge of the tariff." Would *Moch* have come out the same way if its tariff had contained a similar dollar maximum?

SECTION E. SPECIAL RELATIONSHIPS

Restatement (Second) of Torts

§315. GENERAL PRINCIPLE

There is no duty so to control the conduct of a third person as to prevent him from causing physical harm to another unless
(a) a special relation exists between the actor and the third person which imposes a duty upon the actor to control the third person's conduct, or
(b) a special relation exists between the actor and the other which gives the other a right to protection.

NOTE

On the borderland of nonfeasance. In Weirum v. RKO General Inc., 539 P.2d 36, 40-41 (Cal. 1975), the defendant's disk jockey, the Real Don Steele, staged a novel promotional contest. He drove around town announcing that he "had bread to spread" and gave his location on the air. The first contestant to reach that location and answer some simple quiz questions correctly won small prizes. Two teenage drivers got into an 80-miles-per-hour drag race in an effort to reach

Steele at his new location and forced decedent's car off the highway, where it overturned, killing him. The California Court of Appeal, over a dissent, reversed plaintiff's judgment against the radio station, holding that the station "had no control, or right to control, over the conduct of the drivers of other cars on the highway." 119 Cal. Rptr. 468 (1975). The California Supreme Court unanimously reinstated the plaintiff's judgment, insisting that imposing liability here did not open up a Pandora's box:

> We are not persuaded that the imposition of a duty here will lead to unwarranted extensions of liability. Defendant is fearful that entrepreneurs will henceforth be burdened with an avalanche of obligations: an athletic department will owe a duty to an ardent sports fan injured while hastening to purchase one of a limited number of tickets; a department store will be liable to injuries incurred in response to a "while-they-last" sale. This argument, however, suffers from a myopic view of the facts presented here. The giveaway contest was no commonplace invitation to an attraction available on a limited basis. It was a competitive scramble in which the thrill of the chase to be the one and only victor was intensified by the live broadcasts which accompanied the pursuit. In the assertedly analogous situations described by defendant, any haste involved in the purchase of the commodity is an incidental and unavoidable result of the scarcity of the commodity itself. In such situations there is no attempt, as here, to generate a competitive pursuit on public streets, accelerated by repeated importuning by radio to be the very first to arrive at a particular destination. Manifestly the "spectacular" bears little resemblance to daily commercial activities.

The court then rebuffed an effort to limit liability under RST §315, noting that its main purpose was to codify the common law "Good Samaritan rule" applicable to cases of nonfeasance only:

> Here, there can be little doubt that we review an act of misfeasance to which section 315 is inapplicable. Liability is not predicated upon defendant's failure to intervene for the benefit of decedent but rather upon its creation of an unreasonable risk of harm to him. Defendant's reliance upon cases which involve the failure to prevent harm to another is therefore misplaced. . . .

Kline v. 1500 Massachusetts Avenue Apartment Corp.
439 F.2d 477 (D.C. Cir. 1970)

WILKEY, J. The appellee apartment corporation states that there is "only one issue presented for review . . . whether a duty should be placed on a landlord to take steps to protect tenants from foreseeable criminal acts committed by third parties." The District Court as a matter of law held that there is no such duty. We find that there is, and that in the circumstances here the applicable standard of care was breached. We therefore reverse and remand to the District Court for the determination of damages for the appellant.

I

The appellant, Sarah B. Kline, sustained serious injuries when she was criminally assaulted and robbed at approximately 10:15 in the evening by an intruder in the common hallway of an apartment house at 1500 Massachusetts Avenue. This facility, into which the appellant Kline moved in October 1959, is a large apartment building with approximately 585 individual apartment units. It has a main entrance on Massachusetts Avenue, with side entrances on both 15th and 16th Streets. At the time the appellant first signed a lease a doorman was on duty at the main entrance twenty-four hours a day, and at least one employee at all times manned a desk in the lobby from which all persons using the elevators could be observed. The 15th Street door adjoined the entrance to a parking garage used by both the tenants and the public. Two garage attendants were stationed at this dual entranceway; the duties of each being arranged so that one of them always was in position to observe those entering either the apartment building or the garage. The 16th Street entrance was unattended during the day but was locked after 9:00 P.M.

By mid-1966, however, the main entrance had no doorman, the desk in the lobby was left unattended much of the time, the 15th Street entrance was generally unguarded due to a decrease in garage personnel, and the 16th Street entrance was often left unlocked all night. The entrances were allowed to be thus unguarded in the face of an increasing number of assaults, larcenies, and robberies being perpetrated against the tenants in and from the common hallways of the apartment building. These facts were undisputed. . . . The landlord had notice of these crimes and had in fact been urged by appellant Kline herself prior to the events leading to the instant appeal to take steps to secure the building.

Shortly after 10:00 P.M. on November 17, 1966, Miss Kline was assaulted and robbed just outside her apartment on the first floor above the street level of this 585 unit apartment building. This occurred only two months after Leona Sullivan, another female tenant, had been similarly attacked in the same commonway.

II

At the outset we note that of the crimes of violence, robbery, and assault which had been occurring with mounting frequency on the premises at 1500 Massachusetts Avenue, the assaults on Miss Kline and Miss Sullivan took place in the hallways of the building, which were under the exclusive control of the appellee landlord. Even in those crimes of robbery or assault committed in individual apartments, the intruders of necessity had to gain entrance through the common entry and passageways. These premises fronted on three heavily traveled streets, and had multiple entrances. The risk to be guarded against therefore was the risk of unauthorized entrance into the apartment house by intruders bent upon some crime of violence or theft.

While the apartment lessees themselves could take some steps to guard against this risk by installing extra heavy locks and other security devices on the doors and windows of their respective apartments, yet this risk in the greater part could only be guarded against by the landlord. No individual tenant had it within his power to take measures to guard the garage entranceways, to provide scrutiny at the main entrance of the building, to patrol the common hallways and elevators, to set up any kind of a security alarm system in the building, to provide additional locking devices on the main doors, to provide a system of announcement for authorized visitors only, to close the garage doors at appropriate hours, and to see that the entrance was manned at all times.

The risk of criminal assault and robbery on a tenant in the common hallways of the building was thus entirely predictable; that same risk had been occurring with increasing frequency over a period of several months immediately prior to the incident giving rise to this case; it was a risk whose prevention or minimization was almost entirely within the power of the landlord; and the risk materialized in the assault and robbery of appellant on November 17, 1966.

III

In this jurisdiction, certain duties have been assigned to the landlord because of his *control* of common hallways, lobbies, stairwells, etc., used by all tenants in multiple dwelling units. This Court in Levine v. Katz, 407 F.2d 303, 304 (D.C. Cir. 1968), pointed out that:

> It has long been well settled in this jurisdiction that, where a landlord leases separate portions of property and reserves under his own control the halls, stairs, or other parts of the property for use in common by all tenants, he has a duty to all those on the premises of legal right to use ordinary care and diligence to maintain the retained parts in a reasonably safe condition.

While Levine v. Katz dealt with a physical defect in the building leading to plaintiff's injury, the rationale as applied to predictable criminal acts by third parties is the same. The duty is the landlord's because by his control of the areas of common use and common danger he is the only party who has the *power* to make the necessary repairs or to provide the necessary protection.

As a general rule, a private person does not have a duty to protect another from a criminal attack by a third person. We recognize that this rule has sometimes in the past been applied in landlord-tenant law, even by this court. Among the reasons for the application of this rule to landlords are: judicial reluctance to tamper with the traditional common law concept of the landlord-tenant relationship; the notion that the act of a third person in committing an intentional tort or crime is a superseding cause of the harm to another resulting therefrom; the oftentimes difficult problem of determining foreseeability of criminal acts; the vagueness of the standard which the landlord must meet; the economic consequences of the imposition of the duty; and conflict with the public policy allocating the duty of protecting citizens from criminal acts to the government rather than the private sector.

But the rationale of this very broad general rule falters when it is applied to the conditions of modern day urban apartment living, particularly in the circumstances of this case. The rationale of the general rule exonerating a third party from any duty to protect another from a criminal attack has no applicability to the landlord-tenant relationship in multiple dwelling houses. The landlord is no insurer of his tenants' safety, but he certainly is no bystander. And where, as here, the landlord has notice of repeated criminal assaults and robberies, has notice that these crimes occurred in the portion of the premises exclusively within his control, has every reason to expect like crimes to happen again, and has the exclusive power to take preventive action, it does not seem unfair to place upon the landlord a duty to take those steps which are within his power to minimize the predictable risk to his tenants. . . .

In the case at bar we place the duty of taking protective measures guarding the entire premises and the areas peculiarly under the landlord's control against the perpetration of criminal acts upon the landlord, the party to the lease contract who has the effective capacity to perform these necessary acts.

[The court then noted that innkeepers were held liable to their guests for assaults and molestations by third parties, "be they innkeeper's employees, fellow guests or intruders."] Other relationships in which similar duties have been imposed include landowner-invitee, businessman-patron, employer-employee, school district-pupil, hospital-patient, and carrier-passenger. In all, the theory of liability is essentially the same: that since the ability of one of the parties to provide for his own protection has been limited in some way by his submission to the control of the other, a duty should be imposed upon the one possessing control (and thus the power to act) to take reasonable precautions to protect the other one from assaults by third parties which, at least, could reasonably have been anticipated. However, there is no liability normally imposed upon the one having the power to act if the violence is sudden and unexpected provided that the source of the violence is not an employee of the one in control.

We are aware of various cases in other jurisdictions following a different line of reasoning, conceiving of the landlord and tenant relationship along more traditional common law lines, and on varying fact situations reaching a different result from that we reach here. Typical of these is a much cited (although only a 4-3) decision of the Supreme Court of New Jersey, Goldberg v. Housing Authority of Newark [186 A.2d 291 (N.J. 1962)], relied on by appellee landlord here. There the court said:

> Everyone can foresee the commission of crime virtually anywhere and at any time. If foreseeability itself gave rise to a duty to provide "police" protection for others, every residential curtilage, every shop, every store, every manufacturing plant would have to be patrolled by the private arm of the owner. And since hijacking and attack upon occupants of motor vehicles are also foreseeable, it would be the duty of every motorist to provide armed protection for his passengers and the property of others. Of course, none of this is at all palatable.

This language seems to indicate that the court was using the word *foreseeable* interchangeably with the word *possible*. In that context, the statement is quite correct. It would be folly to impose liability for mere possibilities. But we must reach the question of liability for attacks which are foreseeable in the sense that they are *probable* and *predictable*. . . . As between tenant and landlord, the landlord is the only one in the position to take the necessary acts of protection required. He is not an insurer, but he is obligated to minimize the risk to his tenants. Not only as between landlord and tenant is the landlord best equipped to guard against the predictable risk of intruders, but even as between landlord and the police power of government, the landlord is in the best position to take the necessary protective measures. Municipal police cannot patrol the entryways and the hallways, the garages and the basements of private multiple unit apartment dwellings. They are neither equipped, manned, nor empowered to do so. In the area of the predictable risk which materialized in this case, only the landlord could have taken measures which might have prevented the injuries suffered by appellant.

We note that in the fight against crime the police are not expected to do it all; every segment of society has obligations to aid in law enforcement and to minimize the opportunities for crime. . . .

IV

We now turn to the standard of care which should be applied in judging if the landlord has fulfilled his duty of protection to the tenant. Although in many cases the language speaks as if the standard of care itself varies, in the last analysis the standard of care is the same—reasonable care in all the circumstances. . . .

We therefore hold in this case that the applicable standard of care in providing protection for the tenant is that standard which this landlord himself was employing in October 1959 when the appellant became a resident on the premises at 1500 Massachusetts Avenue. The tenant was led to expect that she could rely upon this degree of protection. While we do not say that the precise measures for security which were then in vogue should have been kept up (e.g., the number of people at the main entrances might have been reduced if a tenant-controlled intercom-automatic latch system had been installed in the common entryways), we do hold that the same relative degree of security should have been maintained.

V

[The court then held that liability was "clear" on the face of the record and remanded the case to the district court on the issue of damages only.]

Having said this, it would be well to state what is *not* said by this decision. We do not hold that the landlord is by any means an insurer of the safety of his tenants. His duty is to take those measures of protection which are within his power and capacity to take, and which can reasonably be expected to mitigate the risk of intruders assaulting and robbing tenants. The landlord is not expected to provide protection commonly owed by a municipal police department; but as illustrated in this case, he is obligated to protect those parts of his premises which are not usually subject to periodic patrol and inspection by the municipal police. We do not say that every multiple unit apartment house in the District of Columbia should have those same measures of protection which 1500 Massachusetts Avenue enjoyed in 1959, nor do we say that 1500 Massachusetts Avenue should have precisely those same measures in effect at the present time. Alternative and more up-to-date methods may be equally or even more effective.

Granted, the discharge of this duty of protection by landlords will cause, in many instances, the expenditure of large sums for additional equipment and services, and granted, the cost will be ultimately passed on to the tenant in the form of increased rents. This prospect, in itself, however, is no deterrent to our acknowledging and giving force to the duty, since without protection the tenant already pays in losses from theft, physical assault and increased insurance premiums.

The landlord is entirely justified in passing on the cost of increased protective measures to his tenants, but the rationale of compelling the landlord to do it in the first place is that he is the only one who is in a position to take the necessary protective measures for overall protection of the premises, which he owns in whole and rents in part to individual tenants.

Reversed and remanded to the District Court for the determination of damages.

MACKINNON, J., dissenting. [The dissent first argued that liability was not established on the record, so that the case should, even on the court's view of the substantive law, be retried de novo, because the evidence on the number and frequency of previous criminal attacks was insufficient, given that only one of the 20 incidents involved both an assault and robbery. It also argued that the notice to the landlord was only of theft, and that there was no evidence in the record that the landlord knew of the previous assault upon Leona Sullivan. It continued:]

The evidence introduced by the plaintiff is also deficient in my opinion in not proving that the alleged negligence was the proximate cause of the assault or that it contributed to it in any way. Plaintiff's evidence did not negate that it was a tenant, guest or person properly on the property who committed the offense, and while the panel opinion throughout asserts that an "intruder" committed the offense, there is no proof of that fact. So plaintiff's evidence failed to prove a nexus between the alleged deficiencies of the appellee and the cause of any damage to appellant. . . .

As for the claim that appellant was led to believe she would get the same standard of protection in 1966 that was furnished in 1959, there is obviously nothing to this point. She was not led to expect that. She personally observed the changes which occurred in this respect. They were obvious to her each day of her life. And since her original lease had terminated and her tenancy in 1966 was on a month to month basis, whatever contract existed was created at the beginning of the month and since there was no evidence of any alteration in the security precautions during the current month, there is no basis for any damage claim based on contract. . . .

In my opinion the decision in Goldberg v. Housing Authority of Newark, 186 A.2d 291 (N.J. 1962), answers all appellant's arguments. It is just too much, absent a contractual agreement, to require or expect a combination office-apartment building such as is involved here to provide police patrol protection or its equivalent in the block-long, well-lighted passageways. Yet nothing short of that will meet the second guessing standard of protection the panel opinion practically directs. If tenants expect such protection, they can move to apartments where it is available and presumably pay a higher rental, but it is a mistake in my judgment to hold an office-apartment building to such a requirement when the tenant knew for years that such protection was not being afforded.

NOTES

1. Contract or special relationship? If the defendant landlord could have taken effective steps to prevent crimes in common areas at a lower cost than its tenants, why didn't it assume that liability in its standard residential lease? If it made that promise voluntarily, could it impose a cap on recovery similar to that upheld in *Los Angeles Cellular, supra* at 518, Note 3? In dealing with the contract alternative, should the court in *Kline* take into account administrative costs? Contributory negligence? Error rates in litigation?

Whatever the correct answer to these questions, *Kline* has met with widespread approval insofar as it reverses the older common law rule that imposed no duty on a landlord to shield tenants from criminal attacks. Nonetheless, with stepped-up security precautions, it is now more difficult for plaintiffs to avoid summary judgment under the *Kline* rule. In Beckwith v. Interstate Mgmt. Co., LLC, 82 F. Supp. 3d 255 (D.D.C. 2015), Anthony Lopez "touched Beckwith on the crotch" as they were walking toward the men's room on the lower level of the Hamilton Crowne Plaza Hotel. The hotel had in operation multiple security cameras and was able to apprehend Lopez in its dining room shortly after the incident took place. Contreras, J., granted defendant's motion for summary judgment. It first adopted a "sliding scale analysis" under which this plaintiff did not have to make a "heightened showing of the criminal act's foreseeability" to establish a duty given that the innkeeper-guest relationship imposed a "great duty of protection." Nonetheless, the plaintiff failed to show the minimum level of foreseeability solely by relying on general crime statistics that showed that "[f]rom 2007 to 2009, 542 violent crimes and 4,171 property crimes occurred within a half-mile radius of the hotel. . . . Even assuming that the crime rate cited by Beckwith was extraordinarily high (there is no evidence to this effect), and that an assault by an intruder was foreseeable, the Court finds no evidence suggesting that Lopez was actually an intruder. To the contrary, the fact that the security director found Lopez dining in the hotel's restaurant following the assault suggests that he was an invitee of the hotel." Did the hotel cameras meet the applicable standard of care? What result if Beckwith's assailant had not been identified? Apprehended?

2. Proximate causation. The issues of proximate causation stressed in MacKinnon's, J., dissent explicitly surfaced in Burgos v. Aqueduct Realty Corp., 706 N.E.2d 1163, 1166 (N.Y. 1998). The plaintiff was leaving her apartment unit when she was forced back into it by two men who beat and robbed her. In her action against the landlord for inadequate security, Kaye, C.J., held:

[T]he necessary causal link between a landlord's culpable failure to provide adequate security and a tenant's injuries resulting from a criminal attack in the building can be established only if the assailant gained access to the premises through a negligently maintained entrance. . . . Without such a requirement, landlords would be exposed to liability for virtually all criminal activity in their buildings. By the same token, because victims of criminal assaults often cannot identify their attackers, a blanket rule precluding recovery whenever the attacker remains unidentified would place an impossible burden on tenants.

Kaye, C.J., then held that, although the plaintiff bore the burden of proof on the causation issue, she could reach the jury on the question of proximate causation, when she testified first that the assailants did not wear masks and then that none of the building's entrances had functioning locks. Kaye, C.J., held that the jury could infer that persons known to the plaintiff would have covered their faces, and that access through unlocked doors was easy. What about the possibility that friends of tenants had assaulted the plaintiff?

3. *The procession of liability.*   The new liability first raised in *Kline* has generated a flood of subsequent litigation about institutional responsibilities to protect against crime.

a. Colleges and universities.   In Peterson v. San Francisco Community College District, 685 P.2d 1193, 1197 (Cal. 1984), the California Supreme Court held that a community college district had a duty to protect a college student against a foreseeable criminal assault that took place in broad daylight on campus—here, on a stairway in a parking lot—on the strength of its special relationship with the student. "There is no question that if the defendant district here were a private landowner operating a parking lot on its premises it would owe plaintiff a duty to exercise due care for her protection." The court let the plaintiff reach the jury on two counts of negligence: first, had the defendant properly trimmed the hedge and foliage that concealed the perpetrator before he committed the crime and, second, did the school have a duty to warn the plaintiff about the hazards it left uncorrected. How might such a warning be given? Be updated?

b. Common carriers.   In Lopez v. Southern California Rapid Transit District, 710 P.2d 907, 910-911 (Cal. 1985), the California Supreme Court held that a duty of care in favor of its passengers would not impose "colossal financial burden" on a public transportation district. Even without demanding "an armed security guard on every bus," the district could train drivers to eject unruly passengers who did not heed warnings to quiet down, to radio the police for assistance, or to equip buses with alarm lights to warn of threatened or actual criminal activity. What causal complications are created by each such theory?

c. Condominiums.   In Frances T. v. Village Green Owners Association, 723 P.2d 573 (Cal. 1986), the plaintiff was "molested, raped and robbed" by an unidentified assailant who entered her condominium unit at night after the condominium board refused to allow plaintiff to install lights by her unit for her own self-protection. The court held that the liability imposed on landlords in *Kline* should be extended to condominium boards and to their individual members who function as the de facto landlord of the premises. In dissent, Mosk, J., rejected any parallels between a condominium board and an ordinary landlord and denied the existence of special relationship between a condominium association and its unit members. Will potential liability deter association members from serving gratis on condominium boards?

d. Shopping malls.   In Ann M. v. Pacific Plaza Shopping Center, 863 P.2d 207, 210, 215-216 (Cal. 1993), the court refused to allow the plaintiff, who had been raped inside her place of employment in the defendant's shopping mall, to sue her employer's landlord. The plaintiff's employer had signed a lease that gave defendant exclusive control over all common areas. The plaintiff was raped when she was alone in her shop at around 8:00 A.M. by a customer who entered the store from the mall. There was some evidence that the tenants in the shopping mall had complained of lack of security and the presence of transients, but the merchants association decided not to hire walking guards because the tenants could not afford the prohibitive rent increases that would be passed through under the leases. Instead, alternative arrangements were made for another security company to drive by three or four times a day. Panelli, J., concluded that "a high degree of foreseeability is required in order to find that the scope of a landlord's duty of care includes the hiring of security guards. We further conclude that the requisite degree of foreseeability rarely, if ever, can be proven in the absence of prior similar incidents of violent crime on the landlord's premises. To hold otherwise would be to impose an unfair burden upon landlords and, in effect, would force landlords to become the insurers of public safety, contrary to well established policy in this state."

e. Off-premises liability.   In twin cases, Delgado v. Trax Bar & Grill, 113 P.3d 1159 (Cal. 2005), and Morris v. De La Torre, 113 P.3d 1182, 1188 (Cal. 2005), restaurant patrons were attacked while leaving the premises in plain view of the restaurant employees. In *Delgado*, the defendant's bouncer did not accompany the plaintiffs to their car, and in *Morris*, the employees did not call 911 after a criminal assailant broke into the restaurant to steal a knife that he used to stab one of the plaintiffs. The court allowed both cases to go to the jury. In *Morris*, George, J., explicitly distinguished *Ann M.*:

[A]s we explained in *Delgado*, even if a proprietor, such as the bar in that case, has no special-relationship-based duty to provide security guards or other similarly burdensome measures designed to prevent future criminal conduct (which measures are required only upon a showing of "heightened foreseeability"), such a proprietor nevertheless owes a special-relationship-based duty to undertake reasonable and minimally burdensome measures to assist customers or invitees who face danger from imminent or ongoing criminal assaultive conduct occurring upon the premises. In this regard, we noted in *Delgado* that restaurant proprietors owe a special-relationship-based duty to provide "assistance [to] their customers who become ill or need medical attention and that they are liable if they fail to act."

In any event, . . . foreseeability analysis in a case such as this—involving a proprietor's duty to *respond* reasonably to criminal conduct that is *imminent* or even *ongoing* in his or her presence—contrasts fundamentally with the type of foreseeability at issue in cases such as *Ann M.*, which involve a proprietor's duty to take *preventative* measures to guard against possible *future* criminal conduct.

4. Other duties on occupiers.   Other cases have been reluctant to extend *Kline* in new directions. In Verdugo v. Target Corp., 327 P.3d 774 (Cal. 2014), the court held that Target was under no duty to obtain and make available a defibrillator to a customer who died of a sudden cardiac arrest. The court noted that less than 10 percent of the persons treated for cardiac arrest before they reach a hospital survive. Likewise, in Atcovitz v. Gulph Mills Tennis Club, Inc., 812 A.2d 1218 (Pa. 2002), the defendant tennis club was not required to maintain an automated external defibrillator for the benefit of a paying customer with a history of heart disease who collapsed while playing tennis. Similarly, in Sells v. CSX Transp., Inc., 2015 WL 1963751 (Fla. App. 1 Dist. 2015), the court concluded that "it would be a radical departure from the common law to require employers to ensure that their employees are available, capable, and willing to perform CPR on an injured co-employee while under the instruction of a 911 operator." Finally, in Mastriano v. Blyer, 779 A.2d 951 (Me. 2001), a cab driver who transported a tipsy passenger was only obliged to see that he had a "safe exit" at his chosen destination, but was not required to see that thereafter he did not drive his own automobile while intoxicated.

Tarasoff v. Regents of University of California
551 P.2d 334 (Cal. 1976)

TOBRINER, J. On October 27, 1969, Prosenjit Poddar killed Tatiana Tarasoff. Plaintiffs, Tatiana's parents, allege that two months earlier Poddar confided his intention to kill Tatiana to Dr. Lawrence Moore, a psychologist employed by the Cowell Memorial Hospital at the University of California at Berkeley. They allege that on Moore's request, the campus police briefly detained Poddar, but released him when he appeared rational. They further claim that Dr. Harvey Powelson, Moore's superior, then directed that no further action be taken to detain Poddar. [Elsewhere in the opinion it was noted: "Poddar had persuaded Tatiana's brother to share an apartment with him near Tatiana's residence; shortly after her return from Brazil, Poddar went to her residence and killed her." By way of additional background, Poddar was an "untouchable" Bengali who at that time had little or no contact with women in India. He had come to Berkeley to study naval architecture and found it difficult to adapt to American mores. Tatiana was of Russian heritage, born in China and raised in Brazil, with a much more liberal upbringing. The trouble began when she kissed Poddar on New Year's Eve 1968, but thereafter was unresponsive to his attentions. She in turn had sexual relations with other men, which sent Poddar into a tailspin until his personal life and university work unraveled. He saw Dr. Moore some seven times, who diagnosed his condition as "paranoid schizophrenic reaction, acute and severe." Moore recommended that he be involuntarily committed for the safety of others. Moore's superior may have ordered him not to get further involved in the case. It is clear that no one took any steps to warn Tatiana of any danger. She returned from Brazil in September 1969, making Poddar's pain all the more acute. In late October 1969, Poddar tracked her to her family home, shot her with a pellet gun and stabbed her 17 times with a kitchen knife.*] No one warned plaintiffs of Tatiana's peril.

Concluding that these facts set forth causes of action against neither therapists and policemen involved, nor against the Regents of the University of California as their employer, the superior court sustained defendants' demurrers to plaintiffs' second amended complaints without leave to amend. This appeal ensued. . . .

Plaintiffs' complaints predicate liability on two grounds: defendants' failure to warn plaintiffs of the impending danger and their failure to bring about Poddar's confinement pursuant to the Lanterman-Petris-Short Act (Welf. & Inst. Code, §5000ff.). Defendants, in turn, assert that they owed no duty of reasonable care to Tatiana and that they are immune from suit under the California Tort Claims Act of 1963 (Gov. Code, §810ff.). . . .

2. PLAINTIFFS CAN STATE A CAUSE OF ACTION AGAINST DEFENDANT THERAPISTS FOR NEGLIGENT FAILURE TO PROTECT TATIANA

The second cause of action can be amended to allege that Tatiana's death proximately resulted from defendant's negligent failure to warn Tatiana or others likely to apprise her of her danger. Plaintiffs contend that as amended, such allegations of negligence and proximate causation, with resulting damages, establish a cause of action. Defendants, however, contend that in the circumstances of the present case they owed no duty of care to Tatiana or her parents and that, in the absence of such duty, they were free to act in careless disregard of Tatiana's life and safety.

In analyzing this issue, we bear in mind that legal duties are not discoverable facts of nature, but merely conclusory expressions that, in cases of a particular type, liability should be imposed for damage done. As stated in Dillon v. Legg, 441 P.2d 912, 916 (Cal. 1968): "The assertion that liability must . . . be denied because defendant bears no 'duty' to plaintiff 'begs the essential question—whether the plaintiff's interests are entitled to legal protection against the defendant's conduct. . . . [Duty] is not sacrosanct in itself, but only an expression of the sum total of those considerations of policy which lead the law to say that the particular plaintiff is entitled to protection.' (Prosser, Law of Torts [3d ed. 1964] at pp. 332-333.)"

---

* These and other details are contained in Schuck & Givelber, *Tarasoff v. Regents of the University of California:* The Therapist's Dilemma, *in* Tort Stories 99 (Rabin & Sugarman eds., 2003).

[Tobriner, J., then explicitly relies on the general statements on duties to care from the landmark cases of Rowland v. Christian, *supra* at 494, and Heaven v. Pender, *supra* at 495, to conclude]: We depart from "this fundamental principle" only upon the "balancing of a number of considerations"; major ones "are the foreseeability of harm to the plaintiff, the degree of certainty that the plaintiff suffered injury, the closeness of the connection between the defendant's conduct and the injury suffered, the moral blame attached to the defendant's conduct, the policy of preventing future harm, the extent of the burden to the defendant and consequences to the community of imposing a duty to exercise care with resulting liability for breach, and the availability, cost and prevalence of insurance for the risk involved."

The most important of these considerations in establishing duty is foreseeability. As a general principle, a "defendant owes a duty of care to all persons who are foreseeably endangered by his conduct, with respect to all risks which make the conduct unreasonably dangerous." As we shall explain, however, when the avoidance of foreseeable harm requires a defendant to control the conduct of another person, or to warn of such conduct, the common law has traditionally imposed liability only if the defendant bears some special relationship to the dangerous person or to the potential victim. Since the relationship between a therapist and his patient satisfies this requirement, we need not here decide whether foreseeability alone is sufficient to create a duty to exercise reasonable care to protect a potential victim of another's conduct.

Although, as we have stated above, under the common law, as a general rule, one person owed no duty to control the conduct of another the courts have carved out an exception to this rule[5] in cases in which the defendant stands in some special relationship to either the person whose conduct needs to be controlled or in a relationship to the foreseeable victim of that conduct. Applying this exception to the present case, we note that a relationship of defendant therapists to either Tatiana or Poddar will suffice to establish a duty of care [under RST §315, *supra* at 518].

Although plaintiff's pleadings assert no special relation between Tatiana and defendant therapists, they establish as between Poddar and defendant therapists the special relation that arises between a patient and his doctor or psychotherapist. Such a relationship may support affirmative duties for the benefit of third persons. Thus, for example, a hospital must exercise reasonable care to control

---

5. This rule derives from the common law's distinction between misfeasance and nonfeasance, and its reluctance to impose liability for the latter. (See Harper & Kime, The Duty to Control the Conduct of Another (1934) 43 Yale L.J. 886, 887.) Morally questionable, the rule owes its survival to "the difficulties of setting any standards of unselfish service to fellow men, and of making any workable rule to cover possible situations where fifty people might fail to rescue. . . ." (Prosser, Torts (4th ed. 1971) §56, p. 341.) Because of these practical difficulties, the courts have increased the number of instances in which affirmative duties are imposed not by direct rejection of the common law rule, but by expanding the list of special relationships which will justify departure from that rule.

the behavior of a patient which may endanger other persons.[7] A doctor must also warn a patient if the patient's condition or medication renders certain conduct, such as driving a car, dangerous to others.

Although the California decisions that recognize this duty have involved cases in which the defendant stood in a special relationship *both* to the victim and to the person whose conduct created the danger,[9] we do not think that the duty should logically be constricted to such situations. Decisions of other jurisdictions hold that the single relationship of a doctor to his patient is sufficient to support the duty to exercise reasonable care to protect others against dangers emanating from the patient's illness. The courts hold that a doctor is liable to persons infected by his patient if he negligently fails to diagnose a contagious disease, or, having diagnosed the illness, fails to warn members of the patient's family.

Since it involved a dangerous mental patient, the decision in Merchants Nat. Bank & Trust Co. of Fargo v. United States, 272 F. Supp. 409 (D.N.D. 1967) comes closer to the issue. The Veterans Administration arranged for the patient to work on a local farm, but did not inform the farmer of the man's background. The farmer consequently permitted the patient to come and go freely during non-working hours; the patient borrowed a car, drove to his wife's residence and killed her. Notwithstanding the lack of any "special relationship" between the Veterans Administration and the wife, the court found the Veterans Administration liable for the wrongful death of the wife. . . .

Defendants contend, however, that imposition of a duty to exercise reasonable care to protect third persons is unworkable because therapists cannot accurately predict whether or not a patient will resort to violence. In support of this argument amicus representing the American Psychiatric Association and other professional societies cites numerous articles which indicate that therapists, in the present state of the art, are unable reliably to predict violent acts; their forecasts, amicus claims, tend consistently to overpredict violence, and indeed are more often wrong than right. Since predictions of violence are often erroneous, amicus concludes, the courts should not render rulings that predicate the liability of therapists upon the validity of such predictions. . . .

We recognize the difficulty that a therapist encounters in attempting to forecast whether a patient presents a serious danger of violence. Obviously we do

---

7. When a "hospital has notice or knowledge of facts from which it might reasonably be concluded that a patient would be likely to harm himself *or others* unless preclusive measures were taken, then the hospital must use reasonable care in the circumstances to prevent such harm." (Vistica v. Presbyterian Hospital, 432 P.2d 193, 196 (Cal. 1967).) (Emphasis added.) A mental hospital may be liable if it negligently permits the escape or release of a dangerous patient. Greenberg v. Barbour (E.D. Pa. 1971) 322 F. Supp. 745, upheld a cause of action against a hospital staff doctor whose negligent failure to admit a mental patient resulted in that patient assaulting the plaintiff.

9. Ellis v. D'Angelo, 253 P.2d 675 (Cal. App. 1953), upheld a cause of action against parents who failed to warn a babysitter of the violent proclivities of their child; Johnson v. State of California, 447 P.2d 352 (Cal. 1968), upheld a suit against the state for failure to warn foster parents of the dangerous tendencies of their ward; Morgan v. City of Yuba, 41 Cal. Rptr. 508 (Cal. App. 1964), sustained a cause of action against a sheriff who had promised to warn decedent before releasing a dangerous prisoner, but failed to do so.

not require that the therapist, in making that determination, render a perfect performance; the therapist need only exercise "that reasonable degree of skill, knowledge, and care ordinarily possessed and exercised by members of [that professional specialty] under similar circumstances." Within the broad range of reasonable practice and treatment in which professional opinion and judgment may differ, the therapist is free to exercise his or her own best judgment without liability; proof, aided by hindsight, that he or she judged wrongly is insufficient to establish negligence.

In the instant case, however, the pleadings do not raise any question as to failure of defendant therapists to predict that Poddar presented a serious danger of violence. On the contrary, the present complaints allege that defendant therapists did in fact predict that Poddar would kill, but were negligent in failing to warn.

Amicus contends, however, that even when a therapist does in fact predict that a patient poses a serious danger of violence to others, the therapist should be absolved of any responsibility for failing to act to protect the potential victim. In our view, however, once a therapist does in fact determine, or under applicable professional standards reasonably should have determined, that a patient poses a serious danger of violence to others, he bears a duty to exercise reasonable care to protect the foreseeable victim of that danger. While the discharge of this duty of due care will necessarily vary with the facts of each case,[11] in each instance the adequacy of the therapist's conduct must be measured against the traditional negligence standard of the rendition of reasonable care under the circumstances. . . .

The risk that unnecessary warnings may be given is a reasonable price to pay for the lives of possible victims that may be saved. We would hesitate to hold that the therapist who is aware that his patient expects to attempt to assassinate the President of the United States would not be obligated to warn the authorities because the therapist cannot predict with accuracy that his patient will commit the crime. . . .

We recognize the public interest in supporting effective treatment of mental illness and in protecting the rights of patients to privacy, and the consequent public importance of safeguarding the confidential character of psychotherapeutic communication. Against this interest, however, we must weigh the public interest in safety from violent assault. The Legislature has undertaken the difficult task of balancing the countervailing concerns. In Evidence Code section 1014, it established a broad rule of privilege to protect confidential communications between patient and psychotherapist. In Evidence Code section 1024, the Legislature

---

11. Defendant therapists and amicus also argue that warnings must be given only in those cases in which the therapist knows the identity of the victim. We recognize that in some cases it would be unreasonable to require the therapist to interrogate his patient to discover the victim's identity, or to conduct an independent investigation. But there may also be cases in which a moment's reflection will reveal the victim's identity. The matter thus is one which depends upon the circumstances of each case, and should not be governed by any hard and fast rule.

created a specific and limited exception to the psychotherapist-patient privilege: "There is no privilege . . . if the psychotherapist has reasonable cause to believe that the patient is in such mental or emotional condition as to be dangerous to himself or to the person or property of another and that disclosure of the communication is necessary to prevent the threatened danger."

We realize that the open and confidential character of psychotherapeutic dialogue encourages patients to express threats of violence, few of which are ever executed. Certainly a therapist should not be encouraged routinely to reveal such threats; such disclosures could seriously disrupt the patient's relationship with his therapist and with the persons threatened. To the contrary, the therapist's obligations to his patient require that he not disclose a confidence unless such disclosure is necessary to avert danger to others, and even then that he do so discreetly, and in a fashion that would preserve the privacy of his patient to the fullest extent compatible with the prevention of the threatened danger. (See Fleming & Maximov, The Patient or His Victim: The Therapist's Dilemma (1974) 62 Cal. L. Rev. 1025, 1065-1066.)

The revelation of a communication under the above circumstances is not a breach of trust or a violation of professional ethics as stated in the Principles of Medical Ethics of the American Medical Association (1957) section 9: "A physician may not reveal the confidence entrusted to him in the course of medical attendance . . . *unless he is required to do so by law or unless it becomes necessary in order to protect the welfare of the individual or of the community.*" (Emphasis added.) We conclude that the public policy favoring protection of the confidential character of patient-psychotherapist communications must yield to the extent to which disclosure is essential to avert danger to others. The protective privilege ends where the public peril begins.

Our current crowded and computerized society compels the interdependence of its members. In this risk-infested society we can hardly tolerate the further exposure to danger that would result from a concealed knowledge of the therapist that his patient was lethal. If the exercise of reasonable care to protect the threatened victim requires the therapist to warn the endangered party or those who can reasonably be expected to notify him, we see no sufficient societal interest that would protect and justify concealment. The containment of such risks lies in the public interest. For the foregoing reasons, we find that plaintiffs' complaints can be amended to state a cause of action against defendants Moore, Powelson, Gold, and Yandell and against the Regents as their employer, for breach of a duty to exercise reasonable care to protect Tatiana.

[The court then held that defendant therapists were not immune from liability for their failure to warn under the discretionary function exception to the California Tort Claims Act. It further held that both defendant therapists and defendant police officers were immune from liability for failure to confine Poddar. Finally, the court concluded that the police defendants "do not have any such special relationship to either Tatiana or to Poddar sufficient to impose upon such defendants a duty to warning respecting Poddar's violent intentions."]

WRIGHT, C.J., and SULLIVAN and RICHARDSON, JJ., concur.

MOSK, J., concurring in part and dissenting in part. I concur in the result in this instance only because the complaints allege that defendant therapists did in fact predict that Poddar would kill and were therefore negligent in failing to warn of that danger. Thus the issue here is very narrow: we are not concerned with whether the therapists, pursuant to the standards of their profession, "should have" predicted potential violence; they allegedly did so in actuality. Under these limited circumstances I agree that a cause of action can be stated. . . .

CLARK, J., dissenting. Until today's majority opinion, both legal and medical authorities have agreed that confidentiality is essential to effectively treat the mentally ill, and that imposing a duty on doctors to disclose patient threats to potential victims would greatly impair treatment. Further, recognizing that effective treatment and society's safety are necessarily intertwined, the Legislature has already decided effective and confidential treatment is preferred over imposition of a duty to warn.

The issue whether effective treatment for the mentally ill should be sacrificed to a system of warnings is, in my opinion, properly one for the Legislature, and we are bound by its judgment. Moreover, even in the absence of clear legislative direction, we must reach the same conclusion because imposing the majority's new duty is certain to result in a net increase in violence.

NOTES

1. Tarasoff's *California aftermath.* The duty of reasonable care announced in *Tarasoff* has been widely accepted, and codified in RTT:LPEH §41.

> **Restatement (Third) of Torts: Liability for Physical and Emotional Harm**
>
> **§41. DUTY TO THIRD PERSONS BASED ON SPECIAL RELATIONSHIP WITH PERSON POSING RISKS**
>
> (a) An actor in a special relationship with another owes a duty of reasonable care to third persons with regard to risks posed by the other that arise within the scope of the relationship.
>
> (b) Special relationships giving rise to the duty provided in Subsection (a) include:
>
>   (1) a parent with dependent children,
>
>   (2) a custodian with those in its custody,
>
>   (3) an employer with employees when the employment facilitates the employee's causing harm to third parties, and
>
>   (4) a mental-health professional with patients.

Under the Third Restatement's rationale, is the plaintiff's case easier or more difficult because the defendants were medical professionals instead of ordinary individuals? Should we focus on the competence of psychiatrists to detect dangerous persons or the need for confidentiality in patient-psychiatrist relationships?

How should the law reflect the differences between dangerous persons who are or who are not in custody?

Tarasoff's limits were tested in Beauchene v. Synanon Foundation, Inc., 151 Cal. Rptr. 796 (Ct. App. 1979), which held that a *private* rehabilitation center owed no duty of care to members of the public at large when it accepted convicted individuals referred to it by the state criminal justice system as an alternative to incarceration. The court held that the absence of a duty of care was fatal to both of the plaintiff's claims, to wit, that the assailant had been improperly admitted into the program and that he had been improperly supervised once admitted. Should the same result apply when a private institution treats patients without a criminal conviction?

In the subsequent California Supreme Court case of Thompson v. County of Alameda, 614 P.2d 728, 736 (Cal. 1980), a juvenile with a long and sorrowful personal history of violence and sexual abuse was released into the custody of his mother, even though the county knew that the youth had "indicated that he would, if released, take the life of a young child residing in the neighborhood." Although no particular person was identified, the released juvenile in fact murdered the plaintiff's son in the plaintiff's mother's garage within 24 hours of his release. The plaintiffs argued that warnings should have been issued to (a) the police, (b) the parents in the neighborhood, and/or (c) the juvenile's mother. The contention was rejected by the court:

> Unlike members of the general public, in *Tarasoff* . . . the potential victims were specifically known and designated individuals. The warnings which we therein required were directed at making those individuals aware of the danger to which they were uniquely exposed. The threatened targets were precise. In such cases, it is fair to conclude that warnings given discreetly and to a limited number of persons would have a greater effect because they would alert those particular targeted individuals of the possibility of a specific threat pointed at them. In contrast, the warnings sought by plaintiffs would of necessity have to be made to a broad segment of the population and would be only general in nature. In addition to the likelihood that such generalized warnings when frequently repeated would do little as a practical matter to stimulate increased safety measures . . . such extensive warnings would be difficult to give.

Tobriner, J., dissented on the ground that warnings should have been given to the mother, who "might" have taken additional steps to control the conduct of her son.

The issue of the therapist's care in California is today governed by Cal. Civ. Code §43.92 (West 2015), which provides:

> (a) There shall be no monetary liability on the part of, and no cause of action shall arise against, any person who is a psychotherapist . . . in failing to protect from a patient's threatened violent behavior or failing to predict and protect from a patient's violent behavior except if the patient has communicated to the psychotherapist a serious threat of physical violence against a reasonably identifiable victim or victims.

(b) There shall be no monetary liability on the part of, and no cause of action shall arise against, a psychotherapist who . . . discharges his or her duty to protect by making reasonable efforts to communicate the threat to the victim or victims and to a law enforcement agency.

2. Beyond California.   *Tarasoff's* influence has extended far beyond California. The duties are especially strict on defendants whose steps facilitate attacks by persons within their care on innocent plaintiffs. One particularly chilling example is Lundgren v. Fultz, 354 N.W.2d 25, 29 (Minn. 1984), in which a psychiatrist interceded on behalf of his patient, Fultz, who had been diagnosed and committed as a paranoid schizophrenic, to secure the return of his guns that had been confiscated by the police. Fultz proceeded to shoot Lundgren in "an unprovoked and random attack." The court noted that "a jury could conclude that the psychiatrist's letter caused the police to return these guns and, thus, materially increased the danger that Fultz posed. . . . There is a limit to the protection given the discretion in a professional relationship. That limit is exceeded where a psychiatrist places the gun in a potential assassin's hand under the guise of fostering trust between patient and psychiatrist."

Liability is more closely contested when a psychiatrist has only limited interactions with psychiatric individuals on an outpatient basis. In Long v. Broadlawns Medical Center, 656 N.W.2d 71 (Iowa 2002), the decedent, Jillene Long, was killed by her husband, Gerald, a psychiatric patient who had been released from the defendant medical center. The husband had a long history of spousal abuse. During his commitment, the decedent agreed with hospital officials that she would remain at the marital residence, but that Broadlawns would call her on the day of her husband's discharge. That call was never made, and Cady, J., after extensive consideration of *Tarasoff*, held that the basic issue was "whether Broadlawns failed to exercise reasonable care in performing a promise to warn Jillene of Gerald's discharge thereby increasing the risk of harm to her or resulting in harm to her because of her reliance on the promised warning." "[S]ubstantial evidence exist[ed] to support a finding that Jillene would not have been at the marital residence had she known Gerald was discharged and essentially free to return there himself." Gerald's conduct did not count as a superseding cause because his acts fell "squarely within the scope of the original risk."

For an exhaustive bibliography on these issues, see RTT:LPEH §41, comment *g* and its Reporter's Note.

3. A Tarasoff *retrospective.*   One reason *Tarasoff* has always raised difficult problems is that it is not amenable to easy contractual solutions because, unlike *Long*, the three parties are not in privity with each other. Hence no one doubts the legitimate state interest in seeking to prevent death or serious injury by imposing some form of liability on the psychiatrists and institutions who provide care for seriously deranged patients. Disturbed persons are not easily deterred, and they have few if any resources to answer tort claims. At the same time, the fear that potential disclosure will drive disturbed individuals from the care they so desperately need has placed a brake on the liability. Rosenhan et al., Warning Third Parties:

The Ripple Effects of *Tarasoff*, 24 Pac. L.J. 1165, 1185-1189 (1993), reported that, of 872 surveyed therapists: (i) 50 percent believed they had lost a patient as a result of discussing the need to breach confidentiality should the patient threaten harm; (ii) 18 percent avoided counseling dangerous patients at least in part because of *Tarasoff*; and (iii) 37 percent focused disproportionately on the potential dangerousness of their patients due to *Tarasoff*.

When *Tarasoff* came down in 1976 there were many predictions of systematic professional doom, but these have, on the whole, moderated with time. Alan Stone, an expert in law and psychiatry, first denounced *Tarasoff*, Stone, The *Tarasoff* Decision: Suing Psychotherapists to Safeguard Society, 90 Harv. L. Rev. 358 (1976). But on reflection he later wrote "the duty to warn is not as unmitigated a disaster for the enterprise of psychotherapy as it once seemed to critics like myself." Stone, Law Psychiatry and Morality: Essays and Analysis 181 (1984). And Ginsberg, *Tarasoff* at Thirty: Victim's Knowledge Shrinks the Psychotherapist's Duty to Warn and Protect, 21 J. Contemp. Health L. & Pol'y 1, 2 (2004), concludes: "[T]hirty years of reflection and empirical observation have cast *Tarasoff* in a more optimistic, evolving light."

But why? Three explanations seem relevant. First, many states, like California, have codified the duty in ways that soften its sharpest edges. Second, the courts have tended in practice to be cautious about imposing the duty on persons who are not in custody. Third, the duty tends to bite most powerfully in three situations: (1) where the potential target has been identified by the disturbed person, as in *Tarasoff* itself; (2) where the psychiatrist has somehow facilitated the commission of the crime, as in *Lundgren*; and (3) where the psychiatrist or institution has breached some explicit promise to the future victim, as in *Long*. Not perfect, perhaps. But not a bad application of traditional principles.